Youth and Employment in Sub-Saharan Africa

It is widely acknowledged that youth unemployment is one of the most critical challenges facing countries in Sub-Saharan Africa. This volume brings together an eminent group of international scholars to analyze the extent and complex nature of this joblessness, and to offer a set of evidence-based policy choices that could contribute to solving the problem in the short- and long-run.

Part I reviews the existing literature on youth unemployment and under-employment in Sub-Saharan Africa from microeconomic and macroeconomic perspectives; Part II goes on to present detailed country studies of Ethiopia, Ghana, Kenya and South Africa. These studies offer a deep understanding of the situation on the ground and consider country-specific solutions.

Throughout the book it is argued that the standard International Labour Organization definition of unemployment is too narrow to portray correctly the employment situations in Sub-Saharan Africa. Several alternative measures of unemployment are presented, which show that joblessness is far more pervasive than commonly assumed in the literature.

This volume will be of interest to academics and policymakers involved in African development.

Hiroyuki Hino is Professor of Economics at Kobe University, Japan. He is also Senior Advisor to the Presidency of the Republic of Kenya.

Gustav Ranis was Frank Altschul Professor Emeritus of International Economics at Yale University, USA. After completing this book, he passed away in October, 2013.

Routledge Studies in Development Economics

1 **Economic Development in the Middle East**
Rodney Wilson

2 **Monetary and Financial Policies in Developing Countries**
Growth and stabilization
Akhtar Hossain and Anis Chowdhury

3 **New Directions in Development Economics**
Growth, environmental concerns and government in the 1990s
Edited by Mats Lundahl and Benno J. Ndulu

4 **Financial Liberalization and Investment**
Kanhaya L. Gupta and Robert Lensink

5 **Liberalization in the Developing World**
Institutional and economic changes in Latin America, Africa and Asia
Edited by Alex E. Fernández Jilberto and André Mommen

6 **Financial Development and Economic Growth**
Theory and experiences from developing countries
Edited by Niels Hermes and Robert Lensink

7 **The South African Economy**
Macroeconomic prospects for the medium term
Finn Tarp and Peter Brixen

8 **Public Sector Pay and Adjustment**
Lessons from five countries
Edited by Christopher Colclough

9 **Europe and Economic Reform in Africa**
Structural adjustment and economic diplomacy
Obed O. Mailafia

10 **Post-apartheid Southern Africa**
Economic challenges and policies for the future
Edited by Lennart Petersson

11 **Financial Integration and Development**
Liberalization and reform in sub-Saharan Africa
Ernest Aryeetey and Machiko Nissanke

12 **Regionalization and Globalization in the Modern World Economy**
Perspectives on the Third World and transitional economies
Edited by Alex E. Fernández Jilberto and André Mommen

13 **The African Economy**
Policy, institutions and the future
Steve Kayizzi-Mugerwa

14 **Recovery from Armed Conflict in Developing Countries**
Edited by Geoff Harris

15 **Small Enterprises and Economic Development**
The dynamics of micro and small enterprises
Carl Liedholm and Donald C. Mead

16 **The World Bank**
New agendas in a changing world
Michelle Miller-Adams

17 **Development Policy in the Twenty-First Century**
Beyond the post-Washington consensus
Edited by Ben Fine, Costas Lapavitsas and Jonathan Pincus

18 **State-Owned Enterprises in the Middle East and North Africa**
Privatization, performance and reform
Edited by Merih Celasun

19 **Finance and Competitiveness in Developing Countries**
Edited by José María Fanelli and Rohinton Medhora

20 **Contemporary Issues in Development Economics**
Edited by B.N. Ghosh

21 **Mexico Beyond NAFTA**
Edited by Martín Puchet Anyul and Lionello F. Punzo

22 **Economies in Transition**
A guide to China, Cuba, Mongolia, North Korea and Vietnam at the turn of the twenty-first century
Ian Jeffries

23 **Population, Economic Growth and Agriculture in Less Developed Countries**
Nadia Cuffaro

24 **From Crisis to Growth in Africa?**
Edited by Mats Lundal

25 **The Macroeconomics of Monetary Union**
An analysis of the CFA franc zone
David Fielding

26 **Endogenous Development**
Networking, innovation, institutions and cities
Antonio Vasquez-Barquero

27 **Labour Relations in Development**
Edited by Alex E. Fernández Jilberto and Marieke Riethof

28 **Globalization, Marginalization and Development**
Edited by S. Mansoob Murshed

29 **Programme Aid and Development**
Beyond conditionality
Howard White and Geske Dijkstra

30 **Competitiveness Strategy in Developing Countries**
A manual for policy analysis
Edited by Ganeshan Wignaraja

31 **The African Manufacturing Firm**
An analysis based on firm surveys in sub-Saharan Africa
Dipak Mazumdar and Ata Mazaheri

32 **Trade Policy, Growth and Poverty in Asian Developing Countries**
Edited by Kishor Sharma

33 **International Competitiveness, Investment and Finance**
A case study of India
Edited by A. Ganesh Kumar, Kunal Sen and Rajendra R. Vaidya

34 **The Pattern of Aid Giving**
The impact of good governance on development assistance
Eric Neumayer

35 **New International Poverty Reduction Strategies**
Edited by Jean-Pierre Cling, Mireille Razafindrakoto and François Roubaud

36 **Targeting Development**
Critical perspectives on the Millennium Development Goals
Edited by Richard Black and Howard White

37 **Essays on Balance of Payments Constrained Growth**
Theory and evidence
Edited by J.S.L. McCombie and A.P. Thirlwall

38 **The Private Sector after Communism**
New entrepreneurial firms in transition economies
Jan Winiecki, Vladimir Benacek and Mihaly Laki

39 **Information Technology and Development**
A new paradigm for delivering the internet to rural areas in developing countries
Jeffrey James

40 **The Economics of Palestine**
Economic policy and institutional reform for a viable Palestine state
Edited by David Cobham and Nu'man Kanafani

41 **Development Dilemmas**
The methods and political ethics of growth policy
Melvin Ayogu and Don Ross

42 **Rural Livelihoods and Poverty Reduction Policies**
Edited by Frank Ellis and H. Ade Freeman

43 **Beyond Market-Driven Development**
Drawing on the experience of Asia and Latin America
Edited by Makoto Noguchi and Costas Lapavitsas

44 **The Political Economy of Reform Failure**
Edited by Mats Lundahl and Michael L. Wyzan

45 **Overcoming Inequality in Latin America**
Issues and challenges for the twenty-first century
Edited by Ricardo Gottschalk and Patricia Justino

46 **Trade, Growth and Inequality in the Era of Globalization**
Edited by Kishor Sharma and Oliver Morrissey

47 **Microfinance**
Perils and prospects
Edited by Jude L. Fernando

48 **The IMF, World Bank and Policy Reform**
Edited by Alberto Paloni and Maurizio Zanardi

49 **Managing Development**
Globalization, economic restructuring and social policy
Edited by Junji Nakagawa

50 **Who Gains from Free Trade?**
Export-led growth, inequality and poverty in Latin America
Edited by Rob Vos, Enrique Ganuza, Samuel Morley and Sherman Robinson

51 **Evolution of Markets and Institutions**
A study of an emerging economy
Murali Patibandla

52 **The New Famines**
Why famines exist in an era of globalization
Edited by Stephen Devereux

53 **Development Ethics at Work**
Explorations – 1960–2002
Denis Goulet

54 **Law Reform in Developing and Transitional States**
Edited by Tim Lindsey

55 **The Asymmetries of Globalization**
Edited by Pan A. Yotopoulos and Donato Romano

56 **Ideas, Policies and Economic Development in the Americas**
Edited by Esteban Pérez-Caldentey and Matias Vernengo

57 **European Union Trade Politics and Development**
Everything but arms unravelled
Edited by Gerrit Faber and Jan Orbie

58 **Membership Based Organizations of the Poor**
Edited by Martha Chen, Renana Jhabvala, Ravi Kanbur and Carol Richards

59 **The Politics of Aid Selectivity**
Good governance criteria in World Bank, U.S. and Dutch development assistance
Wil Hout

60 **Economic Development, Education and Transnational Corporations**
Mark Hanson

61 **Achieving Economic Development in the Era of Globalization**
Shalendra Sharma

62 **Sustainable Development and Free Trade**
Shawkat Alam

63 **The Impact of International Debt Relief**
Geske Dijkstra

64 **Europe's Troubled Region**
Economic development, institutional reform and social welfare in the Western Balkans
William Bartlett

65 **Work, Female Empowerment and Economic Development**
Sara Horrell, Hazel Johnson and Paul Mosley

66 **The Chronically Poor in Rural Bangladesh**
Livelihood constraints and capabilities
Pk. Md. Motiur Rahman, Noriatsu Matsui and Yukio Ikemoto

67 **Public–Private Partnerships in Health Care in India**
Lessons for developing countries
A. Venkat Raman and James Warner Björkman

68 **Rural Poverty and Income Dynamics in Asia and Africa**
Edited by Keijiro Otsuka, Jonna P. Estudillo and Yasuyuki Sawada

69 **Microfinance: A Reader**
David Hulme and Thankom Arun

70 **Aid and International NGOs**
Dirk-Jan Koch

71 **Development Macroeconomics**
Essays in memory of Anita Ghatak
Edited by Subrata Ghatak and Paul Levine

72 **Taxation in a Low Income Economy**
The case of Mozambique
Channing Arndt and Finn Tarp

73 **Labour Markets and Economic Development**
Edited by Ravi Kanbur and Jan Svejnar

74 **Economic Transitions to Neoliberalism in Middle-Income Countries**
Policy dilemmas, crises, mass resistance
Edited by Alfedo Saad-Filho and Galip L. Yalman

75 **Latecomer Development**
Innovation and knowledge for economic growth
Banji Oyelaran-Oyeyinka and Padmashree Gehl Sampath

76 **Trade Relations between the EU and Africa**
Development, challenges and options beyond the Cotonou Agreement
Edited by Yenkong Ngangjoh-Hodu and Francis A.S.T. Matambalya

77 **The Comparative Political Economy of Development**
Africa and South Asia
Edited by Barbara Harriss-White and Judith Heyer

78 **Credit Cooperatives in India**
Past, present and future
Biswa Swarup Misra

79 **Development Economics in Action (2nd edition)**
A study of economic policies in Ghana
Tony Killick

80 **The Multinational Enterprise in Developing Countries**
Local versus global logic
Edited by Rick Molz, Cătălin Ratiu and Ali Taleb

81 **Monetary and Financial Integration in West Africa**
Edited by Temitope W. Oshikoya

82 **Reform and Development in China**
What can China offer the developing world?
Edited by Ho-Mou Wu and Yang Yao

83 **Towards New Developmentalism**
Market as means rather than master
Edited by Shahrukh Rafi Khan and Jens Christiansen

84 **Culture, Institutions, and Development**
New insights into an old debate
Edited by Jean-Philippe Platteau and Robert Peccoud

85 **Assessing Prospective Trade Policy**
Methods applied to EU–ACP Economic Partnership Agreements
Edited by Oliver Morrissey

86 **Social Protection for Africa's Children**
Edited by Sudhanshu Handa, Stephen Devereux and Douglas Webb

87 **Energy, Bio Fuels and Development**
Comparing Brazil and the United States
Edited by Edmund Amann, Werner Baer and Don Coes

88 **Value Chains, Social Inclusion and Economic Development**
Contrasting theories and realities
Edited by A.H.J. (Bert) Helmsing and Sietze Vellema

89 **Market Liberalism, Growth, and Economic Development in Latin America**
Edited by Gerardo Angeles Castro, Ignacio Perrotini-Hernández and Humberto Ríos-Bolivar

90 **South–South Globalization**
Challenges and opportunities for development
Edited by S. Mansoob Murshed, Pedro Goulart and Leandro A. Serino

91 **Trade Infrastructure and Economic Development**
Edited by Olu Ajakaiye and T. Ademola Oyejide

92 **Microcredit and International Development**
Contexts, achievements and challenges
Edited by Farhad Hossain, Christopher Rees and Tonya Knight-Millar

93 **Business Regulation and Non-State Actors**
Whose standards? Whose development?
Edited by Darryl Reed and Peter Utting and Ananya Mukherjee Reed

94 **Public Expenditures for Agricultural and Rural Development in Africa**
Edited by Tewodaj Mogues and Samuel Benin

95 **The Global Economic Crisis and the Developing World**
Implications and prospects for recovery and growth
Edited by Ashwini Deshpande and Keith Nurse

96 **The Microfinance Impact**
Ranjula Bali Swain

97 **Gendered Insecurities, Health and Development in Africa**
Edited by Howard Stein and Amal Hassan Fadlalla

98 **Financial Cooperatives and Local Development**
Edited by Silvio Goglio and Yiorgos Alexopoulos

99 **State–Business Relations and Economic Development in Africa and India**
Edited by Kunal Sen

100 **Digital Interactions in Developing Countries**
An economic perspective
Jeffrey James

101 **Migration and Inequality**
Edited by Tanja Bastia

102 **Financing Regional Growth and the Inter-American Development Bank**
The case of Argentina
Ernesto Vivares

103 **Globalization and Development**
Rethinking interventions and governance
Edited by Arne Bigsten

104 **Disasters and the Networked Economy**
J.M. Albala-Bertrand

105 **Microfinance, Debt and Over-Indebtedness**
Juggling with money
Edited by Isabelle Guérin, Solène Morvant-Roux and Magdalena Villarreal

106 **The Universal Social Safety-Net and the Attack on World Poverty**
Pressing need, manageable cost, practical possibilities, favourable spillovers
Anthony Clunies-Ross and Mozammel Huq

107 **Youth and Employment in Sub-Saharan Africa**
Working but poor
Edited by Hiroyuki Hino and Gustav Ranis

Youth and Employment in Sub-Saharan Africa

Working but poor

Edited by
Hiroyuki Hino and Gustav Ranis

LONDON AND NEW YORK

First published 2014 by Routledge

2 Park Square, Milton Park, Abingdon, Oxfordshire OX14 4RN
52 Vanderbilt Avenue, New York, NY 10017

Routledge is an imprint of the Taylor & Francis Group, an informa business

First issued in paperback 2019

British Library Cataloguing in Publication Data
A catalogue record for this book is available from the British Library

Library of Congress Cataloging in Publication Data
Youth and employment in Sub-Saharan Africa : working but poor / edited by Hiroyuki Hino and Gustav Ranis.
pages cm
Includes bibliographical references and index.
1. Youth--Employment--Africa, Sub-Saharan. 2. Youth--Africa, Sub-Saharan--Economic conditions. 3. Youth--Africa, Sub-Saharan--Social conditions. 4. Poverty--Africa, Sub-Saharan. I. Hino, Hiroyuki, 1945- II. Ranis, Gustav.
HD6276.A357Y68 2013
331.340967--dc23
2013015359

ISBN: 978-0-415-85938-7 (hbk)
ISBN: 978-0-367-86826-0 (pbk)

Typeset in Times New Roman
by Taylor & Francis Books

In Memory of Professor Gustav Ranis

Professor Ranis was a pioneer in development economics; his integrity and his insights forever changed both the study and practice of development. He was indeed a dynamic and dedicated scholar, but also an energetic supporter of students and colleagues. In addition, he guided policy and practice of a number of governments and international organizations over the course of his long, illustrative career. Most of all, Gus was a mentor, a motivator, and a dear friend to all of us who joined him in an attempt to untangle the cobweb of ethnic diversity and economic development in Africa, that kept us together for more than three years. Gus departed us on October 15, 2013. He will long be remembered and celebrated for fostering thoughtful, rigorous examination of the complex issues of economic development, and for being a warm and caring individual.

Contents

List of tables

List of figures

List of contributors

Martin Abel is a PhD candidate in public policy at Harvard University. His primary research interests include international development and labor economics with particular interest in labor markets in Sub-Saharan Africa.

Charles Godfred Ackah is Research Fellow at the Institute of Statistical, Social and Economic Research, University of Ghana. His primary research interests include applied trade policy, labour market and poverty analysis, gender and intra-household bargaining, microfinance and consumer demand analysis.

Ernest Aryeetey is Vice-Chancellor and Professor of the University of Ghana, where he has been on the research faculty since 1986. He is also Nonresident Senior Fellow with the Africa Growth Initiative in the Global Economy and Development Program of The Brookings Institution in Washington, DC.

William Baah-Boateng is Labour Economists and Lecturer at the Department of Economics, University of Ghana. He is also a Fellow of International Institute for Advanced Studies in Ghana and Alumnus of University of Ghana and Harvard University. His primary research interests include labour market and industrial relations, poverty, gender and SME analysis.

Marianne Bertrand is the Chris P. Dialynas Professor of Economics of the University of Chicago Booth School of Business. She obtained her PhD in Economics from Harvard University in 1998. Professor Bertrand is an applied microeconomist whose research covers the fields of labour economics, corporate finance and development economics.

Megan Blair is Research Analyst at the Abdul Latif Jameel Poverty Action Lab (J-PAL) Africa. Her work at J-PAL has centered around identifying and setting up evaluations of programs targeting unemployed youth in South Africa.

Nzinga H. Broussard is Social and Behavioral Science Diversity Post-Doctoral Fellow at the Economics Department of the Ohio State University. She obtained her PhD in Economics and Public Policy from University of Michigan in 2008. Her primary research interests include development economics, labour economics and agricultural economics.

Bruno Crépon is Associate Professor at the ENSAE and École Polytechnique. He received his PhD in Economics from Université Paris-I Sorbonne. His research area covers labour economics, microeconometrics, program evaluation and implementation of experimental evaluations.

Raissa Fabregas is a PhD student in public policy at Harvard University. Her research interests are in the fields of development economics, labor economics and political economy.

Tadele Ferede is currently an Associate Dean for Graduate Programs at the Department of Economics, College of Business and Economics, Addis Ababa University. He obtained his PhD in Applied Economics from the University of Antwerp, Belgium. He has long years of teaching experience at university level and a strong track record in research. His research works have been published in internationally reviewed journals.

Douglas Gollin is Professor of Development Economics at the Department of International Development, University of Oxford. Previously he has worked for sixteen years on the faculty of Williams College in the United States. His research focuses on economic development and growth, with particular interests in agriculture and structural transformation.

Kamilla Gumede is Executive Director of the Abdul Latif Jameel Poverty Action Lab (J-PAL) Africa. She has previously worked for the South African National Treasury to promote policy and capacity building in Africa and globally.

Hiroyuki Hino is Senior Advisor to the Presidency of the Republic of Kenya for Strategic Initiates and Economy, Professor at the Research Institute for Economics and Business Administration, Kobe University, and Special Fellow of Japan International Cooperation Agency Research Institute. He held a number of positions at the International Monetary Fund, including the Director of Regional Office for Asia and the Pacific. He was Economic Advisor to the Prime Minister of the Republic of Kenya when he edited this book.

Kim Lehrer is Research Officer at the Centre for the Study of African Economies, Department of Economics, University of Oxford. Her current research is under the program 'Transforming economic policies towards the poor', funded by the Bill and Melinda Gates Foundation.

Murray Leibbrandt holds the NRF/DST Research Chair in Poverty and Inequality Research. He is Director at the Southern Africa Labour and Development Research Unit at the University of Cape Town. He is a past president of the African Econometric Society and the Economic Society of South Africa, and is an IZA Fellow.

William Lyakurwa is Executive Director of the African Economic Research Consortium (AERC). He joined AERC in 1993 from the International Trade Centre based in Geneva, Switzerland, where he held the post of Senior Trade

Promotion Advisor. He received his PhD from Cornell University, USA in 1978. His research interests include trade, regional integration and inclusive growth.

Isaac Mbiti is an Assistant Professor in the Department of Economics at Southern Methodist University and an affiliate of the Jameel Abdul Latif Poverty Action Lab (J-PAL) at MIT. Previously, he was a Martin Luther King Jr Visiting Assistant Professor at MIT and a National Academy of Education/Spencer Foundation Post-doctoral Fellow. His main interests are in the field of economic development, and he is also interested in labor economics and demography. He received his PhD in economics from Brown University in 2007.

Boaz Munga is Policy Analyst at the Social Sector Division, Kenya Institute for Public Policy Research and Analysis. He obtained his MA in Economics from the University of Nairobi, Kenya. His research interests are in socio-economic issues including education, unemployment, and international trade and development.

Germano Mwabu is Professor of Economics at the School of Economics, University of Nairobi. His research interests are health economics, micro-econometrics and development economics. He has served as a consultant for various organizations including the World Health Organization, World Bank and UN Security Council.

Samuel Mwakubo is Manager, Research of the African Economic Research Consortium. He has conducted research in food production and nutrition, horticultural commodity marketing, farming systems development, fertilizer marketing, vegetable oils and protein systems, and soil conservation. His present research interests are in social capital and sustainable use of natural resources. He holds a PhD in environmental economics from Moi University, Kenya.

Othieno Nyanjom is Research Associate in the Social Sector Division, Kenya Institute for Public Policy Research and Analysis. He obtained his doctoral degree in development studies from the University of Sussex and has consulted widely on social sector issues in Kenya and abroad.

Eldah Onsomu is Policy Analyst at Social Sector Division, Kenya Institute for Public Policy Research and Analysis. Her research interests include socio-economic issues notably education, public financial management, labour, inequalities, poverty, gender and health. She holds a Ph.D in economics from the University of Nairobi.

John Page is a Senior Fellow in the Global Economy and Development Program at the Brookings Institution. He was formerly chief economist for Africa and director, poverty reduction at the World Bank, and currently studies industrial development, poverty and migration in Africa. He obtained his PhD from the University of Oxford in 1975.

Gustav Ranis was the Frank Altschul Professor Emeritus of International Economics at the Economic Growth Center, Yale University. He previously held various positions including Assistant Administrator for Program and Policy at USAID, Director of both the Economic Growth Center at Yale as well as the Yale Center for International and Area Studies. He had to his credit more than 20 books and 300 articles on theoretical and policy-related issues of development.

Hansa Teklay Reda is Associate Researcher at the Ethiopian Development Research Institute. Her interests include behavioral and experimental economics, institutional economics and labor economics.

Tsegay Gebrekidan Tekleselassie is a PhD Candidate and Associate Tutor, Department of Economics, University of Sussex, UK. He is also affiliated to the Ethiopian Development Research Institute, Ethiopia.

Foreword

Africa is growing more quickly than many other regions in the world. It has grown more than 5 per cent annually on average since 2000. Endowed with rich natural resources and with the prospect of expanding commodity supply and growing consumer demand, Africa is one of the most promising continents in the world. However, Africa needs to overcome many challenges in order to achieve sustainable development. One of the important challenges is job creation. Unemployment and underemployment, especially of the youth, not only hinder healthy economic growth but also can undermine social stability. Africa is now seeing a rapid expansion of the working-age population. It has to create many more adequate and decent jobs for the youthful population.

This volume is the fruit of a research project that the Japan International Cooperation Agency (JICA) commissioned as part of its contributions to the Fifth Tokyo International Conference on African Development (TICAD), a policy forum held in Japan every five years since 1993. The project is extremely timely and helpful, as current understanding of unemployment issues is indispensable for the constructive discussion of development in Africa. The project was led by Professor Hiroyuki Hino, Economic Advisor to the Kenyan Prime Minister and Professor of Economics at Kobe University. The research team consists of internationally renowned scholars and experts on development in Africa. On behalf of JICA, I would like to thank Professor Hino and the other authors and researchers for their research and valuable findings. I am fully convinced that this book will contribute a great deal to the advancement of the study of unemployment in Africa and provide a strong intellectual foundation for the discussions that will take place in the TICAD process.

Akihiko Tanaka
President
Japan International Cooperation Agency

Preface

It is generally agreed that chronic and pervasive unemployment, especially among the youth, represents one of the most critical challenges faced by policymakers in Sub-Saharan Africa, as well as by bilateral and multilateral agencies working on the continent. While growth has been quite satisfactory over the past decade, income disparities have widened and poverty has remained entrenched. Because of sheer poverty, young people have to find work of some kind to earn whatever they can, even if the employment is of low quality or high risk. Thus the true extent of unemployment—that is, including underemployment and disguised unemployment—is far more pervasive than the official UN/ILO statistics indicate.

This volume represents an effort to pierce the mysteries of youth unemployment in Sub-Saharan Africa. It presents a collection of papers comprising a review of macroeconomic literature and global practices, a survey of microeconomic literature and micro-level interventions, and four intensive country studies (Ethiopia, Ghana, Kenya and South Africa). We want to know why more young people are not gainfully employed, and what policies can be devised to ameliorate the situation.

By examining conditions in the still dominant agricultural sector, the rural non-agriculture sector, and the urban informal and urban formal sectors, as well as interactions among these four sectors, we intend to determine the causes of youth underemployment and develop conceptual as well as empirical frameworks to ameliorate the situation. We investigate nutrition, health, education and other factors that constrain the development of human capital—employability, and also information imperfections, regulatory frameworks and other elements that undermine the functioning of the labour market. We illustrate the nature and extent of open unemployment, underemployment and disguised unemployment in Sub-Saharan Africa, with the presentation of comprehensive and recent data on the four countries.

JICA has supported this effort as part of its contributions to the Fifth Tokyo International Conference on African Development (TICAD V), scheduled for June 2013. The papers contained in this book are intended as background for a full report which JICA hopes to present to TICAD V in collaboration with Kobe University's Research Institute for Economics and Business Administration.

Hiroyuki Hino and Gustav Ranis

Acknowledgement

This book is a collection of papers that the Japan International Cooperation Agency (JICA) commissioned as background papers for its report on youth unemployment in Africa, intended for presentation to the Fifth Tokyo International Conference on African Development to be held during 1–3 June, 2013 in Yokohama, Japan. We are grateful to Dr Rachel Glennerster, Executive Director of J-PAL at MIT, for her contributions in the conceptualization of this project and for her review of the earlier drafts of the papers. We are also thankful to Dr Shanta Devarajan, Chief Economist for the World Bank's Africa Region, and Dr William Lyakurwa, Executive Director of the African Economic Research Consortium, for their respective comments on the papers. The preparation of the papers was coordinated by Innovation for Poverty Action (IPA) under the supervision of Mr Kimiaki Jin, Resident Representative of JICA UK Office. We also would like to express our gratitude to Ms Natalie Tomlinson of Routledge for her encouragement and assistance. Finally, we wish to thank Ms Eva Gladwell Mithamo of the Office of the Economic Advisor of the Prime Minister of the Republic of Kenya, and Ms Takako Kitano of RIEB for their administrative assistance.

Hiroyuki Hino and Gustav Ranis

1 Introduction and summary

Hiroyuki Hino, William Lyakurwa and Samuel Mwakubo

1.1 Aim of this book

This book presents a collection of papers that together show the true extent and complex nature of joblessness among the youth in Sub-Saharan Africa. It also offers a set of evidence-based policy choices that could be expected to contribute to solving the problem in the short- and long-run. The book is composed of full reviews of the macroeconomic and microeconomic literature, and case studies of four major countries in Sub-Saharan Africa (Ethiopia, Ghana, Kenya and South Africa). The reviews provide a theoretical underpinning and broader perspectives drawn from recent and ongoing research projects, while the country studies offer much deeper understanding of the situation on the ground and country-specific solutions.

Throughout the reviews and the country studies, this book argues that the standard International Labour Organization (ILO) definition of unemployment is too narrow to portray correctly the employment situations in Sub-Saharan Africa. The book presents several broader measures of unemployment in each of the country studies—underemployment, vulnerable employment, the working poor, and less stringent conditions to qualify as unemployed—and concludes that joblessness is far more pervasive than commonly assumed in the literature. The book also shows that the essence of joblessness in Sub-Saharan Africa has to do with low productivity and low employability (human capital). Solutions will require a holistic approach combining macroeconomic strategies, interventions to raise productivity and quality of work, public health (especially during early childhood), and education, in addition to conventional labour market measures.

The book stresses that the effectiveness of programs and projects must be tested using randomized controlled trials or other vigorous methods. It reviews measures that have been adopted in Sub-Saharan Africa and elsewhere, and finds that many of them have proven less effective than intended. Finally, it contends that research is fundamental in finding innovative solutions, and suggests areas where further research is promising.

1.2 Challenge of youth and unemployment

It is widely acknowledged among policymakers and observers alike that youth unemployment in Africa is a critical challenge that must be addressed urgently by African countries and the global community. Young people account for the vast majority of Africa's population, and this group is projected to expand at an alarming pace. Most young Africans are not gainfully employed. Chronic and pervasive youth unemployment causes social tension and even conflict. Yet young Africans are dynamic, talented and entrepreneurial. Thus African youth may be either a time bomb that could ignite social unrest and instability—or a reservoir for growth and economic and social transformation. This is the crux of Africa's challenge.

Africa's population is predominantly young, with more than 60 per cent aged under 24 years. It is also estimated that about 40 per cent of the total population are younger than 15. With this age structure and persistently high fertility rates, the proportion of the population under 24 is projected to rise to 75 per cent by 2015. The World Bank estimates that the population of the youth in Africa (ages 15–24) will double from 200 million at present to 400 million by 2045. It is projected that the number of young people in Sub-Sahara will match that in East Asia by 2035, and exceed that in South Asia by 2050. About three-quarters of the youth live in poverty (on under US$2 a day), and a large majority live in rural areas.

Almost all young men and women in Africa, particularly the poor, work in some fashion because poverty forces them to find ways of earning money or taking part in the family's livelihood. But apart from a small educated elite, they rarely have jobs that earn a living wage under decent working conditions. A vast majority of the youth work long hours, usually under poor conditions, but most of them earn little. They have to find some work in order to survive. Even children work, often more than normal full-time hours. The African youth are caught in a poverty trap. They grow up malnourished and in poor health. A significant proportion do not complete even primary education. As a result, their 'human capital' remains underdeveloped, and their productivity is insufficient to earn a decent wage.

The social and economic costs arising from underutilization of Africa's youth are substantial, not only exposing the disenfranchized youth to social exclusion, but also perpetuating poverty through intergenerational transfer of the inadequate development of human capital. As discussed in chapters 5 (Aryeetey *et al.*) and 6 (Munga *et al.*), the lack of employment opportunities could lead to social conflict, violence and juvenile delinquency. Young people are more likely to be recruited into armed groups in civil conflict or insurgency when they are jobless and poor, and see daunting prospects for themselves and their families. The increasing incidence of street hawking and illegal migration abroad are not only symptoms of labour market failures, but also reflect a sense of hopelessness and desperation.

Therefore it is crucial that African governments pursue most vigorously policies and programs that (i) substantially enhance human capital—and hence productivity—of young Africans, particularly those disadvantaged, including women; (ii) create a large number of opportunities for the youth to be gainfully employed, by raising the competitiveness and productivity of the economy, particularly in smallholder agriculture and informal businesses; and (iii) harness the immense talents of the youth, not only for growth and development, but also to demonstrate African heritages in art, music and sports. Such policies and programs must be evidence-based. Their effectiveness must have been proven through randomized control trials and other rigorous research. This book offers a full menu of policy choices that meet this test, as detailed in each of the chapters that follow.

1.3 Gaps in the existing literature

There is a vast volume of literature on the subject of unemployment in Africa. It seems, however, that the literature has yet to capture the reality of joblessness on the ground—at least well enough to resonate with the feeling of ordinary Africans. It also seems that the literature has yet to provide a firm basis for the formulation of policies that are strong and effective enough to address decisively the joblessness among the youth in Africa. There may be two main reasons for this.

First, the literature has predominantly adopted the standard ILO definition of unemployment, which defines unemployment rather narrowly. The ILO defines a person as unemployed if (i) the person is of or above the minimum employment age and is actively looking for a job (as evidenced for example by registration at employment centres); (ii) the person is available for work; and (iii) the person has not worked during a given reference period. In most African countries, many individuals, particularly women, are discouraged from actively looking for a paid job due to social exclusion. And there are not many employment centres in non-urban areas.

But the fact is that, because most of them are poor, and because unemployment compensation and other public social protection schemes are largely absent, almost everyone has to work, even though he or she earns very little or has to work under very poor conditions. It is for these reasons that the standard ILO definition substantially understates the true extent of joblessness in Africa, particularly Sub-Saharan Africa. For example, unemployment is reported at 6 per cent in Ethiopia, 6.5 per cent in Ghana and 13 per cent in Kenya—but these figures do not resonate well with the reality (see Chapters 4–7).

Second, most of the earlier empirical studies on unemployment in Africa have keyed off from labour market theories designed to analyze the classical employment seen in economically developed economies. However, the unemployment dynamics in Africa differs qualitatively from that of the economically developed countries. In Chapter 2, Ranis and Gollin cite the Fei–Ranis model to explain that in an economically developing economy, the labour market is composed of two segments. One is the modern sector where wages adjust to clear the market but unemployment arises from search processes, information asymmetry, etc. The other is the traditional sector (e.g. subsistence agriculture) where all available able-bodied people work with limited land and capital even if there is not enough work to engage everyone fully. They are paid by the average product, rather than marginal product as in the case of classical employment. In this sector no-one is 'unemployed,' but everyone is 'underemployed' from not being engaged fully—some working less than full-time hours while others are working long hours with low productivity.

Although underemployment is far more prevalent than unemployment in Sub-Saharan Africa, there has been little rigorous empirical research geared to understanding the mechanisms of underemployment. Such mechanisms would centrally involve the communal land ownership, the informal social protection based on kinship, and the perpetual supply of a large pool of labour force with limited human capital.

African governments have undertaken a host of interventions that address aspects of underemployment (e.g. low productivity in subsistence farming, inadequate educational attainment). However, most of those interventions appear to have been less effective than intended. In Chapter 3, Bertrand and Crépon introduce a number of recent and ongoing projects that are based on rigorous research and appear to hold good prospects of ameliorating underemployment and unemployment in Sub-Saharan Africa.

Most recently, the World Bank, the African Development Bank, the ILO and other multilateral agencies have issued several major reports that have significantly advanced our understanding of joblessness in the world and in Africa in particular, and of what to do about it. Three of those reports are highlighted below.

World Development Report (2012): Gender Equality and Development (Chapter 5)

Chapter 5 of this report, which is on 'Gender differences in employment and why they matter,' contains discussions directly relevant to employment issues in Sub-Saharan Africa. The chapter focuses on productivity and earnings, and also gender differences in access to employment opportunities. The report argues that participation in market work is not just a simple decision on whether or not to join the labour force, but is about reallocating time across a number of activities, which can be difficult and costly, particularly for women. Despite significant progress in female labour participation, pervasive and persistent gender differences remain in productivity and earnings across different sectors and jobs. Although women's earnings and productivity may be lower, women are not worse farmers, entrepreneurs and workers than men.

The report notes that men's and women's jobs differ, and it appears that women are concentrated in low-productivity jobs. They work in small farms and firms, and are disproportionately involved in unpaid family work and in the informal sector. The interaction of segregation with gender differences in time use, access to inputs and markets, on one hand, and institutional failures on the other hand, trap women in low-paying jobs and low-productivity businesses. Moving out of this trap would require measures that reduce women's time constraints, increase women's access to productive inputs, and deal with market and institutional failures.

The report further notes that the systematic gender differences in productivity and earnings could be explained by differences in characteristics of female and male workers, differences in the types of activities and jobs that women and men do, and also differences in the returns to both worker and job characteristics. Because education and work experience are valuable inputs into production, gender differences in education and work experience contribute to differences in productivity and earnings.

World Development Report 2013: Jobs

This report addresses the critical role of jobs in the development process. About 50 per cent of workers in developing countries are in small-scale farming or self-employment, and these do not provide a regular or steady or stable income. Jobs are instrumental to achieving economic and social development. Besides contributing to wellbeing, jobs contribute to poverty reduction, productivity growth and social cohesion.

The report argues that technological progress expands the possibilities for emerging and even low-income countries to create jobs in higher-skilled production activities, as well as to link to international value chains in services and manufacturing. However, due to changes in technology and the organization of work, permanent jobs are becoming less common. Part-time and temporary wage employment is now a major feature of industrial countries. These countries are focusing on services and knowledge-intensive activities while other activities are outsourced to developing countries. Demography, urbanization, globalization, technological progress and macroeconomic crises are posing major challenges.

The report highlights that even though jobs tend to increase life satisfaction, there are jobs that affect people's health and safety. In addition, some jobs have low earnings (below the poverty line) and hence create working poor. Moreover, work across the developing world is characterized by a high prevalence of informality. Fewer than half of women have jobs compared with almost four-fifths of men, and youth unemployment is generally high. The prospect for employment generation lies with the private sector—about nine out of ten jobs in the world are in the private sector.

The report adds that exchanges and relationships established through jobs can have broader effects on societies, including how they manage tensions between groups and collective decision-making. Some jobs contribute more than others to social cohesion. What matters is not necessarily whether people have a job, but whether the job and its characteristics can contribute to social cohesion. Jobs that influence social identity, build networks and improve transparency and fairness serve to reduce tensions. Thus jobs with the greatest developmental payoffs are those that make cities function better, link the economy with global value chains, protect the environment, enhance trust and civil networks, and reduce poverty.

The report addresses the question of whether countries should focus on growth strategies or job strategies; it is in favour of a growth strategy, but with a stipulation that this may not be sufficient. A job strategy may be more appropriate when potentially important spillovers from jobs are not realized, leading to tensions between living standards, productivity and social cohesion. Entrepreneurship should be fostered not only because markets tend to fail to nurture entrepreneurship, but also because at present the large numbers of unregistered self-employed in developing countries are viewed as subsistence entrepreneurs.

The report argues for adoption of a three-layered policy approach to creating jobs. The first approach is to create a policy environment that is conducive to growth by ensuring macroeconomic stability, an enabling business environment, human capital investments and the rule of the law. The second approach is for governments to ensure that labour policies do not hinder job creation but rather enhance development payoffs from jobs. The third and final approach is to remove market imperfections and institutional failures that prevent the private sector from creating more good jobs for development.

African Economic Outlook 2012: special theme: promoting youth employment

By African Development Bank, OECD, UNDP and United Nations Economic Commission for Africa

This report argues that the continent is facing a youth bulge, which can be positive or negative depending on how it is handled. It could be an opportunity for economic and social development, or a significant risk and threat to social cohesion and political stability. We should focus on youth employment because 60 per cent of Africa's unemployed are young people, and youth unemployment rates are double those of adult unemployment in most African countries. The youth employment challenge has largely been underestimated because past reports on this subject focused on unemployment per se, and did not sufficiently acknowledge the discouraged, inactive, underemployed, vulnerably employed and the working poor.

The report notes that unemployment is, and will persist as, a major issue in Africa. It argues that youth employment is largely a problem of quality in low-income countries and of quantity in middle-income countries. Many of the jobs available in developing countries are of poor quality. Most of the younger workers in Africa are in family-based agriculture, services and sales, while 13 per cent are business owners. The report adds that, given the few prospects for expansion in the public sector, the answer lies with the private sector in creating new jobs. Attention should be focused on informal and rural sectors of the economy as these will be the sources of new employment.

The report addresses the causes of unemployment, which range from insufficient labour demand, inadequate skills, lack of knowledge about where to find a job, insufficient education, skills mismatch, demand–supply matching, labour market regulation, and attitudes of young people, amongst others. The report argues that most governments' programs on promoting youth employment have not been successful. The most common have been those addressing labour supply and skills training.

The report recommends better coordination of government action, improved availability and quality of employment data, addressing bottlenecks constraining labour demand, and helping young people obtain the necessary skills. Other recommended actions include expanding education beyond primary schooling, more rigorous evaluation of programs, and more labour market information.

The above reports largely corroborate findings of this book, particularly as regards the imperative of covering unemployment issues more broadly than hitherto; acknowledgment of the dominance of informal sectors; and the centrality of raising productivity and human capital. Nevertheless, the apparent preference in favour of market principle in the recommendations of World Development Report 2013 must be interrogated in the specific context of Sub-Saharan Africa. *African Economic Outlook* approaches the subject basically as a labour market issue, and hence largely misses macroanalysis. None of the reports draw extensively from recent and ongoing research.

This book, for its part, focuses on Sub-Saharan Africa, building on in-depth studies of four major African countries to show that joblessness in Africa cannot be understood in isolation of poverty itself.

1.4 Organization and summary

This book is composed of two parts. Part I contains two chapters on reviews of literature, global practices, recent and ongoing research, and possible remedies—one on macroeconomic perspectives (Chapter 2), the other on microeconomic perspectives (Chapter 3). Part II consists of four in-depth country studies of youth unemployment—on Ethiopia (Chapter 4), Ghana (Chapter 5), Kenya (Chapter 6) and South Africa (Chapter 7).

In Chapter 2, Ranis and Gollin explore macroeconomic perspectives of youth employment in Sub-Saharan Africa. The authors focus on underemployment rather than classical unemployment because the former is much more prevalent than the latter in Sub-Saharan Africa. They draw on the modern–traditional-sector dual economy models of Fei–Ranis and Harris–Todaro to illustrate the typical structure of labour markets in Sub-Saharan Africa and underemployment that arises from it. The authors then explain that, in most of Sub-Saharan Africa, the labour market structure consists of agriculture, rural household enterprise, the urban informal sector and the urban formal sector. The authors argue that the urban informal sector is not a temporary phenomenon, but a permanent and growing feature. The urban formal sector, on the other hand, is a small but rapidly growing sector that relies on wage employment and is comprised of the private formal sector and the public formal sector. The authors also argue that large fractions of the workforce in Sub-Saharan Africa are engaged in self-employment in which disguised unemployment and underemployment are the norm. Migration patterns, income distribution and other subjects are also discussed as they are crucial to designing macroeconomic policies for addressing economic growth and employment creation.

Ranis and Gollin draw on lessons from Asia and South America and experiences of some projects in Africa, and propose a range of policy recommendations. The authors argue that strong growth is imperative to reducing underemployment and raising wages, and hence should form the pillar of long-term employment policy. Some of the policies include building a supportive environment for entrepreneurship, expanding access to tertiary/vocational education, initiating infrastructure projects, and reducing gender discrimination, amongst others. The authors argue that the government should promote rural household enterprises through microfinance interventions, designing specific programs that enable informal firms to become more productive and increasing the innovative components of the urban informal sector.

In Chapter 3, Bertrand and Crépon give an extensive overview of the microeconomics literature on youth unemployment and low productivity. A number of completed and ongoing studies are reviewed, and concrete and useful findings are offered. Inherent in the chapter is the premise that youth capabilities are fundamental to the problem of low productivity. The authors stress that skills development and education are important for fostering employability. There is a mismatch between the skills needed by employers and the skills provided by the educational systems in many African countries, but there is little empirical evidence on how to address this problem. The primary school literature suggests that provision of inputs alone is inadequate. Thus the need exists to focus on teacher incentives and accountability. The authors note that information flow is critical to linking potential employers and employees. Also, restrictive government regulations and other structural barriers are given as constraints to a well functioning labour market. The authors argue that strong labour market regulations and other distortions due to unionization and collective bargaining are constraining labour market flexibility.

Bertrand and Crépon observe that literature on integration of youth into the labour market is limited. Some of the measures discussed are apprenticeships, temporary or permanent migration to where job opportunities are, and financial literacy training. The available evidence does not find the provision of employment subsidies to be an effective policy. Rigorous evaluations on the impact of providing credit (such as microcredit) have produced disappointing results, although work on promoting savings and more innovative credit instruments are somewhat more encouraging. As regards public works programs, the authors find mixed results, and note that such programs do not necessarily foster long-term employability. The authors recommend randomized evaluations for testing improvements in the design of public work programs. In addition, they recommend some policy measures to reduce information imperfections, such as more effective use of information communication technologies. Little evidence is available on how to integrate youth in post-conflict countries, with the exception of Liberia, where provision of agricultural training to ex-combatants had positive economic effects. Lastly, the authors note that contextual differences between labour markets in North African economies and Sub-Saharan Africa, and between South Africa and the rest of Africa, are important in designing country-specific interventions.

Turning to Part II, the country studies review the conditions and causes of unemployment, and the strategies and policies that have been implemented to address the unemployment problem. The country studies show that 'unemployment' of youth is far more extensive than indicated in previous reports, essentially because those reports were based on the ILO definition of employment. The country studies also show that the issues are far more complex because unemployment or underemployment is fundamentally interwoven with poverty in the country. For example, malnutrition and poor health during early childhood inhibit development of cognitive and non-cognitive skills—the very basis of human capital—as children grow to youth and adulthood. With limited development of human capital, the productivity of a large majority of the youth is adequate only to obtain meagre earnings from any job they can find. Also, because of poverty, a large proportion of children (ages 5–15) work, and many of them work long hours.

The case studies show that labour market characteristics differ significantly between Ethiopia, Ghana and Kenya on one hand, and South Africa on the other. Agriculture remains the chief economic activity in Kenya (25 per cent of GDP), Ethiopia (40 per cent) and Ghana (about 28 per cent), while South Africa has large mining and extractive industries as well as relatively large manufacturing and services sectors. In South Africa, the informal sector is very small (about 6 per cent) in sharp contrast to the situation in Ethiopia (90 per cent), Ghana (86 per cent) and Kenya (81 per cent). Similarly, the extent of labour market regulations and unionization varies among the four countries. In South Africa entry and exit are perceived to be highly rigid, and labour unions are powerful. In contrast, in Ethiopia the large size of the informal sector and low level of wage employment give labour unions low bargaining power. Similarly, in Ghana the large informal sector means that labour regulations are weakly enforced. Much of employment in South Africa could be considered as vulnerable if safety and other working conditions in mining industries are taken into account in judging the quality of work. All the country studies show that men have more employment opportunities than women, even among the youth.

In Chapter 4 (Ethiopia), Nzinga *et al.* stress that Ethiopia's 'employment problem' is a deficiency of good jobs. Ethiopia faces a significant structural deficit—the result of two-and-a-half decades of lack of industrialization. Without an acceleration of structural change, Ethiopia's recent growth turnaround runs the risk of not creating enough good jobs. Investment climate reforms are essential, and Ethiopia's growing infrastructure gap should be addressed. A strategy for industrial development will be needed, focusing on three interrelated objectives—creating an export push, building firm capabilities, and supporting agglomerations—to boost the creation of good jobs for Ethiopian workers. In the short run, active labour market policies can be used to increase the employability of young workers. Such policies could include job-search assistance, employability training, public support for apprenticeship and internship programs, on-the-job training subsidies, and perhaps, entrepreneurship initiatives targeted at the young. In the longer run, labour regulations that determine social insurance contributions and protect job security may need to be changed. The education system must be restructured to build the skills needed to compete globally, largely through further increases in access to post-primary education.

In Chapter 5 (Ghana), Aryeetey *et al.* argue that the real labour market challenges confronting the youth are seen clearly when the discussion goes beyond the traditional measure of unemployment. The success of being able to address the real challenges facing young people depends in large part on the investments that have been made in their health, education and skills development. Looking forward, in the short term the youth with limited or no formal education and employable skills could be absorbed through public works programs, with the opportunity for them to benefit from skill training. Skills mismatches could be reduced by effective collaboration between industrial practitioners and academic and training institutions. Introduction of entrepreneurship in education curricula and effective collaboration between successful entrepreneurs and educational and training institutions will raise entrepreneurial consciousness among the youth. In the medium-to-long term, public investment targeted at high labour-absorption sectors of agriculture, manufacturing and tourism will be essential. In the long term, Ghana should consider the formulation of a long-term national development strategy that emphasizes the generation of decent and productive employment with manufacturing as the focus, with a view to transforming the economy. This should be informed by research to identify relevant and productive industries in manufacturing.

In Chapter 6 (Kenya), Munga *et al.* summarize the youth employment and joblessness challenge as follows: (i) about 24 per cent of youths have ‘poor-quality jobs,’ working either more than 65 hours or less than 29 hours per week; (ii) about 11 per cent of all youth are inactive (excluding those in school); and (iii) about 7 per cent of youth are openly unemployed. The authors also highlight that an estimated 3.8 million children (aged 5–14 years) work, about half of whom work more than 65 hours a week. This implies that a large share of children will grow into youths with little prospect of gaining a decent job. The authors note that in Kenya, the youth rely predominantly on informal channels in job search, which means that those with weak social networks will likely remain continually disadvantaged in accessing decent employment. The authors also point out that education attainment seems to be a good predictor of employment outcome. For example, about 90 per cent of employed primary school graduates were engaged in vulnerable jobs, but this ratio was only 21 per cent for university graduates. The authors offer a full range of policy recommendations, including ‘second-chance education programs’ for the youth who have not completed primary school, and targeted social protection for poor and vulnerable groups so children can attend school, and so young people can acquire the skills required to obtain decent jobs.

In Chapter 7 (South Africa), Abel *et al.* stress that only partial answers can be found to some questions regarding the current knowledge of the nature of South African unemployment, the costs and benefits of current labour regulation, as well as the effectiveness of existing active labour market policies. While there has been a lot of debate over labour market policies, few randomized control trials have been conducted outside the public health sector. This fact stands in contrast to the extensive empirical literature on conditions of unemployment and employment that has been produced in South Africa over the past two decades. The authors recommend that policymakers focus on interventions that target unskilled and semi-skilled, poor workers, and that lend themselves to testing through randomized control trials. They stress that this is important because the most cost-effective ways to improve employment are not always to tackle the biggest obstacle. Comparisons that identify the most cost-effective way of addressing a specific policy objective are particularly useful for policymakers who work within limited budgets. The authors examine a large number of interventions that can be considered for implementation, and group them into three categories according to how firm the knowledge base is (robust, suggestive and limited). They then recommend a small number of concrete, practical, carefully thought-out measures for implementation, in each of the three categories.

The main policy implication arising from the four case studies is that if the challenges of underemployment and disguised unemployment of the youth are to be addressed successfully, African governments would have to adopt a holistic approach that would encompass the following: (i) pro-employment macroeconomic policies (e.g. more emphasis on public investment in small holder agriculture); (ii) encouragement of informal sectors (e.g. more supportive infrastructure, microfinance); (iii) social safety nets for the poor to ensure adequate nutrition and health care in early childhood as well as completion of primary school and beyond (e.g. cash transfer programs); (iv) skills development and education that better match employers' requirements (e.g. curriculum reforms, vouchers for vocational schools, internships); (v) encouragement of diverse talents (e.g. entrepreneurship, art and sports); and (vi) more efficient functioning of the labour market (e.g. financial assistance to facilitate job search). As it may take some time for the above measures to bear fruit, some temporary interventions (e.g. internship programs in private companies facilitated by the public sector) may be required as stop-gap measures to contain rising discontent among the youth.

Part I

Review of literature and global practices

2 Macroeconomic perspectives

*Gustav Ranis and Douglas Gollin**

2.1 Introduction and background

This chapter reviews macroeconomic perspectives on youth underemployment in Sub-Saharan Africa. We focus on underemployment, rather than classical unemployment, because relatively few people in Sub-Saharan Africa fit the standard definitions of unemployment. Almost everyone works in some fashion, but many individuals (including many young people) earn their living from self-employment or family business. This complicates notions of labour force participation and unemployment. Our chapter examines conceptual, theoretical and empirical frameworks for thinking about the causes of youth underemployment, and it discusses some macro and micro policies that may help alleviate the problem.

By some measures, one in five Africans between the ages of 15 and 24 is underemployed, although estimates differ widely.[1] Moreover, many of these youths are experiencing long and persistent spells of underemployment, which are likely to have long-term impacts on their labour market outcomes. Youth underemployment differs significantly between urban and rural areas, between young men and young women, and between those with different educational levels.

Our goal in this chapter is not to duplicate previous efforts. Instead, we seek to focus on the policy challenges that result from the youth employment situation. Our starting point is an understanding that youth unemployment in Africa differs markedly from the problems of unemployment in most advanced countries. In particular, underemployment is far more prevalent than unemployment *per se*, as poverty forces most Africans to find work of some kind. Data show that underemployment is concentrated in rural areas, both in agriculture and rural non-agriculture and in the urban informal sector. Some argue that unemployment has been due to slow growth—but in fact growth has been fairly robust despite recent economic downturns in the developed world.

In our view, youth underemployment in Africa is best viewed as a problem related to the structural characteristics of poor African economies, rather than as a business-cycle phenomenon. As a result, many of the policy responses that are appropriate in advanced economies (e.g. programs designed to address temporary employment shocks) may be less useful in Sub-Saharan countries. As we review policies and programs that might alleviate the problems of youth underemployment, we argue that the principal challenge is to create high-quality jobs through economic growth.

This chapter is organized as follows. Section 1 reviews some background information about youth underemployment in Africa. Section 2 reviews descriptive data on structure, prevalence and characteristics of youth underemployment in Africa through an analytical framework. Section 3 despribes previous macroeconomic experiences and is complemented by Section 4, which introduces micro foundational policy experiences of selected countries that have had different degrees of success in their efforts to limit and manage youth underemployment. Section 5 draws on the lessons learnt from developing countries in Asia and South America. Last but not least, Section 6 offers policy recommendations and Section 7 concludes.

2.1.1 Today's African youth

Africa's youth population is the key to understanding both the continent's current economic difficulties and the best ways to ensure that African economies continue to improve their citizens' standards of living. Over 60 per cent of Africa's population currently falls between the ages of 15 and 24—that number is projected to rise to 75 per cent by 2015, thanks to a high fertility rate (*African Economic Outlook*, 2008). It is estimated that 72 per cent of the youth population subsists on under US$2 a day and, despite continued rural–urban migration, over 70 per cent of the African youth population still lives in rural areas (Zuehlke, 2009).

African labour markets—already hamstrung by poor policymaking, corruption, conflict and diseases such as malaria and HIV/AIDS—have been overwhelmed by the youth bulge and are unable to provide formal employment opportunities for much of today's youth. According to a World Bank report, 6 per cent of young men and over 10 per cent of young women are underemployed in Tanzania, while the average underemployment rate reaches 16 per cent in Burkina Faso (Garcia and Fares, 2008). In Ethiopia, the problem of underemployment is especially serious in rural areas, where the average working time is only 30 hours per week. Overall, according to a Gallup poll, the underemployed constitute 29 per cent of men and 34 per cent of women in Sub-Saharan African countries, where the rate is generally higher for young workers (Marler, 2011). Each year, there will be as many as 8.7 million new labour-market entrants for whom jobs will have to be found (UNECA, 2002).

2.1.2 Theories of employment and unemployment in developing economies

Why do youth unemployment and underemployment exist, and why are they so pervasive in African economies? Neoclassical theory suggests that this kind of unemployment should not exist; fully flexible wages should adjust to clear the labour market, leaving only some short-term structural unemployment among people moving from one job to another. But clearly this is not happening today in African economies. Large numbers of workers find themselves without sufficient work, and many seem to face lengthy spells of underemployment.

How should we conceptualize the types of unemployment that characterize African economies? The literature offers a number of useful conceptual frameworks. A recurring theme is that unemployment in developing countries is typically not viewed as a short-run business-cycle phenomenon, as it is in rich countries; instead, it is seen as a fundamental characteristic of labour markets.

The Fei–Ranis and Harris–Todaro models

Although the literature has grown immensely in the past several decades, it is still strikingly useful to conceptualize employment and unemployment in Africa through the lens of the Fei–Ranis model, which built on the earlier work of W. Arthur Lewis. The Fei–Ranis model represents a poor developing economy as essentially dualistic, with a traditional sector and a modern sector. The traditional sector has very low productivity, and it corresponds roughly to the rural farm and non-farm sector and to the urban informal sector. The modern sector would include any modern formal sector manufacturing and services, plus the government sector. The modern private sector is modelled as an approximately neoclassical sector, in terms of the supply and demand for labour; within the modern private sector, workers are paid their marginal product and the market is competitive.

In contrast, the traditional sector is characterized by a sharing rule in which output is pooled to some degree within households, family networks and even village communities. This suggests that individual workers receive the average product of labour rather than the (substantially lower) marginal product. This in turn suggests that the marginal product in rural areas may be much lower than that in the urban formal sector, even with free labour mobility. A potential migrant compares his or her wage in the modern sector with the *average* product of the traditional sector, rather than with the *marginal* product.

Moreover, in the traditional sector, long-run Malthusian forces will tend to drive the average product close to subsistence levels. As long as the average product is greater than the subsistence level, survival rates will remain high. When average product falls below the subsistence level, Malthusian forces of death and disease, combined perhaps with outmigration, will tend to restore an equilibrium in which the traditional sector operates with average product close to subsistence.

Thus in the Fei–Ranis model underemployment is associated with the traditional sector. Within that sector, labour demand can be highly seasonal, leading to periods of slack. Labour demand may also be spatially uneven, as year-to-year variations in rainfall or market conditions may shift the need for agricultural work from one location to another.

Underemployment also characterizes the urban informal sector, which operates effectively as part of the traditional sector. Families and kinship networks may share output, so it is not uncommon to find some individuals productively and gainfully employed (e.g. as shopkeepers or craftsmen) while others look for work, perform casual labour, or take on self-employment tasks with very low entry costs but also low sales prospects (e.g. shoe shining, food selling or roadside marketing).

In the Fei–Ranis model, growth involves parallel improvements in the traditional and modern sectors. Increases in agricultural productivity can generate surpluses that sustain investment in the modern sector; capital inflows and investments in the modern sector create jobs and labour demand that draw people in from the traditional sector.

This model suggests that underemployment can best be reduced through growth-oriented policies that support the structural transformation of the economy, and ultimately the expansion of the modern sector.

A slightly different, but related, view of unemployment is offered by the Harris–Todaro model, in which migration from a low-productivity rural sector to a high-productivity organized urban sector takes place even with high levels of urban underemployment. In this framework, potential migrants compare the expected payoffs of migration with the certain returns of remaining in rural areas. Because there is some probability that they will (eventually) receive a high-paying job in the urban formal sector, it is rational for individuals to migrate even though they may end up, *ex post*, underemployed. In this model, underemployment is primarily an urban phenomenon that reflects unsuccessful migration. The presumption is that there is some kind of queuing or lottery for jobs in the urban formal sector. A presupposition of this model is that there is some kind of fixed wage in the urban formal sector supported by minimum-wage legislation, unions or government wage-setting, and that those who queue for the limited jobs in this sector occupy themselves while waiting in the urban informal sector.

If the Harris–Todaro model is valid, underemployment could be alleviated by reducing over-regulation and price controls in the labour market. We take up the question of the impact of over-regulation in greater detail below.

An alteration of this model was introduced after observing that migration from rural to urban areas increased while urban–rural wage differentials decreased. Deploying case studies from four Sub-Saharan countries, including Uganda, Tanzania, Nigeria and Sierra Leone, Jamal and Weeks demonstrated a more complex rural–urban interaction mechanism in which the primary distributional relationship of labour is between the rich and poor within both urban and rural sectors (Jamal and Weeks, 1988). They argue that in times of recession, all low-income residents such as unskilled income earners (farmers on smallholdings) suffer from falling real incomes and hence seek employment in other sectors in order to ensure survival. In other words, poor rural households will settle for employment in the urban informal sector while low-income urban residents partially support their livelihoods through agriculture.

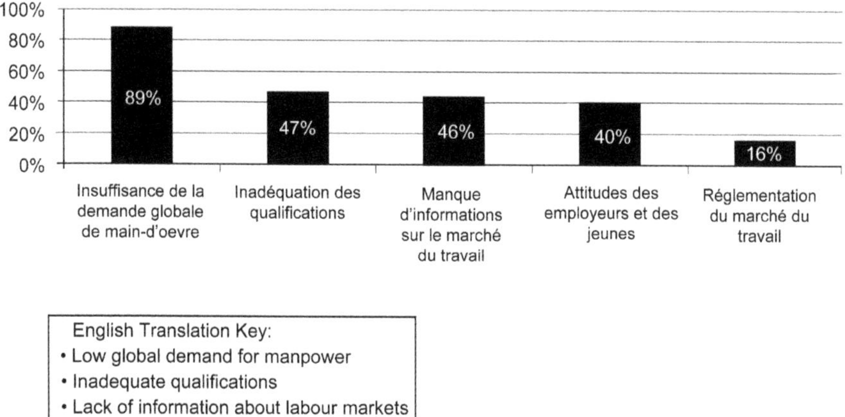

Figure 2.1 Country estimates as the most difficult obstacle (2012)
Source: African Economic Outlook 2012—Promoting Youth Employment, OECD Publishing. http://dx.doi.org/10.1787/aeo-2012-en.

Considering the alternative model, measures to empower the poor and alleviate income inequality between households in general would be the preferred policy.

In practice, evidence from the *African Economic Outlook* Country Experts Study demonstrates that youth face entry barriers, but the biggest obstacle is insufficient aggregate demand for labour (89 per cent; see Figure 2.1).

2.1.3 Demand–supply framework of employment

A simple explanation of the underemployment situation is that economic growth and the induced demand for labour have been insufficient to keep up with the growth in labour supply. Equation 2.1 captures this relationship.

$$\frac{\textit{output growth}}{\textit{total population}} = \frac{\textit{output growth}}{\textit{total employment}} + \frac{\textit{total employment growth}}{\textit{total population}}$$

Creating employment for those willing to work more implies an increase in the ratio of employed persons to the total population, whereas increasing productivity is equivalent to raising output per employed person. Summing these two objectives results in growth in output per capita. This growth indicates that a higher real output per labourer growth provides for a greater capacity for the economy to increase employment and/or increase productivity.

In other words, a strong real growth is imperative to reducing underemployment and raising wages, and should form the pillar of long-term employment policy. According to Equation 2.1, it is of equal importance to maintain moderate levels of population growth to prevent explosive expansion of the labour force to offset growth.

In practice, Sub-Saharan Africa has kept up with the world average annual gross national income (GNI) growth at about 4–5 per cent excluding the period of the 2008–09 global financial crises. Its population growth, however, has been almost double that of the rest of the world, which consequently leads to a significantly lower GNI per capita growth, as shown in Table 2.1.

In the classic growth models of Solow (1956) and Swan (1956), investment in capital affects steady-state income levels. Some empirical studies have also argued that investment rates are a significant determinant of the rate of GDP growth (Ghura and Hadjimichael, 1996; Collier and Gunning, 1999), although the direction of causation is unclear. In the case of Sub-Saharan Africa in particular, international comparison reveals that investment rates are lower than in other regions of the developing world. During the 1990s, investment as a ratio of GDP remained at 17 per cent, which was below both Latin America with 20–22 per cent and Asia with 27–29 per cent (World Bank, 2005). Sub-Saharan Africa had lower levels of private investment as well, with a mere 13.8 per cent relative to 16 and 18 per cent in Latin America and Asia, respectively (World Bank, 2005). Promoting investment, particularly private investment, will create long-run growth and investment in labour-intensive sectors, and can potentially increase employment opportunities, including those for youth.

Consequently, creating an environment conducive to private investment is a key strategy for generating more employment opportunities. One important factor is lowering the economic and political risk for investors and entrepreneurs (Collier and Pattillo, 2000). In addition to maintaining macroeconomic stability, this requires fighting corruption and enhancing microfoundations. These measures are elaborated in later sections.

Table 2.1 Annual growth (percentage) 2002–10

	Region/ year	*2002*	*2003*	*2004*	*2005*	*2006*	*2007*	*2008*	*2009*	*2010*
Population	SSA	2.52	2.51	2.50	2.50	2.49	2.49	2.49	2.49	2.50
	World	1.24	1.22	1.21	1.20	1.19	1.18	1.18	1.17	1.15
GNI	SSA	3.37	3.03	5.19	5.58	5.49	5.10	4.15	1.68	4.19
	World	1.68	2.77	4.27	3.67	4.35	3.49	1.20	−2.57	4.55
GNI per capita	SSA	0.83	0.50	2.62	3.01	2.92	2.55	1.61	−0.80	1.65
	World	0.43	1.53	3.02	2.44	3.12	2.28	0.02	−3.69	3.35

Source: World Bank (2012d).

2.1.4 Categorizing Sub-Saharan African countries

It is impossible to speak of the 'typical' Sub-Saharan African economy—Africa's geography, politics and natural resources vary too dramatically for a one-size-fits-all characterization of the continent's economic prospects. However, it is useful to think of typologies of countries with certain useful similarities that allow for the broad economic analyses that are crucial for policymakers. The challenge, then, is to create a method of categorization that is both reasonably nuanced and plastic enough to be generalizable across different countries.

The Collier–O'Connell classification is a step in the right direction. By distinguishing between resource-rich, coastal and landlocked countries, this approach takes into account the macroeconomic features of geographic location and how natural resource abundance (or lack thereof) influences the labour market structure in terms of modes of employment.

Resource-rich countries

Resource-rich countries are often mineral and petroleum exporters; they potentially attract the lion's share of foreign direct investment. The government may also collect resource rents, providing revenue for undertaking employment and growth-boosting measures.

However, resource rents also provide a means for officials to divert public revenue for their own private spending. In fact, resource rents have been shown to correlate positively with corruption (Collier and Hoeffler, 2005). It is therefore especially important for countries rich in natural resources to develop a strong rule of law that governs the allocation of public spending.

Statistically, Botswana is the only resource-rich country in Sub-Saharan Africa that successfully capitalized on its endowment (Box 2.1), while most other countries have failed to allocate public spending optimally. Consequently, though having the potential for better development, resource-rich countries are, on average, less efficient in generating formal employment and labour absorption.

Box 2.1 Botswana—good economics and good politics

From 1965 through 1995, Botswana was the fastest-growing country in the world. Over three decades it sustained an annual growth rate of 7.7 per cent and developed from being one of the poorest countries to being an upper-middle-income nation.

The unparalleled growth is unlikely to have resulted only from the discovery of diamonds alone as other African countries, such as Nigeria, Sierra Leone and the Democratic Republic of Congo, failed to grow on a similar scale despite their rich endowments. One important distinction is that the Botswana government escaped from the resource curse and practiced good governance. It values property rights, respects the rule of law and maintains a high degree of transparency. This is evident in its continuation of the tribal tradition of consultation, which reinforced people's trust in the government to act in the interest of the people.

Moreover, prudent macroeconomic policies alleviated the pressure of an appreciating exchange rate common to mineral-based countries and prevented the notorious Dutch disease effect. High fiscal savings limited current consumption and curbed domestic price inflation. The savings were partially channeled to develop public goods like human capital and infrastructure, which raised productivity without crowding out private investment. The accumulation of savings itself also served as insurance against negative shocks in mineral production. Consequently, Botswana enjoyed relative macroeconomic stability and growth without the high volatilities of other mineral-rich countries.

Finally, Botswana opted against import substitution policies and maintained a minimal extent of state-owned productive entities, which employ only about 5 per cent of the labour force. This restricted the avenues for rent-seeking and corruption, thereby ensuring the efficiency of resource allocation and the integrity of the government.

Source: Adapted from Lewin (2011)

Coastal countries

Although there are some variations across countries, distance from primary markets and high transport intensities of products are shown to be the main impediments to trade (Esfahani and Ramirez, 2003). This puts landlocked countries at a disadvantage relative to the coastal countries. Limão and Venables (2001) find that a typical Sub-Saharan landlocked country has 50 per cent higher transportation costs and 60 per cent less trade volume than a typical coastal country. Therefore, due to lower transport costs, coastal countries tend to enjoy a net comparative advantage in producing and exporting manufactured goods, which tend to belong to the formal sector. In addition, coastal countries also tend to do better in absorbing labour through sub-coastal contracting, which links formal sector industries to the urban informal sector labour force. Mauritius, for example, successfully followed the Asian example in producing manufactured goods; in doing so, it was able to transform itself from an underdeveloped sugar economy into Africa's richest country (Box 2.2).

Box 2.2 Export-led growth in Mauritius

In spite of its small economic size and low endowment of natural resources, coastal Mauritius has transformed itself from a poor sugar economy into one of the most successful economies in Africa, largely through reliance on trade-led development. Real GDP growth averaged more than 5 per cent between 1970 and 2009, while GDP per capita has increased more than tenfold over the same period.

In the 1970s, Mauritius capitalized on its coastal location to expand the sugar export sector, which once accounted for close to one-third of employment and one-quarter of GDP. With the collapse in international sugar prices, however, Mauritius' policymakers realized the limit of the sugar sector and put forth the idea of developing an export-oriented textile industry following the successful East Asian example. In order to expand export competitiveness on world markets and incentivize manufacturers, new legislations granting duty-free inputs for manufactured exports were passed. Export processing zones (EPZ), with relatively low-cost labour drawn from originally underemployed and unemployed workers, were established. By the 1980s, EPZs accounted for more than 60 per cent of gross export earnings and employed one-third of the labour force. In terms of share of GDP, goods produced in EPZs more than tripled between 1980 and 1988, from 4 per cent to more than 14 per cent. Together with the sugar sector, the textile sector provided the capital accumulation that allowed Mauritius to decrease reliance on foreign capital and start down the path to becoming a middle-income economy. More recently, the Mauritian government has introduced offshore banking and logistics facilities in an effort to boost service exports and transform itself into a trans-shipment center and re-export base.

The development story of the three export-oriented sectors reveals that Mauritius' success was attributable not only to its geographic advantage, but also to the ability to capitalize on the opportunities provided by its favorable coastal location. In addition to promoting export industries, policymakers have early on recognized the vulnerabilities of an export-dependent country to fluctuations in commodity prices and demand. In response, flexible development strategies were devised to ensure successful adaption to a changing world economy.

Last, but not least, proper macroeconomic management—fiscal discipline during boom times, monetary management that kept inflation in the single digits and that produced interest rates that encouraged domestic savings, and an exchange-rate policy that maintained flexibility and competitiveness for exporters—have also been vital for Mauritius' economic success.

Source: Partially adapted from Zafar (2011)

Landlocked countries

For landlocked countries, geographic isolation must not imply economic isolation. They should learn from their European counterpart Switzerland, which successfully exploited its geographic handicap by acting as a transit country for neighboring countries. This will require the development of up-to-date transport and service infrastructure such as railway lines, highways and airports, which in turn create labour demand through public works. The infrastructure upgrade should go hand-in-hand with policy measures reducing port and customs delay. A deeper regional integration through establishing multilateral agreements is an effective means to avoid lengthy clearance procedures, high fees and corruption by customs officials.[2] Eventually, transport costs for exports will be reduced while the logistics sector creates employment opportunities.

Moreover, landlocked countries should adjust trade policies to focus on sectors less constrained by transport costs, such as the labour-intensive service sector. The adoption of information and communications technology (ICT), for example, enables specific services to be traded or off-shored without the need for using traditional transport modes (Box 2.3). Landlocked countries in Sub-Saharan Africa dedicated to developing good ICT frameworks have much potential to follow the successful example of India, where ICT-related industries have increased annual GDP growth by 0.2 to 0.6 per cent (Cali *et al.*, 2008).

Box 2.3 Mobile payment in Uganda

Uganda is a low-income landlocked agricultural country in East Africa, which once had one of the lowest telephone penetration rates in the world. This changed when the government privatized the telecom sector to attract foreign investment and boost economic growth. After the first two private mobile service operators, CelTel and MTN, were introduced in 1995 and 1998, respectively, Uganda's overall telephone density tripled from 0.27 to 0.67 telephone subscribers per 100 people. In December 1999 it became the first African country where the number of mobile phone users surpassed those using fixed telephone lines. The introduction of more competitors and suitable institutional policies has continually increased subscription rates, and at the end of 2006 80 per cent of the population enjoyed mobile signal coverage.

As a result of increased competition, the cost of joining the 'connected' and making phone calls was significantly reduced. This especially benefitted small start-up enterprises in the informal sector, for which access to communication channels was often either unavailable or too costly. Moreover, the boom in mobile service users has also generated new opportunities for a growing number of self-employed complementary service providers. For example, pre-paid air time cards are sold in kiosks, some of which have expanded to provide phone repair and battery charging services.

Capitalizing on the popularization of mobile phone access, providers also introduced an electronic payment system operating through the mobile service network. The Bank of Uganda, commercial banks and businesses have jointly devised an electronic clearing system, which allows real-time gross transfers and settlements of checks. In early 2012, a new system allowing individuals and small businesses to send and receive money by means of a text message was launched. In this regard, the mobile phone network has stepped beyond its traditional role and started to provide access to credit and financial intermediation for many that were once beyond reach of the centralized formal banking system.

Source: Partially adapted from Ndiwalana and Popov (2008)

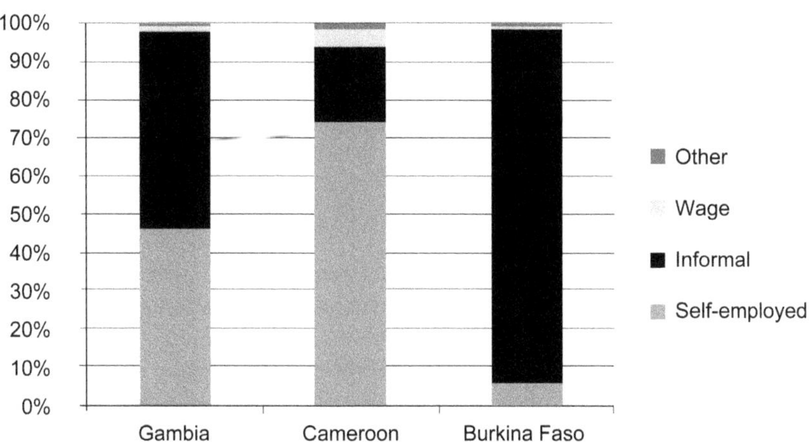

Figure 2.2 Modality of employment of rural youth (2009)
Source: Calculation based on World Bank Standard Files and Indicators—Marito Garcia and Jean Fares, eds, *Youth in Africa's Labor Markets*, Table 5.6, p. 57.

An empirical illustration of the effect of country typology is provided in Figures 2.2 and 2.3. In the urban sector, the coastal country Gambia has the highest proportion of wage employment (42.3 per cent) and the smallest urban informal sector (20.7 per cent). Being a resource-rich country, Cameroon has a larger informal sector (56.9 per cent) and less wage employment (15.3 per cent) than either the landlocked Burkina Faso or the coastal Gambia.

In rural areas, wage employment is rare while self-employment and informal industries are predominant for all three categories.

2.1.5 Defining and measuring underemployment

Underemployment is formally defined as a phenomenon of workers who, during a reference period, were willing to work additional hours, were available to do so, and had worked fewer than a selected number of hours. This

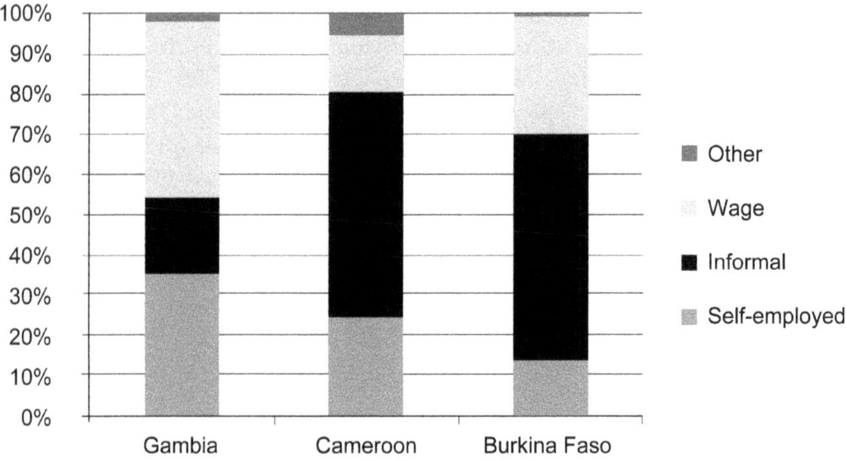

Figure 2.3 Modality of employment of urban youth (2009)
Source: Calculation based on World Bank Standard Files and Indicators—Marito Garcia and Jean Fares, eds, *Youth in Africa's Labor Markets*, Table 5.6, p. 57.

definition is circumscribed to a short reference period, which must be the same as that used to measure employment and unemployment (usually one week).

It is acknowledged that no single definition can capture completely the complexity of the entire labour market, especially in developing regions such as Sub-Saharan Africa. For instance, some workers may work long hours to meet basic living needs, while others suffer poor labour protection and are vulnerable to economic shocks. These are certainly important topics demanding international attention. The International Labour Organization (ILO) has put forward relevant concepts of decent work and vulnerable employment. Nevertheless, they infringe on legal and moral matters and currently lack a systematic means of measurement, which is why this chapter primarily adopts the formal sense of time-based underemployment.

Measuring underemployment according to the above definition is not an easy task. Centralized databases such as the ILO's LABORSTA contain only stand-alone indicators of labour force participation rates, employment rates and unemployment rates, failing to differentiate between unemployment and underemployment. Some countries, however, make a distinction between the unemployed and underemployed in their labour force surveys. Although varying standards for the threshold number of working hours increases the difficulty of obtaining consistent estimates, an attempt is made to record time-related underemployment levels in Tables 2.2 and 2.3.

Table 2.2 shows that apart from Botswana and Kenya, a significant portion of the total labour force is underemployed. In most cases the underemployment rate is more pronounced for rural than for urban areas. This is

Table 2.2 Underemployment rates in urban and rural areas (percentage of labour force, various years)

Country	*Total*	*Urban*	*Rural*
Landlocked			
Uganda	16.9	10.4	17.4
Lesotho	23.8	n.a.	n.a.
Mali	28.2	n.a.	n.a.
Niger	34.6	n.a.	n.a.
Botswana	13.8	n.a.	n.a.
Resource-rich			
Sierra Leone	32.9	30.8	33.8
Coastal			
Tanzania	11.2	12.1	11
Ghana	7.3	5.1	8.8

Source: Lesotho Ministry of Labour and Employment (1998); Kenya Central Bureau of Statistics (1999); Tanzania National Bureau of Statistics (2001); Ghana Statistical Service (2003); Direction Nationale de la Statistique ed de l'Informatique du Mali (2004); Government of Sierra Leone (2007); Uganda Bureau of Statistics (2007); Botswana Central Statistics Office (2008); Burkina Faso Institut national de la statistique et de la démographie (2009); Jütting and de Laiglesia (2009).

Note: Underemployment rate is calculated by dividing the number of underemployed workers, which by standard convention is any person employed less than 40 hours per week, by the total labour force.

Table 2.3 Distribution of the underemployed population by form of employment (percentage of total underemployment, various years)

Country	*Agriculture*	*Unpaid family worker*	*Self-employed*	*Paid employee*	*Total*
Botswana	37.5	5.1	15.3	42.1	100.0
Sierra Leone	47.3	47.3	40.2	12.1	100.0
Tanzania	83.0	4.2	10.5	1.8	100.0

Source: Lesotho Ministry of Labour and Employment (1998); Kenya Central Bureau of Statistics (1999); Tanzania National Bureau of Statistics (2001); Ghana Statistical Service (2003); Direction Nationale de la Statistique et ed l'Informatique du Mali (2004); Government of Sierra Leone (2007); Uganda Bureau of Statistics (2007); Botswana Central Statistics Office (2008); Burkina Faso Institut national de la statisque et ed la démographie (2009); Jütting and de Laiglesia (2009).

consistent with the results in Table 2.3, which show that a large share of the underemployed population is in the agricultural sector found in rural areas.

The results with respect to gender are mixed (Table 2.4). While female underemployment levels are higher than male underemployment in Mali and Niger, other countries such as Sierra Leone and Kenya show contrasting trends. This could in part be due to the difficulty in measuring the size of the female labour force and the underemployed. Homemakers, who are usually female, often split their time between housework and employment. While

Table 2.4 Underemployment rates by gender (percentage of labour force, various years)

Country	*Total*	*Male*	*Female*
Landlocked			
Uganda	16.9	18.9	15.1
Mali	28.2	20.0	39.5
Niger	34.6	32.9	38.3
Resource-rich			
Sierra Leone	32.9	34.2	30.9
Coastal			
Tanzania	11.2	11.7	10.8
Ghana	7.3	7.0	7.5

Source: Lesotho Ministry of Labour and Employment (1998); Kenya Central Bureau of Statistics (1999); Tanzania National Bureau of Statistics (2001); Ghana Statistical Service (2003); Direction Nationale de la Statistique et ed l'Informatique du Mali (2004); Government of Sierra Leone (2007); Uganda Bureau of Statistics (2007); Botswana Central Statistics Office (2008); Burkina Faso Institut national de la statisque et ed la démographie (2009); Jütting and de Laiglesia (2009).

some countries may count them as underemployed due to the low number of hours worked, others may exclude them from the labour force as they are not actively seeking more work.

In a developing country context, however, underemployment is more likely to take the form of individuals working in activities with very low marginal value product—even approaching zero in some cases. Consequently, some workers may work overtime in order to sustain basic living expenses. These workers do not fit the standard definitions for time-related underemployment, but they belong functionally in this category. Therefore, although the explicit classical unemployment is relatively rare in African countries, a more frequent manifestation of inadequate job opportunities is a proliferation of small firms, household enterprises and self-employment. These firms are common in both urban and rural areas, and many households report working in multiple activities.

Another indicator, known as invisible underemployment, is the percentage of the workforce earning less than the hourly minimum wage in the country concerned. A study of seven capital cities in the region (Table 2.5) shows that invisible underemployment rates are often higher than time-related underemployment rates (visible underemployment rate).

Table 2.5 Visible and invisible underemployment rates in capital cities (percentage of labour force, 2005)

Underemployment rate	*Cotonou*	*Quagadougou*	*Abidijian*	*Bamako*	*Niamey*	*Dakar*	*Lome*
Visible	13.4	10.6	12.6	17.1	16.0	16.2	17.1
Invisible	61.1	66.5	53.2	45.4	51.1	57.8	55.8

Source: INSEE, DIAL and AFRISTAT (2005).

In order to ensure consistency and avoid confusion with poverty and other phenomena, we refer to underemployment in the formal sense of time-related underemployment in the following text.

2.2 Sectoral typology of Sub-Saharan African economies

Before advancing to considering policy, it is important first to gain a better understanding of the features of Sub-Saharan countries. The labour market structure, income distribution, migration patterns and other microfoundational factors comprise the building stones of an economy. These are introduced in an analytical framework in this section to build a solid foundation for designing suitable macroeconomic policies to achieve the ultimate aims of real economic growth and employment creation.

2.2.1 Structure of labour markets

An increasing amount of data has become available on youth underemployment in Africa, including relatively detailed information about the process through which young people leave school and enter the labour market, their absorption into employment, the kinds of work available, and the activities of those who are characterized as underemployed. In contrast to rich countries, where employment overwhelmingly consists of wage labour or salaried positions, relatively few individuals in African countries work for a wage. Likewise, while employment growth in the developing world occurs almost exclusively within the formal sector, in Africa (and other developing regions) employment growth in the informal sector dramatically outstrips growth in the formal sector (Barassa and Kaabwe, 2001). Hence most people in Sub-Saharan Africa work as entrepreneurs in household enterprises, as unpaid family labour, or are self-employed.

In rural areas, for families that have access to land, there is almost always some work to be done, but the work will often have a very low marginal product. Many families lack sufficient land or capital, and labour markets do not clear. For families with little land, the problem of underemployment drives many young people to village centers and towns. Here the default option for many individuals, including the young, is self-employment in the rural informal sector. These self-employed are highly heterogeneous. Some operate enterprises that are profitable and growth-oriented, but others earn paltry incomes and find few opportunities for productive work.

As an empirical illustration Table 2.6 gives an overview of youth employment characteristics. Among the four main groups, self- and informal employment account for the overwhelming majority of young workers in both rural and urban areas. The high level of informal employment in most countries may be a sign of labour market entry difficulties.

Table 2.6 Employment characteristics of the young by country (2007)

Country	*Wage*	*Rural Informal*	*Self*	*Other*	*Wage*	*Urban Informal*	*Self*	*Other*
Burkina Faso	0.4	94.8	4.8	0.0	27.9	57.0	14.4	0.7
Burundi	1.8	83.3	14.8	0.1	31.3	19.6	43.3	5.8
Cameroon	6.3	18.1	68.8	6.8	15.3	56.9	22.0	5.9
Ethiopia	55.6	24.8	16.2	3.4	16.2	38.2	23.2	22.3
Gambia	1.2	53.1	45.0	0.8	42.3	20.7	34.7	2.4
Kenya	16.4	40.0	43.6	0.0	21.1	53.3	25.4	0.2
Madagascar	5.9	69.7	34.5	1.0	19.3	58.7	18.2	3.8
Malawi	15.0	7.1	74.5	3.3	63.8	6.8	19.8	9.5
Mozambique	11.8	n.a.	86.7	1.5	40.2	n.a.	53.5	6.3
Sao Tome	59.5	34.3	n.a.	6.2	66.3	24.3	n.a.	9.5
Zambia	3.1	60.4	36.1	0.4	40.9	9.6	46.1	3.5

Source: Cling *et al.* (2007).

We find it useful to consider four major sectors that are represented in most Sub-Saharan African economies:

- agriculture;
- rural non-agricultural enterprise;
- urban informal sector;
- urban formal sector.

In the following sections we describe the characteristics of each sector and how these help us describe the current structure of African youth underemployment. Following this, we discuss other aspects of economies—such as over-regulation, gender divides and health problems—that may also help to explain the persistence of underemployment.

Agriculture

In the rural economy, agriculture remains the predominant activity with up to 90 per cent of the total population. That number reflects the limited progress that has been made among African economies, as a contraction of the agricultural share of the labour force is one of the strongest features of the structural transformation that takes place in the course of development (Njugana, 2008). Africa's rural population density has increased over the past decades, diminishing the land that is available per head. And there is little evidence that that portion of the population that shifted out of agriculture did so due to advances in rural labour productivity.

Youth account for 65 per cent of Africa's agricultural labour force (World Bank, 2012). Much of the underemployment in rural areas is dominated by female youth because many male youth have migrated to the urban areas, with four out of five ending up in the urban formal sector characterized by the same average product, sharing nexus but at somewhat higher income levels.

Besides economic reasons, youth also migrate to avoid ethnic frictions in rural areas and because of the desire to be urbanized (Leibbrandt and Mlatsheni, 2004). Those youth who remain in agriculture often do not possess titles for their land, potentially a significant problem as titles are often required to access credit.

Figures 2.4 and 2.5 show the overall percentages of labour force enrolment in agriculture, industry and services. The agricultural sector employs an average of 65 per cent of the labour force and generates 32 per cent of GDP growth. Services have the second highest labour force enrolment. In most

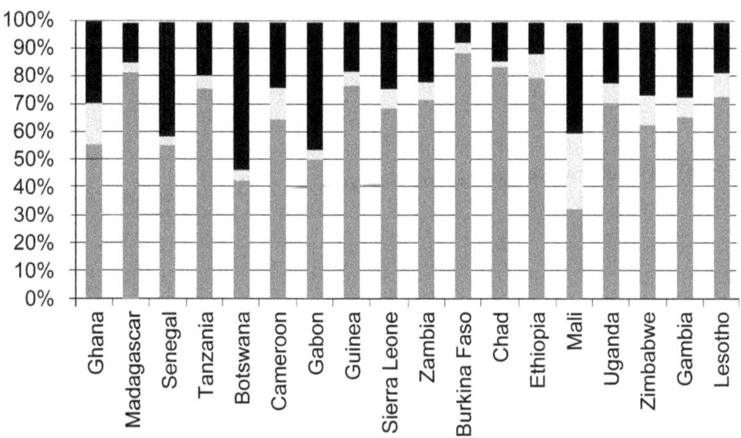

Figure 2.4 Total employment by sector in Sub-Saharan Africa (2011)
Source: The World Bank. African Development Indicators, 2011.

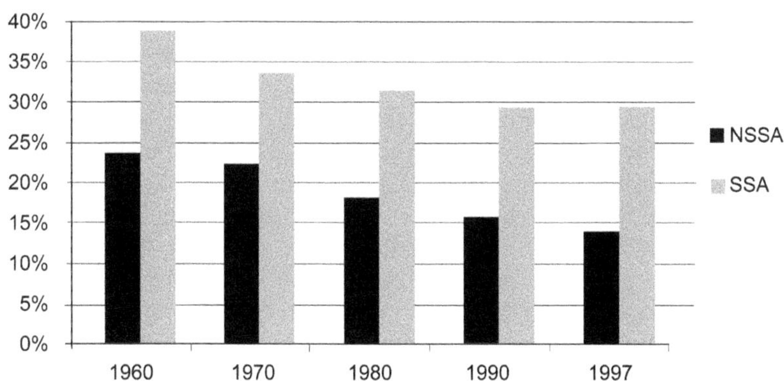

Figure 2.5 Mean agriculture shares of employment for Sub-Saharan African and northern Sub-Saharan African countries (various years)
Source: Barrios, B. and E. Strobl. 'Climate change and rural–urban migration: The case of Sub-Saharan Africa'. World Development, Vol. 19, No.6, pp. 651–670, 2006.

countries, the industrial sector involves less than 10 per cent of the labour population. In terms of GDP share, the size of the agricultural sector remains significant in Sub-Saharan African countries, in contrast to other developing regions and today's rich countries, where agriculture's share of employment has fallen sharply while developed countries have witnessed a sharp decline over time.

Because agriculture is such a large sector in many African economies, agricultural growth plays an obvious role in employment dynamics. But it is not clear whether this role is positive or negative. Some kinds of agricultural growth will demand increased labour; other kinds will reduce the labour in agriculture. For instance, mechanization of ploughing and harvesting can reduce the labour employed in agriculture, potentially exacerbating the employment problems. Other forms of agricultural technology improvement can increase labour demand by increasing the area under cultivation and the physical quantities planted, harvested and processed.

The relationship of agricultural growth to employment creation also depends on countries' ability to import food. For instance, some landlocked countries have little choice but to achieve self-reliance in food; others may have easy access to imports. In countries where food imports are costly or effectively impossible, then the 'food problem' must be solved domestically. In these countries, agricultural productivity increases will tend to release labour into non-agricultural sectors. Urbanization and non-agricultural employment will increase with agricultural productivity (see e.g. Gollin and Rogerson, 2011). However, in this context, increases in agricultural productivity may also move large numbers of unskilled workers from rural areas, where they may be cared for within family networks, to urban areas, where they may become reliant on public services. As a result, the 'disguised unemployment' of traditional agriculture may become more visible as agricultural productivity rises.

This mechanism should be most apparent in those parts of Africa that are landlocked, predominantly rural, and have large fractions of their population living at a considerable distance from coastal cities where they might have access to inexpensive food imports. This might include, for example, Uganda, Congo, Mali, Niger, Ethiopia and Burkina Faso.

Some other countries may be able to rely much more on imported food. Small island economies (e.g. Mauritius or Cape Verde), along with coastal economies with well developed port infrastructure and good access to international markets (e.g. South Africa, much of North Africa and some countries in West Africa), may be able to feed themselves more efficiently from imports than through domestic production. In these countries, increases in agricultural productivity will tend to absorb labour and to create jobs, in the same way that rising productivity in any sector will tend to be employment-enhancing.

These macro effects of agricultural productivity increases will be mediated by a number of social and legal aspects of agricultural economies. For instance, gender roles in many African countries imply that women provide a large fraction of agricultural labour. In these settings, increases in agricultural labour demand will tend to create employment for women relative to men. Conversely, when labour is released from agriculture, it may be disproportionately women's labour.

In the same vein, land rights and access to land will affect the patterns of labour used in agriculture and released to the rest of the economy. Where land rights (either formal or customary) are widely held and smallholder agriculture is the norm, agriculture will absorb more labour than where land-holdings are heavily concentrated (as was the case with colonial agriculture in certain countries).

Another dimension of variation within Sub-Saharan Africa is with respect to land abundance. Some countries, such as Mozambique, have plentiful land available for agricultural expansion. Others, such as the Great Lakes countries, have essentially exhausted the available land. Still others have land available in some locations but face closed frontiers in other locations (e.g. Ethiopia and Uganda). The opportunities for employment creation in agriculture clearly will depend on the availability of land and the techniques used to farm it. As Hayami and Ruttan argued, the direction of agricultural innovation is often related to relative factor abundance. In countries with plentiful land, we might not expect to see labour-intensive farming practices taken up. Instead, agriculture might be introduced as capital and land using, contributing little to employment generation.

Rural non-agricultural enterprise

Most rural households do not limit themselves to agricultural activities but diversify into so-called rural non-agricultural enterprises, providing simple goods and services, generally with a high-income elasticity of demand. Some are forced into non-farm activities due to unfavorable push factors such as sluggish farm income growth and diminishing land availability. Others are voluntarily drawn into non-farm activities by strategic income diversification and maximization as a result of agricultural technology and surplus increases (pull factors).

Rural non-agricultural enterprises perform many economic activities other than the processing and marketing of primary agricultural commodities. Among these is the provision of services (e.g. repair shops and hairdressers), which accounts for 75–80 per cent of the rural non-farm employment. Agro processing (i.e. the transformation of raw agricultural products by milling, packaging and transporting) also forms a key component. The remaining 20–25 per cent is comprised of the production of simple goods such as garments and furniture (Haggblade *et al.*, 2007).

Primary employment data show that that the rural non-agricultural sector accounts for about 10 per cent of the rural workforce. In rural towns, which often depend on the nearby rural regions for inputs and markets, this percentage increases by an additional 10–15 per cent (Hazell and Haggeblade, 1993).

Table 2.7 Share of rural non-agricultural income (percentage of total rural income, various years)

Country	*Year*	*Total RNA income (percentage)*
Ethiopia	1999	20
Ghana	1998	42
Kenya	1994–1996	25
Malawi	2004	64
Mozambique	1991	15
Namibia	1992–1993	56
Rwanda	1999–2000	20
Tanzania	2000	46
Uganda	1999–2000	54
Zimbabwe	1990–1991	38

Source: National household survey data, various.

Especially for women with housework obligations, part-time employment in these enterprises constitutes an important source of income. In comparison, incomes in the urban informal sector might run at 50 per cent over agricultural incomes, but at 25 per cent below the marginal product wages in the urban organized sector (Ruffer and Knight, 2007). However, it should be noted that rural non-agricultural enterprises are riskier than agriculture.

Links between agriculture and rural non-agricultural enterprises

Any serious discussion of employment policies in Africa must take into account agriculture's role in absorbing labour and the potential of the sector to create new jobs. Can the agricultural sector contribute to solving the problem of youth unemployment? Or is agriculture's low productivity and stagnation essentially the cause of the unemployment problem? Would rising productivity in agriculture absorb more labour, or would it conversely lead the sector to shed workers and drive more young people into informal employment?

These are difficult questions, and there is no clear consensus in the macro literature on this point. One extreme view, commonplace in the development literature of the 1950s, is that the agricultural sector is simply a reservoir of unemployed or underemployed labour, with low incomes and living standards, from which people must eventually be moved by economic growth into the non-agricultural economy. To some degree, this assumption was at the heart of Lewis' (1955) model and the work of scholars such as Rosenstein-Rodan (1943) and Rostow (1960). In most of this literature, the agricultural sector was seen essentially as a pool of surplus labour, with a very low shadow wage.

The alternative view is that the agricultural sector itself must generate the growth that will eventually release labour and other resources. The Fei–Ranis model insisted on the need for agricultural productivity increase in a prolonged growth context. This view can be traced equally far back in the development literature. This view held that many poor economies suffered from what T.W. Schultz (1953) characterized as the 'food problem'. Simply put, Schultz argued that many poor countries are in a situation of 'high food drain', in which they have 'a level of income so low that a critically large proportion of the income is required for food'. Schultz took it as given that countries in this situation must produce the bulk of their own food to satisfy subsistence needs, presumably because imports are prohibitively costly and because these countries have few goods or resources to exchange for food. Until they can meet their subsistence needs, Schultz said, they are unable to begin the process of modern economic growth.

Schultz's view was later echoed in a large literature on development, which held that an agricultural surplus is a necessary condition for a country to begin the development process. The hypothesis was a central argument of Johnston and Mellor (1961), Johnston (1970), Johnston and Kilby (1975), Timmer (1988) and Johnson (1997), and it continues to figure prominently in the analyses of many other scholars (e.g. Eswaran and Kotwal, 1993; Mundlak, 2000; Gollin *et al.*, 2002, 2007).

Empirically, a growing agriculture sector has indeed been shown to stimulate the growth of rural non-agricultural enterprises through a number of key linkages. In the input market, much of the government's and private investors' agricultural surpluses have been channelled to the non-farm sector. Conversely, surpluses generated in non-farm activities also provide funding for technology and capital used in agriculture. Equally important is the rising agricultural labour productivity that releases farm workers to undertake non-farm activities. With respect to outputs, there are both backward linkages with rural enterprises supplying inputs for agriculture, and forward distribution and processing links. Empirically, forward linkages are larger than backward linkages by a factor of 17 in Zambia and 2.5 in Kenya, with food processing and distribution and storage the most important in both countries (Freeman and Norcliffe, 1985; Fisseha and Milimo, 1986). Moreover, an increase in per capita farm income increases demand for non-farm products and services, thereby raising employment levels and wage rates (Mellor, 1976).

As a result of both input and output market linkages, regions where agriculture has grown robustly also benefitted from growth in rural non-farm enterprises. Haggblade *et al.* (2007) estimate that in Africa, each dollar of additional value added in agriculture generates an additional rural non-farm income of US$0.3–0.5.

In recent years, a literature in macro and growth economics has revisited the persistence of dualisms. Temple (2005) and Vollrath (2009), among others, have explored multisector models in which unemployment or underemployment is possible in the modern sector as well as in the traditional sector. In these papers, there may be fixed urban wages or other rigidities that prevent the urban labour market from clearing. Other papers (e.g. Caselli and Coleman,

2001) rely on transaction cost wedges that prevent the labour market from equalizing marginal products across sectors. These papers have the feature that the allocation of resources across sectors is inefficient; the social planner would allocate labour and capital differently. A stylized policy implication of this class of models is that policies should focus on removing or reducing the rigidities that lead to inefficient outcomes and over allocation of resources to agriculture.

Urban informal sector

According to the ILO's latest definition, the urban informal economy is comprised of all forms of employment without labour and social protection, both inside and outside informal enterprises, including self-employed in small unregistered enterprises and wage employment in unprotected jobs.

The urban informal sector is not a temporary phenomenon, but a permanent and growing feature. In the urban economy it remains the main employer. A 2002 study showed that two-thirds of urban workers in Kenya were employed in the informal sector, and that the informal share in Kenyan manufacturing employment was at 83 per cent (Bigsten *et al.*, 2004). In Burkina Faso, the share of urban employment in the informal sector is as high as 70 per cent, equivalent to 11 per cent of the workforce (MJE, 2006)

Just as in rural settings, young urban women are significantly worse off than male youth. In Niger for example, men on average earn more than double the amount that women earn. Young women find themselves marginalized socially, culturally and politically in urban settings (Chigunta, 2002)

It would be an oversimplification to assume the entire informal sector will provide lower productivity and less favorable employment. Ranis and Stewart (1999), for instance, differentiate between the modernizing informal sector and the traditional informal sector. With more capital-intensive production, larger size and dynamic technology, the former is found to be more favorably linked to the formal sector while the latter acts like a sponge, absorbing the residual population. Nevertheless, the traditional informal sector still serves the important function of providing a source of subsistence for the urban poor.

In fact, it is important to consider separately informal employment, lower income and underemployment. Some informal own-account workers might be quite well off and not vulnerable at all—a fraction of informal firms are quite successful, enjoying high productivity and growth rates (African Development Bank, 2012). These firms and entrepreneurs actively choose to remain in the informal sector to avoid rigid regulations and to reduce costs (Juetting and Huitfeldt, 2009). For instance, Chigunta (2002) argues that in Kenya, formal firms that try to do business in the country have been faced with government red tape and corruption. Thus, as a result of how the government handles formal sector firms, many businesses take shelter in Kenya's informal sector (Bigsten *et al.*, 2004).

Urban formal sector

This is a small but rapidly growing sector that relies on wage employment. It is comprised of the private formal sector and the public formal sector. Figure 2.6 illustrates the distribution of primary employment between public formal and private formal sectors.

In Tanzania, Uganda and Ghana the growth rate has been as high as 10 per cent. Although the formal sector grew well, its base was not sufficiently large to take on more than one out of five new entrants into the urban labour force, with the other four joining the urban informal sector. According to Gallup World Poll data, this discrepancy is even more pronounced among youth, with 21 per cent employed in the formal public sector compared with 37 per cent among adults (Gallup World Poll 2010, gallup.com/poll/world). One possible reason is that technology is often more capital intensive in the urban formal sector. Since the accumulation of capital and technology can take place only over a longer time span, the short-run labour absorption capacity of the formal sector is limited. Nevertheless, formal sector employment tends to be of higher value added and bears significant potential for development in the long term through increased savings and investment. The Gallup World Poll also predicts that the role of the public sector as an employer will continue to shrink.

Typically, urban African youth with higher levels of education seek entrance into formal sector work—and because of the relatively small number of opportunities in the formal sector, urban youth often find themselves

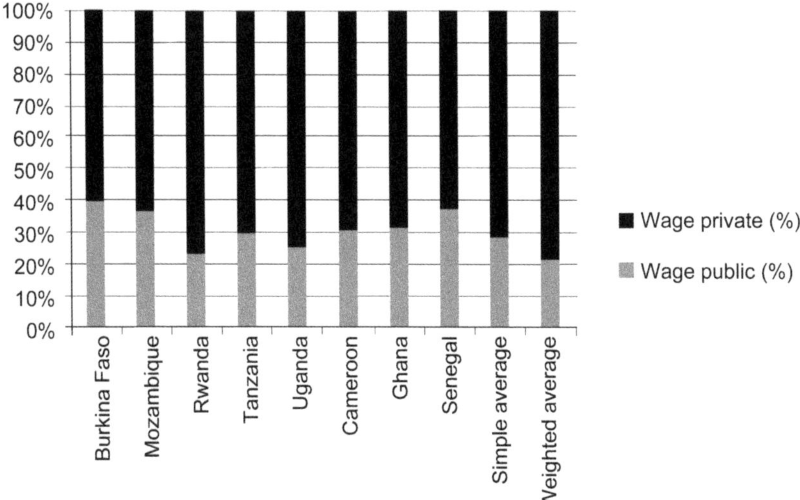

Figure 2.6 Private/public share of urban employment (2012)
Source: African Economic Outlook 2012—Promoting Youth Employment.

underemployed. According to the World Bank, youth underemployment is more prevalent in urban areas and is highest among those with higher formal education attainment.

Underemployment among youth with secondary education or above is three times higher than among those with no educational attainment, and underemployment is twice as high among youth from households in the highest income quintile as compared with those in the first income quintile (World Bank, 2009).

Moreover, moonlighting by formal sector employees in the informal sector is an increasing phenomenon. While the overall poverty level in Africa increased during the period of the reforms (World Bank, 2002), the increases have been particularly high in urban areas (Dhemba, 1999; Monga *et al.*, 2001). The combined effect of the economic reforms and urbanization of poverty is that many salaried employees—the so-called 'protected workers' (Portes and Walton, 1981)—either by necessity or choice have joined the 'marginal workers' in the informal sector in an effort to increase their income-earning opportunities and diversify their sources of income. Thus the informal sector has become an avenue for 'part-time' employment for formal sector employees and a source of additional income for many with full-time employment in the formal sector.

Labour market rigidities and regulations

The majority of the literature still contends that firms are forced to remain in the informal sector due to barriers restricting entry to the formal sector. These regulations typically apply only to a small subset of firms, but these may be the largest and most productive firms in the economy.

Regulations often serve the interests of a labour elite—those workers employed in formal sector firms, multinationals, government and other premium employers. They may also serve the interests of those employers by creating queuing for jobs that can allow them to command loyalty and recruit the highest-quality workers. In other cases, higher cost of firing in the formal sector has also served as disincentive for employers to hire. This has restricted entry for some informal workers to enter the formal sector. It is unclear how much the prevalence of the informal sector is due to these regulations.

The informal sector itself is not shielded from government interference. Both rural and household enterprises pay government license fees and user fees, but do not receive government services or protection in return. But since the revenues from government fees constitute as much as two-thirds of an African government's income, there is a strong disincentive to replace this system with a more efficient one. It should be said that some African countries have been able to improve revenue collection, but these improvements required serious overhauls of tax administration and methods of tax collection—improvements that are still out of reach for many African governments (Njugana, 2008).

Economic reforms and adjustment programs have had a profound and generally negative impact on low-income groups in both rural and urban areas. Sharp reductions in agricultural subsidies have affected small-scale farmers, and while the dismantling of marketing boards has increased their reliance on local markets, access is often hampered by lack of investment in transport infrastructure and storage facilities (Satterthwaite and Tacoli, 2003).

Table 2.8 shows that labour market rigidities are on average higher in Sub-Saharan Africa than in other parts of the world.

Links between the formal and informal sectors

As is true throughout the developing world, there are no hard-and-fast divisions between the formal and informal sectors in Sub-Saharan Africa. Economic activities of production, distribution and employment tend to lie at some point on a spectrum between purely formal and purely informal relations. Workers and enterprise units are known to move along the continuum and even to operate at different points on the continuum simultaneously (e.g. a public sector employee who has an informal job on the side). In some cases, informality can also be used as a 'stepping stone' for formality—entrepreneurs can explore, without significant sunk costs, the potential feasibility of the work they are trying to do by first attempting it in the informal sector.[3]

Most importantly, the formal and informal ends of the economic continuum are dynamically linked.[4] For instance, informal enterprises have production or distribution relations with formal enterprises, supplying inputs, finished goods or services through either direct transactions or sub-contracting arrangements. Also, formal enterprises hire wage workers under informal employment relations. For example, many part-time workers, temporary workers and home workers work for formal enterprises through contracting or sub-contracting arrangements.

Empirically, positive linkages between the formal and informal urban sectors have been verified, but the extent of this articulation seems modest in many countries. Evidence from Burkina Faso, not possessed of a fast-growing organized sector, showed that a 1 per cent increase in formal earning leads to

Table 2.8 Employment rigidity in Africa (2007)

Region of economy	*Difficult of hiring index*	*Rigidity of hours index*	*Difficulty of firing index*
East Asia & Pacific	23.7	25.2	19.6
Europe & Central Asia	34.2	50.7	37.1
Latin America & Caribbean	34.0	34.8	26.5
Middle East & North Africa	29.7	44.7	32.9
OECD	27.0	45.2	27.4
South Asia	41.8	25.0	37.5
Sub-Saharan Africa	44.3	52.0	44.9

Source: Cling *et al.* (2007).

a 0.16–0.20 per cent increase in informal sector earnings, and a 1 per cent increase in formal sector non-labour income leads to informal sector non-labour income increases of 0.48–0.79 per cent (Grimm and Gunther, 2006). These linkages take place mainly through final product markets (forward linkages) and via sub-contracts with formal sector earnings invested in the informal sector.

From a policy perspective, the overall positive linkage shows that developing the formal sector also benefits the informal sector, and vice versa. At the same time, the differences in linkage ratios imply that formal sector growth policies benefit different members and units of the informal sector to a varying extent. This subtlety should be taken into account by policymakers so that informal households are not left out of the overall economic growth process.

Nevertheless, the change in relative importance of the sectors still varies despite the presence of positive linkages. McMillan and Rodrick (2011) argue, for instance, that during the 1990–2000s, structural adjustment and related macro shifts contributed to a movement of workers into low-productivity informal sectors from the formal sector. They perform a decomposition exercise that shows that the reallocation of workers arithmetically reduced overall productivity by 1.27 per cent during this period in Africa. Their argument is consistent with empirical observations in Kenya. Figure 2.7 reveals shrinking formal sector employment and a growing significance of the informal sector over time. It shows that jobs in Kenya have become increasingly informal. The greatest leap took place in 1991 when the formal sector suffered from losses triggered by liberalization policies. In fact, trade liberalization could be damaging to both the urban sectors and the rural non-agricultural sector. Their implementation should therefore be carried out gradually and carefully to minimize the disruption of domestic industries.

Self-employment

Large fractions of the workforce in Sub-Saharan Africa are engaged in self-employment. This is true even outside the agricultural sector. Gollin (2008) documents that levels of self-employment are high even within the manufacturing sector. Self-employment coincides with informality, but the two phenomena are not identical. There are self-employed people who operate formal businesses, and there are certainly many informal firms that have multiple employees. Nevertheless, there may be a high degree of overlap between the two.

The development literature has for many years struggled to understand the persistence and prevalence of self-employment in African economies. One view holds that this sector represents little more than disguised unemployment and underemployment, with many of the self-employed working few hours and earning low returns. An alternative view is that the sector consists of vibrant entrepreneurs who are prevented from expanding their firms by

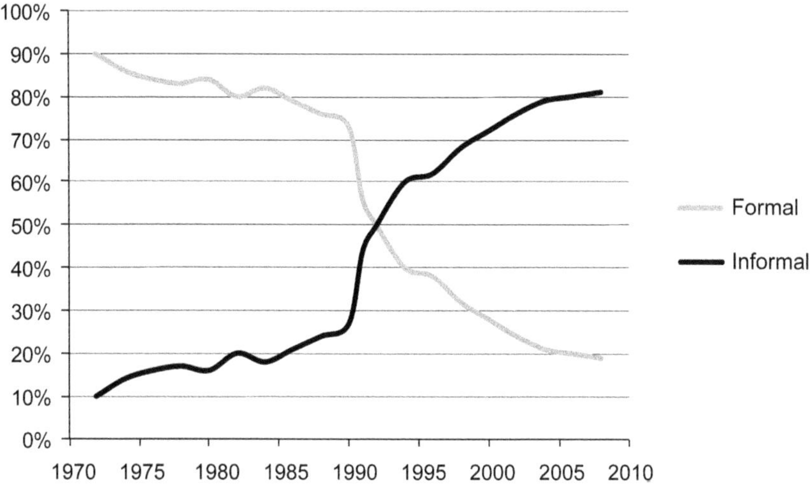

Figure 2.7 Formal and informal sector employment in Kenya (1972–2008)
Source: Omolo, J. "The Dynamics and Trends of Employment in Kenya". Institute of Economic Affaires. IEA paper series No.1. 2010.

high explicit or implicit taxation on larger firms. This is the view popularized by Hernando de Soto, among others. It is a view that has been supported by studies showing the multiple (and often costly) steps faced by a business seeking to enter the formal sector.

Still another view of self-employment is that the efficient scale of operation for most firms in Africa is quite small. In this view, there are relatively modest benefits to firms from expanding, given the technology with which they operate. For example, a tailoring shop that employs five workers with five sewing machines is not much more productive than five separate self-employed tailors, each with a single sewing machine. This is the view articulated by Gollin (2008): the suggestion is that any returns to scale occur at substantially larger firm size, often associated with a change in the type and quality of products. This view is consistent with repeated findings that exporting firms in Africa—even those that are quite small—look quite different from self-employment and other household enterprises.

How much can self-employment absorb the unemployed and underemployed in Sub-Saharan Africa? How much should governments promote self-employment as a strategy for addressing the problems of youth unemployment? And what kinds of policies can stimulate the self-employment sector? In the past, development efforts targeted to this sector have focused on providing training for the self-employed in basic business skills, such as simple accounting (e.g. Karlan and Valdivia, 2009) More recently, micro-credit programs have been seen as a key vehicle for targeting the self-employed and small enterprises.

Bloom *et al.* (2012b) report evidence that many firms in poor countries are hampered by poor management. In experiments, they demonstrate that productivity in some firms can be increased by 15–20 per cent within a year through the implementation of, for example, simple quality-management techniques. In related work, Bloom *et al.* (2012a) hypothesize that family management structures prevent firms from pursuing some efficiency-enhancing measures. Echoing work by Hsieh and Klenow (2009), among others, they argue that market forces do not drive low-productivity firms out of business, leading to the persistence of poorly managed firms with low productivity.

This literature suggests that employment might be enhanced by providing support for the consolidation and rationalization of production in firms that are demonstrably well managed. Supporting inefficient firms (e.g. through credit subsidies) will not, in the end, do much for employment. Instead, linking support to restructuring and to managerial improvements may be the key to promoting increases in the demand for labour.

2.2.2 Demographic factors

Internal migration

The internal migration of young workers is a major characteristic of Sub-Saharan African labour markets. Among the personal and social factors influencing internal migration, economic conditions are generally acknowledged to be a fundamental driver. One survey of internal migration in Ghana revealed that over 80 per cent of respondents gave economic reasons for migrating from their previous location, suggesting that income differentials contribute significantly to internal migration (Anarfi *et al.*, 2003).

In contrast to the rapid urbanization observed during the 1950s and 1960s, the pace of rural-to-urban migration in Africa has slowed since the early 1970s. Rural outmigration rates dropped continually, going from 1.1 per cent per year in the 1960s to 0.8 per cent per year in the 1970s, and then to 0.5 per cent per year in the 1980s. As a share of urban growth, the significance of internal migration also declined from 41 per cent in the 1960s to 25 per cent in the 1980s (Chen *et al.*, 1998). Sub-Saharan Africa is often viewed as urbanizing far more quickly than other parts of the developing world, but Kessides (2005) shows that, in fact, urbanization in the region is not fast when compared with other developing regions. Internal migration also does not account for urban poverty (and the accompanying public health problems). Poverty is instead largely caused by institutional failures that perpetuate social exclusion and inequalities between the urban poor and the urban non-poor (Kessides, 2005).

Rural-to-urban migration appears to be, on balance, favorable for both sending and receiving areas. Instead of viewing migration as a one-way process in which rural poor seek employment opportunities in urban areas, it is more accurate to see urban and rural areas as interlinked, and the migration process as a seasonal/cyclical one that benefits both areas. Access to (urban) markets and services for non-farm production stimulates agricultural productivity and rural incomes, which in turn generate demand and labour supply for more such goods and services. Access to income from non-farm and urban-based activities is associated with reduced rural poverty, and options for such income multiply in proximity to urban markets. Migrants within the urban population do not simply swell the ranks of the poor (as often charged), and much evidence indicates that they do quite well.

Contrary to common assumptions, recent migrants (whether of rural or urban origins) are only slightly more likely to be defined as poor or to suffer from less access to services. A recent poverty study of Ghana found that a major contributor to Ghana's poverty reduction over the 1990s was migration from slower-growing to faster-growing regions. The biggest reduction in poverty was identified among the rural forest residents and was attributed to their receipt of remittances. In addition to income-generating activities, access to services such as health care and education is an important aspect of rural–urban linkages, with 'district' hospitals and secondary schools often located in urban centers from where they also serve the population of surrounding rural areas.

It is important to note that several recent studies have shown that the counter-migratory stream (urban-to-rural migration) has grown and, in some cases, outpaced rural outmigration. In Ghana, for instance, several major cities have experienced a negative migratory balance (Potts, 1995). Zambian population censuses also revealed a greater population growth rate in rural than in urban areas in 1890–2000 and 1990–2000.

Table 2.9 reports the internal migration for selected countries. As part of the Africa Migration Project, six Migration and Remittances Household Surveys were conducted in Burkina Faso, Kenya, Nigeria, Senegal, South Africa and Uganda. A unique feature of these surveys is that they allow for comparison across countries. As the surveys were implemented during the same period, they provide us with a good picture of regional migration and remittances, at the household level, in the six countries surveyed.

The five countries presented in Table 2.9 are migrant-sending countries while South Africa acts as a migrant-receiving country. Migrants are generally male. Most of the migrants (both international and internal) are in the 26–50 years old category.

Migration also has effects on the labour market. As indicated by the Migration Household Survey by the World Bank, in Burkina Faso migration allowed for more full-time and part-time wage activities. In Nigeria, migration allowed a shift from unemployed to self-employment and wage employment. Migration appears to have various implications for women's labour market status in these countries. In Kenya the shift in labour market status is significant for the unemployed, many of whom were able to find wage employment by migrating (Table 2.10).

Table 2.9 Internal migrants' share in representative households (2009)

Countries	*Internal migration rate (percentage)*
Kenya	28.68
Nigeria	38.80
Burkina Faso	31.50
Senegal	33.30
Uganda	12.70

Source: Authors' calculations based on results household surveys as part of Africa Migration Project.
Note: For this survey, a migrant is a person who used to live in a household in the country in which the interview is being conducted, but left before the interview to live abroad, or in another village or urban area within the country, for at least 6 months. Not all the survey samples are nationally representative.

Table 2.10 Labour-market status of migrating individuals from select Sub-Saharan African countries (2009)

(percentage)

Labour market status	*Burkina Faso*		*Senegal*		*Nigeria*		*Kenya*	
	Before	*After*	*Before*	*After*	*Before*	*After*	*Before*	*After*
Self-employed	80	64	42	43	16	26	7	9
Student	10	5	21	8	43	23	31	16
Housewife	3	5	9	8	1	5	2	3
Full-time wage earner	3	9	9	24	14	34	21	53
Part-time wage earner	1	12	3	4	3	4	4	8
Unemployed	2	2	9	3	22	4	33	8
Other	1	3	7	10	2	4	1	3

Source: Authors' calculations based on results household surveys conducted in Burkina Faso, Kenya, Nigeria, Senegal, South Africa, and Uganda in 2009 as part of the Africa Migration Project.

James Knowles and Richard Anker (1980) observed a high relative frequency of rural-to-rural transfers, indicating that a majority of Kenya's migrants were rural-rural migrants (Table 2.11)

International migration

As of 2010 Sub-Saharan Africa had a total of 21.8 million emigrants, comprising 2.5 per cent of the continent's population. The destination breakdown is shown in Table 2.12 below. Table 2.13 depicts the net international migration rates for different Sub-Saharan African countries.

Real incomes in Africa are a fraction of those in Europe and North America, so the incentive to emigrate out of the continent should be

Table 2.11 Kenya's income transfers (1980)

Direction of flows	*Number of transfers*	*Percentage of transfers*	*Percentage of total amount transferred*
Urban to rural	431	37.0	50.4
Urban to urban	119	10.2	15.0
Rural to urban	76	6.5	6.3
Rural to rural	540	46.3	28.3
Totals	1,166	100.0	100.0

Source: James Knowles and Richard Anker (1981), "An analysis of income transfers in a developing country: The case of Kenya," *Journal of Development Economics* 8(2): 205–226.

Table 2.12 Percentage of total emigrants (2001)

Region	*Percentage of total emigrants*
High-income OECD countries	24.8
High-income non-OECD countries	2.5
Intra-regional	63.0
Other developing countries	1.8
Unidentified	7.8

Source: World Bank (2001).

extremely strong. Yet Africa has generated remarkably few emigrants to major labour-scarce countries (roughly a quarter of the total number of African emigrants). Poverty is commonly cited as the most important obstacle to emigration outside Africa.

Labour mobility between Sub-Saharan African countries is higher than emigration to non-African countries—intra-African emigrants account for over 60 per cent of the total. An income difference is a significant factor. One study of rural Botswana, for instance, found a highly elastic and positive migration response to wage rates and employment probabilities in the urban sector, and a negative response to local wage rates and employment probabilities (Lucas and Stark, 1985). Furthermore, the share of the home country population aged 15–29 also has a positive effect, indicating that a rise of five percentage points in the share of the young increases annual out-migration by one per thousand (Hatton and Williamson, 2002).

One recent trend is an increase in migration by women. Stepping beyond their traditional roles as full-time housekeepers, a significant number of females now migrate independently to fulfil their own economic needs. In Côte d'Ivoire, for example, female migration from Burkina Faso has increased, even with slowed economic development (Findley, 1997). One possible explanation is that women become concentrated more in the urban informal sector, which is relatively less affected by economic shocks than the urban formal sector that

Table 2.13 Sub-Saharan international net migration by country (1990 and 2010)

Country	*1990 (percentage)*	*2010 (percentage)*	*Country*	*1990 (percentage)*	*2010 (percentage)*
Angola	n.a.	−7.0	Madagascar	0	0
Benin	−0.1	−3.4	Malawi	6	0
Botswana	0.3	−15.1	Mali	−4	n.a.
Burkina Faso	−1.2	−1.9	Mauritius	−3	n.a.
Burundi	0.0	−2.1	Mozambique	−6	0
Cameroon	0.1	−0.7	Namibia	4	0
Central African Republic	−0.9	−2.8	Rwanda	0	0
Chad	0.0	−1.0	Seychelles	n.a.	21
Comoros	−0.6	−11.3	Somalia	−6	0
D. R. Congo	0.1	−0.1	South Africa	0	0
Djibouti	17.4	−4.6	South Sudan	n.a.	1
Equatorial Guinea	2.4	−3.2	Sudan	−1	0
Eritrea	−0.1	−0.4	Swaziland	2	12
Ethiopia	0.9	0.0	Tanzania	0	1
Gabon	1.3	−1.3	Uganda	1	2
Kenya	0.0	0.0	Zambia	0	n.a.
Lesotho	−2.4	−0.3	Zimbabwe	1	n.a.

Source: World Bank Data, World Development Indicators.

is traditionally male-dominated. As jobs become more difficult to secure and as remittances thin out, many families increasingly rely on women to sustain their incomes.

Another observed phenomenon is migration as a family survival strategy. A family following the survival strategy would sponsor one or more of its members to migrate to, and seek employment in, another country. In return, the migrant remits a substantial proportion of the earned income regularly to support members of the family back home. For many families, the remittance is the lifeline for basic expenses. In some underdeveloped countries such as Senegal, households are highly reliant on remittances from abroad: 30–70 per cent of family needs are covered by incomes remitted by emigrants (ILO, 1995). The deferred pay method practiced in South African mines for labour migrants recruited from Lesotho is another example. Some of these countries, and especially the families of migrants, rely heavily on migrants' remittances, prompting governments to encourage labour migration.

Figure 2.8 depicts the main countries of destination for each of the migrant-sending countries mentioned above. In Burkina Faso there is a predominance of intraregional migration, mainly to Cote d'Ivoire and Mali. For Ghanaians, Nigerians and Kenyans, the United States and United Kingdom are the top two destinations. Senegalese emigrants go to Italy, Spain, France and African countries.

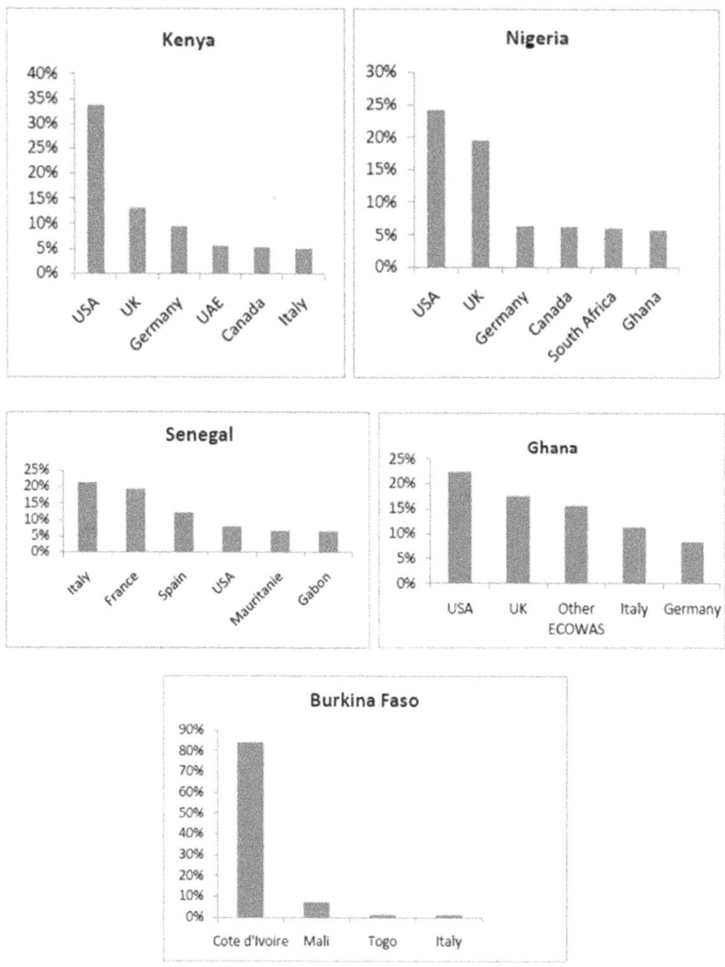

Figure 2.8 Main countries of destination (2011)
Source: Authors' calculations based on results household surveys of the Africa Migration Project.

Box 2.4 A success story of labour exportation—the Philippines

Since the 1970s, the Philippines has supplied all kinds of skilled and low-skilled workers to the world's more developed regions. In 2007, over 8.2 million native Filipinos were working or living in nearly 200 countries and territories, equivalent to almost 25 per cent of the Philippines' total labour force. Remittances from these migrants amounted to about US$17 billion, 13 per cent of the 2007 GDP.

The Philippines has long suffered from high unemployment levels induced by political instability and a lack of sustained economic growth.

Therefore, when the end of the Gulf War created a shortage of labour in the affected countries, the Philippine government was quick to capitalize on the opportunity by implementing a systematic program for the overseas employment of Filipino workers. After decades of development, the program is today coordinated by a comprehensive system of government institutions and private agencies.

On the private sector side, there are more than 1,000 recruitment and manning agencies that match workers with foreign employers. In return, migrant workers are charged placement fees equivalent to a month's salary. Regulation of recruitment is performed by the Philippine Overseas Employment Administration (POEA). The POEA is responsible for licensing private recruitment agencies, providing quality control services through ratings, and publishing a list of overseas job openings through its website. Internationally, the POEA works closely with the Philippine Overseas Labor Offices to monitor the treatment of foreign workers, verify labour documents, and assist workers in employment- and labour-related issues. Following the departure of the workers, the Overseas Workers Welfare Administration provides further support and assistance to migrants and their families.

The success of these policies is evident in the number of overseas Filipino workers. From a few thousand per year in the early 1970s, the flow of overseas workers has grown to hundreds of thousands (933,588 in 2004 alone). Women are very visible in international migration from the Philippines, with a majority employed in domestic work and entertainment. In Hong Kong, for example, more than 90 per cent of the foreign workers from the Philippines are women.

Apart from easing unemployment, remittances from abroad have become an important pillar of the Philippine economy (Box 2.4). In 2004, according to the Central Bank of the Philippines, remittances sent through formal channels amounted to US$8.5 billion. Most of these are made through banks after continuous efforts by the Philippine Central Bank to cut remittance costs to less than 0.5 per cent.

Key policy lessons:

The export of labour has to be balanced with strong development planning in order to maximize the development dividend of remittances. Export of labour is not a substitute for the expansion of employment opportunities in the country of origin.

Women are a key labour resource that needs to be harnessed through labour export. Domestic regulations safeguarding their rights and wellbeing abroad have to be put in place.

Reducing the cost of remittances is important to incentivize overseas employment and for workers to remit through regulated channels.

Source: Adapted from Bakunda and Walusimbi Mpanga (2011)

2.2.3 Income levels and distribution

Income-level disparity by sector

Despite the trend of decreasing urban formal incomes as a result of the oil shocks of the 1970s and the recession in the Western industrial countries (Jamal and Weeks, 1988), Table 2.14 demonstrates that the urban–rural gap still persists, with the urban formal sector providing 3.5 to 6.6 times the average income of the rural sector.[5] Within the urban sector, average income of the urban formal sector is higher than that of the urban informal sector in all countries included, with the only resource-rich country, Botswana, having the highest ratio of 4.6 to 1.[6]

Due to endogenous factors, these figures should not be interpreted simply as a pure causation effect by the sector of employment on average income. For example, Gollin *et al.* (2012) find that the average number of hours worked in the urban sector is 1.2 times that of the rural sector, while the average education attainment (human capital) is relatively higher for urban workers. After these factors are controlled for, the same study finds that the adjusted agricultural productivity gap is lowered but remains significant at approximately 2 to 1. Similarly, observable differences in human capital also account for some, but not all, of the income differences between the urban formal and the urban informal sector (Falco *et al.*, 2011).

In addition, larger firm sizes generally correspond to higher incomes in both formal and informal sectors. Using data from Ghana, Tanzania and Ethiopia, Sandefur and Teal (2007) find that earnings differ little between the

Table 2.14 Per capita income rations between sectors (various years)

Country/ratio	*Urban formal (public) Rural*	*Urban formal (private) Rural*	*Urban informal Rural*	*Urban formal (public) Urban formal (private)*	*Urban formal (public) Urban informal*	*Urban formal (private) Urban informal*
Ghana (1998)	6.6	4.3	3.6	1.6	1.8	1.2
Kenya (1999)	4.0	4.0	1.5	1.0	2.7	2.7
Tanzania (2001)	5.8	3.5	1.7	1.6	3.5	2.1
Madagascar (2000)	n.a.	n.a.	n.a.	1.4	1.5	1.1
Botswana (2007)	5.2	3.5	1.1	1.5	4.6	3.1
Ethiopia (1997)	n.a.	n.a.	n.a.	1.2	2.2	1.8
Burkina Faso (2001)	5.3	4.1	1.3	1.3	4.0	3.1

Source: Central Statistical Agency of Ethiopia (1997); Ghana Statistical Service (1998); Kenya Central Bureau of Statistics (1999); Burkina Faso Institut national de la statistique et de la démographie (2001); Tanzania National Bureau of Statistics (2001); Botswana Central Statistics Office (2007, 2008).

Note: Urban formal sector taken as a whole as individual data for private and public sectors were not available.

self-employed and employees of small private firms, whereas wage earners in large firms on average earn substantially more than the self-employed.

As mentioned in the previous subsection, it is important to note that the rural economy is a heterogeneous collection of both agricultural and non-agricultural activities. On a per capita basis, various case studies show that rural non-farm income exceeds farm income. In Senegal and Rwanda, for example, farm income is half of the average non-farm income (Kelly *et al.*, 1993; Clay *et al.*, 1995). Unsurprisingly, most farm labour is supplied by the poorer households (Peters, 1992; Reardon *et al.*, 1994). Upper-income-strata households are more likely to have members specializing in non-farm employment, and the share of non-farm income in total income is two times higher in upper-income-tercile households than in lower-tercile households (Reardon, 1997).

Income distribution

If one subscribes to a Kuznets type of relationship, then Sub-Saharan Africa, being relatively poor and with a large share of agricultural population, should be enjoying very low levels of income disparity. Empirical evidence suggests, however, that it is in fact both poor and unequal. The average Gini coefficient across 17 Sub-Saharan countries from the late 2000s is 0.42, which is far above Asia's average even after controlling for income levels (Milanovic, 2003).

In addition, resource-rich countries tend to have more unequal income distributions than their landlocked and coastal counterparts (see Table 2.15). This could in part have been driven by the resource-curse effect: mineral rents fund a large number of high-earning public employees while high public spending crowds out small investors and self-employed workers in the informal economy.

Following our sector-by-sector analysis of the labour market, it is also important to transcend aggregate measures of inequality and explore the extent to which inter-regional and intra-regional inequalities are present in the rural and urban areas. Sahn and Stifel (2000) construct a welfare index from households' asset information as a justifiable proxy for income, which is then used to calculate the total and decomposed Theil indexes in Table 2.16.

From the urban–rural decomposition presented in columns two and three, it can be inferred that rural inequality is worse than urban inequality in all countries except Madagascar and Tanzania. The increasing importance of the rural non-agricultural sector, which tends to provide a higher income to relatively rich rural households, is seen by some authors as a contributor to the large rural gaps (Reardon, 1997; Haggblade *et al.*, 2007). From another perspective, however, it also demonstrates the potential for increasing average rural incomes if employment in rural non-farm industries becomes further popularized in the future. An extensive study published by the World Bank, for instance, views the non-farm sector not as a coping strategy, but rather as a growth strategy (Fox and Sohnesen, 2012).

Table 2.15 Change of national Gini coefficients (various years)

Country	*Year (first, second)*	*First Gini index*	*Second Gini index*	*Average annual percentage change*
Landlocked				
Burkina Faso	(1998, 2009)	0.47	0.40	−1.47
Burundi	(1998, 2006)	0.42	0.33	−2.98
Ethiopia	(1999, 2005)	0.30	0.30	−0.09
Malawi	(1997, 2004)	0.50	0.39	−3.57
Mali	(2001, 2010)	0.40	0.33	−1.90
Coastal				
Cote d'Ivoire	(1998, 2008)	0.44	0.42	−0.53
Kenya	(1997, 2005)	0.43	0.48	1.44
Madagascar	(2001, 2010)	0.47	0.44	−0.81
Mozambique	(2002, 2007)	0.47	0.46	−0.62
Tanzania	(2000, 2007)	0.35	0.38	1.18
Senegal	(2001, 2005)	0.41	0.39	−1.27
Resource–rich				
Cameroon	(2001, 2007)	0.40	0.39	−0.63
Nigeria	(2003, 2010)	0.43	0.49	1.86
Mauritania	(2000, 2008)	0.39	0.41	0.45
Swaziland	(2000, 2009)	0.51	0.51	0.18
Zambia	(1998, 2006)	0.53	0.55	0.28
Average second (most recent) Gini index 0.42				

Source: Calculated with reference to PovCal, http://iresearch.worldbank.org/PovcalNet/index.htm.

Table 2.16 Decomposition of inequality (2003)

Country	*Total Theil index*	*Rural inequality*	*Urban inequality*	*Within-sector inequality*	*Between-sector inequality*	*Within-sector percentage share*	*Between-sector percentage share*
Landlocked							
Burkina Faso	0.638	0.403	0.199	0.293	0.345	46.0	54.0
Mali	0.609	0.449	0.281	0.338	0.271	55.5	44.5
Niger	1.185	0.735	0.416	0.508	0.677	42.9	57.1
Uganda	0.484	0.285	0.252	0.272	0.211	56.3	43.7
Coastal							
Ghana	0.345	0.301	0.201	0.244	0.101	70.8	29.2
Kenya	0.362	0.295	0.105	0.204	0.158	56.4	43.6
Madagascar	0.468	0.314	0.370	0.341	0.127	72.9	27.1
Senegal	0.441	0.416	0.198	0.260	0.181	58.9	41.1
Tanzania	0.357	0.215	0.246	0.231	0.126	64.6	35.4
Resource-rich							
Nigeria	0.410	0.421	0.202	0.305	0.105	74.4	25.6

Source: Sahn and Stifel (2003). This table is reproduced here by permission of UNUWIDER, which commissioned the original research and holds copyright thereon.

The fifth and sixth columns further reveal that within-group inequality in rural and urban areas is larger than rural–urban income disparities for all coastal and resource-rich countries, while the shares are more evenly distributed for landlocked countries. This result is coherent with Jamal and Weeks' (1988) observation of a decreasing rural–urban gap and the emergence of both urban and rural poor. The report by Fox and Sohnesen (2012) also shows the importance of non-farm enterprises in providing channels of income smoothing through more diverse livelihoods and eventually acting as a main driver out of poverty for the poor.

Poverty

Over the past 30 years, poverty has become endemic throughout much of Sub-Saharan Africa. In 1993, nearly 40 per cent of the population lived on less than $1.25 a day. In 1997, 31 of the world's least developed countries were in Africa. This trend of poverty deepened in the 2000s—there was a decline in the welfare of Africans due to a fall in real incomes and the decline of per capita social sector expenditure. Africa has higher chronic poverty levels than other developing regions. Despite a general increase in GDP and improvements in macroeconomic stability, the proportion of the population living below the $1.25 a day threshold remains high, at 46 per cent (World Bank, 2004). The unresponsiveness of poverty to economic growth implies that the lack of stable sources of income through employment is an important cause of poverty. Empirical evidence also points to the close association between employment performance and poverty prevalence: poverty rates have remained roughly constant, in the same manner as the recorded unemployment rate, since the 1980s.

One reason, hinted at earlier, is underdevelopment of, and underinvestment in, the agricultural sector, which employs the majority of workers in most African countries. This sector suffers from low productivity growth and has been unable to meet the demands for real employment and income security of the rural population.

There is also a hierarchy of poverty levels among the four sectors mentioned above. Since workers in the informal economy tend to earn less than their counterparts in the formal sector, they face a substantially higher prevalence of poverty. Empirical evidence from five African cities shows historically high proportions of informal sector workers earning less than the minimum wage: 67 per cent in Yaoundé, 43 per cent in Bamako, 33 per cent in Lomé and 23 per cent in Kigali (Charmes, 1990). Moreover, informally employed workers are not provided with risk-coping instruments such as insurance and pensions, further increasing their vulnerability to poverty.

Other causes of poverty include entrenched social norms, failures of public policy, political instability and the worldwide vicissitudes of trade. Due to social pressures, women are often prevented from gaining a decent education—low education rates among women correlate with higher birth rates, and the more children parents have to support, the less parents are able to provide their kin with the educations, immunizations and other resources that could help elevate them out of poverty. Farmers with low education levels are less likely to adopt new, more efficient technologies, and get relatively low returns on their land (World Bank, 2007). Family planning policies and poor government regulation work to limit the opportunities of citizens and often exacerbate poverty. War, civil strife and economic disasters have also contributed to the entrenchment of the continent's impoverishment. Using a wider lens, it is clear that the implementation of economic reform programs has in some cases also worsened the situation of people. The closure of companies, civil service reforms and the retrenchment of workers have all contributed to low standards of living. Finally, Africa is increasingly marginalized by the global marketplace—the continent's share of world trade is less than 3 per cent of the total (and most of the trade that does occur is concentrated in South Africa).

Poverty is especially prevalent among African youth. A high percentage of young people working in the informal sector are poor, and an even larger share of young women (relative to men) working in the informal economy are poor (ILO, 2005). Poverty forces many young Africans to take up unattractive jobs in the informal economy. Overall, average incomes in the informal sector are significantly lower than in the formal economy. The absence or weakness of labour income negatively affects the welfare of young Africans, while their vulnerability to negative shocks increases young people's probability of becoming or staying poor. The number of young working poor in Africa (near 60 per cent of total youth employment) is increasing. In addition to causing a low standard of living, other consequences of youth poverty include delayed social integration and modification of their demographic behavior, disruptive social behavior (such as crime), and participation in armed conflicts (Cling *et al.*, 2007).

Remittances

Remittances are part of a private welfare system that transfers purchasing power from relatively richer to relatively poorer members of a family (or a community), smoothing consumption and affecting labour supply. In Sub-Saharan Africa, migrant workers sending income to their families at home form a significant portion of family incomes. This is part of an overall global trend, although remittances to Sub-Saharan Africa generally increased at a pace slower than to other developing regions. However, the remittance rates shown below are only a small fraction of total remittances to Sub-Saharan Africa. Total remittances are significant in size and are estimated to amount to multiples of foreign aid. Freund and Spatafora (2005) estimate that informal remittances to Sub-Saharan Africa are relatively high at 45–65 per cent of formal flows.

The distribution of remittances from abroad by migrant workers varies by region. Countries in Northern Africa (e.g. Morocco, Algeria and Egypt) are

Table 2.17 Migrant workers and remittances (2006)

Country	*No. of labour migrants (est.)*	*Remittance inflows (US$ million)*	*Remittance percentage of GDP*
Uganda	154,747	814	8.7
Tanzania	188,789	313	2.4
Kenya	427,324	796	3.8
Rwanda	196,104	149	6.0
Burundi	315,477	184	22.8
Nigeria	836,832	5,397	4.7
Ghana	906,698	851	6.6
Senegal	463,403	667	8.5
Algeria	1,783,476	5,399	4.7
Egypt	2,399,251	3,637	3.4
Morocco	2,718,665	6,116	10.7
Tunisia	623,221	1,559	5.1
South Africa	713,104	1,489	0.6
Lesotho	258,589	355	24.1
Mozambique	803,261	565	7.4
Ethiopia	445,926	591	4.4

Source: IFAD Fact Book 2006.

the major recipients. In the East Africa region, annual average remittances per migrant worker reach almost US$1200 and represent 5 per cent of GDP, indicating that these economies are highly dependent on remittance flows.

Remittances to rural areas comprise a large share of total remittances, particularly in West and southern Africa. For example, two thirds of West African migrant workers in Ghana remit to rural areas in their country of origin. Table 2.17 summarizes labour migration and remittance trends in Africa for the year 2006. It further demonstrates that most African countries earned substantial amounts of foreign exchange in the form of remittances, which accounted for between 2 and 24 per cent of their GDP.

A comparison of inward and outward remittance flows for the East African countries show that Uganda's remittance outflows have constituted, on average, about 70 per cent of inward remittances since 2003. Kenya has the lowest level of remittance outflows in the East African Community, whereas remittance outflows exceed the inflows of Rwanda and Tanzania (Table 2.18). This high level of remittance outflows suggests the importance of further increasing

Table 2.18 Trend of remittance flows (2003–07)

Country	*IFS**	*2003 OFS**	*NET*	*IFS*	*2004 OFS*	*NET*	*IFS*	*2005 OFS*	*NET*	*IFS*	*2006 OFS*	*NET*	*IFS*	*2007 OFS*	*NET*
Uganda	306	259	47	371	235	136	423	359	64	814	322	492	856	n.a.	
Kenya	538	7	531	620	34	586	805	56	749	1,128	25	1,103	1,300	n.a.	
Tanzania	9	27	18	11	34	13	18	31	13	14	29	15	14	n.a.	
Rwanda	9	30	21	10	31	21	21	35	14	21	47	26	21	n.a.	

Source: World Bank (2009).

inward remittance to improve the domestic economy and reduce poverty levels through net inward remittances.

2.2.4 Other micro-foundational factors

Education

Opportunities for formal education increased dramatically during Africa's first 50 years of independence. According to UNESCO (2011), during 1970–2008 enrolment in primary education increased 5.5 times, secondary school enrolment grew 8.5 times, and tertiary enrolment increased 22.3 times. The 2000s saw an especially high jump in enrolment figures—the number of primary school enrolees increased from 87 million students in 2000 to 129 million in 2008.

But the increases in the overall youth population mean that educational systems are struggling to enrol as many students as they need to, and the fast rates of enrolment make it more difficult for these systems to satisfactorily educate those who do reach the classroom—many young Africans lack the basic literacy and numeracy skills that are vital to developing a dynamic workforce. This is not due solely to weak educational systems. Poverty prevents families from being able to afford school fees, uniforms and other school-related items, and many children have to stay at home to perform household chores in order to allow their parents to focus on income-generating activities. Child labour is common in African economies, and one study estimates that 25 per cent of children aged between 5 and 14 are working (World Bank, 2009). Child labour and education are not always mutually exclusive activities, and many students are required to perform chores or part-time work while they are in school—but the demands of each activity decreases the energy which the student is able to devote to the other, and the quality of both education and labour are degraded.

The burdens imposed by disease also serve as major impediments to education—children are orphaned by diseases such as malaria or HIV/AIDS, and often have to enter the labour force instead of school. A survey in Tanzania showed that AIDS orphans there were more likely to withdraw from school due to factors such as poverty and the stigmatization of families affected by HIV/AIDS (Garcia and Fares, 2008).

And though the numbers of Africans receiving secondary or tertiary level diplomas and certificates continue to rise, labour markets are not creating skilled job opportunities at the same rates. Hence more high school and college graduates find themselves underemployed, often working unskilled jobs. The resulting dissatisfaction can lead to the radicalization of youth and, sometimes, political unrest (Africa Center for Strategic Studies, 2012).

Health

Young Africans are particularly vulnerable to diseases—such as HIV/AIDS, malaria, tuberculosis and water-borne diseases—and other health problems including malnourishment, birth complications, the consequences of pollution and environmental degradation, and dangerous work environments. These conditions make it more difficult for young people to attain decent levels of education. The conditions often force them, unskilled and vulnerable, out of the classroom and into the workplace, and often decrease the overall productivity of Sub-Saharan African economies.

HIV/AIDS is one of the major health problems affecting the continent, and the problems that result from infection represent the far-reaching negative effects of disease on youth's work productivity. An estimated 10 million young people aged 15–24 are living with HIV/AIDS (United Nations, 2007) and young people account for half of all new infections. According to the African Development Forum[7], AIDS reduces the earning capacity of affected individuals and increases their medical expenses, pushing families and households further into poverty, creating a vicious cycle of material deprivation and health problems. HIV/AIDS is a major burden for affected countries as it reduces the labour supply and productivity levels, which in turn have a negative impact on economic growth. It also severely hampers the efforts of governments to achieve sustainable economic development, in particular by diverting scarce resources from other development priorities.

Young women are particularly vulnerable to health problems, diminishing their opportunities for decent work. According to the United Nations (2007), 76 per cent of youth living with HIV/AIDS in Sub-Saharan African are young women. The burden of HIV means that women in households are forced to drop out of school in order to provide financial support and/or care for their siblings, parents and other family members. According to a British women's health NGO, the common occurrence of early marriage increases the likelihood of child mortality for young women. Girls aged 10 to 14 are five times more likely to die in pregnancy or childbirth than women aged 20 to 24. Young mothers face higher health risks during pregnancies, including complications such as heavy bleeding, fistula, infection, anaemia and eclampsia (FORWARD, 2012).

Gender

Youth underemployment in Africa follows patterns that are highly gender-specific. In rural areas, patterns of land ownership and inheritance may make it difficult for young men to acquire land that they can farm on their own account. In urban areas, rigidly structured apprenticeship systems make it difficult for boys to enter skilled trades. As a result, many boys and young men in urban areas resort to occasional work as porters or hawkers.

Social pressures prevent many women from acquiring the education and skills necessary to find decent work. Young girls are sometimes regarded as economic burdens that must be married off to older men in order to bring economic and social benefits to the girl's family. According to the World Bank (2009), most young African women have already been married before the age of 24, and in many countries they get married even earlier. A 2005 UN

Population Fund study showed that over 70 per cent of girls were married by age 18 in Niger and the Democratic Republic of the Congo, (compared with two of Asia's poorest countries—Afghanistan and Bangladesh—where the rate was approximately 50 per cent) (UNFPA, 2005).

In both rural and urban areas, girls face pressure to provide labour for household production activities, which may leave them unable to work full time in the market. According to UNECA (2005), very few young women engage in establishing and running their own enterprises. For instance, in Zambia only around 5 per cent of females aged 15 to 19 are running enterprises as proprietors compared with 15 per cent among their male counterparts. While 25 per cent of female youth aged 20 to 24 are engaged in running enterprises in Zambia, as many as 40 per cent of male youth are self-employed.

Corruption

Corruption, both large scale at the center and at the micro local level, is well known as a prominent feature of the Sub-Saharan African landscape. It impacts on youth underemployment by giving additional advantage in job-seeking to those with more ample resources, especially in naturally resource-rich countries. It also has an impact on the interaction between agriculture and rural non-agriculture, as well as on the interaction between the urban informal and urban formal sectors. To the extent that transactions are not arms-length but are subject to special pleading and discrimination, the ability of the typical Sub-Saharan African country to move forward is clearly handicapped. To the extent that ethnic differentiations play a role, there is an advantage to decentralization of the vertical variety, which is likely to increase transparency, and of the horizontal variety, which permits local NGOs and other aspects of civil society to supervise local government decision-making and reduce corruption levels.

2.3 Macroeconomic policy

This chapter argues that formal unemployment, as defined in advanced economies, is a relatively rare phenomenon in Sub-Saharan Africa, where almost all people report employment on at least a part-time basis. The more widespread problem is that many people work in activities where they have low productivity and receive little remuneration; this represents a form of (partially disguised) underemployment, whether defined as 'time underemployment' or 'wage underemployment'. Within agriculture and the rural and urban informal sectors, almost all workers are self-employed or contribute unpaid labour to family businesses. This suggests that labour markets are not fully developed or are failing to create productive opportunities for employment.

As a result, underemployment is a structural feature of Sub-Saharan economies, reflecting underlying failures of labour markets. Unlike the unemployment and underemployment of advanced economies, Africa's underemployment is not significantly driven by short-run cyclical fluctuations: it is a long-run phenomenon. This implies that the standard short-run macro toolkit of fiscal and monetary policy does not exert much leverage on the problem. This chapter takes the view that the tools of short-run macro policy will have little impact in reducing the unemployment and underemployment of youth in Africa.

A growing literature recognizes that fiscal and monetary policies are weak tools in many African countries, which are characterized by thin formal sector markets and ineffective institutions, and where central banks and finance ministries have relatively limited reach. In this context, macro policymakers have increasingly focused on achieving macro stability, creating an environment that is conducive to investment and growth, rather than trying to run active countercyclical policies.

These policies have been largely successful over the past 15 years or so in achieving stable macroenvironments in most countries of Sub-Saharan Africa. Until the past year or two, inflation has been modest in most of the region and governments have successfully pursued both internal and external balance. The macro problems of earlier periods—rampant inflation, overvaluation of exchange rates, perennial government deficits and balance of payments crises—have largely been averted as Africa has exhibited sound macro performance.

Altogether, this suggests that most African countries may continue to benefit from a relatively orthodox set of macro policies, in combination with thoughtful programs of social spending and public investment. Employment is not likely to respond greatly to the short-run tools of fiscal and monetary policy; instead, the issue is to create an environment conducive for investment, capital accumulation and employment-enhancing growth.

2.3.1 Monetary policy frameworks and long-term growth

Among the key achievements of macro policy in many African countries has been a general reduction of inflation levels. A new generation of policymakers—often including independent central bank governors—has pragmatically pursued inflation targets and restored monetary stability. This in turn has allowed some countries to maintain reasonably stable exchange rates at competitive levels. Others were less successful and struggled to curb soaring commodity prices, creating Dutch disease pressures. In determining the optimal set of monetary policies, it is important to note the distinct monetary policy frameworks in different Sub-Saharan African countries.

Members of the West African Economic and Monetary Union (*Union économique et monétaire ouest-africaine*, UEMOA) and the Central African Economic and Monetary Community (*Communauté Économique et Monétaire de l'Afrique Centrale*, CEMAC) have adopted a pegged currency regime through a common legal tender. They benefit from a stable nominal anchor and lower transaction cost, which facilitate industry and trade. This is of particular significance for small open economies that are in the process of stabilization (Mussa *et al.*, 2000).

At the same time, however, the rigid exchange rate increases the challenge of adjusting the real exchange rate to external shocks. This can lead to an overvaluation of the currency in the case of domestic inflationary pressures (Edwards, 1988), which decreases the competitiveness of the tradable goods sector relative to the non-tradable goods sector, and thus discourages the development of exports that potentially could provide employment opportunities to low-skilled workers. Allowing a persistent overvaluation has been shown to have a negative impact on long-term growth in a number of developing countries (Gala and Lucinda, 2006). Moreover, given increasing financial integration, external shocks such as credit market crunches would be directly transmitted, increasing vulnerability to fluctuations in the global economy.

As shown in Figure 2.9, most countries with a pegged exchange rate have been maintaining relatively low long-term exchange rates, except for the inflation surge in 1994, which was due to a short-term misalignment of the exchange rate. Inflation rates decreased back to normal levels after adjustment.

Theoretically, the challenges facing fixed exchange rate regimes would be resolved when adopting a managed or independent floating exchange rate coupled with money targeting, which is implemented in most Sub-Saharan countries. However, money demand has been unstable and difficult to predict, rendering the quantity theory of money an unreliable means of attaining price stability (Masson, 2006). Money market uncertainties and policy limitations have caused a significant number of target misses, which are positively related to inflation (IMF, 2008). However, most Sub-Saharan African countries have been able to adhere to realistic flexible exchange rate regimes.

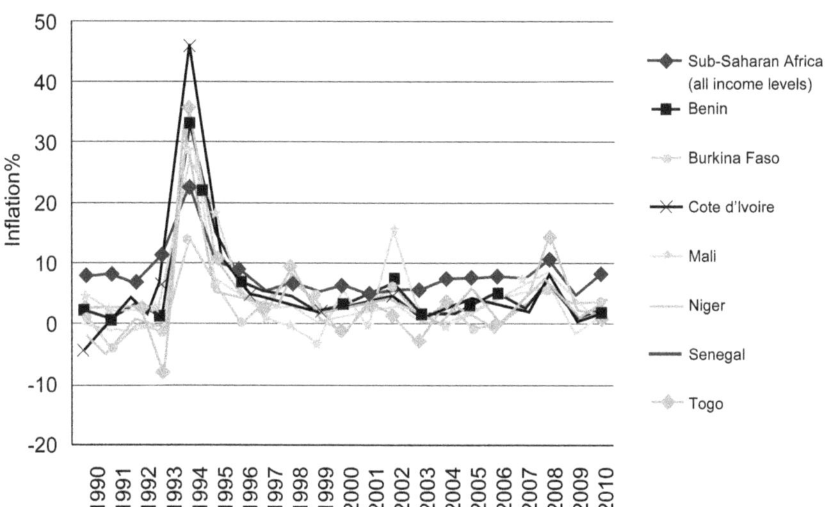

Figure 2.9 Inflation rates in selected countries under pegged exchange rates (1990–2010)
Source: World Bank World Development Indicators.

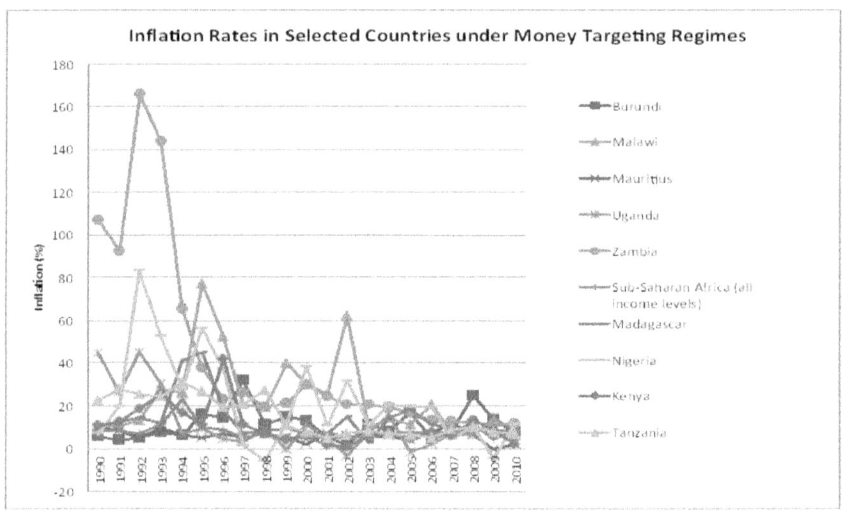

Figure 2.10 Inflation rates in selected countries under money-targeting regimes (1990–2010)

Source: World Bank World Development Indicators.

As observed from Figure 2.10, some countries under money-targeting regimes struggle to control inflation at moderate levels. Malawi and Zambia in particular were able to end runaway inflations only in the early 2000s. Others, such as Kenya and Mauritius, were more successful in their monetary policies and enjoyed consistently low inflation rates.

In response to the view that neither of the above frameworks has succeeded in guaranteeing moderate and stable levels of inflation, Ghana and South Africa have introduced an inflation-targeting framework (Box 2.5). Under this framework, monetary authorities announce medium-term inflation targets with an institutional commitment to achieve this target.

Box 2.5 Inflation targeting in Ghana

The Bank of Ghana Act in 2002 authorized operational independence to the central bank to establish an implicit inflation targeting regime, where the monetary and fiscal institutions are jointly committed to price stability as their primary objective. The numerical target range for inflation is announced in the annual budget, and the Bank of Ghana communicates regularly with the markets about its goals and decisions. First success was achieved when domestic debt levels decreased from 31 per cent of GDP in 2001 to 13.5 per cent in 2006, while inflation decreased from 38 per cent to 12.7 per cent over the same period. In

May 2007 Ghana formally adopted the inflation-targeting framework, and in recent years it has enjoyed much higher levels of growth compared with the 1980s and 1990s.

Source: Adapted from Njugana (2008)

The Ghanaian experience demonstrates the potential benefits of adopting inflation targeting. In fact, although the optimal policy framework is often a combination of components from different regimes depending on the structural features of each individual country, inflation targeting is often seen as the benchmark regime towards which many countries are aiming to progress.

One important reason for its empirical success is a higher capacity for attaining dual targets through effective communication and credible long-term strategies. For example, in response to the recent surges in food prices, a clear and credible public explanation of how food inflation developments alter inflation profiles over the short run, and how the central bank is planning to meet inflation targets over a longer horizon, can help anchor expectations of future inflation surges (IMF, 2008).

With respect to the underemployment issue, focus on a dual mandate of maintaining moderate inflation levels while generating more economic and employment growth is especially relevant because maintaining low inflation levels will not, by itself, increase the rate of economic growth.[8] In some cases, although supply shock-induced inflation brings about a negative growth effect, demand-pull inflation resulting from a process of economic expansion can have a positive impact on growth as long as inflation rates remain moderate (Bruno, 1995). Therefore macroeconomic policy should not focus exclusively on contractionary measures, but should aim comprehensively at decent employment targets coupled with moderate inflation targets over the long run.

Nevertheless, it is important to note that effective inflation-targeting policy requires a set of preconditions with credible central bank instrument independence as a key component (Masson, 2006; IMF, 2008). As Masson further argues, low levels of fiscal deficit, public support for low inflation rates, an effective public communication system, and flexible labour and product markets are conducive to this goal. However, for the minority of countries in which authorities are likely to set prices or interfere with the central bank's polities due to political pressures, inflation targeting would bear little significance.

2.3.2 Fiscal policy and resource allocation

Persistently high levels of fiscal deficits have been the dominant challenge for fiscal policymakers in the past decades, but significant improvements have been made in recent years. As seen from Figure 2.11, oil-exporting countries have recovered from the global crises in the late 2010s and regained their surpluses, while middle-income countries experienced continuous fiscal consolidation.

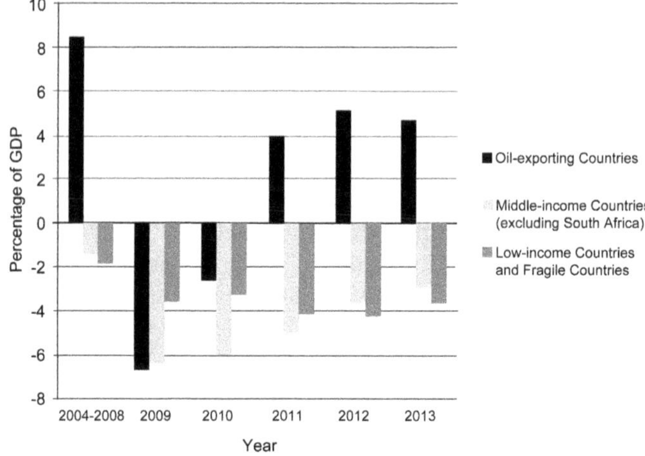

Figure 2.11 Overall fiscal balance by country group (2004–13)
Source: IMF, World Economic Outlook database. http://www.imf.org/external/ns/cs.aspx?id=28.

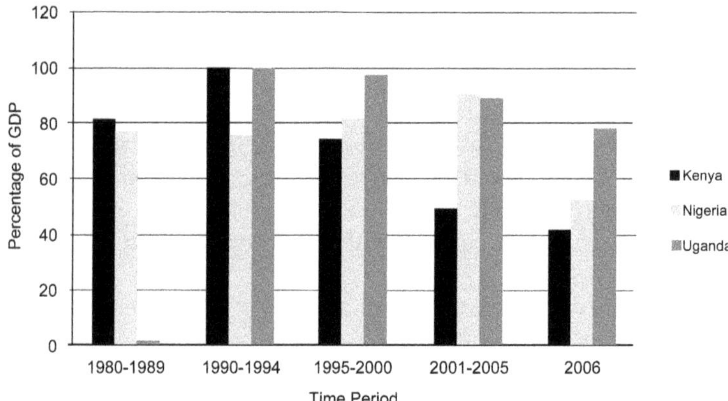

Figure 2.12 Total debt levels of selected countries (1980–2006)
Source: Njugana (2008).

Results for low-income and fragile states remain rather mixed. General economic expansion leads to higher levels of revenue, improvements in revenue collection efficiency through tax reforms, and the relief of debt by the international community—these factors, in turn, contribute to the overall reduction of deficits.

Nevertheless, a significant amount of declining debt is still present in most African economies due to the accumulation of fiscal deficits over time (Figure 2.12).

Theoretically, typical ways of debt financing all have their downsides.[9] In Sub-Saharan African economies, although public sector borrowing does not necessarily crowd out private investment to the extent that it does in rich countries, public sector expansion does tend to drive up wages in the urban formal sector and thereby to squeeze job creation. Higher taxes to fund government spending can also prove burdensome because many countries have a relatively narrow tax base, so that taxes fall heavily on formal sector firms. This can create distortionary patterns and strong disincentives to formal sector investment. Therefore the most sustainable method of achieving low budget deficits and external debt levels is still through responsible fiscal spending and real economic growth.

Box 2.6 Reducing budget deficit without over-reliance on external aid in Kenya

Kenya has come a long way to attain sustainable debt levels in recent years. In 1990–94, Kenya reached the highest total debt ratio of 100 per cent of GDP, while external debt was at 77 per cent of GDP. At the same time, international financing institutions and bilateral donors reduced their development assistance to Kenya towards the mid-1990s. From 1997 onwards, the flow of official development assistance to Kenya shrank to less than 5 per cent of GDP. However, as a result of wise macroeconomic policies, Kenya managed to reduce its total debt to 41 per cent of GDP, while external debt decreased to 22 per cent.

The debt reduction in Kenya can be attributed to fiscal discipline in expenditure and higher revenue collection due to growth of the economy, which jointly led to a reduction in budget deficits. Fiscal tightening was achieved through reducing recurrent and other expenditures, while shifting resources to capital investments while the economy was expanding. Consequentially, fiscal deficits were less than 1 per cent of GDP during 1996–2005. Moreover, an active promotion of the banking sector and an increased demand for financial services led to financial deepening. This allowed the government to borrow more without exerting unsustainable pressure on interest rates.

Source: Adapted from Njugana (2008)

2.3.3 Financial infrastructure

The financial sector is the primary channel through which monetary policies have an impact on real economic outcomes. Sound institutional factors of the financial sector are thus essential in achieving policy goals for a stable macroeconomy. Building on this period of stability to achieve employment and growth-related goals requires optimal allocation of resources as well creating a business-friendly environment conducive to investment.

Unfortunately, the developmental role of the financial sector is undermined by limited access to suitable financial services.[10] Barriers to credit and financial markets pose a particularly serious constraint for agricultural and informal activities operating in remote areas.

Moreover, the cost of credit is relatively high. This discourages investment activities and start-up enterprises, both of which rely on borrowing. It also raises the financial burden and uncertainty of sustaining profitable employment for existing firms with debts. The high costs of borrowing are in part reflected by the large interest rate spreads, which on average fall in the upper portion of the distribution of the spreads in developing countries. One contributing factor is the high risk premium charged to borrowers, which is often based on the misconception that most creditors are high-risk borrowers (Atieno, 2001), as many commercial banks do not make an effort to collect information on the creditworthiness of potential borrowers outside of their original clientele (Kimuyu and Omiti, 2000). In some countries, credit at market rates is not available even for private sector borrowers because banks prefer to hold excess reserves instead of extending loans to perceived high-risk borrowers (Sacerdoti, 2005).

Informal financial institutions and development banks have attempted to fill in the gap where commercial banks have failed to meet the demands for credit, particularly in the rural community. Aryeetey and Udry (1997) have shown that they have a distinct advantage in obtaining more detailed knowledge of local conditions and their clients, leading to lower costs for accessing reliable credit. Policies should recognize and enhance the potential of the informal credit providers in aiding informal and rural enterprises to generate employment opportunities. For example, fostering linkages between formal and informal institutions can increase the amount of financial resources available to improve and expand the service of informal credit providers, with a significant impact on employment outcomes (Amoako-Tuffour, 2002).

2.4 Micro-foundational policy

Though donors and governments are acutely aware of the challenges presented by Africa's youth bulge, their attempts to decrease underemployment—through initiatives such as public works projects, vocational training and promoting entrepreneurship—have not been able to keep pace with the problem. There are many reasons for this failure.[11] One is that effective youth policies require the coordination of various arms of government, as well as government–NGO coordination, and coordination across formal and informal sectors. Such coordination is often stymied by shortfalls in funding, corruption, mismanagement and political conflicts. Another impediment is that governments often do not substantively involve youth in formulating policy, which means that the very people who are affected by government initiatives are not consulted about what they truly need. Finally, for those youth-oriented policies that have been instituted, there have been very few studies done to establish both whether the policies were effective, and whether the initiatives made fiscal sense. Cost–benefit analyses of youth-oriented labour market interventions have been seriously lacking.

The following sections highlight some of the major policy interventions that have been used to try to improve the quality of the Sub-Saharan African work force and increase the number of opportunities for those workers. We overview the benefits and shortcomings of several types of policy intervention, and identify areas that demand more systematic, longitudinal cost–benefit analyses.

2.4.1 Stigmatization of the informal sector

A barrier to better integrating the informal sectors in African economies is the negative perceptions that members of society—and especially African governments—have of the informal sector. Formal primary, secondary and tertiary education, as well as formal apprenticeship programs, are often seen as superior to the informal educational and apprenticeship structures that exist in Sub-Saharan Africa, and social standing is often tied to your level of education. In Nigeria, vocational and technical education have a low public status (Dike, 2010), and in Kenya the assumption exists that many of those who go from school directly into the informal sector are dropouts or school-leavers who have failed to make the grade in formal training institutions (Barassa and Kaabwe, 2001). The presumptions about these informal systems and the people who work in them are often incorrect, and they create stereotypes that ramify throughout policymaking structures. The cementing of popular perceptions can lead policymakers to hold the informal sector in low regard—an unhelpful attitude when it is the mobilization of this large sector that is the key to helping decrease youth underemployment.

2.4.2 Family planning

Efforts to curb Sub-Saharan Africa's dramatically high birth rates have proceeded in fits and starts.[12] Though Sub-Saharan Africa continues to have the youngest populations in the world, family planning efforts have helped most of these countries experience fertility decline, though the degree of this decline varies widely across countries. For example, Eritrea, Namibia and Togo have all succeeded in dramatically lowering their fertility rates; Chad, Cote d'Ivoire and Ethiopia have seen more modest declines; and some countries, such as Niger and Mali, have shown little or no decline.

Given the pressures that Africa's youth bulge continues to exert on already weak labour markets, family planning is one of the more important policy interventions needed by African governments. Effective family planning initiatives can help improve standards of living by decreasing child mortality, decreasing unwanted pregnancies, increasing the educational opportunities of African youth, and increasing young women's access to education and decent work opportunities.

In a study done in Ethiopia, Portner *et al.* (2011) found that access to family planning substantially reduced the number of children ever born by women without education—the reduction is especially pronounced for women younger than 20 and older than 30. Completed fertility, measured as children ever born for women aged 40 to 45, falls by more than one birth with access to family planning. Women younger than 20 with long-term access to family planning have one child fewer than those without access to family planning, indicating postponements of births.

Osili and Long (2008) use economic theory to show how increased education can help lower fertility rates. First, female schooling may increase the opportunity cost of childbearing and rearing among educated women. Second, education may lower fertility through improvements in child health and reduced rates of child mortality, as women need to have fewer births to yield the same desired family size. Finally, female schooling may affect fertility through knowledge and more effective use of contraceptive methods, or by increasing female autonomy and bargaining power in fertility decisions. Osili and Long found that increasing female education by one year reduces early fertility by 0.26 births.

2.4.3 Entrepreneurship

The failure of developing world youth to engage in entrepreneurship can be attributed to an array of factors, including sociocultural attitudes towards youth entrepreneurship, lack of entrepreneurial training in the school curriculum, incomplete market information, absence of business support and physical infrastructure, limited access to technology, regulatory framework conditions, and, in particular, poor access to finance and materials (Garcia and Fares, 2008). In West Africa half of all informal firms report that they have inadequate access to credit, which functions as a significant barrier to creating a sustainable business.[13] In addition, many new small enterprises have difficulties accessing raw materials. The clothing and apparel sector provides an example of the challenges faced by new entrepreneurs (many of whom, it can be assumed, are young people): on one hand, there is the lack of demand (not enough clients, too much competition); on the other hand, there are difficulties in accessing capital in a broad sense (access to credit, savings, lack of locality, lack of machines and equipment).

In response to these factors, many national governments have initiated programs to help spur entrepreneurship, including introducing entrepreneurship training into the curricula of technical education and vocational training centers. In Zambia, the government established the Technical Education Vocational and Entrepreneurship Development Authority, whose purpose is to promote entrepreneurship and self-employment, especially among graduates of technical training institutions (Chigunta, 2002). The Zambian government also has set up a K40 billion Youth Empowerment Fund (Chigunta, 2002). In Kenya, a Micro and Small Enterprise Development Fund used World Bank money to advance entrepreneurship development in the private sector and, more immediately, to overcome barriers to employment and income-generation opportunities in the informal medium and small enterprise sector; and Ethiopia has several employment exchange services, run by both public and private operators (Garcia and Fares, 2008).

2.4.4 Formal education interventions

Despite the increase in the total number of students enrolled in primary school, Leibbrandt and Mlatsheni (2004) highlight how direct and indirect costs of primary schooling continue to constrain enrolment. School fees, mandating that students wear uniforms, and rigid school schedules (which do not take into consideration important events such as the harvest) are some examples of these costs. There are also major cultural impediments to girls' education, including pressure to drop out of school early in order to take care of the home and seek a husband, and school pregnancy policies that discourage women from re-enrolling in school after they give birth. School–community relationships are often weak, and parental involvement and advocacy are lacking. And a dearth of female teachers and administrators means that many girls lack role models and mentors.

Secondary schooling has become more widely available to young Africans. Between 1990 and 2008, the gross enrolment ratio of secondary-level students increased from 11.3 per cent to 34.1 per cent, and some governments have declared for universal secondary education (UNESCO, 2011). But the secondary level requires policies that are more complex than those required for primary schooling, and many African governments are finding it difficult to address these challenges (World Bank, 2012). At the secondary level, teachers need to be hired and trained for a more complex set of subjects; advanced curricula—including sections on science and math—need to be developed and widely promulgated; and secondary schools have to equip students with skills that can match the demands of local labour markets. In addition, many of the challenges that face increasing primary enrolment—pressures to marry, school fees, rigid school schedules and a lack for female teachers—become more acute at the secondary level.

Over the past 50 years, efforts to increase tertiary education in Africa have increased and have become more successful. While the absolute number of students enrolling on the tertiary level is small compared with the primary and secondary levels, its rate increase has been the highest, having risen 22.3 times between 1970 and 2008 (from 0.2 million to 4.5 million students) (UNESCO, 2011). But the World Bank (2012) indicates several key areas that policymakers have to address to continue expanding tertiary education opportunities. These include the need to formulate more sustainable means of financing colleges and universities, encouraging private tertiary education development, increasing the capacity of the education sector (including improving training for administrators), increasing faculty numbers and improving the skills of those teachers, providing mobility for students who wish to go on to advanced degrees, and better orienting students to the needs of local and regional labour markets.

2.4.5 Apprenticeship, training, and skills development

With respect to the rural household and urban informal sectors, technical and vocational education training (TVET) is often viewed as the pre-eminent mode of enhancing the skills and knowledge of the underemployed.[14] In Western Africa, traditional apprenticeships are the most common way for a youth to acquire skills. In Ghana, 80–90 per cent of basic skills training come from traditional apprenticeships (compared with 10–15 per cent from public training institutions and 10–15 per cent from NGOs). In West Africa, it is more common to find apprentices than regular employees in informal sector businesses. According to Cling *et al.* (2007), the advantages of traditional apprenticeships are their relative independence from government funding and regulations, and their cost-effectiveness. On the other hand, they do not reach young women or very poor youth workers, and have a tendency to perpetuate traditional technologies.

Regarding public sector-provided TVET, the consensus is that these programs are usually too rigid and not sufficiently oriented towards problem-solving. They are also expensive, up to 14 times that of ordinary secondary education (World Bank, 2009). Due to these factors, African youth are more likely to participate in traditional apprenticeship schemes than in public training institutions.[15]

Grubb (1995) has argued that work experience schemes alone tend to produce a 'dead-weight effect' where youth who are employed as a result of a scheme replace others who would have been employed in any case. Substitution could also occur where program participants replace other categories of labour, for example older workers. Grubb argues that vocational training schemes alone are less effective because they do not facilitate access to employers and job-specific training, which would increase their value to employers. Additionally, a UNDP report points out that the skills training that is available to youth is not guided by a systematic analysis of current and future market demand (United Nations, 2007).

Private training facilities are seen as preferable, and the best alternative is training via 'learning by doing' within companies. The consensus seems to be that primary education and emphasis on broad numeracy and functional literacy abilities are required, perhaps by adding vocational courses to an academic secondary curriculum. A study by Betcherman *et al.* (2004) argues that job training programs are more likely to be successful if they are one component of a larger package that includes basic education, employment services and social services. A recent review of 19 training programs targeting youth shows that, in the absence of such a package, training programs rarely improve the employment and earnings of young participants.

2.4.6 Public works programs and conditional cash transfers

Although underemployment is ultimately dependent upon real economic performance, immediate needs and inefficiencies do exist and should be addressed as short-term policy goals in addition to the longer-term target of employment generation through growth. For example, labour-intensive public works programs are used as a means of providing immediate-impact jobs for relatively large numbers of unskilled workers, and are often pointed out as an important tool for expanding employment opportunities for underemployed young Africans.[16] In addition to traditional public works program—such as road-building—there are socially beneficial projects that include slum upgrading, building of community centers, schools, health facilities, solid waste management, irrigation systems, anti-erosion works and small dams, and rehabilitation of markets.

Observers point to several limitations of these projects, chief of which is that the jobs serve as mere safety nets, lasting only as long as program funds are available (Betcherman *et al.*, 2004). The short-term nature of these projects means they do not have a sustained impact on local markets, and it also means they often do not provide concurrent initiatives producing skills that can be used beyond a given project. Because many of the programs involve road building or other heavy construction activities, women also face social and cultural barriers to participating.

Without follow-on training or additional employment opportunities, these programs can, paradoxically, increase the prospects for political unrest after they end. Public works projects can form large networks of disaffected workers who might be inclined toward unified protests and other activities that become challenges for politicians and policymakers.

Moreover, given their proven success in Latin America, conditional cash transfers (CCT) have been piloted in 15 African countries. The key characteristic of CCT is that it acts simultaneously upon the short- and long-term dimensions of poverty through cash income transfer and improving human capital through school attendance. A comprehensive study of pilot CCT schemes in all 15 African countries found that the impact of cash transfers is very modest when the budget for the CCT program is set at 0.5 per cent of GDP. The impact increases with simulations using the percentages of the poverty line, especially for the 40 per cent benchmark. However, they achieve a maximum of 3.6 per cent increase in school attendance for Burundi (UNDP, 2005). These results suggest that conditionality is a necessary ingredient of cash transfer programs if the aim is to break the intergenerational cycle of poverty. However, practical constraints of state capacity might limit the scale of the scheme for some underdeveloped countries. In brief, both public works programs and CCTs constitute short-term palliatives and do not tackle the long-term unemployment problem.

2.4.7 Incorporating youth employment into poverty reduction strategy papers

According to Richard Curtain (2004), an increasing number of poverty reduction strategy papers (PRSP) are making reference to decreasing under-employment among young people. Djibouti's PRSP promotes a coherent and comprehensive employment policy that aims to develop, amongst other things, education and literacy, job training programs, and implement targeted employment programs.[17] Senegal's PRSP explicitly recognizes the issue of youth employment, and focuses on increasing the capacities of, and opportunities for, the poor, improving the management and quality of labour, improving efficiency and transparency in the employment market, and promoting independent employment in rural and urban areas. Cameroon's PRSP mentions implementing a 'youth training program', and Zambia's PRSP has many youth employment-focused aspects, including a repeal of laws and regulations that hinder youth and female access to land, credit, trade information and technology, and programs to encourage youth and females to participate in private and public credit schemes. Despite such programs, Curtain argues there is evidence that many of these PRSP initiatives are often piecemeal and hence limited in their scale and potential impact, and there remain many other Sub-Saharan African countries that still have not focused on youth employment in their strategy papers.

2.4.8 Wage subsidies

Evaluations of wage subsidy programs in developing economies are few and far between. In one study, wage subsidies were found to have had significant positive effects on youth in developing and developed countries. According to Olga Susana Puerto (2007), four out of five evaluated programs reported positive impacts on employability or earnings. Puerto has also noted that these programs have been quite successful in improving short-term employment outcomes for youth in developing economies.

However, Betcherman *et al.* (2004) argue that wage and employment subsidies are unlikely to be effective in the long run, with substantial dead-weight loss and substitution risks. Most programs they surveyed revealed that participants were less likely to be employed and earned less than those in the control group after the subsidy ended. And due to the scant number of inquiries into this topic, it is also unclear how much these subsidies would cost if applied on a country-wide or region-wide scale. Studies should be done to investigate these potential costs and weigh them against the benefits of such programs.

2.4.9 Developing ICT

There have been many projects—large and small—to develop Africa's ICT sector, including private sector-driven projects to install marine fibre-optic cables along the coasts. Telecommunications investment in Africa is rising to match the dramatic increase in demand for mobile and other technologies.[18] Currently, this investment is dominated by countries such as Kuwait and South Africa. China has been providing low-cost hardware and credit to state-owned operators, while Indian institutions are building a 53-nation Pan-African E-Network under an African Union initiative. E-trade cooperation with the European Union and the USA is increasingly important to meeting trade regulations. UK and French companies have also been making large telecommunications investments in Africa.

Of course, many African economies still suffer from a lack of connectivity, and deficits in basic education hold countries back from significantly expanding ICT opportunities. With that in mind, governments could sponsor initiatives that expand broadband and general connectivity, and could also increase efforts to integrate ICT into education, which would both improve the skills of the young workforce and also develop a portion of the youth population that specializes in ICT. The ICT sector can become an important means of generating jobs for African youth (Braimah and King, 2006). Youth-friendly jobs in this sector include software engineering, staff for call centers, assembly lines, and the sale and repair of ICT equipment (including computers, television sets, musical instruments, telephones and accessories).

2.5 Some policy lessons from Asia and South America

Youth underemployment is a global phenomenon against which many governments have undertaken different measures. In choosing the optimal policy prescription for Sub-Saharan Africa, it is advisable to bear in mind some of the successes and non-successes of other developing countries, especially as most other regions have tackled the problem more effectively. Sub-Saharan Africa suffered an increase in youth underemployment rate of 18.7 per cent during 1998–2008, compared with the decreases observed in most other places (Table 2.19).

In the section below, emphasis is placed on the developing countries of Asia and Latin America.

2.5.1 Increased investment in the rural economy

The need to give higher priority to rural growth rather than industrialization at the early stages of economic development echoes longstanding arguments

Table 2.19 Changes in youth unemployment and underemployment rates (1998–2008)

Region	*1998–2008 (percentage change)*
World	0.2
Sub-Saharan Africa	18.7
North Africa	–3.7
Developed Economies & European Union	–12.2
Central and South Eastern Europe	–22.5
Latin America & the Caribbean	–9.8
East Asia	–4.7
South Asia & the Pacific	1.4
Middle East	31.9

Source: International Labour Organization (2011).

in the literature. Tiffin and Irz (2006), for example, find evidence that agricultural growth precedes overall growth in developing countries. After the initial stages of development have passed, Ranis (1995) further demonstrates the continued importance of agriculture and the rural non-agricultural sector in the import substitution and export substitution phases of Taiwan and South Korea. By this view, only when agricultural output has risen sufficiently will it be possible to absorb idle rural labour into agriculture and eventually develop the infant non-farm sectors, both of which, if guided by suitable policies, have the potential to generate employment and income.

China's rural development process provides a strong example. Its emphasis on developing agriculture before moving into the service and manufacturing sectors, also known as the 'firing from the bottom' policy, acted as the initial catalyst for economic growth and poverty reduction. Consequently, rural poverty fell rapidly and rural incomes doubled during the 1978–84 period (Fan *et al.*, 2002).

The Chinese agricultural and rural reforms (1978–84) focused on decentralizing rural production, introducing a household responsibility system for securing land rights, and launching a new pricing policy that involved increased procurement prices. The introduction of the household responsibility system alone is estimated to have contributed to 60 per cent of the growth in the early 1980s (Lin, 1992). In addition, the Chinese government has correctly recognized technological improvements as an important driving force for the agricultural sector. Funded by the government, teams of academics and technical specialists have pioneered and spread improved seed varieties such as hybrid rice. Overall, increased investment in research accounted for almost one-fifth of the overall growth in agriculture between 1965 and 1993 (Fan and Pardey, 1997).

Echoing its successful agricultural development, China has also devised a favorable approach toward the rural non-agricultural sector. Responding to insufficient factor and product markets in rural areas, the Chinese government fostered the establishment of township and village enterprises (TVEs) in rural regions that would otherwise have developed in larger towns and industrial regions. The government also provided tax and loan concessions and improved transport and communication systems in remote areas to aid the growth of rural businesses. Although TVEs were initially set up in better-off regions, studies have shown that the poor from worse-off regions also benefitted through migration and other spillover effects, rendering TVEs an important employment-generating and poverty-alleviating tool. Within a decade of 1978, the number of TVEs increased from 1.5 million to 18.7 million, with their labour force tripling to more than 90 million (Findlay and Watson, 1992). They are even seen as the driver of the Chinese economy in the first decade of reforms (Huang and Meng, 1997), but have since shifted to private enterprises.

The Chinese pattern of growth in the early 1980s carries an important lesson for Sub-Saharan Africa, where the vast majority of the population is employed in the rural economy. Although part of the success in agricultural growth stems from country-specific circumstances[19], China's experience is still a convincing illustration of rural development as an effective poverty- and underemployment-combating tool, particularly in the early stages of growth. Resource-rich and export-oriented coastal Sub-Saharan countries should especially bear this lesson in mind, as the abundance of resource rents and profits from export-oriented industrialization are likely to cause undue discrimination against the rural economy.

2.5.2 Strengthening farm and non-farm linkages

The example of China is one of many examples indicating the increasing importance of the rural non-farm sector in developing countries. From a comprehensive review of literature, Reardon *et al.* (2001) show that these activities account for 42 per cent of the rural income in Africa and 40 per cent in Asia. Therefore, in addition to boosting agricultural productivity to release capital and labour, attention should be placed on enhancing the linkages between agriculture and non-agricultural activities.

In Mexico, an empirical study has verified the importance of farm–non-farm linkages, with markets outside villages bearing more linkages than those within.[20] A US$100 increase in exogenous household income stimulates increases in village non-farm production by US$0.3 to US$12, while village demand for outside manufacturers increases by US$88 to US$103. In the village/town region, the same increase in income results in an US$18 increase in village non-farm production and raises demand for outside goods by US$74. These findings illustrate that a large share of rural household demand is supplied by the non-farm sector in villages and provincial towns, which have accounted for much of the country's growth in the past decade (Davis, 2002).

The cooperation of agro-industrial businesses, public agencies and NGOs has been crucial in the success of forging these strong linkages. Most of the time producers such as distributors, pigment-producing companies, and poultry and milk firms initiate the connection through the mechanism of contract agriculture. To compete for business, producers have deployed more and more innovative forms of agreements. Such agreements include, for example, triangular contracts that involve mediation and financial service providers for credit guarantee in addition to the purchasing companies and producers.

Effective policies by the Mexican government have also created a favorable business environment for the development of strong farm–non-farm linkages. Realizing that the paternalistic and interventionist policies were inefficient and unsustainable, the government gradually replaced the official agronomists through subcontracting private agronomy firms and companies under the *Programa de Asistencia Técnica para Apoyar la Producción de Granos Básicos* (PEAT). As a result, the percentage of producers receiving assistance from private companies rose from 1 per cent in 1992 to 40 per cent in 1997 (Davis, 2002).

In order to better link technical assistance with credit and commercialization, the Mexican Development Bank (*Fideicomisos Instituidos en Relación con la Agricultura*, FIRA) has put forward the Credit for Administration Programme (PROCREA) that utilizes the services of integrated firms to interact with and organize groups of producers. For instance, the NGO *Asesoría y Servicios Integrados Agropecuarios* (ASIA)'s *cempasúchitl* (marigold) program provides technical assistance and acts as a mediator in purchase/sale contracts. While ASIA organizes suppliers, provides technical assistance and establishes an agreement for flower cultivation and sales to a purchasing company, FIRA opens a line of credit to finance the sowing of the flower seeds. Finally, ASIA hands the harvest to the purchasing company, pays the producers, and returns credit to FIRA while leaving out a commission for itself.

Nevertheless, room for improvement still exists, especially in terms of protecting the producers. At present, there is no effective evaluation system of technical and credit assistance schemes (which is important for reflecting producers' opinions). It would also provide market information to producers choosing a subcontractor and thus deter contract violations. The establishment of a producer organization acting on behalf of its members will further aid the cause of preventing exploitation. At the same time, the coverage of agricultural insurance programs, which at present cater to fewer than a quarter of producers, should be extended to guard against production risks.

2.5.3 Maintaining macroeconomic stability

Unlike many other developing regions, economies in East Asia have been successful in creating and sustaining a stable macroeconomic environment through managing reasonable levels of inflation, foreign debt and exchange rates.

A steady and moderate inflation rate paves the road for stable interest rates conducive to businesses and industries. The experience of some East Asian countries such as South Korea has verified that low budget deficits with prudent fiscal policies lower the chance of high inflation rates. Countries such as Malaysia and Thailand, on the other hand, although they had relatively higher deficits, were able to avoid periods of high inflation by choosing sustainable means of financing (World Bank, 1993). Apart from having high growth rates, raising the demand for currency and absorbing higher levels of monetary financing, they also enjoyed high savings rates. A significant proportion of the savings were reinvested in the domestic financial system, setting off a ripple effect in the demand for more currency and nominal assets while alleviating the pressure for inflationary financing.

Coupled with moderate inflation levels, proper exchange rate management also helped East Asian countries avoid the severe exchange rate fluctuations experienced in Latin America (World Bank, 1993). Broadly speaking, most countries have moved from a pegged currency to managed floating rate regimes, under which policymakers can influence the exchange rate at a margin to move in parallel with the US dollar. With the United States being a major export partner, East Asian exporters have benefitted from a low foreign exchange risk.

Sub-Saharan African countries should follow the East Asian example of focusing on the fundamentals to create a stable macroeconomic structure, which is at the core of employment issues. This is especially important for resource-rich countries, which are more prone to suffer from short-term inflationary bursts and currency overvaluation when resource rents are not properly managed. It should be understood that only responsible spending and investment in production and agriculture bring about real growth and stability in the long run, which cannot be attained through short-term monetary boosts.

2.5.4 Promoting the development of ICT

The potential of ICTs to provide employment opportunities for youth in developing countries has been illustrated in recent reports (ILO, 2001). Among many examples of ICT-generated employment opportunities, the following section explores a best practice from each of the following categories: youth entrepreneurship, public–private partnerships and informal sector development.

In Asia, young entrepreneurs have often been identified with ventures in the digital economy. Telecenters (small street shops offering internet access and public phones for international calls), for example, involve a relatively low start-up costs and thus are a viable option for young people. In India, for example, equipment costs are about US$10,000 including the telecom service provider's investment in a telephone line of US$1000 (Mitter and Millar, 2001). Being more familiar with new technology, youth also have a particular advantage in setting up these enterprises. In India there are about 300,000 such telecommunication centers that have generated more than 600,000 jobs (ILO, 2001).

In addition to providing employment, these facilities help bridge the gap between the informal and the formal economy. Informal sector and self-employed workers unable to afford their own equipment can now gather market information and publicize their business on the internet at their local telekiosk. The Maharashtra State government in India has also extended the service to farmers by linking 40,000 villages with a specially designed software package offering the latest agriculture trends (Lobo, 2000).

At the same time, young people have the opportunity to gain employment at remote processing ICT facilities for companies outside of their origin countries. Call centers that handle telephone calls, fax, email and other types of customer contact are a typical example. Utilizing the lower operational and labour costs, they have expanded rapidly and constitute important sources of work in Taiwan (China), South Korea, Malaysia and the Philippines (ILO, 2001). ICT remote processing facilities, like call centers, are usually operated by foreign enterprises. Suitable government policy in providing incentives and infrastructure is therefore key in forming partnership arrangements and attracting investment. In China, for instance, the government set up the Ministry of Information Industries in 1998 to establish economic zones devoted to nurturing ICT ventures. A nationwide integrated communication system was also established as supporting infrastructure.

The range of initiatives outlined above demonstrates the potential for ICT to generate employment for young people. Since exporting ICT services does not involve transport costs, like other physical goods, landlocked Sub-Saharan economies should focus particularly on long-term strategies that improve the preconditions for ICT development, namely appropriate infrastructure, human capacity, supportive public policy, support for enterprises and appropriate content (Accenture *et al.*, 2001). Capitalizing successfully on the potentials of ICT industries will allow them gradually to overcome their physical constraints and develop a comparative advantage in the export of services.

2.5.5 Accumulating human capital

The importance of accumulating human capital in enhancing productivity and growth is widely understood, but some countries have been more successful than others in achieving this goal.

In East Asia, while the share of public expenditure in education is similar to that of Latin America and Sub-Saharan Africa, the proportion spent on basic education compared with higher education has been consistently higher. By giving priority to expanding the base of the education pyramid, a large amount of cheap and low-skilled yet efficient and literate youth joined the labour force, which, as Ranis (1995) points out, is an important ingredient for any export-oriented development path. Deploying the example of Taiwan, Ranis further illustrates the benefits of expanding vocational training on the secondary level. Through focusing on a specific skill set, vocational training provided by public institutions and individual firms better prepares workers for tasks in the formal economy, and has been shown to have a more direct effect on labour productivity than pure academic training.

It is important to note that some Sub-Saharan households are not fully aware of the long-run value of education attainment, a value which is entrenched in many Asian cultures. Such undervaluation leads them to make inadequate investment in human capital by forgoing school for work at an early age. Therefore, while the Asian experience of supplying low-cost access to basic and vocational education acts as an important role model, demand-side use of education services should also be fostered. The CCT system first pioneered in Latin America can be taken as a reference.

The educational component of the CCT system rewards schools enrolment and attendance of usually 80–85 per cent for primary school students from low-income families with a monthly stipend. This motivates parents to send their children to school instead of work, thereby inducing more investment in education. Required participation in after-school programs further discourages child labour. Impact evaluation verifies this positive change in behaviour. In

Brazil, for example, the introduction of the Bolsa Família has induced an 11.5 per cent increase in school enrolment rate for families in the lower income deciles (Azevedo and Heinrich, 2006). Empirical studies in Mexico revealed that the PROGRESA system had a higher marginal impact on girls, who are traditionally more prone to dropping out of school to assist with household businesses and housework (Schultz, 2000). Given the association between higher school attainment and lower chances of teenage pregnancy, the CCT system may indirectly lower fertility rates and alleviate the pressure of population growth on labour markets. Nevertheless, Sub-Saharan countries should be careful in designing and implementing similar systems to ensure cost-effective delivery of incentives to the target group while minimizing corruption and misallocation.

2.6 Policy recommendations

This section presents a range of recommendations for policymakers to choose from, depending on their country's specific needs and circumstances. Some have been tested directly through randomized trials; others draw from theory and analytical frameworks in previous sections. Yet none is strictly better than the others, because the most optimal case is for all, or at least a subset of them, to act together and complement each other as part of a bigger policy scheme. After all, only a comprehensive tool set can effectively resolve a problem as complex and multifaceted as youth underemployment.

2.6.1 Sector-specific recommendations

Agriculture

Agriculture and agro-businesses offer strong potential for youth employment. However, ownership of land, access to agricultural inputs, tools and technical training are essential for the successful employment of youth in these activities, particularly in post-conflict situations where farmland is being reclaimed (United Nations, 2007).

To ensure that agriculture—both domestic and export-oriented—experiences productivity change, appropriate growth-oriented macro and exchange rate policies must be in place. Agricultural tax must be further reduced. Remove price and policy distortions that may harm the agricultural sector; refrain from policies that artificially reduce the price of machines and chemicals that may tend to substitute for labour.

There must also be efforts to diversify the types of crops that are produced by agricultural sectors to provide farmers with a broader range of goods to sell.

In addition, we recommend the provision of technical assistance to enhance productivity by means of minor land-saving innovations, and assistance via credit provision plus a continued emphasis on primary education. Some efforts have been made by providing veteran farmers (as in Japan) to cultivators, and apprenticeships to household enterprises and the urban informal sector.

Value added and agro-processing activities should be encouraged. They can provide excellent sources of jobs: fruit and vegetable processing, textiles/garments, leather production, as well as the local manufacturing of basic agricultural tools (United Nations, 2007).

Investment in agricultural research and productivity-enhancing public goods (e.g. rural transportation infrastructure), especially of staple foods. By increasing productivity in these crops, countries can increase real wages even while keeping nominal wages steady or falling. This can help the demand for labour in non-agricultural activities, on both domestic and export markets.

Target agriculture as a key sector for employment expansion in countries where farms can produce for export markets as well as for domestic markets. In these settings, agriculture has the potential to expand employment and to create higher-paying jobs.

Support investments in export-oriented commercial agriculture.

Rural non-agricultural enterprise

The rural non-agricultural enterprise sector is usually neglected in government strategies, which focus mainly on the urban formal sector, yet it is critical for the overall system's growth and poverty reduction. In particular, the government should promote productivity of the agricultural sector to enhance the pull factors to diversify into the rural non-farm economy.

Focus on improving access to the non-farm economy for the rural poor by upgrading their physical and human capital.

Develop and maintain efficient transport and commercial infrastructure to reduce geographic and credit market failure and thereby increase rural non-farm earnings. Further reduce geographic isolation by promoting clustering of population and economic activities in remote areas. Agglomeration allows for more intensive specialization to production activities and lowers the average production cost of rural non-agricultural enterprises.

Urban informal sector

Strengthen the linkages between the formal and urban informal sectors. Provide focused credit and link those provisions to trade opportunities, including export processing zones. The trade and foreign investment climate may need improvement to reduce transactions costs, corruption and insecurity. The African Growth and Opportunity Act of the USA, and similar French initiatives related to the francophone countries, should be a help in this regard. As Bangladesh experience has shown, the dismantling of the Multi Fibre Arrangement in 2005 does not have to hurt competitive exporters if they are able to take advantage of their ample labour supplies.

To bring about informal sector growth and absorption into the formal sector, the government must design its general policies so that they are also relevant for informal firms, and design specific programs targeting informal firms. The skills level and policy environment of the latter need to be improved to make it possible for them to graduate to the formal sector. Since a large part of the population will continue to depend on informal firms for their sustenance for a long time to come, it is important that these firms are helped to become more productive, quite apart from helping them to graduate to the formal sector (Bigsten *et al.*, 2004).

Governments should provide tax incentives to organized sector companies to hire workers from the informal sector.

The business regulation framework must seek to lower the costs of establishing and operating a small business (easier registration procedures, reasonable and fair taxation) and increase the potential benefits of legal registration (access to commercial buyers in the formal economy, more favorable credit markets, legal protection, obtaining foreign exchange). Simpler business rules and lower transaction costs would promote entrepreneurship and facilitate formalization (ILO, 2005).

Urban formal sector

To ensure the small organized urban sector grows, growth-oriented macro and exchange rate policies must be in place.

A friendly business environment should be created through reducing corruption and better financial infrastructure to promote the growth of private firms and encourage private investment and capital accumulation.

It would help to institute initiatives such as export-processing zones, and to provide fiscal encouragement for increasing linkages between the formal sector and the innovative components of the urban informal sector.

2.6.2 Macroeconomic recommendations

Keep public sector debt at a level such that it does not crowd out domestic private sector investment. This requires more disciplined fiscal budget planning instead of financing through monetization (which aggravates inflation) or becoming overdependent on external aid (which crowds out private investment needed for economic growth).

Internally, a well coordinated and gradual decentralization policy (e.g. deregulation and privatization) should be implemented to increase the share of the private sector and improve production and allocation efficiency in the long run.

Improve financial sector and financial intermediation through: strengthening the regulation and enforcement of creditor rights revising institutional infrastructure to make collateralized loans more generally available increasing the sharing of information in credit markets.

Hold the size of the public sector to an appropriate level while maintaining competitive wages to avoid driving up wage rates and to keep taxation rates at modest levels for formal sector firms. Broaden the tax base as much as possible to keep business tax rates low and to prevent heavy and distortionary burdens from falling on any narrowly defined sector.

Promote sustainable development of the export sector through a more stable and correctly valued domestic currency. Overvaluation of exchange rates, as was common in the 1980s, discourages the development of the tradable sector, which arguably has the capacity to create more jobs than any other sector in the long run. This could be achieved by, for example, setting aside commodity-related windfalls as a buffer against private capital inflows, which tend to surge when commodity prices rise. In addition, the central banks ought to adopt a more active accumulation of foreign exchange reserves when net inflows are strong and allow depreciation when these flows weaken.

Trade liberalization policy should be adjusted gradually to improve long-run efficiency while minimizing adjustment costs. In particular, misguided trade policies against agriculture should be adjusted by gradually eliminating trade barriers for manufactured goods and reducing export taxes on agricultural products.

2.6.3 Other recommendations

Public works projects and CCT

Public works, to attract both the rural and urban underemployed, should be an integral part of any policy package. This could be done by guaranteeing 100 working days, as in India. These projects (which are often short-term) should be combined with projects that can help participants attain long-term, sustainable skills, including initiatives that improve literacy, numeracy and skills development (United Nations, 2007).

As many women are prevented from participating in these projects, it is important to provide skills development and micro-credit to women in areas where infrastructure projects are undertaken. This may provide an opportunity for female economic empowerment and participation in the economic activity that is generated by such projects (United Nations, 2007).

Conditionality must be designed and enforced properly to ensure the effectiveness of CCTs. In particular, fulfilment of conditions should be monitored externally (e.g. by schools) instead of solely relying on self-reporting. Also, the scale should be increased when possible, as a larger scale has been shown to bear more favorable returns, while programs below a certain size may not yield results (UNDP, 2005).

Education

On the supply side, primary education should continue to have the highest priority. It is also advisable to increase the repetition rate or reduce dropouts from the earlier years of schooling, and increase the transition rate from earlier to later levels of the education system (Betcherman *et al.*, 2004).

Leibbrandt and Mlatsheni (2004) highlight the importance of cultural impediments to girls attending school and how biases within the family and society in general impact female schooling. One policy to end such biases is to 'strengthen school–community relationships' (as in Tanzania, Malawi, Mali and Uganda), as parental involvement in school governance is often minimal. Increasing the proportion of female teachers is another desirable policy because of the evidence that female primary enrolments are responsive to this. Female role models have been found to be important in motivating parents to send their daughters to school.

Adult non-formal education should also be increased as this has a significant effect on the likelihood of children attending school (Leibbrandt and Mlatsheni, 2004). Work and school attendance go together for many students, though that also means that the efficiency of both activities suffers.

Job training and search programs

Governments should not provide, but should regulate, private and enterprise-based vocational education programs to ensure maximum numeracy and literacy for the underemployed in all three sectors. Training by government is generally too theoretical and too biased toward the small formal sector.

Apprenticeships should be selectively pursued, but with an eye on avoiding older technologies and limited scalability, as well as pro-male bias. As conditions allow, on-the-job training provides more tailor-made skills and should be favored over apprenticeships.

Improve job-search assistance venues and provide information on vacancies in the labour market (Betcherman *et al.*, 2004).

Training should work in conjunction with other instruments, such as fiscal policies, provision of credit and extension of social protection and labour laws, to improve the performance of enterprises and the employability of workers in order to transform what are often marginal, survival activities into decent work fully integrated into mainstream economic life (ILO, 2005).

Create job opportunity programs that specifically target young women. Women engaged in the labour market have lower fertility rates and higher bargaining power, and benefit from an improved allocation of resources at the household level. Therefore targeted job opportunity programs for girls and young women can have positive effects on family size and women's access to resources (UNECA, 2011).

Entrepreneurship

'One way to improve the sustainability of informal enterprises may be to link them in cooperative structures where jointly owned input supply, credit and marketing services can be organized without compromising the autonomy of the individual entrepreneur. Such cooperatives can be registered as legal entities.' (ILO, 2005)

'Employers' organizations can assist the associations of informal entrepreneurs in a number of ways: developing a lobbying agenda specially geared to the needs of micro- and small enterprises, providing business support (developing business plans, project formulation, access to credit) and other relevant services (personnel management, productivity improvement, basic management skills, accounting and entrepreneurship training programs), helping to link micro-enterprises with the formal economy, and providing a range of information which micro- and small enterprises may find difficult to obtain.' (ILO, 2005)

Creating more opportunities in ICT

Integrate ICT into formal education curricula, including computer literacy classes and the purchase of PCs and laptops for staff and students. Also implement ICT modules in technical school curricula. Promote ICT research and development in African universities and companies. Much of Africa is currently a net importer of ICT.

Create centers of excellence in ICT that can train senior level managers, entrepreneurs, government and private sector employees, and university students pursuing advanced ICT studies (African Economic Outlook, 2009a, b).

Create independent regulatory bodies for ICT sectors. In Africa, the number of countries with an ICT regulatory agency has grown from 26 (in 2000) to 44 (in 2007). As most investment comes from the private sector, governments should set the basic goals of telecommunications policy, the regulatory agency should implement and enforce them, and the courts should review them rather than other government branches (African Economic Outlook, 2009a, b).

Creating more opportunities in health services

Increase opportunities in the health services. The potential for young people to work in health services as health professionals, paraprofessionals or emergency assistants in urban and rural areas should be explored through collaboration between national medical services and youth unemployment programs (ILO, 2005).

Promoting family planning

Efforts to reduce fertility rates by discouraging early marriage are important. The legal minimum age for marriage should be raised and thoroughly enforced. Discourage child marriage through severe punishments and improving access to education for girls.[21]

Educate both in-school and out-of-school adolescents about the use and effects of contraception before they become sexually active. This will help to correct the perception that contraception causes infertility and increase the acceptance of using contraceptive methods for family planning (Otoide *et al.*, 2001).

To avoid misunderstanding of religious rules on the use of contraceptive methods, public health professionals should work in partnership with church and spiritual leaders to advocate for effective contraceptive practices.[22]

2.7 Conclusion

This chapter underscores the structural nature of the problem of youth underemployment in Sub-Saharan Africa. The analytical cause of the issue is analyzed through the lens of the Fei–Ranis model, which identifies the problem as a failure of African unskilled labour markets to clear due to workers not having enough land or capital to be fully employed (using the existing technology). The problem in the continent is mainly underemployment, not neoclassical unemployment. The underlying assumptions in this setting differ from those in neoclassical theories— incomes are shared among family members at the average product rather than set equal to marginal productivity. The Fei–Ranis model analyzes the reallocation of labour from traditional underemployed sectors to organized or formal sectors over time via internal labour migration from rural to urban areas. The migrating, mostly young males cannot find urban formal sector jobs, and first find shelter in the urban informal sector while waiting for opportunities to work in the modern sector (which conforms to neoclassical behaviour). Moreover, the Harris–Todaro model contends that excessive regulation and rigidity in urban labour markets hamper the movement of labour from the urban informal to the formal sector. It calls for interventions to stimulate labour mobility through reduction of over-regulation and price controls in the labour market so that structural transformation can be completed more effectively.

We distinguish among four major sectors in the economy: agriculture, rural household enterprises, urban informal sector enterprises, and urban formal sector enterprises. The first three suffer from underemployment. While the urban formal sector is growing rapidly over time, it is small and cannot absorb sufficient numbers of entrants into the urban labour force. Consequently, the growing urban informal sector is much larger than the formal sector. The modest linkage between the urban formal and informal sectors prevents the rapid structural transformation that is required to achieve the 'turning point'—the end of the labour surplus. In the rural economy, agriculture remains the predominant activity for up to 90 per cent of the population, with youth accounting for 65 per cent of Africa's agricultural labour force. The continuing large agricultural share in income and labour shows that limited progress has been made in the necessary structural transformation process.

Gender discrimination, poor education, disease and government corruption are all impediments to the course of development of Sub-Saharan Africa. To this end, we propose policies to be implemented that will increase internal migration and remove the barriers that prevent the informal sector from integrating with the formal sector. After reviewing and evaluating a broad range of policies and programs that contribute to the problem of African youth unemployment, we recommend a multifaceted approach by government and international agencies to address the issue. In general, these policies include building a support environment for entrepreneurship, expanding access to tertiary/vocational education, initiating infrastructure projects, and reducing gender discrimination. Since the majority of young people live in rural areas, development in agriculture and rural non-farm sectors is integral to creating demand for youth labour. Sector-specific recommendations that focus on strengthening the linkage between the three informal sectors and the one formal sector are highlighted. We argue that the government should promote rural household enterprises by microfinance interventions, design specific programs that enable informal firms to become more productive, and increase the innovative components of the urban informal sector. This chapter also emphasizes the need to simplify government labour regulations in order to assist the reallocation process—this will allow African economies to more quickly reach the 'turning point' where they can begin following neoclassical rules.

Youth employment is not an isolated issue. It reflects economic, geographic, demographic and other trends, and is also dictated by the particularities of each country. The main challenge for governments is to determine how best to assist intersectoral reallocation through the implementation of growth-oriented macro policies and the identification and implementation of appropriate policies to encourage the absorption of underemployed youth into the economy.

Notes

* The authors wish to thank Corey Sobel and Yiming Ma, who served as editorial assistants, and research assistants David Carel and Ting Wang.

1 This figure comes from Garcia and Fares (2008). ILO data, however, suggest that the unemployment rate for youth in Sub-Saharan Africa was only 12.5 per cent in 2010, far lower than the rates in North Africa and in many other regions of the globe (International Labour Organization, 2011).

2 The suggestions are partially adapted from Portugal-Perez and Wilson (2008)

3 Bennett and Estrin (2007) provide an example of the deep connections between formal and informal sectors. India's informal sector is, like virtually all Sub-Saharan African countries, large, and accounted for approximately 80 per cent of employment and 20 per cent of value added in Indian manufacturing from 2000 to 2006. A study by Peters *et al.* (2010) found that growth in the modern informal manufacturing sector is positively related to downstream formal sector demand—indicating that a production link exists between the formal and modern informal sector in that country.

4 Although some, like Sethuraman (1976), believe in the informal economy as a distinct disadvantaged sector, the majority of the literature (e.g. Moser, 1978); Portes *et al.*, 1989) agrees on the intrinsic linkages between the two sectors. The underlying theory is that profit-maximizing capitalist firms in the formal economy seek to reduce input costs by promoting informal production and employment relationships with subordinated units.

5 Urban and rural sectors are classified according to the residency status of workers. In the urban sector, workers are further divided into urban formal (public), urban

formal (private), and urban informal, based on their main economic activity. Note that the informal sector is defined as the self-employed plus small and non-registered firms, where the definition of small varies slightly by country. No clear distinction was made between the rural agricultural sector and the rural non-agricultural sector. The effect is discussed further in the following text.

6 All numbers are rounded to the nearest 0.1.

7 The following paragraph is adapted from African Development Forum (2006).

8 This argument and the following explanations are partially adapted from Heintz and Pollin (2008).

9 In particular, monetization of debt increases inflationary pressure and the chance of hyperinflation; privatization of assets is constrained in size and form; internal borrowing drives up interest rates and crowds out internal investment; external borrowing increases currency risk and negatively impacts long-run growth.

10 The following have been partially adapted from Heintz and Pollin (2008).

11 The following points rely heavily on World Bank (2007).

12 The following paragraph is adapted from Shapiro and Gebreselassie (2008).

13 This and the following description of West African entrepreneurs are taken from Grimm *et al.* (2011).

14 The following paragraph is adapted from Cling *et al.* (2007).

15 See Adams (2007). Haan and Serrière (2002) show that in West Africa it is typical to find more apprentices than wage employees in informal sector firms.

16 Much of the language and many of the insights in the following paragraphs are taken from United Nations (2007).

17 This and the Senegal, Cameroon and Zambia profiles are taken from ILO (2005).

18 The following language and insights are taken from *African Economic Outlook* (African Development Bank, 2009b).

19 For example, a more equitable land allocation could be achieved at the time of breaking up the collectives.

20 The following paragraphs adapt insights from Davis (2002).

21 One important source of early marriage is through marrying off young girls for money. Singh and Samara (1996) show that increasing education attainment for girls is one of the most effective means to increase age at marriage and improve women's position in the labour market.

22 Church officials are found to have a positive attitude towards family planning by Nkwo (2011). Moreover, advocacy by spiritual leaders is shown to be an effective means by Orji and Onwudiegwu (2002).

References

Accenture, Markle Foundation and UNDP (2001) *Creating a Development Dynamic: Final Report of the Digital Opportunity Initiative*. www.itu.int/wsis/docs/background/general/reports/26092001_doi.htm.

Adams, A.V. (2007) *The Role of Youth Skills Development in the Transition to Work: A Global Review*. Washington, DC: World Bank.

Addo, V.N. and Tagoe-Darko, E.D. (2009) 'Knowledge, Practices, and Attitudes Regarding Emergency Contraception among Students at a University in Ghana,' *International Journal of Gynecology & Obstetrics*, 105(3): 206–9.

Adepoju, A., ed. (1997) *Family, Population and Development in Africa*. London and NJ: Zed Books.

Africa Center for Strategic Studies (2012) *Preventing Youth Radicalization in East Africa*. National Defense University Program Report. Kigali, Rwanda.

African Development Forum (2006) 'Youth and Economic Development in Africa: An Issues Paper.' Fifth African Development Forum – Youth and Leadership in the 21st Century, Addis Ababa, Ethiopia, 26 October.

African Development Bank (2008) *African Economic Outlook: Developing Technical and Vocational Skills in Africa*. Paris: OECD Publishing.

——(2009a) *African Economic Outlook: Innovation and ICT in Africa*. Paris: OECD Publishing. www.africaneconomicoutlook.org/en/in-depth/ict-africa.

——(2009b) *African Economic Outlook: Human Capacity Building in ICT and Innovation Skills*. Paris: OECD Publishing. www.africaneconomicoutlook.org/en/in-depth/ict-africa/human-capacity-building-in-ict-and-innovation-skills.

——(2012) *African Economic Outlook 2012: Promoting Youth Employment*. Paris: OECD Publishing. www.oecd-ilibrary.org/development/african-economic-outlook-2012_aeo-2012-en.

Amoako-Tuffour, J. (2002) 'Forging Linkages between Formal and Informal Financial Sectors: Emerging Practices in Ghana,' *African Finance Journal*, 4(I): 1–31.

Anarfi, J.K., Kwankye, S., Ofuso-Mensah, A. and Tiemoko, R. (2003) *Migration from and to Ghana: A Background Paper*. Country Background Paper C4, Migration DRC, University of Sussex.

Arnaud, M. (1998) *Dynamique de l'urbanisation de l'Afrique au Sud du Sahara, the Dynamics of urbanization in Sub-Saharan Africa*. Paris: Secrétariat d'État à la coopération et à la francophonie – ISTED.

Aryeetey, E. and Udry, C. (1997) 'The Characteristics of Informal Financial Markets in Sub-Saharan Africa,' *Journal of African Economies*, 8(1): 161–203.

Asiedu, A. (2003) 'Some Benefits of Migrants' Return Visits to Ghana.' Paper presented at an international workshop on migration and poverty in West Africa, University of Sussex.

Atieno, R. (2001) *Formal and Informal Institutions' Lending Policies and Access to Credit by Small-Scale Enterprises in Kenya: An Empirical Assessment*. AERC Research Paper 111. Nairobi: African Economic Research Consortium.

Azevedo, J.P. and Heinrich, C.J. (2006) 'Preliminary Analysis and Impact. Evaluation Strategies for Avaliação de impacto do programa Bolsa Família (AIBF).' Report to Cedeplar, Belo Horizonte, Brazil and Ministry of Social Development, Brasilia, Brazil.

Bakunda, G. and Walusimbi Mpanga, G.F. (2011) *Labor Export as Government Policy: An Assessment of Uganda's Potential for Export of Labor in the Framework of Regional and Multilateral Agreements*. Kampala, Uganda: Private Sector Foundation Uganda.

Barassa, F.S. and Kaabwe, E.S.M. (2001) 'Fallacies in Policy and Strategies of Skill Training for the Informal Sector: Evidence from the Jua Kali Sector in Kenya,' *Journal of Education and Work*, 14(3): 328–53.

Barrios, B. and Strobl, E. (2006) 'Climate Change and Rural–Urban Migration: The Case of Sub-Saharan Africa,' *World Development*, 19(6): 651–70.

Becker, K.F. (2004) 'The Informal Economy,' *Sida Fact Finding Study*. Stockholm: Swedish International Development Cooperation Agency.

Bennett, J. and Estrin, S. (2007) *Informality as a Stepping Stone: Entrepreneurial Entry in a Developing Economy*. Discussion Paper No. 2950. Bonn: Institute for the Study of Labor.

Betcherman, G., Olivas, K. and Dar, A. (2004) *Impacts of Active Labor Market Programs: New Evidence from Evaluations with Particular Attention to Developing and Transition Countries*. Social Protection Discussion Paper Series No. SP 0402. Washington, DC: World Bank.

Betcherman, G., Godfrey, M., Puerto, S., Rother, F. and Stavreska, A. (2007) *A Review of Interventions to Support Young Workers: Findings of the Youth Employment Inventory.* Social Protection Discussion Paper No. SP 0715. Washington, DC: World Bank.

Bigsten, A., Kimuyu, P. and Lundvall, K. (2004) 'What to Do with the Informal Sector?', *Development Policy Review*, 22(6): 701–15.

Bloom, N., Eifert, B., Mahajan, A., McKenzie, D. and Roberts, J. (2012a) 'Does Management Matter? Evidence from India,' manuscript. Stanford University, CA: Department of Economics.

Bloom, N., Mahajan, A., McKenzie, D. and Roberts, J. (2012b) 'Why do Firms in Developing Countries have Low Productivity?' manuscript. Washington, DC: World Bank. http://siteresources.worldbank.org/DEC/Resources/Why_do_firms_in_developing_countries_have_low_productivity.pdf.

Bocquier, P. (2003) 'Analyzing Urbanization in Africa,' in G. Hugo and A. Champion (eds), *New Forms of Urbanisation.* Ashgate, Farnham: IUSSP Group on Urbanisation.

Botswana Central Statistics Office (2007) *Botswana Informal Sector Survey Report 2007.* Gaborone.

——(2008) *Botswana Labour Force Survey 2005/06 Labour Force Survey Report.* Gaborone.

——(2009) *Botswana Labour Force Survey Report 2007.* Gaborone.

Braimah, I. and King, R. (2006) 'Reducing the Vulnerability of the Youth in Terms of Employment in Ghana through the ICT Sector,' *International Journal of Education and Development using ICT*, August 10.

Bruno, M. (1995) 'Does inflation really lower growth?', *Finance and Development*, 32(3): 35–38.

Burkina Faso Institut national de la statistique et de la démographie (2001) *Burkina Faso Annuaire Statistique 2001.* Ouagadougou.

——(2009) *Burkina Faso Annuaire Statistique 2009.* Ouagadougou.

Cali, M., Ellis, K. and te Velde, D.W. (2008) *The Contribution of Services to Development and the Role of Trade Liberalisation and Regulation.* London: Overseas Development Institute.

Caselli, F. and Coleman II, W.J. (2001) 'The U.S. Structural Transformation and Regional Convergence: A Reinterpretation,' *Journal of Political Economy*, 109(3): 584–616.

Central Statistical Agency of Ethiopia (1997) *Ethiopia Labour Force Survey Report 1997.* Addis Ababa.

Charmes, J. (1990) 'A Critical Review of Concepts, Definitions and Studies in the Informal Sector,' in D. Turnham, B. Salomé and A. Schwarz (eds), *The Informal Sector Revisited.* Paris: OECD.

Chen, M. (2000) 'Risk, Insurance, and the Informal Economy,' *Workshop on Risk, Poverty, and Insurance: Innovations for the Informal Economy.* Washington, DC: World Bank, Human Development Network Social Protection and Financial Sector Development Department.

Chen, N., Valente, P. and Zlotnik, H. (1998) 'What Do We Know about Recent Trends in Urbanization?' in R.E. Bilsborrow (ed.), *Migration, Urbanization, and Development: New Directions and Issues.* New York: UNFPA/Kluwer Academic, pp. 59–88.

Chigunta, F. (2002) 'The Socio-Economic Situation of Youth In Africa: Problems, Prospects and Options.' Paper presented at the Youth Employment Summit, Alexandria, Egypt, September.

Clay, D., Byiringiro, F., Kangasniemi, J., Reardon, T., Sibomana, B., Uwamariya, L. and Tardif-Douglin, D. (1995) Promoting Food Security in Rwanda through Sustainable Agricultural Productivity: Meeting the Challenges of Population Pressure, Land Degradation, and Poverty. *International Development Paper No. 17*. East Lansing, MI: Michigan State University.

Cling, J., Gubert, F., Nordman, C.J. and Robilliard, A.-S. (2007) *Youth and Labour Markets in Africa: A Critical Review of Literature*. Paris: Developpement Institutions and Analyses de Long terme (DIAL).

Collier, P. and Gunning, J.W. (1999) 'Explaining African Economic Performance,' *Journal of Economic Literature*, 37(1): 64–111.

Collier, P. and Hoeffler, A. (2005) 'Democracy and Resource Rents,' mimeo. Oxford: CSAE.

Collier, P. and Lal, D. (1984) 'Why Poor People Get Rich: Kenya 1960–79,' *World Development*, 12(10): 1007–18.

Collier, P. and O'Connell, S. (2007) 'Opportunities and choices,' in B.J. Ndulu, S.A. O'Connell, R.H. Bates, P. Collier and C.C. Soludo (eds), *The Political Economy of Economic Growth in Africa, 1960–2000*. Cambridge: Cambridge University Press.

Collier, P. and Pattillo, C. (2000) *Investment and Risk in Africa*. London: Macmillan.

Curtain, R. (2004) 'Strategies for Creating Employment for Urban Youth, with Specific Reference to Africa,' *draft paper for Expert Group Meeting on Strategies for Creating Urban Youth Employment: Solutions for Urban Youth in Africa, Division for Social Policy and Development, Department of Economic and Social Affairs, United Nations in collaboration with UN-HABITAT and the Youth Employment Network*, 21–25 June, Nairobi, Kenya.

Davis, B. (2002) *Promoting Farm/Non-Farm Linkages for Rural Development*. Rome: FAO.

Dhemba, J. (1999) 'Informal Sector Development: A Strategy for Alleviating Urban Poverty in Zimbabwe,' *Journal of Social Development in Africa*, 14(2): 5–19.

Diao, X., Hazell, P., Resnick, D. and Thurlow, J. (2006) 'The Role of Agriculture in Development: Implications for Sub-Saharan Africa.' *DSGC Discussion Paper #29*. Washington, DC: IFPRI.

Dike, V.E. (2010) 'Addressing Youth Unemployment, Underemployment and Poverty in Nigeria: The Role of Technical and Vocational Education in National Development' http://papers.ssrn.com/sol3/papers.cfm?abstract_id=1550555.

Direction Nationale de la Statistique et de l'Informatique du Mali (2004) *Activité, emploi et chômage au Mali premiers résultats de l'enquête emploi permanent auprès des ménages 2004*. Bamako: OEF.

Edwards, S. (1988) *Macroeconomic Policies, Real Exchange Rate Misalignment, and Devaluation*. UCLA Economics Working Paper 509. University of California, Department of Economics.

Ellis, F. and Harris, N. (2004) 'New Thinking about Urban and Rural Development.' Keynote Paper for DFID Sustainable Development Retreat.

Esfahani, H. and Ramirez, M.T. (2003) 'Institutions, Infrastructure and Economic Growth,' *Journal of Development Economics*, 70: 443–77.

Eswaran, M. and Kotwal, A. (1993) 'A Theory of Real Wage Growth in LDCs,' *Journal of Development Economics*, 42(2): 243–69.

Falco, P., Kerr, A., Rankin, N., Sandefur, J. and Teal, F. (2011) 'The Returns to Formality and Informality in Urban Africa,' *Labour Economics*, 18: 21–31.

Fan, S. and Pardey, P.G. (1997) 'Research, Productivity, and Output Growth in Chinese Agriculture,' *Journal of Development Economics*, 53(1): 115–37.

Fan, S., Zhang, L. and Zhang, X. (2002) *Growth, Inequality, and Poverty in Rural China: The Role of Public Investments.* Research Report 125. Washington, DC: IFPRI.

Fei, J.C.H. and Ranis, G. (1964) *Development of the Labor Surplus Economy: Theory and Policy.* Economic Growth Center, Yale University. Homewood, IL: Richard D. Irwin.

Findley, S. (1997) 'Migration and Family Interactions in Africa,' in A. Adepoju (ed.), *Family, Population and Development in Africa.* London and NJ: Zed Books.

Findlay, C. and Watson, A. (1992) 'Surrounding the Cities from the Countryside,' in Garnaut, G. and Liu, G. (eds), *Economic Reform and Internationalization: China and the Pacific Region.* Sydney: Allen and Unwin, pp. 49–78.

Findlay, C. and Watson, A. (2001) 'Surrounding the Cities from the Countryside,' in R. Garnaut and G. Liu (eds), *Economic Reform and Internationalization: China and the Pacific Region.* Canberra: Australia–Japan Research Centre, Australia National University.

Fisseha, Y. and Milimo, J. (1986) *Rural Small-Scale Forest-Based Processing 1986 Enterprises in Zambia: Report of a 1985 Pilot Survey.* Rome: FAO.

FORWARD (2012) 'Child Marriage.' London: Foundation for Women's Health, Research and Development. www.forwarduk.org.uk/key-issues/child-marriage.

Fox, L. and Sohnesen, T.P. (2012) *Household Enterprise in Sub-Saharan Africa – Why they Matter for Growth, Jobs, and Livelihoods.* Washington, DC: World Bank.

Freeman, D.B. and Norcliffe, G.B. (1985) Rural Enterprise in Kenya: Development and Spatial Organization of the Nonfarm Sector. *Research Paper No. 214.* Chicago, IL: University of Chicago, Department of Geography.

Freund, C. and Spatafora, N. (2005) *Remittances: Transaction Costs, Determinants, and Informal Flows.* Policy Research Working Paper No. 3704. Washington, DC: World Bank.

Gala, P. and Lucinda, C.R. (2006) 'Exchange Rate Misalignment and Growth: Old and New Econometric Evidence,' *Revista Economia*, 165–87.

Garcia, M. and Fares, J. (2008) *Youth in Africa's Labor Markets.* Washington, DC: World Bank.

Ghana Statistical Service (1998) *Ghana Living Standard Survey – Report of the Fifth Round.* Accra.

——(2003) *Ghana Living Standards Survey 2003.* Accra.

Ghura, D. and Hadjimichael, M.T. (1996) 'Growth in Sub-Saharan Africa,' *IMF Staff Papers*, 43(3).

Gollin, D. (2008) 'Nobody's Business But My Own: Self Employment and Small Enterprise in Economic Development,' *Journal of Monetary Economics*, 55(2): 219–33.

Gollin, D. and Rogerson, R. (2011) 'Agriculture, Roads, and Economic Development in Uganda.' Mimeo, Williams College Department of Economics.

Gollin, D., Lagakos, D. and Waugh, M.E. (2013) 'The Agricultural Productivity Gap in Developing Countries,' unpublished draft.

Gollin, D., Parente, S.L. and Rogerson, R. (2002) 'The Role of Agriculture in Development,' *American Economic Review: Papers and Proceedings*, 92(2): 160–64.

——(2004) 'Farm Work, Home Work, and International Productivity Differences,' *Review of Economic Dynamics*, 7(4): 827–50.

——(2007) 'The Food Problem and the Evolution of International Income Levels,' *Journal of Monetary Economics*, 54(4): 1230–55.

Government of Sierra Leone (2007) *Core Welfare Indicator Questionnaire Survey (CWIQ) 2007 Final Statistical Report.* Freetown.

Grimm, M. and Gunther, I. (2006) 'Inter- and Intra-household Linkages between the Informal and Formal Sectors: A Case Study for Urban Burkina Faso,' in B. Guha-Khasnobis and R. Kanbur (eds), *Informal Labour Markets and Development*. London: Macmillan.

Grimm, M., Kruger, J. and Lay, J. (2011) 'Barriers to Entry and Returns to Capital in Informal Activities: Evidence from Sub-Saharan Africa,' *Review of Income and Wealth*, 57: S27–S53.

Grubb, W. (1995) *Evaluating Job Training Programmes in the United States: Evidence and Explanations.* Training Policy Studies No. 17. Geneva: ILO.

Gustav, R. and Stewart, F. (1999) 'V-Goods and the Role of the Urban Informal Sector in Development,' *Economic Development and Cultural Change*, 47: 259–88.

Haan, H.C. and Serrière, N. (2002) *Training for Work in the Informal Sector: Fresh Evidence from West and Central Africa*. Geneva: International Training Center/ILO.

Haggblade, S., Reardon, T. and Hyman, E. (2007) 'Technology as a Motor of Change in the Rural Nonfarm Economy,' in S. Haggblade, P. Hazell and T. Reardon (eds), *Transforming the Rural Nonfarm Economy: Opportunities and Threats in the Developing World.* Baltimore, MD: Johns Hopkins University Press, pp. 322–51.

Hatton, T.J. and Williamson, J.G. (2002) 'Out of Africa: Using the Past to Project African Emigration Pressure in the Future,' *Review of International Economics*, 10: 556–73.

Hayami, Y. and Ruttan, V.W. (1971) *Induced Innovation in Agricultural Development*, Discussion Paper No. 3. Center for Economics Research, University of Minnesota.

Hazell, P. and Haggeblade, S. (1993) 'Farm–nonfarm Growth Linkages and the Welfare of the Poor,' in M. Lipton and J. van de Gaag (eds), *Including the Poor*. Washington, DC: World Bank.

Hazell, P., Poulton, C., Wiggins, S. and Dorward, A. (2006) *Future of Small Farms for Poverty Reduction and Growth*. 2020 Discussion Paper #42. Washington, DC: IFPRI.

Heintz, J. and Pollin, R. (2008) *Targeting Employment Expansion, Economic Growth, and Development in Sub-Saharan Africa: Outlines of an Alternative Economic Program for the Region*. Addis Ababa: UN Economic Commission for Africa.

House, W.J. (1984) 'Nairobi's Informal Sector: Dynamic Entrepreneurs or Surplus Labor?', *Economic Development and Cultural Change*, 32(2): 276–302.

Hsieh, C. and Klenow, P. (2009) 'Misallocation and Manufacturing TFP in China and India,' *Quarterly Journal of Economics*, 124(4): 1403–48.

Huang, Y. and Meng, X. (1997) 'China's Industrial Growth and Efficiency: A Comparison between the State and TVE Sectors,' *Journal of the Asia Pacific Economy*, 2(1): 101–21.

Hugo, G. and Stahl, C. (2004) 'Labour Export Strategies in Asia,' in D. Massey and J.E. Taylor (eds), *International Migration: Prospects and Policies in a Globalized context*. Oxford: Oxford University Press.

Huitfeldt, H. and Jütting, J.P. (2009) 'Informality and Informal Employment,' in OECD (eds), *Promoting Pro-Poor Growth: Employment*. Paris: Organisation for Economic Co-operation and Development, pp. 95–108.

IFAD (2007) "Sending Money Home: Worldwide Remittance Flows to Developing and Transition Countries." www.ifad.org/remittances/maps/brochure.pdf.

ILO (1995) *ILO Newsletter*, No. 2, February. Geneva: International Labour Organization.

——(2001) *World Employment Report 2001: Life at Work in the Information Economy.* Geneva: International Labour Organization.

——(2002) 'Decent Work and the Informal Economy.' *International Labour Conference, 90th Session*. Geneva: International Labour Organization.

——(2004) *World Employment Report 2004–2005*. Geneva: International Labour Organization.

——(2005) *Youth: Pathways to Decent Work*. International Labor Conference, 93rd Session. Geneva: International Labour Organization.

——(2011) *Global Employment Trends for Youth: 2011 Update*. Geneva: International Labour Organization.

IMF (2008) *Regional Economic Outlook: Sub-Saharan Africa*. Washington, DC: International Monetary Fund.

INSEE, DIAL and AFRISTAT (2005) *Méthodes statistiques et économiques pour le développement et la transition*. Paris: INSEE.

International Labour Organization Department of Statistics (2011) June.

Jamal, V. and Weeks, J. (1988) 'The Vanishing Rural–Urban Gap in Sub-Saharan Africa,' *International Labour Review*, 127(3): 271–92.

Jensen, R. and Peppard, D. (2003) 'Hanoi's Informal Sector and the Vietnamese Economy: A Case Study of Roving Street Vendors,' *Journal of Asian and African Studies*, 38(1): 71–84.

Johnson, D.G. (1997) 'Agriculture and the Wealth of Nations (Ely Lecture),' *American Economic Review*, 87(2): 1–12.

Johnston, B.F. (1970) 'Agriculture and Structural Transformation in Development Countries: A Survey of Research,' *Journal of Economic Literature*, 3: 369–404.

Johnston, B.F. and Kilby, P. (1975) *Agriculture and Structural Transformation: Economic Strategies in Late-Developing Countries*. New York: Oxford University Press.

Johnston, B.F. and Mellor, J.W. (1961) 'The Role of Agriculture in Economic Development,' *American Economic Review*, 51(4): 566–93.

Jütting, J.P. and de Laiglesia, J.R. (2009) *L'emploi informel dans les pays en développement: une normalité indépassable*. Paris: Centre de Développement de L'organisation de Coopération et de Développement Économiques.

Karlan, D. and Valdivia, M. (2009) 'Teaching Entrepreneurship: Impact of Business Training on Microfinance Clients and Institutions.' Manuscript, Yale University.

Kelly, V., Reardon, T., Fall, A.A., Diagana, B. and McNeilly, L. (1993) 'Final Report of IFPR/ISRA Project on Consumption and Supply Impacts of Agricultural Price Policies in Senegall.' Mimeo. Washington, DC: FPRI.

Kenya Central Bureau of Statistics (1999) *Report of 1998/1999 Kenya Labour Force Survey*. Nairobi.

Kessides, C. (2005) *The Urban Transition in Sub-Saharan Africa: Implications for Economic Growth and Poverty*. Washington, DC: Reduction Urban Development Unit, World Bank.

Kimuyu, P. and Omiti, J. (2000) *Institutional Impediments to Access to Credit By Micro and Small Scale Enterprises in Kenya*. Discussion Paper 26. Nairobi: Institute of Policy Analysis and Research.

Lalnilawma (2009) 'Employment Assurance Scheme: An Impact Assessment,' *International Journal of Rural Studies* [Gramodaya College and Research Institute], 16(1).

Leibbrandt, M. and Mlatsheni, C. (2004) 'Youth in Sub-Saharan Labour Markets. African Development and Poverty Reduction: The Macro–Micro linkage.' *Forum paper for Development Policy and Research Unit/Trade and Industry Strategies Conference*, October 2004.

Lesotho Ministry of Labour and Employment (1998) *Review and Analysis of Special Employment Schemes in Lesotho*. Maseru.
Lewin, M. (2011) 'Botswana's Success: Good Governance, Good Policies, and Good Luck,' in *Yes Africa Can – Success Stories from a Dynamic Continent*. Washington, DC: World Bank.
Lewis, W.A. (1955) *The Theory of Economic Growth*. London: George Allen & Unwin.
Limão, N. and Venables, A.J. (2001) 'Infrastructure, Geographical Disadvantage, Transport Costs and Trade,' *World Bank Economic Review*, 15(3): 451–79.
Lin, J.Y. (1992) 'Rural Reforms and Agricultural Growth in China,' *American Economic Review*, 82: 34–51.
Livingstone, I. (1991) 'A Reassessment of Kenya's Rural and Urban Informal Sector,' *World Development*, 19(6): 651–70.
Lobo, A. (2000) 'Taking IT to the villages,' *ZDNet India*, 6 November.
Lucas, R.E.B. and Stark, O. (1985) 'Motivations to Remit: Evidence from Botswana,' *Journal of Political Economy*, 93(5): 901–18.
Mano, Y., Iddrisu, A., Yoshino, Y. and Sonobe, T. (2011) *How Can Micro and Small Enterprises in Sub-Saharan Africa Become More Productive? The Impacts of Experimental Basic Managerial Training*. Policy Research Working Paper 5755. Washington, DC: World Bank.
Marler, J. (2011) 'World's Women Less Likely to Have Good Jobs.' *Gallup.com*, June 23. www.gallup.com/poll/148175/world-women-less-likely-good-jobs.aspx.
Massimiliano, C., Ellis, K. and te Velde, D.W. (2008) *The Contribution of Services to Development and the Role of Trade Liberalization and Regulation*. London: Overseas Development Institute.
Masson, P. (2006) 'Anchors for Monetary Policy.' Mimeo. Basel: Bank for International Settlement.
McMillan, M. and Rodrik, D. (2011) *Globalization, Structural Change and Productivity Growth*. NBER Working Paper No. 17143. Cambridge, MA: National Bureau of Economic Research.
Mel, S.D., McKenzie, D. and Woodruff, C. (2008) 'Returns to Capital in Microenterprises: Evidence from a Field Experiment,' *Quarterly Journal of Economics*, 113(4): 1329–72.
Mellor, J.W. (1976) *The New Economics of Growth: A Strategy for India and the Developing World*. Ithaca, NY: Cornell University Press.
Mellor, J. (1999) *Faster, More Equitable Growth – The Relation Between Growth in Agriculture and Poverty Reduction*. Research Report No. 4, Agricultural Policy Development Project. Washington, DC: IFPRI.
Milanovic, B. (2003) *Is Inequality in Africa Really Different?* Policy Research Working Paper No. 3169. Washington, DC: World Bank.
Mitter, S. and Millar, J. (2001) 'The Impact of ICT on the Spatial Division of Labour in the Service Sector.' *Background Paper for the World Employment Report 2001*. Geneva: ILO.
MJE (2006) *Rapport sur l'emploi au Burkina Faso en 2006' Janvier 2006, Ouagadougou, Ministère de l'emploi et de la jeunesse*. Ouagadougou: Ministère de la Jeunesse et de l'Emploi.
Monga, C., Tuluy, H. and Fofack, H. (2001) *Household Welfare and Poverty Dynamics in Burkina Faso: Empirical Evidence from Household Surveys*. Working Paper No. 2590. Washington, DC: World Bank.

Mortensen, D. (2005) *Wage Dispersion: Why Are Similar Workers Paid Differently?* Cambridge, MA: MIT Press.

Moser, C.O.N. (1978) 'Informal Sector or Petty Commodity Production: Dualism or Dependence in Urban Development?', *World Development*, 6(9/10): 1041–64.

Mundlak, Y. (2000) *Agriculture and Economic Growth: Theory and Measurement*. Cambridge, MA: Harvard University Press.

Mussa, M., Masson, P., Swaboda, A., Jadresic, E., Mauro, P. and Berg, A. (2000) *Exchange Rate Regimes in an Increasingly Integrated World Economy*. Occasional Paper No. 193. Washington, DC: IMF.

National Population Council (2011) *The Ghana Population Stabilization Report, 2011*. Accra.

Ndiwalana, A. and Popov, O. (2008) 'Mobile Payments: A Comparison between Philippine and Ugandan Contexts,' in Paul Cunningham and Miriam Cunningham (eds), *IST-Africa 2008 Conference Proceedings*. Dublin: International Information Management Corporation.

Njugana, A.E. (2008) *Macroeconomic Policies for Promoting Growth in Africa*. Addis Ababa: Trade, Finance and Economic Development Division, UN Economic Commission for Africa.

Nkwo, P.O. (2011) 'Partnering With Christian Religious Leaders to Increase Contraceptive Coverage: A Viable Option in Enugu Nigeria,' *Internet Journal of Gynecology and Obstetrics*, 14(2).

Omolo, J. (2010) *The Dynamics and Trends of Employment in Kenya*. IEA Paper Series No. 1. London: Institute of Economic Affairs.

Orji, E.O. and Onwudiegwu, U. (2002) 'Prevalence and Determinants of Contraceptive Practice in a Defined Nigerian Population,' *Journal of Obstetrics & Gynaecology*, 22(5): 540–43.

Osili, U.O. and Long, B.T. (2008) 'Does Female Schooling Reduce Fertility? Evidence from Nigeria,' *Journal of Development Economics*, 87(1): 57–75.

Otoide, V.O., Oronsaye, F. and Okonofua, F.E. (2001) 'Why Nigerian Adolescents Seek Abortion Rather than Contraception: Evidence from Focus-Group Discussions,' *International Family Planning Perspectives*, 27(2): 77.

Peters, J. *et al*. (2010) 'Formal – informal production linkages and informal sector heterogeneity: evidence from Indian manufacturing.' Gronigen Growth and Development Centre.

Peters, P.E. (1992) 'Monitoring the Effects of Grain Market Liberalization on the Income, Food Security and Nutrition of Rural Households in Zomba South, Malawi.' Cambridge, MA: Harvard Institute for International Development.

Philippine Overseas Employment Administration (2010) *POEA Annual Report 2009*. Mandaluyong City.

Portes, A. and Walton, J. (1981) *Labor, Class and International System*. New York: Academic Press.

Portes, A., Castells, M. and L.A. Benton, eds (1989) *The Informal Economy: Studies in Advanced and Less Developed Countries*. Baltimore, MD: Johns Hopkins University Press.

Pörtner, C.C., Beegle, K. and Christiaensen, L. (2011) *Family Planning and Fertility: Estimating Program Effects using Cross-sectional Data*. Policy Research Working Paper # 5812. Washington, DC: World Bank.

Portugal-Perez, A. and Wilson, J.S. (2008) *Trade Costs in Africa: Barriers and Opportunities for Reform*. Policy Research Working Paper # 4619. Washington, DC: World Bank.

Potts, D. (1995) 'Shall We Go Home? Increasing Urban Poverty in African Cities and Migration Processes,' *Geographical Journal*, 161(3): 245–64.

Puerto, O.S. (2007) 'International Experience on Youth Employment Interventions: The Youth Employment Inventory.' *Background paper for the World Bank's 2007 Economic and Sector Work*. Washington, DC: World Bank.

Ranis, G. (1995) 'Another Look at the East Asian Miracle,' *World Bank Economic Review*, 9(3): 509–34.

Ranis, G. and Stewart, F. (1999) 'V-Goods and the Role of the Urban Informal Sector in Development,' *Economic Development and Cultural Change*, 47(2): 259–88.

Ravallion, M. and Chen, S. (2007) 'China's (uneven) progress against poverty,' *Journal of Development Economics*, 82(1): 1–42.

Reardon, T. (1997) 'Using Evidence of Household Income Diversification to Inform Study of the Rural Nonfarm Labor Market in Africa,' *World Development*, 25(5): 735–47.

Reardon, T., Fall, A.A., Kelly, V., Delgado, C., Matlon, P., Hopkins, J. and Badiane, O. (1994) 'Is Income Diversification Agriculture-Led in the West African Semi-Arid Tropics? The Nature, Causes, Effects, Distribution, and Production Linkages of Off-Farm Activities,' in A. Atsain, S. Wangwe and A.G. Drabek (eds), *Economic Policy Experience in Africa: What Have We Learned?* Nairobi: African Economic Research Consortium, pp. 207–30.

Reardon, T., Berdegué, J. and Escobar, G. (2001) 'Rural Nonfarm Employment and Incomes in Latin America: Overview and Policy Implications,' *World Development*, 29(3): 411–25.

Rosenstein-Rodan, P.N. (1943) 'Problems of industrialization of Eastern and South-Eastern Europe,' *Economic Journal*, (June–September): 204–7, reprinted in Gerald M. Meier, *Leading Issues in Economic Development*, 6th edn. New York: Oxford University Press, 1995.

Rostow, W.W. (1960) 'The Stages of Economic Growth.' Cambridge: Cambridge University Press.

Ruffer, T. and Knight, J. (2007) 'Informal Sector Labor Markets in Developing Countries.' Oxford Policy Management.

Sacerdoti, E. (2005) *Access to Bank Credit in Sub-Saharan Africa: Key Issues and Reform Strategies.* IMF Working Paper 166. New York: IMF.

Sahn, D.E. and Stifel, D.C. (2000) 'Poverty Comparisons Over Times and Across Countries in Africa,' *World Development*, 28(12): 2123–55.

——(2003) 'Exploring Alternative Measures of Wealth in the Absence of Expenditure Data,' *Review of Income and Wealth*, 49(4): 463–89.

Sandefur, J. and Teal, F. (2007) *Understanding the Informal and Formal Sector In Africa: A Note.* Oxford: Centre for the Study of African Economies, University of Oxford.

Satterthwaite, D. and Tacoli, C. (2003) *The Urban Part of Rural Development: The Role of Small and Intermediate Urban Centres in Rural and Regional Development and Poverty Reduction.* London: International Institute for Environment and Development.

Schiff, M. and Valdes, E. (1992) *The Plundering of Agriculture in Developing Countries.* Washington, DC: World Bank.

Schultz, T.P. (2000) *Impact of PROGRESA on School Attendance Rates in the Sampled Population*. Washington, DC: IFPRI.

Schultz, T.W. (1953) *The Economic Organization of Agriculture.* New York: McGraw-Hill.

Sethuraman, S.V. (1976) 'The Urban Informal Sector: Concept, Measurement and Policy,' *International Labour Review*, 114(1): 69–81.

Shapiro, D. and Gebreselassie, T. (2008) 'Fertility Transition in Sub-Saharan Africa: Falling and Stalling,' *African Population Studies/Etude de la Population Africaine*, 23(1): 3–23.

Singh, S. and Samara, R. (1996) 'Early Marriage among Women in Developing Countries,' *International Family Planning Perspectives*, 22(4): 148–57, 175.

Solow, R. (1956) 'A Contribution to the Theory of Economic Growth,' *Quarterly Journal of Economics*, 70(1): 65–94.

Swan, T. (1956) 'Economic Growth and Capital Accumulation,' *Economic Record*, 32: 344–61.

Tanzania National Bureau of Statistics (2001) *Integrated Labour Force Survey, 2000/01 – Analytical Report*. Dar es Salaam.

Tarantino, G.C. (2003) *Imputation, Estimation and Prediction using the Key Indicators of the Labour Market (KILM) Data Set*. Geneva: ILO, Employment Strategy Department,.

Temple, J.R.W. (2005) 'Dual Economy Models: A Primer for Growth Economists,' *The Manchester School*, 73(4): 435–78.

Tiffin, G. and Irz, X. (2006) 'Is Agriculture the Engine of Growth?' *Agricultural Economics*, 35: 79–89.

Timmer, C.P. (1988) *Agricultural Prices and Stabilization Policy*. Cambridge, MA: Harvard Institute for International Development.

Timmer, C.P. (2003) 'Agriculture and Pro-poor Growth: What the Literature Says.' *Pro-Poor Economic Growth Research Studies*. Washington, DC: USAID.

Uganda Bureau of Statistics (2007) *Report on the Labor Market Conditions in Uganda 2007*. Kampala.

UN (2007) 'Review of National Action Plans on Youth Employment: Putting Commitment into Action.' New York: United Nations.

UNDP (1992) *Human Development Report 1992*. New York: UN Development Programme.

——(2001) *Human Development Report 2001: Making New Technologies Work for Human Development*. New York: Oxford University Press for the UN Development Programme.

——(2005) *Conditional Cash Transfers in African Countries*. Working Paper No. 9. New York: UN Development Programme.

UNECA (2002) 'Youth and Employment in the ECA Region.' *Paper prepared for the Youth Employment Summit*, Alexandria, Egypt, September 7–11. Addis Ababa: UN Economic Commission for Africa.

——(2005) *Youth, Education, Skills and Employment*. Addis Ababa: UN Economic Commission for Africa.

——(2011) *Africa Youth Report: Addressing the Youth Education and Employment Nexus in the New Global Economy*. Addis Ababa: UN Economic Commission for Africa.

UNESCO (2011) *Financing Education in Sub-Saharan Africa: Meeting the Challenges of Expansion, Equity and Quality*. Paris: UN Educational, Scientific and Cultural Organization.

UNFPA (2005) 'Child Marriage Fact Sheet.' *State of the World Population*. New York: UN Population Fund.

UNIDO (2007) *Productive and Decent Work for Youth in the Mano River Union: Guinea, Liberia, Sierra Leone and in Côte d'Ivoire*. Vienna: UN Industrial Development Organization.

UNOWA (2007) *Best Practices, Policy Environment, Tools, and Methodologies for Youth Employment in West Africa*. Dakar: UN Office for West Africa.

Vollrath, D. (2009) 'How Important are Dual Economy Effects for Aggregate Productivity?', *Journal of Development Economics*, 88(2): 325–34.

Wilson, F. (2008) *Challenges and Policy Options Facing the Landlocked.* IDS in Focus 3.6. Brighton: Institute of Development Studies.

World Bank (1993) *The East Asian Miracle.* Washington, DC: World Bank.

——(2001) *Migration and Remittances Factbook*. Washington, DC: World Bank.

——(2002) *World Development Report 2002: Building Institutions for Markets.* Washington, DC: World Bank.

——(2007) *World Development Report 2007: Development and the Next Generation*. Washington, DC: World Bank.

——(2008) *The Growth Report: Strategies for Sustained Growth and Inclusive Development*. Washington, DC: World Bank.

——(2009) *Africa Development Indicators 2008/09: Youth and Employment in Africa – the Potential, the Problem, the Promise.* Washington, DC: World Bank.

——(2011) *Africa Development Indicators 2011*. Washington, DC: World Bank.

——(2012a) *Fact Sheet: The World Bank and Agriculture in Africa*. Washington, DC: World Bank.

——(2012b) 'Secondary Education in Africa.' Washington, DC: World Bank.

——(2012c) 'Tertiary Education in Africa.' Washington, DC: World Bank.

——(2012d) *World Development Indicators 2012*. Washington, DC: World Bank.

Zafar, A. (2011) 'Mauritius: An Economic Success Story,' in *Yes Africa Can: Success Stories from a Dynamic Continent*. Washington, DC: World Bank.

Zuehlke, E. (2009) *Youth Unemployment and Underemployment in Africa Brings Uncertainty and Opportunity.* Washington, DC: Population Reference Bureau.

3 Microeconomic perspectives

Marianne Bertrand and Bruno Crépon

3.1 Introduction

In Chapter 2 in this volume, Ranis and Gollin attribute the bulk of youth labour market problems in Sub-Saharan Africa to demand-side factors. In this chapter, we review the microeconomic evidence regarding the hurdles to better labour market prospects for young Africans. We argue that both supply-side and demand-side factors contribute to this situation.

3.1.1 Supply-side factors

The strongest microeconomic research is concentrated in supply-side causes for youth underemployment, as these supply-side factors more readily lend themselves to rigorous empirical study: it is difficult to conduct randomized controlled trials to vary exposure to demand-side factors, such as corruption, the strength of labour market, or product market regulation. On the other hand, rigorous evaluations of numerous supply-side interventions, such as provision of incentives for continued school attendance, have been conducted across a variety of developed and developing countries, including Africa. More importantly, much of this research suggests that supply-side interventions can be effective in fostering employment.

The first and most obvious supply-side factor we consider is the education and skills of youth. A high level of human capital, typically the outcome of well functioning education system, affects the probability with which young people will find full-time employment. Employers are more likely to hire applicants who can demonstrate a given set of skills, as demonstrated skills are proxy for, and ultimately translate into, higher worker productivity. African youth are more educated now than ever before. Based on current trends, by 2030 the number of individuals aged 20–24 who complete secondary education will reach 137 million (59 per cent) while the number of 20–24-year-olds who complete tertiary education will reach 12 million (AfDB *et al.*, 2012). However, this does not imply that the optimal level of educational attainment has been achieved given the current and future needs of the economy. Moreover, as has clearly transpired from the macro growth literature, a more educated population is a key input into stronger longer-term growth, as it implies more skilled business leaders and a larger pool of potential innovators. Finally, educated youth may also possess the political will to push for the structural reforms that are needed in order to undo the structural constraints that hinder expansion of formal labour demand. While these benefits might materialize only in the long run, we argue that educational improvements will also have immediate benefits.

This latter point gets us to another important, and related, issue: while average educational attainment is important, it is just as important that the right skill sets be taught given the needs of the economy, both in the formal and informal sectors. It is particularly problematic if young people complete more education, but do not acquire the specific skills that match the needs of employers in the formal sector, or do not gain the knowledge that is relevant to running and growing a successful informal microenterprise. This calls for well functioning job training programs, which in Africa often take the form of apprenticeships. The direct aim of such programs would be to improve the labour market relevance of young people's school-acquired skills. Unfortunately, as we discuss below, the current state of knowledge about such job training programs in Africa is poor.

Another source of likely mismatch between youth skills and labour demand are the expectations held by educated youth regarding their future employment prospects. In some parts of Africa, the unemployment rate is highest for college-educated youth. These college-educated workers have unduly high expectations about the wages they should receive, in part because they are targeting public sector jobs that typically pay much more than private sector jobs. However, these public sector jobs have become scarcer over time because many African economies have restructured and downsized their public sector. In this regard, we argue that other promising supply-side interventions might take the form of information policies, which may help young people reset their expectations about the availability of different jobs, readjust their reservation wages, and reconsider the set of skills they want to acquire at school.

Poor physical and mental health affect both human capital attainment when youth are in school, and job search outcomes once youth are ready to transition into the labour market. Malnutrition and illness indirectly harm future employment prospects by shortening years of schooling obtained or decreasing learning while in school. Low health status also directly affects employment outcomes by imposing higher costs on job search and decreasing worker productivity. Youth may have more trouble finding suitable formal sector jobs. And even when they find such jobs, their ability to retain them is compromised. The overall low quality of health delivery services in Africa, and the many epidemics, in particular HIV and AIDS, that have ravaged Africa over the past decades, make health-related issues particularly relevant to the employability of young men and women. A lot of the micro evidence we discuss below has identified effective ways to address health deficits among both young children and young adults.

Women in Africa face a unique set of constraints when it comes to human capital acquisition and labour market success. In developed countries, innovations in household production (e.g. dishwashers, washers and dryers) have decreased the time costs of household production, which in part contributed to the growth in female labour force participation. However, in developing countries household production is still time-intensive, and pregnancy, marriage and child-rearing inhibit the ability of young women to obtain education and transition into well paying jobs. Moreover, strong cultural norms still adversely affect young women in many African countries. Many micro studies have been focused on improving the educational and broader life prospects of African young women.

3.1.2 Demand-side factors

Strong labour market regulations, and other distortions attributable to unionization and collective bargaining, constrain labour market flexibility in some African countries. We argue this has a disproportionately strong negative effect on younger workers. Just as importantly, bureaucratic barriers to firm entry limit product market competition, and a highly corrupt environment makes it difficult for new firms to enter, more productive firms to grow, and less productive firms to be replaced by more productive ones.

Even though these macroeconomic variables influence the labour market prospects of younger workers, robust microeconomic evidence estimating their actual impact is limited. We nevertheless review some of the existing micro literature examining these factors. We also discuss specific policies that have been proposed with regard to lowering the effect of labour market regulation for younger workers, in particular wage subsidy programs. Unfortunately, most of the evidence that exists paints a somewhat pessimistic picture about the long-term effects of such wage subsidies for youth.

In many African countries, the public sector traditionally employed a large share of all workers. However, there is currently little potential for growth in the public sector (in fact, it has been shrinking). For many of the reasons listed above, the private sector is growing too slowly to absorb incoming groups of new workers (AfDB *et al.*, 2012). For the majority of youth, the informal sector is the only option for obtaining employment. Much of the recent micro literature has targeted the many small firms and self-employed workers operating in the informal sector. The two main factors on which these studies have focused are weak access to finance and weak management. Up to now, the evidence provided by existing randomized experiments on micro credit and business training has not been conclusive. More research is needed to understand how to design interventions that will help small informal businesses succeed. Also, more work should go into considering other constraints these businesses may face, such as access to infrastructure. We also discuss new exciting opportunities for small firms in Africa, with particular regard to the spread of information communication technologies.

Because of the large share of the agricultural sector in many African countries, we also review a set of recent micro interventions that aim to improve the productivity of small-scale farms in various African countries. Arguably, a more productive farming sector will translate into more job opportunities for both the younger and the older workforce.

We conclude our review of demand-side factors with a discussion of a popular public policy to address the youth job crisis in several developing countries: public works programs. The lessons we draw from these policies are mixed. While public works programs may (somewhat mechanically) help take some young people out of extreme financial duress, the evidence that public works programs can work as a stepping stone to better long-term job prospects is far from promising.

3.1.3 Contextual differences

While high unemployment rates among youth seem to be common across the continent, it is important to note that economies and cultures vary from country to country in significant ways. Many of the problems, programs and solutions discussed in the following sections will vary according to the specific country's characteristics. While there are a number of important similarities, Africa is a large continent. As demonstrated in the country studies that follow in Chapters 4–7 of this volume, African countries represent a variety of contexts and stages of development. When designing a strategy for targeting youth unemployment, considering the cultural, economic and political context of the individual country is necessary.

Agriculture remains the chief economic activity in countries such as Ethiopia, where agricultural activity accounts for 40 per cent of GDP and employs 85 per cent of the population (Chapter 4). Other countries, particularly South Africa and Nigeria, have large mining and extractive industries. These differences could fundamentally alter the nature of youth unemployment and therefore require distinct solutions. They may affect the type of education, skills or training needed for youth to find employment.

The size and importance of the informal sector varies across different economies as well. According to Schneider *et al.* (2010), Sub-Saharan Africa has the largest informal sector in the world. In 2005 it comprised 38.4 per cent of total GDP. The Middle East and North Africa (MENA) region is not far behind, with 27.3 per cent of total GDP coming from the informal sector. However, South Africa has an extremely small informal sector, with only 6 per cent of South Africans working in informal jobs (Chapter 7). Conversely, the informal sector in Ghana accounts for 86 per cent of total employment in 2010, and in Kenya accounted for 81 per cent of total employment in 2009 (Chapters 5 and 6).

The countries' labour markets, *vis-à-vis* regulations and unionization, vary similarly. In South Africa, entry and exit is rigid and labour unions are powerful (Chapter 7). Conversely, in Ethiopia, the large size of the informal sector and low level of wage employment give unions little bargaining power because employees fear that they will lose their jobs (Chapter 4). Similarly in Ghana, the large informal sector means that existing labour regulations are weakly enforced (Chapter 5).

Poverty levels across the continent differ as well. The *African Economic Outlook* 2012 reported that 15–24 per cent of people in MENA countries live on less than US$2 per day (AfDB *et al.*, 2012). The share was well above one-third for South Africa, half for Ghana, 67 per cent in Kenya, and over three-quarters for Ethiopia.

Health indicators also demonstrate how the challenges some Sub-Saharan countries face differ starkly from their MENA counterparts. In MENA countries, life expectancy is above 60 years. For Africa as a whole, life expectancy is just under 48 years. Additionally, in MENA countries, HIV prevalence is reported as well below 1 per cent in 2009. For countries in Sub-Saharan Africa, HIV and AIDS present more of a widespread public health concern. South Africa has a prevalence of about 18 per cent., Countries such as Botswana and Swaziland face HIV and AIDS prevalence rates of almost 25 per cent (AfDB *et al.*, 2012)

The continent contains a variety of different religious and cultural contexts that have tremendous implications for policies addressing everything from gender and the labour market, to family planning and sexual behavior, to education. All of these differences combine to create unique situations where the reasons for unemployment are different, as are the potential solutions. Context must weigh heavily in any decision to implement a given policy.

This chapter aims to review what has been found regarding youth unemployment and underemployment; to discuss the viable, cost-effective policy options that work to improve youth employment, and to identify key questions that remain unanswered regarding how the labour market problems of youth can be approached in various African contexts. Section 2 sets out to address how to foster employability among youth. Section 3 is related to issues of transition into the labour market. Section 4 reviews the evidence regarding barriers to labour demand. We conclude in Section 5.

3.2 Fostering employability: skills and education

Youth skills development and education is a central policy issue when it comes to addressing youth unemployment and underemployment problems. Many cross-country studies, as summarized by Hanushek and Woessman (2008), have found a strong relationship between the level of cognitive skills in a country and economic growth in that country.

While some may argue that improving the employability of some youth would simply result in the displacement of other less skilled workers, this argument is based on incomplete partial equilibrium reasoning that does not fully incorporate all the positive externalities that result from human capital development. Improving the skills of the workforce may help undo some of the constraints to labour demand in the formal economy by moving the marginal product of workers above the regulated minimum wage. Better education may enable self-employed youth in the informal sector to envision better ideas for new products or better ways to run their businesses, which may in turn create the need to hire additional workers. Broader access to a better educated workforce may be a strong driver of firm productivity and firms' growth; this may subsequently create more dynamism and competition within industries, which have been shown to be strong drivers of growth and job creation. Finally, higher education levels may foster a more politically engaged and informed populace, which eventually may help to change the set of policies and practices that are contributing to the structurally low level of labour demand observed in African countries.

In this section, we review the evidence on policies and interventions targeted at improving skills acquisition and educational achievement in Africa. We identify the constraints to skills acquisition for youth in Africa. They often lack basic health and proper nutrition. Research has convincingly established that this health deficit is an important barrier to learning, especially during early childhood when sensitive periods for skills development occur. Africa has also been affected by epidemics—the most salient being the HIV and AIDS epidemic—which have imposed a particularly strong burden on adolescents who are either still in school or transitioning into the labour market.

When it comes to schooling, credit constraints have unambiguously been identified as a hurdle to school attendance in many African countries. Creative approaches, such as conditional cash transfers (CCTs), have been successfully tested to both relax some of these credit constraints and provide direct incentives for school attendance. On the other hand, the issue of school quality is not as clear. In particular, while we now have fairly good knowledge about how to increase school attendance, our knowledge about how to improve the quality and the labour market relevance of education, particularly when it comes to secondary and post-secondary education, is extremely limited. We conclude this section by reviewing some research regarding the causes of, and remedies for, the educational deficit among African girls.

3.2.1 Health and nutrition

The importance of early childhood health factors

Skills formation during early childhood has been shown to have substantial and sustained effects on future educational attainment and labour market outcomes. For those who have not gained the requisite skills, it is extremely difficult to gain entry and advancement in a desired sector of work. Early childhood investments are especially important in this regard, as human capital acquired at early ages builds on itself and increases the productivity of investments made at later stages (Cunha *et al.*, 2005; Cunha and Heckman, 2008). Moreover, biological research has shown that there are critical and sensitive periods of development during early childhood, and that both cognitive and non-cognitive skills become significantly less malleable as children age. Several studies of early childhood intervention programs conducted in the USA, such as the Perry Preschool program, the Abecedarian program and the Head Start program, have shown that these interventions can have long-lasting positive effects on children born into less advantaged families. Interventions that aim to develop the skills of older children have typically been much less successful. While none of this evidence comes from Africa, the message regarding the critical importance of early childhood in skills development seems generalizable given its biological and mechanical foundations.

In the context of poorer nations, we believe that one critical input into early childhood skills development is access to better health and better food. Nutrition deficiencies are a widespread problem in Africa, with severe consequences for children's learning capabilities. Investing in health during early childhood can substantially expand cognitive function. Offering food in school can improve children's ability to focus in class and provide additional incentives for school attendance. Just as with education interventions, such health interventions might be most productive at early ages, as they stimulate cognitive development during critical periods and can improve children's lifetime productive capacity.

Several studies have demonstrated the health benefits of well designed nutritional and health interventions. For example, Delisle *et al.* (2000) review some cost-effective measures that have been taken to improve health outcomes in children and adolescents in developing countries: iron and folate supplements increased height in stunted adolescents in Nigeria; multi-nutrient fortified snacks and drinks given to South African school children had positive effects on health outcomes; in Tanzania, multivitamin supplements for HIV-infected pregnant women improved immunity rates and reduced the incidence of low birth weights.

Even more importantly, several studies have convincingly demonstrated the positive impact of these interventions for skills development and future labour market outcomes. For example, Field *et al.* (2009) find that intensive in-utero iodine supplementation programs reduced iodine deficiency disorders and dramatically increased cognition and schooling outcomes in Tanzania, especially for females. Treated children completed 0.35 to 0.56 additional years of school relative to comparable children who were not treated.

Several papers have studied the schooling and labour market benefits of deworming programs. In particular, Baird *et al.* (2011) evaluate the impacts of a primary school mass deworming program in Kenya, and find that the sustained benefits of deworming carry over to adulthood. Adults who received deworming treatment as children worked 12 per cent more hours and ate more meals on average. Out-of-school youth enjoyed 20 per cent higher earnings and triple the employment rates in manufacturing jobs relative to those who had not received deworming treatment as children. Ozier (2011a) finds that the school-based deworming program also improved the educational outcomes of younger children who had not been enrolled in primary school but were still able to receive treatment: for children less than one year old at the time of treatment, increases in cognitive performance were on par with gaining 0.5–0.8 additional years of schooling. Miguel and Kremer (2004) report that the program not only reduced absenteeism in treatment schools by a quarter, but also generated positive externalities on neighbouring non-treated primary schools. Because of the size of the impacts, Miguel and Kremer estimate that fully subsidizing the program and paying families to receive treatment would be more cost-effective than other Kenyan programs aimed at increasing school participation directly, such as through teacher incentives or school supply provision.[1] Taken together, the results from the studies reveal a causal effect of better health in childhood on skills development, schooling and employment outcomes in adulthood.

Provision of school meals can also drastically improve educational outcomes for young children through many different mechanisms. First, reducing hunger at school improves children's ability to focus in class and their learning. Second, the provision of school meals may operate as an incentive to attend school. Third, providing school meals generates income effects that offset the opportunity costs of sending children to school. Kremer and Vermeersch (2004) show that randomized provision of school meals to preschools in western Kenya significantly improved children's educational outcomes. Children were 30 per cent more likely to attend school, and learning improved as a result of increased attendance. However, learning improved only in schools with more experienced teachers, indicating that better nutrition alone might not be sufficient for improvement in learning.

Access to proper meals and nutrition has also been shown to increase educational outcomes in primary schools. For example, Adelman *et al.* (2008) study the impact of two Food for Education programs on primary schoolchildren in Uganda. Children were randomized into a control group, the in-school feeding program (where children were given more direct incentives to attend school), or a take-home rations program (where households controlled food allocation and used the rations to smooth consumption over time). Both programs increased the attendance rates of boys in grades 1 and 2 by 9–13 percentage points. The take-home rations program had significantly greater effects than the in-school feeding program for school children in grades 6 and 7. While both programs reduced grade repetition, the reduction in grade repetition rates was greater for children treated by the in-school feeding program. Progression into secondary school was not affected, but there was some evidence that the in-school feeding program was significantly more likely to motivate poor children to delay completing primary school. In a related study, Gelli *et al.* (2007) studied the effect of school-based food provision programs on girls' and boys' enrolment rates in 32 countries in Sub-Saharan Africa. In addition to providing meals during school, some sites also distributed take-home rations to girls. While provision of school meals increased enrolment for both boys and girls by 20 per cent, the enrolment improvements persisted over time only for girls, and only for the sites that also provided take-home rations. Since the cost of attendance for girls increases as they get older, and improvements were more pronounced for girls, the authors conclude that the take-home rations may have produced an income effect that mitigated the opportunity cost of sending girls to school. However, because the design did not balance across treatment and control groups, school-level unobserved factors may confound program estimates.

Overall, there is a general consensus that early childhood health effects induce sustained impacts on skills development, and that programs which provide simple health products have by and large led to significant improvements in educational attainment for African youth. The studies regarding *in utero* or early childhood nutrient supplements demonstrate improved cognitive function and school completion rates. The reported associations are likely to reflect causal estimates given the econometric design of most of the studies discussed above.[2] The studies on primary school deworming programs in Kenya each exploit the randomized program design to arrive at similar conclusions regarding the effectiveness of deworming on education as well as the welfare implications of deworming treatment on young children. Miguel and Kremer (2001) urge full public subsidization of deworming, given its large positive externalities. Finally, the picture on school feeding programs is also favorable for both preschool and primary school students. Using take-home rations as opposed to in-school feeding appears to be more effective in increasing school attendance rates, although the results differ slightly across studies, suggesting a need for more research to settle this question.

Future work in this area may also focus on how best to deliver health services and who to target given public budget constraints. Tanaka (2010) shows that simply providing needed health services is not sufficient to guarantee that benefits will reach all children. In particular, Tanaka examines the effect of a national health policy that improved access to health infrastructure in South Africa. He finds that increased access to free health services improved the nutrition of boys who had not yet reached primary school age. However, these effects were not found for girls. His results suggest that gender discrimination against girls within households may require more child-specific delivery of health services. There should be greater consideration as to how health product provision can be designed to bring about improvements for both boys and girls.

While our discussion of the early childhood literature above suggests that interventions targeted at very young children have the highest returns, more research is still needed to uncover the age gradient in the relationship between health improvement and skills acquisition. Evaluations that vary child age when investigating the effect of health service provision may help guide the design of more cost-effective interventions. In addition, it would probably be erroneous to assume that health interventions aimed at improving children's educational prospects should focus only on the health of the child. The health of adult family members may have dramatic and sustained consequences for the wellbeing and skills formation process of young children. As an extreme example, Bhargava (2005) examines the socio-emotional wellbeing and school participation of Ethiopian orphans whose mothers died from AIDS or other illnesses.

He finds that maternal death from illness severely hindered children's school participation and harmed socio-emotional wellbeing, with girls significantly less likely to continue schooling and scoring lower on measures of social and emotional wellbeing relative to boys. However, household income, access to food and clothing, and the attitudes of the fostering family significantly mediated these effects. In Kenya, Evans and Miguel (2007) find that parental death substantially reduced school participation, with the largest reductions for children with low baseline academic performance and for children who had experienced maternal death.

Youth's exposure to health risks: HIV and AIDS

HIV and AIDS are the leading causes of death in Sub-Saharan Africa and have devastating long-term consequences for human capital investment (Akbulut-Yuksel and Turan, 2010). As such, the true effect of AIDS will not materialize until decades into the future. Bell *et al.* (2006) use simulated models to estimate that in South Africa, where HIV prevalence was over 20 per cent in 2006, the economy would shrink to half its current size in four generations in the absence of effective interventions.

Diseases that affect primarily young adults, HIV and AIDS reduce human capital acquisition in a self-perpetuating cycle. They lower the productivity of infected prime-age adults and severely reduce the value of those adults' human capital. Prevalence of HIV and AIDS disproportionately affects the attendance and grade progression rates of young girls and the poor. These young people are in turn less capable of investing in the human capital of their own children. Akbulut-Yuksel and Turan (2010) show that children with HIV-positive mothers were half as likely to attend school and exhibited slower progress at school. Even if mothers were not infected, high HIV prevalence in the community shortened the child's expected lifespan and decreased the returns from transferring human capital to children. Using structural modelling and simulations, Bell *et al.* (2006) demonstrate that in Kenya, combating AIDS would increase future social gains not only through enhancing health and mortality, but also through improving family resources and the expected return from additional schooling. While the expected increase in education could be small at first, Bell *et al.* predict that the gains will increase exponentially over generations due to the persistent increases in household resources and the better educational opportunities that result from having a healthier populace.

There has been a great deal of research targeted at developing policies to reduce the incidence of risky sexual behavior among young people in Africa. Several papers have shown that incentive-based policies can be effective. In a recent study, De Walque *et al.* (2012) gave youth cash rewards conditional on testing negative for sexually transmitted infections (STI) tests. In a randomized intervention in Tanzania, they find that high-value cash rewards (US$20) caused a 19 per cent decrease in STI infection, compared with increases in STI infection rates of 19 per cent and 13 per cent in the low-value cash rewards group (US$10) and the control group, respectively. The effects took 12 months to materialize, possibly because it took time to remove oneself from sexual relationships or to trust that the program will actually follow through on its payments.

In African countries, it is common for adolescent girls to enter into sexual relationships with older men in order to gain economic security. Such economic dependence is problematic as older men are more likely to transmit STIs to young girls. In a randomized intervention conducted in Malawi, Baird *et al.* (2012) evaluate whether providing financial incentives to stay in school would reduce such risky behavior. Girls aged 13 to 22 were randomly selected to receive small cash transfers (US$1–5) that were either conditional on school attendance or unconditional. Despite the fact that the transfers did not condition directly on sexual behavior, girls who were selected to receive unconditional and CCTs experienced substantially lower rates of HIV and herpes infection relative to the control group in the 18 months following the start of the program. The study presents strong evidence that greater financial security decreases risky sexual behavior among adolescent girls.

In a separate randomized evaluation, where people were given HIV testing at home and the results were processed in a testing centre, Thornton (2008) finds that even small financial incentives to learn about one's HIV status double the proportion of people who go to the centre to receive their test results. Sexually active individuals who learn that they are HIV-positive are three times more likely to purchase condoms than HIV-positive individuals who did not learn their results.

Another intervention that discourages risky sexual behavior involves supporting greater access to contraceptives. A randomized evaluation reveals that giving non-monetary incentives, namely social recognition, to distributors of female condoms leveraged distributors' intrinsic motivation to promote the social good and substantially increased sales above those achieved by distributors who received monetary incentives. While researchers worry that financial incentives might crowd out intrinsic motivation for socially beneficial tasks, there was no evidence of that effect in this case (Ashraf *et al.*, 2012).

Although these studies are promising, more studies regarding the most effective incentive-based methods to curtail risky sexual behavior among youth are urgently needed. There remains much to learn about how best to structure incentives; about the effectiveness of unconditional cash transfers (UCTs), which are typically much cheaper to implement; and about the best use of non-monetary incentives. Moreover, due to the dependence of sexual norms (risky or not) on cultural context, it is necessary to test potential incentive programs across different regions within Africa.

Information campaigns are another widely explored method that has proven to be effective in reducing STIs and teenage pregnancies. Using a randomized experiment in Kenya, Dupas (2011) finds that when given information about the relative risks of HIV infection, pregnancy rates among teenagers decreased by 28 per cent. In contrast, abstinence-only HIV instruction led to no change in teen pregnancy rates. The results suggest that information dissemination campaigns can be effective, but that risk-reduction messages may be more successful than risk-avoidance messages.

Higher educational attainment has also been shown to increase the effectiveness of policies aiming to curtail the spread of HIV and AIDS through information campaigns. De Walque (2004) shows that educated youth displayed greater increases in condom usage, visits to counselling centres and visits to testing centres as a result of the campaigns. The greater responsiveness of educated individuals to information campaigns indicates that education helps individuals incorporate health-related information. In fact, in the 1990s, the decline in HIV and AIDS prevalence was twice as high for well educated individuals. Gregson *et al.* (2006) report that Zimbabwe experienced similar decreases in HIV prevalence from changes in sexual behavior. Again, HIV prevalence fell most for youth and the well educated.

The existing evidence suggests that information-based policies can successfully reduce risky behavior, and that information on risk-reduction strategies is more effective than information on risk-avoidance strategies. While providing youth with financial incentives is another effective way to reduce risky behavior, the cost of financially rewarding youth for desirable behavior is typically much higher than the cost of implementing information campaigns. Better evidence on the relative benefits of these different policies is needed. For example, in an ongoing study, Duflo, Dupas and Sharma are testing whether lack of resources or lack of access to information contributes more to risky sexual behavior in youth, by providing randomly selected youth in Kenya with free condoms, access to a voluntary counselling and testing centre, or both.

There must be further study regarding the type of information that would be most effective in containing the spread of HIV and AIDS. In particular, insight from psychology may help correct the short-term biases and self-control problems that often drive risky behavior, especially among young people. Additionally, evaluations of these policies need to be tested over a greater variety of social and geographical contexts; as discussed above, different cultures could have different norms associated with risky sexual behavior. Additionally, different programs may be more effective for different types of individuals. For example, McLaren (2011) finds that in South Africa, government provision of free AIDS treatment drugs significantly increased labour force participation and employment for black men but not for black women.

3.2.2 Credit constraints and education

Constrained credit is perhaps one of the most pressing problems facing African youth who seek to obtain more skills and education in order to improve their employment prospects. The alleviation of credit constraints is also one of the most appropriate areas for policy intervention, as low access to credit markets prevents youth with both the ability and the interest in greater schooling from attaining the necessary skills to realize their economic potential. As greater skill sets increase economic productivity and income, policies that relax credit constraints improve both private utility and societal welfare.

The literature on education and credit constraints is extensive and very rigorous. The main finding is that policies that increase household resources allow families to invest in education and improve future formal employment outcomes. For example, Edmonds (2006) studies the impact of receiving social pension transfers for the first time on schooling outcomes in South African black families. He finds that boys' attendance rates increase and work hours decrease only at the point when the first pensioner in the household becomes eligible for the transfer, which indicates that household investment decisions were credit-constrained. The effects found for girls were less significant and smaller in magnitude. Edmonds explains that as girls' attendance was higher than boys' attendance in the sample at baseline, the scope for growth in boys' attendance was larger. In another example, a study that randomized provision of school uniforms, which are mandatory to attend school, found increased school participation and improved test scores in both the short and the long term among treated students (Evans *et al.*, 2009). Also, both Bhargava (2005) and Evans and Miguel (2007) argue that one of the mediating factors for lower school participation rates among orphaned children is the loss in family income due to the death of a parent.

Another likely sign that credit constraints are a barrier to education is the prevalence of child labour. Children are frequently taken out of school to work full-time or are required to work in addition to attending school. Guarcello and Rosati (2007) report that Ethiopia's low school enrolment is primarily because many children live in rural areas, the majority of whom participate in child labour. Future labour market outcomes are typically the worst for former child labourers, who have had limited access to human capital acquisition opportunities. According to Guarcello and Rosati (2007), for many economically distressed families in Ethiopia, household survival greatly depends on children's labour market contributions. The results reported by Guarcello and Rosati (2007) indicate that improving households' financial positions may both decrease demand for child labour and increase school attendance. There is, however, also some suggestive evidence that child labour may not be exclusively due to low financial resources, as child labour occurs more frequently in areas with few educational opportunities.

Some of the ongoing research in this area has been concerned with exploring the potential side effects of alleviating credit constraints in education. Lucas and Mbiti (2012a) find that abolishing primary school fees increased primary school completion rates, but also changed the composition of students by inducing higher-income households to choose private schooling for their children. Hence a negative side-effect of abolishing school fees was increased overcrowding among public primary schools, which caused rich households to substitute for private schools and which indirectly decreased the average performance on test scores. This further suggests that lowering the cost of education without complementary investment in school infrastructure may harm learning.

More work also must address the relevance of credit constraints at different levels of education. The research discussed above focuses on reducing the cost of primary education. It is *a priori* less clear whether subsidizing secondary or post-secondary education would also significantly increase educational attainment. Duflo, Dupas, and Kremer (forthcoming a, b) are conducting a randomized evaluation in which students who could not attend secondary school because of financial distress are randomly selected to receive scholarships for secondary school attendance. By measuring improvements in employment and educational outcomes across treatment and control groups, they hope to obtain an estimate of the causal impacts of secondary school attendance.

Schultz (2003) argues that public subsidies for post-secondary education are unnecessary and serve only to entrench existing intergenerational inequalities. Subsidies might disproportionately favor enrolment of students from well educated families, as such students are the most likely to enrol in post-secondary education in the first place. Further research is needed to assess whether methods to expand higher education for low-income children, such as targeted education subsidies, would be effective.

There is also a growing literature evaluating sponsorship programs, where a private donor agrees to send a monthly cash transfer to a low-income child in a developing country. Wydick *et al.* (2011) find that in Kenya and Uganda, sponsorship on average increased formal education by 1.75 (Kenya) and 3.12 (Uganda) additional years, increased the probability of white-collar employment by 17.3 percentage points, and decreased the proportion of females who bore at least one child by age 20 by 11.8 percentage points. Even though only 4.2 per cent of the control population held a university degree at baseline, sponsorship increased the probability of obtaining a university degree by a remarkable 5.1 percentage points. The authors attribute the success of these programs to a focus on developing children's intrinsic motivation and nurturing their aspirations regarding education and employment instead of enforcing extrinsic incentives to keep children in school. They present evidence that sponsored children demonstrated more self-esteem and higher self-expectations than control children. The large impacts of sponsorship may also be from the strong complementarities between stronger educational aspirations and the relaxation of credit constraints. This research hints that the returns to initiatives that lower the cost of education could be greatly enhanced by complementary activities aimed at motivating students, suggesting a greater policy and research focus on developing students' economic aspirations while simultaneously giving them greater resources to fulfil those aspirations.

3.2.3 Financial incentives for education

Conditional cash transfer programs have seen considerable success in improving schooling outcomes, particularly in developing countries. By doling out financial rewards to participating households based on the attendance, enrolment or achievement of their children, CCT programs increase the present rate of return on schooling and decrease the cost of school. Most of the current research on CCTs is targeted at outstanding questions regarding the optimal design of a CCT. The majority of CCTs target young children, but a few have been implemented for adolescents. This section focuses on the CCTs that belong to the latter group.

If the elasticity of behavioral response to transfer amount is high, then increasing the transfer amount could increase the return on each dollar transferred. However, if the elasticity is low, then decreasing the transfer amount could save substantial program costs. Another important question pertains to the role of conditionality in inducing behavior changes. If UCTs are just as effective as CCTs, then the observed improvements in educational outcomes occur mostly through a relaxation of credit constraints (see previous section), and there is no need for the policymaker to incur the extra monitoring costs associated with CCTs. Baird *et al.* (2011) explore such questions using a randomized cash transfer program in Malawi that varied transfer amount and conditionality. Although dropout rates decreased among those who received UCTs, the decrease was only 43 per cent of the size of the decline in the CCT group. The CCT group scored higher than the UCT group in tests of English reading comprehension, but teenage pregnancy and marriage rates were significantly lower in the UCT group. Baird *et al.* explain that the UCT program benefitted those female youth who dropped out of school and were the most susceptible to teenage pregnancy and teenage marriage. Enrolment and English test scores in the CCT group appeared unresponsive to any increase in transfer amount above the minimum (US$5 per month), whereas enrolment and marriage likelihoods were highly responsive to increases in transfer amount. The authors conclude that offering CCTs with low transfer amounts would be more cost-effective than offering UCTs with higher transfer amounts in improving schooling outcomes, especially in poor countries such as Malawi. They estimate that the program would have to offer over US$10 per month under a UCT intervention to achieve the same gains in enrolment as a US$5 per month CCT, and that the increase in cost per transfer outweighed any additional monitoring costs that the CCT program would have to incur.

Another way to improve skills acquisition among youth is to condition the cash transfers on school achievement. Through a randomized controlled trial, Kremer *et al.* (2009) find that rewarding female students for academic performance significantly increased test scores as well as teacher attendance and parental monitoring. Moreover, because the program improved teacher attendance and teacher effort, improvements in achievement were observed for the entire class, including those not targeted by the program. Conditioning on achievement has not been as widely explored as conditioning on attendance. It would be useful to conduct more studies like that of Kremer *et al.* (2009) across a greater variety of contexts.

Current research is also investigating the best way to structure incentives to increase the cost-effectiveness of CCTs. For example, Blimpo (2010) experiments with individual, team and tournament-type incentive structures, and measures their effect on student performance in Benin. He finds that individual incentives motivated students only just below the target to work harder. With team incentives where the entire group of students received rewards if their average test score exceeded a target, low-performing individuals often free-rode off their high-performing teammates. In the 'tournament' set-up, where groups of students were rewarded if they outcompeted other groups, Blimpo finds that the free-riding problem was substantially reduced and that even low-performing individuals exerted greater effort and improved their test scores. Overall, while all incentive structures performed better than the control group, the tournament set-up exhibited the highest gains in test scores.

Overall, there is a large body of literature on the effectiveness of financial incentives in education, in part because of the ease with which financial incentives lend themselves to experimentation. Cash transfers that condition on school attendance have been consistently demonstrated to be effective in increasing schooling for both children and adolescents. The greater effectiveness of CCTs over UCTs indicates that low human capital acquisition stems from low motivation and high discount rates among youth, not only from low credit market access. While fewer studies examine the effect of conditioning on achievement, the evidence that does exist is also strong and favorable. Conditional cash transfers stand out as a promising method for improving educational outcomes among youth, both in Africa and in other parts of the developing world. Future research in this area should concentrate on investigating the most cost-effective design of CCTs, in the spirit of the work by Baird *et al.* (2011) and Blimpo (2010), particularly examining the effects of conditioning on achievement.

3.2.4 School quality and the returns to education

It is a mistake to focus only on school attainment and to ignore the quality and content of what is being taught at school (Hanushek and Woessman, 2008). After all, no matter how many years of schooling young people complete, it is the skills that they acquired at school that will ultimately determine their employability. Instead, schools must effectively promote learning, and the skills they teach must match the demands of the local economy. Otherwise, policies that increase schooling attendance will not effectively help youth acquire the skills they need to obtain formal employment.

For instance, in many countries in North Africa, unemployment rates are highest among the most educated youth since they typically have high reservation wages but are not adequately trained with the skills desired by employers. In Egypt, there exists a mismatch between the proportion of jobs available in different fields and the proportion of students studying in those fields, especially in higher levels of education. Many schools are overcrowded and have insufficient resources, which further contributes to the problem of low education quality. Finally, there is high variation in the quality of vocational training institutions, which makes imperfectly informed employers generally hesitant to employ new graduates (van Eekelen *et al.*, 2001). While these findings are reported only for North Africa, these problems (too few resources, too many students, labour market skill mismatches and high variation in quality across establishments) presumably extend to Sub-Saharan Africa as well. In order to improve labour market outcomes for Africa's youth, it is important to ensure that schooling adequately prepares them for skilled work. Various interventions to address these problems have been attempted, yielding varying degrees of success. Most of those interventions have taken place only in primary schools.

Some programs are designed to improve education quality through increasing school resources. Among the best known are interventions implemented in Kenya to provide more textbooks to schools (Glewwe *et al.*, 2004, 2009). The results of these resource-based interventions were somewhat disappointing: more access to textbooks and flip charts did not improve test scores, reduce grade repetition or decrease dropout rates. The provision of textbooks helped only those students who were already academically strong, without helping weaker students in lower grades progress to higher grades. Given the extreme heterogeneity of backgrounds and abilities among Kenyan students, more effective interventions may need to provide instruction or materials that are better tailored to the specific needs and abilities of different schoolchildren.

More successful interventions with respect to primary school quality are reported by Duflo *et al.* (2011). They find that giving primary school funds to hire teachers on short-term contracts lowered the pupil–teacher ratio and improved student performance in Kenya. Training the school hiring committee to select better teachers and to monitor those teachers also generated improvements in student performance. Finally, tracking students—assigning them to different classrooms based on their initial academic achievement—allowed teachers to tailor their instruction to meet the needs of their students more effectively. Consistent learning improvements were observed for all students, no matter their initial performance. This study illustrates that there exist simple but effective methods to improve learning in primary schools.

Other interventions have looked at whether providing teachers with financial incentives improves student outcomes. Glewwe *et al.* (2010) assess the impact of teacher incentives on test scores in Kenya, and find that while test scores improved, teacher attendance, student dropout rates and student repetition rates did not change. Rather than improve teaching methods, the incentives caused teachers to conduct test-preparation sessions, which did not promote learning. The improvements in student performance were not sustained at the end of the intervention. Glewwe and Jacoby (1994) use data from Ghana to find that alternative policies may bring about larger per-dollar impacts than financially incentivizing teachers. In particular, they argue that projects that repair school buildings can be more cost-effective in improving student outcomes.

Our assessment is that this literature is incomplete. This subject is ripe for further study. We know much more about how to get youth to school than about how to improve the quality of schooling. Although all of the primary school studies individually provide strong evidence for their conclusions, together they do not reach a consensus as to what works and what does not in improving school quality. On one hand, improving classroom equipment and building quality promotes the ability of schools to strengthen skill formation. On the other, provision of textbooks enhances the achievement only of those who were high-performing anyway, and does not help low-income students. Hiring more teachers through a selective process, monitoring teachers and tracking students significantly improves achievement outcomes. But incentive-based teacher contracts only increase 'teaching to the test' without improving actual learning. When it comes to improving school quality, there must be greater attention to the details. Further research on program design will help determine why certain policies work while apparently similar policies fail.

Furthermore, the bulk of the evidence appears to be concentrated among primary schools. We know much less about the quality of secondary and post-secondary education. One exception is presented by Lucas and Mbiti (2011), who estimate the causal effect of attending elite secondary school on student achievement.[3] Another exception is Ozier (2011b), who finds that attaining secondary education decreases the probability that male youth will enter low-skill self-employment by 50 per cent and increases the probability that they will be formally employed by 30 percentage points. While such research is informative about the value of current secondary schools, it provides only limited guidance about the constraints that hinder these schools from becoming places for more effective learning. It is not clear that the issues that are relevant to primary school (such as wide heterogeneity in student quality) are also relevant to secondary and post-secondary education as well. More work on how to improve the quality and labour market relevance of instruction in secondary and post-secondary schools, which more directly feed youth into higher skilled jobs, is crucially needed.

3.2.5 Post-secondary education

As mentioned above, there is a scarcity of research regarding post-secondary education in African countries. Research in this area could also be the most valuable in increasing youth underemployment in the short term, as technical and vocational schools more directly prepare youth with skills for the labour market. In a study of six Sub-Saharan African countries,[4] Schultz (2003) finds that the returns to education are highest at secondary and post-secondary levels. Recent reviews of the African youth labour market corroborate the view that returns to education are convex, with significantly higher returns to post-primary schooling (AfDB *et al.*, 2012). If primary and secondary education equip youth with basic cognitive and non-cognitive skills, then post-secondary schooling builds upon those general skills to develop more advanced, sector-specific expertise. A well functioning post-secondary school system consequently may improve the probability of formal employment by improving the skills most salient to potential employers.

In order to understand how to increase enrolment in post-secondary schooling, it is necessary to identify both the factors that prevent youth from obtaining more post-secondary schooling, and the steps that can be taken to ensure greater rates of return on post-secondary schooling. Hicks *et al.* (forthcoming) currently are evaluating the impacts of a randomized voucher program for technical and vocational schools in Kenya. Eligible youth who had left school were chosen to receive either a restricted voucher, which they could redeem at a public institution, or an unrestricted voucher, which they could redeem at a public or private institution. Hicks *et al.* find that the voucher system increased demand for vocational training, which indicates that policies to alleviate credit constraints can substantially increase uptake for vocational training. The unrestricted vouchers proved to be more effective than the restricted vouchers in terms of take-up rates and coursework completion. The authors hypothesize that this could be due to either the higher quality of private institutions, as they were able to offer more flexible and relevant training as well as better resources, or the increased choices available for those with unrestricted vouchers, which result in better individual–institution matches.

The results presented by Hicks *et al.* indicate that vouchers for vocational training are an effective way to increase demand for vocational schools, and that unrestricted vouchers are more effective than restricted vouchers at creating better individual–institution matches. Policies aimed at expanding the supply of private vocational institutions also may increase returns from vocational education, as demand for vocational training increased under the unrestricted voucher, and as dropout rates were lower for private institutions. Increasing the share of private vocational institutions not only enhances choice but also may place greater competitive pressure on public vocational institutions to provide better education quality. Consequently, expanding the market for vocational institutions may help increase the rate of return on education.

While the Hicks *et al.* study presents a compelling case for post-secondary school vouchers, there must be more research to better inform policymakers of other viable ways in which improvements can be made in both youth enrolment and education quality in post-secondary schools. More work also must be done to link post-secondary schooling to employment outcomes—while post-secondary schooling improves labour market outcomes in both developed and developing countries in general, to what extent does this occur in Africa? Finally, there is essentially no microeconomic research on college education in Africa. Are colleges providing the expected skills? Are they providing the leadership skills that we know to be so crucial to the creation and development of successful businesses? Are they fostering the spirit of initiative-taking and entrepreneurship that we know to be so crucial to a dynamic and healthy economy? If not, what are the binding constraints? Is it poor infrastructure, or a lack of financial resources, or a lack of properly trained instructors? We believe all these understudied areas deserve much more attention in the future.

3.2.6 Gender gaps in education

Rectifying gender gaps in educational attainment, student performance and returns to education is by no means an easy task, especially given the different priorities and cultural norms for girls and boys, as well as society's different attitudes toward their continued education and chosen occupation. Understanding how gender gaps arise, why they persist, and how to narrow them in a cost-effective manner is an especially important first step towards decreasing marginalization and promoting the wellbeing of both young men and young women.

Gender gaps in school choice arise from different preferences or differential responses to certain environments. Ajayi (2009) finds that when students select secondary schools in Ghana, girls are less likely to choose technical programs, more likely to choose single-sex schools, and more likely to choose public schools than boys are. Lee and Lockheed (1990) find that, with respect to achievement and sexist attitudes regarding maths, single-sex schools benefit girls but adversely affect boys. Girls in single-sex schools perform better at maths than girls in co-educational schools, but boys in single-sex schools perform worse than boys in co-ed schools. Lee and Lockheed present evidence that girls' schools are less prone to instil sexist views of maths as a male discipline compared with co-educational schools, while boys' schools are more likely to instil the idea of maths as a male-biased subject.

Lloyd *et al.* (2003) find that in Egypt, boys and girls have different motivations for dropping out: boys' likelihood of exiting school depends on family socioeconomic characteristics, whereas girls' likelihood of exiting school depends more on the quality of teaching. While boys and girls are both more likely to drop out of schools with a higher ratio of temporary to full-time teachers, girls' likelihood of school exit depends on quality of school facilities, share of recently trained teachers, and whether or not there exist classes tailored to provide their desired skill sets. On the other hand, boys' school retention rates depend more on the income and education of parents. It is unclear as to how these results generalize to the rest of Africa. In Egypt, parents emphasize investment in girls' human capital so as to ensure that their daughters will marry educated men. Teachers express a preference for teaching girls over boys, since girls tend to have better behavior in the classroom than boys.

These preferences are different in Kenya, where traditional female roles are seen as inferior to male roles and teachers favor male over female students (Lloyd *et al.*, 2003). Teachers regularly exhibit discriminatory behavior against girls. As such, while the rate of primary school completion is high for both genders, girls are significantly more likely than boys to drop out of school during their teenage years. Girls are more likely to exit school if their school's treatment of girls relative to boys is especially unequal. In contrast to the results in Egypt, family background is a more significant factor in girls' likelihood of school exit than boys' (Lloyd *et al.*, 2000).

Previous evaluations of policy interventions help us better understand the differential factors affecting girls' and boys' schooling outcomes. Lucas and Mbiti (2012b) examine the effect of Kenya's free public primary school program on the gender gap in schooling outcomes. Before the program, boys had higher enrolment rates than girls. While the program increased absolute enrolment levels for both boys and girls, it widened the gender gap as boys were more responsive to free primary schooling than girls were. Since the widening gap is in part driven by boys and girls older than 17, Lucas and Mbiti posit that the lower responsiveness of older girls could be due to the higher propensity of girls to leave school due to pregnancy or marriage. Girls were also more likely to drop out of school in order to take care of younger siblings. Lokshin *et al.* (2004) find that older daughters are substitutes for mothers in childcare. An increase in the mother's wages increased the attendance of older boys but decreased the enrolment of older girls, who exited school in order to take care of their younger siblings when their mothers worked longer hours.

Schools can be an especially important medium for policies aimed at solving problems unique to young women. In a paper that expands on the results of Evans *et al.* (2009) described above, Duflo *et al.* (2006) find that providing free school uniforms increased enrolment length and reduced the rate of teen marriage and pregnancy. When school uniform provision was combined with training sessions for teachers on teaching about HIV in the classroom, school dropout rates and incidences of teen pregnancy decreased even further. The incidence of STIs also decreased significantly. Increased access to schooling significantly reduced risky sexual behaviors among women. Ozier (2011b) corroborates this conclusion. Using regression discontinuity methods, he finds that secondary schooling significantly decreased the rate of teenage pregnancies of Kenyan young women.

Suboptimal human capital acquisition renders young women unable to support themselves or to convince their parents to finance secondary school enrolment. Often, they turn to male partners who support them but demand sex in return, which increases the probability of HIV infection and unwanted pregnancy. Ashraf *et al.* (forthcoming) examine the impact of negotiation skills training and health information sessions on eighth-grade girls in Zambia. The forthcoming results will shed light on whether better negotiation skills affect school participation rates, STI infection rates, incidence of unplanned pregnancies, or parents' willingness to pay for post-primary education.

Given the high rate of teenage pregnancies in Africa, substantial welfare gains may arise if teenage mothers are given greater opportunities to continue schooling. In South Africa, where the rate of teenage pregnancy is especially high, girls are permitted to go back to school after having a child. In this context, girls' parents are usually supportive of additional investment in schooling, as educated girls bring in greater bride wealth. However, re-enrolling in school and keeping up academically with peers is difficult for young mothers. Further research is needed to determine the most effective ways for policy to help them generate supportive and accepting social networks (Kaufman *et al.*, 2001).

3.3 The integration of youth into the labour market

This section reviews the micro evidence regarding youth's transition into the labour market. One overarching finding is that, in contrast with issues of health and human capital formation discussed in the previous section, there is little systematic evidence on the topics discussed below. Yet we view many of these topics as crucially important, and urge more research effort on them. We start with a review of work on job training and school-to-work transition programs, which might be particularly crucial in terms of reducing the mismatch between the skill set young people acquire and the skills desired by employers. We then discuss issues related to the spatial mismatch that may exist in many African countries between job-seeker location and firm location, and explore policies to address that mismatch. One of the implications of spatial mismatch is that young people often possess poor information about the availability of jobs, and wrong expectations about the distribution of wages in the economy. We discuss possible policies to address these information imperfections. We then review a set of micro interventions related to young people's saving behavior. This literature is relevant to labour market integration in that some savings will typically be needed to facilitate the job search process. Our final section relates to the specific labour market hurdles faced by young people who live through, or participate in, conflicts—a topic of great importance for many African countries.

3.3.1 Job training and school-to-work transition programs

Job training programs are typically used to combat skill mismatch, in which the skills youth possess are not the skills desired by employers. However, job training programs can serve an additional purpose in Africa, where the informal sector accounts for a substantial fraction of all employment. If effective, job training could allow informally employed youth to develop microenterprises and create jobs. Indeed, workers who enter the informal sector overwhelmingly possess low levels of education and skills, which prevents the informal sector from expanding beyond small enterprises. Haan and Serrière (2002) report that many entrepreneurs cite low capital, insufficient managerial and entrepreneurial skills, and a lack of information about training programs as crucial impediments to the expansion of their small and microenterprises. They mention the need for training programs to focus on developing job-relevant skills as well as on book-keeping, management and marketing knowledge.

Apprenticeship is the primary avenue of job training for youth. It has strong social and cultural roots in several parts of Africa, in particular in West and Central Africa. In West Africa, apprenticeships constitute over 90 per cent of all training programs. Their popularity stems from the fact that they focus on the practical training desired by youth, and are much more accessible to children and adolescents than other training programs. In Ghana, apprenticeship training accounts for 80–90 per cent of youth training programs compared with 5–10 per cent by public vocational training programs, and 10–15 per cent by private vocational training programs. In Cameroon, most training comes from apprenticeships as training institutions and technical colleges are extremely underdeveloped and fail to provide meaningful ways for youth to acquire skills.

Despite their popularity, traditional apprenticeships do not appear to be adequately structured to guarantee skills acquisition for the trainee. In Niger, as master craftsmen typically receive annual fees for each apprentice, they have incentives to delay training as much as possible and to prevent apprentices from learning the trade. In order to avoid future competition, masters have also been known to send an apprentice away on an errand when they perform the most crucial element of their craft (Haan and Serrière, 2002).

Training programs are much more accessible to males than to females, even though women make up a larger share of the informal sector workforce. In Senegal's clothing sector, training for boys lasting 5–8 years is provided free of charge, while training for girls taking only 2–3 years must be paid for. Of those attending training institutions in Ghana, fewer than one fourth are girls (Haan and Serrière, 2002).

Small fees, transportation costs and the opportunity cost of time also often prevent the poorest from enrolling in vocational training programs. Haan and Serrière (2002) present evidence that the opportunity cost of time is the most relevant cost of enrolment into vocational programs, as most informally employed workers lose sales and risk jeopardizing their business if they leave it unattended for an extended period of time. In this regard, short skills training courses have been shown to have a higher rate of take-up and do not seem to be less effective than longer courses. Based on this evidence, Haan and Serrière conclude that optimal vocational training programs and apprenticeships should focus on short courses centering around the technical skills required for the craft. More rigorous research in better-controlled environments should be performed to confirm the validity of this insight.

Overall, in its current state, the evidence on job training programs in Africa is too meagre and too weak to inform any policy. What little work exists in this area lacks rigor, is mostly descriptive, and does not offer clear policy implications regarding what can be done to improve job training. One exception is a recent randomized evaluation in Uganda that gives youth funds for vocational training and business investment, and finds improved labour force attachment for youth (Blattman *et al.*, 2011). However, in this study it is difficult to extricate the effect of vocational training from business investment.

More work must be done to test whether the results of experimental job training programs conducted in other developing countries extend to the case of Africa. Overall, the randomized evidence from other developing countries offers some mixed evidence about the success of youth training. A randomized evaluation conducted in the Dominican Republic reported a short-term positive effect on wages, although the effect attenuated in the long run, with no effect on employment rate (Card *et al.*, 2011). Another randomized evaluation in Colombia (Attanasio *et al.*, 2009) finds increased average wages and probability of employment, especially for women; however, because the program had multiple components besides job training, it is difficult to tease out the effect of the job training component.

All in all, we have extremely limited knowledge of what makes for an effective job training program, whether in Africa or outside Africa. The prevalence of the apprenticeship system in many African countries makes studies about this system, and ways to improve it (access, content, optimal duration, incentives for both student and master), particularly urgent. More work could also be done to help youth who have undergone informal job training to communicate their skills to formal sector employers. While apprenticeships have the highest take-up in most African countries, formal sector employers lack systematic methods to recognize that informally trained youth may possess additional skills that make them better candidates. Offering a certification for apprenticeships, as has been done in Benin (AfDB *et al.*, 2012), may facilitate recognition of skills acquired during informal training and rectify this information asymmetry.

3.3.2 Spatial mismatch

One obvious issue related to integration into the labour market is physical access to areas where employment opportunities exist. The spatial mismatch hypothesis attempts to explain minority low-skilled workers' underemployment by the fact that they are physically disconnected from job opportunities. Longer distances to jobs induce bigger costs to become employed. High transportation costs to reach employment areas or employment agencies may exceed the benefits of searching for a job. The costs of relocation near job opportunities may also prevent the unemployed from searching actively. Getting information on jobs can also be costly, and information frictions are likely to increase with physical distance.

When the likelihood of finding high-quality employment is higher elsewhere, members of households (most commonly rural) who lack sufficient income may send a household member of working age to live and work, permanently or seasonally, in another area (usually urban), whether inside their home country or internationally. That household member, once work is found, would send remittances back to their family. As Ranis and Gollin discuss in Chapter 2 of this volume, migration is commonly used in Africa to generate income necessary for survival in the presence of high local unemployment or underemployment. Money received through remittances is also used for investing in education, health, housing and businesses (Ratha *et al.*, 2011).

As Ranis and Gollin (Chapter 2) point out, while migrants benefit both host urban areas and rural areas that send them, research suggests that some households that would benefit greatly from receiving remittances face credit and childcare constraints that often prevent them from sending members to find work elsewhere. This may be especially difficult for unemployed youth, as they have had less time to build up savings to finance relocating, and may have young children. Ardington *et al.* (2009) find that for multi-generational households in rural South Africa, relaxing credit constraints significantly increases the likelihood of migration and employment for prime-aged workers. They examine the effect of a household member receiving old-age pension from the South African government on the migration likelihood of job searchers. The introduction of additional income means that the household now has additional financial resources to support the household member who is conducting the initial search process. These results are supported by Posel *et al.* (2006). The results hold for developing countries outside of Africa as well, as Bryan *et al.* (2012) find that providing incentives to seek work elsewhere during seasonal famines in Bangladesh increases migration. According to Bryan *et al.*, the additional income makes migration in the face of uncertainty possible for households that otherwise would not be able to support the migrant job searcher.

This body of work presents evidence that relaxing the credit constraints that hinder migration improves the allocation of workers to jobs and helps address the spatial mismatch that exists between labour supply and demand. Other policies should also be investigated to reduce that mismatch. Access to a better public transportation system, improving roads, or transportation subsidies should also be considered.

3.3.3 Information imperfections

Related to the spatial mismatch problem discussed above are issues related to information imperfections. Youth and employers alike face substantial barriers to information. Formal sector firms often struggle to fill vacancies. For example, even though 1.5 million youth are unemployed in Egypt, there are 600,000 open positions in the formal sector (AfDB *et al.*, 2012). Unemployed youth may lack information about the types of jobs available and the skills desired by employers; as a result, they may prepare poorly for the labour market (van Eekelen *et al.*, 2001; AfDB *et al.*, 2012). Information barriers may also affect the take-up of programs designed to help youth prepare better for jobs: in a large-scale youth survey conducted in Egypt, only 18 per cent of respondents report being aware of projects to help the unemployed (van Eekelen *et al.*, 2001).

Interventions targeted at improving access to information about the labour market could facilitate faster entry into the labour market for youth, especially when there is a strong spatial or social mismatch between firms and workers. Providing youth with more information about wages, necessary skills, jobs and training opportunities available could help facilitate entry into the labour market. For example, with the spread of cellular phones, better information systems could be developed to help guide job seekers living in remote locations about the location of job vacancies. More evidence is needed in this area to identify effective policies that reduce barriers to obtaining information for labour market entrants and labour market participants.

Developing the proper labour market institutions that promote information flow between employers and youth could substantially help in this regard. Public employment services currently exist in only 23 African countries. Most of these services reach, at most, half of the youth who are seeking formal sector employment. In Morocco, public employment services have found employment for only 9 per cent of those registered with the service. In Algeria, only 11 per cent of those registered have found employment through public employment services (AfDB *et al.*, 2012). While public employment agencies have so far failed to demonstrate much success for youth, it is unclear whether private provision would be better. There is some evidence that private employment services prioritize those whose employment probabilities are the highest (AfDB *et al.*, 2012). Given the information asymmetries and lack of job experience that characterize young job applicants, they may be placed at the back of the line. It is important to investigate how better incentive structures could be designed to make employment agencies, public or private, more effective intermediaries for young people's labour market transition.

Another manifestation of information problems involves reservation wages. In particular, there is evidence from several African countries that young people, especially the most educated, have unduly high reservation wages which may slow their entry into the workforce. Using structural modelling, Levinsohn and Pugatch (2009) find that educated youth in Cape Town, South Africa tend to value their own abilities more than potential employers do, and choose to remain unemployed if their reservation wage exceeds their offered wage. Arguably, providing these educated young people with better information about the typical level of compensation of their peers should prompt them to adjust their reservation wages downward and reduce their sub-optimally lengthy job search.

One factor that explains why youth have unnecessarily high reservation wages is the gap in compensation between public and private sector jobs. In Tunisia, employment for college graduates is driven primarily by jobs in public administration. The availability of such jobs relies on budgetary allocations. Additionally, there has been an overall decline in the number of public sector jobs. College graduates often remain unemployed for long periods, preferring to wait for a high-status job in the public sector rather than settle for a job below their expectations (Stampini and Verdier-Chouchane, 2011). Boudarbat (2005) uses labour supply data and structural estimation to arrive at the same conclusions regarding the high unemployment rate of educated youth in Morocco, where the unemployment rate was 5.6 per cent among uneducated workers but 32.2 per cent for university graduates. He finds that university graduates, as in Tunisia, largely preferred employment in the public sector even though employment opportunities in the public sector were more scarce than in other sectors. The unemployment duration of university graduates increased when the wage differential between the public and private sectors increased.

At the macro level, these data suggest that reducing public sector wages could substantially improve employment conditions for highly educated youth. Reduced public sector wages would contribute to an increase in the demand for more educated workers in the private sector, which currently cannot match the high pay rates in the public sector. At the micro level, information campaigns that re-set young, educated people's expectations about public sector jobs could be particularly beneficial. Such information campaigns would help adjust reservation wages down and may also lead young people to select their course of study in college more wisely. This may shift skills acquisition away from the skills valuable for the public sector and toward the skills necessary for working in the private sector. We are not aware of any systematic evaluation of such policy interventions, indicating that this as a valuable topic for future research. Note, however, that given the distinct contexts represented by South Africa and MENA countries, it would be useful to know more about the wage and job expectations of the highly educated youth in other countries more representative of Sub-Saharan African labour markets.

3.3.4 Youth and the trap of the present: savings behavior

Youth systematically exhibit behaviors that further disadvantage them in the labour market. Their demonstrated greater impulsivity and present-biased preferences are likely to prevent them from saving responsibly, when saving could increase their ability to meet the costs of job search or finance additional schooling. Exacerbating the problem is the fact that young people in developing countries have had little or no training in financial literacy and may not be properly informed about the importance of saving. Developing a consistent ethic of saving early on could also improve their economic position and give them greater latitude to participate in job training programs. Youth who save more are better equipped to smooth consumption over time and make productive but costly investments in their future labour market value.

Various impact evaluations have analysed the effectiveness and desirability of different programs aimed at encouraging savings. Specifically, interventions are testing two broad approaches to promoting savings among youth. The first is through using financial education programs, which are more likely to work if the low rate of saving among youth is due to a lack of information regarding financially responsible behavior. The second is through increasing access to savings accounts, which are more likely to work if low savings rates are due to a lack of formal savings devices.

Berry *et al.* (forthcoming) are examining the impact of two financial education programs on savings behaviors and financial knowledge of primary and junior high school students. Despite non-significant effects on academic achievement, time preferences and total amount saved, the program increased expected education expenditures, measures of student risk aversion and the percentage of students who report saving. One of the interventions improved students' self-reported attitudes about saving and public health behavior, as well as self-reported measures of wellbeing.

Bandiera *et al.* (forthcoming) observe that women in Uganda and Tanzania hold limited financial knowledge and these women usually cannot procure bank loans. The researchers examine whether such disadvantages can be rectified early on with school-based interventions. In particular, they analyse whether the adolescence development program, which provides 14–20-year-old females with opportunities for education and financial literacy training, can have a beneficial impact on girls' educational attainment, financial independence, probability of employment and behavioral outcomes. Results will inform whether there exist gender-based differences in the response of savings behavior to financial education.

Work on savings behavior has clearly demonstrated that providing formal savings accounts to self-employed women substantially increased savings and productive investments (Dupas and Robinson, 2012), but it is still unclear whether youth will respond in the same way. Jamison *et al.* (forthcoming) are evaluating an ongoing intervention aimed at encouraging savings behavior among Ugandan youth. The program provides two treatments. In one, youth are randomly selected to participate in educational sessions on financial literacy. In the other, youth are given access to savings group accounts. The comparative effectiveness of one group compared with the other will shed light on whether the low savings rate among Ugandan youth is motivated by a lack of information, or by a lack of access to formal savings accounts.

Alternative formal savings devices may better promote educational investments than traditional bank accounts do. Karlan and Linden (forthcoming) are studying the impact of a savings program in primary schools. The program randomly offers students either a savings account or a savings voucher. Both treatments allow students to access their savings only at the beginning of year. However, one group receives savings in cash, while the other receives savings in the form of a voucher that can be used only for education expenditures. The results will inform whether school-based savings programs are effective in encouraging savings behavior and decreasing the likelihood of dropout.

A number of evaluations conducted with farmers may also be effective for youth, especially those employed informally in the agricultural sector. Brune *et al.* (2011) conducted a field experiment in Malawi, where farmers were assigned to two savings treatments: a regular savings treatment that provides farmers an ordinary savings account, and a 'commitment treatment' that provides farmers an ordinary savings account as well as an account that restricts access to funds until a future date of their choosing. Farmers in the commitment treatment increased bank deposits, agriculture input use, crop sales and household expenditures over those levels achieved by farmers in the regular savings treatment. The effect did not occur through limiting control over disposable income, as the savings were concentrated in the ordinary savings account. Rather, Brune *et al.* hypothesize that farmers increased savings through decreasing the amount of money they shared in their social network or through mental accounting effects. Similarly, Karlan *et al.* (forthcoming) find that simple psychological savings tools, namely labelling a savings account for a specific goal, increased savings rates by 31.2 per cent. Using pilot evaluations that apply these methods specifically to youth will improve understanding regarding what is effective in improving youth savings behavior.

As the literature on promoting savings behavior presented in this chapter includes only randomized controlled trials, the causal validity of each study is quite strong. The evaluations that focus on encouraging savings behavior among youth primarily involve financial education programs held in schools. However, many of these evaluations are ongoing and conclusive results have yet to be published. What evidence does exist strongly favors financial literacy training as an effective means of improving the proportion of students who save, as well as total investment in education. Interventions that target adults show similarly successful results: financial education programs increased productive investments among self-employed women. The simple use of commitment savings devices and labelled savings accounts increased savings and improved the economic position of farmers. Similar research that draws from results in behavioral economics and applies them to youth could improve understanding regarding whether the interventions that work for adults could also work for youth.

3.3.5 The effect of conflict areas on youth labour force participation

Youth in post-conflict environments are extremely vulnerable to remaining unemployed and impoverished, as they have experienced disruption in their education and could have been victims or perpetrators of violence associated with conflict. Social stigma as well as a lack of skills may keep conflict-affected youth out of the formal, legal labour market, even in post-conflict settings. More evidence is needed to determine what aspects of rehabilitation and reintegration programs work at healing some of the social wounds that come from conflicts.

War and conflict scenarios have enormous destructive impacts on individual wellbeing and community cohesion. Liberia's 14-year civil war was responsible for 'displacing the majority of Liberia's three million inhabitants, halting economic activity, deepening poverty, and depriving a generation of basic education' (Annan and Blattman, 2011). Youth in post-war Liberia have faced numerous frustrations, few available jobs and persistent poverty. Opportunities to acquire skills and to garner employment are bleak for everyone, but especially for youth. Due to poor infrastructure and the limited functionality of the labour market, many turn to illegal activities for their livelihood. The Liberian government has labelled youth disempowerment one of its two major threats to durable peace, as frustrated youth are often responsible for riots, civil conflict, revolutions and organized crime (Blattman *et al.*, forthcoming).

Given the dearth of resources and opportunities in post-conflict settings, research is urgently needed on how to reintegrate youth, to prepare them for employment, and to nurture their mental and physical wellbeing. Youth either grew up as bystanders in highly charged conflict scenarios or were combatants themselves. The ethical norms and behavioral conduct that made them survivors may in fact impede their integration into civilian society. In war and conflict settings, an individual can maximize the probability of survival by focusing on the present and taking risks. But in post-conflict scenarios, the same tendencies typically lead to criminal behavior, heavy drug use, low savings rates and suboptimal human capital accumulation.

Reintegration of ex-combatants into society is a daunting task, and there is very little knowledge surrounding successful programs that facilitate reintegration. Humphreys and Weinstein (2007) use data from Sierra Leone to determine the characteristics of ex-combatants that affect ease of reintegration into civilian life. They find that social reintegration was most difficult for individuals who fought in especially abusive military factions or were ranked highly in their faction. Men, younger combatants, and those who joined the faction out of political support for the cause were most likely to maintain connections to former military factions, which retarded the process of reintegration. Proponents of demobilization and reintegration programs argue that participation in such programs dissolves factional networks, improves employment prospects and facilitates reconciliation with family and friends. However, Humphreys and Weinstein find no evidence that funded programs significantly helped the process of demobilization and reintegration for ex-combatants. They admit that their causal effect estimates may not be cleanly identified, and advocate the use of randomized evaluations to assess the effectiveness of reintegration programs rigorously.

A number of different agricultural projects are aiming to provide sustainable legal employment and feasible reintegration strategies for ex-combatants. Agricultural projects have been touted as successful in other contexts and the agricultural sector can employ ex-combatants in large numbers. Agricultural projects are also useful in developing the infrastructure necessary to support an efficient labour market, as agricultural production can help turn lands ravaged by war into arable fields (Peters, 2006).

Annan and Blattman (2011) conduct a randomized evaluation of agricultural training's effect on employment outcomes for young ex-combatants in Liberia, and find promising results. Survey data indicate that ex-combatant youth viewed agricultural production as a lucrative means of legal employment. Eighteen months after the completion of the program, individuals in the treatment group were at least 25 per cent more likely to be engaged in agriculture and 37 per cent more likely to have sold crops. While both youth in the treatment and control groups continued to participate in illegal activities, treatment youth spent far fewer hours on illegal activities than those in the control group. The program induced substantial increases in household wealth for the treatment group, but did not significantly reduce aggressive or criminal tendencies. It is exceedingly difficult for a short training program to shift deeply entrenched behaviors and mindsets, but the program's substantial economic improvements indicate that agricultural training programs are a promising tool for economic reintegration.

Blattman *et al.* (forthcoming) are conducting a randomized evaluation that explores whether, and to what extent, credit constraints and risky preferences contribute to the persistent poverty plaguing Liberia's street youth. Street youth selected for their high-risk behavior (who typically engage in organized crime, violence, drug abuse and excessive alcohol consumption) are randomized into groups in which they are to receive cognitive behavioral therapy and life-skills training, an unconditional cash grant, both, or neither. The forthcoming results will shed light on effective strategies to help garner sustainable employment for high-risk youth in post-conflict scenarios.

Annan *et al.* (forthcoming) are conducting an ongoing intervention targeting vulnerable young women in northern Uganda, another area devastated by civil conflict. They study the effects of a program that gave women training in business skills and group dynamics. Annan *et al.* find that women in the treatment group experienced twice the cash income, three times the savings amounts, and 39 per cent gains in consumption levels relative to the control group. However, the program did not improve feelings of empowerment, psychological wellbeing or social integration; it remains an open question as to whether such a female-focused program enhanced or undermined women's empowerment.

3.4 Labour demand

In this section, we review evidence from the micro literature related to the structural barriers to labour demand in Africa. We start with a review of two potentially key macroeconomic factors affecting labour demand, particularly in the formal sector: labour market regulation and corruption. We also discuss a particular macro policy that has received wide interest, both inside and outside of Africa, in terms of improving labour demand for young workers: employment subsidies. We then continue with a discussion of the informal sector and self-employment, which, given the limited number of formal sector jobs in many African countries, is where many youth are employed or underemployed. We discuss factors that may help these microenterprises grow and succeed, with special attention to programs that provide better access to credit and better managerial skills. We also discuss promising opportunities for these microenterprises related to firm clustering and information technology. We also include a section specific to micro-interventions in the agricultural sector, given the large size of this sector in many African countries. We conclude with a section on public sector labour demand, and in particular the use of public works programs as a source of labour market opportunities for young people.

3.4.1 Macroeconomic factors

Labour market regulation

Strong labour market regulations in Africa segment the labour market by protecting employment for incumbent workers (typically adult workers) at the expense of prospective entrants (the majority of whom are young). The duration of contracts, the costs of hiring and dismissal, and the legal provisions regarding contract termination all affect the number and type of hires in significant ways (AfDB *et al.*, 2012). Employment protection reduces labour market turnover as increased hiring or dismissal costs make employers more likely to retain inefficient workers rather than hire potentially more productive workers. A separate but related effect is that pro-worker employment legislation may increase employers' reluctance to hire riskier applicants, of whom youth constitute a sizable share. Because labour market regulation tends to increase barriers to hiring and firing workers in the private sector, and decreases the demand for labour, many youth must seek employment through the informal sector or to become self-employed (AfDB *et al.*, 2012).

Labour market regulations in Africa are ranked the most rigid in the world, with greater *de jure* rigidity in Sub-Saharan Africa than in North Africa, exacerbating the problems posed by the growing oversupply of young job-seekers, as that rigidity places further constraints on the ability of formal sector firms to expand employment capacity. However, rigidity is not regarded as a first-order concern for most African countries, as many other factors contribute more significantly to youth underemployment, and a weak rule of law makes enforcement of labour market regulations difficult (AfDB *et al.*, 2012).

Rigidity is identified to be more important for MENA economies than for Sub-Saharan African economies. Despite the higher measured rigidity of the Sub-Saharan Africa region, North African governments possess stronger capacity to enforce regulations and face greater pressure from organized labour groups to pass pro-worker legislation. For example, labour markets in Morocco and Egypt are ranked among the least efficient in the world. In these countries, not only do high dismissal costs make employers reluctant to hire youth to permanent positions, but employment protection severely limits employers from arranging internships and short-term contracts, which could otherwise provide youth with much-needed job experience and skills development opportunities (AfDB *et al.*, 2012).

There is a paucity of research regarding labour employment regulation and its effect on youth employment in Africa, but evidence from a variety of countries has consistently demonstrated the significant detrimental effect of labour market regulation on permanent hires. Kugler and Pica (2008) find that increasing dismissal costs in small firms reduced labour market turnover for small firms relative to large firms in Italy. Besley and Burgess (2004) find that pro-worker employment legislation in India led to lower output, employment and productivity in the formal sector. Besley and Burgess also find that the stringent regulatory measures placed on the formal sector led output in informal firms to increase. Similarly, Magruder (2012) finds that in South Africa, extending centralized agreements made by unionized firms to small firms decreased employment among small firms and start-up companies.

More stringent employment regulation leads formal sector firms to rely more heavily on temporary contracts, which have lower firing and hiring costs, when temporary contracts are legally introduced. In theory, temporary contracts could provide a stepping stone to permanent employment, as they allow firms to ascertain worker productivity more effectively and offer productive workers permanent contracts. In addition to rectifying information asymmetries, temporary contracts may offer youth the job experience and skills development they need to signal productivity to prospective employers. On the other hand, another possibility is that, instead of serving as a stepping-stone to permanent employment, temporary contracts may function merely as a low-cost substitute for permanent contracts. Moreover, temporary contracts are often accompanied by lower investment in training, lower wages and lower job security.

Consistent with the more negative view, the empirical evidence suggests that temporary contracts fail to help youth obtain permanent employment. Instead, temporary contracts might trap youth in a series of short-term positions where skills development is low and the tasks are not meaningful. Evidence from France and Spain demonstrates that relaxing labour market regulation for temporary contracts did not decrease unemployment duration or help workers transition to permanent employment, but merely increased the share of temporary workers (Blanchard and Landier, 2002; Dolado *et al.*, 2002). The results indicate that, instead of using temporary contracts to resolve information asymmetries regarding worker productivity, employers used temporary contracts to avoid the increased hiring costs of permanent contracts. Little work has been done in Africa on this front, and Africa-specific evaluations that adopt the approach of Blanchard and Landier (2002) and Dolado *et al.* (2002) would benefit our understanding of labour market regulations as they apply to African youth employment. Since labour market regulations are more reliably enforced in France and Spain than in African countries, it is unclear what the results of similar policies will be when exercised in an African context.

An alternative approach, which has proven to be more effective, is to designate that employment regulation be relaxed for youth hires. Reducing dismissal costs for young workers on long-term contracts improved long-term employment among youth in Spain (Kugler *et al.*, 2003). However, one potential drawback of this approach is that it may lead firms to decrease their demand for older workers, who cost more to hire and fire than younger workers, and simply result in displacement effects with no net job creation. Again, given the sharp contextual differences between developed and African countries, it is difficult to determine with the evidence available whether such an approach will effectively increase youth hires in African countries.

To address the effect of labour market regulations on youth employment, one approach is to take existing policies and test them in African countries. The other approach, which might require more creativity but may prove more effective, is to devise specific solutions to this problem in Africa. Provisions regarding severance pay are reported to have the highest adverse impacts for youth employment in Africa (AfDB *et al.*, 2012). As with most pro-worker regulation, severance pay provisions hinder the ability of the labour market to be flexible and hire additional workers when needed. Because most African countries lack social safety nets for unemployed workers, there is increased pressure among African firms to provide generous severance pay (AfDB *et al.*, 2012), which reduces labour market turnover and decreases the rate of hiring. Just as with other labour market regulations, severance pay provisions have disproportionate adverse impacts on youth. Therefore providing greater social safety nets (e.g. unemployment benefits provided by the government) may ease the pressure on firms to provide generous severance pay, which would in turn decrease dismissal costs, improve labour market turnover and improve the probability that youth will land permanent jobs.

There is still no clear vision as to what is effective in alleviating the disproportionate effects of labour market regulation on youth employment, and few studies have explored the subject at length for the case of Africa. A greater variety of methods must be employed over a larger array of contexts to determine whether temporary contracts can be structured to improve permanent employment probabilities for youth, whether alternative methods work better in fostering long-term labour force attachment, and whether policies that relax employment regulations for youth will generate long-term improvements in economic outcomes.

Corruption

Corruption increases the costs of economic development by promoting inefficiency among firms and the misallocation of technology, talent and capital from socially productive uses (Murphy *et al.*, 1991). High levels of corruption within a country will induce firms to devote resources to overcoming extra-legal obstacles and obtaining preferential market access. By raising operational costs and increasing uncertainty, corruption deters productive investment (Shleifer and Vishny, 1993), thereby decreasing labour demand for all workers, young and old.

The problem with studying corruption is the lack of accurate data: due to the nature of the topic, measurement error is a persistent concern. Surveying firms usually collect data on corruption by asking about perceptions and experiences regarding corrupt practices. However, the corruption is likely to be correlated with various firm attributes that also affect investment and economic success. Moreover, as corruption is a sensitive topic, respondents may choose to give deceptive or evasive answers that would hinder precise estimation of the impacts.

Using data from a range of countries, Mauro (1995) finds that corruption lowered productive investment and economic growth. Controlling for GDP per capita, corrupt and unstable governments tended to invest less in education and skills acquisition, which would indirectly retard economic growth even further. Overall, Mauro's analysis finds that a one standard deviation increase in the bureaucratic efficiency index is associated with a 1.8 percentage point increase in the GDP per capita yearly growth rate.

A few studies have investigated the impact of corruption at the micro level. Using linear probability models and data from surveys of firms in South Africa and Mozambique, Sequeira and Djankov (2010) find that real efficiency losses in firms' production are created through corruption. In particular, 46 per cent of South African firms more than doubled their transport costs by using a longer route in order to avoid bribe payments. The firms exhibited high aversion to the ambiguity and uncertainties posed by bribe payments, as they chose to incur re-routing costs that were eight times the amount of the actual bribe payments. Such corruption-induced costs can significantly affect a firm's ability to grow. Fisman and Svensson (2007) use survey data from Uganda and instrumental variables methodology to estimate large negative impacts of corruption on firms' growth. A 1 percentage point increase in bribery rates decreased growth by 3.3 percentage points, while a comparable increase in tax rates decreased growth by only 1.5 percentage points. While neither Sequeira and Djankov (2010) nor Fisman and Svensson (2007) use randomized controlled trials to arrive at their results, their econometric specifications make a strong case that their findings represent causal impacts. The evidence strongly suggests that corruption is an important barrier to firms' growth, and hence a damper to labour demand, for both younger and older workers.

Although corruption is difficult to investigate in a randomized setting, there is a growing body of literature that demonstrates the adverse impacts of corruption. The results appear to hold not only in African countries, but in contexts beyond Africa. Given these findings, it is likely that the effect of corruption will be consistent across a variety of settings. To our knowledge, there is no rigorous study that examines the specific effects of corruption on youth employment outcomes.

Employment subsidies

By definition, young workers have less experience than older workers and are less capable of signalling their productivity to potential employers. If they are aware of these disadvantages, young people should be willing to accept lower wage offers in order to secure full-time employment. However, minimum wage regulations and other sources of wage rigidity, such as those attributable to collective bargaining agreements and powerful unions, will eject from the formal labour market those youth who would have otherwise been employed at a wage below the minimum wage. Those regulations therefore place structural barriers on labour demand and generate deadweight losses that disproportionately affect young people (Freeman and Freeman, 1991). Possible policies to address this inefficiency include instituting a separate minimum wage for youth, lowering labour taxes for hiring youth, and providing employment subsidies to promote greater hiring of youth in the formal sector.

Employment subsidy programs for young workers aim to increase work opportunities for targeted beneficiaries by transferring subsidies to the firms that employ eligible workers. The subsidy is intended to compensate the firm for screening, orientation and training costs, as well as any losses in firm productivity that result from hiring a young worker instead of a more senior job applicant. Some employment subsidy programs also provide training for youth in addition to the training provided by firms. Through temporarily increasing the proportion of youth hired, employment subsidy programs ideally would alleviate information asymmetries regarding young people's productivity. High-ability youth who were hired due to the subsidy would be better able to communicate their productivity to employers and increase their chances of obtaining long-term employment. Through increasing work experience, employment subsidies may also improve the employability of youth and better enable them to find jobs on their own after the end of the program. Finally, employment subsidies could generate a scale effect. As long as hiring subsidized workers decreases labour costs, firms would have more funds available for investment, which could encourage expansion and increase demand for workers in future (Burns *et al.*, 2010).

Overall, the available evidence suggests that employment subsidy policies are difficult to implement and only weakly effective in helping youth access stable and durable employment. While they may show positive effects in the short run, these effects vanish after the program ends (Groh *et al.*, 2012). Also, wage subsidy programs can be especially costly: most of the programs that saw positive effects subsidized half the entire wage rate for at least a year. More evidence is needed on the precise effect of these policies and on their cost–benefit balance, especially in the African context. Indeed, most of the evidence we have on this policy comes from outside of Africa.

The only Africa-based study of employment subsidies we are aware of is an ongoing study in South Africa by Levinsohn and co-workers, This study is based on randomized provision of hiring vouchers for firms, which could only be used if youth were hired. The take-up rate from firms is very low, which further highlights the difficulty of implementing such programs. Yet youth who received the vouchers were significantly more likely to be employed one year after the start of the program. There was also evidence that individuals in the treatment group were more likely to move in order to expand their job search, perhaps because they believed that the vouchers improved their probabilities of obtaining employment.

A few studies also report positive effects of employment subsidies on youth employment in other countries. Katz (1998) examined the Targeted Jobs Tax Credit, a two-year US program that offered substantial wage subsidies (50 per cent in the first year, 25 per cent in the second year) to vulnerable and disadvantaged workers. The program increased employment for youth by 7.7 per cent. Galasso *et al.* (2001) evaluated a randomized controlled trial in Argentina that subsidized 50 per cent of wages for the first 18 months of employment. The program significantly improved probability of employment for women and youth. However, as in South Africa, implementation was imperfect and the take-up rate of the policy was very low.

There are many possible reasons as to why employment subsidy programs might fail to translate into longer-term employment gains for beneficiaries. Each entails a distinct set of solutions. First, the magnitude of the subsidies in many cases may not have been enough to make young workers attractive to formal employers. If that is the case, increasing the quality, intensity or duration of training that often accompanies the wage subsidy, or further increasing the level of the subsidy, may help improve the success of these programs. Second, beneficiaries may not be sufficiently motivated to perform well at the subsidized job, thereby limiting the chance that the job will turn into longer term employment. Tying the employment subsidy to greater incentives, such as renewal of the subsidized job conditional on performance, may address this problem. Finally, if beneficiaries remain unable to signal their job experience to potential future employers, employment subsidy programs may be combined successfully with formal referral and counselling processes, which may reduce any remaining information asymmetries regarding worker productivity.

A crucial concern with wage subsidy programs is the extent to which they are associated with displacement effects. It is unclear whether employment subsidy programs are actually effective in creating employment. Rather, wage subsidies may induce substitution effects in labour market demand and displace incumbent workers (Gustman and Steinmeier, 1988). A randomized evaluation of employment subsidies in Jordan (Groh *et al.*, 2012) revealed large displacement effects. Employment subsidy programs could also subsidize employment positions for those youth who would have already been hired, although the deadweight loss effect would be small given the low employment rate of African youth in the formal sector.

Despite these limitations, one potentially underappreciated benefit of subsidy programs is that they may encourage the formalization of informal jobs. Subsidizing wages decreases the labour costs for firms and may incentivize informal firms to transition into the formal sector. Betcherman *et al.* (2010) show that such a dynamic had occurred with two subsidy programs in Turkey. While this also does not create new jobs, it may be effective in spurring competition in the formal private sector and incentivizing more efficient wage adjustments among formal sector employers. Also, because of easier access to credit and other government benefits, formal firms typically grow at a faster pace than informal firms.

Overall, we believe there is a strong need to undertake more rigorous evaluations of such programs. These evaluations should be designed to measure displacement effects better. They should also aim to provide information about the full costs and benefits, including the firms' formalization process described above. Also, while the evidence that exists suggests only short-term benefits for beneficiaries, we recommend testing alternative models that may combine the subsidies with other policies (including additional training, referrals and counselling, and financial incentives for good performance) that may improve the chance that stable and durable jobs will be created.

3.4.2 The informal sector and self-employment

The informal sector makes up a considerable share of the overall economy in Africa. Schneider *et al.* (2010) find that the informal sector in Sub-Saharan Africa constitutes a larger share of the total economy than anywhere else in the world. They estimate that in 2005, the share of the informal sector was 38.4 per cent of total GDP in Sub-Saharan Africa and 27.3 per cent of total GDP in the MENA region. As of 2006, 82.6 and 30.7 per cent of all employed men, and 92.1 and 39.0 per cent of all employed women, worked in the informal sectors of Kenya and South Africa, respectively (UNRISD, 2010).

Informal sector work was previously seen as low-status manual labour as it has mostly been performed by poorly educated workers. However, educated youth have increasingly opted for work in the informal sector due to their inability to find jobs in the public and private formal sectors. The increase in skills and education among informal sector workers has diminished some of the stigma against informal sector work. Women typically make up a greater share of informal sector workers than men. The gender inequality in work across the formal and informal sectors is especially pronounced in Cameroon, where 82 per cent of formal sector jobs went to men, and 95 per cent of all working women were employed in the informal sector (Haan and Serrière, 2002). Even within the informal sector, men tend to work in high-level jobs—that is, they tend to be employers of formal work—while women are overrepresented at bottom-tier occupations (UNRISD, 2010).

Given the importance of the informal sector and self-employment in many African countries, it is important to discuss the factors that may constrain the ability of the firms in those sectors to expand and succeed. We identify two core factors: access to credit and managerial skills. We also discuss the opportunities created by new information technologies, which we argue might be particularly promising for microenterprises, as well by geographic clustering policies.

Access to credit

In theory, microfinance should directly address the structural labour demand problems identified by Ranis and Gollin as the primary cause of youth under-employment (see Chapter 2 in this volume). Providing greater access to credit enables youth to invest in the capital and labour inputs that are necessary to start or maintain their small businesses. The profit earned from business activities could be allocated to make loan payments for additional investments in business production. In this way, microcredit could allow youth to counteract the problems of low demand in the formal sector directly by creating demand for labour themselves. Under microfinance, successful microenterprises could have a greater wealth of financial resources to expand their businesses and employ a larger number of workers. Microfinance therefore enhances the productive potential of the informal sector and facilitates the expansion of profitable microenterprises into businesses that would employ more job-seekers in gainful full-time work. However, microfinance programs, as they are currently structured, can promote microenterprise expansion only to a certain point, and alone are insufficient to fuel the expansion of small and medium enterprises (SMEs).

While microfinance has been extensively studied in the developing world, few randomized controlled trials have specifically examined its effect on African youth. This chapter synthesizes the current state of knowledge and presents implications for African youth based on the effects of microcredit programs on the general population. We do so with the disclaimer that, while it is likely that the general results will apply to African youth, it is also possible that the features that distinguish Africa and the characteristics that set youth apart may lead to different program effects on African youth. There are significant differences in microcredit uptake rates among youth relative to adults, partly due to the fact that, although youth represent a significant share of the underemployed in Africa, microfinance institutions view youth as riskier clients, given their lack of experience and the sharp information asymmetries regarding their productivity. Youth also represent a small market for microfinance institutions, so the potential profit gains may not justify the costs involved if special services must be developed for youth (e.g. structuring special credit products appropriate for youth). There is also political opposition to microcredit for adolescents, as child labour might increase and as adolescents may be more likely to exit school as a result (Nagarajan, 2005).

Overall, the empirical literature on microcredit shows mixed and inconclusive results on employment outcomes and enterprise development. Bauchet *et al.* (2011) review recent randomized evaluations in developing countries and report that results are heterogeneous among targeted populations, with benefits to some and losses to others. Crépon *et al.* (forthcoming) find that microcredit slightly improved business development, increased self-employment and increased formal employment in Morocco. Desai *et al.* (2011) find that even though take-up was high, the impact of microcredit on economic activity in Ethiopia was inconclusive. There were, however, significant increases in the school enrolment rate of borrowers' children. In another study conducted in South Africa, Fernald *et al.* (2008) report that the pressure to pay back loans on time and avoid being trapped in a never-ending cycle of debt increased stress among borrowers, particularly men.

The design and structure of a microcredit program are important in determining its success or failure. Fafchamps *et al.* (2011) find that female-owned microenterprises in Ghana cannot be stimulated by capital alone. In-kind grants were much more important than cash for female entrepreneurs, as only in-kind grants increased profits. For men, both in-kind and cash transfers improved profits. The evidence presented by Fafchamps *et al.* suggests that credit constraints may not be the only problem faced by female entrepreneurs, and that lack of self-control or knowledge regarding how to properly handle cash transfers may hinder the development of female-owned enterprises. The study also demonstrates that different conditions and stipulations must be applied for different target populations, as what is effective for one group may not be effective for another. Consequently, if youth and the adult populations differ significantly, what has been found for adults may not apply for youth. If this is the case, more research must be conducted on whether it is cost-effective to design separate microfinance components tailored to youth. There also must be further study of whether the program components that are effective for young men are just as effective for young women.

A study that corroborates these ideas is one conducted by Akhmisse *et al.* (2008), which finds that significant changes must be made to microfinance program structure if the services are to be appropriate for youth. For example, youths' savings decisions and ability to plan for the future are closely linked to their family environment. In Morocco, parents are burdened with heavy stigmas regarding entrepreneurial work and pressure their children to wait for high-paying but scarce jobs in the public sector. Close communication with parents may resolve prejudices regarding informal work and improve both the uptake and economic impact of microcredit programs targeted at youth. Additionally, Akhmisse *et al.* (2008) argue that more flexible loan options need to be created for youth, as current loan terms make it difficult for youth to qualify for microcredit. For instance, microloans typically require applicants to rent or own their own business, an unrealistic criterion for young people just beginning their careers. Current microfinance arrangements generate low uptake among youth, which prevents clear assessment of the true impact of credit access on youths' business outcomes.

While microcredit theoretically could be a feasible short-term solution to rectifying the problem of low formal labour demand, it is unclear what its capacity for creating gainful employment is relative to the formal sector. According to Ranis and Gollin (Chapter 2), most youth employed in the informal sector do not have full-time work and are not making use of their full productive potential. Does microcredit have the potential to alleviate such problems and improve employment in the informal sector? Rigorous empirical research comparing the benefits of micro-entrepreneurship and formal employment is scarce, especially when it comes to youth. Blattman and Dercon (forthcoming) are evaluating an intervention in which 15–20 new Ethiopian factories randomly hired qualified applicants. The rest of the applicants were randomized into either a micro-enterprise treatment or a control group. Once the program is complete, Blattman and Dercon hope to assess the comparative welfare effects of microenterprise treatment and industrial employment based on measures of poverty levels, health, household income, political behavior and social behavior.

While the general lessons from the microcredit literature can be applied to youth, it is possible that the causes of unemployment that are particular to youth also affect their entrepreneurship potential and their ability to take advantage of microfinance. Questions as to what these factors are, and how they affect microfinancing for youth, cannot be reasonably addressed without more youth-specific research. Microfinance is a subject that lends itself very well to randomized evaluations, and the numerous evaluations in both Africa and the rest of the developing world have generated mixed and inconclusive findings (Fernald *et al.*, 2008; Bauchet *et al.*, 2011; Desai *et al.*, 2011; Crépon *et al.*, forthcoming).

There is a possibility that microfinance programs might be improved if they were better tailored to address the needs of specific subgroups. For example, there is strong evidence from randomized evaluations that what works for male entrepreneurs does not work for female entrepreneurs (Fafchamps *et al.*, 2011). Therefore researching detailed project components that better address the specific needs of the targeted population may generate better economic impacts. In particular, designing specific program components to address the unique needs of youth may generate higher take-up rates and improve youth business outcomes better than simply offering them the loan packages that worked best for adults. Akhmisse *et al.* (2008) determine that allowing more flexible loan terms and involving the parents of youth would help improve take-up, but such suggestions have not been tested in a randomized setting.

Management skills

One factor likely to be important to the success of a microenterprise is its owner's collection of management skills. There are currently several randomized evaluation devoted to measuring the effects of programs designed to increase management skills.

Fischer *et al.* (forthcoming) evaluate whether lack of managerial human capital may be limiting the expansion of SMEs in Uganda, especially those owned by women (40 per cent of SMEs in Uganda are run by women). In particular, they study the impacts of an ongoing intervention that provides entrepreneurship training services to female entrepreneurs. The program randomly assigns women to a control group, a less-intensive entrepreneurial training program, or a more-intensive entrepreneurial training program. The forthcoming results will shed light as to the most cost-effective level of training intensity, and whether lack of managerial human capital is indeed limiting the growth of female-owned SMEs.

A similar evaluation is being conducted by Karlan and Udry (forthcoming a, b), who are investigating the impact of business consulting and cash transfers on small enterprises and microenterprises in Ghana. Half of 170 tailoring businesses were randomly selected to receive business consultations, training sessions on business topics (such as costing and record-keeping), and individual mentorship. At the end of the treatment half of the control group and half of the treatment group were given a US$133 grant to use in their business. The forthcoming results will reveal the impact on business outcomes of consulting services, cash transfers, and the combination of the two. It is possible that incorporating business training would enhance the effectiveness of microcredit programs. Our understanding could be improved substantially if future interventions extended the ideas of Karlan and Udry in other contexts.

There is very little literature on management skills training and micro-enterprise development, particularly for African youth. Based on forthcoming results, we would be able to better assess whether training programs, coupled with a simultaneous increase in credit access for poor youth, would generate greater impacts than providing credit access alone. In general, future randomized evaluations could explore how programs aiming to foster microenterprise development can be augmented so as to generate better outcomes for youth.

Geographic clustering

Physical clustering facilitates joint decision-making, cost-sharing, cooperative investments and the exchange of production information. Ayele *et al.* (2009) study the impact of grouping entrepreneurs within one industry into close proximity ('clustering'). They focus on handloom weavers in Ethiopia, and find clustering to be a flexible approach that is adaptive to both urban and rural areas. Because clustering can adapt to even the most restrictive environments, it allows workers with low levels of capital to participate in the handloom weaving business. Clustering changes the production structure and allows entrepreneurs on the margin to circumvent the constraints that would have otherwise made their business prohibitively expensive: through sharing rent, service costs and equipment, more handloom weavers are able to participate in the labour force. The results indicate that clustering can improve employment outcomes for youth in areas where capital is low and financial resources are few.

An ongoing randomized evaluation in Uganda by Schoar and Zia (forthcoming) examines if and how business and financial knowledge spread within clusters of industrial microenterprises. The intervention seeks to determine whether entrepreneurs within a cluster function as collaborators who share information, or as competitors who withhold information from each other. The forthcoming results may support or challenge the conclusions reported by Ayele *et al.* (2009).

While only nascent, this research suggests that grouping informal workers in one industry and allowing them to share certain resources may help reduce costs and increase entry, thereby fostering more labour demand. Schoar and Zia's research will tell us more about how individual entrepreneurs within these clusters interact, whether competitively or collaboratively. This additional research is needed to determine conclusively whether or not clustering expands informal opportunity.

Infrastructural improvements might be especially useful in magnifying the benefits of clustering. In clusters with access to electricity, workers work longer and more productively than those in clusters without access to electricity. More generally, access to infrastructure and basic utilities is a basic input into firms' growth. Lack of access to electricity has been identified as one of the biggest obstacles to firms' growth in Sub-Saharan Africa (AfDB *et al.*, 2012). Sub-Saharan Africa is also a place where getting an electrical grid connection is extremely expensive and time-consuming. Surprisingly, there have been few rigorous studies about the effects of infrastructure development on firms' growth in Africa. One exception is that of Dinkelman (2011), who studies the effect of electrification in South Africa. Using several identification strategies, Dinkelman shows that electrification significantly increased female employment, and hours of work for men and women.

Information communication technology

ICT presents a large opportunity for development. As Ranis and Gollin discuss (Chapter 2 in this volume), youth are particularly well positioned to capitalize on the rapid developments in this sector, which could improve youth employment prospects and propel economies forward. For example, according to Aker and Mbiti (2010), mobile phone networks have expanded from covering 10 per cent of Africa's population in 1999, concentrated in North Africa, to covering 60 per cent of the continent's population in 2009. This sort of rapid expansion is positioned to continue, and could present unemployed youth, as early adopters, with increased economic opportunities (Aker and Mbiti, 2010; Ranis and Gollin, Chapter 2). ICT development could improve the labour prospects for youth through two channels: increasing the productivity and profitability of informal activities, and expanding employment opportunities by helping formal sector businesses operate more efficiently.

Small entrepreneurs and self-employed individuals in the agriculture sector face significant costs, in terms of time and money, for obtaining the information necessary to maximize productivity and profit. Recent research has attempted to quantify the potential gains to agricultural commodity traders from using mobile phones to communicate price information. Aker (2010) studies the effect of cellular phone network expansion on price differences between grain markets in Niger. Mobile phone networks were first introduced in Niger in 2001. By 2006, more than three-quarters of grain markets had service. Before the introduction of mobile phones, grain traders in Niger had to travel to markets to find out the day's trading price on their commodity. Theoretically, introducing mobile phones would allow traders to access information on prices before they spent time on travelling, and would give them better information regarding the markets that offered higher prices for that day. The study found that extension of mobile phone coverage accounted for a 10–16 per cent reduction in the size of price differences between markets. Easier access to better information on prices allowed traders to maximize the price they received with minimal search costs.

Building on a similar concept, Casaburi *et al.* (forthcoming a) plan to test the effects of using mobile phones to deliver reminders through text messages to farmers on when to water and feed crops, when to apply fertilizer, and other crop management techniques. The findings of this research could further support mobile phone use as an inexpensive way to improve information access for informal sector workers, raising output and increasing profit. Access to this technology could encourage the expansion and growth of informal enterprises, which could employ more youth or increase the attractiveness of informal sector jobs.

The second way in which ICT development could improve prospects for youth's economic output is through providing new jobs. Aker and Mbiti (2010) argue that mobile phone companies depend on individual shop owners or kiosk operators to sell airtime and to sell, repair or even charge mobile phones. These are suitable positions for youth to fill. Klonner and Nolen (2008) study the employment effects of expanding mobile phone networks in South Africa during 1995–2000. They find that mobile phone coverage increases employment by 15 percentage points on average, and that women account for a large part of that increase.

Based on the current research, ICT development could help expand job opportunities for youth and increase the productivity of informal sector jobs. However, there exists little research on how to target these programs to benefit youth specifically. Additionally, the studies largely focus on use of mobile phones. More research is needed on the potential benefits to the labour market that other ICT media could bring, and how productivity gains from ICT will also benefit formal sector jobs. Greater knowledge regarding how to leverage the expansion of ICT technology in Africa to benefit youth is crucial, as innovation and development are among the most effective ways to promote business efficiency and expand employment in the long run.

3.4.3 The agricultural sector

As of 2009, agriculture makes up 13 per cent of the GDP across all of Africa, although agriculture as a percentage of GDP varies greatly from country to country. Half of all females and 30 per cent of all males are employed in the agricultural sector in North African countries (World Bank, 2012). As the agricultural sector continues to contribute significantly to the economy of African countries, it is important to conduct further research on how best to improve agricultural productivity and also how best to facilitate youth employment in agricultural work.

It would be naïve to believe that one could simply encourage young unemployed people to start their own farm. For example, van Eekelen *et al.* (2001) describe a program implemented in Egypt in which unemployed youth are given the opportunity to cultivate 5 acres of land in the desert. The program was unsuccessful because youth lacked both the agricultural experience and the capital needed to invest in the land. Furthermore, due to the heavy cultural stigma against rural and blue-collar work, most youth decided to remain unemployed rather than take up low-status work. The stigma youth hold against agricultural work extends across most of Africa, in part due to the low productivity of the agricultural sector in Africa (Proctor and Lucchesi, 2012).

Such a program remains one of the few agricultural projects that exclusively targeted unemployed youth. There have, however, been a multitude of micro-evaluations over the past few years targeted at understanding the constraints to investment and productivity in African farms. Understanding those constraints helps provide some information about these farms' labour demand and growth constraints, which are directly relevant to youth employment. We review some of this micro evidence in the remainder of this section.

Adopting simple productivity-enhancing technologies as well as agronomic techniques, such as pruning tree crops or using the correct combination of fertilizers, could dramatically increase output and move farmers out of subsistence living. Assuming that lack of information is the main explanation behind the low rates of adoption of these practices, Duflo, Keniston and Suri are currently conducting a study in rural Rwanda to assess the impact of training and information programs on small-scale farm output (Duflo *et al.*, forthcoming c). Results will inform the structure of future policies designed to improve business outcomes and information uptake for subsistence farmers. In a similar vein, Beaman *et al.* (forthcoming a) are conducting a randomized evaluation in Malawi that analyses the effectiveness of social networks in disseminating information about productive agricultural techniques. Based on the forthcoming results, Beaman *et al.* will assess whether policies can harness social networks to dissolve information barriers in a cost-effective way. Similarly, BenYishay and Mobarak (forthcoming) are conducting a randomized evaluation in Malawi on the effect on farmers' income of providing information on technology and agricultural techniques. They vary the information farmers receive (information regarding how to use fertilizers properly versus information regarding techniques to conserve the biodiversity of the farm ecosystem) as well as the methods through which the information is disseminated.

Duflo *et al.* (2011) find that due to the inability to save money from harvest time to the next planting season, farmers use little or no fertilizer, which constrains agricultural output in Kenya. Giving farmers the option to prepay for fertilizer when they had cash on hand, combined with a very small incentive (free delivery), was sufficient to increase fertilizer usage significantly above baseline levels. To build on these findings, ongoing interventions in Mozambique and Kenya randomize provision of vouchers for discounted fertilizer, provision of savings accounts, and assignment into farmers' cooperatives to assess possible interactions between credit constraints, savings constraints and lack of information on low fertilizer usage (Carter *et al.*, forthcoming; Duflo *et al.*, forthcoming d). Another ongoing intervention in Mali measures the importance of credit constraints by randomizing access to loans and grants for agricultural purposes (Beaman *et al.*, forthcoming b).

In another ongoing study, Karlan and Udry (forthcoming a, b) are testing whether underinvestment in agricultural inputs is due to limited capital or to risk aversion. If the latter were true, then farmers may be hesitant to borrow to finance profitable investments if high weather variation increases the uncertainty that they will repay their loan on time. Under the intervention, randomly selected farmers in Ghana will receive a capital grant, free rainfall insurance, rainfall insurance at varying prices, both a capital grant and rainfall insurance, or nothing. If risk aversion partly explains low agricultural investment, then the rainfall insurance treatments will generate improvements in the levels of profitable investments made by farmers.

Additionally, a lack of storage space constrains farmers' abilities to withhold selling their crop until a more profitable season of the year. Casaburi, Glennerster and Suri are currently conducting an intervention in Sierra Leone, in which farmers are randomly selected to receive access to storage, access to credit, both, or neither (Casaburi *et al.*, forthcoming b). Forthcoming results of household income and sales volume across time will reveal the comparative importance of storage and credit access to smallholder farmers.

Many farmers grow only crops for personal consumption or local markets, even though involvement in export markets is more profitable. When farmers in Kenya were randomly offered services that help them manage savings, connect to transportation services and reach exporters, income increased by 32 per cent for first-time growers of export crops a year after the start of the program. However, a year after the program began, farmers failed to meet new EU production requirements, defaulted on their loans and switched back to selling in local markets. The failure of the program highlights the extensive risks small-scale farmers face in producing for an export market (Ashraf *et al.*, 2009).

While most interventions focus on crop-based agriculture, livestock agriculture faces a unique set of problems. Jamison and Karlan (forthcoming) are conducting an ongoing study in northern Namibia, where many rely on cattle production as a source of income. They plan to address farmers' lack of information regarding appropriate cattle production techniques as well as the tragedy of the commons problem these farmers often face, wherein each individual farmer is reluctant to reduce his own herds' grazing out of the fear that the herds of competing farmers will use more of the shared rangeland.

While there is already a large body of literature on agricultural participation and productivity, more research is needed on programs that facilitate youth entry into the sector. There also must be greater effort to recruit more youth to work in agriculture, as the agricultural sector can employ youth in large numbers. On one hand, there must be more studies on how to improve the negative attitudes youth have about agricultural work. Simultaneously, researchers must determine how to improve the productivity of the agricultural sector so that youth will perceive agricultural work as profitable employment. A good amount of research is being done to address the latter concern, but we still lack information on how to improve youths' perceptions of agricultural employment.

3.4.4 Public works programs

Public works programs aim to promote long-term employment by enlisting the unemployed to work on short-term projects related to economic and social infrastructure development. Projects include work on irrigation, drainage, protection of agricultural land, roads and building restoration. Conceptually, the idea is the same as with subsidized jobs in the private sector: providing young people with valuable labour market experience will improve their labour market prospects in the long run (in this case, after the completion of the public work project). In addition, the development of local infrastructure is predicted to create new jobs and grant rural communities greater access to basic necessities. Finally, public programs can provide an alternative form of welfare assistance for the society's most needy. Besley and Coate (1992) present theoretical motivations for the preference of public works programs over other forms of social assistance such as cash transfers. They argue that public works programs can be designed to provide employment only for those who truly need the assistance, and screen out those who would otherwise reduce their work hours in order to become eligible for some government cash transfers.

Three main concerns have been raised about public works programs. First, structuring public works programs to target the poorest of the poor has produced little success. Adato and Haddad (2002) report on results from seven community-based public works programs conducted in South Africa. They find that the programs did not target the poorest individuals. Their study highlights the difficulties of enacting programs designed to undertake demand-driven projects (projects that the community needs) while simultaneously employing those who need employment assistance the most. Teklu and Asefa (1999) find that public works programs conducted in Kenya and Botswana employed a large amount of non-poor, which further indicates the need for more effective screening measures, which would exclude the non-poor without screening out those in the lowest income groups. More research is needed to understand why these programs often fail in their targeting goals. One hypothesis is that these programs are likely subject to strong political influences, and that the use of social connections and other corrupt means strongly distort targeting.

Second, both researchers and policymakers are also concerned that public works projects may crowd out employment by the regular workforce, with no net effect on employment (van Eekelen *et al.*, 2001). Imbert and Papp (2011) study a public works program in India and find that the public works program crowded out private sector work on a one-to-one basis.

Finally, while there is not a great deal of literature in this area, the evidence that exists suggests that public works programs typically fail in their longer-term goal of fostering future employability. Kluve (2010) and Betcherman *et al.* (2004) review the evidence on public employment programs in European and developing countries, respectively, and find that they are rarely effective beyond the length of the public work period. However, a few evaluations of programs in developing countries such as Colombia and India do find sustained gains in household income and wages as a result of public works programs (Attanasio *et al.*, 2007; Imbert and Papp, 2011). This suggests that these programs may work under specific circumstances, but unfortunately we have no guidance from the literature as to how to identify those favorable circumstances or detailed features of implementation.

A recent study in Africa worth featuring is one by Andrews *et al.* (2011), which uses a before/after methodology to study the impact of a recent public works program in Liberia. They find that the public works project employed a considerable number of females (46 per cent overall, 30–70 per cent depending on the country) and youth (60 per cent). While the program showed success in employing the poor, it was not able to elicit the participation of the lowest income groups, who remained more socially and geographically isolated than their more wealthy peers. The program experienced a 21 per cent decline in the poverty gap relative to baseline, and exhibited gains in soft skills as a result of program participation, with benefits in the surrounding community from the project's infrastructural improvements. Participants also reported that they saved their earnings or used their earnings to invest in the education of their children. In the short term, it cost US$1.96 to pay a participant US$1, but this estimate ignores potential gains in market activity due to infrastructural improvements as well as possible impacts on participants' future labour market success. Andrews *et al.* (2011) also find that the program appeared to benefit women more than alternative job options would have. The long-term impacts of this program remain to be studied.

Overall, while the literature reveals that public works programs can be effective at increasing short-term employment for some groups (a rather trivial finding, given the nature of public works programs), more research is needed regarding how to design programs to target certain groups effectively. Also, it is important to note that many of the existing studies on public works programs do not involve randomized evaluations, which suggests that these studies often cannot adequately account for selection and unobserved heterogeneity in program participation. Individuals targeted by such programs typically have low labour-market prospects, so estimates obtained in the absence of randomization are likely to be biased downwards. Hence there is a great need to engage in randomized evaluations to assess the causal effect of public works programs accurately. Additionally, little has been done to date to assess the cost-effectiveness of public works programs: truly informative results must incorporate the projected costs and benefits of prolonging such programs. There is a considerable amount of political appeal to public works programs, which can drastically increase employment rates in the short-term. Consequently, rigorous research as to how to make these programs more cost-effective is urgently needed.

3.5 Conclusion and policy recommendations

Although there exists some evidence surrounding the effectiveness of programs targeting youth labour market outcomes in Africa, our policy recommendations could be strengthened by greater evidence from across contexts in order to flesh out precisely what works, what does not work, what program components contribute to the success of a policy, and what country-specific factors make a policy work in one setting but fail in another. As discussed in the Introduction, Africa is a vast continent spanning many different country contexts. Some countries and environments have been more conducive than others to research regarding certain topics. There is stronger evidence on some topics in Sub-Saharan Africa than in North Africa, and *vice versa*. In addition, some issues with a high potential for improving youth employment have been studied only outside of Africa (e.g. wage subsidy programs, job training programs) and will need to be rigorously studied within African contexts. Finally, despite the effort we put into isolating all of the relevant research, a lot of the most convincing evidence reviewed in this chapter is not on programs targeted specifically at youth. There should be more research on whether these programs will affect youth in the same way as they affected the general population.

Table 3.1 presents a review of the main themes discussed throughout this chapter. In particular, we have identified three broad areas of interest: improving skills and human capital formation; improving young people's transition into the labour market; and increasing labour demand. In the remaining section, we attempt to organize our findings based on the strength of the evidence that has been produced so far, which leads us into recommendations for future work and future micro-interventions.

Of the policies discussed in this chapter, a few stand out as very promising given their repeatedly demonstrated success across various contexts. We believe the strongest evidence is that related to skills acquisition. Again, this does not mean we believe these are the most important policies to implement in Africa right now in order to improve the employment of youth. Instead, this means that various policies aimed at improving schooling outcomes have been shown to be effective and have often translated into better labour outcomes for the targeted group. In other words, the strength of the evidence comes from the enormous volume of literature on the topic and the general consistency of the findings.

In particular, CCT programs have been the most widely studied, especially when it comes to primary education, and have been the most widely successful. Part of their success is attributed to the fact that they couple the use of extrinsic financial incentives with a simultaneous relaxation of credit constraints. They attack the problem of low human capital investment on multiple fronts through combating simultaneously the problems of low household resources and low motivation for schooling.

CCTs have been most widely implemented to condition on attendance and enrolment; but solely focusing on schooling misses the point when it comes to

Table 3.1 Policies to decrease youth underemployment

Improving skills and human capital	*Improving transition to labour market*	*Increasing labour demand*
Conditional cash transfers	Information regarding the location and types of jobs available to youth	Addressing detrimental impacts of labour market regulations
Improving health status	Educating youth regarding realistic labour market wages	Reducing corrupt practices
Reducing risky sexual behaviour	Improving access and quality of vocational training institutions	Increasing credit access to informal firms
Improving access and quality of post-secondary education	Implementing more effective job training programs	Providing managerial skill training to micro-entrepreneurs
Improving access and quality of vocational training institutions	Addressing spatial mismatch and alleviating migration costs	Increasing agricultural sector productivity
Implementing effective job training programs	Promoting savings behavior to meet costs of search	Developing ICT, providing access to formal and informal firms
Alleviating credit constraints to human capital investment	Youth reintegration in post-conflict areas	Employment subsidies
		Public works projects Infrastructure development Promoting geographic clustering

creating more employment. Rather, Hanushek and Woessman (2008) provide strong evidence that models which account for cognitive skill level explain the variation in economic growth much more precisely than models that examine only the effect of number of years of schooling. Conditioning on achievement has been successful across different contexts, but more work must be conducted in Africa to determine the specific program components that would maximize the returns of CCTs for African youth.

The micro literature on the learning and cognition benefits of better health is also extremely strong and conclusive. This is especially true of young children, for whom the benefits of better health are magnified across their entire life cycle. If health status and skills acquisition are complementary and build upon each other across various stages of life, then policies that improve the health of youth are all the more important.

In addition, various policies have been successful in reducing young people's risky sexual behavior and protecting them from the severe labour and life consequences of contracting potentially fatal diseases. Given their immediate beneficial impacts, many of these programs could and should be implemented on a larger scale soon. Among young women, the likelihood of teenage pregnancy or early marriage represents a substantial impediment to continuing their education. Across many developing country contexts, the use of financial incentives to reduce risky sexual behavior has been shown to decrease pregnancy rates among youth. Other successful interventions have involved improving the resources adolescent girls have to finance their education, and providing classroom-based education regarding STIs and risky sexual behavior. Both have increased school enrolment and decreased irresponsible sexual behaviors. Such interventions are especially important in rectifying the persistent gender gaps in schooling attainment and employment opportunities that characterize so much of Africa today.

While the evidence from policies targeted at improving human capital acquisition is the richest and the most conclusive so far, we have repeatedly argued that such policies may not bring about as much short-run job creation as is currently needed in many parts of Africa. However, the longer-run effects of these policies could be extremely large. The students of today will be the entrepreneurs and innovators of tomorrow. Moreover, a highly educated population is more likely to be better equipped to stand against the structural hurdles to job creation in Africa, such as corruption and other political inefficiencies.

While the micro-evidence on education is strong, most of the evidence comes from primary education. The biggest weakness of this part of the literature so far is that it neglects post-primary, and especially post-secondary, education. Yet the fact that several African countries, especially in North Africa, face very high levels of unemployment among their college-educated youth strongly suggests that more of the education literature should be devoted to how secondary and post-secondary schools are functioning, and to the (mis)match between the skills of their graduates and the skills currently demanded in the labour market. Issues related to the cost and financing of higher education urgently need more investigation. Finally, while vocational schools are the most apt at tailoring young people's skills to the needs of the labour market, we know very little about the supply of these schools, access to these schools, and the quality of the learning that happens in these schools. On a related note, job training programs, which take the form of apprenticeships in many African countries, are a direct tool to reduce the mismatch between the skills with which young people enter the labour market and the demands of the economy. Yet our knowledge about the impact of such job training programs in Africa is extremely limited. We believe many of these questions are very well suited to, randomized, microeconomic studies.

There are multiple constraints to labour demand in the formal sectors of many African countries. We highlighted the role of labour market regulations and corruption. Other likely culprits include product market regulation, bureaucratic barriers to domestic firm entry, and barriers to foreign investment. Given these constraints, the lifting of which would require much more macro-based or political change, we strongly believe that more energy should be devoted to understanding the informal sector and to developing policies and programs that address the needs of the microenterprises and self-employed workers that dominate this sector. In particular, several micro-evaluations are addressing how easier access to credit and improvements in managerial skills may help grow these firms. Some of this research is appropriately targeting the specific needs of small farms, which remain a main source of jobs for young workers in many rural parts of Africa. We strongly encourage more work in this direction, which will help to account for the various circumstances that exist across different African countries. We also encourage more thinking about how to help microenterprises leverage the power of new ICTs, or better share limited infrastructure by adequately clustering their activities. Also, puzzles remain about the relative size of the informal sector across African countries. One extreme example is South Africa, where informal employment is close to non-existent despite a lack of formal sector jobs. The specific constraints to informal employment growth in South Africa remain unknown and should be investigated.

We also strongly recommend more interventions targeted at reducing information imperfections. Information campaigns are typically quite cheap to implement, so even slight benefits may justify their cost-effectiveness. We identified a set of areas where information barriers might be particularly constraining. Specifically, we believe the job-search process could be substantially improved if young workers had better information about the nature and location of jobs available, and the wages they might expect at those jobs. A spatial mismatch between employee location and firm location in many African countries may enhance these information asymmetries. ICTs could be used effectively to facilitate information flows between firms and prospective workers.

Finally, we discussed a few public policies that might potentially be effective ways of promoting youth employment without formally undoing core labour market regulations. In particular, some countries have shown political interest in introducing wage subsidies for youth. In addition, large-scale public works programs have been proposed as a way to offer the most needy in the population some form of assistance. There is no robust evidence on the potential impacts of such policies in Africa. The evidence that exists outside of Africa is somewhat bleak. While these programs provide benefits to the targeted groups, the benefits appear to last only as long as the programs last; there is little evidence that those programs serve as stepping stones into longer-term employment. Moreover, these programs have been shown to exhibit substantial crowding-out effects, which casts doubt on whether or not they can create real jobs. Nevertheless, given the political interest in these programs, especially in public works programs, we strongly believe that more should be done to understand how these programs might be reshaped (such as by combination with job training, or a referral system, or stronger incentives for job performance) to deliver long-term benefits for participants.

Notes

1 Miguel and Kremer (2001) find the introduction of a small fee for deworming treatment reduced treatment rates by 80 per cent. Thus socially beneficial programs with low private benefits may not spread unless treatment is fully subsidized.

2 The exception is the Delisle *et al.* (2000) study, which claims to find associations only between health products and better educational outcomes.

3 Studies of the effect of attendance at elite schools in countries outside of Africa have shown mixed results. Pop-Eleches and Urquiola (2011) find that attendance at a better school significantly improves students' academic performance in Romania. Jackson (2010) finds that studying with better peers improves one's learning, and that the effect of high-quality peers on own achievement is greater within high-quality schools. On the other hand, Zhang (2009) finds that attending a magnet school in China had few significant benefits for students' academic performance on exams or future enrollment status.

4 The study included Ghana, Cote d'Ivoire, Kenya, South Africa, Burkina Faso and Nigeria.

References

Adato, M. and Haddad, L. (2002) 'Targeting Poverty through Community-Based Public Works Programmes: Experience from South Africa,' *Journal of Development Studies*, 38(3): 1–36.

Adelman, S., Alderman, H., Gilligan, D.O. and Lehrer, K. (2008) 'The Impact of Alternative Food for Education Programs on Learning Achievement and Cognitive Development in Northern Uganda.' *Draft working Paper.* http://paa2009.princeton.edu/papers/91265.

AfDB, OECD, UNDP and UNECA (2012) *African Economic Outlook 2012: Promoting Youth Employment.* Paris: OECD.

Ajayi, K. (2009) 'Gender and Demand for Schooling: Lessons from School Choice and Admission Outcomes in Ghana.' Preliminary Draft, University of California.

Akbulut-Yuksel, M. and Turan, B. (2010) *Left Behind: Intergenerational Transmission of Human Capital in the Midst of HIV and AIDS.* IZA Discussion Paper 5166. Bonn: Institute for the Study of Labor.

Aker, J. (2008) *Does Digital Divide or Provide? The Impact of Mobile Phones on Grain Markets in Niger.* BREAD Working Paper 177. Durham, NC: Duke University, Bureau for Research and Economic Analysis of Development. http://ipl.econ.duke.edu/bread/papers/working/177.pdf.

——(2010) 'Information from Markets Near and Far: Mobile Phones and Agricultural Markets in Niger,' *American Economic Journal: Applied Economics*, 2(3): 46–59.

Aker, J. and Mbiti, I. (2010) 'Mobile Phones and Economic Development in Africa,' *Journal of Economic Perspectives*, 24(3): 207–32.

Akhmisse, L., Conklin, S., Derdari, B. and Torres, V. (2008) *Linking Youth with Knowledge and Opportunities in Microfinance (LYKOM) Project, Morocco: A Youth Livelihoods Program Case Study.* Washington, DC: USAID, Save the Children, SEEP Network and Foundation Zakoura Microcredit. http://pdfusaid.gov/pdf_docs/PNADN073.pdf.

Alderman, H., Hoddinott, J. and Kinsey, B. (2006) 'Long term consequences of early childhood malnutrition,' *Oxford Economic Papers*, 58(3): 450–74.

Andrews, C., Backiny-Yetna, P., Garin, E., Weedon, E., Wodon, Q. and Zampaglione, G. (2011) *Liberia's Cash for Work Temporary Employment Project: Responding to Crisis in Low Income, Fragile Countries.* Washington, DC: World Bank. http://siteresources.worldbank.org/SOCIALPROTECTION/Resources/SP-Discussion-papers/Safety-Nets-DP/1114.pdf

Annan, J. and Blattman, C. (2011) *Reintegrating and Employing High Risk Youth in Liberia: Lessons from a Randomized Evaluation of a Landmine Action Agricultural Training Program for Ex-Combatants, Innovations for Poverty Action.* Evidence from Randomized Evaluations of Peacebuilding in Liberia: Policy Report 2011.1. New Haven, CT: Yale University and Innovations for Poverty Action. www.poverty-action.org/sites/default/files/blattman_annan_ex-com_reintegration_ipa_liberia_1.pdf.

Annan, J. and Gupta, J. (forthcoming) 'Reduction of Gender-Based Violence Against Women in Cote d'Ivoire.' New Haven, CT: Innovations for Poverty Action. www.poverty-action.org/project/0506.

Annan, J., Blatttman, C., Green, E. and Jamison, J. (forthcoming) *Enterprises for Ultra-Poor Women after War: The WINGS Program in Northern Uganda.* New Haven, CT: Innovations for Poverty Action. www.poverty-action.org/project/0104.

Ardington, C., Case, A. and Hosegood, V. (2009) 'Labor Supply Responses to Large Social Transfers: Longitudinal Evidence from South Africa,' *American Economic Journal: Applied Economics*, 1(1): 22–48.

Ashraf, N., Gine, X. and Karlan, D. (2009) 'Finding Missing Markets (and a Disturbing Epilogue): Evidence from an Export Crop Adoption and Marketing Intervention in Kenya,' *American Journal of Agricultural Economics*, 91(4): 973–90.

Ashraf, N., Bandiera, O. and Jack, K. (2012) *No margin, No Mission? A Field Experiment on Incentives for Pro-Social Tasks.* CEPR Discussion Paper No. DP8834. Cambridge, MA: Harvard Business School.

Ashraf, N., Low, C. and McGinn, K. (forthcoming) 'The Impact of Teaching Girls Negotiation Skills on Health and Educational Outcomes in Zambia.' Unpublished.

Asiedu, E. and Freeman, J. (2009) 'The Effect of Corruption on Investment Growth: Evidence from Firms in Latin America, Sub-Saharan Africa, and Transition Countries,' *Review of Development Studies*, 13(2): 200–214.

Attanasio, O.P., Meghir, C. and Vera-Hernandez, M. (2007) 'Investigating Different Benefits of Workfare Programs,' *paper presented at Second IZA/World Bank Conference on Employment and Development*, Bonn, June 8–9.

Aryeetey, E., Baah-Boateng, W., Ackah, C.G., Lehrer, K. and Mbithi, I. (2013) 'Chapter 5: Youth Employment and Unemployment Challenges in Africa: The Case of Ghana,' in this volume.

Attanasio, O.P., Kugler, A.D. and Meghir, C. (2009) *Subsidizing Vocational Training for Disadvantaged Youth in Developing Countries: Evidence from a Randomized Trial.* IZA Discussion Paper 4251. Bonn: Institute for the Study of Labor.

Ayele, G., Chamberlain, J., Moorman, L., Wamisho, K. and Zhang, X. (2009) *Infrastructure and Cluster Development: A Case Study of Handloom Weavers in Ethiopia.* Discussion Paper ESSP2 001, Ethiopia Strategy Support Program 2. Washington, DC: IFPRI.

Aziken, M.E., Ande, A.B.A., and Okonta, P.I. (2003) 'Knowledge and Perception of Emergency Contraception among Female Nigerian Undergraduates,' *International Family Planning Perspective*, 29(2): 84–87.

Baird, S., Hicks, J.H., Kremer, M. and Miguel, E. (2011a) *Worms at Work: Long-run Impacts of Child Health Gains.* Working Paper. Berkeley, CA: University of California. http://elsa.berkeley.edu/~emiguel/pdfs/miguel_wormsatwork.pdf.

Baird, S., McIntosh, C. and Ozler, B. (2011b) 'Cash or Condition? Evidence from a Cash Transfer Experiment,' *Quarterly Journal of Economics*, 126(4): 1709–53.

Baird, S., Garfein, R.S., McIntosh, C.T. and Ozler, B. (2012) 'Effect of a Cash Transfer Programme for Schooling on Prevalence of HIV and Herpes Simplex Type 2 in Malawi: A Cluster Randomised Trial,' *Lancet*, 379(9823): 1320–29.

Bandiera, O., Burgess, R., Goldstein, M., Gulesci, S., Rasul, I. and Sulaiman, M. (forthcoming) 'Human Capital, Financial Capital, and the Economic Empowerment of Female Adolescents in Uganda and Tanzania.' New Haven, CT: Innovations for Poverty Action. www.poverty-action.org/project/0392.

Banerjee, A.V., Banerji, R., Duflo, E., Glennerster, R. and Khemani, S. (2010) 'Pitfalls of Participatory Programs: Evidence from a Randomized Evaluation in Education in India,' *American Economic Journal: Economic Policy*, 2(1): 1–30.

Bauchet, J., Marshall, C., Starita, L., Thomas, J. and Yalouris, A. (2011) *Latest Findings from Randomized Evaluations of Microfinance*, 2nd edn. Access to Finance Forum. Washington, DC: Consultative Group to Assist the Poor.

Beaman, L. and Dillon, A. (forthcoming) 'Irrigation and Property Rights for Farmers in Mali.' New Haven, CT: Innovations for Poverty Action. www.poverty-action.org/project/0078.

Beaman, L., BenYishay, A., Fatch, P., Magruder, J. and Mobarak, M. (forthcoming a) 'Making Networks Work for Policy: Evidence from Agricultural Technology Adoption in Malawi.' New Haven, CT: Innovations for Poverty Action. www.poverty-action.org/project/0402.

Beaman, L., Karlan, D., Thuysbaert, B. and Udry, C. (forthcoming b) 'Agricultural Microfinance in Mali.' New Haven, CT: Innovations for Poverty Action. www.poverty-action.org/project/0167.

Becker, G.S. (1976) 'A Theory of the Allocation of Time,' *Economic Journal*, 75(299): 493–517.

Bell, C., Bruhns, R. and Gersbach, H. (2006a) 'Economic Growth, Education and AIDs in Kenya Model: A Long-Run Analysis.' *Background paper for World Development Report 2007*. Washington, DC: World Bank.

Bell, C., Devarajan, S. and Gersbach, H. (2006b) 'The Long-run Economic Costs of AIDS: A Model with an Application to South Africa,' *World Bank Economic Review*, 20(1): 55–89.

BenYishay, A. and Mobarak, M. (forthcoming) 'Promoting Sustainable Farming Practices in Malawi.' New Haven, CT: Innovations for Poverty Action. www.poverty-action.org/project/0227.

Berry, J., Karlan, D. and Pradhan, M. (forthcoming) 'Evaluating the Efficacy of School Based Financial Education Programs with Children in Ghana.' New Haven, CT: Innovations for Poverty Action. www.poverty-action.org/project/0465.

Bertrand, M., Mullainathan, S. and Miller, D. (2003) 'Public Policy and Extended Families: Evidence from Pensions in South Africa,' *World Bank Economic Review*, 17(1): 27–50.

Bertrand, M., Djankov, S., Hanna, R. and Mullainathan, S. (2007) 'Obtaining a Driver's License in India: An Experimental Approach to Studying Corruption,' *Quarterly Journal of Economics*, 122(4): 1639–76.

Besley, T. and Burgess, R. (2004) 'Can Labor Regulation Hinder Economic Performance? Evidence from India,' *Quarterly Journal of Economics*, 199(1): 91–134.

Besley, T. and Coate, S. (1992) 'Workfare versus Welfare: Incentive Arguments for Work Requirements in Poverty-Alleviation Programs,' *American Economic Review*, 82(1): 249–61.

Betcherman, G., Olivas, K. and Dar, A. (2004) *Impacts of Active Labor Market Programs: New Evidence from Evaluations with Particular Attention to Developing and Transition Countries*. Social Protection Discussion Paper No. 0402. Washington, DC: World Bank.

Betcherman, G., Daysal, N. and Pagés, C. (2010) 'Do Employment Subsidies Work? Evidence from Regionally Targeted Subsidies in Turkey,' *Labour Economics*, 17(4): 710–22.

Bhargava, A. (2005) 'AIDS Epidemic and the Psychological Well-being and School Participation of Ethiopian Orphans,' *Psychology, Health and Medicine*, 10(3): 263–75.

Binzel, C. (2011) *Decline in Social Mobility: Unfulfilled Aspirations among Egypt's Educated Youth*. IZA Discussion Paper 6139. Bonn: Institute for the Study of Labor.

Blanchard, O. and Landier, A. (2002) 'The Perverse Effect of Partial Labour Market Reform: Fixed-Term Contracts in France,' *Economic Journal*, 112(480): F214–44.

Blattman, C. and Dercon, S. (forthcoming) 'Ethiopia: More Sweatshops for Africa? An Experimental Study of Firms, Factory Labor, and Poverty Alleviation.' New Haven, CT: Innovations for Poverty Action. www.poverty-action.org/project/0203.

Blattman, C., Blair, R. and Hartman, A. (2011a) *Can we Teach Peace and Conflict Resolution? Results from a randomized evaluation of the Community Empowerment Program (CEP) in Liberia: A Program to Build Peace, Human Rights, and Civic Participation*. Evidence from Randomized Evaluations of Peacebuilding in Liberia: Policy Report 2011.2. New Haven, CT: Yale University and Innovations for Poverty Action. www.poverty-action.org/sites/default/files/blattman_hartman_blair_can_ we_teach_ peace_ipa_liberia_0.pdf.

Blattman, C., Fiala, N. and Martinez, S. (2011b) *Employment Generation in Rural Africa: Mid-term Results from an Experimental Evaluation of the Youth Opportunities Program in Northern Uganda*. Social Protection and Labor Discussion Paper 1120. Washington, DC: World Bank.

Blattman, C., Jamison, J. and Sheridan, M. (forthcoming) 'Roots and Remedies: Persistent poverty and violence amongst urban street youth in Liberia.' New Haven, CT: Innovations for Poverty Action. www.poverty-action.org/project/0166.

Blimpo, M. (2010) *Team Incentives for Education in Developing Countries: A Randomized Field Experiment in Benin*. Working Paper. Stanford, CA: Stanford University. www.stanford.edu/~mpblimpo/TeamIncentives_Blimpo032010.pdf.

Boudarbat, B. (2005) 'Job-search Strategies and the Unemployment of University Graduates in Morocco,' *paper presented at the IZA/EBRD International Conference on Labor Market Dynamics*, Bologna, May 05–08.

Brune, L., Gine, X., Goldberg, J. and Yang, D. (2011) *Commitments to Save: A Field Experiment in Rural Malawi*. Policy Research Working Paper 5748. Washington, DC: World Bank.

Bryan, G., Chowdhury, S. and Mobarak, A.M. (2012) *Seasonal Migration and Risk Mitigation*. Discussion Paper No. 8739. London: Centre for Economic Policy Research.

Burns, J., Edwards, L. and Pauw, K. (2010) *Wage Subsidies to Combat Unemployment and Poverty: Assessing South Africa's Options*. Working Paper 45. Cape Town: University of Cape Town, Southern Africa Labour and Development Research Unit.

Card, D., Ibarraran, P., Regalia, F., Rosas-Shady, D. and Soares, Y. (2011) 'The Labor Market Impacts of Youth Training in the Dominican Republic,' *Journal of Labor Economics*, 29(2): 267–300.

Carter, M., Laajaj, R. and Yang, D. (forthcoming) 'Savings, Subsidies, and Sustainable Food Security in Mozambique.' New Haven, CT: Innovations for Poverty Action. www.poverty-action.org/project/0384.

Casaburi, L., Kremer, M. and Mullainathan, S. (forthcoming a) 'Contract Farming, Technology Adoption and Agricultural Productivity: Evidence from Small Scale Farmers in Western Kenya.' New Haven, CT: Innovations for Poverty Action. www. poverty-action. org/project/0235.

Casaburi, L., Glennerster, R. and Suri, T. (forthcoming b) 'Providing Collateral and Improving Product Market Access for Smallholder Farmers: A Randomized Evaluation of Inventory Credit in Sierra Leone.' New Haven, CT: Innovations for Poverty Action. www.poverty-action.org/project/0467.

Cilliers, J., Dube, O. and Siddiqi, B. (forthcoming) 'Reconciliation, Conflict and Development: A Field Experiment in Sierra Leone.' New Haven, CT: Innovations for Poverty Action. www.poverty-action.org/project/0534.

Crepon, B., Devoto, F., Duflo, E. and Pariente, W. (forthcoming) 'Impact of rural microcredit in Morocco.' New Haven, CT: Innovations for Poverty Action. www. poverty-action.org/project/0097.

Cunha, F. and Heckman, J.J. (2008) 'Formulating, Identifying and Estimating the Technology of Cognitive and Non-cognitive Skill Formation,' *Journal of Human Resources*, 43(4): 738–82.

Cunha, F., Heckman, J.J., Lochner, L. and Masterov, D.V. (2005) *Interpreting the Evidence on Life Cycle Skill Formation*. NBER Working Paper 11331. Cambridge, MA: National Bureau of Economic Research.

De Walque, D. (2004) *How Does the Impact of an HIV and AIDS Information Campaign Vary with Educational Attainment? Evidence from Rural Uganda*. Policy Research Working Paper 3289. Washington, DC: World Bank.

——(2005) *Parental Education and Children's Schooling Outcomes: Is the Effect Nature, Nurture, or Both? Evidence from Recomposed Families in Rwanda*. Policy Research Working Paper 3483. Washington, DC: World Bank.

De Walque, D., Down, W.H., Nathan, R., Abdul, R., Abilahi, F., Gong, E., Isdahl, Z., Jamison, J., Jullu, B., Krishnan, S., Majura, A., Miguel, E., Moncada, J., Mtenga, S., Mwanyangala, M.A., Packel, L., Schachter, J., Shirima, K. and Medlin, C.A. (2012) 'Incentivising Safe Sex: A Randomized Trial of Conditional Cash Transfers for HIV and Sexually Transmitted Infection Prevention in Rural Tanzania,' *BMJ Open*, 2012(2).

Delisle, H., Chandra-Mouli, V. and de Benoist, B. (2000) *Should Adolescents Be Specifically Targeted for Nutrition in Developing Countries? To Address Which Problems, and How?* Geneva: World Health Organization.

Desai, J., and Tarozzi, A. (2011) 'Microcredit, Family Planning Programs, and Contraceptive Behavior: Evidence From a Field Experiment in Ethiopia,' *Demography*, 48(2): 749–82.

Desai, J., Johnson, K. and Tarozzi, A. (2011) 'On the Impact of Microcredit: Evidence from a Randomized Intervention in Rural Ethiopia.' Unpublished, Durham, NC: Duke University.

Dinkelman, T. (2011) 'The Effects of Rural Electrification on Employment: New Evidence from South Africa,' *American Economic Review*, 101(7): 3078–108.

Dolado, J.J., Garcia, C. and Jimeno, J.F. (2002) 'Drawing Lessons from the Boom of Temporary Jobs in Spain,' *Economic Journal*, 112(480): F270–95.

Duflo, E., Dupas, P., Kremer, M. and Sinei, S. (2006) *Education and HIV/AIDS Prevention: Evidence from a randomized evaluation in Western Kenya*. Policy Research Working Paper 4024. Washington, DC: World Bank.

Duflo, E., Dupas, P. and Kremer, M. (2011a) 'Peer Effects, Teacher Incentives, and the Impact of Tracking: Evidence from a Randomized Evaluation in Kenya,' *American Economic Review*, 101(5): 1739–74.

Duflo, E., Kremer, M. and Robinson, J. (2011b) 'Nudging Farmers to Use Fertilizer: Theory and Experimental Evidence from Kenya,' *American Economic Review*, 101: 2350–90.

Duflo, E., Dupas, P. and Kremer, M. (forthcoming a) 'Returns to Secondary Schooling in Ghana.' New Haven, CT: Innovations for Poverty Action. www.poverty-action.org/project/0077.

Duflo, E., Dupas, P. and Sharma, V. (forthcoming b) 'HIV Prevention Among Youths: Evidence from a Randomized Controlled Trial in Kenya.' New Haven, CT: Innovations for Poverty Action. www.poverty-action.org/project/0086.

Duflo, E., Keniston, D. and Suri, T. (forthcoming c) 'Technology Adoption and Diffusion through Social Networks – Evidence from a Coffee Training Program in Rwanda.' New Haven, CT: Innovations for Poverty Action. www.poverty-action.org/project/0462.

Duflo, E., Kremer, M. and Robinson, J. (forthcoming d) 'Barriers to Fertilizer Use: Evidence from a Field Experiment in Kenya.' New Haven, CT: Innovations for Poverty Action. www.poverty-action.org/project/0193.

Dupas, P. (2011) 'Do Teenagers Respond to HIV Risk Information? Evidence from a Field Experiment in Kenya,' *American Economic Journal: Applied Economics*, 3(1): 1–34.

Dupas, P. and Robinson, J. (2012) *Savings Constraints and Microenterprise Development: Evidence from a Field Experiment in Kenya*. NBER Working Paper 14693. Cambridge, MA: National Bureau of Economic Research.

Edmonds, E. (2006) 'Child Labor and Schooling Responses to Anticipated Income in South Africa,' *Journal of Development Economics*, 81(2): 386–414.

Evans, D.K. and Miguel, E. (2007) 'Orphans and Schooling in Africa: A Longitudinal Analysis,' *Demography*, 44(1): 35–57.

Evans, D., Kremer, M. and Ngatia, M. (2009) *The Impact of Distributing School Uniforms on Children's Education in Kenya*. Working Paper. www.poverty-action.org/sites/default/files/169_new_paper_november_2009.pdf.

Falco, P. (2011) 'Determinants of Income in Informal Self-Employment: New Evidence from a Long African Panel,' *paper presented at Sixth IZA/World Bank Conference: Employment and Development*, Mexico, May 30–31.

Fafchamps, M. and Moradi, A. (2011) *Referral and Job Performance: Evidence from the Ghana Colonial Army*. CEPR Discussion Paper 7408. Washington, DC: Center for Economic and Policy Research.

Fafchamps, M., McKenzie, D., Quinn, S. and Woodruff, C. (2011) *When is Capital Enough to Get Female Microenterprises Growing? Evidence from a Randomized Experiment in Ghana*. CSAE Working Paper WPS/2011–11. Oxford: Centre for the Study of African Economies.

Fernald, L.C.H., Hamad, R., Karlan, D., Ozer, E.J. and Zinman, J. (2008) 'Small Individual Loans and Mental Health: A Randomized Controlled Trial among South Africa Adults,' *BioMed Central Public Health*, 8: 409.

Field, E., Robles, O. and Torero, M. (2009) 'Iodine Deficiency and Schooling Attainment in Tanzania,' *American Economic Journal: Applied Economics*, 1(4): 140–69.

Fischer, G., Karlan, D. and Startz, M. (forthcoming) 'The Impact of Entrepreneurship Training for Women in Uganda.'

Fisman, R. and Svensson, J. (2007) 'Are Corruption and Taxation Really Harmful to Growth? Firm Level Evidence,' *Journal of Development Economics*, 83(1): 63–75.

Freeman, A.C. and Freeman, R.B. (1991) *Minimum Wages in Puerto Rico: Textbook Case of a Wage Floor?* NBER Working Paper 3759. Cambridge, MA: National Bureau of Economic Research.

Galasso, E., Ravallion, M. and Salvia, A. (2001) *Assisting the Transition from Workfare to Work: A Randomized Experiment*. Policy Research Working Paper 2738. Washington, DC: World Bank.

Gelli, A., Meir, U. and Espejo, F. (2007) 'Does Provision of Food in School Increase Girls' Enrollment? Evidence from Schools in Sub-Saharan Africa,' *Food and Nutrition Bulletin*, 28(2): 149–55.

Glewwe, P. and Jacoby, H. (1994) 'Student Achievement and Schooling Choice in Low-Income Countries: Evidence from Ghana,' *Journal of Human Resources*, 29(3): 843–64.

Glewwe, P., Kremer, M., Moulin, S. and Zitzewitz, E. (2004) 'Retrospective vs. Prospective Analyses of School Inputs: The Case of Flip Charts in Kenya,' *Journal of Development Economics*, 74(1): 251–68.

Glewwe, P., Kremer, M. and Moulin, S. (2009) 'Many Children Left Behind? Textbooks and Test Scores in Kenya,' *American Economic Journal: Applied Economics*, 1(1): 112–35.

Glewwe, P., Ilias, N. and Kremer, M. (2010) 'Teacher Incentives,' *American Economic Journal: Applied Economics*, 2(3): 205–27.

Glick, P. and Sahn, D.E. (2008) 'Cognitive Skills among Children in Senegal: Disentangling the Roles of Schooling and Family Background,' *Economics of Education Review*, 28(2): 178–88.

Gregson, S., Garnett, G.P., Nyamukapa, C.A., Hallett, T.B., Lewis, J.J.C., Mason, P.R., Chandiwana, S.K. and Anderson, R.M. (2006) 'HIV Decline Associated with Behavior Change in Eastern Zimbabwe,' *Science*, 311(5761): 664–66.

Groh, M., Krishnan, N., McKenzie, D. and Vishwanath, T. (2012) *Soft Skills or Hard Cash? The Impact of Training and Wage Subsidy Programs on Female Youth Employment in Jordan*. Policy Research Working Paper 6141. Washington, DC: World Bank.

Grosskurth, H., Mosha, F., Todd, J., Mwijarubi, E., Klokke, A., Senkoro, K., Mayaud, P., Changalucha, J., Nicoll, A., ka Gina, G., Newell, J., Mugeye, K., Mabye, D. and Hayes, R. (1995) 'Impact of Improved Treatment of Sexually Transmitted Diseases on HIV Infection in Rural Tanzania: Randomized Controlled Trial,' *Lancet*, 346(8974): 530–36.

Guarcello, L. and Rosati, F. (2007) *Child Labor and Youth Employment: Ethiopia Country Study*, Social Protection Discussion Paper 0704. Washington, DC: World Bank.

Gustman, A.L. and Steinmeier, T.L. (1988) 'A Model for Analyzing Youth Labor Market Policies,' *Journal of Labor Economics*, 6(3): 376–96.

Haan, H.C. and Serrière, N. (2002) *Training for Work in the Informal Sector: Fresh Evidence from West and Central Africa*. Turin: International Training Centre of the International Labour Organization.

Hanushek, E.A. and Woessman, L. (2008) 'The Role of Cognitive Skills in Economic Development,' *Journal of Economic Literature*, 46(3): 607–68.

Heady, C. (2003) 'The Effect of Child Labor on Learning Achievement,' *World Development*, 31(2): 385–98.

Hicks, J.H., Kremer, M., Mbiti, I.M. and Miguel, E. (forthcoming) 'Vocational Education Voucher Delivery and Labor Market Returns: A Randomized Evaluation Among Kenyan Youth,' *Report for Spanish Impact Evaluation Fund (SIEF) Phase II.*

Humphreys, M. and Weinstein, J. (2007) 'Demobilization and Reintegration,' *Journal of Conflict Resolution*, 51(4): 531–67.

Imbert, C. and Papp, J. (2011) 'Government Hiring and Labor Market Equilibrium: Evidence from India's Employment Guarantee,' *paper presented at the Indian Statistical Institute's Seventh Annual Conference on Economic Growth and Development*, New Delhi, December 15–17.

Jackson, C.K. (2010) *Peer Quality or Input Quality? Evidence from Trinidad and Tobago*, NBER Working Paper 16598. Cambridge, MA: National Bureau of Economic Research.

Jamison, J. and Karlan, D. (forthcoming) 'Community Based Rangeland Management in Namibia.' New Haven, CT: Innovations for Poverty Action. www.poverty-action.org/project/0253.

Jamison, J., Karlan, D. and Zinman, J. (forthcoming) 'Starting a Lifetime of Saving: Teaching the Practice of Saving to Ugandan Youth.' New Haven, CT: Innovations for Poverty Action. www.poverty-action.org/project/0113.

Kabbani, N. and Kothari, E. (2005) *Youth Employment in the MENA Region: A Situational Assessment*, Social Protection Discussion Paper 0534. Washington, DC: World Bank.

Karlan, D. and Linden, L. (forthcoming) 'Smoothing the Cost of Education: Primary School Saving in Uganda.' New Haven, CT: Innovations for Poverty Action. www.poverty-action.org/project/0079.

Karlan, D. and Thuysbaert, B. (forthcoming) 'The Impact of Malaria Education on the Health of Microfinance Clients in Benin.' New Haven, CT: Innovations for Poverty Action. www.poverty-action.org/project/0001.

Karlan, D. and Udry, C. (forthcoming a) 'Returns to Capital and MSE Management Consulting in Ghana.' New Haven, CT: Innovations for Poverty Action. www.poverty-action.org/project/0068.

——(forthcoming b) 'Examining Underinvestment in Agriculture: Returns to Capital and Insurance among Farmers in Ghana.' New Haven, CT: Innovations for Poverty Action. www.poverty-action.org/project/0072.

Karlan, D., Kutsoati, E., McMillan, M. and Udry, C. (2011) 'Crop Price Indemnified Loans for Farmers: A Pilot Experiment in Rural Ghana,' *Journal of Risk and Insurance*, 78(1): 37–55.

——(forthcoming) 'Savings Account Labeling and Financial Literacy Training in Ghana.' Poverty Action Lab. www.povertyactionlab.org/node/5602.

Katz, L. (1998) 'Wage Subsidies for the Disadvantaged,' in *Generating Jobs: How to Increase Demand for Less Skilled Workers*, Peter Gottschalk and Richard B. Freeman (eds), New York: Russell Sage Foundation, pp. 21–53.

Kaufman, C.E., de Wet, T. and Stadler, J. (2001) 'Adolescent Pregnancy and Parenthood in South Africa,' *Studies in Family Planning*, 32(2): 147–60.

Klonner, S. and Nolen, P. (2008) 'Does ICT Benefit the Poor? Evidence from South Africa,' draft paper, University of Essex. http://privatewww.essex.ac.uk/~pjnolen/KlonnerNolenCellPhonesSouthAfrica.pdf.

Kluve, J. (2010) 'The Effectiveness of European Active Labor Market Programs,' *Labour Economics*, 17(6): 904–18.

Kremer, M. and Vermeersch, C. (2004) *School Meals, Educational Achievement and School Competition: Evidence from a Randomized Evaluation*, Policy Research Working Paper 3523. Washington, DC: World Bank.

Kremer, M., Miguel, E. and Thornton, R. (2009) 'Incentives to Learn,' *Review of Economics and Statistics*, 91(3): 437–56.

Kugler, A. and Pica, G. (2008) 'Effects of Employment Protection on Worker and Job Flows: Evidence from the 1990 Italian Reform,' *Labour Economics*, 15(1): 78–95.

Kugler, A.D., Jimeno, J.F. and Hernanz, V. (2003) *Employment Consequences of Restrictive Permanent Contracts: Evidence from Spanish Labor Market Reforms*, IZA Discussion Paper Series No. 657. Bonn: Institute for the Study of Labor.

Kwak, S. and Smith, S.C. (2011) *Multidimensional Poverty and Interlocking Poverty Traps: Framework and Application to Ethiopian Household Panel Data*, IIEP Working Paper 2011–04. Paris: International Institute for Educational Planning.

Lee, V. and Lockheed, M. (1990) 'The Effects of Single-Sex Schooling on Achievement and Attitudes in Nigeria,' *Comparative Education Review*, 34(2): 209–31.

Levinsohn, J. and Pugatch, T. (2009) 'The Role of Reservation Wages in Youth Unemployment in Cape Town, South Africa: A Structural Approach.' Unpublished, University of Michigan.

Lloyd, C.B., Mensch, B.S. and Clark, W.H. (2000) 'The Effects of Primary School Quality on School Dropout among Kenyan Girls and Boys,' *Comparative Education Review*, 44(2): 113–47.

Lloyd, C.B., El Tawila, S., Clark, W.H. and Mensch, B.S. (2003) 'The Impact of Educational Quality on School Exit in Egypt,' *Comparative Education Review*, 47(4): 444–67.

Lokshin, M., Glinskaya, E. and Garcia, M. (2004) 'The Effect of Early Childhood Development Programs on Women's Labor Force Participation and Older Children's Schooling in Kenya,' *Journal of African Economies*, 13(2): 240–76.

Lucas, A.M. and Mbiti, I. (2011) 'Effects of School Quality on Student Achievement: Discontinuity Evidence from Kenya,' *Southern Methodist University working paper.*

Lucas, A.M. and Mbiti, I.M. (2012a) 'Access, Sorting, and Achievement: The Short-Run Effects of Free Primary Education in Kenya,' *American Economic Journal: Applied Economics*, 4(4): 226–53.

Lucas, A.M. and Mbiti, I.M. (2012b) 'Does Free Primary Education Narrow Gender Differences in Schooling Outcomes? Evidence from Kenya,' *Journal of African Economies*, 21(5): 691–722.

Magruder, J. (2012) 'High Unemployment Yet Few Small Firms: The Role of Centralized Bargaining in South Africa,' *American Economic Journal: Applied Economics*, 4(3): 138–66.

Mauro, P. (1995) 'Corruption and Growth,' *Quarterly Journal of Economics*, 110(3): 681–712.

McLaren, Z.M. (2011) 'The Effect of Access to AIDS Treatment on Employment Outcomes in South Africa,' *University of Michigan working paper.* www.personal.umich.edu/~zmclaren/mclaren_aidstreatment.pdf.

Miguel, E. and Kremer, M. (2001) *The Illusion of Sustainability*, NBER Working Paper 10324. Cambridge, MA: National Bureau of Economic Research.

——(2004) 'Worms: Identifying Impacts on Education and Health in the Presence of Treatment Externalities,' *Econometrica*, 72(1): 159–217.

Murphy, K., Shleifer, A. and Vishny, R. (1991) 'The Allocation of Talent: Implications for Growth,' *Quarterly Journal of Economics*, 106: 503–30.

Nagarajan, G. (2005) 'Microfinance, Youth and Conflict: Emerging Lessons and Issues,' *MicroNote #4*. Washington, DC: USAID.

Nyqvist, M.B., Corno, L., Svensson, J. and de Walque, D. (2013) 'Evaluating the Impact of Short Term Financial Incentives on HIV and STI Incidence among Youth in Lesotho: A Randomized Trial,' *poster presented at 7th International AIDS Society Conference*, Kuala Lumpur, 30 June–3 July. http://pag.ias2013.org/abstracts.aspx?aid=553.

OECD, AfDB, UNDP and UNECA (2009) *African Economic Outlook*. Paris: OECD.

Ozier, O. (2011a) 'Exploiting Externalities to Estimate the Long-Term Effects of Early Childhood Deworming,' *Working Paper*. Partnership for Child Development. Berkeley, CA: University of California. www.dewormtheworld.org/sites/default/files/pdf/Owen%20Ozier%20-%20Early%20Deworming.pdf.

——(2011b) 'The Impact of Secondary Schooling in Kenya: A Regression Discontinuity Analysis,' *Job Market Paper*. Berkeley, CA: University of California. http://economics.ozier.com/owen/papers/ozier_JMP_20110117.pdf.

Page, J., Broussard, N.H., Tekleselassie, T.G., Ferede, T., and Reda, H.T. (2012) 'Chapter 4: Youth Unemployment: Ethiopia Country Study,' in this volume.

Peters, K. (2006) 'Footpaths to Reintegration: Armed Conflict, Youth and the Rural Crisis in Sierra Leone,' *PhD thesis*, Wageningen University.

Pop-Eleches, C. and Urquiola, M. (2011) 'Going to a Better School: Effects and Behavioral Responses,' *NBER Working Paper 16886*. Cambridge, MA: National Bureau of Economic Research.

Posel, D., Fairburn, J. and Lund, F. (2006) 'Labour Migration and Households: A Reconsideration of the Effects of the Social Pension on Labour Supply in South Africa,' *Economic Modelling*, 23(5): 836–53.

Proctor, F. and Lucchesi, V. (2012) 'Small-scale Farming and Youth in an Era of Rapid Rural Change.' *International Institute for Environment and Development (IIED)/HIVOS*. http://pubs.iied.org/pdfs/14617IIED.pdf.

Pugatch, T. (2010) 'Bumpy Rides: School to Work Transitions in South Africa,' *Job Market Paper*. Princeton, NJ: Princeton University. http://paa2011.princeton.edu/papers/111004.

Ratha, D., Mohapatra, S., Özden, Ç., Plaza, S., Shaw, W. and Shimeles, A. (2011) *Leveraging Migration for Africa: Remittances, Skills, and Investments*. Washington, DC: World Bank.

Schneider, F., Buehn, A. and Montenegro, C.E. (2010) *Shadow Economies All over the World: New Estimates for 162 Countries 1999–2007*, Policy Research Working Paper 5356. Washington, DC: World Bank.

Schoar, A. and Zia, B. (forthcoming) 'Network Effects in SME Clusters: An Experiment to Differentiate the Diffusion Paths of Business and Technical Training in Uganda.' New Haven, CT: Innovations for Poverty Action. www.poverty-action.org/node/4742.

Schultz, T.P. (2003) *Evidence of Return to Schooling in Africa from Household Surveys: Monitoring and Restructuring the Market for Education*, Growth Center Discussion Paper No. 875. New Haven, CT: Economic Growth Center, Yale University.

Sequeira, S. and Djankov, S. (2010) *An Empirical Study of Corruption in Ports*, MPRA Paper 21791. Munich: University Library of Munich.

Shleifer, A. and Vishny, R.W. (1993) 'Corruption,' *Quarterly Journal of Economics*, 108(3): 599–617.

Stampini, M. and Verdier-Chouchane, A. (2011) *Labor Market Dynamics in Tunisia: The Issue of Youth Unemployment*, Working Paper No. 123. Abidjan: African Development Bank.

Tanaka, S. (2010) *Access to Health Infrastructure and Child Health Development: Evidence from Post-Apartheid South Africa*, ISER Discussion Paper 0768. Colchester: Institute for Social and Economic Research.

Teklu, T. and Asefa, S. (1999) 'Who Participates in Labor-Intensive Public Works in Sub-Saharan Africa? Evidence from Rural Botswana and Kenya,' *World Development*, 27(2): 431–38.

Thornton, R.L. (2008) 'The Demand for, and Impact of, Learning HIV Status,' *American Economic Review*, 98(5): 1829–63.

UNRISD (2010) 'Gender Inequalities at Home and in the Market,' in *Combating Poverty and Inequality: Structural Change, Social Policy and Politics*, UNRISD Flagship Report. Geneva: United Nations Research Institute for Social Development.

van Eekelen, W., de Luca, L. and Ismail, N. (2001) *Youth Employment in Egypt. InFocus Programme on Skills, Knowledge, and Employability Skills.* Skills Working Paper 2. International Labour Organization.

World Bank (2012) *World Development Indicators 2012*. Washington, DC: World Bank.

——(forthcoming) *The World DataBank*. http://databank.worldbank.org/ddp/home.do?Step=1&id=4.

Wydick, B., Glewwe, P. and Rutledge, L. (2011) *Does International Child Sponsorship Work? A Six-Country Study of Impacts on Adult Life Outcomes*, Working Paper, University of San Francisco. http://usf.usfca.edu/fac_staff/wydick/csp.pdf.

Zhang, H.L. (2009) *Magnet Schools and Student Achievement: Evidence from a Randomized Natural Experiment in China*, Job Market Paper. Cambridge, MA: Massachusetts Institute of Technology.

Part II

Country studies

4 Ethiopia

Nzinga H. Broussard, John Page and Tsegay Gebrekidan Tekleselassie with Tadele Ferede and Hansa Teklay Reda[1]

4.1 Introduction

Ethiopia has enjoyed more than 15 years of sustained economic growth. Per capita income is rising steadily, and it has been famously singled out by *The Economist* as one of the best-performing economies in Africa (Economist, 2012). Between 2005 and 2010 the economy grew on average by 11 per cent. Yet there are signs that this growth has not resulted in robust growth of 'good' jobs—those offering higher wages and better working conditions—especially for the young. Youth employment presents a particular challenge to Ethiopia; the country faces growing landlessness among the young in rural areas and slow rural job creation, leading to increasing pressures for migration to urban areas (World Bank, 2007).[2]

Driven by a delayed demographic transition, the share of youths (aged 15–24) in Ethiopia has been rising steadily over time. This demographic bulge offers the possibility of a growth dividend, if—as in the case of East Asia—a rapidly growing workforce can be combined with capital and technology.[3] But it can also represent a major threat. The question is whether there will be sufficient growth and job creation in urban areas to absorb new labour market participants into productive employment.

This paper argues that Ethiopia's 'youth employment problem' is a symptom of a larger employment problem brought about by its lack of structural change. Despite rapid growth, Ethiopia has had very little structural change. Eighty per cent of its working population remains in agriculture, although the sector produces only about 40 per cent of GDP. Differences in output per worker across sectors are huge. The failure of high-productivity sectors such as manufacturing to grow robustly has meant that while measured unemployment rates are relatively modest, a large informal sector and widespread self-employment condemn many workers to vulnerable employment and working poverty.

Seen from this perspective, youth employment policies cannot focus only on the supply side of the labour market. Indeed, while labour market reforms and active labour market policies can make a contribution to solving the employment problem, the greatest traction is likely to come from policies and public actions designed to accelerate the growth of sectors with high value added per worker: in short, from a strategy for structural change.

The following section summarizes recent literature on growth, demography and employment in Ethiopia within an African regional context. It makes the case that the youth employment problem is a subset of a larger employment problem arising from limited growth of good jobs and a very large informal sector: a problem that affects a large number of low-income African economies. Section 4.3 describes the data used in the analysis. This chapter uses nearly nationally representative data collected at four times—1999–00, 2004–05, 2009 and 2011—to provide a comprehensive description of the main characteristics of rural and urban youth labour market participants in Ethiopia.

Effective youth employment policies and interventions require a thorough understanding of who are the employed and unemployed, where they are located, and in what types of jobs they are engaged. Section 4.4 describes the extent and characteristics of unemployment, underemployment and informal employment in Ethiopia. To the extent possible, we focus on the quality of jobs as well as on their quantity. Section 4.5 places youth employment outcomes in the context of the larger labour market. We pay particular attention to rural versus urban labour market dynamics, gender and the role of education. Section 4.6 focuses attention on the role of education in youth employment.

Sections 4.7–4.10 turn to public policy. Section 4.7 provides a review of existing employment policies, programs and laws. Section 4.8 begins the discussion of employment policy by examining potential labour market interventions. Among these we consider short-term initiatives to create employment for the young, technical and vocational education and training (TVET), and reforms in education and labour market policies. Where relevant, we discuss existing government programs to reduce the barriers to youth participation in the labour market. The analysis leads us to the conclusion that the youth employment problem in Ethiopia is largely the result of insufficient labour demand rather than labour market distortions. This in turn leads us to focus on the evolution of Ethiopia's economic structure. Section 4.9 turns to policies to accelerate structural change and employment creation. It deals with the conventional wisdom of the need for improvements in the 'investment climate'—the institutional, regulatory and physical environment within which firms operate. Section 4.10 offers some unconventional wisdom in the form of a strategy for structural change, and Section 4.11 concludes.

4.2 Growth, demography and employment in Ethiopia

This section briefly surveys recent trends in economic growth and employment in Ethiopia. Its main purpose is to place these issues in a broader regional context. It also briefly describes the nature of the demographic challenge faced by Ethiopia and some key elements of Ethiopia's development strategy.

4.2.1 Record of impressive growth

In recent years Ethiopia has experienced remarkable economic growth and substantial decreases in poverty. Between 1994 and 2011 the economy grew at

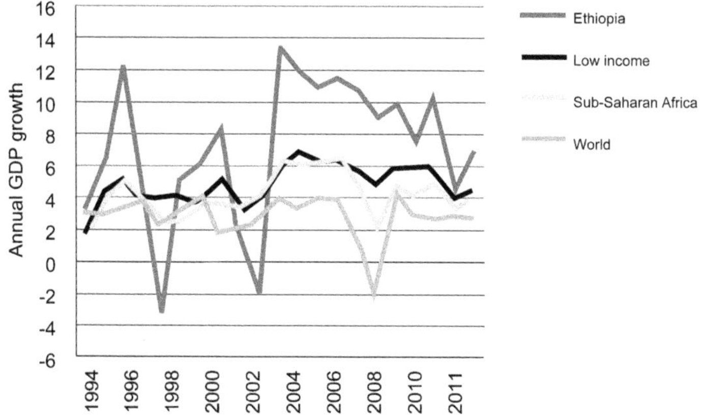

Figure 4.1 GDP growth rates 1994–2011
Source: WDI 2012; authors' calculations.

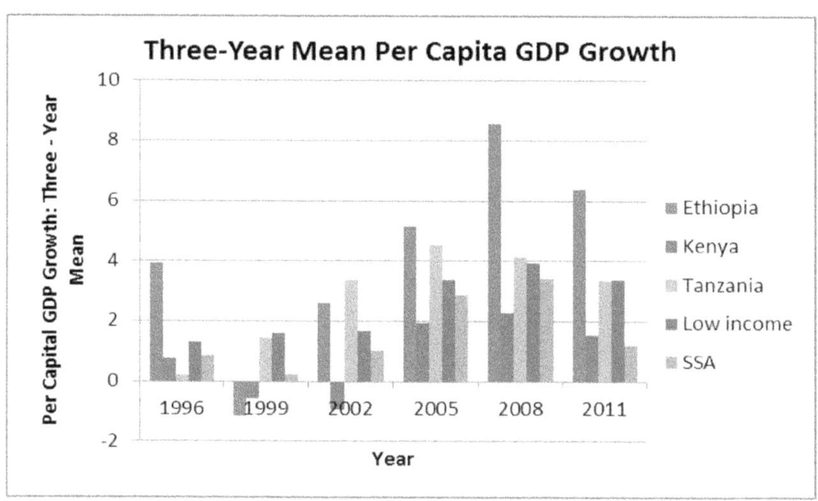

Figure 4.2 Per capita GDP Growth in Ethiopia and neighboring countries

a rapid pace with only two breaks, in 1998 (due to war with Eritrea) and in 2003 (due to drought). GDP growth for 1994–2011 averaged close to 7 per cent. Growth, exceeding the Sub-Saharan Africa average and the average rate for low-income countries (Figure 4.1). Growth in the past seven years (2003–11) has been even more impressive, averaging 10.5 per cent. Despite rapid population growth, per capita GDP growth has been similarly rapid, in comparison to both neighbouring economies and developing countries overall (Figure 4.2).

Rapid growth has translated into encouraging results in reducing poverty (Woldehanna *et al.*, 2008). The poverty head count ratio at $1.25 a day (percentage of population, PPP) declined from 60.5 per cent of the population in 1995 to 39 per cent in 2005. The intensity of poverty as measured by the poverty gap index at $2 a day (PPP) declined from about 41 per cent in 1995 to 29 per cent in 2005 (World Bank, 2012).

A recent challenge to both growth and poverty reduction has been the acceleration of inflation since 2007 (Figure 4.3). Rapid increases in public investment in infrastructure and social services, accompanied by a construction boom in the private sector, have put pressure on urban wages.

Despite rapid growth, the structure of the Ethiopian economy has not fundamentally changed over the past two decades. It is still a hugely agrarian economy, even in comparison with other economies in Africa (Figure 4.4). Figure 4.5 shows the five-year moving average growth rates of GDP and for respective sectors. Since 1995, services and industry have generally grown faster than agriculture. Until quite recently, the service sector has been the main driver of growth. The industrial sector has grown at about the same rate as the economy overall but accounts for only a very small share of total output (Figure 4.5).

The share of international trade (exports and imports) in GDP has doubled from 20 per cent in 1994 to about 40.5 per cent in 2011. However, the change is mainly due to doubling of import shares in GDP while the share of export has remained largely unchanged. The increase in imports is a positive sign of Ethiopia's access to foreign capital, mainly in the form of development assistance (aid), but the lack of export dynamism is a worry.

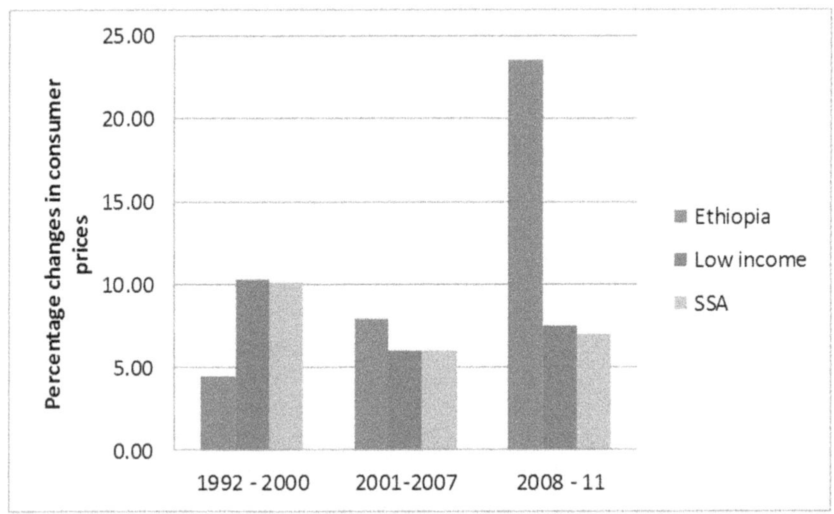

Figure 4.3 Percentage changes in consumer prices: annual average change for the period
Source: WDI 2012; authors' calculations.

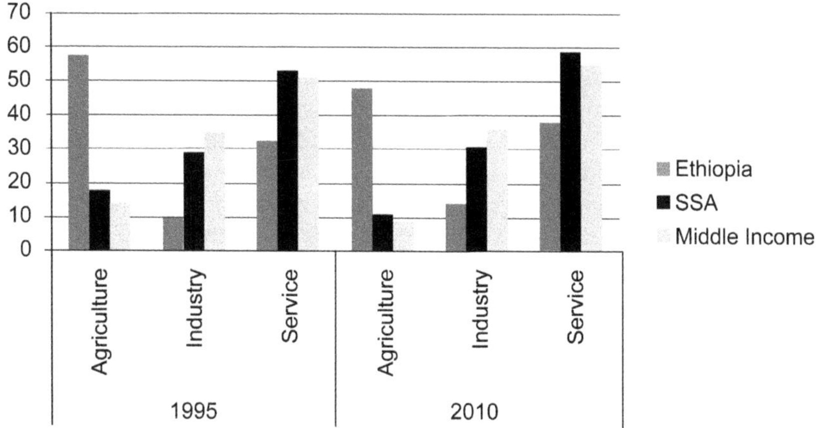

Figure 4.4 Sectoral structure of value added 1995 and 2010
Source: WDI 2012; authors' calculations.

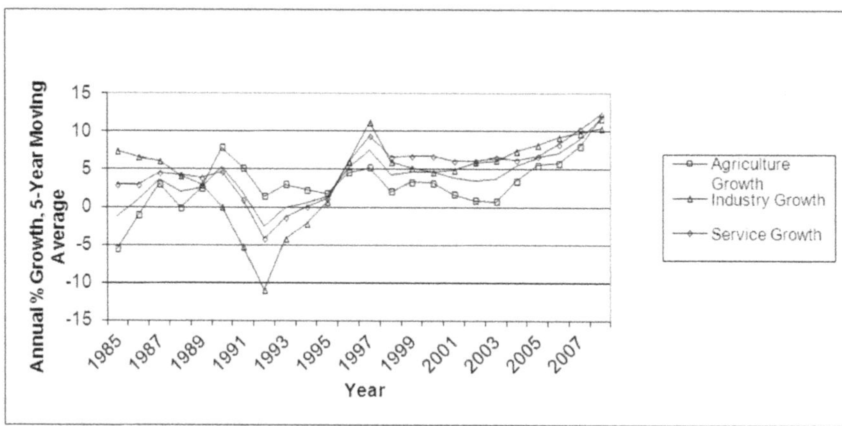

Figure 4.5 Five-year moving average growth rates of GDP by sector
Source: WDI 2012; authors' calculations.

4.2.2 Unorthodox development strategy

In Ethiopia, the five-year economic plans guide both the overall economic development strategy and the public investment program. It is therefore relevant to ask to what extent the Ethiopian economy has conformed to planners' expectations. Under Ethiopia's 'Agriculturally-led Industrialization Strategy' of 1993–2010, increasing smallholder agricultural productivity was the principal objective of public policy.

The strategy was based on an interpretation, championed by John Mellor and others, of the Industrial Revolution in Britain and of the East Asian miracle. It is grounded in the closed, dual-economy model, and in its simplest form follows these lines. Agricultural growth is driven by productivity improvements in smallholder agriculture, either in the form of new technologies for the production of existing crops, as in the Green Revolution, or the introduction of new higher value-added crops, such as fruits and vegetables. The increases in agricultural productivity raise farm household incomes and, in turn, lead to higher expenditures on non-agricultural goods, stimulating the growth of the industrial and services sectors. In the absence of international trade, productivity growth is also needed to restrain increases in the price of food, the urban wage good, as the urban economy expands (Mellor, 1995; World Bank, 2008).

This view of the role of agriculture in development leads to seemingly paradoxical policy advice. For industrialization to succeed, it is necessary first to focus on an agricultural transformation, raising land productivity and creating more efficient market links between urban and rural areas. Only after these public actions have taken place should governments turn to industrial development.

There are several flaws in the agriculturally led industrialization paradigm, perhaps most prominent among them the fact that openness to trade fundamentally changes a key assumption underpinning the strategy (Page, 2012b). For a large, landlocked agrarian economy such as Ethiopia, however, the logic of the agriculture-first strategy cannot be dismissed out of hand, although as Dercon and Zeitlin (2009) point out, the evidence for Ethiopia supporting such an approach is not wholly persuasive.

In practice, the strategy did not lead to accelerated industrial development. Rapid increases in agricultural yields during more than 10 years failed to generate corresponding increases in industrial production (Dercon and Zeitlin, 2009). Between 2005 and 2010, the service sector experienced rapid growth (far more than the planned target), but the industrial sector underperformed and failed to achieve its base case target (Table 4.1). Table 4.2 shows targets and achievements in key subsectors between 2005 and 2010. The results

Table 4.1 Growth in GDP and main sector share in PASDEP: planned versus performance

Sector	*Planned average growth target (2005/6–2009/10)*		*Average growth achieved 2005/6–2009/10)*	*Percentage share of real GDP (2009/10)*
	Base case	*High case*		
Real GDP	7.0	10.0	11.0	100.0
Agriculture	6.0	6.4	8.4	41.6
Industry	11.0	18.0	10.0	12.9
Services	7.0	10.3	14.6	45.5

Source: MoFED (2010).

Table 4.2 PASDEP key sub-sector performance: target versus. achievement (2005/6–2009/10)

Sub-sector	*Unit and main purpose*	*Target (millions)*	*Achievement (millions)*	*Percentage achievement*
Agriculture products	US$, export	1550.0	1517.0	97.9
Coffee production	TON	0.4	0.3	81.0
Horticulture	QTS	27.2	12.8	47.1
Cement	TON*	4.7	1.7	36.2
Leather and leather products	US$, export	221.0	75.7	34.3
Textile and Garment	US$, export	500.0	21.8	4.4

Source: MoFED (2010).

clearly reveal the pro-agriculture bias of the strategy. Agricultural export targets were largely achieved, while the performance in industry was far from the planned results. For example, achieved results were less than 5.5 per cent of the target for textiles and garments, 34 per cent for leather, and 36 per cent for cement.

Beginning in 2010 with the new 'Growth and Transformation Plan', the government has shifted its strategic focus in two new directions. First, it has reduced the emphasis on smallholder agriculture in favour of more rapid commercialization of the sector, including large commercial farms. Second, it has introduced more active industrial policies targeted at raising the rate of growth of manufacturing.

4.2.3 Stiff demographic challenge

With an estimated population of about 84 million in 2012 (based on the 2007 Census), Ethiopia is the second most populous country in Africa (after Nigeria). Population growth is high. The annual population growth rate was 2.6 per cent between 1994 and 2007, a rate that was slightly lower than the 2.8 per cent annual growth registered between the 1984 and 1994 censuses (CSA and FPCC, 2008). Recent World Bank (2012) estimates of population dynamics show that Ethiopia's population growth will slowly decelerate toward the average rate for low-income countries. The estimated birth rate is about 31.5 for every 1000 people. The death rate is close to 10 for every 1000 people. Both figures are slightly lower than the low-income and Sub-Saharan Africa averages.

The national censuses show an overwhelmingly young population, one of the youngest in Africa (Table 4.3). This is particularly true for the rural population as reflected in the broad-based population pyramids constructed from the two censuses (Figure 4.6). The pyramids for urban population show a large proportion of youths between the ages of 10 and 29, presenting a tough challenge of job creation.[4]

Table 4.3 Percentage of population under the age of 15

Country	*Percentage under 15*		
	1992	*2000*	*2011*
Burundi	45.14	46.17	37.51
Ethiopia	45.42	45.94	40.80
Kenya	48.09	44.29	42.44
Sudan	43.62	42.28	39.79
Tanzania	45.79	44.74	44.79
Sub-Saharan Africa	45.05	43.90	42.28
Low income	43.44	41.95	38.96
Middle income	33.91	31.14	26.63

Source: World Bank (2012).

This challenge is not unique to Ethiopia; other low-income African economies face similar demographic challenges. With almost 200 million people aged between 15 and 24, Africa has the youngest population in the world. In a majority of African countries, the young account for more than 20 per cent of the population. At the projected rates of population growth, the number of young people in Africa will double by 2045 (AfDB, 2012). While the proportion of young people (15–24) is projected to decline globally, it will stay at the same level in Africa for the foreseeable future.

Urbanization has been slow in Ethiopia. The proportion of the population living in urban areas according to the three national censuses was 11.4 per cent in 1984, 14 per cent in 1994, and 16 per cent in 2007. The country has a single metropolis. The capital city, Addis Ababa, holds about a quarter of the national urban population. It is eight times bigger than the second biggest city, Dire Dawa. Regions with high proportions of urban population, such as Addis Ababa, Dire Dawa, Gambella and Harari, also have high proportions of incoming migrants. At the national level about two-thirds of migrants come from rural areas.

4.2.4 Shared 'employment problem'

The African Development Bank (AfDB) has recently completed an analysis of household and labour force surveys in 16 African countries (AfDB, 2012). This represents the most comprehensive picture to date of the performance of African labour markets. The headline news from the African Bank is that, on the face of it, Sub-Saharan Africa does not appear to have a severe 'employment problem'. In 2009 the overall unemployment rate for the continent was 6.4 per cent compared with a global average of 4.7 per cent.[5] The regional unemployment rate has been stable since 2000 and ranks third, behind the Middle East and North Africa (MENA), and Europe and Central Asia. Ethiopia conforms closely to the all-Africa pattern: in 2005—the last year for which we have comprehensive data—Ethiopia's unemployment rate was 5.5 per cent.

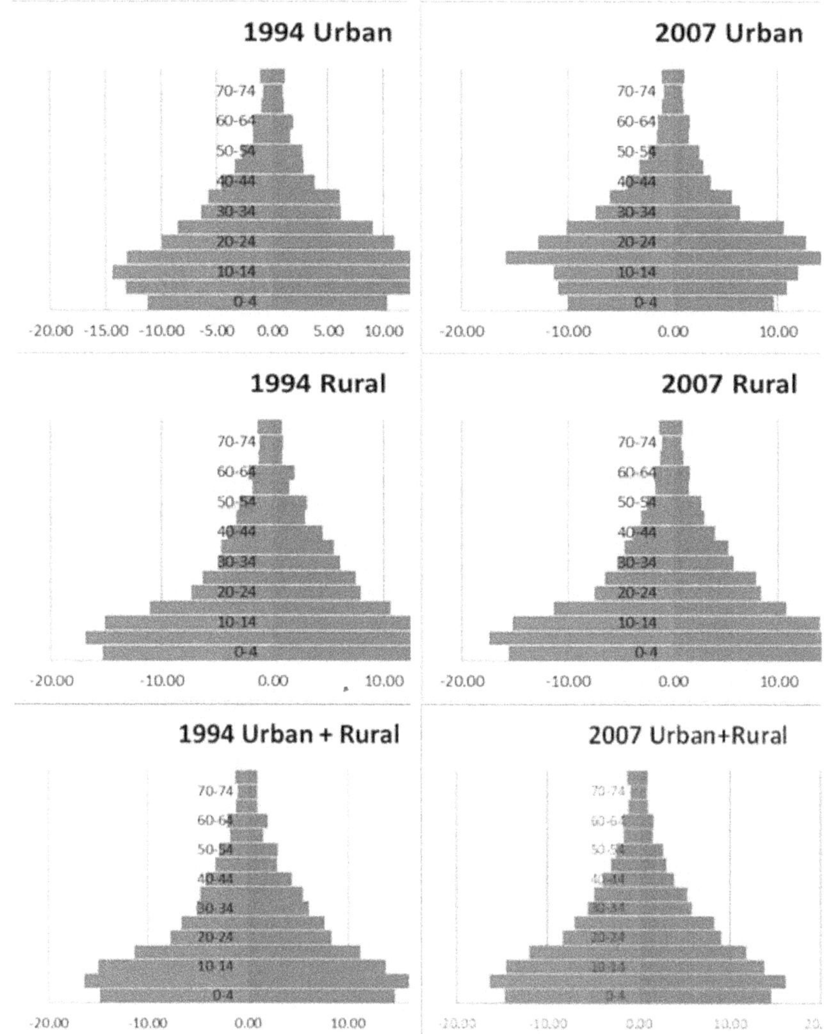

Figure 4.6 Population pyramids for Ethiopia, 1994 and 2007 Census
Source: Constructed from the 1994 and 2007 Census Reports.

Youth unemployment rates in many Sub-Saharan African countries are low compared with world averages. Worldwide, there is a fairly regular relationship between the overall rate of unemployment and the unemployment rate of the young. Sub-Saharan Africa's youth unemployment rate is below that which would be predicted from the region's overall rate of unemployment (Page, 2012c). The ratio of youth to adult unemployment rates in Sub-Saharan Africa is 1.9 compared with 2.7 globally. Not surprisingly, the youth unemployment rate for African countries north of the Sahara (North Africa) substantially exceeds its predicted value. Here again, Ethiopia does not stand out from the regional pattern. Its youth unemployment rate in 2005 was 7.4 per cent, about one-third higher than the adult unemployment rate.

There is considerable heterogeneity in Africa's labour markets. While, on average, neither overall nor youth unemployment rates in Sub-Saharan Africa stand out globally, the variation across countries is significant. Broadly, countries fall into three groups. In African countries with well structured labour markets and a large formal sector, measured unemployment tends to be high. This is particularly true of the southern cone of Africa, where unemployment rates exceed 15 per cent in Botswana, Namibia and South Africa. Lesotho has both a large informal sector and high unemployment. Unemployment is also high by international standards in North Africa—especially in Algeria and Tunisia.

Unemployment is relatively low in lower-income countries—falling in the range 1–5 per cent—while the informal sector is large. Ethiopia is among a cluster of countries—among them Burkina Faso, Ghana, Tanzania and Uganda—which share similar labour market structures. Kenya, Mali, Zambia and Zimbabwe comprise a third group with large informal sectors and unemployment rates in the range 5–15 per cent (Figure 4.7).

Across Africa, low unemployment rates—both overall and for the young—coexist with high levels of working poverty and vulnerable employment (AfDB, 2012). The ILO (2011a) estimates that three out of four jobs in Sub-Saharan Africa can be labelled 'vulnerable' due to workers working on their own account or as unpaid family workers. The poor quality of employment in most of Sub-Saharan Africa is also reflected in the large share of working poor in total employment. In 2011, 81.5 per cent of workers in Africa were

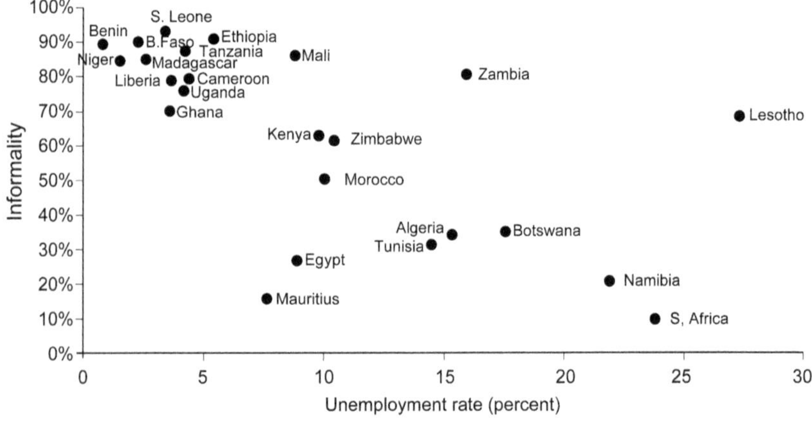

Figure 4.7 Unemployment and informality
Source: AfDB (2012).

classified as working poor, compared with the world average of 39.1 per cent (ILO, 2011a).

Between 2004 and 2008, Africa had some of the most employment-intensive growth in the world. Average employment elasticities of growth were 0.7 and 0.5, respectively (AfDB, 2012). Globally, the employment elasticity of growth is estimated to be about 0.3, and it ranges from a low of 0.2 in eastern Asia to a high of 0.9 in the Arab Middle East (Kapsos, 2005). There is, however, a strong negative relationship between the rate of growth and the employment intensity of growth across Africa (Figure 4.8). The region's fastest-growing economies—Ethiopia, Rwanda, Tanzania and Uganda—have its lowest elasticities of employment creation with respect to growth.

When younger African workers find a job, it is likely to be of low quality in terms of wages, benefits and job security. In many African countries, self-employment and informal employment account for the overwhelming majority of young workers in both rural and urban areas. With the exceptions of Botswana, Nigeria and South Africa—all of which have high youth unemployment rates—fewer than 20 per cent of Africa's young workers find places in wage employment. Over 70 per cent of young workers in Congo, Congo DR, Ethiopia, Ghana, Malawi, Mali, Rwanda, Senegal and Uganda are either self-employed or contributing to family work (AfDB, 2012). Most of these jobs offer low wages, few benefits and few opportunities to build skills. For the great majority of African economies, the employment problem is more about the quality of the job than the absence of a job.

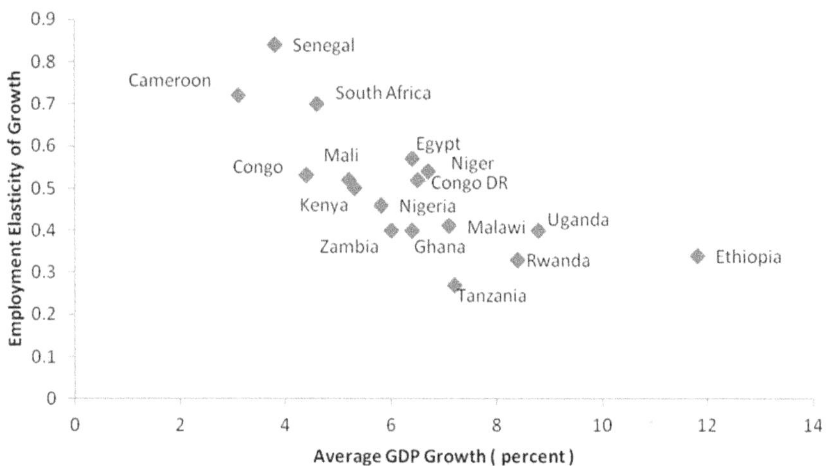

Figure 4.8 Growth elasticity of employment
Source: AfDB (2012).

4.3 Data and definitions

Ethiopia—unlike many countries in low-income Africa—has a rich stock of data on economic activity and employment. In this section we describe the main data sources used in this chapter.

4.3.1 Data sources

Our main data come from the 1999/2000 and 2004/2005 labour force surveys, and the 2009 and 2011 urban employment and unemployment surveys. The 1999/2000 and the 2004/2005 labour force surveys are nationally representative surveys covering both the rural and urban areas of all regions.[6] The 2009 and 2011 urban employment and unemployment surveys covered all urban parts of the country. The surveys provide information on the size and characteristics of the economically active and the non-active population aged 10 years and over.

The study in 1999 consisted of 1423 Enumeration Areas (EAs) and 49,614 households in rural areas, and 911 EAs and 31,859 households in urban areas. In 2005 the size of the study decreased to 830 rural EAs with 24,861 households, and 720 urban EAs with 21,420 households. For the urban employment and unemployment survey in 2009, 525 EAs were sampled with 15,575 households. In 2011, 660 EAs were sampled with 19,730 households.

Our sample, drawn from the surveys, consists of all household members between the ages of 15 and 65. Most international organizations and countries classify individuals aged between 15 and 24 as youths. The Ethiopian government, however, defines youths as those between the ages of 15 and 29. To maintain compatibility with the Ethiopian government definition we also use the 15–29 year age range as one definition of youth.

The two labour force surveys give us a final sample size of 189,919 individuals in 1999; 99,196 of whom are youths. In 2005 the sample consists of 128,389 individuals, of whom 70,217 are youths. The samples drawn from the urban employment and unemployment surveys give 46,943 individuals in 2009 (26,636 youths) and 47,180 individuals in 2011 (26,768 youths).[7] We apply population weights to the data to make them nationally and regionally representative.

4.3.2 Definitions

Economically active individuals were defined as those who reported being engaged in production of goods and/or services for sale or exchange, the production of certain products for own consumption, or were available to be engaged in any economic activity seven days prior to the date of interview.[8] Individuals in the surveys who reported being employed were also asked if they were available and ready to work additional hours. Those who responded yes were coded as underemployed.[9]

The international standard definition of unemployment is based on the following three criteria that must be satisfied simultaneously: 'without work', 'currently available for work' and 'seeking work' (ILO, 1982). However, this definition of unemployment, with its emphasis on seeking work, has been criticized as overly restrictive in many developing countries, including Ethiopia. Hence we relax the requirement that the respondent must be actively seeking work. An individual is classified as unemployed if the individual is without work and is available for work.[10]

The informal sector plays an important role in employment in Ethiopia. The surveys included three questions to identify the sector of the economy in which employed persons were engaged as their main activity. A person is classified as working in the informal economy when 'the person is engaged in a business or enterprise that does not keep books of account, has fewer than 10 workers, and has no business/enterprise license'.

4.4 Ethiopia's labour market

In order to understand youth employment issues, it is essential to place them in the context of the labour market as a whole. In this section we use data from our four samples to provide a picture of the labour market in Ethiopia. We turn to the labour market for young people in the next section.

Table 4.4 provides a summary picture of the Ethiopian labour market. Table 4.5 gives more detail on labour force participation (LFP) rates, employment-to-population ratios (the employment rate), unemployment rates,

Table 4.4 Summary view of the Ethiopian labour market

	Ethiopian labour force					
	Urban (15–65)				*Rural (15–65)*	
	1999	*2005*	*2009*	*2011*	*1999*	*2005*
	LFS	*LFS*	*UEUS*	*UEUS*	*LFS*	*LFS*
Labour force	3,373,619	4,028,586	5,444,461	5,971,862	19,101,383	23,146,354
Wage employment	1,069,676	1,425,460	2,273,007	2,492,255	771,163	857,911
Self-employment	1,412,257	1,747,844	2,038,973	2,386,462	17,327,058	21,636,179
Informal employment	1,377,634	1,206,172	1,462,764	1,525,382	17,553,429	21,538,616
Formal employment	1,074,554	1,695,579	2,491,709	2,806,638	514,234	839,972
Unemployment	887,741	854,141	1,122,450	1,091,951	984,884	646,966
Real earnings in wage employment			380	359		
Real earnings in wage employment (formal sector)			436	409		

Source: Central Statistical Agency (1999, 2005) Ethiopian Labor Force Survey, Addis Ababa, Ethiopia; (2009, 2011) Urban Employment Unemployment Survey, Addis Ababa, Ethiopia.

Table 4.5 Labour market characteristics for total population and for youth population

	National					*Rural*					*Urban*				
	LFP	*EMP*	*UNEMP*	*UNDEREMP*	*INF SECT*	*LFP*	*EMP*	*UNEMP*	*UNDER EMP*	*INF SECT*	*LFP*	*EMP*	*UNEMP*	*UNDER EMP*	*INF SECT*
Ages 15–65															
1999	0.82	0.76	0.08	0.48	0.92	0.84	0.79	0.05	0.47	0.97	0.77	0.57	0.26	0.54	0.56
2005	0.86	0.81	0.06	0.28	0.90	0.89	0.86	0.03	0.27	0.96	0.73	0.58	0.21	0.34	0.42
2009											0.70	0.56	0.21	0.50	0.37
2011											0.71	0.58	0.18	0.48	0.35
Ages 15–24															
1999	0.78	0.69	0.12	0.50	0.94	0.81	0.76	0.07	0.49	0.98	0.64	0.39	0.38	0.54	0.65
2005	0.79	0.73	0.08	0.25	0.91	0.84	0.81	0.04	0.25	0.96	0.57	0.41	0.29	0.30	0.45
2009											0.52	0.37	0.29	0.48	0.39
2011											0.51	0.37	0.28	0.47	0.38
Ages 15–29															
1999	0.81	0.72	0.11	0.51	0.93	0.83	0.78	0.07	0.51	0.97	0.71	0.47	0.34	0.56	0.60
2005	0.82	0.76	0.07	0.27	0.90	0.87	0.83	0.04	0.27	0.96	0.65	0.48	0.27	0.33	0.43
2009											0.62	0.46	0.26	0.51	0.35
2011											0.62	0.47	0.24	0.49	0.34

Sources: Labour Force Surveys (CSA, 1999, 2005); Urban Employment and Unemployment Surveys (CSA, 2009, 2011); authors' calculations.

Notes: Employment rates are a proportion of the total population. The labour force participation (LFP) rate is given as the number of employed (EMP) and unemployed (UNEMP) population as a proportion of the adult/youth population. The unemployment rate is given as the proportion of the labour force that is unemployed. The underemployment rate (UNDEREMP) and the informal sector rate (INF SECT) is given as a proportion of the employed population.

underemployment rates and informal sector employment rates for Ethiopia as a whole and separately for rural and urban areas. Data are provided for the total population between the ages of 15 and 65 and for the youth population. For the youth population, we provide data for youths between the ages of 15 and 24, and also for the broader group of youths between the ages of 15 and 29, who are the object of interest of Ethiopian policymakers. The national and rural data are given for 1999 and 2005; the urban data are provided for the years 1999, 2005, 2009 and 2011.

4.4.1 Labour force participation

In 2005, 86 per cent of Ethiopians participated in the labour market.[11] Labour force participation rates were higher in rural than in urban areas: 89 and 73 per cent, respectively. This is one of the highest LFP rates in the world (sixth). High LFP rates are not unusual for poor countries, which tend to have an absence of social security systems, and low wages and household incomes (ILO, 2011b). In 2009, the average LFP rate for Sub-Saharan Africa and East Asia was 71 per cent, the average for the least-developed countries was 74 per cent, and for high income countries 61 per cent (World Bank, 2012).

Between 1999 and 2005, LFP in Ethiopia went up due to an increase in LFP in rural areas. Between 1999 and 2005, rural LFP rates increased by 5 percentage points. However, in urban areas, LFP declined by four percentage points. The fall in participation rates in urban areas was primarily due to increases in access to education. Urban LFP rates continued to fall through 2009, decreasing by a total of seven percentage points from 1999.

4.4.2 Unemployment and underemployment

As discussed in Section 4.2, Ethiopia, like much of Sub-Saharan Africa, does not appear to have a severe 'employment problem'. The measured unemployment rate for the country as a whole was 6 per cent in 2005, driven almost entirely by unemployment in urban areas. The urban unemployment rate in 2005 was 21 per cent. Between 1999 and 2005, unemployment at the national level decreased by 2 percentage points, driven by reductions in unemployment in both rural and urban areas. Urban unemployment fell from 21 to 18 per cent of the urban labour force between 2005 and 2011.

Although unemployment is low, a high fraction of Ethiopian workers consider themselves to be underemployed. In 2005, 28 per cent of employed Ethiopians[12] reported being underemployed, 27 per cent in rural areas and 34 per cent in urban areas. There was a sharp fall of 20 percentage points in underemployment nationally between 1999 and 2005, shared equally in urban and rural areas. However, underemployment in urban areas appears to have increased since 2005. The urban employment and unemployment surveys report urban underemployment of 45 per cent in 2006, 50 per cent in 2009 and 48 per cent in 2011.

The high level of urban underemployment is an area of concern. Individuals who report themselves as underemployed include those who are working part-time but who would prefer to work full-time, those who are earning less than they feel they should be, and individuals who are employed in jobs where they do not utilize their skills or training. Unfortunately, the data are not very informative with respect to the sources of urban underemployment. In the private sector, underemployment may reflect the inability of workers to find full-time employment. Workers may choose to work fewer hours than desired, or in a job that does not fully utilize their skills, because the alternative, not working, means living in poverty. Long spells of underemployment due to a skills mismatch can have negative implications for future employment and productivity. In the public sector, underemployment could also be a form of disguised unemployment if public and parastatal firms hire workers who are not productive.

4.4.3 Informal employment

In 2005, the share of employed persons working in the informal sector nationally was 90 per cent.[13] Informality is predominant in rural areas, where 96 per cent of the working population reported being informally employed in 2005. But even in urban areas, the informal sector employed 42 per cent of the working population in 2005. In 2011, 35 per cent of employed Ethiopians in urban areas were working in the informal sector.

There was little change in the degree of informality of work between 1999 and 2005. In both 1999 and 2005, 84 per cent of all working Ethiopians were employed in informal activities (Table 4.4). Informal employment increased from 92 to 93 per cent of the rural working population between 1999 and 2005. This translates into a substantial increase in the number of rural workers in the informal sector. In 1999, 17.3 million rural Ethiopians were engaged in informal employment, the vast majority on farms. By 2005 this number had increased to 21.6 million.

In urban areas a reduction in informal employment has taken place, from 41 per cent of the workforce in 1999 to 30 per cent in 2005, and further to 25 per cent in 2011. In 1999, of the 3.4 million employed Ethiopians between the ages of 15–65 living in urban areas, 1.4 million were employed in the informal sector. In 2011, of the 4.0 million employed Ethiopians living in urban areas, 1.2 million were employed in the informal sector. Put another way, while there are still a large number of Ethiopians employed in the urban informal sector, it has not grown significantly since 1999.

4.4.4 Regional labour market outcomes

The regional distribution and trends in employment-to-population ratios and unemployment rates are shown in Table 4.6. The table provides rates for 1999 and 2005 for both rural and urban areas, and rates for 2011 for urban areas. In

Table 4.6 Employment-population ratios and unemployment rates by region

Region	*1999*			*2005*			*2011*	*1999*			*2005*			*2011*
	Total	*Rural*	*Urban*	*Total*	*Rural*	*Urban*	*Urban*	*Total*	*Rural*	*Urban*	*Total*	*Rural*	*Urban*	*Urban*
Tigray	0.75	0.78	0.57	0.79	0.84	0.60	0.55	0.10	0.04	0.21	0.11	0.03	0.21	0.19
Affar	0.72	0.76	0.62	0.69	0.78	0.59	0.59	0.09	0.05	0.22	0.12	0.07	0.19	0.15
Amhara	0.75	0.77	0.59	0.85	0.88	0.60	0.57	0.12	0.06	0.21	0.10	0.02	0.21	0.20
Oromiya	0.79	0.81	0.64	0.82	0.85	0.61	0.61	0.09	0.04	0.18	0.11	0.03	0.20	0.17
Somali	0.73	0.80	0.54	0.70	0.80	0.48	0.47	0.12	0.06	0.30	0.17	0.05	0.32	0.20
Benishangul-Gumz	0.77	0.79	0.64	0.82	0.83	0.69	0.65	0.06	0.04	0.17	0.07	0.03	0.12	0.09
SNNP	0.80	0.81	0.63	0.85	0.87	0.62	0.64	0.07	0.03	0.16	0.10	0.03	0.20	0.14
Gambella	0.64	0.66	0.57	0.45		0.45	0.62	0.13	0.10	0.19	0.26		0.26	0.09
Harari	0.62	0.70	0.57	0.65	0.80	0.54	0.69	0.18	0.11	0.29	0.16	0.07	0.27	0.14
Addis Ababa	0.47	0.69	0.47	0.51	0.75	0.51	0.52	0.38	0.07	0.38	0.29	0.10	0.32	0.25
Dire Dawa	0.61	0.84	0.51	0.61	0.86	0.53	0.55	0.16	0.03	0.35	0.18	0.03	0.33	0.24
Total	0.76	0.79	0.57	0.81	0.86	0.58	0.58	0.11	0.05	0.22	0.14	0.03	0.24	0.18

Sources: Labour Force Surveys (CSA, 1999, 2005); Urban Employment and Unemployment Surveys (CSA, 2009, 2011); authors' calculations.
Notes: Employment rates are a proportion of the total population.

2005, Gambella (45 per cent), Addis Ababa (51 per cent) and Dire Dawa (61 per cent) had the lowest employment-to-population ratios and the highest unemployment rates at 18, 26 and 29 per cent for Dire Dawa, Gambella and Addis Ababa, respectively. The low employment-to-population ratios and high unemployment rates for Addis Ababa and Dire Dawa are not surprising. Both are chartered cities with over 60 per cent of their populations living in urban areas.[14]

Given the growth in the number of Ethiopians migrating to urban areas, it is also interesting to look at regional unemployment trends in urban areas. Regional urban unemployment rates fell between 5 and 53 per cent in every region between 1999 and 2011. The fall in urban unemployment holds even if we look at the shorter period of 2005–11.

4.4.5 Summing things up

The labour force surveys give us a picture of the 'average' Ethiopian worker aged 16–65 in 2005. The overwhelming probability is that the worker is of rural origin, employed in the informal economy, and self-employed. In that year, a worker had an 85 per cent chance of working in a rural area, an 84 per cent chance of working in the informal sector, and an 86 per cent chance of being self-employed. They had about an 8 per cent probability of finding wage employment and a 6 per cent probability of being unemployed.

Since 2005 we know little about changes in the rural labour market, but the urban labour market trends are encouraging. Between 2005 and 2011, the urban labour force grew by 48 per cent, reflecting increasing movement from rural to urban areas. Urban wage employment grew at nearly double that rate (75 per cent) and unemployment grew by only slightly more than half the rate of growth of the urban labour force (18 per cent). Both informal employment and self-employment grew at less than the overall rate for the urban labour force. Thus, in 2011, 42 per cent of urban workers found themselves in wage employment. Forty per cent were in self-employment and 18 per cent of urban labour force participants were unemployed.

We can combine our data on demographic trends with the urban labour force data to arrive at a back-of-the-envelope calculation of the probability a member of the labour force in Ethiopia will find a place in wage employment. Depending on the assumptions made with respect to the growth of wage employment in rural areas, the estimated share of wage employment in the Ethiopian labour force in 2011 falls in the range 10–13 per cent. Despite nearly 15 years of rapid growth, the average Ethiopian worker still has only about a 1 in 10 chance of finding a wage-paying job.

The urban labour force surveys also provide a modest insight into the quality of the jobs offered. In 2011 real earnings in wage employment in the formal sector exceeded those in all wage employment by about 15 per cent. Perhaps reflecting the acceleration of inflation discussed in Section 4.2, real earnings in both formal wage employment and all urban wage employment declined between 2009 and 2011 (Table 4.4).

4.5 Labour markets and the young

How do younger Ethiopians fit into the broader labour market? Ethiopian youths in the labour market are also overwhelmingly rural, self-employed and working at an informal job (Table 4.7). Youths have lower LFP and employment-to-population ratios than the country as a whole. They are more likely to be unemployed than the national average, but less likely to be underemployed. A slightly larger share of young people are employed in the informal sector.

When we look at rural and urban areas separately, we notice some major differences. The first is that there is a much higher share of rural youths participating in the labour market compared with urban youths. The second is that youths in rural areas face very similar labour market outcomes to the adult rural population. In urban areas, however, young people encounter quite different labour market outcomes from those faced by the adult urban population.

4.5.1 Labour force participation

In 2005, 79 per cent of Ethiopian's between the ages of 15 and 24 participated in the labour market (Table 4.4). If we include those up to the age of 29, the youth LFP rate was 82 per cent. The employment-to-population ratios were 73 and 76 per cent for youths aged 15–24 and youths aged 15–29, respectively.

Urban youths have lower LFP rates and employment-to-population ratios. In 2005, 84 per cent of the rural population between the ages of 15 and 24 participated in some form of economic activity compared with only 57 per cent of the urban youth population. The differences in urban and rural labour

Table 4.7 Summary view of Ethiopia's labour market for youths (15–29)

	Summary of the Ethiopia labour force					
	Urban (15–29)				*Rural (15–29)*	
	1999	*2005*	*2009*	*2011*	*1999*	*2005*
	LFS	*LFS*	*UEUS*	*UEUS*	*LFS*	*LFS*
Labour force	1,779,680	2,095,084	2,718,658	2,929,689	9,514,748	11,418,620
Wage employment	522,358	704,925	1,150,395	1,246,054	429,834	507,754
Self-employment	644,446	824,002	854,165	989,429	8,444,063	10,467,630
Informal employment	691,215	565,873	618,458	654,919	8,616,807	10,460,689
Formal employment	458,452	758,768	1,125,908	1,257,476	239,154	441,778
Unemployment	610,912	565,100	707,969	693,071	631,607	439,494
Real earnings in wage employment			293	283		
Real earnings in wage employment (formal sector)			351	337		

Source: Central Statistical Agency (1999, 2005) Ethiopian Labor Force Survey, Addis Ababa, Ethiopia; (2009, 2011) Urban Employment Unemployment Survey, Addis Ababa, Ethiopia.

market participation by the young are primarily due to educational opportunities and income. With fewer opportunities for education and higher levels of poverty in rural areas, rural youths are more likely to participate in the labour force (Denu *et al.*, 2005).

There is little difference in LFP between the young and the average worker for rural areas. In 2005 the 15–24 and 15–29 LFP rates in rural areas were 84 and 87 per cent, respectively, compared with an overall average of 89 per cent. In urban areas the story is quite different. In 2011 youths between the ages of 15 and 24 had LFP rates that were 20 percentage points lower than the urban average, and a substantial difference remains (nine percentage points) when we include youths aged 25–29.

Tables 4.8 and 4.9 give LFP rates, unemployment rates, unemployment durations, underemployment rates and employment in the informal sector for men and women in three subsamples: youths between the ages of 15 and 19

Table 4.8 Urban male youth labour market by age group and education (2011)

Age group	*Educational level*	*LFP*	*UNEMP*	*UNEMP DUR*	*UNDEREMP*	*INF SECT*
Ages 15–19	No schooling	0.73	0.19	11.41	0.52	0.48
	Primary or less	0.34	0.15	9.16	0.39	0.53
	Not completed lower secondary	0.22	0.28	13.89	0.40	0.43
	Completed lower secondary	0.38	0.38	9.73	0.62	0.24
	Higher education	0.26	0.44	7.76	0.46	0.14
	Other	0.19	0.00		0.00	1.00
	Total	0.33	0.23	9.96	0.44	0.45
Ages 20–24	No schooling	0.87	0.08	14.42	0.52	0.64
	Primary or less	0.80	0.14	11.60	0.53	0.41
	Not completed lower secondary	0.56	0.23	18.92	0.46	0.29
	Completed lower secondary	0.79	0.26	14.66	0.54	0.25
	Higher education	0.72	0.28	14.15	0.55	0.10
	Other	0.78	0.00		1.00	1.00
	Total	0.75	0.21	14.16	0.53	0.30
Ages 25–29	No schooling	0.92	0.06	6.21	0.58	0.58
	Primary or less	0.94	0.09	10.47	0.51	0.39
	Not completed lower secondary	0.83	0.13	10.56	0.52	0.20
	Completed lower secondary	0.93	0.15	13.54	0.48	0.18
	Higher education	0.93	0.10	14.90	0.53	0.04
	Other	0.86	0.02	24.00	0.68	0.47
	Total	0.93	0.11	12.37	0.52	0.24

Note: Lower education includes grades 9–12 under the old educational system (prior to 1994) or grades 9–10 under the new system (1994 and later).

Source: Table 4.19 in Urban Employment and Unemployment Surveys (2011). Authors' calculations.

Table 4.9 Urban female youth labour market by age group and education (2011)

Age group	*Educational level*	*LFP*	*UNEMP*	*UNEMP DUR*	*UNDEREMP*	*INF SECT*
Ages 15–19	No schooling	0.71	0.20	7.86	0.32	0.68
	Primary or less	0.32	0.23	11.27	0.34	0.69
	Not completed lower secondary	0.14	0.36	10.36	0.38	0.56
	Completed lower secondary	0.44	0.46	11.67	0.62	0.45
	Higher education	0.30	0.49	10.88	0.36	0.17
	Other	0.74	0.49	6.00	0.00	1.00
	Total	0.34	0.30	10.80	0.38	0.59
Ages 20–24	No schooling	0.71	0.25	16.79	0.46	0.71
	Primary or less	0.66	0.33	13.13	0.50	0.57
	Not completed lower secondary	0.47	0.51	12.72	0.49	0.34
	Completed lower secondary	0.71	0.42	14.51	0.51	0.27
	Higher education	0.74	0.31	10.33	0.48	0.08
	Other	0.89	0.18	6.00	0.00	0.00
	Total	0.68	0.34	13.05	0.49	0.35
Ages 25–29	No schooling	0.74	0.27	11.91	0.51	0.75
	Primary or less	0.71	0.28	14.02	0.54	0.57
	Not completed lower secondary	0.69	0.42	19.76	0.53	0.31
	Completed lower secondary	0.79	0.33	19.58	0.50	0.25
	Higher education	0.88	0.16	18.85	0.43	0.04
	Other	0.69	0.30	12.00	0.60	0.73
	Total	0.76	0.27	15.98	0.50	0.39

Source: Table 4.19 in Urban Employment and Unemployment Surveys (2011). Authors' calculations.

(teenage youths), youths aged 20–24 (young adults), and youths aged 25–29. Labour force participation increases for both men and women as they age. The LFP rates are as low as 33 per cent for teenagers, and rise to 93 per cent for men and to 76 per cent for women between the ages of 25 and 29.

Between 1999 and 2005, LFP among the young increased in rural areas and fell in urban areas. The trend of falling LFP for urban youths continued through 2011, when the urban LFP rate for those between 15 and 25 reached 51 per cent (63 per cent of those aged 15–29). The decline in the share of young workers in the labour force is attributable mainly to a reduction in LFP by the young as more educational opportunities have become available and younger workers have delayed entry into the labour force (O'Higgins, 2001, 2003).

4.5.2 Unemployment and underemployment

The national youth unemployment rate in 2005 was slightly higher than the national average at 8 per cent for youths 15–24 and 7 per cent for youths 15–29. As with LFP, differences between unemployment rates for the young, regardless of definition, and the average worker are small for rural areas. In urban areas the 15–24 unemployment rate is 10 percentage points higher than the urban average. For young men, unemployment falls as they age.

Youth unemployment has fallen since 1999 in both rural and urban areas. Indeed, unemployment among the young has actually been declining more rapidly than the average for the economy. The decline has been particularly sharp in urban areas where youth unemployment rates under either definition of the relevant age group declined by 10 percentage points between 1999 and 2011.

In 2005 national youth underemployment rates were lower than the national average, with 25 per cent underemployment for those aged 15–24, and 27 per cent underemployment for youths aged 15–29. About 25 per cent of rural youths and 29 per cent of urban youths were classified as underemployed. Differences in underemployment between the young and the average worker are quite small in the rural economy. Underemployment rates for youths in urban areas are essentially the same as those for the average worker. There are some indications that the 2005 labour force survey understated the degree of urban underemployment for both groups. In 2011 the extent of urban underemployment among the young was nearly 50 per cent.

4.5.3 Labour market outcomes in urban centers

Understanding labour markets in major urban centers has important implications for analyzing youth employment issues, for two reasons: urban centers create a disproportionate number of jobs, and youths are the most likely population to migrate to urban areas. Addis Ababa and Dire Dawa are Ethiopia's two largest urban regions. Over 40 per cent of urban youths participating in the labour market reside in these two cities. Both cities have youth employment rates below the urban average and unemployment rates above the urban average. However, the gap between these rates with the urban average has been falling (Table 4.10).

In 1999 the youth employment-to-population ratios in Addis Ababa and Dire Dawa were 38 and 42 per cent, respectively, compared with the urban average of 47 per cent. While the youth unemployment rate in all urban areas was 29 per cent, they were 47 and 43 per cent for Addis Ababa and Dire Dawa. By 2011 the situation had improved and there was a modest increase in the youth employment ratios for Addis Ababa and Dire Dawa. More importantly, between 1999 and 2011 youth unemployment in both cities fell compared with the urban average for youths. In 2011, the national urban unemployment rate for youths was 23 per cent. In Addis Ababa and Dire Dawa, the rates were 28 and 29 per cent, respectively.

Table 4.10 Youth employment-population ratios and unemployment rates by region

Region	*Unemployment rate*													
	1999			*2005*			*2011*	*1999*			*2005*			*2011*
	Total	*Rural*	*Urban*	*Total*	*Rural*	*Urban*	*Urban*	*Total*	*Rural*	*Urban*	*Total*	*Rural*	*Urban*	*Urban*
Tigray	0.70	0.74	0.47	0.74	0.81	0.50	0.43	0.15	0.06	0.29	0.16	0.04	0.29	0.27
Affar	0.69	0.77	0.49	0.61	0.73	0.49	0.41	0.12	0.06	0.33	0.16	0.09	0.24	0.22
Amhara	0.73	0.76	0.47	0.81	0.86	0.49	0.46	0.16	0.07	0.30	0.14	0.03	0.27	0.27
Oromiya	0.76	0.80	0.55	0.77	0.82	0.50	0.50	0.13	0.06	0.25	0.14	0.04	0.26	0.22
Somali	0.69	0.80	0.44	0.64	0.78	0.35	0.31	0.15	0.09	0.37	0.21	0.07	0.41	0.26
Benishangul-Gumz	0.72	0.74	0.53	0.77	0.80	0.60	0.52	0.09	0.04	0.26	0.10	0.04	0.17	0.13
SNNP	0.75	0.78	0.53	0.79	0.83	0.50	0.52	0.10	0.04	0.22	0.14	0.04	0.25	0.18
Gambella	0.54	0.57	0.47	0.33		0.33	0.52	0.19	0.15	0.24	0.34		0.34	0.13
Harari	0.56	0.71	0.47	0.54	0.72	0.42	0.58	0.22	0.12	0.36	0.22	0.09	0.37	0.18
Addis Ababa	0.38	0.68	0.38	0.43	0.69	0.43	0.44	0.46	0.08	0.47	0.35	0.12	0.38	0.28
Dire Dawa	0.54	0.83	0.42	0.53	0.82	0.44	0.45	0.21	0.04	0.43	0.22	0.06	0.39	0.29
Total	0.72	0.78	0.47	0.76	0.83	0.48	0.47	0.15	0.06	0.29	0.18	0.05	0.30	0.23

Source: Labour Force Surveys (1999; 2005); Urban Employment and Unemployment Surveys (2009; 2011). Authors' calculations.

Notes: Employment rates are a proportion of the total population.

4.5.4 Duration of unemployment and finding a job

Unemployment duration is an important measure of how well youths are able to transition from school to work. It also provides an indication of how the skills youths acquire in school or through training are perceived in the labour market. While youths in Ethiopia tend to have the highest unemployment rates, they tend to spend a shorter amount of time unemployed. There has been a substantial decrease in the average duration of unemployment experienced in urban areas in recent years. In 2011 the average duration of unemployment in urban areas was 14 months. For youths (aged 15–29) the average duration was 13 months; for people aged 30–65 the average duration was 16 months. Corresponding figures for 1999 were 24 months for youths and 26 months for adults (Tables 4.8 and 4.9).

Unemployment durations tend to be shorter in rural areas. In 1999 the average duration of unemployment was 13 months:- youths spent 14 months on average unemployed, while adults spent 11 months on average unemployed. In 2005, the average unemployment spell was 7 months for both youths and adults. Among young men, the duration of unemployment peaks for the age group 20–24 at about 14 months. For young women, the age group 24–29 has the longest duration of unemployment, nearly 16 months. For male and female teenagers, the average length of time spent unemployed is generally shorter than for older youths.

Table 4.11 provides information on the methods used by unemployed urban youths to find work. The primary sources used in seeking employment are searching vacancies, seeking assistance of friends, and checking at work places. Between 1999 and 2011, youths have increased the use of more formal methods to find jobs by searching vacancies and through newspaper advertisements. They reduced the reliance on the practice of checking at work places, but still rely on assistance from friends or family members to identify employment opportunities. One of the most interesting observations from Table 4.11 is the

Table 4.11 Search method distribution for unemployed urban youths, 1999–2011

Search method	*1999*	*2011*	*1999*	*2011*
Produced unemployment card	6.83	1.44	8.27	2.00
Direct application	6.52	0.00	7.09	0.00
Searching vacancies	27.52	44.39	32.13	48.85
Through newspaper	2.60	7.69	3.27	5.59
Seeking assistance of friends	18.05	23.90	18.84	24.20
Checking at workplace	28.18	16.49	15.89	12.56
Trying to establish own enterprise	8.82	4.43	12.43	3.29
Others	1.47	1.65	2.07	3.50
Total	100.00	100.00	100.00	100.00

Source: Labour Force Survey (1999); Urban Employment and Unemployment Surveys (2011). Authors' Calculations.

Notes: Samples consist only of unemployed youths who report having searched for employment.

decrease in the number of unemployed youths attempting to start their own business as a means to obtain employment.

4.5.5 Informal employment

Young Ethiopians are overwhelmingly employed in informal activities. Nationally, 82 per cent of workers aged 15–29 were engaged in the informal sector in 2005 (Table 4.7). Thus the share of the youth labour force working in the informal sector is roughly the same as the national average. Informal employment of the young has fallen nationally since 1999, but much more quickly in urban than in rural settings. In urban areas in 1999, 65 per cent of workers aged 15–24 were engaged in informal employment, as were 60 per cent of workers aged 15–29. By 2011 the informal employment rates among the urban young had fallen to 38 and 34 per cent, respectively.

The fall in the share of youths employed in the informal sector in urban areas is driven almost entirely by growth in formal sector employment. In 1999, 691,000 youths (aged 15–29) were employed in the informal sector; by 2011 the number had fallen to 655,000. Formal sector employment among the young almost tripled between 1999 and 2011. In 1999, 458,000 urban youths were employed in the formal sector. In 2011, the number of youths employed in the formal sector rose to 1.26 million (Table 4.7).

The relative decline in informal sector employment suggests an important improvement in labour market outcomes for urban youths. However, urban youths are still overwhelmingly self-employed or unemployed. In 2011, over 34 per cent of youths (19–29) were either self-employed or worked as unpaid family labourers. Another 24 per cent were unemployed.

4.5.6 Differences between men and women

Table 4.12 replicates Table 4.8 separately for young men and women aged 15–29. It shows that labour market outcomes for young male and female Ethiopians differ substantially from each other. Young men in Ethiopia have higher LFP rates and lower unemployment rates than young women. Men are more likely to be underemployed, but less likely to be found in the informal sector.

In 2005, 79 per cent of Ethiopian women between the ages of 15 and 29 were participating in the labour force compared with 86 per cent of Ethiopian men in the same age group. For men this was a slight decrease from 87 per cent participation in 1999, whereas for women it was an increase from 75 per cent in 1999. Urban LFP rates have fallen substantially both for young men and women, a product of increased participation in education. The decline in LFP for young urban women, however, has been greater than for young urban men.

Gender differences in unemployment rates are more pronounced. Nationwide, young males had an unemployment rate of 4 per cent in 2005, compared with an unemployment rate of 11 per cent for young females. In rural areas in the

Table 4.12 Youth labour market characteristics by gender

	National					*Rural*					*Urban*				
	LFP	*EMP*	*UNEMP*	*UNDEREMP*	*INF SECT*	*LFP*	*EMP*	*UNEMP*	*UNDEREMP*	*INF SECT*	*LFP*	*EMP*	*UNEMP*	*UNDEREMP*	*INF SECT*
Men															
1999	0.87	0.82	0.06	0.56	0.92	0.90	0.87	0.03	0.56	0.97	0.73	0.54	0.25	0.58	0.51
2005	0.86	0.83	0.04	0.30	0.88	0.91	0.90	0.01	0.30	0.94	0.64	0.52	0.19	0.35	0.36
2009											0.66	0.54	0.17	0.53	0.33
2011											0.66	0.55	0.16	0.51	0.29
Women															
1999	0.75	0.63	0.16	0.45	0.94	0.77	0.69	0.11	0.44	0.98	0.70	0.41	0.42	0.53	0.69
2005	0.79	0.71	0.11	0.24	0.93	0.83	0.77	0.06	0.23	0.98	0.66	0.44	0.33	0.30	0.51
2009											0.59	0.39	0.34	0.48	0.38
2011											0.58	0.40	0.30	0.47	0.41

Source: Labour Force Surveys (1999; 2005); Urban Employment and Unemployment Surveys (2009; 2011). Authors' calculations.
Notes: Youths aged 15–29. Employment rates are a proportion of the total population.

same year, the male youth unemployment rate was 1 per cent and the female rate 6 per cent. In urban areas, the male and female youth unemployment rates in 2005 were 19 and 33 per cent, respectively. Although urban unemployment had fallen to 16 and 30 per cent by 2011, the large gender differential remained.

Differences in labour market outcomes for young men and women are not unique to Ethiopia. The employment prospects of young women vary considerably across countries in Africa. In nine out of 14 countries with relevant data, LFP rates are lower among young females than among young males. Out of 15 countries, the female youth unemployment rate is higher in eight. In the seven remaining countries the opposite is true (AfDB, 2012).

Across Africa, gender inequalities manifest themselves primarily in the much higher share of women in vulnerable employment in comparison with men. The rate of working poor for females exceeded that of male rates in 22 out of 27 sub-Saharan countries according to available data (ILO, 2011a). Ethiopia is no exception. In 2011, 41 per cent of young urban women were employed in the informal sector, compared with 29 per cent of men.

Table 4.13 gives the educational and gender composition of the urban unemployed youth population for 1999 and 2011. The young urban unemployed are disproportionably female and their share of the unemployed has not changed over time. While women made up approximately 52 per cent of the youth labour force in both 1999 and 2011, 67 per cent of all unemployed youths were women. The preponderance of women among the young unemployed appears at all educational levels. Women with the least amount of education fare worse in the labour market relative to men with the same level of educational attainment.

4.5.7 Who are the working youth?

Table 4.14 gives the industry distribution of employed youths. Male youths are employed primarily in manufacturing, construction, and wholesale and retail trade. Female youths are primarily employed in wholesale and retail trade, hotels and restaurants, and private household services. Nearly a third of employed young men and women are engaged in wholesale or retail trade or 'other services'. Many of these activities are likely to be in the informal sector. Construction and education are two industries that have expanded in terms of providing more employment opportunities for youths.

Table 4.15 reports the occupational distribution of employed youths by sector. Public sector employment combines government, NGO and parastatal employment; private sector employment includes private sector employee and private sector employer; self-employment includes the self-employed and unpaid family labour. Between 1999 and 2011 there was an increase in the incidence of employment in jobs that require some skill (columns 10 and 11). A higher proportion of young people were employed as professionals and clerks in 2011 than in 1999, which is consistent with the rising levels of

Table 4.13 Educational and gender composition of urban unemployed youths (1999–2011)

Educational level	*1999*			*2011*		
	Male	*Female*	*Share female*	*Male*	*Female*	*Share female*
No schooling	5.22	15.99	0.86	4.47	16.11	0.88
Primary or less	39.92	40.23	0.68	28.17	32.32	0.70
Not completed lower secondary	21.19	17.60	0.63	10.76	9.45	0.64
Completed lower secondary	28.31	22.95	0.63	28.04	23.13	0.62
Higher education	4.47	2.29	0.51	28.53	18.75	0.57
Other	0.88	0.94	0.69	0.02	0.25	0.96
Total	100.00	100.00	0.67	100.00	100.00	0.67

Source: Labour Force Surveys (1999); Urban Employment and Unemployment Surveys (2011). Authors' calculations.

Notes: Lower education includes grades 9–12 under the old educational system (prior to 1994) or grades 9–10 under the new system (1994 and later).

Table 4.14 Industry distribution for employed urban youths, 1999–2011

Industry	*Male*		*Female*	
	1999	*2011*	*1999*	*2011*
Agriculture, fishing, and forestry	12.90	7.66	5.78	5.62
Manufacturing	13.90	13.22	11.78	11.12
Construction	6.78	12.41	1.73	3.76
Wholesale and retail trade	27.80	19.85	23.66	20.00
Hotels and restaurants	4.44	4.61	23.60	13.78
Transportation and communications	8.57	8.86	0.57	0.64
Public administration and defence	5.87	5.78	4.34	4.26
Real estate and business services	1.50	2.48	0.53	1.98
Education	2.79	6.40	2.63	7.21
Health and social work	1.82	2.49	1.92	4.10
Other services	9.09	11.64	3.65	9.17
Private household services	2.49	1.02	18.37	14.57

Source: Labour Force Surveys (1999; 2005); Urban Employment and Unemployment Surveys (2009; 2011). Authors' calculations.

educational attainment in the economy, especially among the youth. However, the majority of youths are employed as service workers and craft workers, and between 20 and 30 per cent of youths are employed in elementary occupations. Elementary occupations consist of simple and routine tasks and often require no more than a primary education. These occupations account for a large number of informal sector jobs.

4.5.8 *Quality of jobs*

The urban labour force surveys provide a glimpse of evidence on the quality of jobs held by young people (Table 4.16). Real monthly earnings in the public sector exceeded those for the private sector in both 2009 and 2011 for men and women. For men in 2011, the monthly earnings in public sector employment were 74 per cent higher than those of private sector employment. For women, public sector earnings were double monthly earnings in the private sector. There were significant gender differences in monthly earnings between males and females in both public and private employment, but they were greater in the private sector than in the public sector.

To a great extent, these differences in earnings reflect different characteristics of workers in the two sectors, mainly in educational attainment. We return to this subject below. But it also appears that the public sector remains the 'wage leader' in the formal sector labour market. This is why there appears to be a heavy preference among better-educated young Ethiopians for public employment. It also raises the risk that, as has happened in a number of other African economies, if the private sector cannot take up the slack, then increasing numbers of educated young people might queue for extended periods awaiting a public sector job.

Table 4.15 Occupational distribution for urban youths by sector of employment, 1999–2011

(a) Male workers

Occupation	*Public sector*		*Private sector*		*Self-employed*		*Other*		*Total*	
	1999	*2011*	*1999*	*2011*	*1999*	*2011*	*1999*	*2011*	*1999*	*2011*
Legislators, senior officials and managers	4.87	9.18	0.86	1.17	0.36	0.30	1.48	0.57	1.33	2.47
Professionals	6.62	26.46	0.72	3.35	0.10	0.54	0.46	3.62	1.46	7.05
Technicians and associate professionals	22.33	23.33	4.06	4.08	2.64	1.28	18.90	6.05	6.92	7.03
Clerks	13.57	9.56	3.35	3.77	0.65	1.81	1.65	0.77	3.75	4.08
Service workers and shop and market sales	9.54	7.94	14.87	13.42	39.69	34.55	6.80	10.33	26.59	20.92
Skilled agricultural and fishery workers	1.86	0.62	1.54	1.90	11.33	12.55	3.94	5.14	6.71	6.15
Crafts and related trades workers	12.12	7.38	30.71	29.43	16.26	21.80	44.18	35.55	20.16	21.83
Plant and machine operators and assemblers	6.74	5.52	10.53	16.09	2.28	4.31	2.54	7.23	5.41	8.69
Elementary occupations	20.75	9.81	33.37	26.68	26.70	22.86	20.04	30.75	27.37	21.68
Armed forces	1.59	0.20	0.00	0.11	0.00	0.00	0.00	0.00	0.29	0.08
Total	100.00	100.00	100.00	100.00	100.00	100.00	100.00	100.00	100.00	100.00

(*continued on next page*)

Table 4.15 (continued)

(b) Female workers

Occupation	*Public sector*		*Private sector*		*Self-employed*		*Other*		*Total*	
	1999	*2011*	*1999*	*2011*	*1999*	*2011*	*1999*	*2011*	*1999*	*2011*
Legislators, senior officials and managers	2.57	3.98	0.38	0.47	0.15	0.09	0.59	0.00	0.56	0.96
Professionals	2.83	19.38	0.29	3.87	0.05	0.11	0.00	3.25	0.50	5.22
Technicians and associate professionals	24.04	24.27	1.94	2.81	0.12	0.60	1.23	6.59	3.97	5.99
Clerks	26.36	27.98	5.69	8.50	0.51	0.52	9.15	7.99	5.78	8.89
Service workers and shop and market sales	6.36	5.21	11.87	20.92	43.31	53.86	6.43	17.73	28.01	31.23
Skilled agricultural and fishery workers	1.40	0.68	0.32	2.40	2.60	7.56	0.00	2.03	1.69	4.15
Crafts and related trades workers	5.21	3.04	8.20	8.31	43.83	20.80	15.22	22.17	27.20	12.70
Plant and machine operators and assemblers	3.11	0.65	0.87	2.01	0.06	0.10	0.10	2.15	0.73	0.99
Elementary occupations	28.08	14.78	70.44	50.72	9.36	16.35	67.27	38.09	31.55	29.86
Armed forces	0.04	0.03	0.00	0.00	0.00	0.00	0.00	0.00	0.00	0.01
Total	100.00	100.00	100.00	100.00	100.00	100.00	100.00	100.00	100.00	100.00

Source: Labour Force Surveys (1999; 2005); Urban Employment and Unemployment Surveys (2009; 2011). Authors' calculations.

Table 4.16 Real earnings and hours worked, urban youths, 2009, 2011

	Real monthly earnings		*Hours worked per week*	
	2009	*2011*	*2009*	*2011*
(a) Male workers				
Public sector	496.28	480.62	43	46
Private sector	278.67	276.97	50	52
Self-employment			43	46
Total	362.40	355.76	47	50
(b) Female workers				
Public sector	369.69	352.27	39	39
Private sector	138.67	134.23	53	54
Self-employment			38	37
Total	219.03	205.43	48	50

Source: Urban Employment and Unemployment Surveys (2009; 2011). Authors' calculations.

4.5.9 Summing things up

What do these data tell us about the transition to work of young Ethiopians? Male or female young workers are entering a labour market that is still mostly informal. In 2005 the share of employed persons working in the informal sector was about 85 per cent. Unemployment—as measured by the relaxed definition—is low, about 6 per cent of the labour force in 2005, and almost entirely in urban areas. But a large number of Ethiopian workers feel underemployed. In 2011 nearly half of all urban workers reported being underemployed. Despite more than 15 years of robust economic growth, young labour force entrants confront a labour market that has generated few wage jobs and a substantial share of workers wish they could work more.

Against this background, young Ethiopians are less likely than the average worker to participate in the labour market. To a great extent, this is true because they have more educational opportunities available to them than ever before, and they delay entering the labour market until they have completed their education. But once in the labour market, young people face somewhat dimmer employment prospects than the average worker, especially in cities. In urban areas the unemployment rate of youths aged 15–29 is 24 per cent. The corresponding figure is even higher for women aged 15–29. About 43 per cent of young Ethiopians in urban areas find wage employment.

Informal on-farm employment is the fate of the overwhelming majority of young workers in rural areas. In urban areas, 34 per cent of workers aged 15–29 were in self-employment in 2011, while about two-thirds were in the informal sector. More than a quarter of young Ethiopians are underemployed. In urban areas this figure rises to nearly one half. Most of those jobs offer low wages, few benefits and few opportunities to build skills. For a great majority of Ethiopia's young, the employment problem is more about the quality of the job than the absence of a job.

4.6 Education and labour market outcomes for the young

In this section we discuss the relationship between educational attainment and labour market outcomes for young labour force participants. The education system in Ethiopia has three levels: (a) general education, comprising primary (grades 1–8, ages 7–14) and lower secondary (grades 9–10, ages 15–16); (b) college/university preparatory (grades 11–12, ages 17–18) for those who pass the grade 10 national school leaving exam or 1–3 years of vocational training for those who do not score sufficient grades to start preparatory education; and (c) university education for those who pass a national university entrance examination in grade 12.

4.6.1 Rising educational attainment

Table 4.17 shows the educational attainment of urban Ethiopian youths in 1999 and 2011. The educational attainment of the youth population rose between 1999 and 2011. In 1999, 61 per cent of Ethiopians between the ages of 15 and 29 had no more than a primary education, and only 18 per cent completed lower secondary education. In 2011, the proportion of youths with no more than a primary education fell to 51 per cent. The proportion completing at least secondary education rose to 37 per cent in 2011. Women are more likely to have no education and are less likely to complete lower secondary or obtain some form of higher education.

The most impressive change in educational attainment has occurred among individuals acquiring some form of higher education. In 1999, only 4 per cent of Ethiopian youths had some form of higher education; in 2011 this share had reached 20 per cent. This trend is observed for both men and women. Improvements in educational attainment in rural areas have lagged behind those in urban areas. Between 1999 and 2005, literacy rates went up and the share of rural youths obtaining some primary education increased. However,

Table 4.17 Educational attainment for urban youth population

Educational level	*1999*			*2011*		
	Male	*Female*	*Total*	*Male*	*Female*	*Total*
No schooling	8.85	22.78	16.77	6.05	15.46	11.25
Primary or less	46.25	43.19	44.51	40.01	39.44	39.70
Not completed lower secondary	21.97	17.13	19.22	13.06	11.32	12.10
Completed lower secondary	16.09	12.83	14.24	18.18	15.77	16.85
Higher education	5.52	3.00	4.08	22.48	17.82	19.91
Other	1.32	1.08	1.18	0.21	0.18	0.20
Total	100.00	100.00	100.00	100.00	100.00	100.00

Source: Labour Force Survey (1999); Urban Employment and Unemployment Surveys (2011). Authors' calculations.

there was no substantial improvement in educational attainment in rural areas beyond primary education.

4.6.2 Education and unemployment

Figure 4.9 shows the relationship between educational attainment and unemployment for urban male and female youths in 1999 and 2011. The downward trend in unemployment for both young men and women is apparent over time. However, the unemployment rates for young women are substantially higher than those for men at all educational levels. The gender employment gap is least for young women with university education. It is largest for those with no schooling. This is consistent with evidence from other African countries both north and south of the Sahara (Page, 2012c).

In Ethiopia there is an inverted U-shaped relationship between education and unemployment for both men and women. Unemployment peaks at the secondary level. Those of both genders with university education have unemployment rates that exceed those of primary school graduates, but are less than those of secondary school leavers, which is not altogether surprising. In most African countries, those with higher educational attainment tend to take longer to search for a job and have higher unemployment rates than those who are less well educated. Except for Niger and South Africa, youth unemployment rates tend to be lowest among those with either no or basic education (AfDB, 2012; Page, 2012c). In six out of 14 countries for which data were available, the unemployment rate for those with tertiary education was the highest of all.

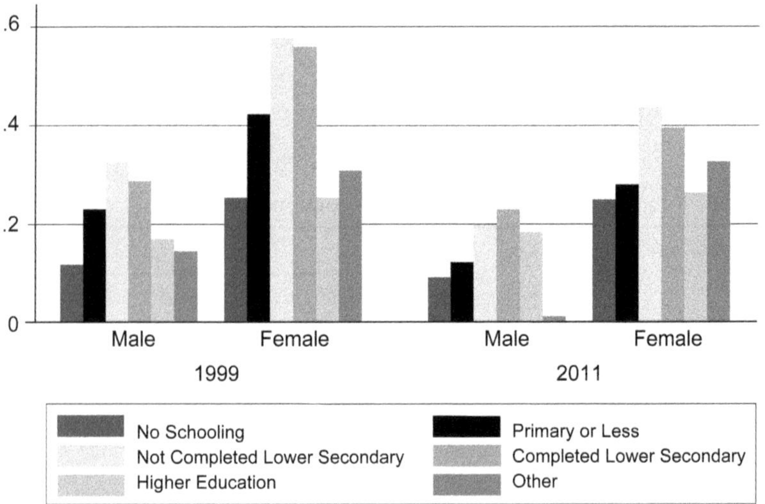

Figure 4.9 Urban youth unemployment rates by educational level and gender, 1999–2011
Source: Central Statistical Agency (1999) Ethiopian Labour Force Survey, Addis Ababa, Ethiopia; (2011) Urban Employment Unemployment Survey, Addis Ababa, Ethiopia.

The share of the unemployed who were better educated increased between 1999 and 2011 (Tables 4.9 and 4.10). In 1999, 66 per cent of unemployed men and 74 per cent of unemployed women had less than a lower secondary education. By 2011, 43 per cent of unemployed men and 58 per cent of unemployed women had less than a lower secondary education. The increase in the share of the better educated unemployed is most marked in higher education. In 1999 only 4.5 per cent of young unemployed men and 2.3 per cent of young unemployed women received higher education. By 2011 the shares of the tertiary educated unemployed had risen to 28.5 and 18.8 per cent, respectively. In an interview, the Ethiopian Federation of Employers cited lack of appropriate skills of university graduates for announced vacancies as one of the reasons for high educated unemployment. Employers also indicated that they perceived the quality of university education to be poor.

There does not appear to be a consistent relationship between educational attainment and the duration of unemployment. Among men aged 15–24, the duration of unemployment is highest for those who have not completed secondary school. In the 25–29 age group, the average duration of unemployment is highest among men with tertiary education. Among women the relationship between age, education and duration of unemployment is even more muddled. One consistent finding does emerge: across educational levels, young women experience somewhat longer periods of unemployment than young men.

Figure 4.10 shows the probability of being unemployed in 2011 for male and female youths adjusting for age, household characteristics and region of

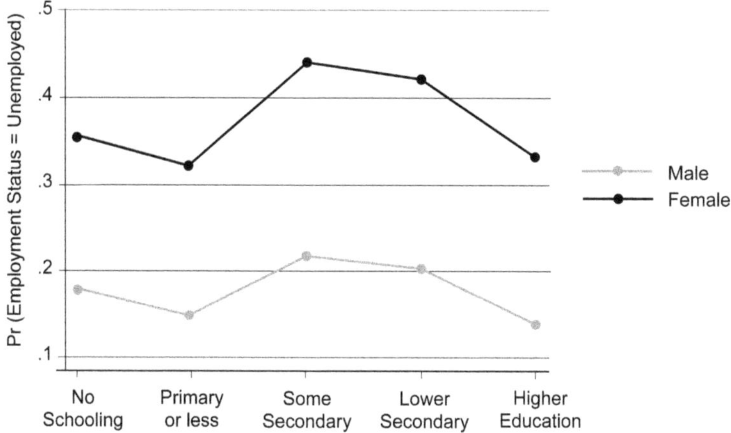

Figure 4.10 Adjusted probabilities of unemployment for male and female youths by educational attainment, 2011

Notes: Probabilities are from a multinomial logit. Additional controls include: age, age squared, number of children under the age of 5 living in the household, number of children between the age of 5 and 14 liviing in the household, number of adult women living in the household, number of adult men living in the household, number of elderly adults living in the household, and regional dummies. The adjusted probabilities are calculated by setting each of the control variables to their mean outcomes.

residence, obtained from a multinomial logit regression.[15] After adjusting for age and household characteristics, the probability of being unemployed for male youths with higher education is lower (14 per cent) compared with the unadjusted mean of 19 per cent (Figure 4.10). However, the probability of being unemployed for female youths with higher education is higher at 33 per cent compared with an unadjusted mean of 27 per cent.[16]

For highly educated youths, the labour force decision is simply a decision between unemployment and formal sector employment. Less than 5 per cent of youths with a higher education are employed in the informal sector; this is true for both men and women. This is partly driven by the high returns to public sector employment (Table 4.16), which encourages highly educated youths to queue for public sector employment. For the other educational groups, the labour force decision is a decision between formal sector employment, informal sector employment or unemployment.[17]

4.6.3 Education and informality

The share of young men and women engaged in informal employment declines as education increases. Across all educational levels, however, women have a higher share of employment in informal activities than men. Informal employment shows the same pattern as for young men, declining with age. Figures 4.11 and 4.12 present adjusted probabilities of being employed in the formal and informal sectors by educational attainment for youths in 2011. The adjusted probabilities are from a multinomial logit regression (see note 12).

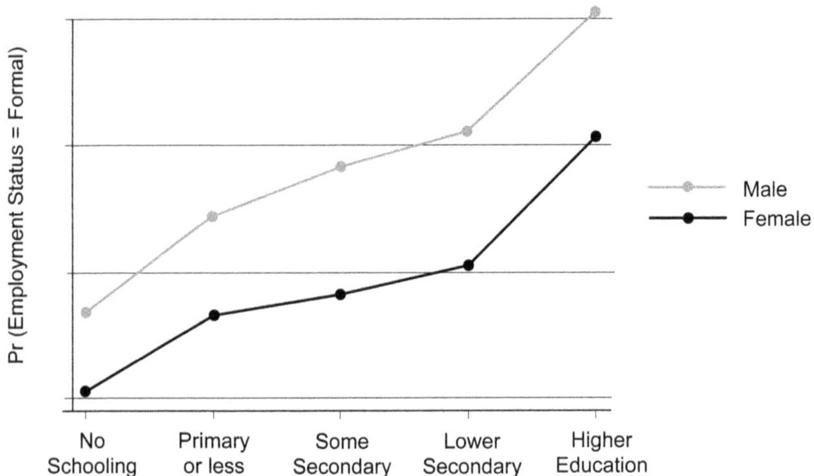

Figure 4.11 Adjusted probabilities of formal sector employment for male and female youths by educational attainment, 2011

Notes: Refer to Figure 4.10.

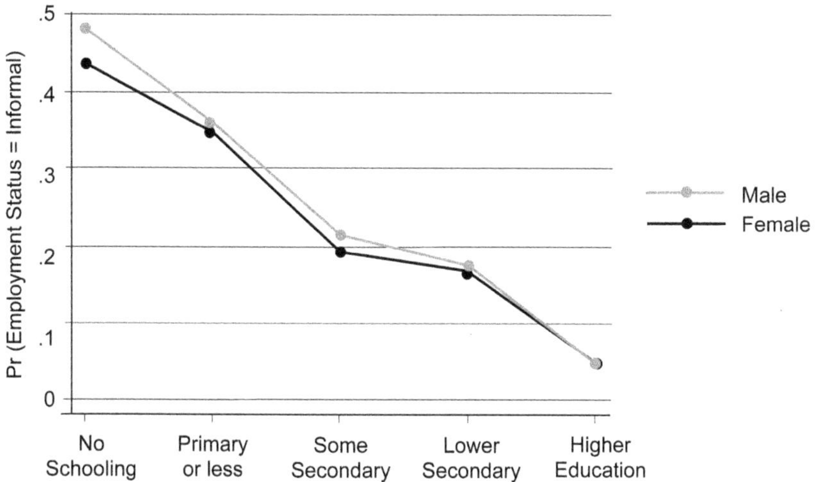

Figure 4.12 Adjusted probabilities of informal sector employment for male and female youths by educational attainment, 2011

Notes: Refer to Figure 4.10.

The figures highlight the importance of education in obtaining formal sector employment. The probability of formal sector employment increases with education for both men and women. The probability of informal sector employment decreases with educational attainment.

Figure 4.11 shows that there is no gender gap in obtaining informal sector employment. However, women are much more likely to be unemployed than employed in the formal sector relative to men at all educational levels. Figures 4.10–4.12 provide some insight into how the labour force decision is made across educational groups and across gender.

The high rates of unemployment and informal sector employment among youths with less than a secondary education are of particular interest. The informal sector absorbs the surplus labour that the formal sector is unable or unwilling to hire (Dasgupta and Ray, 1986). The fact that some workers are choosing unemployment over informal sector employment suggests either that the informal sector is undesirable, or that there are barriers to entry in the informal sector. Another explanation could be that the chances of finding formal sector employment are higher if the job search is done while not employed in the informal sector.

4.6.4 Education and occupational choice

Interestingly, in light of the many gender differences in the youth labour market, the pattern of employment is quite similar among highly educated men and women (Table 4.18). Individuals with higher education are most likely to work for the government. In 2011, approximately 50 per cent of

Table 4.18 Employment status distribution for employed urban male youths by education

(a) Male workers

Employment status	*No schooling*		*Primary or less*		*NC lower Secondary*		*C lower Secondary*		*Higher education*		*Other*		*Total*	
	1999	*2011*	*1999*	*2011*	*1999*	*2011*	*1999*	*2011*	*1999*	*2011*	*1999*	*2011*	*1999*	*2011*
Employee-govt	0.85	2.18	5.53	2.84	12.67	8.05	22.93	13.78	62.82	54.38	2.29	0.00	13.23	17.94
Employee-NGO	1.31	0.08	1.31	0.73	1.59	0.35	4.91	0.74	7.22	3.11	2.75	2.06	2.45	1.23
Employee-parastatal	0.27	0.40	1.54	1.35	3.19	1.94	4.29	2.46	4.92	2.70	0.59	0.00	2.34	1.85
Employee-private	32.69	36.70	27.74	37.97	26.72	35.41	28.70	36.31	16.86	22.56	29.73	25.71	27.65	33.51
Employer	0.61	0.52	0.38	0.78	0.63	1.33	0.60	0.86	0.28	0.26	0.23	0.00	0.48	0.69
Self-employed	40.34	47.82	41.86	40.68	32.91	33.58	26.56	33.50	5.99	11.32	45.64	56.48	35.03	32.18
Unpaid family	22.96	10.70	19.53	12.27	18.86	14.74	9.92	7.29	1.30	3.64	16.21	5.09	16.76	9.27
Apprentice	0.07	0.00	0.86	0.29	2.25	0.61	0.77	0.65	0.26	0.33	0.00	0.00	0.89	0.36
Cooperative	0.05	0.88	0.16	1.12	0.28	1.06	0.02	1.78	0.00	0.90	0.00	0.00	0.12	1.16
Other	0.87	0.72	1.10	1.96	0.91	2.92	1.30	2.63	0.34	0.80	2.56	10.66	1.05	1.80
Total	100.00	100.00	100.00	100.00	100.00	100.00	100.00	100.00	100.00	100.00	100.00	100.00	100.00	100.00

(continued on next page)

Table 4.18 (continued)

(b) Female workers

Employment status	*No schooling*		*Primary or less*		*NC lower Secondary*		*C lower Secondary*		*Higher education*		*Other*		*Total*	
	1999	*2011*	*1999*	*2011*	*1999*	*2011*	*1999*	*2011*	*1999*	*2011*	*1999*	*2011*	*1999*	2011
Employee-govt	1.06	1.25	4.17	2.53	12.46	5.36	29.70	15.85	65.77	52.49	2.21	0.00	10.09	15.73
Employee-NGO	0.61	0.29	1.12	0.35	3.47	1.70	5.13	1.64	6.19	4.80	3.42	0.00	1.95	1.61
Employee-parastatal	0.41	0.78	1.80	0.71	2.66	1.06	3.13	2.66	3.63	1.66	0.82	0.00	1.66	1.25
Employee-private	39.21	43.69	27.50	42.85	20.99	41.35	24.90	38.63	16.90	26.04	39.79	35.26	30.12	38.49
Employer	0.05	0.10	0.22	0.08	0.57	0.00	0.01	0.26	0.00	0.53	0.00	0.00	0.16	0.21
Self-employed	36.34	38.88	39.37	33.72	33.71	33.54	22.82	27.87	5.56	8.36	30.75	36.28	33.99	28.17
Unpaid family	20.21	12.86	23.95	17.08	25.27	12.42	11.66	11.15	1.28	4.50	17.91	28.45	20.09	12.23
Apprentice	0.01	0.00	0.27	0.01	0.26	0.00	1.34	0.07	0.65	0.69	0.00	0.00	0.33	0.17
Cooperative	0.07	0.11	0.04	0.59	0.40	1.78	0.09	0.88	0.00	0.41	0.00	0.00	0.09	0.56
Other	2.03	2.04	1.55	2.06	0.21	2.79	1.22	0.99	0.02	0.53	5.10	0.00	1.53	1.58
Total	100.00	100.00	100.00	100.00	100.00	100.00	100.00	100.00	100.00	100.00	100.00	100.00	100.00	100.00

Source: Labour Force Survey (1999); Urban Employment and Unemployment Surveys (2011). Authors' calculations.
Notes: NC, not completed; C, completed.

individuals with higher education were employed by the public sector. This is a decline from the approximately 60 per cent who were employed by the government in 1999. Roughly another quarter of highly educated youths find employment in the private sector. In contrast to the employment patterns for all youths, only a small fraction—about 15 per cent—of highly educated youths are self-employed or work as unpaid family labourers.

Employed youths with less education are very likely to be self-employed or unpaid family labourers. In 2011, about half of the young Ethiopians with a primary education or less were either self-employed or unpaid family workers. Even among youths who had completed lower secondary school, some 40 per cent were self-employed or unpaid family workers. The less educated have also benefited from a growing private sector. While self-employment shares between 1999 and 2011 have remained broadly similar, shares in the private sector have increased for each educational group.[18] The data suggest that women are benefiting the most from the growing private sector.

4.6.5 Returns to schooling

In this section we investigate the returns to education for wage labour.[19] We conducted two sets of regression analyses for men and women separately. The first set of regressions is a basic Mincer wage regression; we assume log hourly earnings are a linear function of education and age (Mincer, 1974).

$$LogW = \beta_o + \beta_1 S + \beta_2 age + \beta_3 age^2 + \varepsilon$$

The coefficient β_1 stands for the market return to an additional year of schooling.[20]

The second set of regressions investigates whether the returns to education increase discontinuously at different levels of completed education (Hungerford and Solon, 1987).

$$LogW = \beta_o + \beta_1 S + \beta_2 age + \beta_3 age^2 + \beta_4 D_8 + \beta_5 D_8 \cdot (S - 8) \\ + \beta_6 D_{12} + \beta_7 D_{12}(S - 12) + \varepsilon$$

We allow for the return to schooling to differ at $S = 8$ and 12. D_8 is a dummy showing whether the respondent has more than eight years of schooling. D_{12} is a dummy showing whether the respondent has more than 12 years of schooling. β_1 gives the return to the first seven years of schooling, $\beta_1 + \beta_4$ gives the return to completing primary school, $\beta_1 + \beta_5$ gives the return for completing grades 9–11, $\beta_1 + \beta_5 + \beta_6$ for completing secondary school, and $\beta_1 + \beta_5 + \beta_7$ gives the return for each year of education after secondary school.

Table 4.19 reports the results from the ordinary least-squares regressions. Columns 1 and 2 report the results for men; columns 3 and 4 report the

Table 4.19 Log wage regression, urban, 2011

	Men		*Women*	
	1	*2*	*3*	*4*
Age	0.061	0.056	0.057	0.046
	(0.008)***	(0.007)***	(0.010)***	(0.010)***
Age squared	–0.001	–0.001	0.000	0.000
	(0.000)***	(0.000)***	(0.000)***	(0.000)***
Years of schooling	0.118	0.034	0.124	0.045
	(0.003)***	(0.010)***	(0.003)***	(0.011)***
Completed primary		0.100		–0.080
		(0.061)		(0.081)
8–11 years of schooling		0.021		0.142
		(0.025)		(0.032)***
Completed secondary		0.224		0.059
		(0.064)***		(0.083)
12 + years of schooling		0.164		0.031
		(0.024)***		(0.033)
Constant	–1.988	–1.380	–2.296	–1.713
	(0.137)***	(0.141)***	(0.167)***	(0.165)***
Regional dummies	Yes	yes	yes	yes
R^2	0.38	0.43	0.45	0.50
N	7113	7113	3938	3938

Notes: Standard errors in parentheses. Sample consists of formal sector wage employees aged 15–65. Hourly wages are constructed by dividing monthly reported earnings by four times reported weekly earnings.

results for women. The sample consists of all individuals aged 15–65 who report working for the government, an NGO, a parastatal corporation or in the private sector in 2011. We exclude individuals who were employed in the informal sector. All the regressions include regional dummies. Columns 1 and 3 report the results from basic Mincer wage regressions for men and women, respectively. The return to an additional year of schooling is 11.8 per cent for men and 12.4 per cent for women. This is in accordance with what has been reported in the literature (Psacharopoulos, 1994; Psacharopoulos and Patrinos, 2002).

Columns 2 and 4 report the results from equation 4.2, where we allow for discontinuities in the return to completed years of schooling. Recent evidence has shown that the returns to education are not linear, but increase with higher levels of completed education (Bigsten *et al.*, 2000; Schultz, 2004). Figure 4.13 plots the corresponding returns. For men the returns for an additional year of schooling is 3.4 per cent for years 1–7. The return for completing primary school education jumps to 13.4 per cent. The return for each additional year in secondary school falls to 5.5 per cent, and then jumps again to 27.9 per cent for completing secondary education. The return for each additional year of education after secondary education is 21.9 per cent.

For women, the pattern is similar although, strikingly, the returns to completing primary education only are negative and are not statistically

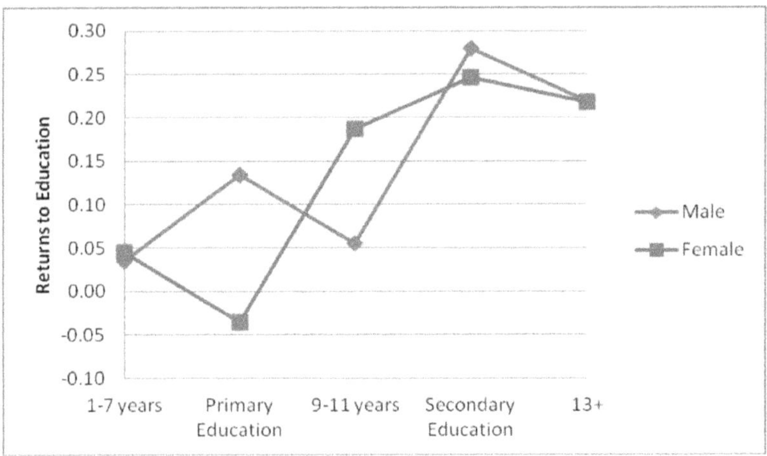

Figure 4.13 Returns to education, 2011

Notes: Estimates are from the estimated coefficients from regression equation (2) and reported in Table 4.11. The reported return to education provides the average increase

significant.[21] However, for each additional year of secondary school education, the returns are 18.7 per cent. The returns to women for completing secondary school education jump to 24.6 per cent. The returns for each additional year of education after secondary education are 21.8 per cent.

These results are similar to findings in other parts of Africa. Bigsten *et al.* (2000) report private returns of 3 per cent at the primary level, 10 per cent at the secondary level, and 35 per cent for tertiary using panel data from manufacturing firms in Cameroon, Ghana, Kenya, Zambia and Zimbabwe. Using household surveys from Ghana, Cote d'Ivoire, Kenya, South Africa, Nigeria and Burkina Faso, Schultz (2004) finds returns of 3–10 per cent for primary education and 10–15 per cent for higher education.

4.7 Labour market laws, regulations and institutions

We turn now from analysis to policy. Ethiopia's labour market institutions and laws focus mainly on the formal and wage employment sector. The informal sector and self-employment, despite being huge employers of youths, receive minimal attention in legislation or administrative regulations. This section surveys the relevant policies and institutions governing Ethiopia's formal labour market.

4.7.1 Labour legislation and regulations

In 1963, Ethiopia introduced for the first time a Labour Relations Proclamation, which coincided with the adoption of the civil code. This proclamation provided rules for the employment relationship and authorized the creation of workers' and employers' organizations. Proclamation No. 42/1993, which replaced the Labour Proclamation of 1975, brought significant change in the labour market. Changes included abolishment of central public sector employment, the end of guaranteed employment in the public sector for college and university graduates, the easing of conditions allowing temporary employment, the shortening of probation contracts from 90 to 45 days, and widening the range of cases where dismissal is not unlawful (De Gobbi, 2006).

The 1993 Labour Proclamation was amended by Labour Proclamation No. 377/2003, which is the act currently regulating the employment relationship. It differs from Proclamation No. 42/1993 in areas such as international labour standards and constitutional provisions. While Proclamation No. 377/2003 regulates the employment relationship in the private sector, Federal Civil Servants Proclamation No. 262/2002 contains rules on the employment relationship in the public sector. In addition to the national Labour Proclamations, since joining the International Labour Organization (ILO) in 1923, Ethiopia has also ratified a number of international labour market conventions.[22]

Under Proclamation No. 377/2003, a labour contract can be made for a definite or indefinite period, or for a specific task. A labour contract is presumed to be for an indefinite period unless specific conditions are met. Since the proclamation does not specify a time limit for which a temporary contract can be written, employers can repeatedly recruit employees for a limited duration, thereby avoiding the application of the higher protection standards provided to workers recruited with contracts for an indefinite period. According to the Federal Civil Servants Proclamation, employees in the public sector can be hired either temporarily or for an indefinite period.

Apprenticeship contracts are particularly important for the recruitment of young unemployed people. The Labour Proclamation establishes that the written contract must specify the nature and duration of the training, remuneration due to the trainee, and the conditions of work. According to the Federal Civil Servants Proclamation, permanent appointment requires a probation period of six months with a possible extension of three additional months in the public sector. The proclamation also provides provisions for temporary employment in the public sector for jobs that are not permanent in nature, or jobs are offered when the need arises.

Regarding the termination of employment contracts, Proclamation No. 377/2003 provides the legal basis for terminating employment contracts, which relates to the conduct of the employee, the ability of the worker to perform a task, and operational requirements of the undertaking. Lawful dismissal requires a notice period of 1–3 months, depending on the number of years of service of the employee in the organization.[23] The proclamation does not have provisions for a minimum wage. It stipulates that wages are to be negotiated between employers and employees at enterprise level.[24]

4.7.2 Labour market institutions

Ethiopia has very low unionization (MoLSA, 2009). The number of member-workers of the Confederation of Ethiopian Trade Unions (CETU) represents only 1 per cent of the total labour force. Labour unions of private employees and public enterprise employees (outside the civil service) are eligible to be members of CETU. Public workers under the civil services institutions (workers under government ministries) are not eligible to be members of CETU.

The predominance of agriculture as an employer and the informal nature of much of the economy are cited as the major reason for low levels of unionization (World Bank, 2007). Another reason for the low level of unionization, especially in the formal private sector, is that excess supply of labour diminishes the bargaining power of employees in favour of employers due to the risk of job loss. There is also very little enforcement of the collective bargaining provisions of the Labour Proclamation, especially in the private sector. According to the World Bank's 2002 firm-level Investment Climate Survey, labour regulations and relations are not regarded by firms as major business impediments (World Bank, 2007).

Institutions involved in the labour market in Ethiopia, apart from workers' and employers' groups, include the Ministry of Labour and Social Affairs (MoLSA), the Ministry of Youth Sports and Culture (MYSC), the Ministry of Education (MoE), the Ministry of Trade and Industry (MoTI), and the Central Statistical Agency (CSA). MoLSA is involved mainly in industrial relations, occupational safety and health for the employed. However, only public sector employees benefit from MoLSA's activities due to its capacity problems and workers' willingness to accept harsh work conditions, which is a result of high unemployment in urban areas. MoLSA's involvement in providing information to job seekers and employees is minimal. Job seekers have to rely on vacancy announcements on notice boards and in newspapers, and on family/friendship networks. Job centers that provide training and job market information to the unemployed are non-existent in Ethiopia.

The MYSC is involved in promoting youth development and participation in the country. The MYSC prepared the Youth Policy in 2004 to ensure youth participation in the country's development. The MoTI (recently divided into two as the Ministry of Trade and the Ministry of Industry) plays a key role in employment creation through the Micro and Small Enterprise Development Strategy of 1998, and the establishment of the Federal Micro and Small Enterprises Development Agency in 1998. The MoE plays an important role in employment creation by preparing youths for the labour market through general education, TVET and higher education. The TVET program is specifically tailored to the needs of micro and small enterprises (MSEs) and preparing youths for self-employment.

The Central Statistical Agency, the country's main data collection, organization and dissemination center, conducts various socio-economic surveys. The labour force surveys, urban employment/unemployment surveys, and household income and welfare surveys are useful sources of information on the labour market. However, there is no indication that policymakers are making adequate use of the outputs from the surveys. A study by the Ethiopian Economic Association (EEA, 2012) identifies lack of capacity in terms of human resources and information technology, as the main problems in proper collection, storage, dissemination and use of data on labour market outcomes.

4.7.3 Labour policy

In an attempt to align labour market policies with the national economic growth and poverty reduction strategies, the government prepared the National Employment Policy Strategy (NEPS) in 2009. The NEPS provides a framework to guide interventions aimed at improving employment and poverty outcomes (MoLSA, 2009). It seeks to address problems of unemployment; underemployment, poor working conditions and the lack of job protection—particularly in the informal sector—through a coordinated employment policy.

The Ethiopian government has introduced various policy reforms over the past two or so decades, which continue to impact on the country's economic performance and business environment, with significant bearing on the labour market. In particular, in 2010 the government issued two proclamations with important implication for market competition as well as for business entry, operation and exit: The Trade Practices and Consumer Protection Proclamation (TPCPP) No. 685/2010 and the Commercial Registration and Business Licensing Proclamation (CRBLP) No. 686/2010. Except for a few provisions (e.g. those dealing with price caps and hoarding), the TPCPP has not been implemented because the authority in charge of enforcing the law is not yet in place.

The CRBLP repealed an earlier version that had been introduced in 1997. The new proclamation was put into effect in 2011, requiring that all business activities have both a registration certificate and business license to undertake any business. This requirement is intended to promote formalization of business activities by encouraging self-employed businesses to register, which, in turn, has a direct impact on informal sector employment.

4.7.4 Employment policy in the five-year plans

We argued above that in Ethiopia, the five-year development plans are the main guidelines of government policy. Since 2005 the country's development plans have focused considerable attention on employment issues, especially for the young. The 2005/06–2009/10 Plan for Accelerated and Sustained Development to End Poverty (PASDEP) explicitly addressed labour market outcomes and unemployment, particularly youth unemployment. It stressed the need to create employment and income-earning opportunities for younger workers by incorporating into the plan the Education, Training and the Employment of Youth sections of the 2004 National Youth Policy (FDRE, 2004).

The PASDEP focused on job creation through the private sector. It placed particular emphasis on MSEs as an instrument of job creation based on their assumed potential to create employment opportunities. The plan also addressed improving the quality of education and integrating TVET with the job requirements of the economy. These were identified as key problems leading to rising unemployment, particularly in urban areas. Other initiatives included special efforts to provide skills training to the unemployed and to generate employment through public works (MoFED, 2006).

The current (2010/11–2014/15) development plan—the Growth and Transformation Plan—does not directly address the issue of youth unemployment. Rather, it deals with labour demand implicitly by targeting improved performance of the various sectors in the economy. The plan also addresses the economic and social challenges faced by women and youths. Private sector development continues to receive special attention as a strategy for tackling unemployment. As in the PASDEP, MSEs are singled out as potential employment creators and poverty reduction mechanisms. The plan also emphasizes tailoring TVET programs to the demands of the economy (MoFED, 2010).

4.8 New approaches to jobs and skills

Ethiopia has a youth 'employment problem'. Despite more than a decade of growth, the prospects of finding a job that can pay good wages and offer decent working conditions are slim, especially for the young. In this section we discuss a number of initiatives designed to boost the employment prospects of young Ethiopians. These are mainly 'supply-side' initiatives, although we discuss some temporary programs to address open unemployment. In the following section we turn to policy reforms designed to increase the demand for labour.

4.8.1 Addressing unemployment

Although open unemployment among Ethiopia's young is modest and confined to urban areas, accelerating rural–urban migration among the young will increase competition in urban labour markets and may increase pressures to address open unemployment—especially in light of the Arab Spring. The government can target young workers in employment-intensive activities such as tourism and construction with programs that offer cash for work. It can also experiment with increasing budget allocations to labour intensive public works. Public works programs provide good opportunities for young workers, particularly rural residents and people with low skills, to acquire initial work experience.

In Ethiopia the Integrated Housing Development Program aims to alleviate a pressing housing problem by deploying and supporting MSEs to construct low-cost houses. The program targets the unemployed poor indirectly, in that the MSE construction enterprises tend to be labour-intensive and to employ low-skilled workers. The participating MSEs are usually established by youths who have either graduated from technical training in construction, or have had some experience in the construction sector. The regional housing development offices give various forms of assistance to the firms participating in the program. They provide or subsidize a place to work, they provide training, and they subsidize machinery purchases.

The program was commissioned in 2004 and set an ambitious goal of constructing 400,000 low-cost condominium homes, creating job opportunities for 200,000 people, and promoting more than 10,000 MSEs all over the country by 2010. The intervention has not been rigorously evaluated but its early results are encouraging. By 2010, the program had constructed 171,000 houses, created 176,000 new jobs, raised the technical capacity of the construction sector, and enhanced the number and capacity of MSEs (UN-Habitat, 2011).

The Productive Safety Net Program (PSNP), started in 2005, is part of the Food Security Program of Ethiopia. It targets the most food-insecure and vulnerable areas with cash-for-work programs. Labour-deficient households (the elderly and disabled) receive unconditional transfers, while households with labour are offered employment in public works that benefit the community—such as building irrigation schemes and repairing schools and health centers—contributing to asset creation at the community level. PSNP exists mainly to address the food insecurity of households in rural Ethiopia, but it is also a labour-intensive public works program. The PSNP employs a significant number of workers in the areas where it operates. It is estimated that more than 1.2 million workers participate in the PSNP annually, making it the largest single employer in Ethiopia (Lieuw-Kie-Song, 2011).

4.8.2 Helping the young find better jobs

One way to deal with the early transition to work among those aged 15–19 would be to put in place programs to ease the income constraints of poor families, allowing students to remain in school. In Ethiopia, school attendance in rural areas rose after the introduction of a flexible school calendar that took into account the agricultural cycle. Conditional cash transfers—which transfer funds to poor families as long as their children attend school or after-school programs—have been shown to increase school enrolment and reduce child labour in Brazil and Mexico (Raju, 2006).

Active labour market policies—such as job search assistance, employability training, public support for apprenticeship and internship programs, and on-the-job training subsidies—can be used to increase the employability of young workers. The Cobblestone Project is an example of an employability program. It was initiated by the Engineering Capacity Building Program (ECBP), a government program supported by the German Development Cooperative (GTZ). Since 2007 the ECBP has been training men and women (mostly youths) in traditional crafting of cobblestone paving with the dual objective of creating jobs for youths and creating clean, attractive pavement in Ethiopian towns.

The program is based on the principle of using local resources in a labour-intensive manner to pave roads and public spaces using environmentally friendly techniques. The jobs created include quarrying, chiseling, transporting, laying of cobblestones and the production of tools. The construction of pavements in towns and cities increases mobility and housing investment. To date the project has created more than 2000 paving MSEs and has employed more than 90,000 (primarily young) workers in 140 towns.[25]

4.8.3 Technical and vocational education and training

An important feature of the new education and training policy introduced in 1994 was the attention given to TVET (MoE, 2002). Prior to 1994, education was generally perceived among the public as a means to obtain public sector employment.[26] The new education policy, on the other hand, in addition to addressing general education and higher education, identifies TVET in the various sectors of the economy as important avenues for enhancing productivity and employment generation, particularly in MSEs. The important feature of TVET in the new education system is its integration with MSEs. Not only is the TVET designed to meet the demands of MSEs, trainees are strongly encouraged to start their own MSEs.

The number of TVET institutions providing formal non-agriculture training increased from 17 in 1996–97 to 199 in 2004–05, and enrolment increased from 3000 to 106,305 (MoE, 2008). Little evaluation of the TVET scheme has taken place. Data from the labour force surveys show that between 1999 and 2005, there was an increase in vocational training and in the number of individuals obtaining specialized training. In 1999, only 12 per cent of youths reported having received a certificate for professional training. In 2011, the share receiving professional training was 23 per cent. For men there is a clear relationship between unemployment and certificate-holding in both years. Within each educational group (except for youths with no schooling in 1999), individuals who received a certificate for professional training had lower unemployment rates. For women, this relationship was less pronounced. Interviews with representatives from the Ethiopian Federation of Employers suggested that graduates of TVET centers were generally a better fit for posted jobs than graduates from universities. Vocational training may also play a significant role in innovation (Gebreeyesus, 2007). However, studies by the MoE indicate that, despite success in terms of high enrolment, many graduates remained unemployed. For this reason the 2008 National TVET Strategy emphasized quality and relevance of TVET, not just the number of graduates (MoE, 2008).

The experience of other countries in trying to equip young job seekers with better labour force skills may offer some guidance. Job training programs for early labour force entrants are more likely to be successful if they are part of a package that includes basic education, employment services and social services. A recent review of 19 training programs targeting youths shows that in the absence of such a package, training programs rarely improve the employment and earnings of young participants (World Bank, 2008). Well targeted and comprehensive training programs, such as Proyecto Joven in Argentina, Chile and Peru, have been successful in reaching the most vulnerable youths and improving their earnings and employment (World Bank, 2006).

In the longer term, the technical education system must be structured to teach the skills needed for the global marketplace. This argues for changes in curriculum and in teaching practices that are likely to be resisted by incumbent teachers. It also argues for increased provision by the private sector. A more market-oriented approach to training, that allows employers to shape the training they need with financial support from the government, is needed. This could be done through the use of training vouchers that can be redeemed with accredited private sector training providers, or through industry-led training centers (Adams, 2007). In Mauritius, for example, the Industrial Vocational Training Board has split the financing and provision of training and adopted a competitive model for procuring training services. Building program evaluation into such initiatives is essential.

4.8.4 Targeting young entrepreneurs

A more speculative area for public action would be to develop entrepreneurship initiatives targeted at the young. Young entrepreneurs face several constraints to creating a venture and making it grow. Some lack entrepreneurial skills, others lack access to information and networks, and almost all have difficulty accessing credit. Some type of prize competition that provides a small start-up grant to applicants with a viable business plan might serve as a complement to cash-for-work programs—especially among the more educated—and as a substitute for existing public employment programs. Programs that provide access to networks and information have been launched in some countries in Latin America and seem promising (e.g. Endeavour in Argentina, Brazil, Mexico and Uruguay). These programs would need to be time-bound, in the first instance to, say, three years, and be rigorously evaluated to prevent them from degenerating into permanent transfer programs.

4.8.5 Reforming education

Despite the increase in enrolments in Ethiopia—especially at the primary level—the out-of-school population has very low educational attainment (World Bank, 2008). Fifty-one per cent of the 15–24-year-olds in Ethiopia have a primary school education or less. Only 17 per cent have completed secondary school. This means that almost two-thirds of all young workers in the labour market lack the basic skills needed to be competitive in the labour force. At the post-primary level, employer surveys report that graduates are weak in problem-solving, business understanding, computer use and communication skills (World Bank, 2007).

The high rates of return to post-primary schooling clearly indicate that the labour market is rewarding increases in educational attainment beyond primary school completion. In the short run this suggests that the government should increase its focus on post-primary education. However, increasing education budgets for post-primary education will not be popular with Ethiopia's development partners, who remain transfixed by the Millennium Development Goal (MDG) of universal primary education. It would be appropriate for Ethiopia to open a dialogue with its development partners on a broader definition of educational attainment than the current MDG. The high private returns also suggest that private provision of post-primary education can be a viable alternative to increased public provision.

In the longer term, the education system must be restructured to teach the skills needed for the global marketplace. To address skills mismatch in labour supply and demand, the Ethiopian government recently introduced the 70/30 system, which allocates 70 per cent of all new public university entrants to natural science and engineering programs. The remaining 30 per cent are placed in the social sciences and business programs. This will require changes in curricula and teaching practices that are likely to be resisted by incumbent teachers. At present, individuals with higher education are most likely to work for the government, but over time the private sector has also taken an increasing share of educated youths. In 2011, approximately 50 per cent of individuals with higher education were employed by the public sector and another quarter by the private sector. To equip students to compete in the private sector, the quality of teachers and instruction must be raised.

4.9 Policies for job creation

For Ethiopia, the key to solving the youth employment problem is to solve its overall employment problem: the need for more rapid growth of good jobs. If the history of those countries that have successfully sustained growth, job creation and poverty reduction is any guide, creating such good jobs will require significant structural change (Kuznets, 1955; Chenery *et al.*, 1986).

4.9.1 Ethiopia's structural deficit

One of the most striking aspects of Ethiopia's recent economic history is how little structural change has taken place. Services constitute the second largest component of GDP, also contributing slightly over 40 per cent. Industry's share of GDP has remained essentially constant since 1981. A way to measure the extent of the structural change needed for more rapid job creation is to compare Ethiopia to a benchmark middle-income country, constructed from those economies that have been successful in sustaining growth and creating jobs. Such a benchmark economy was constructed using the sectoral shares of value added and employment in a sample of countries that have succeeded at sustained growth and job creation at the time when they crossed the World Bank defined lower-middle income threshold.[27]

Ethiopia's economic structure is far from that of a benchmark middle-income country, and reflects its very early stage of structural transformation. Agriculture is the largest sector in the economy, contributing over 40 per cent to GDP and 60 per cent of exports (World Bank, 2012). While the share of agriculture in GDP has declined since the mid-1990s, it still employs over 80 per cent of Ethiopians. The most striking differences occur in the shares of value added and labour in manufacturing. With a value added share of only 5 per cent of GDP, the share of manufacturing in total output is less than a quarter of the benchmark economy. Manufacturing's employment share is about half the benchmark value.

The structural gap between the benchmark country and Ethiopia is a measure of the potential for income growth through structural change. Table 4.20 summarizes the results of the following simple simulation. Assume that sectoral productivity levels in the African countries shown remain unchanged, but that the inter-sectoral distribution of employment changes to match that of the benchmark. The potential productivity gains from such a reallocation are substantial. On average, economy-wide productivity for the low income African countries in the sample would increase 1.3 times. Ethiopia's productivity would increase 1.6 times. If the structure of the Ethiopian economy were to shift to that of Africa's own middle-income countries, output per worker would more than double (Page, 2011). These numbers are indicative of the extent of dualism that marks the Ethiopian economy.

There is some potentially good news for Ethiopia as it attempts to close its 'structural deficit'. Margret McMillan and Dani Rodrik (2011) decompose labour productivity growth into within-sector and structural change—across-sectors—components and show that large differences in patterns of structural change across countries and regions account for much of the difference in their growth rates.[28] In particular, they demonstrate that since 1990, while Asian countries have had productivity-enhancing structural change, structural change in Africa has reduced overall productivity (Table 4.21). The movement of workers from higher-productivity to lower-productivity employment offset productivity improvements within sectors, reducing the overall rate of productivity growth.

Ethiopia is an exception to the African pattern. It has a relatively modest rate of productivity change within sectors, mainly reflecting the slow pace of productivity improvements in agriculture, but a substantial contribution to productivity growth from structural change. In fact, of the 1.9 per cent overall rate of productivity growth in the economy between 1990 and 2005, 1.5 per cent is due to shifts in employment from lower- to higher-productivity sectors. The challenge of creating good jobs, therefore, is primarily one of sustaining and accelerating the pace of structural change in the Ethiopian economy.

Table 4.20 Ethiopia's structural deficit, 2005

	VASH AGR	*VASH IND*	*VASH MFG*	*VASH SER*	*LSH AGR*	*LSH IND*	*LSH MFG*	*LSH SER*	*REL PROD AGR*	*REL PROD IND*	*REL PROD MFG*	*REL PROD SER*
BMK MIC	21.7	12.2	21.9	44.2	45.2	6.6	11.6	36.6	0.48	1.85	1.89	1.21
Ethiopia	43.9	7.8	5.1	43.2	80.3	1.5	4.8	13.4	0.55	5.2	1.06	3.22
Africa low-income sample	27.8	11.8	11.1	49.3	63.1	5.1	6.6	25.2	0.44	2.31	1.68	1.96
Africa middle-income sample	4.8	10.9	17.1	67.2	8.6	11.9	16.8	62.7	0.56	0.92	1.02	1.07
Africa resource-rich economies	17.8	29.6	8.3	21.1	45.4	4.8	6.5	43.4	0.39	6.17	1.28	0.49

Sources: McMillan and Rodrik (2011); World Development Indicators, http://data.worldbank.org/data-catalog/world-development-indicators; author's calculations.

Notes: Africa low-income sample: Ethiopia, Malawi, Ghana, Kenya, Madagascar, Mozambique, Senegal, Tanzania.
Africa middle-income sample: Mauritius, South Africa.
Africa resource-rich economies: Botswana, Lesotho, Nigeria, Namibia, South Africa.

Table 4.21 Role of structural change in productivity growth

Country/region	*Labour productivity growth (percentage)*	*Productivity growth within sectors (percentage)*	*Productivity growth due to structural change (percentage)*
Ethiopia	1.87	0.39	1.48
Asia	3.87	3.31	0.57
High-income	1.46	1.54	–0.09
LAC	1.35	2.24	–0.88
Africa	0.86	2.13	–1.27

Source: McMillan and Rodrik (2011); authors' calculations.

4.9.2 Structural change and private investment

Ethiopia's slow pace of structural change mainly reflects a failure of its economy to industrialize. Boosting the rate of growth of high value-added 'industries' in Ethiopia means increasing private investment in such industries. Domestic private investment has remained quite stable in Ethiopia since 2000 at less than 10 per cent of GDP, well below the levels found in East Asia, especially during periods of rapid structural change (Table 4.22). For Ethiopia, then, the crucial challenge in creating jobs for the young is increasing private investment in high value added per worker industries.

Ethiopia potentially can benefit from an opportunity that was not available to early industrializers: industry no longer needs 'smokestacks'. Falling transport and communication costs have created a class of economic activities in agriculture and services that more closely resemble manufacturing than the sectors to which they are assigned in economic statistics. This is potentially

Table 4.22 Private investment as a share of GDP, 1990–2009

	1990–94	*1995–99*	*2000–04*	*2005–09*
Ethiopia	6.1	7.2	9.0	7.0
Africa low-income countries	10.2	11.2	11.1	11.8
Africa middle-income countries	14.6	14.5	13.8	15.8
East Asia	24.9	19.9	12.4	16.8
Low-income countries	10.0	11.5	12.9	15.4
All developing countries	13.7	14.5	14.0	16.6

Sources: World Bank National Accounts Data *Open Data Catalogue*, http://datacatalog.worldbank.org; OECD National Accounts Statistics, http://www.oecd-ilibrary.org/economics/data/oecd-national-accounts-statistics_na-data-en; World Development Indicators, http://data.worldbank.org/data-catalog/world-development-indicators; authors' calculations.

Note: Entries are five-year averages in percentages.

good news. Agro-based industry and tradable services broaden the possibilities for growth-enhancing structural change.

Information and communications technologies have made many services tradable and separable from previously vertically integrated production. The range of business processes that can be globalized and digitized—including communication, banking, insurance and business-related services—is constantly expanding. Since the 1980s, the global trade in services has grown faster than the global trade in merchandise goods. The global agricultural value chain in flowers and horticultural crops is another industry without smokestacks.

Industries without smokestacks have many features in common with manufacturing. Like manufacturing, they benefit from technological advances that generate productivity growth. They exhibit similar tendencies for scale and agglomeration economies. The relationship between export and innovation activities is similar to that of manufacturing. But there are also differences. Tradable services, for example, are more skill-intensive than other types of economic activity. This makes them highly sensitive to education policies. High-value horticultural crops require excellent transportation infrastructure.

4.9.3 Targeting micro and small enterprises

The Ethiopian government has identified MSEs as key elements of its pro-poor economic growth strategy. The government has tried to adopt best practices from other countries to help transform existing small enterprises into medium-level enterprises. Efforts have also been under way to facilitate production, create market linkages and help value-chain development among small enterprises. With support from the government of Germany, the Federal Micro and Small Enterprises Development Agency (FeMSEDA) has started providing industry extension services and business development services (consulting, training, etc.) to MSEs.

Ethiopia is not alone in this. Small firms are big business in the aid industry. Why? In a word: jobs. When a cut-off of 100 employees is used, MSEs employ about 50 per cent of workers in the median country worldwide and nearly 60 per cent of workers in low income countries. In the median African country, about 47 per cent of gross new jobs were created in firms with 5–19 workers (Page and Soderbom, 2012). In their recent paper, John Page and Mans Soderbom ask whether programs targeted to MSEs are the best way to create jobs in Africa.[29] To answer the question, they use in part an almost unique (for Africa) panel of data on Ethiopian firms.

Attempts to assess the job-creating potential of small firms are bedeviled by a number of important problems. The first and most critical is to distinguish between gross and net job creation. Small firms indisputably create new jobs, but evidence—mainly from high-income countries—shows that they can also destroy jobs through higher failure rates. If small firms have higher mortality rates, ignoring firms' exits will tend to exaggerate their role in creating net new jobs. Understanding net job creation for firms of any size requires longitudinal (panel) firm-level data that record exit and entry. Unfortunately, for developing countries in general, and for Africa in particular, such data are very scarce.

The focus on job creation also begs another important question: what is the quality of jobs created? High failure translates into high job turnover, and there is a large body of empirical evidence from developed and developing countries showing that large firms offer much higher wages than small firms, even when differences in worker education and experience and the nature of the industry are considered (Page and Soderbom, 2012). If the objective of policy toward MSEs is not just to create any job, but to create a *good* job—in terms of wages, employment duration and working conditions—the quality of jobs is also relevant.

Unlike most other African countries, Ethiopia has collected a lot of data on performance and employment in the manufacturing sector across all sizes of firms. Most of the data derive from surveys conducted by the CSA. The most comprehensive dataset is that based on the Large and Medium Manufacturing Industries Survey (LMMS), which attempts to cover all manufacturing establishments in the country that engage 10 persons or more and use power-driven machinery. The survey is conducted every year. In 2007–08 it covered a total of 1930 firms, 71 per cent of which had fewer than 50 employees (CSA, 2010).

By international standards, most firms included in the LMMS would be categorized as small firms. Total employment was 133,673 individuals, which amounts to only about 0.4 per cent of Ethiopia's total workforce and 7 per cent of those employed in the formal sector. Although from the point of view of 'where the jobs are' this class of firms currently plays a small role in Ethiopia, the LMMS is the only dataset that contains information on firms and their development over several years.[30] From the point of view of employment policy, where it is critical to shed light on the employment dynamics of small and large firms, the LMMS data are unique.

Page and Soderbom (2012) combine all LMMS datasets from 1995/06 to 2006/07. This yields nearly 10,000 firm-year observations. To tackle the survival problem, they focus exclusively on the subsample of new entrants over the 1995/06–2005/06 period. There is enormous diversity in the growth outcomes of Ethiopian firms. The most common outcome, however, is to go out of business relatively soon after start-up, especially for small firms. Firms that survive often grow—especially smaller firms—and smaller firms grow faster than large firms. On the face of it this is apparently good news for proponents of MSE programs.

But in fact the results of Page and Soderbom (2012) provide a cautionary tale for enthusiasts of MSEs. Although they find that those small firms that survive grow faster than large firms, when they take into account the significantly lower survival rates of small firms, they find that expected job growth for large and small firms is essentially the same. Put another way, a job created today in a new small firm is more likely to disappear in six to eight years than a job created in a new large firm, but because those small firms that survive create more jobs, the number of new workers hired by small and large firms over the same period will be about the same.

Their results suggest quite clearly that the view, common in Ethiopia, that small firms grow employment faster than large ones can be very misleading if survival rates are not taken into account. Because of higher rates of firm mortality, MSEs in Ethiopia are not a superior source of job creation. Moreover, the jobs that small firms in Ethiopia create are less attractive than those in larger enterprises. Small firms have higher job turnover and persistently lower wages than larger firms.

Employment policy must target those firms that are successful at creating 'better' jobs. Page and Soderbom (2012) tell us—not surprisingly—that growing firms regardless of size are the ones that create net new employment and offer the potential for wage growth. But size alone cannot predict which firms will grow. We know that a small firm is more likely to fail than a larger one, despite the fact that if the small firm survives, it will grow faster. This argues in the first instance for policies and programs that reduce the constraints to the growth of firms, regardless of size.

4.9.4 Improving the investment climate

In Ethiopia, job growth—whether in manufacturing or industries without smokestacks—depends on the rapid expansion of competitive firms of all sizes. One set of public actions to support industrial development is largely non-controversial and size-neutral. It includes mainly policies and investments directed at improving the 'investment climate'—the regulatory, institutional and physical environment within which firms operate.

Regulatory reform

Since the 1990s, private sector development efforts in Africa have focused on improving the investment climate. The high costs of doing business in Africa have been well documented in a decade of comparative research reports sponsored by the World Bank and the World Economic Forum.[31] Overall, these reports conclude that the cost of doing business in Africa is 20–40 per cent above that for other developing regions. Investment climate reforms are therefore central to the success of any strategy to create jobs.

Ethiopia is no exception. In 2012, Ethiopia's rank in the World Bank's *Doing Business* indicators was 111 (where 1 = best and 183 = worst). Ethiopia must do better at doing business. However, some donors—notably the World Bank—have focused their policy dialogue with individual countries in Africa on the narrow range of regulatory issues embodied by *Doing Business*, and this has diverted both the international community and policymakers from deeper diagnosis of the constraints to faster industrial growth.

Doing Business was not designed to be used as a country-level diagnostic tool; it is a 'league table' or cross-country benchmarking exercise. Moreover, seven of its nine indicators 'presume that lessening regulation is always desirable' (World Bank, 2008; p. xv). Changes in the *Doing Business* rankings are properly viewed as an outcome of a regulatory reform process, not as a guidebook. A more informed analysis of the regulatory constraints to private investment is urgently needed—one based on structured feedback from the private sector.

Ethiopia has a successful example of such close coordination in its cut flowers sector. It was a late entrant into East Africa's cut flower export industry, but it has achieved notable success. Government action in the industry's early days contributed substantially to its ability to break into global markets and enhanced medium-term growth prospects. Monthly meetings, involving representatives of the firms then involved, took place with both the Minister of Industry and the Prime Minister present. Firms were free to identify barriers to their growth and development, and action points were agreed upon. The action points led to prompt and effective action. Implementation of agreed actions was monitored in succeeding meetings, and a public record of actions taken by government was available to all firms (Sutton and Kellow, 2010).

Replication of the successful experience of close coordination in cut flowers should be possible, but it is not guaranteed. A similar program in metals and plastics failed to spur more rapid development of the sector.

Closing the infrastructure gap

Like much of low-income Africa, Ethiopia suffers from a large infrastructure deficit. Evidence from enterprise surveys suggests that infrastructure constraints are responsible for an estimated 50 per cent of the productivity handicap faced by Ethiopian firms. Power is the infrastructure constraint that weighs by far most heavily on Ethiopian firms. Nearly 80 per cent of the firms surveyed by the World Bank in its Enterprise Survey ranked availability and reliability of power as the most binding constraint to enterprise growth. Transport ranked second, considered as the binding constraint by 10 per cent of firms (Escribano *et al.*, 2010).

In recent years, Ethiopia has made significant progress in infrastructure. Its infrastructure indicators compare relatively well with low-income country peers. Ethiopia's infrastructure spending as a share of GDP is among the highest in Africa. It currently devotes 10 per cent of GDP to infrastructure, which is higher than the average for low-income countries and for its East African neighbours. In recent years it has dedicated 3 per cent of GDP to road investments. This is one of the highest GDP shares in Africa, although the absolute value of this spending (approximately \$5 per capita annually) is comparable with what other East African countries are investing (Foster and Morella, 2010).

Ethiopian Airlines is one of the three main African airlines, and has fostered the development of an associated regional air transport hub. The government has launched an ambitious investment program to upgrade its network of trunk roads and is establishing a modern funding mechanism for road maintenance. But much remains to be done. The country's greatest infrastructure challenge lies in the power sector, where a doubling of current capacity will be needed over the next decade, both to serve a growing national market and to permit exports of hydro-power to neighbouring countries. In transport, the key challenge is to improve Ethiopia's exceptionally low levels of rural roads and to ensure that recent investments in the road network receive adequate maintenance (Foster and Morella, 2010).

Coverage of information and communications technology (ICT) services in Ethiopia is the lowest in Africa. GSM signals cover barely 10 per cent of the population, compared with 48 per cent for the low-income country average. International call charges are substantially higher than the African average. Ethiopia has failed to modernize its institutional and regulatory framework in ICT. The central challenge is to introduce competition to the sector. By awarding a second mobile license alone, the country could rapidly expand its mobile penetration rates and raise an estimated $0.5 billion in revenue (Foster and Morella, 2010).

The Infrastructure Consortium for Africa estimates that closing Ethiopia's infrastructure deficit will require sustained annual expenditure of $5.1 billion over the next decade. This level of investment is more than 40 per cent of GDP and is three times the current infrastructure spending of around $1.3 billion. The power sector alone would require $3.3 billion per year.

4.10 Strategy for structural change

Improving the investment climate is a major step toward generating growth and jobs, but private investment will also need to flow into high value-added activities. As the successful experience of East Asia demonstrates, once a critical minimum threshold is crossed, industrial growth can be explosive. But industry is lumpy in size, space and time, and threshold effects are important. Below the threshold, marginal changes in policies and investments—the centerpiece of investment climate reform—may not yield results. Ethiopia needs an industrialization strategy to complement efforts to reform labour markets and improve the investment climate. Three important strategic initiatives appear to offer some promise. These are: pushing exports, building capabilities, and supporting industrial clusters.

4.10.1 Pushing exports

For Ethiopia—as for the vast majority of Africa's economies—the export market represents the only option for rapid growth of manufacturing, agro-industry and high value-added services. More than two-thirds of Ethiopia's

Table 4.23 Share of light manufactures in exports

Country/region	*Manufactured exports as a share of total exports*		*Light manufactures as a share of total exports*	
	1990–94	*2005–09*	*1990–94*	*2005–09*
Ethiopia	22	13	10	9
Cambodia	22	90	21	89
China	81	90	56	35
India	51	54	41	29
Indonesia	27	38	19	16
Lao PDR	33	34	32	22
Vietnam	23	58	21	43

Source: UNIDO (2011).

exports are primary commodities, mainly coffee. It has had little success in manufactured exports. Table 4.23 compares Ethiopia's manufactured and light manufactured export performance with that of a number of African and Asian economies. Ethiopia has very low shares of manufactured exports in total exports (13 per cent), and light manufactured exports in total exports (9 per cent), in comparison with the Asian economies that have succeeded in rapid creation of good jobs. What may be more disturbing is that the share of manufactured exports in total exports actually declined between 1990–94 and 2005–09.

Ethiopia's apparel sector currently generates only US$8 million in exports and 9000 jobs, compared with US$2.3 billion exports and 600,000 jobs in Vietnam, a country of similar size. Only a handful of large firms (employing about 1000 workers) have managed to export apparel—mostly non-time-sensitive, low-value items. But detailed comparative value-chain analysis shows that Ethiopia has the potential to become globally competitive in apparel (Dinh *et al.*, 2012). Despite having some of the best hides in the world due to climate conditions, performance in the leather products industry is as poor as in apparel. Exports in 2010 were US$8 million and employment is only 8000, mostly in small firms producing low-quality items for the domestic market.

Breaking into export markets will require an export push: a concerted set of public investments, policy and institutional reforms focused on increasing the share of non-traditional exports in GDP. The distinguishing feature of an export push is that it must be a whole-government initiative. Macroeconomic policy must play a key role. While it is unlikely that Ethiopia will find it possible to undertake exchange rate protection of the tradables sector, it would be good to encourage policy debate within the government on the pros and cons of such a policy.[32] At a minimum, coherent macro-policies designed to prevent excessive appreciation are essential for a globally competitive export sector. Public expenditure programs need to be evaluated and prioritized in terms of their contribution to achieving global competitiveness, and the structure of incentives must be tilted to the extent possible in the direction of export promotion, through institutional, regulatory and trade policy reforms.

Trade policy reforms are the first area for attention in developing an export push. Anti-export bias arising from tariff and non-tariff protection of domestic producers acts an implicit tax on exports. Here there is some good news: since the early 1990s, at the border policy reforms in Ethiopia have significantly reduced anti-export bias. But surveys of manufacturing firms highlight a number of areas in which regulatory or administrative burdens fall especially hard on exporters. In leather and footwear, for example, the most binding constraint is the shortage of quality processed leather. With full liberalization of leather imports, Ethiopia would already be in a position to be globally competitive. Enabling import of high-quality processed leather would be a quick and easy solution to the acute shortage of leather in the industry. Removing restrictions on exports of leather would increase the incentives to invest in the Ethiopian leather supply chain.

Improving trade logistics is vital. Trade in tasks has greatly increased the importance of 'beyond-the-border' constraints to trade. Because new entrants to task-based production tend to specialize in the final stages of the value chain, 'trade friction costs'—the implicit taxes imposed by poor trade logistics—are amplified. Ethiopia ranks of 141 out of 155 countries in the recently compiled World Bank (2012) Trade Logistics Index. There is a correlation between income level and trade logistics performance. As one of Africa's poorest countries, Ethiopia might be expected to perform poorly relative to higher income countries, but it also performs poorly relative to its predicted performance based on income. Ethiopia scores poorly on all major dimensions of trade logistics performance, but it scores worst on the dimensions of quality and competence, and tracking and tracing.

These constraints directly reduce Ethiopia's ability to compete. The binding constraint to Ethiopia's global competitiveness in apparel is poor trade logistics, which nearly eliminate Ethiopia's wage advantage. Poor trade logistics also exclude Ethiopia from the higher value time-sensitive segments of the market—elapsed time between order and delivery exceeds 90 days and remains unpredictable (Dinh *et al.*, 2012).

4.10.2 Attracting and building capabilities

In most industries, capability is the tacit knowledge or working practices possessed jointly by the individuals who comprise the firm's workforce (Sutton, 2005). These are the know-how or behaviours that are used either in the course of production or in developing new products. Most often, capability is not codified in a piece of knowledge that can be embodied in a blueprint or technology, and the process of acquiring and building capabilities consists of two phases. The first phase involves the introduction of a higher level of capability to some firm or group of firms. The second phase consists of the spillover of capabilities to firms within and outside the host industry, mainly through supply-chain relationships.

Globally, firms are competing in capabilities. Firms are able to enter global markets when their capabilities reach a level that allows them to compete successfully with other producers in price and quality. To succeed in industrialization, Ethiopia will need to attract and build more capable firms. Public policy has a role to play in acquisition and transfer of the knowledge of the working practices and organization needed to compete in global industry.

The initial introduction of a higher level of capability is often a result of foreign direct investment (FDI). An 'Enterprise Map' of the 50 most successful industrial firms in Ethiopia revealed, for example, that half of the successful enterprises were owned by foreigners who brought the required capabilities with them (Sutton and Kellow, 2010). Ethiopia's record in attracting FDI has generally been poor. The amount of FDI flowing into the country has been very small, both in per capita terms and as a share of the total FDI inflow into Sub-Saharan Africa. The share of FDI inflows to Ethiopia as a share of the total FDI inflows to Sub-Saharan Africa in 2001 was just 0.2 per cent. Of the FDI-financed projects licensed in Ethiopia, a significant majority (estimated at more than four-fifths) have not been implemented (Dinh *et al.*, 2012).

Policies and institutions for attracting FDI are therefore a key tool in capability building. The work of Ireland's Industrial Development Authority in the 1960s provided an institutional model for attracting and keeping FDI that has become international best practice over the past 20 years. Approaches similar to that used in Ireland have been central to FDI policy in a wide range of countries from Jordan to Singapore; they are not yet found in Ethiopia. Reform of the Foreign Investment Authority to global standards of good practice should receive high priority.

In some international markets—apparel and agro-industry, for example—exchanges of information between suppliers and buyers with a reputation for high quality are well developed and add to the capabilities of supplying firms. For this reason, an export push is strongly complementary to the process of acquiring capabilities. Demanding buyers and repeated relationships are characteristic of many global markets in industry, and promote learning by exporting.

Transmission of capabilities to other firms within an economy most often takes place through vertical supply-chain relationships. In many industries there is a close and continuing contractual relationship between buyer and supplier, which often involves a two way movement of technical and engineering personnel between their respective plants. Removing obstacles to the formation of vertical value-chain relationships is therefore a critical task for government.

4.10.3 Supporting agglomerations

Manufacturing and service industries tend to concentrate in geographical areas—usually cities—driven by common needs for inputs and access to markets, knowledge flows and specialized skills. A large empirical literature has documented the significant productivity gains to firms from industrial agglomeration. One major contribution to this literature documents the productivity-enhancing impact of industrial clusters in Ethiopia (Siba *et al.*, 2012).

Because of the productivity boost that agglomerations provide, starting a new industrial location is a form of collective action problem. If a critical mass of firms can be persuaded to locate in a new area, they will realize productivity gains, but no single firm has the incentive to locate in a new area in the absence of others. Because Ethiopia has few large-scale, modern industrial agglomerations, it is more difficult for its existing firms to compete, and more difficult to attract new industry.

For this reason, spatial industrial policies should be a third, complementary area of public action. Case studies indicate that governments can foster industrial agglomerations by concentrating investment in high-quality institutions, social services and infrastructure in a limited physical area—such as a special economic zone (SEZ). Spatial policies may also play a role in the transfer and diffusion of firm capabilities. High-capability firms tend to locate among other high-capability firms (Krugman and Venables, 1995). Countries that have been successful in building firms' capabilities through their SEZ programs have had an ongoing exchange between the domestic economy and activities based in the zone, through investment in the zone by domestic firms, forward and backward linkages, and the movement of skilled labour and entrepreneurs between the zone and the domestic economy.

To date, Ethiopia's experience with spatial industrial policy has been largely unsuccessful. The SEZs have failed to reach the critical threshold levels of physical, institutional and human capital needed to solve the collective action problem of industrial location. Existing SEZs have low levels of investment and exports, and their job-creation impact has been limited. The zones have few links with the domestic economy, and they have a much lower density of enterprises within the geographical boundaries of the SEZ than the zones in Asia or Latin America. Ethiopia has recently embarked on a major policy and legal reform agenda for SEZs, with technical support from the World Bank and the IFC.

China's Ministry of Commerce is supporting the development of six economic and trade cooperation zones in five African countries, of which Ethiopia is one. In addition to contributing to China's Africa Initiative, the zones are intended to help China's own restructuring by encouraging labour-intensive industries, such as textiles, leather goods and building materials, to move offshore. The official zones involve three parties: the Chinese government, Chinese developers and the host government. The Chinese government has not involved itself in the design or direct operation of the zones, but it has organized marketing events in China to promote investment in them. The Chinese Eastern Industry Zone outside of Addis Ababa is one of the six official zones. If successful, it may point the way toward a more effective design for spatial industrial policy in Ethiopia.

The zone in Ethiopia is 100 per cent Chinese-owned. The Chinese zone developers are obliged to construct high-standard infrastructure, promote the zone, and bring in world-class professional management. The Ethiopian government is expected to provide infrastructure outside the zone, including guaranteed supplies of electricity, water and gas, roads leading up to the zones, and improved port services (Brautigam and Tang, 2011a, b).

It is too early to evaluate whether this new initiative will succeed. Originally, the park planned to attract 80 projects in five years and create 10,000–20,000 jobs for Ethiopians. The Ethiopian zone was probably the slowest of the six zones in Africa to get going. It suffered through a number of changes in ownership structure and a financial restructuring, but it is moving ahead more quickly now. The single factory on the site (producing cement) is owned by the zone developers. Apparently profits from the factory are helping them overcome capital shortages experienced in earlier years, enabling accelerated infrastructure development. Eleven enterprises with US$91 million total investment have signed letters of intent to move in. These enterprises cover such industries as construction materials, steel products (plates and pipes), home appliances, garments, leather processing and automobile assembly (Brautigam, 2011a, b).

There are some warning signs, however, that point to the possibility that the potential of the new SEZ may not fully be realized. For example, there is no evidence that the Ethiopian government has made efforts to develop supplier programs or other close links between the domestic private sector and the zones. In contrast to trends in China, no efforts appear to have been designed specifically to encourage synergies with local universities or technology institutes (Brautigam and Tang, 2011b).

4.11 Conclusions

Ethiopia's 'employment problem' is a deficiency of good jobs. Rapid population growth has resulted in rapid growth of the labour force and increasing pressures on the job market, especially for the young. In Ethiopia, the way in which this pressure is felt is through a combination of low unemployment coupled with underemployment and high informality. In such a case, the solution to the employment problem cannot be found in employment policies alone.

In the short run, active labour market policies such as job-search assistance, employability training, public support for apprenticeship and internship programs, and on-the-job training subsidies can be used to increase the employability of young workers. A more speculative area for public action is to develop entrepreneurship initiatives targeted at the young. In the longer run, labour regulations that determine social insurance contributions and protect job security must be addressed.

Improving the skills and problem-solving capacity of Ethiopia's workers will require education reforms. The education system must be restructured to build the skills needed to compete globally, largely through further increases in access to post-primary education. This argues for changes in curricula and in teaching practices. It also argues for changes in TVET, including increased provision by the private sector.

On the labour demand side, Ethiopia faces a structural deficit—the result of two-and-a-half decades of lack of industrialization. Without an acceleration of structural change, Ethiopia's recent growth turn-around runs the risk of not creating enough good jobs. Meeting the challenge of industrialization will need new thinking. Investment climate reforms need to be prioritized and refocused. Urgent action is needed to address Ethiopia's growing infrastructure gap.

Investment climate reforms alone may not be enough to overcome the advantages of the world's existing industrial locations. A strategy for industrial development also will be needed. Public policy should focus on three interrelated objectives—creating an export push, building firm capabilities and supporting agglomerations—to boost the creation of good jobs for Ethiopian workers, young and old.

Notes

1 Funding for some of the work was provided by the International Growth Centre.
2 Under the current land tenure system, land is under government ownership and households are granted usufruct rights. Households migrating to urban areas are required to abandon their rights to agricultural land. This, coupled with scant work opportunities in urban areas, has resulted in low rural–urban migration in Ethiopia compared with elsewhere in Africa (Dorosh and Schmidt, 2010).
3 All regional groupings of countries used in this paper (e.g. East Asia) conform to the World Bank standard regional definitions.
4 According to the 2007 census, about a third of the population are 9 years or younger. In urban areas youth (15–29 years of age) account for well over a quarter of the population.
5 Unemployment rates in Africa are likely to be underestimated because the ILO excludes people who were not working, were not actively looking for work, but say they would take a job if one were offered.
6 The exceptions being that in 1999 only three zones were covered in the Affar Region and only three zones in the Gambella Region. In 2005, only the urban area was covered in the Gambella Region and only two zones in the Affar Region. In 1999 and 2005, only three zones in Somali Region were covered.
7 The larger sample size in the 1999 and 2005 samples are due to the inclusion of both the rural and urban parts of the country surveyed in the labour force survey, whereas the 2009 and 2011 urban employment and unemployment survey sample covers only the urban parts of the country.
8 Unpaid household chores, such as preparing food, cleaning the house, taking care of children and collecting firewood for own consumption, are not considered in the category of economic activity.
9 The formal definition of underemployment as defined by ILO (1997) requires the respondent not only to be available and ready to work, but also to have worked less than the normal duration of work. We exclude the latter requirement in our definition of underemployment.
10 Availability in this situation is tested by asking the willingness to take up work for wage or salary in locally prevailing terms, or readiness to undertake self-employment activity, given the necessary resources and facilities.
11 Because we use a broad definition of unemployment, discouraged workers are included as labour force participants if they are available to work.

12 In this chapter 'Ethiopians' refers to people residing in Ethiopia.

13 In the 1999 labour force survey, most rural individuals who reported their employment status as self-employed or unpaid family worker were coded as informal sector workers, as most had not met the requirements for formal sector employment (book of accounts, more than 10 employees and business with a license). However, in 2005 most self-employed and unpaid family workers reported that their place of employment was in the formal sector (i.e. meeting at least one of the requirements for formal sector employment). We have recoded all rural self-employed and unpaid family workers as being employed in the informal sector. As not all self-employed and unpaid family workers in 1999 were informal sector workers, the national and rural informal sector rates may slightly overestimate the share of informal sector workers.

14 Based on the 2007 census, 16 per cent of Ethiopia's residents live in urban areas. Harari, Addis Ababa and Dire Dawa regions each had urban population shares greater than 50 per cent. In Gambella Region, approximately 25 per cent of residents live in urban areas.

15 The multinomial logit regression models the labour force participation decision as a multi-choice decision instead of a binary choice decision. We model the labour force participation decision as a choice between working in the formal sector, working in the informal sector, or being unemployed.

16 The regressions do not control for non-labour income or the wage offer, which are important factors affecting the decision to work.

17 David Mains' (2011) ethnographic study on urban youth unemployment details the perceptions held by many youth that education opened up opportunities for employment. In particular, the author details the social stigma associated with working in the informal sector for educated youth and youth from well off families.

18 Haile (2008) suggests that self-employment in Ethiopia is largely a route out of unemployment.

19 Monthly earnings are not available for self-employed workers.

20 According to convention we refer to the estimated coefficient as the return to schooling, but it is not the true rate of return as it is not compared with the cost of education. The coefficient actually provides the average increase in wages that someone with an extra year of education earns.

21 The negative return to completing primary education should be interpreted with caution, as the point estimate on the dummy for completing primary education is not significantly different from zero.

22 Ethiopia has ratified the eight fundamental ILO conventions that are considered key principles and rights at work. It has not yet ratified the four 'priority ' instruments that consist of Labour Inspection Convention, Employment Policy Convention, Labour Inspection (Agriculture) Convention, and Tripartite Consultation (International Labour Standards) Convention.

23 The 2003 Labour Proclamation was amended slightly in 2006 with Labour (Amendment) Proclamation No 494/2006.

24 Wages of public workers under the civil service institutions (government ministries) are determined by the Federal Ministry of Civil Services.

25 Mains (2012) provides a brief discussion of the cobblestone project and how it has been perceived by urban youth.

26 The previous government had established job guarantees for all university graduates. In 1983 the public sector employed 73 per cent of those in wage employment (Krishnan *et al.*, 1998).

27 China (2000), India (2007), Indonesia (2004), Korea (1968), Malaysia (1968), Philippines (1976) and Thailand (1987).

28 We are grateful to Margaret McMillian for making the data available.

29 Page and Soderbom (2012) are not able to deal with microenterprises because the Ethiopian statistical office does not collect panel data on them. However, the periodic surveys of microenterprises conducted suggest that the findings for small enterprises carry over to microenterprises.

30 Other surveys exist too. Manufacturing enterprises that use power-driven machinery and engage fewer than 10 people are covered in the Small-Scale Manufacturing Industries Survey. To date, three rounds of this survey are available, generating data for 2001/02, 2005/06 and 2007/08. Estimates are that a total number of 43,338 such microenterprises existed in 2007/08, employing 139,000 people, which corresponds to 0.4 per cent of Ethiopia's workforce. Unfortunately there is not enough information in these data to enable researchers to construct a panel dataset; hence the data are not well suited for analysis of enterprise dynamics. In addition, there exist enterprises that do not use power to produce output. Such enterprises form the cottage and handicraft sector, which is the technologically least sophisticated segment of manufacturing in Ethiopia. This sector engages substantially more people than manufacturing firms with power-based production. The latest available figures, which are for 2002, indicate that there are 974,676 cottage and handicraft establishments engaging a total of 1,306,865 individuals (CSA, 2003, cited by Gebrehiwot and Wolday, 2006). Fewer data are available for non-farm sectors outside manufacturing. No comprehensive survey of the service or trading sectors appears to have been fielded to date.

31 See for example the *Doing Business* surveys of the World Bank or the *World Competitiveness Report* of the World Economic Forum.

32 See Page (2012a) for a discussion of the pros and cons of exchange rate protection as a means of subsidizing African exports.

References

Adams, A.V. (2007) *The Role of Youth Skills Development in the Transition to Work A Global Review.* Washington, DC: Human Development Network, Children and Youth Department, World Bank.

AfDB (2012) *Youth Employment in Africa.* Tunis: African Development Bank.

Bigsten, A., Collier, P., Dercon, S. *et al.* (2000) 'Rates of Return on Physical and Human Capital in Africa's Manufacturing Sector,' *Economic Development and Cultural Change*, 48(4): 801–27.

Bigsten, A., Collier, P., Dercon, S. *et al.* (2004) 'Do African Manufacturing Firms Learn from Exporting?', *Journal of Development Studies*, 40(3): 115–41.

Brautigam, D. (2011) *Economic Statecraft in China's New Overseas Special Economic Zones.* Washington, DC: International Food Policy Research Institute. www.ifpri.org/publication/economic-statecraft-china-s-new-overseas-special-economic-zones.

Brautigam, D. and Tang, X. (2011a) 'African Shenzhen: China's Special Economic Zones in Africa', *Journal of Modern African Studies*, 49(1): 27–54.

——(2011b) 'China's Investment in Special Economic Zones in Africa', in Thomas Farole and Gokhan Akinci (eds), *Special Economic Zones: Progress, Emerging Challenges and Future Directions.* Washington, DC: World Bank.

Chenery, H.B., Robinson, S., Syrquin, M., World Bank *et al.* (1986) *Industrialization and Growth: A Comparative Study.* New York: Oxford University Press.

CSA (1999) *Ethiopian Labor Force Survey.* Addis Ababa: Central Statistical Agency.

——(2005) *Ethiopian Labor Force Survey.* Addis Ababa: Central Statistical Agency.

——(2011) *Urban Employment Unemployment Survey.* Addis Ababa: Central Statistical Agency.

——(2009) *The 2007 Population and Housing Census of Ethiopia: Statistical Report at Country Level.* Addis Ababa: Central Statistical Agency.

——(2011) *Urban Employment Unemployment Survey.* Addis Ababa: Central Statistical Agency.

CSA and FPCC (2008) *Summary and Statistical Report of the 2007 Population and Housing Census* – draft report. Addis Ababa, Ethiopia: Statistical Report, Central Statistical Agency.

Dasgupta, P. and Ray, D. (1986) 'Inequality as a Determinant of Malnutrition and Unemployment: Theory', *Economic Journal*, 96(4): 1011–34.

De Gobbi, M.S. (2006) '*Labor Market Flexibility and Employment and Income Security in Ethiopia: Alternative Considerations*', Employment Strategy Papers 2006/1. Geneva: ILO.

Denu, B., Tekeste, A. and van der Deijl, H. (2005) *Characteristics and Determinants of Youth Unemployment, Underemployment and Inadequate Employment in Ethiopia.* Geneva: ILO.

Dercon, S. and Zeitlin, A. (2009) 'Rethinking Agriculture and Growth in Ethiopia: A Conceptual Discussion', *paper prepared as part of a study on Agriculture and Growth in Ethiopia.* London: Department for International Development.

Dinh, Hinh T., Palmade, V., Chandra, V. and Cossar, F. (2012) *Light Manufacturing in Africa.* Washington, DC: World Bank.

Dorosh, P. and Schmidt, E. (2010) *The Rural–Urban Transformation in Ethiopia*, IFPRI ESSP2 Working Paper 13. Washington, DC: International Food Policy Research Institute.

Economist (2012) 'Investing in Ethiopia: Frontier Mentality,' *The Economist,* May 12. www.economist.com/node/21554547?zid=304&ah=e5690753dc78ce91909083042ad12e30.

EEA (2012) *Developing Labour Market Information and Analysis Systems (LMIAS) in Africa: Country LMIAS Assessment for Decent Work (DW) Measurement: Ethiopia.* Addis Ababa: Ethiopian Economic Association.

Escribano, A., Guasch, J.L. and Pena, J. (2010) *Assessing the Impact of Infrastructure Quality on Firm Productivity in Africa*, Policy Research Working Paper 5191. Washington, DC: World Bank.

Fagin, L. and Little, M. (1984) *The Forsaken Families: The Effects of Unemployment on Family Life.* Harmondsworth: Penguin.

Farole, T. (2011) *Special Economic Zones in Africa: Comparing Performance and Learning from Experience.* Washington, DC: World Bank.

FDRE (1993) *Labour. Proclamation no. 42/1993.* Addis Ababa: Federal Democratic Republic of Ethiopia.

——(2004) *National Youth Policy.* Addis Ababa: Federal Democratic Republic of Ethiopia.

Foster, V. and Morella, E. (2010) *Ethiopia's Infrastructure: A Continental Perspective.* Washington, DC: World Bank.

Fujita, M.P., Krugman, P.R. and Venables, A.J. (1999) *The Spatial Economy: Cities, Regions and International Trade.* Cambridge, MA: MIT Press.

Gebreeyesus, M. (2007) *Growth of Micro-Enterprises: Empirical Evidence from Ethiopia*, EDRI Working Paper. Addis Ababa: Ethiopian Development Research Institute.

Gebrehiwot, A. and Wolday, A. (2006) Micro and Small Enterprises (MSEs) Finance in Ethiopia: Empirical Evidence, *Eastern Africa Social Science Research Review,* 22(1): 63–86.

Haile, G.A. (2008) Determinants of Self-employment in Urban Ethiopia: Panel Data Based Evidence, *Ethiopian Journal of Economics*, 17(1): 22–42.

Hungerford, T. and Solon, G. (1987) 'Sheepskin Effects in the Returns to Education', *Review of Economics and Statistics*, 69: 175–77.

ILO (1982) *Resolution Concerning Statistics of the Economically Active Population, Employment, Unemployment and Underemployment*. Adopted by the Thirteenth International Conference of Labour Statisticians. Geneva: International Labour Organization.

——(1997) *Underemployment: Concept and Measurement*. Prepared for the Meeting of Experts on Labour Statistics, 14–23 October. Geneva: International Labour Organization.

——(2011a) *Global Employment Trends*. Geneva: International Labour Organization.

——(2011b) *Key Indicators of Labor Market*, 7th edn. Geneva: International Labour Organization.

Kapsos, S. (2005) *The Employment Intensity of Growth: Trends and Macroeconomic Determinants*. Geneva: ILO.

Krishnan, P., Tesfaye, G.S. and Dercon, S. (1998) *The Urban Labour Market During Structural Adjustment: Ethiopia 1990–97*, CSAE Working Paper Series 1998–09. Oxford: Centre for the Study of African Economies, University of Oxford.

Krugman, P. and Venables, A. (1995) 'Globalization and the Inequality of Nations', *Quarterly Journal of Economics*, 110(4): 857–80.

Kuznets, S. (1955) Economic Growth and Income Inequality, *American Economic Review*, 45(1): 1–28.

Lieuw-Kie-Song, M. (2011) *Integrating Public Works and Cash Transfers in Ethiopia: Implications for Social Protection, Employment and Decent Work*, Working Paper 84. Brasilia: International Policy Centre for Inclusive Growth.

Mains, D. (2011) *Hope Is Cut: Youth, Unemployment and the Future in Urban Ethiopia*. Philadelphia, PA: Temple University Press.

——(2012) 'Blackouts and Progress: Privatization, Infrastructure, and a Developmentalist State in Jimma, Ethiopia,' *Cultural Anthropology*, 27(1): 3–27.

McMillan, M.S. and Rodrik, D. (2011) *Globalization, Structural Change and Productivity Growth*, NBER Working Paper 17143. Cambridge: National Bureau of Economic Research.

Mellor, J.W. (1995) *Agriculture on the Road to Industrialization*. Baltimore, MD: Johns Hopkins University Press.

Mincer, J.A. (1974) *Schooling, Experience, and Earnings*. New York: Columbia University Press for National Bureau of Economic Research.

MoE (2002) *The Education and Training Policy and its Implementation*. Addis Ababa: Ministry of Education.

——(2008) *National Technical and Vocational Education and Training Strategy*, 2nd edn. Addis Ababa: Ministry of Education.

MoFED (2006) *Ethiopia: Building on Progress A Plan for Accelerated and Sustained Development to End Poverty (PASDEP)(2005/06–2009/10)*. Volume I: Main text. Addis Ababa: Ministry of Finance and Economic Development.

MoFED (2010) *Growth and Transformation Plan (2010/11–2014/15)*. Volume I: Main text. Addis Ababa: Ministry of Finance and Economic Development.

MoLSA (2009) *National Employment Policy and Strategy of Ethiopia*. Addis Ababa: Ministry of Labour and Social Affairs.

O'Higgins, N. (2001) *Youth Unemployment and Employment Policy: A Global Perspective*, MPRA Paper 23698. Munich: University Library of Munich.

——(2003) *Trends in the Youth Labour Market in Developing and Transition Countries*, Social Protection Discussion Paper Series 0321. Washington, DC: World Bank.

Page, J. (2011) *Aid, Structural Change, and the Private Sector in Africa*, WIDER Working Paper 2012/21. Helsinki: UNU-World Institute for Development Economics Research.

——(2012a) 'Can Africa Industrialise?', *Journal of African Economies*, 21(2): 86–124.

——(2012b) 'Should Africa Industrialize?' in L. Alcorta, W. Naude and E. Szrmy (eds), *Industrial Policy: New Directions for the 21st Century*. Oxford: Oxford University Press.

——(2012c) *Youth, Jobs, and Structural Change: Confronting Africa's "Employment Problem"*. Tunis: African Development Bank.

Page, J. and Soderbom, M. (2012) *Is Small Beautiful? Small Enterprise, Aid and Employment in Africa*, WIDER Working Paper. Helsinki: UNU-World Institute for Development Economics Research.

Psacharopoulos, G. (1994) 'Returns to Investment in Education: A Global Update,' *World Development*, 22(9): 1325–43.

Psacharopoulos, G. and Patrinos, H.A. (2002) 'Returns to Investment in Education: A Further Update,' *Education Economics*, 12(2): 111–34.

Raju, D. (2006) *The Effects of Conditional Cash Transfer Programs on Child Work: A Critical Review and Analysis of the Evidence*, Working Paper. Washington, DC: World Bank.

Schultz, T.P. (2004) 'Evidence of Returns to Schooling in Africa from Household Surveys: Monitoring and Restructuring the Market for Education,' *Journal of African Economies*, 13(AERC Supplement): ii95–ii148.

Siba, E., Söderbom, M., Bigsten, A. and Gebreeyesus, M. (2012) 'Enterprise Agglomeration, Output Prices, and Physical Productivity: Firm-Level Evidence from Ethiopia,' *WIDER Working Paper 2012/85*. Helsinki: UNU-World Institute for Development Economics Research.

Sutton, J. (2005) *Competing in Capabilities: An Informal Overview*. London: London School of Economics.

Sutton, J. and Kellow, N. (2010) *An Enterprise Map of Ethiopia*. London: International Growth Centre.

UN-Habitat (2011) *Condominium Housing in Ethiopia: The Integrated Housing Development Programme*. Housing Practices Series. Nairobi: United Nations Human Settlements Programme.

UNIDO (2009) *Industrial Development Report, 2009*. Vienna: United Nations Industrial Development Organization.

——(2011) *Industrial Development Report, 2011: Industrial Energy Efficiency for Sustainable Wealth Creation*. Vienna: United Nations Industrial Development Organization.

Woldehanna, T., Hoddinott, J. and Dercon, S. (2008) *Poverty and Inequality in Ethiopia: 1995/96–2004/05*. Social Science Research Network. www.ssrn.com.

World Bank (2006) *World Development Report 2007: Development and the Next Generation*. Washington, DC: World Bank.

——(2007a) *Expanding the Possible in Sub-Saharan Africa: How Tertiary Institutions Can Increase Growth and Competitiveness*. Washington, DC: World Bank.

——(2007b) *Urban Labor Markets in Ethiopia: Challenges and Prospects*, Vol. I: Synthesis Report 38665, Poverty Reduction and Economic Management Unit, Africa Region. Washington, DC: World Bank.

——(2008) *Youth in Africa's Labor Market*. Washington, DC: World Bank.

——(2012) *World Development Indicators*. Washington, DC: World Bank.

5 Ghana

Ernest Aryeetey, William Baah-Boateng, Charles Godfred Ackah, Kim Lehrer and Isaac Mbiti

5.1 Introduction

5.1.1 Background

Ghana's economic growth performance has been easily one of the better known in Sub-Saharan Africa over the past three decades. The country's annual growth performance averaged 5.1 per cent between 1984 and 2010. A rebasing of the country's national accounts in 2006 pushed the country from being lower-income to the ranks of lower-middle-income countries with an annual average real GDP growth of about 8.5 per cent during 2006–11. The good growth performance has not, however, been reflected in the generation of productive, decent and sustainable employment. It is estimated that the employment elasticity of output dropped from an average of 0.64 in 1992–2000 to 0.52 and 0.4 in 2001–04 and 2005–08, respectively (ILO, 2008a).

Employment growth has tended to lag behind economic growth, as reflected in the divergence of growth of national output and employment. An annual average growth of real GDP of 5 per cent between 1992 and 2008 could translate into only a 2.7 per cent annual average employment growth over the same period. Estimates from the last three rounds of the Ghana Living Standards Surveys (GLSS3, 4 and 5) indicate that total employment increased from 5.79 million in 1992 to 7.07 million and 9.14 million in 1999 and 2006, respectively (Figure 5.1). These represent average annual employment growth of 3.94 and 2.69 per cent over 1992–99 and 1999–2006, respectively, with projected total employment at about 10.05 million in 2010 against actual total employment of 10.24 million, based on the 2010 population and housing census.

The slow response of employment generation to growth of the economy is largely linked to the slow growth of the labour-intensive sectors of the economy, such as manufacturing and agriculture, as against remarkable growth of low labour-absorption sectors of mining, finance, telecommunication and cocoa. Estimates from National Accounts indicate that during 2000–10, while agriculture and manufacturing grew annually on average at 4.7 and 3.7 per cent, respectively, mining and quarrying, finance, insurance and business, and

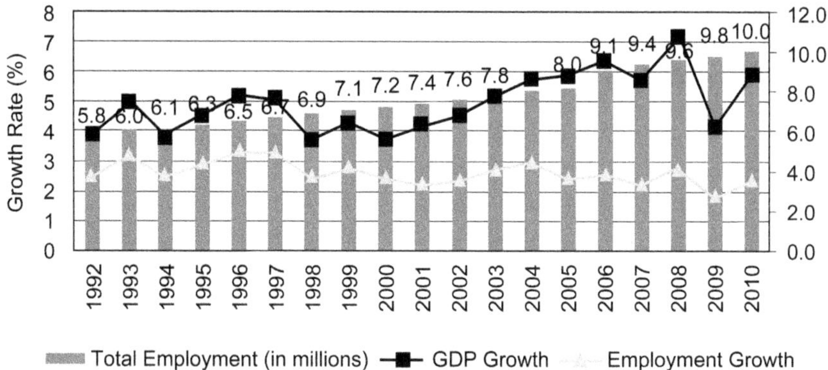

Figure 5.1 Trend of total employment, and growth of employment and GDP, 1992–2010

Source: Computed by Author from KILM, 2008 and GLSS3,4&5 and National Accounts.

transport, storage and communication grew on average between 5.4 and 7.8 per cent. In 2011, the economy grew by 14.4 per cent, of which half emanated from production of oil, which commenced in that year. These have culminated in the continuous decline in the share of agriculture and manufacturing in GDP (Table 5.1).

Aside from the slow growth of employment, another major problem is the low quality of employment in the country. For example, about three-quarters of workers in Ghana were in vulnerable employment[1] in 2006 (Baah-Boateng and Sparreboom, 2011), while only 17.5 per cent worked in wage employment during the same period (Ackah and Baah-Boateng, 2012). There is also a growing concern about the incidence and duration of unemployment, particularly among the youth. Although the challenges of youth unemployment and low quality of employment are not new, the increasing incidence of this among the educated youth, relative to the uneducated or less educated, is the main source of concern. Many young people who have completed tertiary

Table 5.1 Sectoral growth performance and composition of GDP, 1990–2010

Sector	*1990–94*	*1995–99*	*2000–04*	*2005–09*	*2010*
Agriculture	42.2	40.5	39.7	38.1	35.6 (30.2)
Industry	27.8	27.8	27.4	27.9	28.3 (18.6)
Manufacturing	*10.7*	*10.1*	*10.0*	*9.0*	*8.3 (8.1)*
Service	30.0	31.7	32.8	34.0	36.1 (51.1)

Source: Computed from Quarterly Digest of Statistics various Issues, Ghana Statistical Service.

Note: Based on 1993 Constant prices.

Figures in parentheses are based on rebased GDP at 2006 constant prices.

education and those with secondary education continue to struggle with the problem of getting employed, with many spending long spells in unemployment.

Politicians often use the lack of adequate and sustainable employment for the youth as a tool to solicit votes from citizens, but the problem always remains unresolved after their tenure of office. New governments often criticize their predecessors for doing little or nothing to address the problem of youth unemployment in the country. However, after a period in power, criticisms turn against them for neglecting the youth and making them jobless.

5.1.2 Why a special focus on youth?

Africa's population is very young, with more than half aged under 25. The World Bank (2009) puts the population of young people in Africa aged 15–24 years at 200 million. In Ghana, about 20 per cent of the population in 2006 was estimated to be young people within the age bracket 15–24, while children under the age of 15 account for about 40 per cent. The 2010 population and housing census puts the number of people aged 15–24 at 2.412 million, representing 20.1 per cent of the population. The future of the country within the next two decades rests on this segment of the population. In effect, the failure of the country to enact policies and programs to utilize their potential could be detrimental to the economy. The youth represent a particular opportunity and simultaneously a threat to national security and social tension. On one hand, they are a potential resource for growth and development if they are gainfully and productively engaged. On the other hand, they could also be a source of civil conflict and social tension if this untapped resource is poorly managed or left to waste. Youth without education, jobs or the prospect of a meaningful future could be a source of future instability, migration, radicalization and violent conflict.

There is a significant social and economic cost associated with underutilization of the skills and time of the youth. Young people often suffer from social exclusion in the face of underutilization of their skills, which has the effect of creating chronic poverty through the intergenerational transfer of poverty. The youth are more likely to accept recruitment into fighting forces when they face a high incidence of joblessness and poverty. As noted by Coenjaerts *et al.* (2009), lack of employment opportunities may result in social conflicts, including violence and juvenile delinquency, which in turn lead to high social costs. The increasing incidence of street hawking, and the migration of Ghanaian youth across the Sahara Desert and the Mediterranean in search of economic opportunities in Europe, with its attendant risks, are not only symptoms of labour market challenges facing people, but also reflect a sense of hopelessness.

In Ghana and many other African countries, the degree to which the youth can contribute to the development effort of their country is constrained by the lack of job opportunities. Young people face particular challenges in accessing the labour market, and this tends to lower their chances of finding decent, gainful and productive employment. Young people are more likely to lose their jobs during economic downturns. They face specific barriers to entry, largely due to the lack of experience and no networking (Clark and Summers, 1982; Freeman and Wise, 1982). A comprehensive analysis of labour market challenges confronting the youth in Ghana is therefore required to find a long-term solution to youth employment challenges in the country.

5.1.3 Who are the youth?

The classification of a group of people as youth differs from country to country, and according to the purpose of the classification. Generally, the period between childhood and adulthood is the 'youthful period' during which a person prepares to be an active and fully responsible member of society (Ministry of Youth and Sports, 2010). It is also a period of transformation from family-dependent childhood to independent adulthood and integration into society as a responsible citizen. Youth as an economic and social concept refers to a separate stage in the life cycle between childhood and adulthood (Curtain, 2001). From a legal perspective, the minimum age of youth varies in terms of marriage, criminal responsibility, voting rights, access to alcoholic beverages, consent to medical treatment, military service, etc. In Ghana, the legal definition of adulthood in terms of marriage, voting rights and the right to drive is 18 years. The minimum age for admission into employment in the country is 15 years, in line with the minimum age limit suggested by International Labour Organization (ILO) Convention No. 138.

There are variations in the definition of youth from a statistical perspective. The United Nations (UN) refers to individuals within the age range 15–24 as youth, compared with the Commonwealth definition of 15–29 years. The African Union defines youth as individuals within the age range 15–35 years, which has been adopted by Ghana's National Youth Policy. The age range for youth also varies for policy purposes. The African Youth Charter defines youth as persons aged 18–35 years. The National Youth Employment Programme (NYEP) adopts the African Union definition of 15–35 years. In this chapter we classify the youth into two groups—15–24 and 25–35 years—to account for both the UN and African Union definitions of youth, and also to conform to the definition of youth in the Ghana National Youth Policy and the NYEP. In Ghana, the minimum age of completing tertiary education plus one year national service is about 23 years. The adoption of a maximum limit of 35 years for the youth would therefore help to capture those who spend more than three years in unemployment.

5.1.4 Conventional theories and definitions of unemployment are inadequate

For about a century, various theories have attempted to explain variations in unemployment across space and time. While some of these theories need revision in order to become suitable to the current economic situations, others have maintained their old forms in explaining unemployment in the labour market. More recently, Farm (2012) argued that because hires are not instantaneous, and are actually preceded by job vacancies, search theory should be the standard theory for explaining unemployment caused by job vacancies. As Stigler (1962) notes, searching for bargains or jobs should be considered an economically important problem.

Another theory that explains variation in unemployment is efficiency wage theory. It posits that, in some markets, wages are determined by more than supply and demand. For instance, managers sometimes use wage as incentive to increase the efficiency of their employees by paying them more than the market-clearing wage. In such a situation, potential employees are kept out as the increased wage bills and the workers' higher productivity would not make it appealing to engage more hands. This theory was applied first in the late 1950s, to developing economies. It was argued that higher wages would enable poor workers to improve their diets and thus to become more productive. However, the efficiency wage theory has almost lost its relevance.

The insider–outsider theory started with the models of Lindbeck and Snower (1984, 1988) and the hysteresis model of Blanchard and Summers (1986). This theory explains how unemployment can arise when working conditions, and wages in particular, are determined by taking into account only the interests of employed insiders without regard to the interests of unemployed outsiders. According to Blanchard and Summers:

> When some external shock reduces employment, so that some insiders become outsiders, the number of insiders decreases. This incentivizes the insiders to set even higher wages when the economy again gets better, as there are not as many insiders remaining as before, instead of letting the outsiders to again get jobs at earlier wages. This causes hysteresis, that is, the unemployment becomes permanently higher after negative shocks.
>
> (Blanchard and Summers, 1986)

The above and other theories were developed mostly in the context of the developed economies. Similarly, there are a limited number of empirical studies on unemployment in developing countries, compared with the developed countries. Moreover, such studies often focus on the supply side, drawing on theoretical models intended for the developed countries. They suggest, for example, that unemployment is a queuing phenomenon, where the unemployed are waiting for a good job, and that it is concentrated among the better-educated middle classes (see Serneels, 2007). In this study, queuing is explained in a dual economy in the spirit of the standard job search model as set out by Mortensen (1986).

The concept of unemployment in developed economies is substantively different from that in the developing world, particularly Sub-Saharan Africa. However, policy in the developing world has always depended on definitions and concepts that originate from the advanced world. Some scholars argue that the concept of unemployment (as defined by the ILO) should be supplemented with other concepts, such as visible and invisible underemployment, time-related underemployment and inadequate employment, extended unemployment, labour shortage and labour reserve (e.g. Baah-Boateng, 2011). There is therefore a need to review the concept of unemployment to capture adequately the realities of developing world labour markets. As long as unemployment statistics are highly criticized by ordinary citizens as misleading and by experts for failing to reflect the true extent of the employment problem (Mehran *et al.*, 2008), the current policy on unemployment in the developing world might not be effective.

This chapter augments the theoretical expositions of unemployment in developing countries by highlighting economic and social exclusion of segments of the population as an important factor discouraging them from seeking employment. The chapter also presents a more realistic picture of employment problems in Africa, with particular reference to Ghana, by presenting several measures of unemployment based on broader and more diverse definitions.

5.1.5 Organization of this chapter

This chapter is organized into five main sections. The theoretical and conceptual issues of unemployment are discussed in section 2, and a comprehensive description of the current state of youth unemployment, quality of employment and working poverty is provided in section 3, which also reviews government policies on youth unemployment and the effectiveness of development strategies on alleviating this challenge. Section 4 focuses on quantitative analyses of determinants of incidence and duration of unemployment of the youth. Section 5 reviews recent and ongoing research and interventions that are effective in creating jobs, improving employability of the youth and raising productivity. The main conclusion and recommendations are presented in section 6.

5.2 Theoretical and conceptual issues regarding unemployment

5.2.1 Unemployment: concept and definition

The ILO, through the International Conference of Labour Statisticians, has provided a standard framework to guide the conceptualization and definition of unemployment (Liu and Wu, 1999). Based on this framework, a person of working age (e.g. 15 years) is classified as unemployed if, during a specified reference period (either a day or a week), the person had been:

- 'without work', not even for one hour in paid employment or self-employment of the type covered by the international definition of employment;
- 'currently available for work', whether for paid employment or self-employment; and
- 'seeking work', by taking active steps in a specified recent period to seek paid employment or self-employment.

According to this definition, for an individual without work to qualify as unemployed, the individual must not only be available to work, but should also be seeking work. Seeking work means taking active steps to look for work, such as registration at public or private employment exchanges, direct application to employers, checking at work sites, farms, factory gates, markets or other assembly places, placing or answering newspaper advertisements, seeking assistance of friends or relatives, or looking for financial resources, land, building, machinery or equipment, or permits or licenses, to establish their own enterprise (ILO, 2008a). However, the facilities to estimate the number of people seeking work are limited or non-existent in the developing world (Baah-Boateng, 2011), resulting in the underestimation of unemployment rates in developing countries including Ghana.

5.2.2 Economic exclusion and labour underutilization

The ILO definition could also involve a conceptual problem, as a significant portion of the population in Africa may be discouraged from seeking employment on account of economic exclusion. The theory of economic exclusion as an aspect of the theory of social exclusion seeks to explain how an individual could either be partially or fully excluded from economic production processes (Bradshaw, 2003). The theory rightly focuses on both the processes by which social and economic institutions exclude groups, and the multidimensional nature of the adverse consequences experienced by those who are excluded (Thorat, 2007). In other words, demographic characteristics of the worker and the institutional, environmental, cultural and legal framework of the labour market can determine whether a person qualifies to work at all, or should work for only a few of the stipulated labour hours. While those who suffer complete economic exclusion are often referred to as unemployed in the labour market, the partially excluded can appropriately be described as underemployed.

Factors that promote economic exclusion among workers have been classified as both group-based and individual-based. The caste system in India[2] is a good example of how group-based factors could render an individual worker either unemployed or underemployed. Thorat (2007) explains the exclusion for scheduled castes (those at the very bottom of the caste hierarchy) as involving:

- limited access to markets such as those for labour, agricultural land, inputs, capital, goods and social services;
- differences between prices charged to, or received from, them in market transactions;
- exclusion from certain categories of jobs and discrimination in hiring;
- exclusion from the sale of certain consumer goods, such as vegetables or milk, due to the notion that scheduled castes are considered impure or 'polluting';

- discrimination in the use of public services, such as roads and bodies of water;
- physical or residential exclusion that prevents contact with other community members and full participation in community life.

Under such practices, society denies certain groups of people the right to employment through limited access to labour market, land, capital, use of public resources and exclusion from certain categories of jobs. Combination of all or some of these factors would lead to labour underutilization.

Typically, discrimination based on ethnicity is a good example of a group-based economic exclusion that explains underemployment. For instance, Blackaby *et al.* (1999) found the unemployment rate among Britain's ethnic minority population to be twice that of the majority white population. They explained that characteristics such as schooling, discrimination and different responses to such discrimination by the individual minority workers may contribute to the high unemployment rate among this category of people. Other studies have also found discrimination to be the main reason why white applicants are much more likely to be successful when similar individuals undertake job searches (Smith, 1974, 1981; Brown, 1984; Brown and Gay, 1985).

Individual-based exclusion is caused by a failure to meet standard characteristics required by production processes as prescribed by the labour market. Individual-based characteristics are better explained by the human capital theory, which links stock of individual knowledge, capability, and skills to employment. Even though other demographic factors, such as age, ethnicity and residential status, can explain why an individual is either unemployed or underemployed, knowledge and skills stand out as the most important factors in the context of labour underutilization. Therefore human capital development through knowledge acquisition and training could be the best way to avoid labour slack. Human capital is just a factor of an individual-based economic exclusion. It is described in the labour market as the stock of competencies, knowledge, social and personality attributes, including creativity, embodied in the ability to perform labour so as to produce economic value. Human capital is an important determinant of demand for labour by firms, and therefore has implications for the incidence of unemployment.

The working poor usually suffer from both group-based and individual-based exclusion. Apart from poverty, discrimination can also result in inefficiency by reducing the magnitude of investments in human capital. According to Figueroa (1999), exclusion from the economic process means exclusion from market exchange:

> Conventional economic theory assumes that all markets are 'Walrasian,' in the sense that individuals can buy or sell a good or a service as much as they want at the prevailing market price. In such markets, rationing

> operates through prices, and the amount to be exchanged is just a matter of money. In these markets no one willing and capable of buying or selling could be excluded from exchange. People may be excluded from exchange in some particular markets, but this is because their real income, or productive capacity, is too low.
>
> (Figueroa, 1999: 3)

5.2.3 Inadequacy of the conventional definition of unemployment

As explained above, the ILO defines the unemployed as persons who are available and looking for paid employment, and have registered at an employment center (ILO, 1989). The application of this definition to most countries in Africa, including Ghana, seems quite problematic considering the peculiar nature of the labour market in Africa. For example, given two economies, one with a comprehensive social protection scheme and the other little or no social protection scheme, unemployment outcomes from the two countries would be misleading for comparison and policy purposes. That is, individuals in the countries with adequate insurance coverage can afford to remain unemployed, while those in countries with limited or no unemployment insurance coverage must do something to make a living, no matter how inadequate.

In Ghana, a considerable number of jobless people may be available for work but fail to look for work, partly as a result of inadequate and under-resourced employment placement and registration centers for jobseekers. In addition, many people drop out of the labour force as discouraged workers due to the perception of no jobs, and the absence of unemployment insurance benefits and other social protection measures as an incentive to attract jobless people to employment registration centers. In effect, the high 'discouraged worker' effect tends to understate the true unemployment situation in the country. As noted by AfDB *et al.* (2012), the weakness of using youth unemployment rate as the main measure of negative labour market outcomes is that it excludes many young people who are not in employment, who would be ready to work but have given up looking for a job. These discouraged young people are often worse off than the unemployed, and should be in the forefront of policymakers' thinking.

Moreover, the high degree of informality provides a safety net for many jobseekers who are unable to endure the challenges of remaining unemployed for a long time. Many jobseekers, especially those with limited employable skills required in the formal labour market, are compelled to seek refuge in the informal economy as a survival strategy. Underemployment, vulnerable employment and working poverty are widespread in many Sub-Saharan African countries. Focusing on the unemployment rate fails to take this reality into account (AfDB *et al.*, 2012). As shown in Figure 5.2, while the unemployment rate in Ghana for adults aged 15+ has remained virtually within single digits, the informal economy accounts for over 86 per cent of

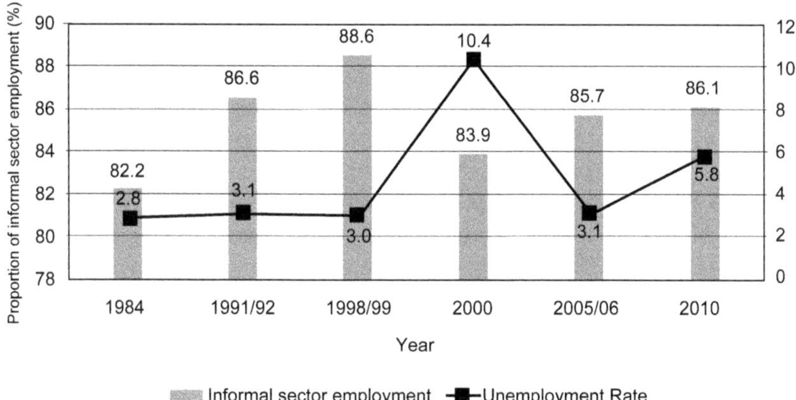

Figure 5.2 Unemployment rates and informal sector employment as a percentage of total employment

Source: Ghana Living Standards Survey 3, 4, & 5 and Population and Housing Census.

Note: The GLSS figures (1991/92, 1998/99 & 2005-06) were computed by the authors.

total employment. The implication is the low unemployment rate, which stands at 5.8 per cent for those aged 15+ in Ghana in 2010, should be viewed against the backdrop of street hawking and many other informal economic activities performed by the employed population, especially young people.

A trade-off between vulnerable employment, which is largely informal in nature, and unemployment in Africa (AfDB *et al.*, 2012) is also evident in Ghana. In many developing countries where farming and self-employment are prevalent and safety nets are modest at best, unemployment rates can be low.[3] Baah-Boateng (2011) observed a significantly negative correlation between unemployment rate and vulnerable employment based on a sample of 31 African countries.

Clearly, the conventional ILO definition tends to produce low rates of unemployment, which do not present the true labour market challenges in the country. Consequently, the conventional unemployment definition is increasingly seen as inadequate to characterize low-income countries' labour markets (Fares *et al.*, 2006; World Bank, 2006; Cling *et al.*, 2007). In effect, unemployment in developing countries is usually described in terms of disguised unemployment or underemployment, while in the developed countries unemployment is explained in terms of labour demand–supply gaps. As a result, some countries have relaxed this conditional phrase in their measure of unemployment. Hong Kong showed the way by adding the category of 'discouraged workers' to the 'unemployed'.

As long as the ILO's conventional definition for unemployment is continuously employed in the developing world, unemployment statistics will be persistently misleading. A unique and appropriate definition of unemployment is needed for the developing economies, including Ghana. As an alternative to the conventional or traditional definition of unemployment, AfDB *et al.* (2012) suggest counting all those who are not in employment, education, or training (NEET) as a proportion of the total youth population. In this study, we use three measures to assess the labour market challenges of the youth: the traditional narrow youth unemployment rate; the broad youth unemployment rate; and NEET as a proportion of the youth population as suggested by AfDB *et al.* (2012). The study also analyzes the type of employment engaged in by the youth to ascertain the extent of quality of youth employment in terms of access to wage employment *vis à vis* vulnerable employment.

5.3 Current state of youth employment and unemployment, and policies

5.3.1 Incidence of youth unemployment

Table 5.2 reports narrow and broad unemployment rates as well as NEET for 1991–2006. The youth unemployment rate in Ghana in 2006 was estimated at 6.5 per cent among youth aged 15–24 years based on the narrow definition, and 15.8 per cent when discouraged workers are accounted for. NEET, which sums up jobseekers, discouraged workers and the inactive, net of those who are in school and sick, suggests a more realistic labour market challenge for the youth. About 34.2 per cent of young people aged 15–24 were estimated to be jobless but not in any education and training institutions in 1998–99; subsequently this figure dropped to 26.9 per cent in 2006.

Generally, there has not been much variation in youth unemployment rates in Ghana since 1991. The narrow ILO definition of unemployment indicated a 1.1 percentage point increase among youth aged 15–24 during 1991–2006, as against no change in the rate for youth aged 25–35 (Table 5.1). Based on the broader definition that accounts for discouraged workers, the rate inched up by 5.5 percentage points for those aged 15–24 years as against 2 percentage points for their older counterparts. Similarly, the proportion of youth (15–24 years) in NEET rose by about 4 percentage points between 1991 and 2006

Table 5.2 Pattern of youth unemployment rates and overall joblessness 1991–2006

Year	*Narrow ILO Definition*			*Broader Definition*			*NEET*		
	15–24	*25–35*	*15–35*	*15–24*	*25–35*	*15–35*	*15–24*	*25–35*	*15–35*
1991/92	5.4	3.7	4.5	8.0	5.0	6.4	23.0	18.0	20.8
1998/99	5.4	4.0	4.5	15.8	9.2	11.5	34.2	26.0	20.4
2005/06	6.5	3.7	4.8	13.5	7.0	9.6	26.9	17.6	22.9

Source: Computed by Authors from the GLSS3, 4&5, GSS.

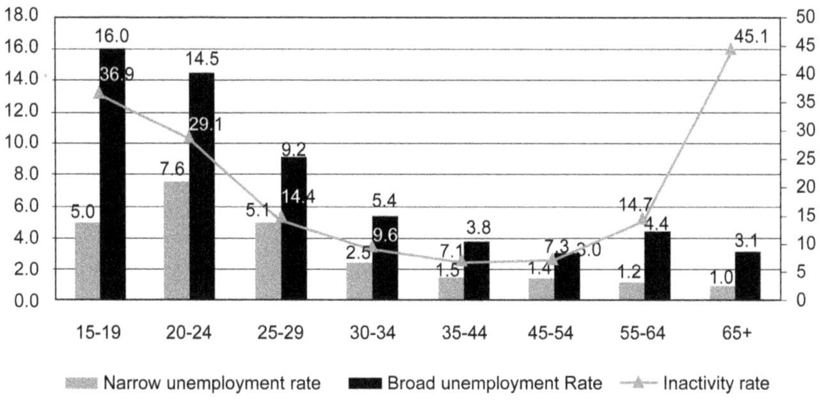

Figure 5.3 Unemployment and inactivity rates by age group (percentage) in 2005–06
Source: Computed by authors from the GLSS5, Ghana Statistical Service.

compared with less than 1 percentage point drop in the proportion of youth aged 25–35 years in NEET over the same period.

The high NEET is a result of high rate of inactivity (net of those in school), which is substantially higher than narrow and broad unemployment rates (Figure 5.3). Essentially, the high rate of inactivity may not be a matter of choice, but reflects limited employment opportunities as a result of slow expansion of the high labour-absorption sectors of agriculture and manufacturing.

Unemployment rates, regardless of the definition and inactivity rates, are estimated to be generally higher among the youth than adults (Figure 5.3). As noted by Baah-Boateng (2008), unemployment is more of a youth than an adult phenomenon, and declines with age. Estimates by the ILO (2012) indicate that the youth unemployment rate in Sub-Saharan Africa is twice as high as the adult unemployment rate. Inactivity rate is also shown to decline with age up to age 54, before rising to a high rate of 45 per cent for those aged 65+ years.

The high unemployment and inactivity rate of young people emanates from a number of factors. First, young people often face labour demand barriers such as observed discrimination due largely to limited or no job experience and insufficient exposure to a working environment. Second, they also lack job-search experience to facilitate their job acquisition. In times of economic downturn, lack of work experience combined with a lack of social capital puts the youth at a disadvantage for new job opportunities (UNECA, 2005). When employers face the challenge of executing layoff policies, the adoption of a last-in-first-out strategy disproportionately affects the youth. The situation becomes worse in Africa, where many countries lack properly functioning employment and placement centers, compelling the youth to resort to job search through friends and family members, which is clearly less effective. Many of these young people become frustrated as a result of the difficulty in securing jobs and fall out of the labour force as discouraged workers. Information gaps between potential employers and jobseekers, and limited information about the creation and development of businesses, especially in gaining access to financial, physical and social capital, continue to pose a barrier to the youth in gaining access to employment. In addition, in situations in which job openings are created, skills mismatch (both soft and hard skills) between young jobseekers and skill requirements of available jobs makes it difficult for them to secure employment.

The youth unemployment rate is established as an urban phenomenon, particularly among the youth. The youth are often attracted to cities in search of non-existent jobs, finding rural life unattractive largely due to the lower earnings in agriculture, the main economic activity in the rural areas. Table 5.3 reports on rural–urban and sex disparities in youth unemployment in 2005–06, and indicates that the unemployment rate (based on the ILO definition) among the youth aged 15–24 is about six times higher in Accra, the national capital, and at least three times higher in other urban areas than in rural areas. Similarly, the rate among the youth aged 25–35 years is found to be more than eight times higher in Accra and seven times higher in urban areas than in rural areas. Youth unemployment rates based on a broader definition and NEET follow the same pattern. With the increasing urbanization and limited job opportunities in the cities and big towns, the urban unemployment rate among the youth is likely to escalate. On the other hand, the very low rural youth unemployment rate relative to the rate in urban areas is explained by the dominance of agricultural activities in rural areas, which is characterized by low earnings but does tend to keep many youth away from unemployment.

The gender dimension of youth unemployment indicates higher rates for men than women based on the narrow ILO definition of unemployment. In contrast, a higher rate for women than men is reported when the definition is broadened to cover discouraged workers and the inactive. The rates based on the ILO definition are reported to be 0.8 and 0.4 percentage points higher among men than women for those aged 15–24 and 25–35, respectively. In contrast, a higher proportion of young women than men are found to be

Table 5.3 Youth unemployment rates by sex and location, 2006

Demographic Group	*ILO Definition*		*Broader Definition*		*NEET*	
	15–24	*25–35*	*15–24*	*25–35*	*15–24*	*25–35*
Male	6.9	3.9	13.2	6.3	22.5	13.7
Female	6.1	3.5	13.9	7.7	31.2	20.8
Accra	20.3	8.2	34.3	14.5	40.0	29.3
Urban	10.7	7.1	18.4	11.0	30.4	21.5
Rural	3.4	1.0	8.9	3.4	22.0	12.6

Source: Computed by authors from the GLSS5, Ghana Statistical Service.

unemployed if the 'seeking work' criterion of the conventional ILO measure of unemployment is relaxed. The gender difference of NEET is much wider, with 8.7 and 7.1 percentage point differences for youth aged 15–24 and 25–35 years, respectively. The implication is that a greater proportion of jobless young women than men who are available for work refuse to seek work for various reasons, suggesting a greater discouraged worker effect and higher inactivity rates of women than men.

An emerging dimension of youth employment in Ghana in recent times is the increasing unemployment among the educated. Figure 5.4 provides evidence to show that youth unemployment increases with the level of education. Only 3.0 per cent of young people aged 15–24 years in the labour force with no formal education were estimated to be unemployed in 2005–06 compared with 6.1 per cent of those with basic education, and 15.4 per cent and 33.0 per cent of those with secondary and tertiary education, respectively. A similar situation is reported for the youth aged 25–35 years (Figure 5.4a). This pattern is also reported if the broader definition of unemployment is used (Figure 5.4b).

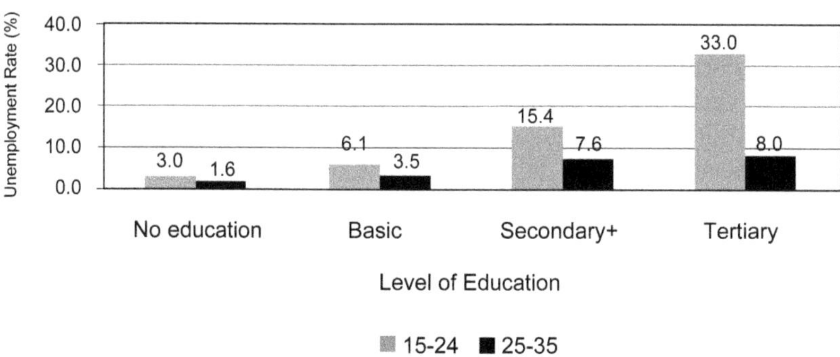

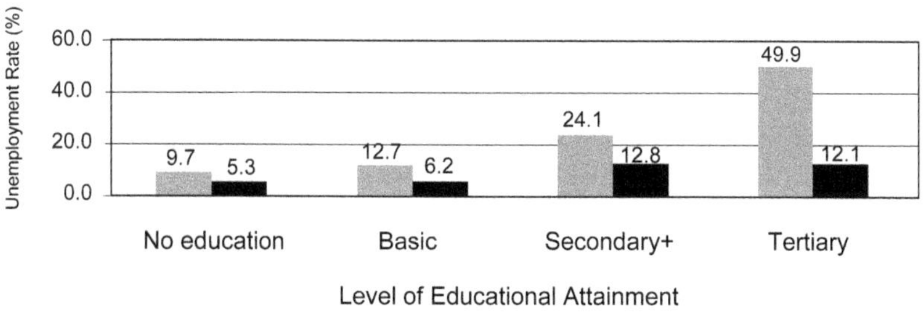

Figure 5.4 Unemployment rates by level of educational attainment, 2005–06
Source: Computed by authors from the GLSS5, Ghana Statistical Service.

A number of factors account for this phenomenon. The lower youth unemployment rate among those with no education or, at best, basic education is explained largely by the fact that they have limited or no requisite employable skills to access formal employment. They clearly have no choice other than to settle for informal agricultural and non-technical jobs, which do not require any formal education. On the other hand, young people with secondary education who are unable to obtain the required examination grade or score to access tertiary education also face difficulties in securing formal employment due to their inability to meet the skill requirements of the sector. The situation is exacerbated by the slow growth of the formal sector over the past two decades. For instance, recruitment into the security services, teaching and nursing training, among others, requires a pass in mathematics and English language, which are the same requirements for gaining admission into any tertiary institution in Ghana. These young secondary school-leavers do not seem to find the informal sector attractive, leaving them with no option other than to continue to seek employment in the formal sector.

The lack of appropriate skills produced by academic and training institutions for the labour market cannot escape blame for the high rate of unemployment among the educated in the country. Invariably, programs pursued at tertiary and second-cycle institutions in Ghana are biased in favour of the humanities (arts, social sciences and business) as against science, medicine, engineering and technology. Currently, Ghana has at least 50 public and private universities and 10 polytechnics, few of which are running courses in medicine, science, engineering and technology, for which skills are in short supply. In contrast, the increasing supply of human resources in business administration, arts and social sciences, in excess of what the economy requires, tends to create the problem of educated joblessness. In addition, the design of training curricula of educational and training institutions does not seem to have any place for the involvement of industry, making the skills produced alien to industry. There is also very little opportunity, if any, for trainers or instructors to retool through practical attachment to industry, to be in tune with changing demands in the labour market. Instructors therefore become ill-equipped to deliver effectively in class, to the detriment of students.

Furthermore, the emphasis on examination as the main tool for assessing students and trainees, coupled with reverence for certificates rather than ability to deliver on the job, has the effect of undermining the ability of the educated youth to cope with changing demands of the labour market. In recent times, library patronage in tertiary institutions by students has reduced considerably. In addition, those who visit the library mostly go there to read their lecture notes. The effect is undoubtedly low quality of those thrown into the labour market by academic and training institutions.

The inherent weakness in the current education system, which produces a considerable number of school-leavers at all levels of education, is a major source of labour market challenges facing the youth in Ghana. A considerable number of junior high school-leavers fail to make the grade to move up the education ladder, and therefore enter the labour market with no employable skills. Estimates from the Ghana Education Service indicate that during 2008–11, over 675,000 Basic Education Certificate Examination (BECE) leavers could not make the grade to enter senior high school. Many of these people surprisingly do not find vocational and technical training attractive. The option is to seek refuge in the informal economy or to remain as unemployed, discouraged worker or inactive. Similarly, fewer than 50 per cent of senior high school-leavers manage to secure admission into tertiary institutions. In 2010, out of about 351,000 pupils who sat for the BECE, about 49 per cent obtained the grades required to enter senior high school, with about 179,000 entering the labour market as new entrants with few or no employable skills. Also, about half of 157,500 senior high school-leavers in 2010 could not manage to meet the admission requirements of any tertiary institution due to their poor performance and were cast into the labour market with limited employable skills. Furthermore, there were over 40,000 tertiary graduates produced by public tertiary institutions in the same year, suggesting that at least 300,000 new labour market entrants overall were recorded in 2010, with limited job opportunities. The outcome is the high incidence of joblessness, particularly among the youth.

From the demand side, the limited formal sector jobs for graduates due to slow expansion of the sector, coupled with no consideration for employment in the informal economy, continues to be the major driving force for the high youth unemployment among university and other tertiary graduates in Ghana. The lack of entrepreneurship culture among young graduates, due to the limited or inadequate entrepreneurial content and creativity of university curricula, tends to make them look for someone to employ them rather than creating jobs for themselves.

5.3.2 Duration of youth unemployment

An additional factor to the structure and degree of the problem of unemployment is its duration. This refers to the period during which an individual remains unemployed continuously. It constitutes a signal about how long one must seek a job before finding one or abandoning the search altogether. The length of time one spends in searching for jobs has a reinforcing effect on discouragement. A long duration in search for employment may result in some jobseekers abandoning the search, thereby pushing them out of the labour force and raising the level of discouragement in the labour market. Equally important is the relationship between duration and demographic characteristics of jobseekers in order to understand the individual profiles that influence chances of securing employment and shortening the unemployment duration. This study is unable to analyze the duration of inactivity, and thus NEET, because available household survey datasets do not have any information to that effect.

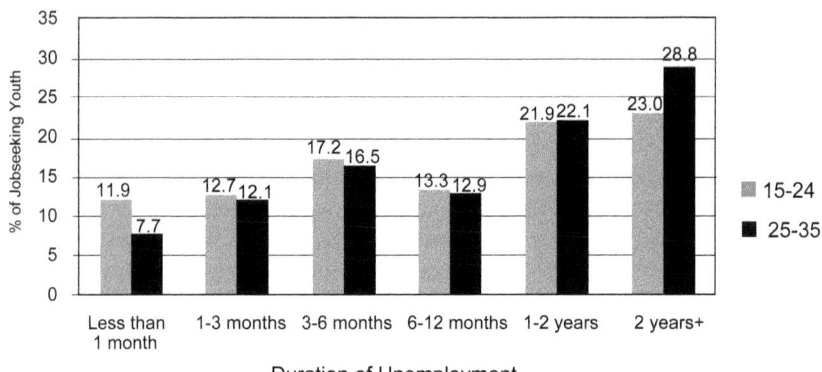

Figure 5.5 Duration of unemployment by the youth
Source: Computed by authors from the GLSS5, Ghana Statistical Service.

Figure 5.5 shows the duration of unemployment (or jobseeking) among young people, and indicates that a higher proportion of youth aged 25–35 spent a longer time in search for jobs than their younger counterparts aged 15–24. Specifically, about 51 per cent of the youth aged 25–35, compared with about 45 per cent of younger youth (15–24), spent at least a year in search for employment in 2005–06. On the other hand, about 36 per cent of youth (25–35) as against 42 per cent of their younger counterparts spent less than 6 months in search of a job over the period. These observations contrast with the expectation that a higher proportion of younger people would spend much longer searching, considering the labour market challenges they often faced.

One possible explanation for this observation may be the types of job being sought by these young jobseekers. Evidently, a greater proportion of the youth aged 25–35 were too specific about the type of employment they were seeking compared with to their younger counterparts, causing them to spend longer period in employment search. As reported in Figure 5.6, while about 44 per cent of young jobseekers aged 15–24 were looking for any type of job and thus improving their chances of becoming successful, fewer than a quarter of jobseekers aged 25–35 were general in the type of job they sought. In contrast, over three-quarters of the jobseekers aged 25–35 compared with 56 per cent of those aged 15–24 were specific about the type of job they were looking for. In addition, about 27 per cent of the 25–35-year-olds, compared with 18 per cent of their younger counterparts, were looking for formal sector employment, which, coupled with the slow expansion of the formal sector, implies longer duration of employment search in that sector.

The gender dimension of unemployment duration suggests a longer duration of employment search for young men aged 25–35 than for their female counterparts, while no significant gender difference in unemployment duration is observed among those aged 15–24. From Table 5.4, about 56 per cent of young men aged 25–35 as against 49 per cent of young women within the

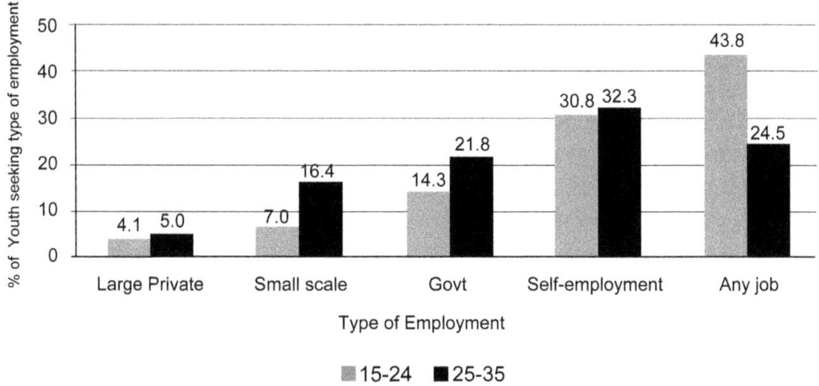

Figure 5.6 Type of employment sought by young jobseekers in 2005–06 (percentage)
Source: Computed by authors from the GLSS5, Ghana Statistical Service.

same age category spent at least one year searching for employment. In contrast, 41.4 per cent of young men and 44.8 per cent of young women aged 15–24 were estimated to spend more than one year in search of employment, suggesting a marginal difference between the two sexes. However, a higher proportion of women than men within the 25–35 age group spent two years or more in search of employment, while the reverse was the case with regard to employment search within a period of one year.

The rural–urban difference in employment search also indicates a longer duration of search for urban young jobseekers than for those in rural areas. About 60 per cent of young jobseekers aged 25–35 in urban areas, compared with about 32 per cent in rural areas, spent more than one year in search of a job (Table 5.4). With regard to young people aged 15–24 years, a less than 1 percentage point difference in the proportion of urban and rural young jobseekers spending more than one year in search of employment was recorded. In effect, the disparity in unemployment duration between urban and rural jobseekers and sex differences depends largely on the age group under consideration.

Table 5.4 Duration of unemployment by location and gender, 2006

Duration	*15–24 years*				*25–35 years*			
	Male	*Female*	*Rural*	*Urban*	*Male*	*Female*	*Rural*	*Urban*
Less than 1 month	15.3	10.3	10.9	14.3	7.1	8.0	18.3	3.6
1–3 months	15.2	11.9	14.9	12.3	10.0	13.7	13.6	11.6
3–6 months	18.3	18.5	21.2	16.0	14.3	17.2	24.1	13.0
6–12 months	9.8	17.4	13.1	14.3	12.3	12.2	12.7	12.0
1–2 years	21.9	19.0	18.0	22.5	19.6	25.2	13.7	26.5
2 years +	19.5	22.8	22.0	20.7	36.8	23.8	17.8	33.2

Source: Computed by authors from the GLSS5, Ghana Statistical Service.

5.3.3 Quality of employment

The youth face not only a high rate and duration of unemployment, but also the problem of quality employment if they manage to secure a job. Employment is defined within the ILO context as any economic activity that generates income through wages, profit or family gain, in kind or in cash, during a specified period. Thus the 'employed' comprise all persons above a specific age who, during a specified brief period, either one week or one day, were in paid employment or self-employment or contributing to family work. Generally, employment could be categorized into different forms: full-time or part-time, temporary or permanent, decent or vulnerable. From a statistical angle, based on the International Standard Classification, it can also be classified into occupation (professional, technical, clerical etc.), industry/economic sector (agriculture, industry and service) or type/status (wage or regular employment, self-employment, etc.), formal (public and private) or informal. Labour statistics also differentiate between current employment and usual employment. The former refers to any lawful economic activity engaged in by an individual above a specific age for pay in kind or in cash or for family gain for at least an hour during seven days, as against the latter, which looks at 12 months prior to the survey period.

Available statistics indicate a lower proportion of young people than adults in both current and usual employment. The high rate of inactivity on account of schooling or the high rate of unemployment largely account for this observation. Table 5.5 reports a lower employment-to-population ratio for the youth aged 15–24 than other age groups. Specifically, 37.7 per cent of young people aged 15–24 years as against 81.2 per cent of youth aged 25–35 years; 81.7 per cent of adults aged 36 years and above were engaged in different forms of economic activity within seven days prior to the survey. Similarly, 42.2 per cent of the youth within the 15–24 age group compared with 89.8 and 87.8 per cent of those aged 25–35 and 36+ years, respectively, were engaged in various economic activities for more than one week within a year.

The lower employment-to-population ratio among the youth, particularly within the 15–24 range, is reflected in the lower current and usual inactivity rate of 59.6 and 85.6 per cent, respectively, among this group (Table 5.5).

Table 5.5 Employment-to-population and inactivity rate by age group, 2005–06

Age Group	*Employment-to-population ratio*		*Inactivity rate*	
	Current	*Usual*	*Current*	*Usual*
15−24	37.7	42.2	59.6	85.6
25−35	81.2	89.8	15.7	34.4
36+	81.7	87.8	17.2	42.4

Source: Computed by authors from GLSS5

Note: Current refers to 7 days prior to the survey; usual refers to employed or inactive for at least 1 week within the year.

Generally, the employment-to-population ratio is one of the measures of a country's ability to provide jobs (see Sparreboom and Baah-Boateng, 2011). A lower ratio for the youth therefore suggests that they are not benefiting as much as their adult counterparts from increased job openings in the country. It can also be explained by the fact that, besides the high inactivity rate, employment prospects for the youth are also weak relative to their adult counterparts considering the labour market challenges they often face.

In addition to the low level of employment openings for the youth is the issue of the quality of employment engaged by young people. The employment-to-population ratio as a measure of the employment-generation performance of a country is limited because it cannot show the type and nature of jobs created. For instance, a higher employment-to-population ratio in rural than in urban areas may give a misleading indication of better job-creation performance in the former than the latter, because it falls short of showing the quality of jobs being created. The low quality of youth employment is reflected in the lower proportion of young people in waged employment and in self-employment with employees (i.e. employers), where earnings are high. Indeed, the youth are found to be mostly engaged in contributing family work with virtually no earnings.

From Table 5.6, over half of the youth aged 15–24 and 18.3 per cent of those aged 25–35 were engaged in contributing to family work, compared with 11.6 per cent of adults (36–60) engaged in a similar type of employment. In contrast, only 13.3 per cent of youth aged 15–24 compared with 21.1 and 18.9 per cent of the youth aged 25–35 and adults aged 36–60 were engaged in wage employment where earnings are better. In addition, only 1.0 per cent of the youth in the 15–24 age group, as against 4.3 per cent of their counterparts aged 25–35 and 2.5 per cent of adults aged 36–60, were engaged as employers (i.e. self-employed with employees). These have culminated in low average basic hourly earnings for young workers. In 2005–06, the average hourly pay of the youth (15–24 years) was estimated as equivalent to 0.42 Ghana cedis (GH¢) compared with GH¢0.67 for their older counterparts (25–35 years) and GH¢0.91 for adults (36–60 years). Clearly, the basic hourly earnings of youth

Table 5.6 Employment type, earnings and working poverty rate by age group, 2005–06

Indicator	*15–24*	*25–35*	*15–35*	*36–60*
Type of employment				
Wage employment	13.3	21.1	18.3	18.9
Employer	1.0	4.3	3.2	2.5
Own account work, non-agric	12.9	27.2	22.0	24.5
Own account work, agric	12.2	26.9	21.9	39.1
Contributing family work	50.4	18.3	29.7	11.6
Mean hourly earnings (GH)	0.42	0.67	0.60	0.91
Working poverty rate (%)	27.1	22.4	25.1	10.3

Source: Computed by authors from GLSS5.

aged 15–24 and 25–35 years were 38 and 74 per cent, respectively, of that of adults aged 36–60 years. Overall, the youth (15–35 years) were estimated to earn 66 per cent of the earnings of adults aged 36–60 years. The implication is high youth working poverty rates, estimated at 27.1 and 22.4 per cent for youth aged 15–24 and 25–35, respectively, compared with 10.3 per cent of adults aged 36–60 (see Table 5.4).

Generally, the youth are more affected than their elders in terms of poor quality of employment considering the barriers they face in the labour market, including lower education and skills as well as limited labour market experience. The high proportion of young people in informal or vulnerable economic activity, particularly in the area of contributing family and own-account work, is a sign of labour market entry difficulties for young people. In addition, it symbolizes low employment quality as informal jobs are generally less secure with limited application of labour and safety regulations. Limited access of youth to wage and regular employment tends to expose them to high levels of poverty, which has implications for their level of confidence in the labour market and ability to escape from that situation.

Clearly, the youth in Ghana face not only high rate and long duration of unemployment, but also low quality of employment and lower earnings. The most affected are the youth aged 15–24 years, who have lower skills, and limited labour market experience and networking. It is therefore important that policy strategies designed to address labour market challenges are not only targeted at addressing the high rate and long duration of unemployment among the youth, but also consider the problem of high rate of inactivity outside the school system and low quality of employment of young people in the labour market.

5.3.4. Review of labour market regulations and employment policy interventions

Labour market characteristics and regulation

The structure of the Ghanaian labour market largely mirrors the structure of the entire economy because labour is an input into the production process. Consequently, the demand and supply of labour respond to the changing growth pattern of the national economy. A common feature of the Ghanaian labour market is the dominance of agriculture and other rural economic activities, which are mostly organized on informal basis. The informal sector accounts for 86.1 per cent of total employment in 2010, the majority of whom are self-employed. Agriculture remains the main source of employment for the growing labour force in Ghana, even though its share in total employment has shrunk by about 11 percentage points in favour of services during 2000–10. Available statistics from the Population and Housing Census indicate that the share of agriculture in total employment has dropped substantially from 53.1 per cent in 2000 to 41.6 per cent in 2010, while the services sector's share has surged from 31.4 to 43.2 per cent over the same period,[4] with industry's share dropping marginally from 15.5 to 15.2 per cent. The share of the informal sector has also inched up by at least 2 percentage points from 83.9 to 86.1 per cent during 2000–10, while the share of both public and private formal sectors recorded a decline in their employment share.

The Ghanaian labour market is governed by the Labour Act of 2003, Act 651, which regulates the behaviour of actors in the market. It stipulates the rights and duties of employers and workers, sets general conditions of employment, and promotes freedom of association of workers and employers by providing regulations for the establishment of employers' organizations and workers' union. The Act also establishes a Labour Commission with the responsibility of adjudicating disputes between employers and workers' union. A National Tripartite Committee is also established by the Act to, among other things, to determine the national daily minimum wage and advise government on employment and labour market issues.

The effectiveness of labour market regulation in Ghana is observed to be quite weak, largely on account of its high degree of informality, which is a common feature of the market. Clearly, with a majority of the Ghanaian workforce engaged in the informal economy, with the formal sector accounting for only 14 per cent of total employment, labour market regulation covers only 14 per cent of the market. The inability of the Labour Department to enforce some regulations (such as the minimum wage legislation) in the informal sector implies that a higher proportion of workers in the labour market do not benefit from such social protection programs such as the minimum wage. In addition, employment and labour market policies targeted at the formal sector tend to exclude a greater proportion of the workforce. For instance, public sector pay policy, including the Single Spine Pay Policy targeted at improving the incomes of public sector workers, benefited only 6 per cent (the size of the public sector) of the total workforce in the country. The implication is that any public policy aimed at improving labour market performance must be chosen in light of the greater proportion of actors who operate within the informal segment of the market.

Review of employment policy interventions

The failure of the labour market to ensure a reasonable and sustainable growth of productive employment in the economy often necessitates the presence of government in the market. Although critics are often quick to raise concerns about the distortions and rigidities in the labour market arising out of government intervention, there seems to be no disagreement that the formulation and implementation of public policy targeted at protecting the vulnerable and the weak in the labour market could help address inequality. The absence of a well coordinated and harmonized national development strategy that focuses on employment-oriented growth has been the bane of the Ghanaian economy in relation to employment generation. Ghana is yet to have any comprehensive national strategy that focuses primarily on employment. A draft employment policy presented to Cabinet in 2008 is yet to be approved and adopted for implementation. Historically, employment issues in the country have often been treated as residual or passive outcomes of sectoral and macroeconomic policies. Policies on employment in particular, and labour market issues in general, have been mostly uncoordinated.

Prior to the launch of economic reform in Ghana in 1983, the government's economic policies were characterized by direct state involvement and control of economic activity, which resulted in an expansion of public sector employment in the 1960s and 1970s. For instance, a considerable improvement in formal sector employment occurred in the first half of the 1960s through the promotion of state enterprises, and also in the mid-1970s under the Operation Feed Yourself program (Baah-Boateng, 2008). A change in economic policy strategy from direct state involvement to private sector-led economic strategy caused a shift of labour from the public to the private sector, particularly the informal sector. A public sector retrenchment exercise, pursued as part of the reform, resulted in the layoff of many public sector employees. Indeed, between 1985 and 1991, employment in the public sector declined by 59.7 per cent, with about a third of this decline emanating from the public sector retrenchment program (Baah-Boateng and Turkson, 2005). Most of the public sector workers affected were at the lowest echelon of the job ladder and lacked the appropriate skills to enable them secure alternative placement in the private formal sector. Consequently, most of these people took refuge in the informal sector, resulting in a surge in informal sector employment from 83.8 per cent in 1984 to 88.4 per cent in 1991/92 (Baah-Boateng and Turkson, 2005).

The adverse implications of the reform measures in the labour market (including a high degree of joblessness and a high incidence of poverty, which stood at 51.7 per cent in 1991/92) prompted the introduction of a number of interventions in the 1990s to reverse the employment challenges in the economy. Among such interventions are the Programme of Action to Mitigate the Social Cost of Adjustment (PAMSCAD), the Alternative Employment Programme (AEP), and some programs in the agricultural sector. Under the PAMSCAD, a number of community projects were set up to generate employment for rural households, particularly in northern Ghana. These projects were targeted mainly at low-income households, unemployed and underemployed urban households, and retrenched workers. The AEP was introduced to accommodate displaced public sector workers who were affected by the Public Sector Management Reform Programme. The agricultural sector also initiated a program aimed at achieving food security and also generating employment and incomes in the rural areas through agricultural research and extension, smallholder credits and provision of other services.

A number of projects have also been carried out at different times over the past two decades to promote employment generation for the youth and other vulnerable groups in the country. These include Priority Public Works projects, Food for Work projects, the Labour Based Feeder Road Rehabilitation and Maintenance project, the Feeder Road project, Priority Public Works projects and Special Employment Schemes. The government in 2002 also undertook the Skill Training and Employment Placement program for the unemployed who were registered in 2001. The main weakness of these projects in terms of employment generation is that jobs created by them were not sustainable because they were largely limited to the life of the project.

In 1995, the government initiated a 25-year long-term economic development strategy called 'Vision 2020'. The Vision, designed to propel the country to achieve middle-income status by year 2020, introduced some employment-generation considerations into all macroeconomic and production policies to address the problems of unemployment and underemployment. It was, however, truncated in 2001 after a change of government, with the reason that the formulation and implementation was *ad hoc*.[5] Since 2003, Ghana has put in place three medium-term strategy frameworks—Ghana Poverty Reduction Strategies I and II[6] and the four-year Ghana Shared Growth and Development Agenda 2010–13—to promote growth and poverty reduction. In all these medium-term policy frameworks, employment generation was not seen to be the main focus of the strategy. The evidence is the absence of any initiative to generate regular labour market data to monitor the employment-generation response to the policies on the basis of these policy frameworks.

The National Service Scheme, which has been in existence for over three decades, has also been used to provide a one-year opportunity for tertiary school-leavers to render service to the nation. The scheme provides a sort of platform to facilitate the transition of youth from school to work, offering opportunities for young school-leavers to be exposed to the world of work. Most of these young people are posted into educational institutions to carry out teaching activities. At the end of the one-year program, some of them are absorbed by the institutions where they had their national service, while many others enter the labour market as new jobseekers,[7] with few of them pursuing further studies.

One major policy initiative that is directly targeted at providing job opportunities for young people aged 15–35 years is the NYEP. This program, initiated by the government in 2006, was meant to address the youth employment challenges facing the country at the time and their implications for national security. The program seeks to provide opportunities for young people, regardless of their level of education, to be engaged temporarily and acquire skills to facilitate their transition into permanent work. One major criticism of the program, however, is that the youth engaged under the NYEP do not contribute to social security, making it fall short of meeting the tenets of decent work. The dominance of management of the program by political appointees has also been a major source of criticism to the effect that some critics perceive it as being used as a tool for political advantage by the ruling government. In addition, delays in payment of a monthly allowance to the youth engaged, and the absence of any proper exit plan after a period on the program, remain major concerns for the viability of the program.

5.3.5 Employment-oriented development strategies

Labour market outcomes are generally influenced by policy strategies in the labour market in particular and the economy in general. Labour market policies are of two kinds: active and passive. Active labour market policy is a deliberate action by government to influence the workings of the labour market with a view to achieving desirable employment and wage outcomes. It generally involves implementation of labour market programs such as retraining, small business assistance, wage subsidies, apprenticeship and public works programs, as well as job placement and counselling services. Passive labour market policies simply provide support (e.g. compensation) to the unemployed and other vulnerable actors in the market, and rely on market forces to alter equilibrium level of employment and income. Some passive labour market interventions include unemployment benefits, unemployment assistance and disability benefits.

Employment is the outcome of demand for, and supply of, labour. Effective employment policies involve measures to stimulate the desire of enterprises to engage jobseekers through employment-oriented economic growth and to enhance the productivity of jobseekers through effective and efficient human resource development and control of population growth. The first step towards addressing employment-generation challenges, particularly for the youth in the country, requires a strong recognition and understanding that employment is central to achieving an improved standard of living and poverty reduction. In this regard, mainstreaming employment in all policy initiatives is one major way of addressing the employment-generation challenges facing young people in the economy. It could take the form of incorporating and assessing the job-creation effect of all policy initiatives at macroeconomic and sectoral levels.

In the short term, the adoption of labour-intensive initiatives through a public works program, targeted at the youth with limited or no skills or formal education, is one major way of absorbing the uneducated jobless youth. A public works program is a useful means of creating employment opportunities for new labour market entrants to 'taste' work and gain some experience. It can be a useful means of drawing the youth away from the streets and helping them to pursue other goals, such as environmental cleanup and afforestation programs. Agriculture and road maintenance modules under the NYEP are public works initiatives that have the effect of halting joblessness among the youth, particularly for those with low or no education, in the short term.

In the medium to long term, more employment-friendly public investment that aims at facilitating the growth and expansion of agriculture and manufacturing is one major way of creating jobs and addressing unemployment challenges. Obviously, unemployment is a component of joblessness arising largely out of deficiency in aggregate demand, and cannot be tackled unless economic growth is sufficient and employment-friendly. Investment in infrastructure, effective agricultural marketing strategy, affordable credit support and deepening of sectoral linkages could facilitate the creation of productive and quality jobs for the growing labour force, particularly the youth. The problem of skills mismatch, which tends to set jobseekers and employers apart even where job openings are created, must be tackled head-on through the design of appropriate curricula that meet the requirement of industry. Moreover, vocational and technical skills training must also be designed in line with the demands of the economy. Clearly, investment in education must be geared towards providing students with the knowledge needed to compete in the job market, not to just pass examinations. Effective collaboration between industry and academic and training institutions must be harnessed to address the problem of skills mismatch. Such initiatives can take the form of the involvement of industrial practitioners in curriculum design and teaching, internship opportunities for trainees, and retooling the skills of trainers in education. Teaching methods and assessment of students through classroom examination also need to be reviewed at all levels to infuse practically oriented assessment and to avoid examination-focused learning and training.

Slow growth of wage employment opportunities, coupled with the growing youth population in the country, require reorientation of the youth from 'jobseeking' to 'job provision'. Given the right combinations of motivation, opportunities and ideas, the youth are capable of establishing productive and creative enterprises that would shift them from being jobseekers to job creators. Many young people tend to shy away from entrepreneurship for a number of reasons: absence of business support, physical infrastructure and regulatory framework conditions; poor access to finance; lack of entrepreneurial training in school curricula; and sociocultural attitudes towards youth entrepreneurship. Removal of these constraints would provide a fertile ground for entrepreneurship to strive for the creation of productive jobs. This should be accompanied by efforts to expand the productive segment of the economy through aggregate demand measures to create effective demand for entrepreneurial activities.

A long-term national development strategy that emphasizes the generation of decent and productive employment for all, particularly the youth, must engage the attention of policymakers. This will make it possible for employment to be fully integrated into all sectoral and macroeconomic policies as well as human capital development strategy. From the demand side of the employment equation, agriculture and manufacturing, that are deemed to have greater job-creation potential and strong backward and forward linkages, could be used as the lead sectors, supported by construction, energy and the services sectors, in the long-term national vision. This must be backed by macroeconomic policies: fiscal, monetary, exchange rate and trade policies that are in tune with the dictates of the long-term national agenda.

The demand-side initiatives would elicit appropriate supply responses through enactment of appropriate human capital development strategies to train and develop the required skills to promote the growth of targeted sectors. It would require academic and training institutions to design programs and curricula to supply the skills required by the lead sectors of agriculture and manufacturing. Equally important is investment in the development of reliable, accurate, timely and regular labour statistics, necessary for regular monitoring of job-creation outcomes of the long-term national vision for periodic review of strategies within the broader long-term national strategy.

5.4 Empirical analysis of determinants of incidence and duration of youth unemployment

5.4.1 Introduction

In this section we analyze the determinants of the incidence and duration of youth unemployment in Ghana, relying mainly on a quantitative approach. Studies on determinants of incidence and duration of unemployment have often focused on the impact of personal or demographic and productive characteristics such as age, ethnicity, education, previous work experience, etc., all of which are supply-side factors on the probability of being unemployed or leaving unemployment. In addition to supply-side factors, demand-side factors such as growth performance of the economy and the sources of growth are also relevant considerations in the determination of incidence and duration of the phenomenon. We begin with theoretical and empirical analyses of unemployment, and adopt appropriate quantitative techniques to assess the sources and duration of youth unemployment in Ghana.

5.4.2 Model specification and estimation technique

The question as to why young people remain unemployed is an empirical issue. The empirical literature has concentrated heavily on supply-side explanations of unemployment as a function of unemployment incentives and personal characteristics. One reason may be that most data sources are not suitable for investigating demand-side influences at the level of the individual worker. Demand-side explanations of individual unemployment (usually based on profit-maximizing decisions of firms) have therefore been ignored in favor of supply-side discussions of utility maximizing labour/leisure choices.

This section investigates the determinants of an individual's incidence and duration of unemployment. The methodology follows Osberg *et al.* (1986). The basic model is seen in the following equation:

$$U_i = F(S_i) + g(D_j)$$

where U_i is the incidence or duration of individual unemployment, S_i refers to the incentives faced by individual workers to become or remain employed, and D_j measures the incentives to employing firms to employ workers. One would suspect, in advance, that the incidence and duration of individual unemployment is affected by both supply and demand variables.

Determinants of incidence of unemployment and joblessness

Based on this, we specify and estimate a probit model with exogenous individual characteristics that classically explains labour supply and demand as control variables to explain the incidence of youth unemployment. The model is of the form:

$$Y_i = \alpha_0 + \alpha_i AgeD + \beta_i EduD + \delta_i female + \phi_i LocD + \\ \theta_i \mathrm{Res}W + \lambda_i WorkD + \omega_i EmplD + \varepsilon_i$$

where Age$D$ is a vector of the age dummy (ages 15–19, 20–24, 25–29, 30–36), Edu D is a vector of the education dummy (basic, secondary+, tertiary education), 'female' represents the female dummy (female 1: male 0), Loc$D$ is the location dummy (Accra, other urban, rural areas), Res$W$ denotes log of reservation wage, Work$D$ is a dummy of type of work being sought (full-time, 1; part-time, 0); Empl$D$ denotes a vector of dummy of type of employment the individual is looking for (government, large private enterprise, small-scale enterprise, self-employed, any job), and ε is the random error term. The dependent variable Y measures the incidence of jobseeking (narrow unemployment); available for work regardless of whether one is seeking (broad unemployment); or NEET. The implication is that three different types of model are estimated. For the determinants of unemployment based on the ILO narrow definition we measure Y as (narrow unemployed, 1; employed, 0), while under the broader definition we measure Y as (broad unemployed, 1; employed, 0). In estimating the model of determinants of NEET, we measure Y as (NEET, 1; employed, 0).

We use the dummies of type of work and employment to capture the demand side of the determinants of incidence of jobseeking. Thus positive marginal effects of the full-time dummy, dummies of government work, and large private enterprise suggest that slow growth of these sectors (that provide quality employment) would raise the probability of young people in the labour force who target these sectors being unemployed. In contrast, accounting for determinants of broad unemployment and NEET, these variables could not be included because they are not relevant in this context and the survey instrument did not capture them. Other variables, such as the vector of education, age and location, and female dummy are used to capture the supply-side of the determinants of the incidence of unemployment.

Estimating determinants of unemployment duration

To estimate a model of the determinants of duration of unemployment, we specify a model similar to that above which takes into account the demand

and supply sides of the labour market. The focus is on duration of jobseeking, which was appropriately captured by the dataset. We follow the standard methods in analyzing the determinants of individual unemployment durations by employing the reduced form hazard function to estimate the probability of leaving unemployment. The reason is the two unique features of unemployment duration data: censoring and time-varying explanatory variables. The Cox proportional hazard model particularly is used to estimate the determinants of youth unemployment duration. We use the type of work (full-time or part-time) and type of employment (government, large private enterprise, small-scale enterprises, self-employment, or any job) targeted by jobseekers to capture the exit states from unemployment. We hypothesize that the effect of a covariate on unemployment duration will be different across the different exit states because different processes govern them. The individual jobseekers' demographic and productive characteristics (including age, sex and education) and location are used to capture the supply-side factors.

Source of data for estimation

The main data source for estimating the incidence and duration model of unemployment is individual-level data from the most recent nationwide household survey (the fifth round of GLSS5) conducted in 2005–06. It is a nationwide survey, which collected information on issues including demographic characteristics of the population, education, health employment and time use, migration, housing condition, agriculture, and welfare or poverty status. The fieldwork covered a one-year period between September 2005 and September 2006. It is a nationally representative survey covering a sample of 8687 households containing 37,128 household members in 580 enumeration areas The dataset available did not permit the panel analysis to investigate the labour market dynamics, which has yet to be explored well in the context of Ghana.

5.4.3 Discussion of empirical results

The empirical results of determinants of incidence and duration of unemployment are reported in Tables 5.5 and 5.6, respectively. In both tables we show estimation results for young people aged 15–24 years, 25–35 years, and a pool of the two samples (15–35 years).

Determinants of incidence of youth unemployment and joblessness

The estimation results of the determinants of incidence of narrow and broad unemployment and NEET, as reported in Table 5.7, were quite robust with statistical significance of the Wald chi^2 suggesting overall significance of the estimated model. The results also indicate a predicted probability on overall average of the regressors, ranging from 0.048 in terms of the estimated broad unemployment model for the 25–35-year age group and 0.447 with regard to the estimated NEET model for the 15–24-year group.

The empirical results suggest that individual demographic and productive characteristics such as sex, education, location or residence, and the type of work and employment being sought matter in determining the incidence of jobseeking or narrow unemployment, broad unemployment and joblessness in different directions depending on the age group. Among the youth aged 15–24 years, the results suggest a higher probability of those within the 15–19 age bracket becoming jobless outside education and training (NEET), but less likely to be unemployed in a broader sense. Furthermore, while women aged 15–24 are less likely to be jobseekers in narrow unemployment, they are found to be more likely to be jobless outside education and training. The implication is that women are less likely to seek work when they are jobless and available for work. Within that age group, those with secondary education have a higher probability of becoming jobseekers or NEET, while those with tertiary education are more likely to be broad unemployed or NEET. There is also a higher probability of these youth (15–24) in Accra and other urban areas to be broad unemployed or NEET relative to their counterparts in rural areas, with no marked effect of rural–urban location on narrow unemployment. The poor within this age group are observed to be more likely to join the broad unemployed.

Among the youth aged 25–35 years, the younger ones aged 25–29 are found to have a higher probability of being broad unemployed or NEET relative to their older colleagues. In addition, while women are less likely to be jobseekers (narrow unemployed), they are observed to have a higher probability of becoming NEET or unemployed from a broader perspective. Also, while the level of education has no effect on narrow unemployment for the youth aged 25–35, those with secondary education are more likely to be broad unemployed but less likely to be NEET, including those with basic education. There is a higher probability of those living in Accra and other urban areas to fall into broad unemployment and NEET relative to their rural counterparts, with only those in other urban areas found to be more likely to be jobseekers (narrow unemployment). There is also a higher probability of the poor being broad unemployed or NEET.

From the demand side of the determinants of unemployment, there is a higher probability of young jobseekers whose main employment focus is the government sector to be unemployed regardless of age group. This finding confirms the observation of slow expansion of the public sector on account of implementation of policies to reduce the government wage bill, which reduces the incidence of job openings in the public sector. In addition, those who seek full-time as against part-time work are more likely to be unemployed, with statistically significant marginal effect for those aged 15–24 and 15–35 years. The high proportion of jobseekers seeking full-time work—estimated at more than 80 per cent regardless of age group—against the limited availability of full-time work largely accounts for this observation. Young jobseekers aged

Table 5.7 Results of binary regression model (probit-marginal effect) of determinants of incidence of youth unemployment (dependent variable: unemployment)

Variable	*Narrow ILO Unemployment*			*Broader Unemployment*			*NEET*		
	15–24	*25–35*	*15–35*	*15–24*	*25–35*	*15–35*	*15–24*	*25–35*	*15–35*
Age 15–19	0.082	–	–0.055	–0.043***	–	–0.006	0.179***	–	0.458***
Age 20–24	–	–	0.024	–	–	0.037***	–	–	0.310***
Age 25–29	–	0.018	0.021	–	0.024***	0.030***	–	0.090***	0.116***
Female	–0.101**	–0.114*	–0.106***	0.002	0.015**	0.007*	0.066***	0.066***	0.078***
Basic education	0.072	0.068	0.082*	–0.010	0.002	–0.002	–0.011	–0.098***	–0.071***
Second education+	0.179**	0.050	0.115**	–0.016	0.033***	0.004	0.195***	–0.058***	0.036***
Tertiary education	0.036	0.015	0.027	0.071**	0.039**	0.043**	0.321***	–0.112***	–0.069*
No education (reference)									
Urban Accra	–0.024	0.058	–0.013	0.068***	0.114***	0.087***	0.284***	0.255***	0.279***
Other urban	0.082	0.215**	0.142***	0.028***	0.085***	0.051***	0.154***	0.141***	0.153***
Log of reservation wage	0.012	0.038	0.025	–	–	–	–	–	–
Poor	0.021	0.045	0.003	0.027***	0.056***	0.038***	–0.037	0.046***	0.010
Fulltime employment	0.169**	0.127	0.146***	–	–	–	–	–	–
Government work	0.326***	0.251**	0.273***	–	–	–	–	–	–
Large private enterprise	–0.139	0.030	–0.076	–	–	–	–	–	–
Small scale enterprises	–0.137	0.200**	0.023	–	–	–	–	–	–
Self-employment	0.037	–0.017	0.010	–	–	–	–	–	–
Any type of job (reference)									
Pred. Probability (at x-bar)	0.366	0.418	0.390	0.052	0.048	0.052	0.447	0.162	0.273
Pseudo R^2	0.087	0.104	0.0808	0.042	0.078	0.050	0.075	0.071	0.128
Wald chi^2	45.58***	51.64***	85.11***	100.8***	170.8***	205.6***	339.9***	272.5***	1,189.1***
Number observations	2,979	4,546	7,525	3,247	4,744	7,991	4,361	5,321	9,682

Note: * 10% significance level **5% significance level ***1% significance level.

15–24 targeting large private enterprises and small-scale enterprises are less likely to be unemployed relative to those seeking any job.

In effect, demographic and human capital factors such as sex and education are observed to be supply-side factors that can contribute significantly to unemployment and joblessness in Ghana. On the demand side, slow expansion of the public sector and full-time work, coupled with the number of young jobseekers in that area, can be blamed for youth unemployment in Ghana.

Determinants of duration of youth unemployment

Table 5.8 provides empirical results on the determinants of duration of youth unemployment (defined by jobseeking) in Ghana. Overall, the statistical significance of hazard ratio of P = 1.829 (or ln$P$ = 0.604) implies positive duration dependence. The estimated Weibull regression results indicate that age, education, urban–rural location, reservation wage, poverty status, and jobseekers in government and large private sector are relevant in the determination of duration of unemployment, depending on the age bracket under consideration. Specifically, the educated youth, regardless of the level of education (except those aged 25–35, with tertiary as the only education dummy found not to be statistically significant), are more likely to transition from unemployment than the uneducated. The implication is that the educated youth are more likely than the uneducated to spend short spells in unemployment.

In terms of age effect on duration of unemployment, the results show that the youth aged 15–19 years are more likely than their older counterparts (aged 20–24, 25–29 and 30–35) to escape from unemployment. The main explanation of this observation is that, due to their low level of education (maximum level is secondary education), the youth aged 15–19 compared with their older counterparts may want to take refuge in the informal sector. The youth aged 25–35 who live in urban Accra and other urban areas are less likely to transition from unemployment than their counterparts in rural areas.

Reservation wage is also found to matter in duration of unemployment or jobseeking, such that a high reservation wage is less likely to result in the youth (except those aged 25–35) to transition from unemployment, confirming a long-held expectation. In addition, the poor are observed to be less likely than the better-off to escape unemployment, indicating a longer duration of unemployment for the poor.

Young jobseekers (excluding those aged 15–24) who seek only full-time work are found to be more likely to transition from unemployment than those who seek part-time work, contrary to expectation. Thus, although full-time jobseekers are more likely to be unemployed, they are more likely than part-time jobseekers to escape from unemployment. In addition, young jobseekers in the government sector are less likely to escape unemployment than those seeking any job, indicating that jobseekers in the public sector are more likely to have a longer unemployment duration than those seeking any job. In addition, young jobseekers aged 25–35 seeking a government job or employment in

Table 5.8 Weibull regression—log relative hazard form of unemployment duration for three different age groups

Variable	*15–24 years Hazard Ratio*	*25–35 years Hazard Ratio*	*15–35 years Hazard Ratio*
Age 15–19	1.214**	–	1.229**
Age 20–24	–	–	1.042
Age 25–29	–	1.078	1.032
Female	0.996	1.039	1.047
Basic education	1.278***	1.098	1.153**
Secondary education+	1.289**	1.108	1.208**
Tertiary education	1.719***	1.541**	1.524***
No education (reference)			
Urban Accra	1.030	0.576***	0.881
Other Urban	1.064	0.552***	0.878
Log of reservation wage	0.894**	0.964	0.919**
Poor	0.851**	0.684***	0.813
Fulltime employment	1.073	1.430**	1.152*
Government work	0.777**	0.809*	0.794***
Large private enterprise	1.282	0.730**	0.985
Small scale enterprises	1.083	1.053	1.029
Self-employment	1.003	1.192	1.047
Any type of job (reference)			
Ln_p	0.604***	0.873***	0.708***
p	1.829	2.393	2.030
l/p	0.547	0.418	0.493
Ward Chi^2	49.55***	50.69***	58.23***
Number observations	535	423	958

Source: Based on GLSS5, 2006.
Note: * 10% significance level ** 5% significance level *** 1% significance level.

large enterprises are estimated to be less likely than those seeking any job to escape unemployment.

5.5 Interventions to create jobs and to improve the employability of youth

5.5.1 Introduction

In this section we review existing and ongoing research projects that address issues related to employment creation, skills development and the employability of youth. Evidence from these studies regarding the effectiveness of interventions towards addressing unemployment and underemployment in the country are critically discussed and summarized. Such interventions include primary education, vocational training, public health, the promotion of small-scale agriculture, and microfinance.

This section identifies the key issues currently facing the labour market, suggests potential solutions based on lessons learned from rigorous quantitative research, and summarizes promising solutions that may be important for the Ghanaian labour market but are yet to be rigorously evaluated. It also highlights a subset of proven high-impact and cost-effective policies that could improve the functioning of the labour market. This section also identifies new programs that are currently being implemented in Ghana to address unemployment and underemployment and to improve the quality of jobs, specifically interventions aimed at youth. It focuses on the role of health and education in the labour market. It also assesses issues pertaining to gender and youth, and the importance of the informal sector and self-employment in the labour market.

5.5.2 Key issues in the Ghanaian labour market

The Government of Ghana is making employment a priority for poverty reduction and as an underpinning for economic growth (World Bank, 2009). This is reflected in both the government's Second Poverty Reduction Strategy (2006–09) and the recent establishment of the Council for Technical and Vocational Education and Training (COTVET), which coordinates job training programs across nearly 10 ministries. The establishment of COTVET will hopefully streamline and unify technical and vocational education and training (TVET) policy in Ghana. Prior to the introduction of COTVET, several ministries conducted their own training programs and developed their own policies on training, with inefficiencies due to duplicated effort and initiatives across the various ministries. Although COTVET is a body under the Ministry of Education, it coordinates and oversees training programs across the Ghanaian government and is responsible for reforming the TVET system. In particular, COTVET aims to modernize the TVET sector and move toward a competency-based training system that focuses on certification that trainees have acquired market-relevant skills.

Two major initiatives launched by COTVET are the Skills Development Fund, aimed at promoting training in the public and private sectors; and the National Apprenticeship Programme, aimed at providing disadvantaged youth with a path to acquiring employable skills. Mbiti *et al.* are currently undertaking a randomized evaluation of the National Apprenticeship Programme, while ISSER is working with COTVET to evaluate the Skills Development Fund.

According to the World Bank (2008), the unemployment rate among Ghanaian youth with no education is 70 per cent. For those with primary education it is nearly 75 per cent, while for youth with secondary education it is approximately 80 per cent. These are the highest rates among the 14 Sub-Saharan African countries analyzed in the report. The unemployment rate of Ghanaian youth with tertiary education is nearly half that of those with less education. These statistics highlight the extent of unemployment among youth in Ghana, and how education and skills may play an important role in its determination.

Given the seriousness of youth unemployment in Ghana, various government and non-governmental agencies have put in place interventions hoping to address this issue. These range from health and education interventions to harnessing the potential of the informal sector for job creation and skills development. The interventions are described in the following section along with existing evidence of their impacts. Several ongoing research studies are described that, once completed, will provide reliable estimates of the impacts of several interventions on youth labour market outcomes. Finally, findings from evaluations of job interventions in other countries are summarized and their implications for Ghana are discussed.

5.5.3 Findings of randomized evaluations and other research

Health and labour markets

We provide a general overview of the health environment faced by Ghanaian workers. While we are unable to focus exclusively on youth, a general overview of the constraints faced by workers should be informative for youth. Data from the 2008 GLSS show that, on average, approximately one in five Ghanaians of working age reported being ill in the two weeks prior to being interviewed. The data further show that those living in Accra had the lowest rates of illness, while those in rural areas had significantly higher rates of self-reported illness. The difference in illness rates could reflect unequal access to healthcare or high prevalence of endemic illnesses in rural compared with urban areas. In addition, the data show that close to 60 per cent of those who were ill missed work due to the illness episode. While women were more likely to report illness, men were more likely to miss work due to illness.

Health-seeking behaviour of workers is on a par with other countries in Sub-Saharan Africa, where 63 per cent of those who reported being ill in Ghana visited a health practitioner. While the proportions for those who visit a health practitioner are high throughout Ghana, the quality of care differs. Outside Accra, people are more likely to buy drugs without consulting a doctor. This percentage varies from 40 per cent in rural coastal regions to 20 per cent in the rural savannah region, while in Accra it is below 5 per cent (GLSS5, 2008). People outside Accra are also more likely to consult a nurse than a doctor, suggesting regional differences in the availability of quality of care.

The World Bank (2012b) report on Health Equity and Financial Protection highlights the low physician density in Ghana and attributes it to the migration of trained personnel to developed countries. Between 1985 and 1994, up to 61 per cent of the physicians who graduated from medical institutions in Ghana migrated abroad. The low density is further exacerbated by uneven distribution. The report states that 69 per cent of physicians in Ghana operate in the two biggest cities in the country. This is highlighted by the differences in the physician-to-population ratio, which stands at 1:5000 in Accra compared with 1:92,000 in the rural Northern region.

There are also differences in distribution based on wealth. Ghana offers more subsidies for healthcare to the rich, except in the utilization of health centers and posts, which account for only 16.6 per cent of healthcare spending. The poor also fare worse in terms of health outcomes: under-5 mortality, diarrhea, acute respiratory infection and fever are higher among the poor than the rich (World Bank, 2012a). Surprisingly, the study also shows lower intake of fruit amongst richer households, indicating a lack of information regarding dietary needs and nutrition.

The National Health Insurance Scheme (NHIS), introduced in 2004, has had an effect on reducing these disparities. The NHIS financing accounts for 40 per cent of the health expenditure in Ghana and covers approximately 60 per cent of the population. However, the system is still plagued with issues of fraud and administrative failure (World Bank, 2012).

Ghana also faces a crisis in the availability of drinking water, particularly in urban areas (Stoler *et al.*, 2012). Despite receiving enough rainfall to provide all its citizens with water, uneven distribution of rainfall and inadequate water infrastructure leads to local shortages. Higher population densities in urban areas worsen these shortages. Drinking water sources also suffer from pollution due to cross-contamination and inadequate infrastructure. The shortage in water supply also affects poorer households disproportionately, leading to higher incidences of illnesses such as diarrhea.

Overall, infectious diseases such as malaria, HIV, tuberculosis, diarrhea and perinatal conditions are the biggest challenges facing Ghana, accounting for 50 per cent of all deaths and 68 per cent of deaths among children under 14 years. Sanitation-related illnesses are also major challenges, where reports suggest that 80 per cent of cases treated under the NHIS were sanitation-related (*Public Agenda*, 2008). Illnesses such as diarrhoea have a significant effect on the health of children. Healthier children are more likely to grow up to be healthier adults, acquire more education and skills, and perform better in the labour market. There is evidence of a high prevalence of micronutrient deficiencies in Ghana. According to the Micronutrient Initiative (2011), 65 per cent of children under 5, and 40 per cent of women aged 15–49, suffer from iron-deficiency anaemia. A further 60 per cent of children under 5 are deficient in vitamin A, and 18 per cent of the population suffer from goiter. Overall, these statistics reveal the need to address micronutrients both at an early age, as a way to promote the physical and cognitive development of the next generation, and for current youth, as a way to improve health and labour market productivity.

Evidence

Investment in health not only increases labour productivity but also increases workers' income. Taller people with higher body mass indices are likely to earn higher wages (Strauss and Thomas, 1998). Research from that paper also indicates that a diet with a higher level of protein, after controlling for calorie intake, height and body-mass index (BMI), leads to an increase in wages. The implication is that policies promoting better nutrition can lead to contemporaneous increases in labour productivity.

Furthermore, in a randomized evaluation of iron supplements in Indonesia, researchers found that men assigned to the treatment group performed better than those in the control group in terms of various outcomes. They are more likely to be working, sleep less, are more energetic and are able to undertake physically arduous tasks. The self-employed men in the treatment group also experienced a significant improvement in hourly wage (Thomas *et al.*, 2006). In China, preliminary results from a study of the efficacy of iron-fortified soy sauce indicated dramatic reductions in iron deficiency (from 50 to 10 per cent in one year among young women). Iron-fortified fish sauce has also been tested in Vietnam, where its introduction saw a 33 per cent reduction in anaemia among women over the course of six months. The cost of iron fortification islow. It is estimated that the marginal cost of fortifying fish sauce is about US$6 per person per year (Thomas *et al.*, 2004). Fortifying Ghanaian staples may be one approach to promote better health and increased productivity.

Asenso-Okyere *et al.* (2011) review the various ways in which farm labour productivity, health and nutrition are linked. They find that poor farm households tend to be vulnerable to malnutrition and poor health, which lead to reductions in agricultural productivity. In addition to the direct impacts due to lost labour, illness undermines long-term agricultural productivity in a number of ways, as it may lead to the withdrawal of savings, the sale of important assets, withdrawal of children from school, or reducing the nutritional value of food consumption. Thus severe illness can lead to perpetual poverty traps.

Given the current mineral boom in Ghana, it is important to highlight the negative externalities that may arise from mining activities. Aragon and Rud (2012) find that mining pollution reduced agricultural productivity by almost 40 per cent during 1998–2005 in Ghana. Additionally, they find that the pollution externality from mining was associated with increases in poverty, child malnutrition and respiratory diseases.

While there is evidence for unequal distribution of health spending and resources across regions and wealth categories, the NHIS has taken an important step towards reducing these disparities. Nguyen *et al.* (2011) use data from two rural districts in Ghana to show that the NHIS has had an effect in reducing the often catastrophic financial burden of illness among the poor. They also show that the insurance scheme has not been able to eliminate out-of-pocket expenditure on illnesses due to inefficiencies in the quality of care and supply-side constraints, which limit access. As a result, the insured often end up paying for informal care and medical services that should be covered by the scheme. The implication is that reforms should be enacted to improve access to care and to reduce administrative inefficiencies to improve the effectiveness of its insurance scheme.

There is also evidence that, in the absence of public services, private entities step in to fill the gap. Stoler *et al.* (2012) discuss how private water providers have bridged the gaps in access to water in urban areas through water sachets. These sachets serve an important role in providing poorer households access to safe drinking water, which has reduced waterborne illnesses such as diarrhoea. The effect, however, is the high cost borne by households, which have to pay higher prices for water from private companies.

Access to safe drinking water is a critical element in ensuring the health of working adults and of children. There also is evidence that improving the health of children has an effect on future labour market outcomes. A wealth of evidence from health interventions in Kenya shows that children who are healthier do better in school and earn more as adults (Miguel and Kremer, 2004; Miguel *et al.*, 2011; Ozier, 2011). Glewwe and Jacoby (1995) show that early childhood malnutrition causes delayed enrolment. Better-nourished children tend to start school earlier and have better education outcomes. Thus early childhood nutrition interventions can lead to substantial increases in lifetime wealth. Schultz (2003b) estimates the effects on log wages of adult health/nutrition (proxied by body mass index) and child nutrition (proxied by height) for Ghana from household surveys collected during the late 1980s. He finds that the overall returns of adult health/nutrition and child nutrition to productivity are similar for men and women, and the wage effects of child nutrition are greater in poorer, more malnourished Ghana. Higgins and Alderman (1997) find that the physical labour performed by Ghanaian women, especially in agriculture, appears to have a significant negative effect on their nutritional status. These negative effects on maternal malnutrition can negatively affect the health and survival probabilities of future children and their future labour productivity (Martorell and Gonzalez-Cossio, 1987).

Current evidence demonstrates the substantial effects of health and nutrition on productivity. However, more research is needed to determine the most cost-effective ways to improve the health of youth. Research that focuses on innovative ways to promote health should be conducted and the cost-effectiveness of various options computed. Further, there is very little known about health dynamics over the life-course in developing countries, particularly in response to negative economic shocks and aging (Strauss and Thomas, 1998).

Recommendations

IMPROVE THE NATIONAL HEALTH INSURANCE SCHEME

The NHIS has reduced the cost of healthcare for poorer households and thereby improved access to medical facilities. The government should focus on eliminating fraud and administrative limitations, while working concurrently on supply side constraints. These steps would ensure the benefits of the NHIS can be fully realized, leading to a healthier and more productive workforce. There is little evidence concerning the impacts of health insurance schemes, and this is one area where more research is urgently needed.

IMPROVE ACCESS TO SAFE DRINKING WATER

Safe drinking water is essential for reducing illnesses and labour lost due to illnesses. Ghana faces chronic water shortages due to uneven distribution of rainfall and inadequate infrastructure. It is imperative to find a solution to this problem, particularly in urban areas, by laying out infrastructure to expand access to and reliability of drinking water. The country also has high levels of water pollution leading to waterborne ailments such as diarrhoea. An ongoing project in Kenya by Innovation for Poverty Action, which provides premeasured chlorine doses at communal water sources, has proven effective in reducing water contamination. The government should investigate the use of similar inexpensive means to sanitize water.

ADVOCATE FOR BETTER NUTRITION

Awareness among the population about dietary needs and nutrition appears to be low. The government should consider awareness campaigns regarding the nutritional value of food sources such as fruit. The government should also invest in promoting fortified food targeted at poorer households to reduce nutrient deficiencies and improve health and labour productivity.

PROVIDE INCENTIVES FOR PHYSICIANS

A high proportion of trained doctors leave the country to pursue opportunities abroad. The government should explore incentive schemes that encourage doctors and trained medical professionals to stay in the country. These incentives should also encourage them to move to rural regions with lower physician-to-population ratios.

INCREASE VACCINATION COVERAGE

In certain regions such as the rural savannah, up to 5 per cent of children younger than age 5 have not been vaccinated. The most commonly cited reason is distance to a health center (GLSS5, 2010). The government should therefore identify villages or communities that are cut off from health centers, and hold vaccination camps or deliver vaccines directly to them to attain closer to full coverage. Recent research by Banerjee *et al.* (2010) shows that providing small incentives to families that vaccinate their children can significantly boost vaccination rates. Other methods that boost vaccination rates can be tested.

INVEST IN CHILD HEALTH

Research has shown that investing in child health is very cost-effective. Programs that focus on reducing malaria incidence, deworming and providing better nutrition for children should be prioritized, in conjunction with youth-focused health programs such as iron supplementation. There is a large body of literature describing the importance of early childhood investments. Overall, this literature finds that the returns to early child investments are extremely large. The programs in this area should be assigned priority.

Education and labour markets

There is a large literature in economics linking education to labour market outcomes in both developing and developed countries. The Millennium Development Goal of universal primary education has focused attention on education worldwide and in Ghana. The Government of Ghana instituted the Free Compulsory Universal Basic Education in 1996, and is currently discussing the possibility of pursuing a policy of free secondary education. In order to evaluate these policies, it is important to understand the link between education outcomes and socioeconomic outcomes, including labour market outcomes.

Table 5.9 provides an overview of the education sector in Ghana. During 2005–11, gross enrolment rates in primary, secondary and tertiary education have increased by 10.9, 17.0 and 6.5 per cent, respectively. During this period, the ratio of female-to-male enrolment has increased by 6.3, 3.1 and 5.8 per cent in the primary, secondary and tertiary sectors, respectively (World Bank, 2011).

Evidence from Ghana demonstrates an increase in earnings associated with higher levels of education. Teal (2007) uses data from the Ghana Manufacturing Enterprise Survey,[8] and finds that skilled workers have, on average, higher monthly wages when compared with unskilled workers in manufacturing firms, as demonstrated in Figure 5.7.

Teal (2007) also shows an increase in monthly wages associated with years of education. Figure 5.8 presents these findings and demonstrates that the largest increases in wages accrue to those with higher levels of education. In the sample of firm workers, the average duration of education is 9.5 years. At this level of education, the rate of return of an additional year of schooling is under 5 per cent and the monthly wage for a worker with average characteristics

Table 5.9 Summary of education in Ghana, 2005–11

Education	*Value*
Public expenditure on education (% of GDP)	5.4
Expected years of schooling (of children)	10.5
Adult literacy rate, both sexes (% aged 15 and above)	66.6
Mean years of schooling (of adults)	7.1
Combined gross enrolment in education (both sexes) (%)	63.3
School enrolment, primary (% gross)	99.8
School enrolment, secondary (% gross)	90.5
School enrolment, tertiary (% gross)	12.1
Ratio of female to male primary enrolment (%)	99.8
Ratio of female to male secondary enrolment (%)	90.5
Ratio of female to male tertiary enrolment (%)	61.9

Source: World Bank (2011); UNDP (2011).

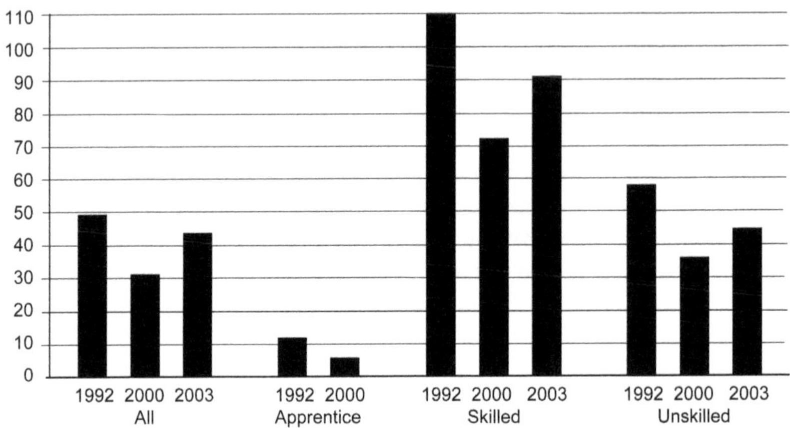

Figure 5.7 Wages and skills
Source: Teal (2007).

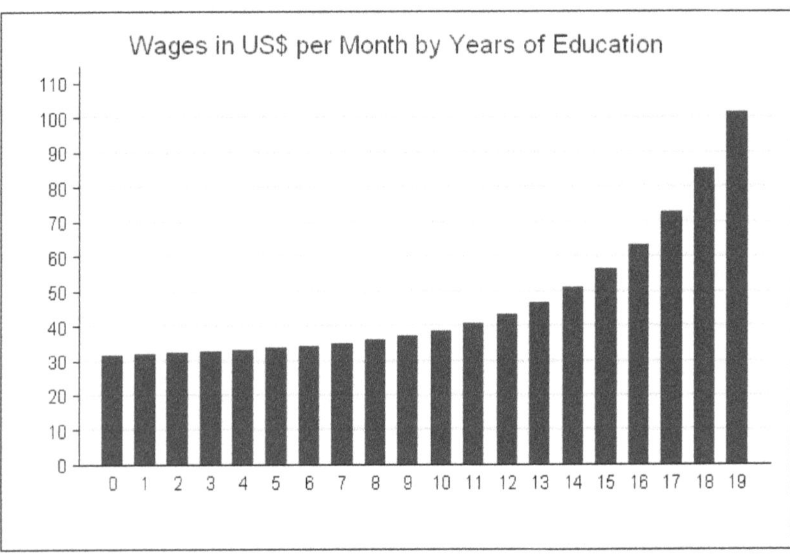

Figure 5.8 Wages and years of education
Source: Teal (2007).

is approximately US$40, less than US$10 more than workers with less than primary education. However, in contrast, those with the longest duration of schooling have wages more than twice as high as the average.

Canagarajah *et al.* (1997) and Kingdon and Söderbom (2007) also find that the (private and social) returns to upper secondary are greater than the returns to lower levels of educational attainment. Kingdon *et al.* (2007) use data from the 1998–99 GLSS, and find suggestive evidence that education raises earnings indirectly by helping individuals gain entry into high-paying occupations, but leads to only modest increases in earnings, with these gains exclusively in the wage employment sector. In contrast, the authors do not find an increase in earnings for the large majority of workers in Ghana, because returns to education in self-employment and agriculture are very low, and because these two occupations together constitute 82.5 per cent of the employed workforce.

Jolliffe (2003) estimates the returns to education in farm and off-farm work, and finds that the returns to schooling are much higher in off-farm work than in farm work. Though different studies have produced different estimates of the returns to education in Ghana, the findings suggest that there are positive returns to education. However, these returns are concentrated largely at high levels of education and outside self-employment and agriculture.

In addition to differences in wages, education may also be associated with differences in unemployment rates and sectors of employment, particularly whether an individual is self-employed or wage-employed. We use data from the 2009 wave of a longitudinal labour market survey, conducted by the Centre for the Study of African Economies at the University of Oxford in collaboration with the Ghana Statistical Office, to investigate these associations in urban Ghana. The sample is a stratified random sample of urban households in the four largest urban centers of Ghana: Greater Accra (including Tema), Kumasi, Takoradi and Cape Coast. The sample was drawn from the Ghanaian Census of 2000.

Figure 5.9 shows that for individuals aged 15–55 there is no strong relationship between the likelihood of employment and years of schooling. However, for those individuals who are employed, those with more education are significantly more likely to be wage-employed rather than self-employed, as seen in Figure 5.10. Given the importance of education in determining labour market outcomes and firm success, finding successful cost-effective policies that improve education outcomes is of vital importance. Moreover, given the non-linear relationship between education and earnings, how best to allocate limited education resources between primary, secondary and post-secondary education is an important policy question.

Programs aimed at improving access to education and increasing enrolment rates have been used in many developing countries, particularly at the primary school level. They include school-building campaigns (Indonesia), conditional cash transfers (Mexico), and programs aimed at improving child health (Kenya).

Costs of schooling can be a major impediment to educational attainment. Numerous studies have shown that price is a major deterrent to educational investment (Holla and Kremer, 2008). Fee-reduction schemes such as vouchers and scholarships are promising avenues for increasing educational investments. In addition, programs that reduce the burden of ancillary and indirect costs of schooling can also be effective policy options. Programs that provide school uniforms or reduce the distance to school can lead to increases in education, especially for girls (Duflo *et al.*, 2011; Burde and Linden, 2012). Duflo (2001)

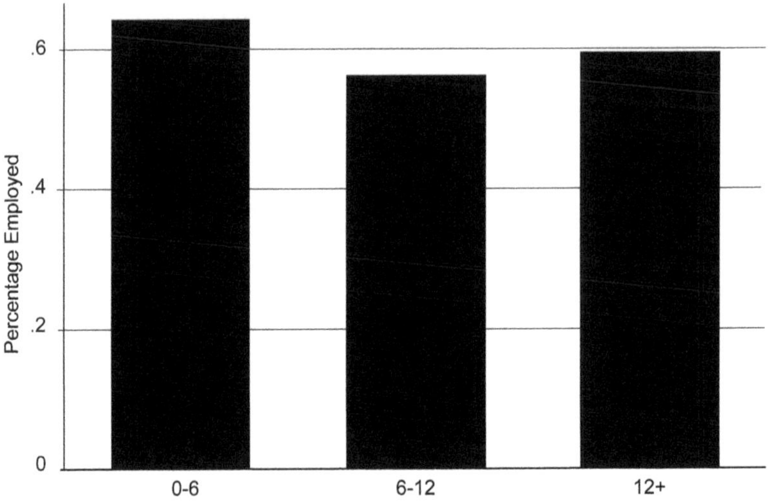

Figure 5.9 Employment status and years of schooling
Source: Author's calculations.

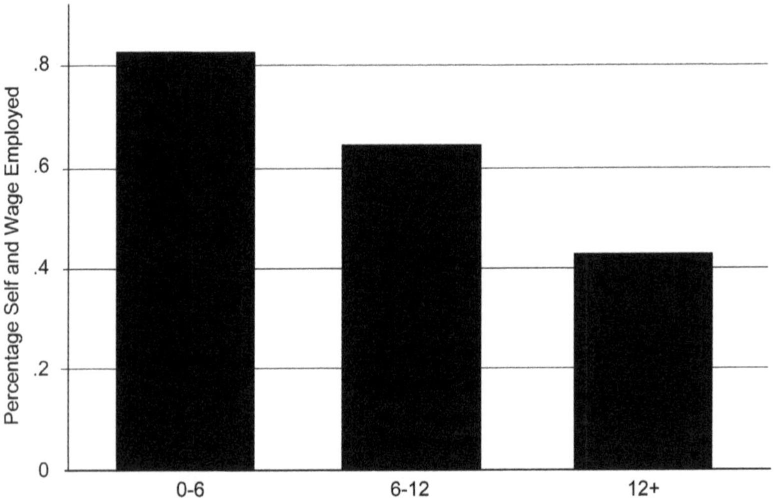

Figure 5.10 Employment type and years of schooling
Source: Author's calculations.

studies a major school-construction program in Indonesia in which more than 61,000 primary schools were built, and argues that increasing physical access to schools leads to increases in educational attainment.

Health can also be a constraint on educational access. Miguel and Kremer (2004) show that students who were dewormed (and thus saw health improvements) were more likely to attend and participate in school. While that study was based in Kenya, several studies from other settings support the generalizability of the relationship between poor health and low school attendance.

How best to improve the quality of education is another important policy question. Increasing educational inputs such as textbooks, flipcharts and computers is one method. Another is improving teaching through better training of teachers, more supervision of teachers by parent–teacher associations, the hiring of contract teachers, changes in the structure of teachers' pay, or reductions in class size. The impacts of these interventions have been investigated in both Kenya and Uganda (Glewwe *et al.*, 2004; Zeitlin *et al.*, 2011; Bold *et al.*, 2012; Duflo *et al.*, 2012). However, further education research in Ghana is necessary.

Several government and non-governmental programs have been introduced in Ghana to expand educational access and improve education quality. The introduction of the National Early Childhood Development Strategy was associated with an increase in kindergarten enrolment by 38.5 per cent in 2005 compared with the previous academic year (Ministry of Education, 2006). Akyeampong *et al.* (2007) and Akyeampong (2011) argue that the introduction of School Capitation Grants, which replaced school fees with grants, successfully pulled a large group of out-of-school children back into education. During the 2005–06 school year, primary school gross enrolment rose by nearly 10 per cent while overall enrolment in basic school increased by 16.7 per cent (UNICEF, 2006). GETFund support has been used to expand academic and physical facilities in the tertiary education sector, allowing institutions to increase their intake. Despite this progress, the enrolment rate of students aged 17–21 is very low, at less than 5 per cent, compared with developed countries, where it averages over 50 per cent (Akyeampong *et al.*, 2007).

Current research by Ksoll and Lehrer is investigating the transition of youth from senior high schools in Ghana into the activities they undertake immediately after leaving senior high school and in the years following. The focus of the research is on the transition from secondary school to post-secondary education and into the labour market. The research follows students from 136 randomly selected senior high schools throughout Ghana who completed senior high school in 2008, 2009, 2011 and 2012, and will investigate the determinants of post-secondary educational attendance and achievement. Given the high returns to education that are found only at the post-secondary level in Ghana (Teal, 2007), this ongoing research will inform the policy debate in Ghana regarding access to post-secondary attendance. Moreover, the research will focus on the determinants of youth unemployment of senior high school graduates.

Recommendations

EXPAND ACCESS TO EDUCATION FOR THE RURAL POOR

Education resources in Ghana are distributed unevenly. Rarieya and Fentiman (2012) find that enrolment in the north of the country lags seriously behind the south. Akyeampong (2005) shows there is better-quality provision in traditional boarding schools located mostly in cities and towns than in community day secondary schools that are found mainly in rural or peri-urban areas. Moreover, traditional schools attract more qualified teachers than the community schools. Teacher shortages in technical and vocational education are constraining the sector, perhaps undermining student interest. Limited access and the low quality of education in rural areas result in low tertiary enrolment rates. Although there has been an increase in tertiary enrolment, the growth in the sector has disproportionally benefited students from selected urban secondary schools. For example, 60–90 per cent of students selected to various degree programs at the University of Ghana came from the top 50 senior high schools in Ghana. These 50 schools constitute fewer than 10 per cent of senior high schools in Ghana (Addae-Mensah, 2000).

Overall, the literature clearly demonstrates that fees hinder schooling access. Conditional cash transfers (CCTs), scholarships and vouchers have been shown to be effective at boosting schooling in various settings. These could be implemented in Ghana. In addition, reducing the distance to schools, especially in underserved rural areas, may be an important policy option.

IMPROVE THE RATES OF TRANSITION FOR GIRLS

Rarieya and Fentiman (2012) show that although more girls enter school earlier than boys, a higher proportion of girls drop out and do not make the transition from primary school to junior high school. This is especially significant in rural areas where school children are also working, and a considerable number of girls migrate in search of wage labour. The pioneering PROGRESA CCT program in Mexico provided cash grants for poor mothers whose children attended school at least 85 per cent of the time. This program significantly increased the transition rate from elementary school to junior secondary school (Schultz, 2004). There may be potential for a CCT program in Ghana, perhaps with a focus on girls, to improve educational attainment.

IMPROVE THE QUALITY OF EDUCATION

International evidence suggests that the 'quality of secondary education, especially in maths and science, has a stronger impact on economic growth than years of schooling' (World Bank, 2007). Low returns to education in Ghana suggest that curriculum reform and programs that improve teaching quality should be prioritized. Akyeampong *et al.* (2007) argue that teachers in secondary education are not able to generate enough interest in science and mathematics through innovative teaching. Of the approximately 14,000 secondary teachers in public schools in Ghana, approximately one-fifth are not professionally qualified, and an even smaller number of teachers of science and mathematics subjects are qualified (NPT/GHA PRACTICAL project,

2007). Meanwhile, the expansion in secondary education has focused predominantly on the general arts subjects, while enrolment in technical, vocational and agricultural streams have all declined (NPT/GHA PRACTICAL Project, 2007).

Overall, the literature points to the efficacy of reforming pedagogy in a manner that allows teachers to focus on the needs of their students. Programs such as teacher incentives and remedial education have the potential to improve teaching, and should be piloted.

Gender and the labour market

Though Ghana has made great strides in achieving gender equality in many spheres, significant gaps remain. In 2001, the adult literacy rate (aged 15 and over) of women was 64.5 per cent compared with 81.1 per cent for men (Chant and Jones, 2005). Though net primary enrolment rates for boys and girls are almost equal, with a ratio of girls to boys of 0.95, for net secondary enrolment this ratio falls to 0.86, and for gross tertiary enrolment further to only 0.40 (Chant and Jones, 2005).

There is also evidence of gender discrimination in earnings in the Ghanaian informal sector. Addai (2011) uses the 1998/99 GLSS and finds that women in the Ghanaian informal sector labour market are, on average, 36 per cent more skilled than their male counterparts. However, a man with the same characteristics as the female sample average earns, on average, 87 per cent more in log monthly wages.

We use data from the 2009 and 2010 waves of the longitudinal labour market survey conducted by the Centre for the Study of African Economies at the University of Oxford in collaboration with the Ghana Statistical Office to summarize the employment characteristics of men and women in urban Ghana.

Table 5.10 presents employment status by gender for both years of the survey, for both the full sample of respondents and the subset of youth aged between 15 and 24. In both 2009 and 2010, men and women were equally likely to be employed. This is true both for the full sample and for youth. However, youth are much less likely to be employed. The youth employment rate in the sample is 21.89 per cent in 2009 and 25.40 per cent in 2010, compared with 77.96 and 74.74, respectively, for those aged 25 or older.

Though employment rates among urban men and women are approximately equal, the type of employment in which they are engaged differs considerably. Respondents are classified as being either self-employed or wage-employed. Table 5.11 presents the summary statistics of these categories by gender. Conditional on being employed, women are more likely to be engaged in self-employment compared with men. This observation holds true for both the full sample and the youth subsample. As in Table 5.10, both male and female youth are less likely to be self-employed compared with those over the age of 25.

Table 5.10 Employment status

Gender	2009		2010	
	Employed (%)	*Unemployed (%)*	*Employed (%)*	*Unemployed (%)*
Full sample				
Male	57.07	42.93	59.13	40.87
Female	60.13	39.87	59.47	40.53
Youth (15–24)				
Male	22.73	77.27	25.69	74.31
Female	21.20	78.80	25.15	74.85

Source: Authors' calculations.

Table 5.11 Job type

Gender	2009		2010	
	Self-employed	*Wage-employed*	*Self-employed*	*Wage-employed*
Full sample				
Male	40.54	59.46	38.70	61.30
Female	75.89	24.11	75.62	24.38
Youth (15–24)				
Male	20.00	80.00	18.92	81.08
Female	48.72	51.28	47.62	52.38

Source: Authors' calculations.

Table 5.12 further distinguishes the activity type of the sample by gender and by year. There is a substantial amount of segregation of activity types between genders, with men much more likely to be involved in, for example, manufacturing and construction, while women are more likely to be involved in, for example, hairdressing and trade.

Heintz (2005) also examines gender differences in employment using the fourth round of the GLSS. The findings are in line with those above, and show substantial labour force segmentation by gender in Ghana. Women's employment was largely restricted to agriculture, manufacturing, trading and services. These sectors, excluding services, are those with some of the highest overall poverty rates in Ghana. Within these sectors, women were largely employed as own-account workers and informal wage workers.

Furthermore, Heintz (2005) shows that women are disproportionately represented in more precarious forms of employment; women's employment is concentrated in activities for which earnings are low and where the risks of poverty are high (unpaid workers on family enterprises and informal self-employment). Poverty rates among working women remain higher than those of working men.

Table 5.12 Activity choice

	(1)	(2)	(3)	(4)	(5)	(6)
	All		*Male*		*Female*	
	2009	*2010*	*2009*	*2010*	*2009*	*2010*
Wage work						
Accounts/finance	6	4	4	3	2	1
Cashier/teller	1	3	–	–	1	3
Manual work	88	79	60	54	28	25
Manufacturing	3	5	3	2	–	3
Office/secretarial/clerical	20	22	10	11	10	11
Official/technical/managers/supervisors	12	24	11	18	1	5
Other jobs involving money	4	7	2	5	2	2
Other jobs not involving money	61	53	31	33	30	20
Sales/shop assistants	25	33	11	15	14	18
Number of observations	220	230	132	141	88	88
Self employed						
Manufacturing						
Agriculture, fishing, livestock	2	2	–	2	2	–
Arts and crafts	1	2	1	1	–	1
Carpentry	8	4	8	4	–	–
Processed food	40	55	–	1	40	54
Metal/welding	5	6	5	6	–	–
Sewing/tailoring	33	36	7	8	26	28
Other	8	8	5	4	3	4
Number of observations	97	114	26	26	71	87
Services						
Building, construction, plumbing, carpentry	3	11	3	11	–	–
Driving taxis, buses, etc.	3	5	3	5	–	–
Electrician	7	7	7	7	–	–
Hairdressing	20	14	2	1	18	13
Mechanic	6	7	6	7	–	–
Other	16	8	7	6	9	1
Number of observations	55	52	28	37	27	14
Trade						
Clothes	32	29	6	3	26	26
Electronics	1	19	1	6	–	13
Processed food	47	11	1	–	46	11
Unprocessed food	66	31	7	1	59	30
Household items	31	77	5	7	26	70
Tools/building materials	3	1	2	1	1	–
Water	9	11	1	1	8	10
Fuel	4	4	–	–	4	4
Jewelry	5	5	3	3	2	2
Phone products	11	2	5	2	1	4
Other	6	6	5	1	6	1
Number of observations	215	196	36	25	179	171
Unpaid workers	23	43	6	15	17	28
Total	610	635	228	244	382	388

Source: Aslam and Lehrer (2012).

Moreover, within forms of employment, Heintz (2005) shows that women earn less in every category except for unpaid family workers (imputed wages). Within the formal sector (public wage employees and formal self-employed) and within the informal sector (informal self-employed, self-employed agriculture, informal public wage worker), women, on average, earn less per hour than men. Lower average earnings and labour force segmentation combined mean that employed women earned 76 per cent of male earnings. Moreover, women tend to work fewer hours per week compared with men.

Canagarajah *et al.* (2001) investigated the distributional aspects of poverty reduction in the late 1980s and early 1990s in rural Ghana and Uganda. The authors used data from the GLSS from 1987–88 and 1991–92, and found that being a female household head had positive effects on non-farm income. This positive effect (55 per cent) outweighed the negative effect of being female in 1988. However, in 1992 the positive effect of being a female household head fell to 27 per cent and no longer outweighed the negative effect of being female. The authors also found that women made about 40 per cent less than men during this period.

The employment outcomes of women have important implications for other socioeconomic outcomes, including marriage and fertility. Jensen (2012) analyzed a randomized control trial, which provided three years of job-recruiting services for the business process outsourcing industry to young women aged 15–21 in randomly selected rural Indian villages. The intervention effectively increased women's labour force opportunities in the 160 treatment villages in which it was implemented. An additional 160 villages acted as control villages. Twenty households were interviewed per village. The author found that women in treatment villages were 5–6 percentage points less likely to get married or have children during the period of study, during September–October 2003 to September–October 2006. They chose instead to enter the labour market or obtain additional schooling or training. Women also reported wanting to have 0.35 fewer children and to work more steadily throughout their lifetime. These changes are consistent with increased career aspirations.

Though labour force participation rates among women in Ghana are higher than those of India, the findings of Jensen (2012) do have important implications for Ghanaian policy. That paper demonstrates that improved career aspirations and opportunities can have significant impacts not only on labour market outcomes, but additionally on other important life-cycle outcomes including marriage and fertility. These issues are relevant for Ghanaian women and can have important intergenerational impacts on the transmission of poverty.

Understanding the gender differences in employment outcomes and the mechanisms through which they are generated is necessary to implement policies aimed at closing the gaps that exist between Ghanaian men and women in labour market outcomes.

One possible explanation for these gender differences is differential rates of technological adoption between men and women, leading to differences in incomes, productivity and hours of work. Morris and Doss (2001) investigate this channel in agriculture, but the findings probably apply to other sectors in Ghana. The authors investigate whether differential adoption rates are attributable to inherent characteristics of the technologies themselves, or rather to gender-linked differences in access to other key inputs. The distinction is crucial for policymaking because each mechanism implies different policies to ensure gender equality in technology adoption. The authors suggest that if gender directly affects technology adoption, research and extension strategies may be modified. However, if the differential rates of adoption are caused by unequal access to complementary inputs, then improving women's access to these inputs may be an important policy tool.

Their findings suggest that gender differences in the adoption of modern maize varieties and chemical fertilizer are not attributable to the inherent characteristics of the technologies themselves, but result from gender differences in access to associated inputs (Morris and Doss, 2001). However, the appropriate policy intervention remains less clear. One policy option would be to increase women's access to the associated resources which they lack. Alternatively, the authors suggest that it may be desirable to target technologies that are particularly suited for the resources that are already available to women.

Information can play an important role in finding employment and in human capital investment decisions. Access to such information may differ by gender and may explain some of the differences in labour market outcomes between men and women that we observe in Ghana. Jensen (2012) found that in 2003 women from Indian villages aged 15–21 exposed to the recruiting intervention described previously were 4.6 percentage points more likely to work in the business process outsourcing industry than women in control villages, and 2.4 percentage points more likely to work at all for pay outside the home. They were also significantly more likely to enroll in computer or English language courses at fee-paying training institutes. These findings suggest a willingness to invest in human capital in order to find a job when suitable opportunities are available.

The author also found that younger school-aged girls were affected by the intervention. Such girls showed increased school enrolment rates and greater BMI, reflecting better nutrition and health investments. These results suggest that parents are willing to invest in girls' human capital when labour market opportunities exist for girls.

Jensen (2012) notes that the goal of the intervention was not to investigate recruiting services as a policy instrument, and that recruiting services do not actually create any new jobs. However, the study does highlight the importance of information regarding labour demand and labour market returns both for women's employment and education decision-making, and for the decision-making of girls' parents. However, there are likely to be more cost-effective means of doing so than recruiting services, such as through the use of mass media. This is the case for India and likely remains true for Ghana as well. Policies and interventions aimed at informing women, girls, and parents of girls about labour market opportunities and returns may have significant impacts on employment and education outcomes.

In addition to information, the importance of networks in influencing schooling choices and employment outcomes can be substantial. Munshi and Rosenzweig (2006) studied the importance of networks in Bombay, India. Their findings demonstrate the importance of networks in a changing economy and may be relevant for women's outcomes in Ghana. They found that having fewer existing networks may actually benefit women as opposed to hindering them in the labour market. Using data from a sample of 4900 households in Bombay in 2001–02, they found that male lower-caste networks continued to direct boys into local language schools that led to traditional working-class occupations, despite the fact that returns to non-traditional white collar occupations rose substantially during that period. In contrast, lower-caste girls, who historically had low labour market participation rates and so did not benefit from the network, took advantage of the opportunities that had become available by switching to English schools.

Evidence from an ongoing randomized control study on vocational education in Kenya highlights the importance of credit and information constraints on youth educational investments (Hicks *et al.*, 2011). Among winners of a voucher for vocational education, the authors did not find statistically significant differences in the take-up rates by gender. However, among the young women who did not take up the voucher, childcare was the primary reason cited for non-enrolment. This highlights the importance of addressing childcare concerns in programs targeting young women.

In addition, the authors found that students were often uncertain about the most lucrative vocational trades, reflecting the presence of information constraints. The randomized provision of information regarding the labour market returns to female-dominated trades (e.g. beauty and tailoring) and male-dominated trades (e.g. construction, mechanics/driving and computing) led to a 6 per cent increase in female enrolment in male-dominated trades. The high levels of occupation segregation suggest that simple information campaigns can encourage women to depart from traditional gender roles and enter into more potentially lucrative male-dominated trades.

While the authors are currently collecting follow-up data, some preliminary data analysis reveals that vocational education increases the profits of men in self-employment, but has no impact on women in self-employment or on formal wage-employed individuals. More research is required to show the labour market impacts of training and the drivers of the documented effects.

The findings of the *World Development Report 2012: Gender Equality and Employment* (World Bank, 2012a) demonstrate that the same pattern of gender differences in labour market outcomes in Ghana also exists more broadly. The authors found gender differences in productivity and earnings across sectors and jobs. They argue that these differences arise primarily from employment segregation: differences in the economic activities of men and women. However, as in Ghana, the authors note that gender differences in human capital also play a role.

The authors of the report list the following three factors in explaining gender segregation in employment: differences in time use, access to productive inputs (particularly land and credit), and gender differences arising from market and institutional failures. They explain that there is a feedback loop between employment segregation and its causes. Many women worldwide appear to be caught in this trap, where employment segregation reinforces gender differences in time use and in access to inputs, which further perpetuate market and institutional failures.

The report concludes that breaking out of this productivity trap requires addressing all three of its causes: interventions that reduce time constraints, increase productive inputs, and those that correct market and institutional failures. The authors further note that successful interventions will depend on identifying the binding constraint in each context while acknowledging the existence of multiple constraints. They recommend the possibility of sequencing policies to address all constraints.

Recommendations

CONSIDER GENDER

Ghana has yet to achieve gender equality in education and labour market outcomes. Gender should be considered when discussing possible labour market interventions as well the possibility of differential impacts by gender. Some interventions may require modifications by gender in order to achieve their desired outcomes. While there are many potential ways to promote gender equality, the policy options will depend on the economic sector.

PROVIDE INFORMATION

The provision of information on technologies, job opportunities and returns to different types of employment can be inexpensive interventions, especially using mass media such as radio, television, newspapers and the internet, to reduce information gaps, particularly among young women when they are making education and labour market decisions. A growing body of rigorous research shows the effectiveness (and cost-effectiveness) of information provision. There may be more research needed to evaluate the best way to deliver information to girls. For example, studies suggest that information provision through role models may be particularly effective for girls.

IMPROVE ACCESS TO HUMAN AND PHYSICAL CAPITAL

Ghanaian women remain less educated and more capital constrained than Ghanaian men. Many interventions to eliminate these differences are possible.

The impacts and cost-effectiveness of such policies in Ghana should be analyzed. These include microfinance, education scholarships, vouchers for vocational training, business training and cash transfers, among others. There is a large body of rigorous evidence that points to potentially cost-effective programs. Overall, programs that provide girls with scholarships, CCTs, and programs that reduce distance to schooling are effective policy options.

ADDRESS MULTIPLE CONSTRAINTS

Successful interventions must address all constraints facing women in the labour market. Interventions should reduce time constraints, increase productive inputs, and correct market and institutional failures. Policies may be sequenced in order to address all constraints.

Self-employment and the role of the informal sector

Ghana's economy has seen steady growth over the past decade as it has responded to the government's strategy of encouraging the private sector. Agriculture continues to be the highest contributor to the economy at 38 per cent, though its share has been steadily falling with the growth in services (33.4 per cent share of the economy) and the industrial/manufacturing sector (28.6 per cent share). Ghana has also improved its business environment over the past decade. Data from the World Bank Enterprise Surveys show that it took 5 days to register a business in 2007 compared with 14 in 2005, and the ease of doing business ranking improved from 94 in 2005 to 87 in 2007.

Despite its efforts to formalize the economy, the informal sector in Ghana is large and growing, and is bigger than in other countries in Sub-Saharan Africa (World Bank, 2007). Appiah-Kubi (2007) estimates that the informal sector accounts for approximately 20–40 per cent of national output. The informal sector is arguably even more important as a source of employment. In 2010, the proportion of workers in this sector stood at 86.1 per cent, while self-employment constituted 64.8 per cent of total employment. Adams (2009) also suggests that an increasing number of individuals in Sub-Saharan Africa view employment in the informal sector as their first option, rather than a formal sector job.

Given the importance of the informal sector to the economy and especially to employment, it is critical to understand the constraints faced by this sector. As noted by La Porta and Shleifer (2008: 328), the productivity of the informal sector lags behind that of the formal sector. They find that '[o]n average, based on the Informal sample, the productivity of small firms in the Enterprise Survey is around 154, 180, or 314 per cent higher than for unregistered firms depending on whether we look at value added, sales per employee, or real output per employee, respectively'. Informal firms, on average, are also younger than registered firms, export very rarely, own lower-quality assets, and own fewer assets in total. Registered firms very rarely start as unregistered firms. La Porta and Shleifer (2008) also note that tax evasion is a large benefit for informal firms. Tax liability and regulatory burdens increase with firm size. Finally, the authors find substantial differences in human capital between formal and informal firms. Formal firms are run by much better-educated managers: only 6.1 per cent of informal firms operate with a top manager with some college education, compared with 15.9 per cent for registered firms.

Data from the World Bank Enterprise surveys show that the lagging productivity of the informal sector relative to the formal sector is particularly salient in Ghana (Figure 5.11). The productivity (measured by sales growth and labour productivity growth) in Ghana's informal sector is particularly low relative to other countries in the region. Thus boosting the productivity of this sector could have important implications for Ghana's economy and for the labour market outcomes of youth, as a large share of youth would be employed by this sector.

More than 70 per cent of Ghanaian firms identify access to finance as a major constraint (more than twice the average ratio of firms surveyed across the world), suggesting that the lack of access to credit may hinder the productivity of the informal sector in Ghana (World Bank Enterprise Survey, 2007). Close to 44 per cent of all Ghanaians and 55 per cent of rural Ghanaians do not have access to any kind of financial service. In addition, 33.9 per cent of the businesses have no access or do not use any kind of financial products (FinScope survey, 2010). Overall, banks finance only about 11 per cent of small Ghanaian firms' investments, and it is likely that firms in the informal sector have even less access to bank financing. Moreover, only 78.3 per cent of small firms have a checking or savings account compared with 95.2 and 97.1

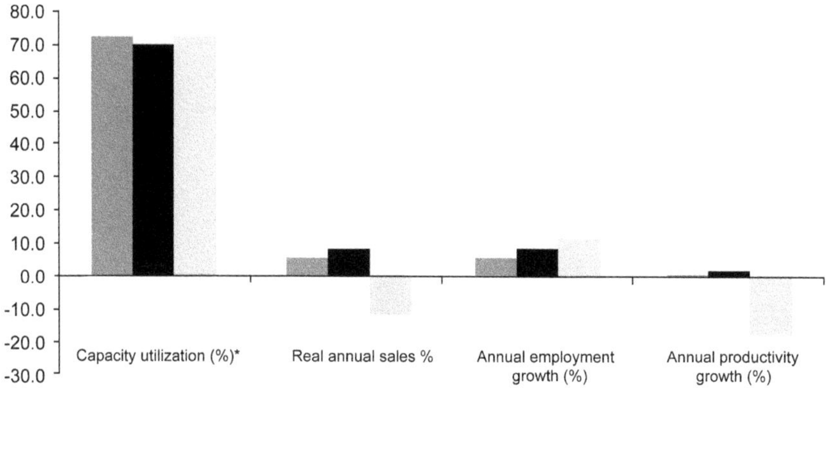

Figure 5.11 Low productivity in the informal sector
Source: World Bank Enterprise Survey 2007.

per cent, respectively, for medium-sized and large firms (World Bank Enterprise Survey, 2007).

Udry and Anagol (2006) found that while credit constraints were prevalent in Ghana, the returns to capital in the informal sector were substantial. They showed that the annual returns to investments in new technology (pineapple cultivation) were 205–350 per cent, while returns in 'regular technology' (staple food crops) were between 30 and 50 per cent. They also found returns to capital among used car-part traders to be approximately 60 per cent. This is consistent with recent experimental evidence from Sri Lanka by De Mel *et al.* (2007), which found high rates of return to capital in the informal sector. They found that average real returns to capital for microenterprise firms were 5.7 per cent per month, or at least 68 per cent per year, substantially higher than the market interest rate. They also found that the returns were highest for entrepreneurs with more ability and with fewer workers who were household members.

Access to reliable infrastructure is an additional challenge that hinders the productivity of the informal sector in Ghana. Figure 5.12 shows that the level of access to reliable electricity and water is much lower in Ghana relative to other African countries in the survey. 86.2 per cent of firms in Ghana identified electricity as a major constraint, compared with 49.2 per cent for firms across Sub-Saharan Africa (World Bank Enterprise Survey, 2007).

There is a notion that the informal sector is the employer of last resort, perhaps attracting a disproportionate number of 'low-productivity' individuals. This notion suggests that part of the productivity lag may be driven in part by the (lower) abilities and characteristics of the individuals who enter the informal sector. However, evidence from Günther and Launov (2012)

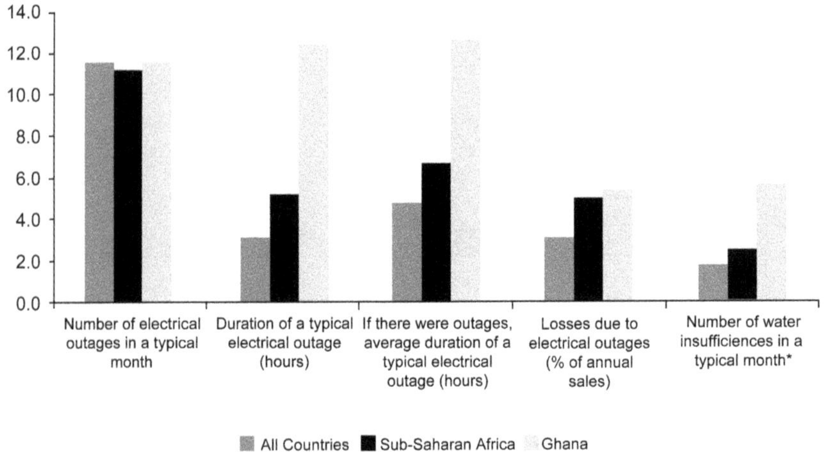

Figure 5.12 Infrastructural challenges
Source: World Bank Enterprise Survey 2007.

suggests that approximately 55 per cent of those employed in the informal sector have a comparative advantage in the sector and choose to enter it voluntarily. The implication is that encouraging those with a comparative advantage to enter the sector and improving their training and access to capital could increase the productivity of the sector.

A recent paper by Falco *et al.* (2010) highlights the importance of unobservable factors on the type of employment that individuals select. Using panel datasets from urban markets in Ghana and Tanzania, they show that skills levels of workers and unobservable factors linked to the size and sector of employment are important determinants of wages. Moreover, they find that unobservable distributions between workers who are self-employed with no employees and those who are self-employed with some employees are very different, suggesting that these are fundamentally different types of enterprise. Their results suggest that policymakers should differentiate informal sector firms by their size and not treat the informal sector as homogeneous.

Human capital constraints are also prevalent in the informal sector. The education levels of those employed in the informal sector are generally lower than those in the formal sector (Liimatainen, 2002). Moreover, those working in the informal sector acquire most of their skills outside of the formal education sector, and mainly through traditional apprenticeship training (Haan, 2002). While apprenticeships are common in many African countries, they are particularly prevalent in West African countries such as Ghana and Cote d'Ivoire (Frazer, 2006). It is estimated that apprenticeships in Ghana are by far the most important source of skills for those working in the informal sector, responsible for some 80–90 per cent of all skills development in the country. Other skills providers account for a much smaller share: 5–10 per cent through public sector vocational training centers and 10–15 per cent by private non-profit training providers (Korboe, 2001). Monk *et al.* (2008) show that the importance of apprenticeships may be increasing in Ghana. Using a variety of nationally representative data sources, they show that the share of apprentices in the labour force has increased from about 4 per cent in 1984 to 10 per cent in 2000. They further show that apprentices account for 25 per cent of working age adults in Ghana, with a slightly higher share of apprentices found in urban areas. While in many countries the apprenticeship period varies with the trade, the traditional apprenticeship system in Ghana is standardized at 3–4 years (Haan, 2002).

The effects of apprenticeships vary across skills, education and vocation. While there are currently no experimental estimates on the returns to apprenticeships in Ghana, an ongoing randomized evaluation conducted by Mbiti *et al.* is expected to provide some empirical evidence.

Existing evidence from non-randomized studies in Ghana and in other countries does show that apprenticeships have positive impacts on earnings. Using data from Ghana, Frazer (2006) argues that apprenticeships provide firm-specific skills that increase an individual's productivity in their current firm, but less so in any other firm. Due to this form of skills acquisition, Frazer

(2006) argues that the returns to apprenticeship are in self-employment, where a former apprentice replicates both the technology and business practices of the apprenticeship firm.

Monk *et al.* (2008) find that the returns to apprenticeships in Ghana vary by the (formal) education attainment of the apprentice. They estimate that training increases earnings by 50 per cent for currently employed individuals who completed apprenticeships but have no formal education. However, this return declines as education levels rise. There is additional evidence from earlier research by Monk *et al.* (2007) showing that apprenticeships increase the probability of informal employment relative to having no job. Overall, these studies show that apprenticeships are an important way to provide employable skills for the informal sector.

The smaller size of informal sector firms, combined with the lack adequate institutional support and quality human resources, raises the risks for firms in this sector. Some of this risk can be mitigated through trade associations of informal sector firms based on relevant sectors. Such associations can facilitate information transfer, marketing services and employee training. Strengthening these associations can play a critical role in defining training needs, delivering short courses, setting competency standards and skills certification, thereby addressing issues related to human capital development (Johanson and Adams, 2004). There is, however, very little evidence of the effect of associations on skills development in the informal sector (World Bank, 2008). Industry associations also have a greater ability to inform policy decisions. This in turn would improve the productivity and output of these firms (Alila and Pedersen, 2001; Fafchamps, 2004).

There is also an argument for encouraging informal sector firms to join the formal sector. La Porta and Shleifer (2008) used several World Bank firm-level surveys[9] to uncover a strong negative relationship between income per capita and the informal economy. By one measure, the informal economy is 18 per cent larger in poor countries than in rich ones. The authors suggest that the decline of informal firms has important implications for development.

Recommendations

INCREASE FINANCIAL ACCESS

Access to credit is a major barrier to increasing the productivity of informal sector firms. Given the rates of return documented by Udry and Anagol (2006) and De Mel *et al.* (2007), providing credit or grants to self-employed individuals in the informal sector could have significant effects on informal sector productivity. Recent work by Fafchamps *et al.* (2012) shows that cash grants and in-kind grants have different effects for men and women in the informal sector. While there were no statistically different effects between the returns (in terms of profits) to cash grants versus in-kind grants for men, women benefited more from in-kind grants. By implication, self-control issues are likely to interfere with investment decisions, especially in female microenterprises. The authors argue that microcredit may be effective in this setting, as regular meetings and repayment schedules help individuals overcome self-control issues.

Overall, there is a large body of evidence that supports this recommendation. However, more research is needed to ascertain optimal ways to increase financial access. These include incorporating lessons from behavioural economics, such as the recent study by Fafchamps *et al.* (2012) which demonstrated the importance of providing mechanisms to overcome self-control problems.

FACILITATE FORMALIZATION

One potential benefit of formalization is the protection of property rights. Increased property rights for microenterprises can increase investments and subsequently lead to productivity gains. Belsey (1995) shows that investments in agriculture increased with land titling in Ghana. Field (2007) showed that introducing well defined land titles in urban Peru led to substantial growth, an increase in the number of hours worked per person by 13.5–23.3 hours. Taken together, these results imply that firms may be encouraged to invest more if they were protected from eviction from their current location through a formal process.

Such policies need to go beyond merely encouraging firms to register formally with government agencies. Experimental evidence by De Mel *et al.* (2012) in Sri Lanka finds that information and reimbursement for the modest direct costs of registration are not effective at increasing firm registration. They show that registration is spurred only when the information is combined with incentive payments of approximately two months' profit. While about half the firms registered because of the incentive payment, formalization did not provide firms with benefits such as increased access to credit, obtaining government contracts or participating in government programs. The authors did, however, find an increase in trust in the government because of formalizing.

While there is evidence for the general benefits of formalization, it is not clear how to best promote formalization in the informal sector in Ghana. Given the findings in the literature, programs probably should focus on securing property rights through a variety of mechanisms. Given the importance of trade associations in Ghana, pilot programs can be developed that work with and through trade associations to increase the property rights of the informal sector.

PROVIDE SHORT-TERM WAGE SUBSIDIES

One potential way for informal sector firms to grow is to encourage them to hire workers. With limited access to credit and limited information, firms may be unable to hire workers even when the marginal productivity of an additional unit of labour in microenterprises is higher than the market wage. De Mel *et al.* (2010) show that a wage subsidy equivalent to approximately half the cost of hiring a low-skilled worker induced 22 per cent of eligible microenterprise owners to hire a worker in Sri Lanka. Among those hiring workers, 64 per cent of the owners reported that this was the first paid employee they had ever hired, and 86 per cent expected to continue to employ the worker after the subsidy was removed. The median enterprise expected sales to increase by 25 per cent as a result of hiring the employee. If these expectations are realized, they suggest that a short-term wage subsidy could have long-term effects on enterprise size and productivity. Even though this has not been tested empirically, a program that subsidized the hiring of youth workers could be piloted and evaluated in the Ghanaian informal sector. More research is needed to understand how best to design and implement wage-subsidy programs in countries like Ghana.

INCREASE ACCESS TO VOCATIONAL TRAINING

Insufficient funds to pay fees are a barrier for many youth aiming to acquire skills at vocational training centers or through apprenticeships. Master trainers charge between $75 and $150 for training and often demand this payment up front. Recent work by Hicks *et al.* (2011) in Kenya shows that reducing fee barriers to training (through vouchers) enabled youth to enroll in vocational courses of their choice, demonstrating the negative effect of credit constraints on youth human capital investments. The authors found that youth who were randomly chosen to receive a voucher for vocational education were almost 70 percentage points more likely to enroll in a course compared with the control group. Programs that either provide loans for training or completely (or partially) subsidize training could have large effects on the skills of youth.

Hicks *et al.* (2011) also show the importance of information in assisting youth in making informed decisions. As suggested by Aryeetey (2011), introducing guidance and counselling coordinators to provide career advice to young people could help youth make optimal decisions about training.

Overall, there is clear evidence that fees are a barrier to take-up of training. It is less clear, however, how best to structure programs to mitigate this barrier. The voucher system used in Kenya was found to be effective and could be piloted in Ghana. Other mechanisms could also be piloted. Evidence also points to the importance of information. There are different models to provide information, such as counselling schemes (currently being evaluated in France). The preliminary evidence shows that counselling programs for youth were effective in increasing employment outcomes for youth. Similar programs could be piloted in Ghana.

STRENGTHEN VOCATIONAL TRAINING

As the most important source of vocational training in the informal sector, master craftspeople (who train apprentices) constitute a critical mass of professionals with potential that can be harnessed to enhance the quality of training. Aryeetey (2011) argues that policies that develop a common platform for industry and training institutions are a potential way to narrow the gap between the supply of skills and the demand of industry.

Capacity training for master craftspeople can improve the effectiveness of apprentices. For instance, training programs could be implemented that assist master craftspeople in providing quality apprenticeship training with relevant curricula and improved pedagogy (Adams, 2007; Aryeetey, 2011). Ongoing research by Mbiti *et al.* aims to understand whether financial incentives to trainers can increase the effectiveness of training. However, more research on methods of improving the efficacy of apprenticeship training is needed.

The Skills Development Fund is a new $70 million scheme launched by the government and administered by the COTVET. The fund provides financial support to private and public sector enterprises to engage in training activities. Enterprises submit training proposals to COTVET, and proposals that are deemed high quality are funded. While the fund may lead to greater training and perhaps encourage innovation in this sector, it may have no impact as companies already have an incentive to train their workers. Similar schemes, such as the UK's 'Train to Gain' program, have been launched and their impacts were found to be minimal (Abramovsky *et al.*, 2011). A comprehensive evaluation of this program is needed. In addition, the program provides a platform to pilot various schemes that can be incorporated. For example, a scheme that focused on encouraging innovations in training (e.g. a prize tournament for trainers), or one that worked with firms to provide internships for youth, could be tested.

Industrial partnerships are important in improving the relevance of vocational training. Attanasio *et al.* (2011) used a randomized study of the *Jovenes en Accion* program in Columbia to show that those who participated in the technical training program through industrial partnerships had higher levels of employment and wages. A similar industrial training program in Ghana would help formally educated students to transition smoothly into the labour market and improve the overall productivity of the informal sector.

STRENGTHENING TRADE ASSOCIATIONS

Trade associations are important institutions in the informal sector in Ghana. Associations are composed of various stakeholders including retailers, resident wholesalers, traders and master craftspeople, who pay a registration and membership fee (Ortiz *et al.*, 2010). These associations have 'self-identified objectives that are flexible and fluid' and have clear leadership structures (Lyon, 2003). Associations provide oversight for apprenticeship training and, in some trades, they also certify examinations. They are important vehicles for the dissemination of information and could be leveraged to increase the productivity of their members (Lyon, 2003; Porter *et al.*, 2007). Programs that strengthen their training oversight and certification programs could help them produce workers with greater and more employable skills. Acemoglu and Pischke (2000) provide theoretical insights into the importance of certification in the market for training. However, there is little empirical work that quantifies the impact of certification.

5.6 Conclusion and recommendations

The labour market situation facing Ghanaian youth today is a challenging one. It is based on the fact that a significant proportion of them are jobless outside the school system. Those who are fortunate to be engaged in some form of economic activity find themselves in poor quality jobs with low earnings. Quite clearly, the use of 'unemployment' based on the traditional ILO definition as a measure of labour market challenges facing the youth is misleading. The high rate of inactivity and considerable number of youth who fall out of the labour force to join the discouraged worker group tends to underestimate the real labour market challenges in the country. Indeed, the real labour market challenges confronting the youth are seen clearly when the discussion goes beyond the traditional measure of unemployment to cover joblessness outside school and training and the quality of jobs engaged in by the youth.

Success in addressing the real challenges facing young people in the country depends in large part on the investments that were made in their health, education and skills development up to now. In part, their success will be determined by their ability to find formal wage employment or by their success in self-employment, which is highly dependent on access to capital and business skills. Many policy interventions aimed at improving labour market outcomes have already been tried in developing and developed countries alike. Ghana can learn from the findings of the impacts of these policies, in addition to those that have already been implemented in the country. Such policies include health interventions for children, such as vaccinations and deworming; and health interventions that affect the working-age population, including access to safe drinking water and affordable, accessible healthcare. Educational interventions include increasing access to education through fee reductions, transfers, scholarships, grants and school construction. Improvements in the quality of education can be made through increasing inputs and improving teaching. Self-employed individuals can benefit from transfers, skills development and access to capital.

In a broader perspective, the labour market challenges can be addressed from short-, medium- and long-term perspectives. In the short term, the youth with limited or no formal education and employable skills could be absorbed through labour-intensive public works programs, with the opportunity for them to benefit from skill training. In the medium to long term, public investment targeted at facilitating rapid growth of high labour absorption sectors of agriculture, manufacturing and tourism would be a major step of creating employment opportunities for the growing youth population. Strong support for agriculture in the area of credit, extension services and marketing could help reverse the declining performance of agriculture and make it attractive to the youth. The declining growth and employment in the manufacturing sector can also be addressed by creating a conducive business environment through public investment in power generation and road infrastructure, and implementation of appropriate macroeconomic policies to enable the private sector to borrow at affordable rates to raise their competitiveness.

The problem of skills mismatch, which tends to set jobseekers and employers apart even where job openings are created, must be tackled seriously through the design of appropriate curricula that meet the requirements of industry. This requires effective collaboration between industrial practitioners and academic and training institutions in the form of the involvement of industrial practitioners in curriculum design and teaching, opportunities for internships for trainees, and retooling the skills of trainers in education. A review of teaching methods and assessment of students to infuse practically oriented assessment requires particular attention. Policy measures to address constraints on the growth of small businesses (poor access to affordable credit, poor infrastructure, lack of entrepreneurial culture, etc.) would motivate and encourage jobseekers to develop an interest in entrepreneurship. The introduction of entrepreneurship in curricula, and effective collaboration between successful entrepreneurs and educational and training institutions, would raise entrepreneurial consciousness in the youth as a major means of addressing the key problem of joblessness facing them.

In the long term, Ghana should consider the formulation of a long-term national development strategy that emphasizes the generation of decent and productive employment, with manufacturing as the focus, with a view to transforming the economy. This should be informed by research to identify relevant and productive industries in manufacturing that have strong linkages with other sectors and provide direction for the development of appropriate human resources in line with the strategy.

Notes

1 Vulnerable employment is the sum of own account work (i.e. self-employment without employees) and contributing family work (i.e. unpaid family work).
2 The caste system is based on the division of people into social groups whereby each group's occupations and property rights are inherited.
3 See *World Development Report 2013* (World Bank, 2013).
4 See 2000 and 2010 Population and Housing Censuses.
5 The absence of legal backing to the vision provided no legal restraint for the new government to truncate it.
6 GPRS I is Ghana Poverty Reduction Strategy; GPRS II is Growth and Poverty Reduction Strategy.
7 Estimates from the 2010 Population and Housing Census report 79.4 per cent of the 632,994 jobseekers were doing so for the first time.
8 These data include firms in the following sectors: food processing, textiles and garments, wood products and furniture, metal products and machinery.
9 The surveys are the Enterprise Survey, which covers formal firms and is available for 105 countries; the Informal Survey, for 13 countries; and the Micro Survey, for 14 mostly African countries.

References

Abramovsky, L., Battistin, E., Fitzsimons, E., Goodman, A. and Simpson, H. (2011) 'Providing Employers with Incentives to Train Low-Skilled Workers: Evidence from the UK Employer Training Pilots,' *Journal of Labour Economics*, 29: 153–93.

Acemoglu, D. and Pischke, J.S. (2000) 'Certification of Training and Training Outcomes,' *European Economic Review*, 44(4–6): 917–27.

Ackah, C.G. and Baah-Boateng, W. (2012) 'Trends in Growth, Employment and Poverty in Ghana,' in Ackah, C.G. and Aryeetey, E. (eds), *Globalisation, Trade and Poverty in Ghana*. Legon-Accra: Sub-Saharan Publishers.

Adams, A. (2009) *Skills Development in the Informal Sector of sub-Saharan Africa*. International Handbook of Education for the Changing World of Work: Bridging Academic and Vocational Learning, 1. Bonn/Dordrecht: UNESCO-UNEVOC/ Springer.

Addae-Mensah, I. (2000) 'Education in Ghana: A Tool for Social Mobility or Social Stratification,' *The J.B. Danquah Memorial Lectures*. Accra: Ghana Academy of Arts and Sciences.

Addai, I. (2011) 'An Empirical Analysis of Gender Earnings Gap in the Ghanaian Informal Sector Using the 1998/1999 Ghana Living Standards Survey,' *Current Research Journal of Social Sciences*, 3(4): 347–52.

AfDB, OECD, UNDP and UNECA (2012) 'Promoting Youth Employment,' *African Economic Outlook 2012*, www.africaneconomicoutlook.org

Akyeampong, K. (2005) *Whole School Development In Ghana*. EFA Monitoring Report Commissioned Study.

——(2011) *Educational Access: (Re) Assessing the Impact of School Capitation Grants on Educational Access in Ghana*, Research Monograph No. 71. Falmer: Consortium for Educational Access, Transitions and Equity (CREATE), University of Sussex.

Akyeampong, K., Djangmah, J., Oduro, A., Seidu, A. and Hunt, F. (2007) *Access to Basic Education in Ghana: The Evidence and the Issues*, CREATE Country Analytic Review. Winneba and Brighton: University of Education at Winneba and University of Sussex.

Alila, P.O. and Pedersen, P.O. (eds) (2001) *Negotiating Social Space: East African Microenterprises*. Asmara: Africa World Press.

Appiah-Kubi, A. (2007) 'Poverty Reduction, GPRS and the Informal Sector in Ghana,' *paper presented at the ISSER/Merchant Bank Development Seminars Series*, Accra, February.

Aragon, F. and Rud, J.P. (2012) *Mining, Pollution and Agricultural Productivity: Evidence from Ghana*, Discussion Papers 12–08. Burnaby: Department of Economics, Simon Fraser University.

Aryeetey, E., Baah-Nuakoh, A., Duggleby, H., Hettige, H. and Steel, W.F. (1994) *The Supply and Demand for Finance among SMEs in Ghana*, Africa Technical Department Discussion Paper 251. Washington, DC: World Bank.

Asenso-Okyere, K., Chiang, C., Thangata, P., Andam, K. and Mekonnen, D.A. (2011) 'Understanding the Interaction between Farm Labour Productivity, and Health and Nutrition: A Survey of the Evidence,' *Journal of Development and Agricultural Economics*, 3(3): 80–90.

Aslam, M. and Lehrer, K. (2012) *Learning by Doing: Skills and Jobs in Urban Ghana*, Working Paper. Oxford: Oxford University, Centre For Study of African Economies.

Attanasio, O., Kugler, A. and Costas, M. (2011) 'Subsidizing Vocational Training for Disadvantaged Youth in Colombia: Evidence from a Randomized Trial,' *American Economic Journal: Applied Economics*, 3(3): 188–220.

Baah-Boateng, W. (2008) 'Employment Generation for Poverty Alleviation,' in Amoako-Tuffour and Bartholomew Armah (eds), *Poverty Reduction Strategies in Action: Perspectives and Lessons from Ghana*. Lanham, MD: Lexington Books, pp. 223–42.

——(2011) 'Unemployment in Ghana: How appropriate is the current definition for policy purposes,' unpublished paper presented at Faculty of Social Sciences Colloquium in November at the University of Ghana, Legon.

Baah-Boateng, W. and Turkson, E.F. (2005) 'Employment,' in Aryeetey E. (ed.), *Globalisation, Employment and Poverty Reduction: A Case Study of Ghana*. Legon-Accra: University of Ghana, Institute of Statistical, Social and Economic Research, pp. 104–39.

Banerjee, A.L., Duflo, E., Glennerster, R. and Kothari, D. (2010) 'Improving Immunization Coverage in Rural India: A Clustered Randomized Controlled Evaluation of Immunization Campaigns With and Without Incentives,' *British Medical Journal*, 340: c2220.

Belsey, T. (1995) 'Property Rights and Investment Incentives: Theory and Evidence from Ghana,' *Journal of Political Economy*, 103(5): 903–37.

Blanchflower, D. and Freeman, R.B. (1999) *Youth Employment and Joblessness in Advanced Countries*, NBER Comparative Labour Markets Series. Chicago, IL: University of Chicago Press.

Bentolila, S., Juan, J.D. and Jimeno, J.F. (2011) *Reforming an Insider – Outsider Labour Market: The Spanish Experience*. Bonn: IZA.

Bin-Obaid, A.S. (1997) 'Classical, Keynesian and Monetarist Theorist of Unemployment: Are they Adequate to LDCs?', *Journal of Economic and Administrative Sciences*, 13: 151–72.

Blackaby, D., Leslie, D., Murphy, P. and O'Leary, N. (1999) 'Unemployment among Britain's Ethnic Minorities,' *The Manchester School*, 67(1).

Blanchard, O.J. and Summers, L.H. (1987) *Hysteresis and the European Unemployment Problem*, NBER Working Paper No. 1950 (also Reprint No. r0808). Cambridge: National Bureau of Economic Research.

Bold, T., Kimenyi, M., Mwabu, G., Ng'ang'a, A. and Sandefur, J. (2012) *Interventions & Institutions: Experimental Evidence on Scaling Up Education Reforms in Kenya*. Stockholm: Institute for International Economic Studies, Stockholm University.

Bortei-Doku Aryeetey, E., Doh, D. and Andoh, P. (2011) *From Prejudice to Prestige: Vocational Education and Training in Ghana*. Accra: City and Guilds Centre for Skills Development and Council for Technical and Vocational Education and Training.

Bradshaw, J. (2003) 'How Has the Notion of Social Exclusion Developed in the European Discourse?' *Plenary Address to the 2003 Australian Social Policy Conference*, Social Policy Research Centre. Sydney: University of New South Wales.

Brown, C. (1984) *Black and White Britain: The Third PSI Survey*. London: Policy Studies Institute.

Brown, C. and Gay, P. (1985) *Racial Discrimination: 17 Years After the Act*. London: Policy Studies Institute.

Burchardt, T. (2000) 'Social Exclusion: Concepts and Evidence,' in Gordon, D. and Townsend P. (eds), *Breadline Europe. The Measurement of Poverty*. Bristol: Policy Press, pp. 385–406.

Burchardt, T., Le Grand, J. and Piachaud, D. (2002) 'Degrees of Exclusion: Developing a Dynamic, Multidimensional Measure,' in Hills, J., Le Grand, J. and Piachaud, D. (eds), *Understanding Social Exclusion*. Oxford: Oxford University Press, pp. 30–43.

Burde, D. and Linden, L.L. (2012) *The Effect of Village-Based Schools: Evidence from Randomized Controlled Trial in Afghanistan*, NBER Working Paper No. 18039. Cambridge: National Bureau of Economic Research.

Canagarajah, S., Mazumdar, D. and Ye, X. (1998) *The Structure and Determinants of Inequality and Poverty Reduction in Ghana, 1988–92*, Policy Research Working Paper. Washington, DC: World Bank.

Canagarajah, S., Newman, C. and Bhattamishra, R. (2001) 'Non-Farm Income, Gender, and Inequality: Evidence from Rural Ghana and Uganda,' *Food Policy*, 26(4): 405–20.

Chant, S. and Jones, G.A. (2005) 'Youth, Gender and Livelihoods in West Africa: Perspectives from Ghana and The Gambia,' *Children's Geographies*, 3(2): 185–99.

Clark, K.B. and Summers, L. (1982) 'The Dynamics of Youth Unemployment,' in Freeman, R. and Wise, D. (eds), *The Youth Labour Market Problem: Its Nature, Causes and Consequences*. Chicago, IL: University of Chicago Press, pp. 199–234.

Cling, J.-P.G., Nordman, F., Christophe, J. and Robilliard, A.-S. (2007) *Youth and Labour Markets in Africa: A Critical Review of Literature*, Document de Travail No 49. Paris: Agence Française de Développement.

Coenjaerts, C., Ernst, C., Fortuny, M., Rei, D. and Pilgrim, M. (2009) 'Youth Employment,' in OECD (ed.), *Promoting Pro-Poor Growth: Employment*. Paris: OECD.

Curtain, R. (2001) 'Youth and Employment: A Public Policy Perspective,' *Development Bulletin*, (55): 7–11.

De Mel, S., McKenzie, D. and Woodruff, C. (2007) *Returns to Capital in Microenterprises: Evidence from a Field Experiment*, World Bank Policy Research Working Paper 4230. Washington, DC: World Bank.

——(2009) *Innovative Firms or Innovative Owners? Determinants of Innovation in Micro, Small, and Medium Enterprises*, Policy Research Working Paper Series 4934. Washington, DC: World Bank.

——(2010) 'Wage Subsidies for Microenterprises,' *American Economic Review*, 100(2): 614–18.

——(2012) *The Demand for, and Consequences of, Formalization among Informal Firms in Sri Lanka*, Policy Research Working Paper Series 5991. Washington, DC: World Bank.

DIAL (2007) *Youth and Labour Market in Africa: A Critical Review of Literature*, DT/2007–02. Développement Institutions et Analysis de Long terme.

Dickens, W.T. and Lang, K. (1995) 'An Analysis of the Nature of Unemployment in Sri Lanka,' *Journal of Development Studies*, 31(4): 620–36.

Duflo, E. (2001) 'Schooling and Labour Market Consequences of School Construction in Indonesia: Evidence from an Unusual Policy Experiment,' *American Economic Review*, 91(4): 795–813.

Duflo, E., Dupas, P. and Kremer, M. (2011) 'Peer Effects, Teacher Incentives, and the Impact of Tracking: Evidence from a Randomized Evaluation in Kenya,' *American Economic Review*, 101(5): 1739–74.

——(2012) *School Governance, Teacher Incentives and Pupil–Teacher Ratios: Experimental Evidence from Kenyan Primary Schools*, NBER Working Paper 17939. Cambridge: National Bureau of Economic Research.

Fafchamps, M. (2004) *Market Institutions in Sub-Saharan Africa*. Cambridge, MA: MIT Press.

Fafchamps, M., McKenzie, D., Quinn, S. and Woodruff, C. (2012) *Female Microenterprises and the Fly-paper Effect: Evidence from a Randomized Experiment in Ghana*, Discussion Paper. Oxford: Centre for the Study of African Economies, University of Oxford.

Falco, P., Kerr, A., Rankin, N., Sandefur, J. and Teal, F. (2010) *The Returns to Formality and Informality in Urban Africa*, Working Paper 2010–03. Oxford: Centre for the Study of African Economies, University of Oxford.

Fares, J., Montenegro, C.E. and Orazem, P.F. (2006) *How are Youth Faring in the Labour Market? Evidence from Around the World*, Policy Research Working Paper Series 4071. Washington, DC: World Bank.

Farm, A. (2012) *Vacancies, Labour Demand, and Unemployment*. Stockholm: Swedish Institute for Social Research, Stockholm University.

Feldman, D.C. (1996) 'The Nature, Antecedents and Consequences of Underemployment,' *Journal of Management*, 22(3): 385–407.

Field, E. (2007) 'Entitled to Work: Urban Property Rights and Labour Supply in Peru,' *Quarterly Journal of Economics*, 122(4): 1561–1602.

Figueroa, A. (1999) 'Social Exclusion and Rural Underdevelopment,' *paper prepared for the World Bank Conference on Evaluation and Poverty Reduction*, Washington, DC, June 14–15.

Frazer, G. (2006). 'Learning the Master's Trade: Apprenticeship and Human Capital in Ghana,' *Journal of Development Economics*, 81(2): 259–98.

Freeman, R. and Wise, D. (eds) (1982) *The Youth Labour Market Problem: Its Nature, Causes and Consequences*. Chicago, IL: University of Chicago Press.

Genre, V., Gomez-Salavador, R. and Lamo, A. (2003) 'European Women: Why Do (Not) They Work?', *ECB-CEPR Labour Workshop*, June. European Central Bank and Centre for Economic Policy Research.

Glewwe, P. and Jacoby, H.G. (1995) 'An Economic Analysis of Delayed Primary School Enrollment in a Low Income Country: The Role of Early Childhood Nutrition,' *Review of Economics and Statistics*, 77(1): 156–69.

Glewwe, P., Kremer, M., Moulin, S. and Zitzewitz, E. (2004) 'Retrospective vs. Prospective Analyses of School Inputs: The Case of Flip Charts in Kenya,' *Journal of Development Economics*, 74(1): 251–68.

Görg, H. and Strobl, E. (2001) *The Incidence of Visible Underemployment: Evidence for Trinidad and Tobago*, CREDIT Research Paper No. 01&10. Nottingham: Centre for Research in Economic Development and International Trade, University of Nottingham.

GSS (various dates) *The Datasets of the 3rd, 4th and 5th Rounds of the Ghana Living Standards Surveys, 1991/92, 1998/99 and 2005/06 (GLSS3,4 and 5)*. Accra: Ghana Statistical Service.

Günther, I. and Launov, A. (2012) 'Informal Employment in Developing Countries: Opportunity or Last Resort?', *Journal of Development Economics*, 97: 88–98.

Haan, H.C. (2002) *Training for Work in the Informal Sector: New evidence from Kenya, Tanzania and Uganda*, International Training Center Occasional Paper. Turin: ILO.

Hamermesh, D.S. (1993) *Labour Demand*. Princeton, NJ: Princeton University Press.

Heintz, J. (2005) *Employment, Poverty, and Gender in Ghana*. Amherst, MA: Political Economy Research Institute, University of Massachusetts.

Hicks, J., Hjort, J., Kremer, M., Mbiti, I., McCasland, J. and Miguel, E. (2011) *Vocational Education Voucher Delivery and Labour Market Returns: A Randomized*

Evaluation Among Kenyan Youth, Strategic Impact Evaluation Fund Report. Washington, DC: World Bank.

Higgins, P.A. and Alderman, H. (1997) 'Labour and Women's Nutrition: The Impact of Work Effort and Fertility on Nutritional Status in Ghana,' *Journal of Human Resources*, 32(3): 577–95.

Holla, A. and Kremer, M. (2008) 'Pricing and Access: Lessons from Randomized Evaluations in Education and Health,' in Easterly, W. and Cohen, J. (eds), *What Works in Development: Thinking Big and Thinking Small*. Washington, DC: Brookings Institution.

ILO (2008a) *Global Employment Trends for Youth*. Geneva: International Labour Organization.

ILO (2008b) *Key Indicators of the Labour Market*. Geneva: International Labour Organization. www.ilo.org/klim.

——(2011) *Global Employment Trends 2011*. Geneva: International Labour Organization.

——(2012) *The Youth Employment Crisis: Time for Action*, report prepared by youth for the Youth Employment Forum, 23–25 May. Geneva: International Labour Organization.

Jaumotte, F. (2003) *Female Labour Force Participation: Past Trends and Main Determinants in OECD Countries*, Dec., ECO/WKP (2003)30. Paris: OECD.

Jensen, R. (2012) 'Do Labour Market Opportunities Affect Young Women's Work and Family Decisions? Experimental Evidence from India,' *Quarterly Journal of Economics*, 127(2): 753–92.

Johanson, R. and Adams, A.V. (2004) *Skills Development in Sub-Saharan Africa. Regional and Sectoral Studies*. Washington, DC: World Bank.

Jolliffe, D. (2003) 'The Impact of Education in Rural Ghana: Examining Household Labour Allocation and Returns on and off the Farm,' *Journal of Development Economics*, 73(1): 287–314.

Kanyenze, G., Mhone, G. and Sparreboom, T. (2000) *Strategies to Combat Youth Unemployment and Marginalisation in Anglophone Africa*, Discussion Paper 14. Harare: ILO.

Kingdon, G. and Knight, J. (1991) *Unemployment and Wages in South Africa: A Spatial Approach*, CSAE Working Paper WPS/99.12. Oxford: Centre for the Study of African Economies, University of Oxford.

Kingdon, G. and Söderbom, M. (2007) 'Education, Skills and Labour Market Outcomes: Evidence from Pakistan and Ghana,' *paper written for the World Bank Human Development Network*. Washington, DC: World Bank.

Korboe, D. (2001) 'Government of Ghana: Vocational Skills and Informal Sector Support Project,' *Project Evaluation Report* (draft, 30 June).

La Porta, R. and Shleifer, A. (2008) *The Unofficial Economy and Economic Development*, NBER Working Paper No. 14520. Cambridge: National Bureau of Economic Research.

Lam, D. (2006) *The Demography of Youth in Developing Countries and its Economic Implications*, Policy Research Working Paper No. 4071. Washington, DC: World Bank.

Leibbrandt, M. and Mlatsheni, C. (2004) 'Youth in Sub-Saharan Labour Markets,' *paper presented at African Development and Poverty Reduction: The Macro–Micro Linkage Forum*, October 13–15, Somerset West, South Africa.

Liimatainen, M.-R. (2002) *Training and Skills Acquisition in the Informal Sector: A Literature Review*, InFocus Programme on Skills, Knowledge and Employability, Informal Economy Series. Geneva: ILO.

Lindbeck, A. and Snower, D.J. (1984) *Involuntary Unemployment as an Insider–Outsider Dilemma*, Seminar Paper 309. Stockholm: Institute for International Economic Studies.

——(1988) *The Insider–Outsider Theory of Employment and Unemployment.* Cambridge, MA: MIT Press.

Liu, E. and Wu, J. (1999) *Minimum Wage Systems.* Hong Kong: Research and Library Services Division, Legislative Council Secretariat.

Lyon, F. (2003) 'Trader Associations and Urban Food Systems in Ghana: Institutionalist Approaches to Understanding Urban Collective Action,' *International Journal of Urban and Regional Research*, 27(1): 11–23.

Mankiw, G.N. and Taylor, M.P. (2008) *Macroeconomics*, European edn. New York: Worth Publishers, pp. 181–82.

Marito, G. and Fares, J. (2008) *Youth in Africa's Labour Market.* Washington, DC: World Bank.

Martin, J.P. (2000) *What Works among Active Labour Market Policies: Evidence from OECD countries' Experience.* OECD Economic Studies No. 30. Paris: OECD.

Martorell, R. and Gonzalez-Cossio, T. (1987) 'Maternal Nutrition and Birth Weight,' *Yearbook of Physical Anthropology*, 30: 195–220.

McCall, J.J. (1970) 'Economics of Information and Job Search,' *Quarterly Journal of Economics*, 84(1): 113–26.

Mehran, F., Bescond, D., Hussmanns, R. and Benes, E. (2008) 'Beyond Unemployment: Measurement of Other Forms of Labour Underutilization,' *18th International Conference of Labour Statisticians Geneva*, 24 November–5 December. Geneva: ILO Bureau of Statistics.

Miguel, E. and Kremer, M. (2004) 'Worms: Identifying Impacts on Education and Health in the Presence of Treatment Externalities,' *Econometrica*, 72(1): 159–217.

Miguel, E., Hicks, J., Kremer, M. and Mbiti, I. (2011) 'Vocational Education Voucher Delivery and Labour Market Returns: A Randomized Evaluation Among Kenyan Youth,' *Report to World Bank Spanish Impact Evaluation Fund.* Washington, DC: World Bank.

Ministry of Youth and Sports (2010) *National Youth Policy of Ghana: Towards an Empowered Youth, Impacting Positively on National Development.* Accra: Ministry of Youth and Sports.

Mkandawire, R. (2000) 'Alienated, Criminalized and Stigmatized Youth Sub-cultures of South Africa,' *paper presented at the Kopano Southern Africa Regional Exchange Conference*, Dikhololo, North West Province, 20–25 July.

Monk, C., Sandefur, J. and Teal, F. (2008) 'Does Doing an Apprenticeship Pay Off? Evidence from Ghana,' *CSAE Working Paper Series 2008–08.* Oxford: Centre for the Study of African Economies, University of Oxford.

Morris, M.L. and Doss, C.R. (2001) 'How does gender affect the adoption of agricultural innovations? The case of improved maize technology in Ghana,' *Agricultural Economics*, 25(1): 27–39.

Morris, M.L., Tripp, R. and Dankyi, A.A. (1999) *Adoption and Impacts of Improved Maize Production Technology: A Case Study of the Ghana Grains Development Project.* El Batan: International Maize and Wheat Improvement Center (CIMMYT).

Mortensen, D.T. (1986) 'Job Search and Labor Market Analysis,' in Ashenfelter, O. and Layard, R. (eds), *Handbook of Labor Economics.* Amsterdam: North Holland, pp. 849–920.

Munshi, K. and Rosenzweig, M. (2006) 'Traditional institutions meet the modern world: caste, gender, and schooling choice in a globalizing economy,' *American Economic Review*, 96(4): 1225–52.

Nguyen, H.T.H., Rajkotia, Y. and Wang, H. (2011) 'The financial protection effect of Ghana National Health Insurance Scheme: evidence from a study in two rural districts,' *International Journal for Equity in Health*, 10(1): 1–12.

Nickell, S.J. (1986) 'Dynamic models of labour demand,' in Ashenfelter, O. and Layard, R. (eds), *Handbook of Labour Economics.* Amsterdam: North-Holland.

Nsowah-Nuamah, N., Teal, F. and Awoonor-Williams, M. (2010) *Jobs, Skills and Incomes in Ghana: How was Poverty Halved?* Oxford: Centre for the Study of African Economies, University of Oxford.

Nunziata, L. (2003). 'Labour market institutions and the cyclical dynamics of employment,' *Labour Economics*, 10(1): 31–53.

Ortiz, N., Campbell, C. and Hyman, B. (2010) *Analyzing Market Reforms and Food Distribution Systems in Accra, Ghana*. Cambridge, MA: Massachusetts Institute of Technology, Department of Urban Studies and Planning.

Osberg, L., Apostle, R. and Clairmont, D. (1986) 'The Incidence and Duration of Individual Unemployment: Supply Side or Demand Side?', *Cambridge Journal of Economics*, 10: 13–33.

Ozier, O. (2011) *Exploiting Externalities to Estimate the Long-Term Effects of Early Childhood Deworming*. Washington, DC: Development Economics Research Group, World Bank.

Pissarides, C.A. (2000) *Equilibrium Unemployment Theory*, 2nd edn. Cambridge, MA: MIT Press.

Porter, G., Lyon, F. and Potts, D. (2007) 'Market institutions and urban food supply in West and Southern Africa: a review,' *Progress in Development Studies*, 7(2): 115–34.

Rarieya, J. and Fentiman, A. (2012) *Gender in East Africa: Women Role Models in Kenya*, Gender Report 4/CCE Report No. 9. Centre for Commonwealth Education.

Rogerson, R., Shimer, R. and Wright, R. (2005) 'Search-theoretic models of the labour market: a survey,' *Journal of Economic Literature*, 43: 959–88.

Sackey, H.A. and Osei, B. (2006) *Human Resource Underutilization in an Era of Poverty Reduction: An Analysis of Unemployment and Underemployment in Ghana.* Malden, MA: African Development Bank/Blackwell Publishing.

Schultz, T.P. (2003b) 'Wage rentals for reproducible human capital: evidence from Ghana and the Ivory Coast,' *Economics & Human Biology*, 1(3): 331–66.

——(2004) 'School subsidies for the poor: evaluating the Mexican Progressa poverty programme,' *Journal of Development Economics*, 74(1): 199–250.

Serneels, P. (2007) *The Role of the Labour Market for Shared Growth in Ghana*, Country Labor Study. Washington, DC: World Bank.

Smith, D.J. (1974) 'Racial disadvantage in employment,' *Political and Economic Planning*, 11: 547.

Smith, D. (1981) 'Discrimination against applicants for white-collar jobs,' in Braham, P., Rhodes, E. and Pearn M. (eds), *Discrimination and Disadvantage in Employment.* London: Harper & Row.

Sparreboom, T. and Baah-Boateng, W. (2011) 'Ghana – Economic Growth and Better Labour Market Outcomes, but Challenges remain,' in Sparreboom, T. and Albee, A. (eds), *Towards Decent Work in Sub-Saharan Africa: Monitoring MDG Employment Indicators.* Geneva: International Labour Office.

Stigler, G.J. (1962) 'Information in the labour market,' *Journal of Political Economy*, 70(5): 94–105.

Stoler, J., Fink, G., Weeks, J.R., Appiah Otoo, R., Ampofo, J.A. and Hill, A.G. (2012) 'When urban taps run dry: sachet water consumption and health effects in low income neighbourhoods of Accra, Ghana,' *Health and Place*, 18: 250–62.

Strauss, J. and Thomas, D. (1998) 'Health, Nutrition, and Economic Development,' *Journal of Economic Literature*, 36(2): 766–817.

Tasci, M.H. (2006) 'Recent trend in underemployment and determinants of in Turkey,' *Iktisadi, veldari Bilimler Fakultesi, Turkiye*, C.11: 299–319.

Teal, F. (2000) *Employment and Unemployment in Sub-Saharan Africa: An Overview*. Oxford: Centre for the Study of African Economies, University of Oxford.

——(2007) *Labour Demand in Ghana for Skilled and Unskilled Workers*. Oxford: Centre For Study of African Economies, University of Oxford.

Thomas, D. *et al.* (2006) 'Iron deficiency and the well-being of older adults: early results from a randomized nutrition intervention,' *Population Association of America Annual Meetings*, Minneapolis, MN, April and International Studies in Health and Economic Development Network meeting, San Francisco, CA, May.

Thomas, D. and Strauss, J. (1997) 'Health and wages: evidence on men and women in urban Brazil,' *Journal of Econometrics*, 77(1): 159–85.

Thomas, D., Frankenberg, E., Friedman, J., Habicht, J.P., Jones, N., McKelvey, C. *et al.* (2004) *Causal Effect of Health on Labour Market Outcomes: Evidence from a Random Assignment Iron Supplementation Intervention*. Los Angeles, CA: UC Los Angeles, California Centre for Population Research.

Thorat, S. (2007) *Economic Exclusion and Poverty in Asia: The Example of Castes in India*, 2020 Focus Brief on the World's Poor and Hungry People. Washington, DC: International Food Policy Research Institute.

Udry, C. and Anagol, S. (2006) 'The Return to Capital in Ghana,' *American Economic Review*, 96(2): 388–93.

UNAIDS (2004) *Report of the Global AIDS Epidemic*. Geneva: United Nations Programme on HIV/AIDS.

UNDP (2004) *Human Development Report 2004: Cultural Liberty in Today's Diverse World*. New York: United Nations Development Programme.

UNECA (2011) *Addressing the Youth Education and Employment Nexus in the New Global Economy*, African Youth Report. Addis Ababa: United Nations Economic Commission for Africa.

——(2006) *Youth and Economic Development in Africa*, an Issues Paper for the Fifth African Development Forum. Addis Ababa: United Nations Economic Commission for Africa.

——(2005) *Economic Report on Africa 2005: Meeting the Challenges of Unemployment and Poverty in Africa*. Addis Ababa: United Nations Economic Commission for Africa.

United Nations (2007) *World Youth Report 2007: Young People's Transition to Adulthood: Progress and Challenges*. New York: United Nations, Department of Economic and Social Affairs.

Valletta, R. and Kuang, K. (2011) 'Why Is Unemployment Duration So Long?' Federal Reserve Bank of San Francisco, Economic Letter.

Van Ours, J.C. and Ridder, G. (1992) 'Vacancies and the Recruitment of New Employees,' *Journal of Labour Economics*, 10: 138–55.

Wasmer, É. (2006) Links between Labour Supply and Unemployment: Theory and Empirics, *Working Paper 06-15*. Montreal: UQAM (Centre interuniversitaire sur le risque, les politiques économiques et l'emploi), IZA and Center for Economic and Policy Research.

World Bank (2009) *Youth and Employment in Africa: The Potential, the Problem, the Promise.* Washington, DC: World Bank.

——(2007) *World Development Report 2007: Development and the Next Generation.* Washington, DC: World Bank.

——(2006) *Labour Diagnostics for Sub-Saharan Africa: Assessing Indicators and Data Available.* Washington, DC: World Bank.

——(2008) *Youth in Africa's Labour Market.* Washington, DC: World Bank.

——(2009) *Ghana Job Creation and Skills Development.* Washington, DC: World Bank.

——(2012a) *World Development Report 2012: Gender Equality and Employment.* Washington, DC: World Bank.

——(2012b) *Health Equity and Financial Protection Report – Ghana.* Washington, DC: World Bank.

——(2013) *World Development Report 2013: Jobs.* Washington, DC: World Bank.

Zeitlin, A., Bategeka, L., Guloba, M., Kasirye, I. and Mugisha, F. (2011) *Management and Motivation in Ugandan Primary Schools: Impact Evaluation Final Report.* Poverty and Economic Policy Research Network.

6 Kenya

Boaz Munga, Othieno Nyanjom, Eldah Onsomu and Germano Mwabu

6.1 Introduction

6.1.1 Background

The generation of adequate employment opportunities has remained a top agenda for most governments across the world, most notably among the poorer countries with no unemployment or other welfare benefits. High unemployment remains one of the greatest challenges facing Sub-Saharan Africa today, with the youth bearing the brunt of the burden. High rates of unemployment and underemployment present multiple challenges, such as exacerbation of poverty and delinquency among the youth.

According to Kenya's most recent household survey, the 2005–06 Kenya Integrated Household Budget Survey (KIHBS 2005/06), the overall rate of open unemployment is estimated at 12.7 per cent, but open unemployment among the youth aged 15–24 is nearly twice as large at 24 per cent. Although measured open unemployment is low, the majority of individuals remain underemployed—or employed in low-productivity jobs—and therefore cannot meet their subsistence needs.

Although most of the labour force might be classified as employed (using the conventional definition of unemployment by the International Labour Organization, ILO), nearly half of the working persons are the 'working poor.' Specifically, of those who work 40 or more hours a week, about 46.1 per cent are classified as poor. Among those working between 1 and 27 hours a week, 69.8 per cent live below the poverty line, while among those working 28–39 hours a week, 65.6 per cent are poor. Nearly 65.9 per cent of the labour force without any form of employment live in poverty.

There are disparities in the types of employment opportunities available among the working-age population. A very high proportion of the labour force has little access to quality employment opportunities or decent work.[1] Although current studies use hours worked as a measure of underemployment, there is limited analysis on the earnings levels for this category of workers.

Even with the increasing unemployment rates and growth in youth population, the economy has not been able to create enough jobs to accommodate the growing labour force. For instance, the economic recovery strategy target of creating 500,000 jobs per year was not met, despite the tremendous GDP growth rates generated by the strategy (Ministry of Labour, 2008). An average of 467,000 jobs were created annually during 2003–07, yet most of these new jobs, over 80 per cent, were created in the informal sector, which is characterized by poor-quality jobs, low earnings, underemployment, personal and property insecurity, and hazardous environments (Manda and Odhiambo, 2003; Manda, 2004). There was a need to create 1 million jobs to absorb the current and new entrants into the labour market.

Youth employment prospects in the formal sector have been generally low. If these prospects are measured by the ratio of the expansion in formal sector employment each year to the number of graduates from the secondary and tertiary institutions, assuming all secondary school graduates join the labour market, only about 19 and 13 per cent of all graduates could have been absorbed in formal sector jobs in 1980 and 1990, respectively. The prospects declined to about 1 per cent in 2000 before rising to about 14 per cent in 2009. Thus, as currently structured, the formal sector may not produce the number of jobs required to absorb the large number of young people entering the labour market annually, even if the target growth rate of 10 per year stated in *Kenya Vision 2030* were to be achieved.

In order to understand better the functioning of the labour market in Kenya, besides analyzing open unemployment, there is a need to analyze the quality of work available and the characteristics of the employed and unemployed. There is a need to define 'decent work' and to measure the productivity of the working population. One objective of this chapter is to provide a profile of types of jobs in Kenya. The chapter provides a synthesis of the extent of unemployment and underemployment in the country, with special reference to the youth. In addition, the main factors associated with unemployment and the characteristics of both the unemployed and underemployed are analyzed.

6.1.2 Why focus on youth?

In 2009, about 30 per cent of the Kenyan population was estimated to be young people aged 15–29 years. The future of the country—certainly in the context of its *Kenya Vision 2030*—rests critically on this age group.

The youth represent a particular opportunity and, if not tapped productively, may become a threat to national development and security. The youth could be a source of civil conflict and social tension if this untapped resource is poorly managed. Undoubtedly, youth without education, jobs or the prospect of a meaningful future may fuel instability, radicalization and violent conflict. On the positive side, the youth are a potential resource for fast and sustained growth and development if they are gainfully and productively engaged. Their transformational capacity might be what is necessary for societies to move away from the inherited development bottlenecks, such as adverse cultural practices, negative ethnicity and corruption.

In many African countries, including Kenya, the degree to which the youth can contribute to the development effort of their country in particular, and the continent in general, is constrained by a lack of job opportunities. Young people face particular challenges in accessing labour markets, and are more likely to lose their jobs during economic downturns. They face specific barriers to entry into labour markets, due largely to lack of experience and social networks (see Clark and Summers, 1982; Freeman and Wise, 1982; Leo, 2012).

There is a significant social and economic cost associated with underutilization of the skills and time of the youth. The youth are not only exposed to social exclusion in the face of underutilization of their skills, but can also trigger intergenerational poverty, thus worsening social cohesion across generations. The youth are more likely to accept recruitment into fighting forces when they face high incidence of poverty. As noted by the Organization for Economic Co-operation and Development (OECD), lack of employment opportunities may result in social conflicts such as violence and juvenile delinquency (OECD, 2009). A comprehensive analysis of labour market challenges confronting the youth in Kenya is therefore necessary to identify long-term solutions to the challenges of youth underemployment and joblessness (inactivity or unemployment).

6.1.3 Who are the youth?

Youth as an economic and social concept refers to a distinctive stage in the life cycle between childhood and adulthood (Curtain, 2001). From a legal perspective, the minimum age of youth varies in terms of marriage, voting rights, employment and political office-holding. In Kenya, the minimum legal age for marriage and voting rights is 18 years. However, the minimum age of 15 is used for admission into employment, as stipulated by ILO Convention No. 138.

In practice, there are differing conventions for classifying youths. The United Nations (UN) classification refers to individuals within the age range of 15–24 years, while the African Union and Kenya define them to be 15–35 years. In most employment studies, the UN classification is used. However, the Kenya definition of youth (15–35 years) is adopted for this chapter.

6.1.4 Defining unemployment

According to the ILO, a person is unemployed if the person is older than the minimum employment age, is actively looking for a job, is available for work, and has not worked during a given reference period. To be considered as 'actively looking' for a job, the unemployed person must take specific steps, including registration at a public or private employment exchange or centre, application to employers, checking at worksites, farms, factory gates, market or other assembly places, placing or answering newspaper advertisements, seeking assistance of friends or relatives, looking for land, building, machinery or equipment to establish own enterprise, arranging for financial resources, and applying for permits and licenses. In effect, the ILO statistical sources define the unemployed as 'persons who are available and looking for paid employment, who have registered at any of the employment centres' (ILO, 1989).

The application of the ILO definition of unemployment to most countries in Africa, including Kenya, seems quite problematic considering the peculiar nature of the labour market in Africa. A considerable number of jobless people in many African countries, Kenya included, may be available for work but may fail to look for work because there are few or limited employment placement and registration centres to record jobseekers. Even where these facilities exist, people stay away from them because of a lack of adequate jobs or the perception of no jobs, coupled with an absence of unemployment benefits as an incentive to attract jobless people. This contributes to a large number of discouraged workers, who are not counted as unemployed.

Moreover, a high degree of informality in the continent's work environment provides a safety net for many jobseekers. Indeed, many jobseekers—especially those with limited employable skills required in the formal labour market—are compelled to seek refuge in the informal economy as a survival strategy. The low unemployment rates registered in African countries are due to the application of conventional ILO definitions of unemployment in an environment with extensive non-formal economic activities, such as street hawking, and farm workers who in most cases earn little from their labour.

Discussions of unemployment in developing countries, particularly in Africa, usually focus on the extent of disguised unemployment or underemployment, in contrast to the developed country context in which unemployment is viewed in terms of the mismatch between labour demand and supply (Boateng, 2000). Clearly, the analysis of unemployment of the youth in Africa must include both the conventional unemployment and underemployment (using ILO definitions), as well as those who do not look for a job because of the lack of realistic opportunity, or those who are involved in indecent work.

6.1.5 Organization of the chapter

This chapter is organized as follows: section 6.2 provides an overview of macroeconomic context and a detailed review of current state of employment in Kenya with a special focus on the youth. Section 6.3 provides further analyses of unemployment, underemployment and the working poor. Section 6.4 reviews recent and current government policies and interventions on youth employment. Section 6.5 provides a quantitative analysis of determinants of unemployment of the youth. Section 6.6 offers simulation analyses to assess the effectiveness of alternative development strategies on employment creation. Summary and policy recommendations are presented in the concluding section.

6.2 Current state of youth employment and unemployment

6.2.1 Data

This chapter is based on data from primary and secondary sources. The data from the literature is drawn from government policy documents, and publications produced by local and international agencies such as the Kenya Institute for Public Policy Research and Analysis (KIPPRA), ILO, United Nations Development Programme (UNDP), National Economic and Social Council (NESC) and the World Bank, among others. This is supplemented with information from stakeholders' fora. The existing nationally representative datasets, notably KIHBS 2005/06 and the 2009 census data, are used extensively.

6.2.2 Macroeconomy and population structure

Kenya experienced economic recovery as measured by the GDP growth rate beginning in the year 2003. Economic growth peaked at 7.0 per cent in 2007 and declined sharply in 2008, following the overlapping effects of the post-election violence in early 2008, the global financial crisis, drought, and high global energy and food prices (see Table 6.1). The GDP growth averaged 4.6 per cent between 2003 and 2012.

During the 2003–10 period, the employment-to-population ratio increased from 0.22 to 0.28, implying that total employment increased faster than the population growth. However, as will be evident later, most of the growth in employment was in the informal sector, which is characterized by poor-quality jobs.

Kenya's population is largely made up of young people, with individuals aged 35 or less constituting nearly 80 per cent of the total population. Kenya's young population structure is captured by the 2009 census, as illustrated in Figure 6.1. The share of population under 15 is 43 per cent, while that of the youth aged 15 to 34 is 35.3 per cent. A similar distribution is repeated across all the provinces,[2] North Eastern's highest provincial total fertility rate of 5.9 per cent being reflected in its greatest share of population under age 15.

The annual population growth rate increased steadily from 2.5 per cent in 1948 and peaked in 1979 at a rate of 3.8 per cent. Albeit still high, the annual

Table 6.1 Selected socio-economic indicators for Kenya, 2003–10

Indicator	*2003*	*2004*	*2005*	*2006*	*2007*	*2008*	*2009*	*2010*
Annual growth of GDP	2.9	5.1	5.7	6.1	7.0	1.6	2.6	5.6
Total employment (millions)	7.33	7.99	8.51	8.99	9.48	9.95	10.46	10.96
Population (millions)	32.7	32.8	35.1	36.1	37.2	38.3	38.6	39.8
Employment to population ratio	0.22	0.24	0.24	0.25	0.25	0.26	0.27	0.28

Source: Kenya National Bureau of Statistics (KNBS) (2002–2011).

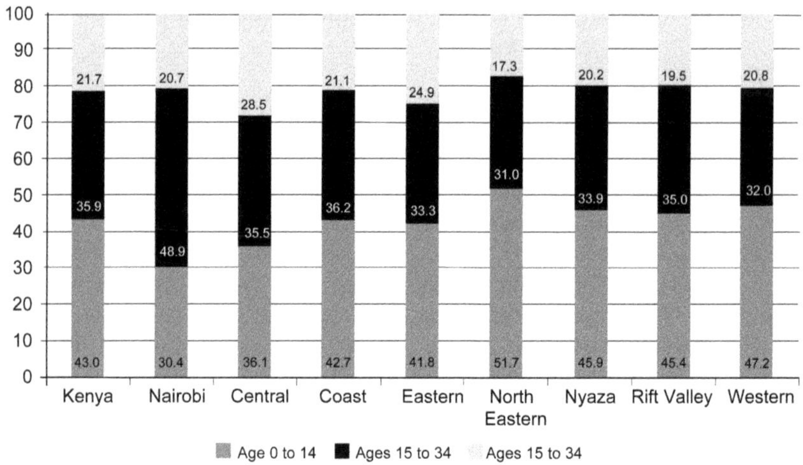

Figure 6.1 Structure of the population in Kenya and its provinces, 2009
Source: Census, 2009.

population growth rate began to decline, reaching 3.4 per cent in 1989 and further to 2.5 per cent in 1999. The 2009 census indicates that the 1999–2009 inter-census population growth rate was 3.0 per cent a year, still among the highest in the world.[3]

Another feature of Kenya's population structure is that the proportion of children (age 0–14) in the total population is high, estimated at 43 per cent in 2009. This meant that the proportion of working-age population (age 15–64) is only slightly larger than that of the child population, even though the share of the elderly (age 65 and above) is extremely small. As a consequence, the child dependency ratio (the number of children per one working age person) is quite high in Kenya: 0.78 in 2009.

In addition to the high population growth and the dominance of children and youth in the total population, regional migration is a significant factor affecting employment in Kenya. Relevant data are provided by the National Council for Population and Development, as shown in Figure 6.2. The data

Table 6.2 Age distribution of the population (percentage), 2009

Total population (millions)	39.8
Population (0–14) – children	43
Population (15–64) – working-age population	55
Population (65+) – aged population	3
Child dependency ratio (under-15s as percentage of working-age population)	78
Elderly dependency ratio (aged as percentage of working-age population)	5
Overall dependency ratio	82.4

Source: World Bank (2011).

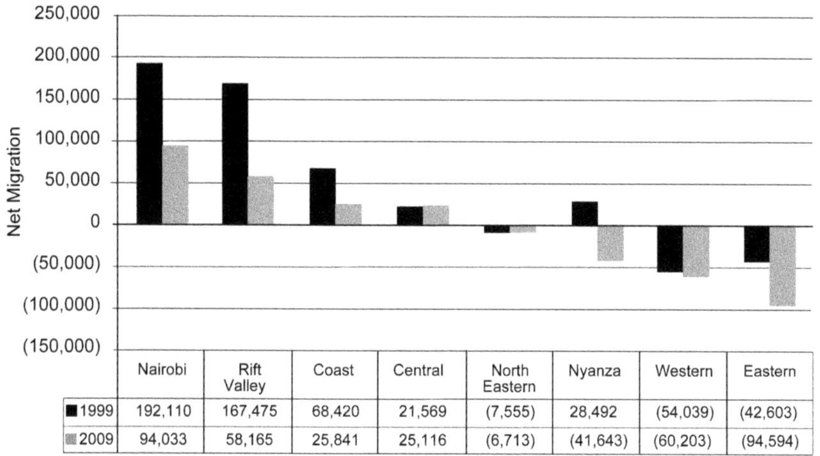

	Nairobi	Rift Valley	Coast	Central	North Eastern	Nyanza	Western	Eastern
1999	192,110	167,475	68,420	21,569	(7,555)	28,492	(54,039)	(42,603)
2009	94,033	58,165	25,841	25,116	(6,713)	(41,643)	(60,203)	(94,594)

Figure 6.2 Net migration by province, 1999 and 2009
Source: NCPAD (2011: 72).

show that four provinces—Nairobi, Rift Valley, Coast and Central provinces—were net receivers of migrants during the inter-census period (1999 and 2009). The largely arid and semi-arid lands of Eastern and North Eastern provinces are net losers of people through migration. This is not surprising given the large share of these provinces in national poverty in a country of vast inequalities.[4] Western province is also a net loser, probably due to the severe land constraints juxtaposed with poor alternative livelihood opportunities in that region.[5] Nyanza's change from net inflow to net outflow over the period is interesting. This change is probably explained by the dismal performance of the region's key industries, including the sugar industry and textile factories.[6]

6.2.3 Trends and characteristics of employment

Despite the strong economic growth that characterized the post-2002 period, growth of formal sector jobs (good quality jobs) has been minimal, as most jobs created were in the informal sector. Figure 6.3 represents trends in the shares of various categories of employment. The data show that between 1989 and 2010, total employment grew from under 2 million to over 11 million. The share of formal sector employment declined steadily to less than 20 per cent by 2010 from 22.1 per cent in 2004.

The share of formal employment in total employment fell during 2003–10, the period of the country's more recent economic boom. Thus, in the formal sector, Kenya experienced minimal growth in jobs, which is underscored for example by KIPPRA's evidence (2010: 26) that 90 per cent of new jobs in 2008 were created in the informal sector.

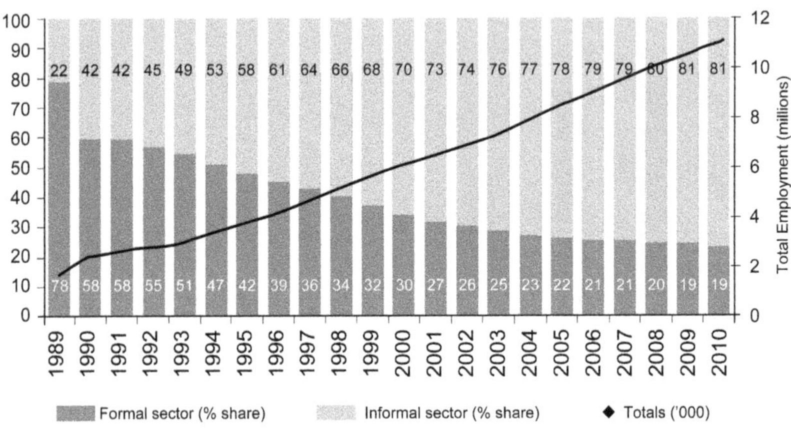

Figure 6.3 Total employment and formal and informal sector shares (percentage), 1989–2010
Source: Republic of Kenya, *Economic Survey*, various issues.

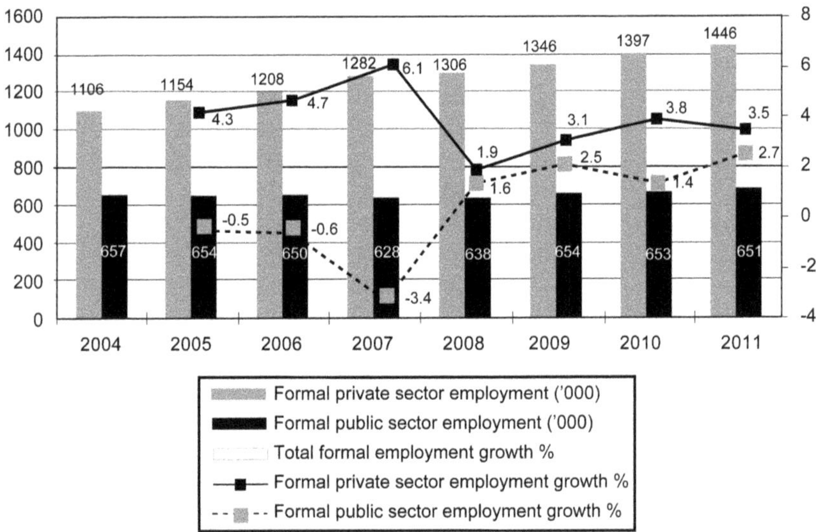

Figure 6.4 Formal private and public sector employment levels and total growth, 2004–11
Source: Republic of Kenya, *Economic Survey*, various issues.

In the formal sector, since 2007 the private sector has employed about twice as many workers as the public sector (see Figure 6.4). The rate of growth of formal private sector wage employment has been increasing since 2008 to stand at 3.5 per cent in 2011. The formal public sector employment growth rate is lower and unsteady, but has nevertheless increased relative to its pre-2008 negative growth rates.

Table 6.3 Share of employment by sector to total formal employment

	2006	*2007*	*2008*	*2009*	*2010*
Community, social and personal services	40.3	39.6	39.8	40.9	40.9
Agriculture and forestry	18.0	17.8	17.5	17.0	16.7
Manufacturing	14.0	13.9	13.6	13.3	13.0
Wholesale and retail trade, restaurants and hotels	10.0	10.3	10.4	10.8	11.0
Transport and communications	7.1	8.1	8.1	7.3	7.3
Building and construction	4.3	4.3	4.4	4.7	4.9
Finance, insurance, real estate and business services	5.0	4.9	4.9	4.9	4.8
Electricity and water	1.1	1.0	1.0	1.0	1.0
Mining and quarrying	0.3	0.3	0.3	0.3	0.3
Total	100.0	100.0	100.0	100.0	100.0

Source: KIPPRA computations based on: Kenya National Bureau of Statistics (KNBS) (2006–2011).

As summarized in Table 6.3, manufacturing industry shares in total wage employment did not change markedly during the 2006–10 period, after declining by 1 per cent during those five years. The largest source of wage jobs remained the community, social and personal services sector at 41 per cent of total wage employment in 2010, followed by agriculture and forestry with a share of about 17 per cent.

Table 6.4 presents the national and regional structure of the labour force and inactivity based on data from the 2009 census. While at the national level the employed constituted 61.7 per cent of the working-age population (15–64 years), those working for pay—including those on sick leave and regular leave—accounted for only 22.7 per cent of the total cohort. The dominant employment category is that of own family agriculture holdings, with a 27.3 per cent share of employment, while own family business accounts for 11.2 per cent of employment. The provincial employment rates range from North Eastern province's rate of 48.7 per cent to Western province's 65 per cent.

Table 6.5 exhibits the dominance of the private sector in the formal sector, accounting for 74.2 per cent of the total employment. Under the formal sector, central government and the Teachers Service Commission have dominant equal shares of employment (33 per cent) while the local authorities had the smallest share (12 per cent)

In the census data, those classified as employed included individuals who (i) worked for pay, (ii) were on leave, (iii) were on sick leave, (iv) worked in own family business, (v) worked in own family agriculture holding, (vi) interns/apprentices, and (vii) volunteers. As is apparent from the data represented in Table 6.5, a comparatively large percentage of the working-age population is employed. However, the overall employment rate, exceeding 60 per cent across all recent national datasets, may mask the precarious nature of most of the jobs.

Table 6.4 Employment and joblessness by province (15–64 years), 2009 (percentage of total)

	Kenya	*Nairobi*	*Central*	*Coast*	*Eastern*	*North Eastern*	*Nyanza*	*Rift Valley*	*Western*
Employed	61.7	63.2	64.7	54.6	60.7	48.7	64.3	62.6	65.0
Unemployed	7.4	10.6	5.7	9.2	5.3	22.7	4.8	6.4	5.2
Inactive	30.5	25.9	29.5	36.0	33.7	27.1	30.7	30.5	29.6
Other	0.4	0.3	0.1	0.3	0.3	1.4	0.2	0.5	0.2
Total	20,557,010	2,133,640	2,577,470	1,782,360	3,003,560	1,063,820	2,730,330	5,145,200	2,120,630

Source: Census, 2009.

Table 6.5 Distribution of formal sector employment (15–64 years), 2009

Private sector employment	2,074,680
Public sector employment:	722,920
central government (33.9 per cent) local authorities (11.7 per cent) Teachers' Service Commission (33.4 per cent) state-owned enterprises (20.9 per cent)	
Total	2,797,600

Source: Census, 2009.

Even though the majority of the youth (about 63 per cent) fall in the category of the employed, it is important to gauge the quality of jobs they hold. This is done by determining the proportion of 'vulnerable jobs' to total employment. The vulnerable employment rate is defined as the percentage of own account workers and unpaid family labour in total employment (United Nations, 2011). Vulnerable employment is characterized by informal working arrangements, lack of adequate social protection, low pay and difficult working conditions. In the Kenyan context, vulnerable jobs would encompass the informal sector (*jua kali*), self-employed (informal), small-scale agriculture, pastoralist activities and so on, as detailed in Figure 6.5. Thus non-vulnerable jobs are seen to be those of a permanent nature primarily in the formal sector. Since the 2009 census required individuals to indicate their 'main employer,' the foregoing characterization allows an approximation of the numbers of youths and other individuals engaged in vulnerable as opposed to non-vulnerable jobs. As Figure 6.5 shows, about 77 per cent of all employed youth and 79 per cent of those aged above 35 years were engaged in vulnerable employment.

The vulnerable/non-vulnerable dichotomy might suggest a direct link to the levels of earnings, whereby vulnerable employment is linked to low incomes, while non-vulnerable jobs are linked to high incomes. Since the 2009 census did not explore earnings, this study developed an indicative wealth index based on household access to various assets: radio, TV, mobile or landline telephone and computer.[7] The wealth index enabled an examination of the quintile distribution of vulnerable employment, presented in Figure 6.6. The analysis shows that 89 per cent of the quintile 1 employees aged 15 and above were in vulnerable employment, compared with 67 per cent for quintile 5 (the richest). While the extent of vulnerable employment is remarkable, this reality is consistent with the employment distribution of Figure 6.3, for which the formal sector share of employment was a modest 19 per cent.

A further analysis is undertaken of the quintile distribution of vulnerable employment by age categories, the results being presented in Figure 6.7. The figure shows that rising wealth status is associated with a reduction in the incidence of vulnerable employment for all employed persons, those aged 36 and above (36+), and for the youth (ages 15–35). Thus while 92 per cent of all

Main Employer	Total Workers (Ages 15 and above)	Ages 15-35 years (youth)	Above 35 years
Private Sector	Non-vulnerable employment (3,342,770) 18% of the total workers	Non-vulnerable employment (2,024,320) 23% of the employed youth	Non-vulnerable employment (1,291,480) 21% of those above 35 years
Local Authorities			
Central Government			
Teachers Service Commission			
State Owned Enterprise			
International NGO			
Local NGO			
Faith Based Organization			
Self Modern			
Informal Sector (Jua Kali)	Vulnerable employment (15,545,160) 82% of the total workers	Vulnerable employment (6,914,490) 77% of the employed youth	Vulnerable employment (4,920,220) 79% of those above 35 years
Self Employed - Informal			
Small Scale Agriculture			
Self Small Scale Agriculture			
Pastoralist Employed			
Self Pastoralist			
Private Household			
Other	Other (22,120)	Other (17,920)	Other (7,240)
Total	18,910,050	8,956,730	6,218,940

Figure 6.5 Vulnerable and non-vulnerable employment by age group
Source: 2009 Census.

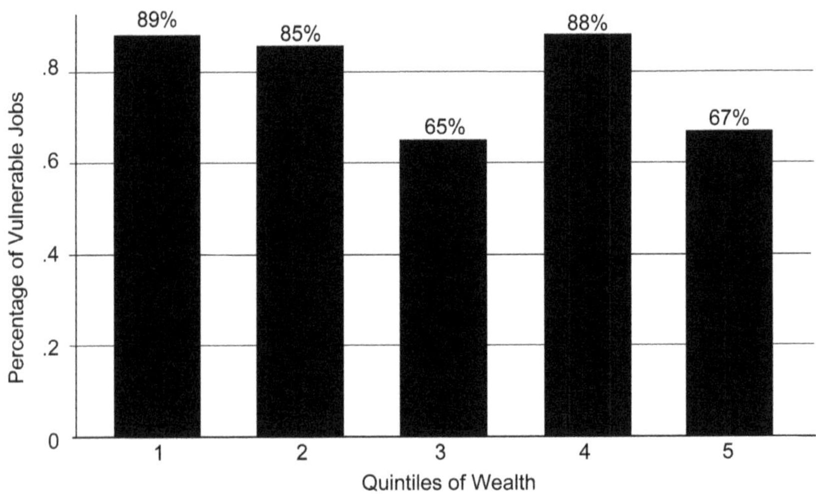

Figure 6.6 Quintile distribution of vulnerable employment for age 15+, 2009
Source: Calculated from Census 2009.

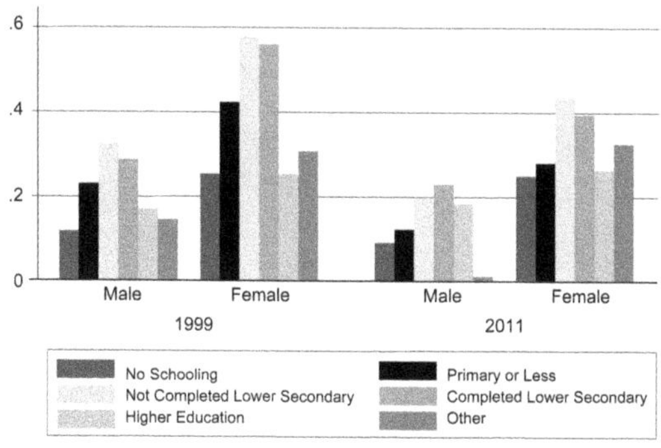

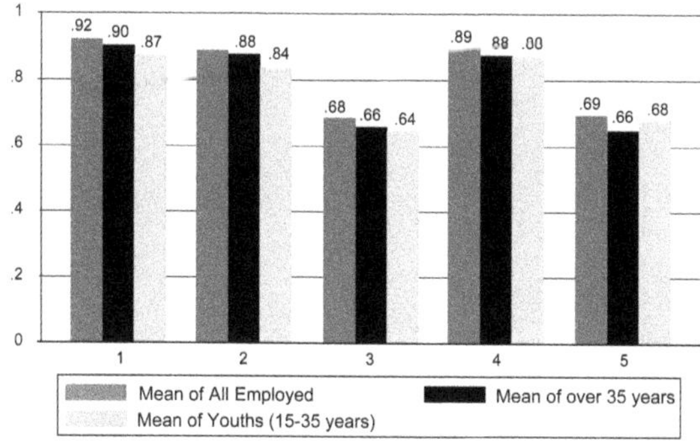

Figure 6.7 Quintile distribution of vulnerable employment
Source: Census 2009.

employed persons in quintile 1 had vulnerable jobs, the share was only 69 per cent in quintile 5. Comparable figures for the 36+ category were 90 and 66 per cent. For the youths, the comparable shares were 87 and 68 per cent. Quintile 4 presents a curious blip in the trend across the wealth divide. An interesting aspect of Figure 6.7 is that the share of youths in vulnerable employment is generally lower than that for older people for all the quintiles. However, given the age structure of the population—with youths accounting for 35.3 per cent compared with those 36+ accounting for 21.7 per cent (Figure 6.1)—the numbers of the youth in vulnerable employment in all the quintiles are invariably much higher in the 36+ group.

Figure 6.8 portrays the magnitude of the labour market challenge, with a focus on the youth. Approximately 60 per cent of the youth are employed, but 78 per cent of them are in vulnerable employment. The figure illustrates the fact that besides inactivity and open unemployment, there is also a need to focus policy attention on the nearly half of the total youth population who are employed in vulnerable jobs.

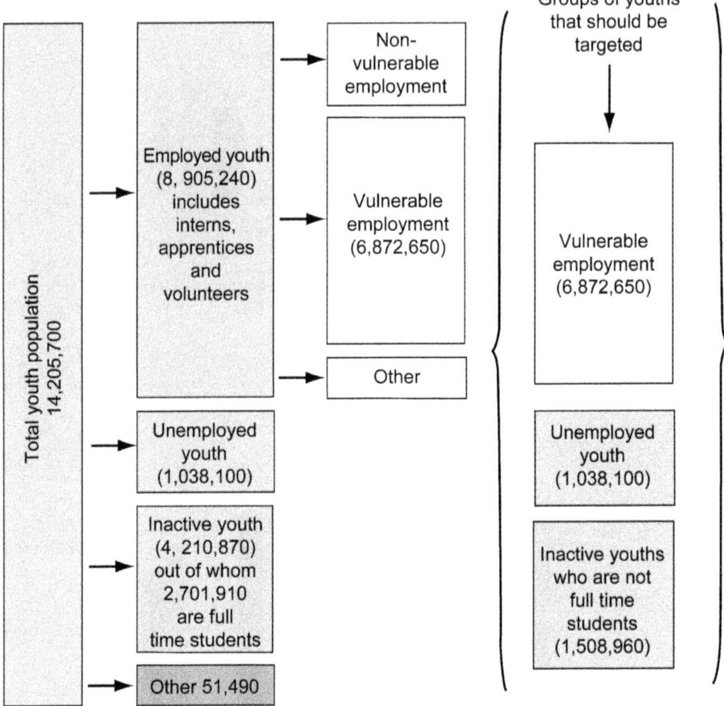

Figure 6.8 Youth employment and joblessness, 2009
Source: Census 2009.

Due to the absence of income data in the census, this analysis chose to use a time criterion to evaluate the quality of jobs in the labour market. The premise is that individuals who reported working 'very long hours'—more than 65 hours in the previous week—are likely to be engaged in low-paying (per work unit) and therefore low-quality jobs. In contrast, those who reported working very few hours (less than 29 hours) are likely to desire more hours as they likely attract low wage incomes.[8]

As summarized in Table 6.6, analysis of the recent census data shows that out of the nearly 19 million employed individuals, only about 18 per cent worked between 36 and 45 hours in the previous week, a time frame that is close to the expected work week of 40 hours (assuming an eight-hour day for five days). The corresponding ratio for the youth who worked between 36 and 45 hours was about 19 per cent. About 18 per cent of all workers and 16 per cent of the youths were underemployed, that is, worked fewer than 29 hours in the past seven days. A significant number of the employed individuals worked for over 65 hours in a week. Specifically, nearly 18 per cent of all workers and 22 per cent of youths worked beyond 65 hours. If the underemployed are included, about two out of every five jobs could be of poor quality on account

Table 6.6 Percentage distribution of employment by hours worked in the seven pre-census days

Hours worked	*All workers**	*Workers aged <15 years*	*Youth (15–35 years)*	*Workers >35 years*
0–29	17.8	25.5	15.7	16.2
29–35	11.2	7.9	11.5	12.7
36–45	17.6	7.2	19.2	21.8
46–55	13.8	4.1	16.0	16.5
56–65	13.0	3.9	15.6	14.9
66+	26.5	51.3	22.1	17.9
Total number	18,910,050	3,785,870	8,905,240	6,218,940

Source: 2009 Census.
Note: * includes individuals who reported working aged five years and above.

of weekly work hours alone. Quality of work—employment terms—could also be gauged by provision of medical allowance and/or insurance, house allowance and leave entitlement. On medical insurance, data from Kenya's pre-eminent medical insurer, the National Hospital Insurance Fund, show a total insurance membership of 2.8 million, with members and their dependents amounting to 6.6 million.[9] Juxtaposing this coverage against the Table 6.6 employment level of 18.9 million suggests that access to medical assurance is low, implying low quality of work.

A different issue arising from Table 6.6 concerns the high level of employment of workers aged less than 16 years, who by all the definitions listed above—UN, ILO, African Union and Kenya—have not graduated into the youth category. The rate of their employment diminishes with an increase in working hours, and then abruptly rises to 51 per cent for those working more than 65 hours per week—which is more than eight hours per day. This fact suggests that a large proportion of school-age children are not in school, drawing petty earnings that encourage the long hours spent at work. Indeed, analysis of the data shows that 99 per cent of this category are in vulnerable employment. This relatively large group of children will, in the near future, graduate into youths who enter the labour market with no meaningful education and consequently few or no labour market skills that can result in gainful employment.

The census data also enable an analysis of the distribution of hours worked as a proxy for quality of work across the vulnerable/non-vulnerable divide. The results summarized in Table 6.7 show that nearly half of those employed in vulnerable jobs (48 per cent) were either underemployed (worked fewer than 29 hours in the past week) or worked for 66 hours or more per week. The distribution of hours worked is better for those in non-vulnerable jobs, for whom those underemployed plus those working for over 66 hours accounted for 25 per cent of that employment category.

Figure 6.9 continues the analysis of Figure 6.8, providing a more general view of the state of employment and joblessness in Kenya. It illustrates the

Table 6.7 Hours worked in non-vulnerable and vulnerable jobs (percentage of total)

Number of hours worked	*Non-vulnerable job*	*Vulnerable job*
0–29 (underemployed)	6.8	20.2
29–35	5.2	12.5
36–45	23.9	16.3
46–55	21.3	12.2
56–65	23.9	10.7
66+	18.9	28.1
Total	100.0	100.0

Source: 2009 Census.

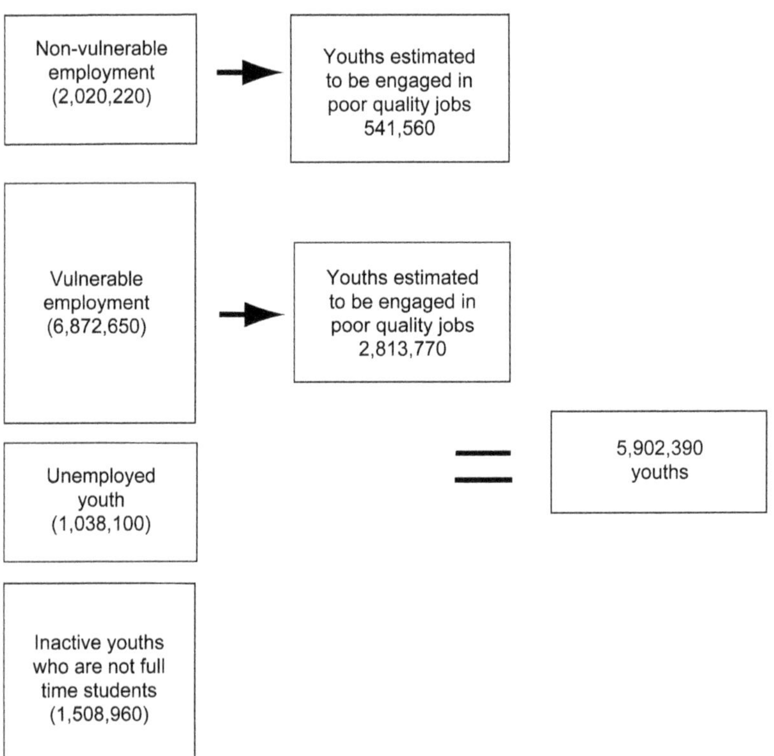

Figure 6.9 Youth employment status: unemployed, inactive and poor quality jobs
Source: 2009 Census.

extent of open unemployment, inactivity, and numbers of employed youths who are in poor-quality jobs based on the time criterion. Based on this figure, the youth labour market challenge may be summarized as follows:

Approximately 38 per cent of youth are engaged in vulnerable jobs that take either fewer than 29 hours weekly or more than 65 hours weekly. These are about 2.8 million youths.

Nearly 11 per cent of all youth (about 1.5 million youths) are inactive: those who were not searching for jobs, the incapacitated and homemakers.
About 1 million youths are openly unemployed, accounting for about 7 per cent of the total youth population (note that this is not the unemployment rate).
Additionally, over half a million youths are engaged in non-vulnerable, yet poor quality jobs—jobs that take up either fewer than 29 hours or more than 65 hours weekly. These youths account for nearly 4 per cent of the total youth population.

In addition to these four groups, policy attention should be paid to the youth engaged in vulnerable jobs, although their jobs are not classified as being of 'poor quality'—with respect to total work hours per week—numbering about 4.1 million. However, they could also be in poor-quality work because of the earning rate. The overriding message is that although the openly unemployed youth may number just about a million, their relatively small number hides a much more complex labour market challenge. The preceding analysis, as illustrated in Figures 6.8 and 6.9, implies that a focus on open unemployment would have limited impact in remedying the labour market challenge. Apart from addressing open unemployment, labour market interventions will also need to focus on: (i) vulnerable employment; (ii) inactive youth; (iii) non-vulnerable yet poor-quality jobs; (iv) 'working children,' among whom the majority could be out of school; and (v) those in vulnerable jobs that are not classified as poor quality on account of time spent working.

6.2.4 Employment characteristics of the youth

To inform policy prescriptions, Table 6.8 outlines some key characteristics of the various groups of youth isolated above: (i) youths engaged in vulnerable

Table 6.8 Various groups of youths and their characteristics

Selected categories	*Percentage of youths who never attended school*	*Mean age (years)*	*Percentage of females*	*Percentage residing in rural areas*
All youth	10.6	24	51.3	62.2
Employed youth	11.2	26	48.5	63.4
Vulnerable jobs (neither underemployed nor working >65 hours)	12	26	51.3	74.9
Vulnerable jobs (either underemployed or working >65 hours)	16.9	24	52.5	68.2
Inactive youth	17.6	24	81.6	57.5
Openly unemployed youth	21.2	23	47.2	51.5

Source: 2009 Census.

jobs that are of poor quality; (ii) inactive youths (excluding full time students); (iii) the openly unemployed youths; (iv) youths in non-vulnerable yet poor quality jobs; and (v) the youths engaged in vulnerable jobs that are not of poor quality. Key information from the table is the extent to which the youth of various categories have not been to school, meaning they have a low stock of skills.

The concern with low educational attainment is further highlighted in Figure 6.9, which shows that 62 per cent of the youth have below secondary-level education, 34 per cent have secondary education, and only 1 per cent have a university education. Other data show that those with low educational attainments are predominantly female. The level of educational attainment of the working population provides a good measure of the stock of human capital and skills in a country. According to this measure, Kenya's skill level is still low.

The findings illustrate that the worst-off groups—the openly unemployed and inactive youths—have a higher ratio of individuals who 'never went to school.' This is supported by the evidence of Table 6.8: educational attainment seems to influence whether or not an individual falls in the vulnerable category of the employed. About 90 per cent of all employed individuals whose highest level of education is primary schooling are engaged in vulnerable jobs, compared with 61 and 21 per cent for those with at least secondary and university qualifications, respectively. On average, the youths with some form of employment tend to be older, and females tend to be more inactive. Although about 62 per cent of all youth reside in rural areas, a lower proportion of these rural youth are openly unemployed, but a larger proportion are engaged in vulnerable jobs.

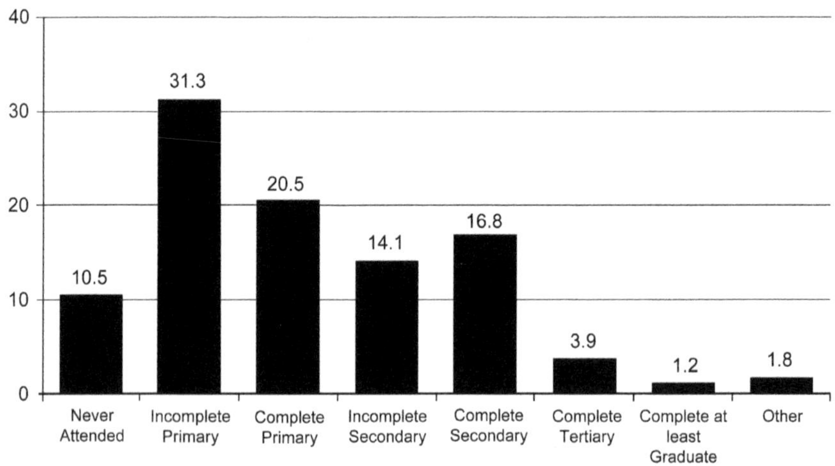

Figure 6.10 Highest level of education attainment by youths, 15–35 years, 2009
Source: Census 2009.

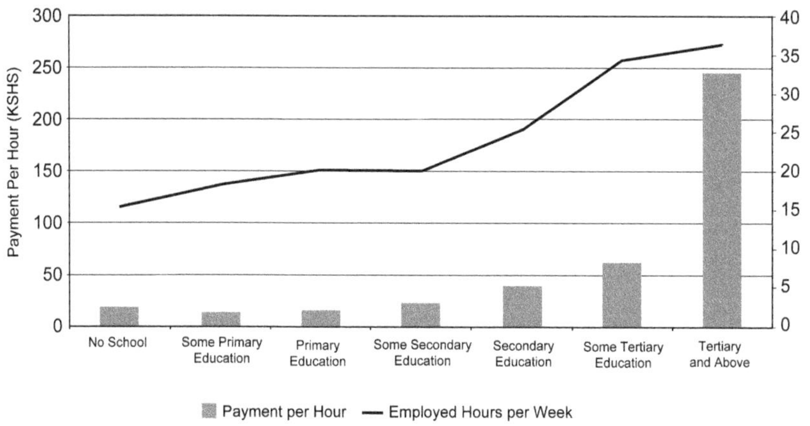

Figure 6.11 Weekly hours worked and earnings by level of education
Source: KIHBS 2005–06.

The majority of the youth (64 per cent) reside in rural areas where they are employed in the agriculture sector, which is expected as the bulk of them have low educational attainment. In terms of marital status, about 55 per cent of the Kenyan youth population is single. As found elsewhere (Van *et al.*, 2005), we hypothesize that perhaps the desire for higher education and employment have encouraged young people in Kenya to delay marriage. On average, each household has about six members, two of whom are employed. The average monthly total household consumption expenditure per capita is Ksh3121 (approximately US$36).[10]

There exists an insidious gap between levels of education, numbers of hours worked and the earning rate per hour, as illustrated by KIHBS 2005–06 data in Figure 6.11. The data show that youths with no schooling work about 15 hours per week and earn an average Ksh20 (US$0.24) per hour, resulting in a weekly income of about Ksh300 (US$3.5). Conversely, youths with secondary education work an average 25 hours a week at an average Ksh45 (US$0.53) per hour, amounting to about Ksh1125 (US$13.2) weekly. The few youths with tertiary education and above work 37 hours a week at Ksh250 (US$2.9) per hour, earning a weekly Ksh9250 (US$108.8). This education-driven transformation in earnings and hours worked probably explains Kenyans' growing demand for university degrees, reflected in the explosion of rural-based constituent campuses of existing universities.[11]

6.3 Youth unemployment, underemployment and working poor

The unemployed are defined to include (i) those who have taken action in seeking work and have not found work; and (ii) those for whom no work is available. This definition is akin to the narrow definition of unemployment. The 'wide' definition of unemployment includes those who have taken

Table 6.9 Unemployment rates (percentage) in Kenya by age and gender, 1978–2009

Age bracket	*1978**	*1986**	*1998–99**	*1998–99*			*2005–06*			*2009*		
				Total	*Male*	*Female*	*Total*	*Male*	*Female*	*Total*	*Male*	*Female*
15–19	26.6	36.2	47.0	24.3	21.8	26.4	19.0	19.2	18.8	15.8	16.5	15.1
20–24	18.5	29.2	47.3	27.1	19.0	33.9	32.6	31.1	33.8	13.1	13.6	12.6
25–29	4.8	8.6	25.1	15.5	8.2	21.6	20.9	20.2	21.5	8.5	8.7	8.3
30–34	2.0	2.7	14.3	10.8	4.8	16.8	8.3	8.1	8.5	6.4	6.5	6.3
35–39	1.8	2.1	12.0	8.4	5.0	11.8	6.6	6.6	6.6	5.4	5.7	5.1
40–44	0.7	0.7	11.2	9.1	7.8	10.6	5.0	5.6	4.5	5.3	5.7	4.9
45–49	1.1	2.0	14.7	8.2	4.9	12.5	3.5	3.5	3.5	4.8	5.1	4.4
50–54	1.4	0.9	18.9	8.7	6.3	11.1	2.1	2.6	1.7	5.4	5.8	4.8
55–59	1.5	4.1	40.6	13.5	14.2	12.7	1.4	2.0	0.9	5.4	5.7	5.0
60–64	3.2	—	45.2	11.7	7.5	15.7	0.6	1.1	0.2	6.4	6.4	6.3
Total	6.7	9.7	25.1	14.6	9.8	19.3	12.7	11.2	14.3	8.6	8.8	8.3

Sources: Vandermoortele (1991); Republic of Kenya (2003, 2008); Census 2009.
Notes: * is urban unemployment; the rest reflect total unemployment rates (urban plus rural).

action in seeking work, plus those who have not taken any action to seek work.

Kenyan unemployment rates estimated in various studies and surveys over time are presented in Table 6.9. Earlier studies, in the 1970s and 1980s, show modest unemployment rates, with Vandermoortele (1991) reporting urban rates below 10 per cent compared with an urban rate of 25.1 per cent from the 1998–99 labour force survey. The 1998–99 labour force survey also reflected an aggregate (rural plus urban) unemployment rate of 14.6 per cent, after which the rate declined by the time of KIHBS 2005–06 and the 2009 population census, standing at 12.7 and 8.3 per cent, respectively. By 2009, the urban rate had fallen to 11 per cent, hence the lowering of the aggregated rate. That the inclusion of rural unemployment reduces the national rate is consistent with the dominance in rural areas of the household enterprise over individual employment (see Chapter 2 in this volume).

Unemployment in 1998–99 was characterized by higher rates among the youngest and oldest individuals, compared with the middle-aged population. Thus the respective rates in the age categories from 35–39 to 50–54 were about one-third of those among the lowest age categories, and just under a half of those of the higher age categories. A remarkable transformation occurred between the 1998–99 and 2005–06 survey periods: while unemployment among urban youths and the middle-aged more or less mapped the 1998–99 levels, that among the older members of the labour force (aged 50 and above) dropped drastically—from an average 35 per cent to an average 6 per cent in the later period (Wambugu *et al.*, 2012: 76). The same transformation is discernible in the aggregate data for the older people—from an unemployment rate of 11 per cent for 1998–99 to about 3 per cent for 2005–06. The unemployment decline reflected in the latter surveys, especially among the older age groups, is likely a factor of the various reforms under the government's *Economic Recovery Strategy for Wealth and Employment Creation 2003–07*, which, for example, launched the Women's Enterprise Fund.

Table 6.9 also captures the gender dimension of unemployment. According to ILO (2005), female unemployment rates may often be underestimated for various reasons, including their disproportionate engagement in unpaid home production, which means they are excluded from the labour force, and the greater likelihood of their being discouraged workers. However, while the Kenyan open unemployment rate for females was nearly twice that for males during the 1998–99 survey, the gap narrowed in 2005–06 and was lower than that for males in 2009.

The educational dimension of unemployment in Kenya shows that, relative to the attainment of only primary education, unemployment rate generally decreases with the level of education. However, individuals with secondary education exhibit a higher chance of being openly unemployed, which could be interpreted as a reflection of preference for wage employment among the more educated individuals in an environment characterized by restricted expansion of formal sector jobs (KIHBS, 2005–06; Kabubo-Mariara, 2003).

6.3.1 Spatial distribution of unemployment

Regional unemployment for the working-age population is further reflected in Table 6.10, which introduces a 'peri-urban' category in 2009, besides the 'traditional' rural/urban divide of Table 6.9. The peri-urban category's 11 per cent rate for 2009 likely reflects a transition between the individual and household nature of urban and rural employment.

There was a substantial variation in unemployment rates across regions. Urban areas recorded higher levels of unemployment (19.9 per cent) compared with

Table 6.10 Regional unemployment rates for ages 15–64, 1998–99, 2005–06 and 2009

Region/province	*Unemployment rates*		
	1998–99	*2005–06*	*2009*
Rural	9.4	9.8	5.6
Urban	25.1	199.9	11.0
Peri-urban	–		8.1
Province:			
Nairobi	23.9	16.0	11.1
Central	6.2	12.1	5.1
Coast	23.4	11.7	9.7
Eastern	6.8	12.3	5.4
North Eastern	34.7	6.0	16.5
Nyanza	12.2	8.3	4.7
Rift Valley	12.1	23.9	6.3
Western	27.5	9.6	4.8
Total	14.6	12.7	8.6

Source: CBS (2003); Republic of Kenya (2008); Census 2009.

rural areas (9.8 per cent) in 1998–99. In 2009, unemployment for urban and rural areas was 11.0 and 5.6 per cent, respectively. Nairobi province had one of the highest unemployment rates across the three periods, which is consistent with the distinction between rural and urban employment made in Chapter 2 of this volume. The unemployment rates across the provinces were rather erratic, an example being North Eastern province's rate of 6.0 per cent in 2005–06 having declined from 34.7 per cent in 1998–99. The fourfold gap between Nairobi and neighbouring Central and Eastern provinces suggests the latter were exporting unemployment into a constrained Nairobi market. North Eastern province's pre-eminent rate across the provinces is surprising as its dominant pastoralist livelihoods are expected to engage all members in the household.

6.3.2 Underemployment

Underutilization of human resources manifests itself in 'underemployment' or the 'working poor,' whom UNECA (2005) defines as individuals working full-time in agriculture or the informal sector and having very low earnings. However, a more nuanced attention to underemployment should move beyond hours worked and wages earned to work in relation to existing capacity. Such a consideration is important in highlighting the efficiency of public and private spending on education and human capital formation. This is especially important for a country such as Kenya, where the informal sector has increasingly dominated employment (see Figure 6.2): it is conceivable, for example, that the peers of graduate middle-level managers are operating informal sector enterprises. These concerns could be addressed by the government's recent national manpower survey.

Table 6.11 summarizes the numbers and rates in total and by gender of underemployment defined as persons working for fewer than 29 hours a week. According to the data, slightly over half a million Kenyan workers were classified as underemployed by the 1998–99 labour force survey, rising to

Table 6.11 Underemployment by gender and average weekly hours worked, age 15–64

Hours of work	*1998–99*				*2005–06*				*2009*			
	M (%)	*F (%)*	*Total*	*%*	*M (%)*	*F (%)*	*Total*	*%*	*M (%)*	*F (%)*	*Total*	*%*
<6	63.4	36.6	21,420	4	52.3	47.7	258,407	9	45.9	54.1	170,440	5.1
6–9	52.1	47.9	51,076	10	44.5	55.5	265,306	10	48.7	51.3	278,180	8.3
10–13	56.2	43.8	70,771	14	43.9	56.1	336,758	12	47.5	52.5	344,670	10.2
14–17	67.7	32.3	60,943	12	38.5	61.5	284,014	10	45.2	54.8	379,300	11.3
18–21	65.5	34.5	115,983	23	43.3	56.7	589,588	22	42.6	57.4	874,640	26.0
22–25	69.2	30.8	139,194	28	43.2	56.8	721,243	27	42.9	57.1	658,680	19.6
26–28	76.7	23.3	46,631	9	50.9	49.1	265,932	10	44.0	56.0	622,130	19.7
Total	65.1	34.9	506,017	100	44.6	55.4	2,721,248	100	44.4	55.6	3,368,040	100

Source: CBS (2003); Republic of Kenya (2008); Census 2009.

2.7 million by the time of the 2005–06 household budget survey. By the time of the 2009 census, the absolute numbers of the underemployed had increased to over 3.3 million. In relative terms, the ratio of the underemployed to the total employed persons was about 5 per cent in 1998–99, 21 per cent in 2005–06, and 18 per cent in 2009.

Most of the underemployed worked for between 18–21 and 22–25 hours per week across the three periods. Based on the 2005–06 household budget survey, Pollin *et al.* (2007) reported that a large proportion of the underemployed are poor (70 per cent) compared with a poverty rate of 46 per cent for the overall population. An interesting transformation in the character of underemployment is the shift from the extensive male dominance for all time categories in the 1998–99 surveys to female dominance in the later surveys.

The other remarkable characteristic of the unemployment landscape is the comparatively high rates of inactivity: 30 per cent for the country, and between 27 and 36 per cent across the provinces. Inactive labour includes full-time students, homemakers and the incapacitated.

6.4 Employment interventions, programs and policies

Employment—and the labour market in general—has a significant place in Kenya's history. The economy of colonial Kenya depended extensively on the steady supply of adequate labour to European settler farms (van Zwanenberg, 1975). Investment in education during the colonial era (mainly by Christian missionaries) was designed to create a small cadre of clerical officers for the colonial service (Mwiria, 1991). A majority of the remaining working-age population of Kenyans constituted a labour reserve that was induced to avail itself to settler farms through a variety of taxes payable in cash (which could only be earned as wages) (Gardner, 2009). Beyond the settler farms, the railway corporation and other agencies of the East African Common Services Organisation also became major employers. The colonial labour context was characterized by forms of racial discrimination, which carried over into early independence. In 1964, for example, there was a simultaneous army mutiny across the three newly independent East African states over racially prescribed working conditions.

Into the early independence decade, the government grossly undermined the trade unions to stifle their political potential. Meanwhile, the failure to undertake extensive land reforms meant that the bulk of a Kenyan population experiencing among the highest growth rates globally—4.8 per cent in the early 1970s—would be confined to crowded former native reserves, even as expanded freedoms of movement and access to education created the urge for alternative livelihoods, notably in urban destinations. While economic growth averaged an impressive 6.5 per cent between independence and the mid-1970s, the growth was driven by smallholder agriculture rather than Kenya's import-substituting manufacturing and industry sectors. Mwega and Ndung'u, (2008: 236) argue that despite its coastal location, cheap labour and market-friendly policies; Kenya never took advantage of globalization to expand manufacturing and industry. Consequently, the independence government initially had been averse to the trickle of youthful labour into underemployment in the emerging urban informal sector. It was not until 1972 that the recommendations of an ILO Mission caused the government to acknowledge the emerging informal sector as a potential solution to the actual and anticipated unemployment problem (Chapter 2 in this volume).

However, the government did not subsequently undertake any substantive policy measures to integrate the Kenyan informal sector into the national economy. On the contrary, the existence of minimum wage guidelines that favoured urban over rural/agriculture areas over the years (see Table 6.12), and the persisting comparative marginalization of rural areas, has meant there has been a sustained flow of youthful labour in search of urban employment. Further, owing partly to governance challenges into the 1980s, there seemed to be a conscious informalization of key areas of the economy: for example, there appeared to be a systematic displacement of formal urban public transport by the unregulated *matatu* industry; and the failure to expand low cost housing pushed peripheral households into urban informal accommodation.

The recent significance of the informal sector—which is no longer an exclusively urban phenomenon—is best illustrated by its role in employment creation during the implementation of the NARC government's Economic Recovery Strategy of 2003–07. While the strategy aimed to create 500,000 new jobs per year, most of these were created in the informal sector, the

Table 6.12 Trends in minimum monthly wage differentials (Ksh), 1995–2010

	1995	*1996*	*1997*	*1998*	*1999*	*2000*	*2001*	*2002*
Nairobi, Mombasa and Kisumu	2993	3293	3722	4241	4538	4809	5122	5534
Municipalities	2776	3054	3420	3934	4209	4462	4796	5132
Other towns	2366	2599	2911	3347	3582	3797	4081	4367
Agriculture	1168	1238	1362	1567	1676	1777	1910	2199
Nairobi to agriculture ratio	2.6	2.7	2.7	2.7	2.7	2.7	2.7	2.5
	2003	*2004*	*2005*	*2006*	*2007*	*2008*	*2009*	*2010*
Nairobi, Mombasa and Kisumu	6142	6818	7295	8171	8171	8171	9641	10606
Municipalities	5697	6323	6766	5578	5578	5578	8942	9836
Other towns	4818	5381	5756	6447	6447	6447	7607	8368
Agriculture	2529	2870	3060	3396	3396	3396	4076	4483
Nairobi to agriculture ratio	2.4	2.4	2.4	2.4	2.4	2.4	2.4	2.4

Source: Republic of Kenya, *Economic Survey*, various issues.

period 2004–08 seeing employment rise by 1,763,800 persons with only 10 per cent of this number being wages (Wambugu *et al.*, 2012). Yet the informal sector has never received due attention. For example, not much came from a 1992 sessional paper proposal of facilitating the sector's entry into the public procurement domain (Moyi *et al.*, 2006). That sessional paper's concerns were repeated in a 2005 sessional paper, *On Micro and Small Enterprises for Wealth and Employment Creation for Poverty Reduction*, yet nothing substantive has been done to integrate the sector into the formal national economy into which it could offer linkages, as was done for small and medium enterprises (SMEs) in Malaysia.

Since independence, the government has been part of three Tripartite Agreements also involving the Federation of Kenyan Employers and the Central Organisation of Trade Unions (COTU). The agreement secured periodic pro-rata increases in employment across the private and public sectors. While this created employment, it was essentially a strategy to rein in labour activism during a period in which the government often strove to influence the choice of COTU office-holders. However, the period also saw a disproportionate growth in public sector employment—in the civil service and state corporations—as jobs were created through political patronage. While the beneficiaries of these measures earned wages, the underlying inefficiencies meant such wages were unrepresentative of the labour's marginal product. Kenya's mid-1980s adoption of structural adjustment programs ended the Tripartite Agreement, imposed a moratorium on public sector employment even as it pruned existing employees through retrenchment and early retirement schemes, and liberalized the labour market so that private sector employers could declare redundancies that were unacceptable during the Tripartite Agreement era. Heintz and Pollin (2003) have argued that one effect of liberalization was the informalization of the economy, which in turn lowered the quality of jobs.

Kenya is only now developing an employment policy and strategy. Over the years, however, there have been many interventions that have sought to influence employment. Wambugu *et al.* (2012) distinguish between policies that prevent formal education graduates from falling into unemployment from causes of unemployment, such as market failure and the lack of investment capital. They use Godfrey's (2003) framework incorporating six intervention areas to analyze Kenya's history of employment interventions.

6.4.1 Making labour markets work better for the poor

Under this heading, Wambugu *et al.* (2012) identify public works programs (PWP) and improvements to the job-search infrastructure. Kenya has a long history of PWPs, the pre-independence ones involving forced labour. Into independence, however, PWPs have been used to manage potential crises related to food shortages and famine, as well as to provide low-cost infrastructure, such as through the Dutch-sponsored, labour-intensive Rural Access Roads

Programme of the 1970s. Under the latter scheme, household members maintained road portions adjacent to their homesteads for a fee. More recent programs have included the Kenya Youth Empowerment Programme and the Trees for Jobs Initiative. The National Accord (2008) mandated interventions to provide youth employment, resulting in a number of initiatives including the World Bank-sponsored *Kazi kwa Vijana* scheme. A similar initiative includes the Youth Employment for Sustainable Development Project (launched in 2012), in which youths will be trained in road-maintenance skills and thereafter engaged in road rehabilitation and maintenance across the country.

The Ministry of Labour, through its labour offices, historically offered registration and placement services for jobseekers. However, the efficiency with which this was done was undermined by the mismatch between economic and population growth, and the resulting influx of jobseekers into the towns. More recently, the ministry's range of services was expanded to include registration of employment agencies. One of the remaining challenges is that job placement services are well established in urban areas compared with rural areas, which remain underserved. In addition, survey evidence indicates that most jobseekers search for work through friends and relatives, a factor that may undermine equity in employment among other labour market outcomes.[12]

6.4.2 Improving the environment for entrepreneurship

After independence, Kenya instituted various measures to empower and enhance opportunities for hitherto disadvantaged racial groups. As an example, the Kenyanization of Personnel Bureau prioritized the accession of indigenous Kenyans to key public positions.[13] However, the government also championed a number of other employment-generating opportunities through state corporations in various sectors. The agriculture initiatives included credit and technical services from the Agriculture Finance Corporation and the Agriculture Development Corporation. This occurred hand-in-hand with land resettlement schemes and a network of village-based extension workers. In industry, the Industrial and Commercial Development Corporation and the Kenya National Trading Company were designed to facilitate the entry of Africans into commerce and industry. These initiatives may have had limited efficiency and national outreach as they were undermined by governance challenges related to nepotism and ethnic parochialism.

One important area of improved chances for entrepreneurs over the years has been microcredit and related activities. The cooperative movement has spawned savings and credit facilities, of which low-cost borrowing might have alleviated the capital constraint for grassroots investments. It is necessary to determine the extent to which these initiatives have been successful in alleviating unemployment and generating or augmenting incomes. Even so, the absence of a favourable policy framework undermined exploitation of the potential of the SME sector—such as in terms of backward and forward linkages to the formal sector. However, there have been various short-term initiatives that apparently have not been evaluated to enable policy formulation (Wambugu *et al.*, 2012). Among these initiatives are the government-sponsored 2006 Youth Enterprise Development Fund (YEDF), the International Finance Corporation-sponsored Grassroots Business Initiative, and UNDP's Growing Sustainable Business Initiative of 2005–08. Others include K-Rep's Youth Saving and Credit Project and Micro-Leasing Project, and the government's SME Solutions Centre. Information on the impacts of these government and non-government initiatives is necessary to inform policy formulation.

A key theme in the Kenyan context would be to support individuals involved in entrepreneurship activities to escape informality. A key intervention would be to transform the motivation for entrepreneurship from being necessity-driven to being opportunity-driven. Wambugu *et al.* (2012: 46) report that global studies conclude that high-growth and high-expectation entrepreneurship is positively correlated with, among others, government regulations, education support for entrepreneurs, physical infrastructure, intellectual property rights protection and market openness. The macro-level instability may dampen the role of entrepreneurship.

6.4.3 Skills development and training programs

The mismatch between skills needs and supply continues to be perceived as a problem bedeviling the labour market. The education system is often viewed as having an academic bias. This explains why successive commissions of enquiry into Kenyan educational needs—Gachathi; Ominde; Mackay; and most recently, Odhiambo—have made recommendations for reforms. The country has expanded all levels of education, including the university level. Yet the latter has been achieved partially through the transformation of medium-level colleges into constituent colleges or regional campuses of public universities.

The mismatch between skills needs and supply is attributable to the lack of a coherent policy on technical education and skills development, leading to an initiative to develop a National Training Strategy (Wambugu *et al.*, 2012). One means by which to close the gap would be to encourage private sector participation in developing curricula for technical and vocational education and training and university education, and in financing the same, as public education funding already focuses on formal (academic) education. There is also a very urgent need to regulate the numerous private institutions that currently offer skills development, which will improve intra-sector mobility for their graduates. There is a further need for ongoing learning and relearning among trainers, as the contexts within which they provide education services respond to technological changes.

6.4.4 Making training systems work better for young people

Training systems would work well if a number of factors were present, including the recipients' ability to pay; yet this is seldom the case in a poor country like

Kenya. Those in need of training may not be able to pay for it. In addition, more so in the informal sector, training is usually neither assessed nor certified. Such training is likely to limit the benefits to the trainee. Other challenges may undermine the training systems: (i) absence of or outdated curriculum, (ii) no framework for identifying training needs, (iii) lack of either an industrial training and policy framework or a national qualification framework, (iv) poor coordination of activities between or among industry, training and research institutions, and (v) inadequate, dilapidated or obsolete training facilities.

One of the initiatives by the government to make training systems work better was the *Kenya Jua Kali* Voucher Programme. Launched as a 1997 pilot scheme under the Micro and Small Enterprise Training and Technology Project, the initiative focused primarily on disadvantaged youths whose training costs were subsidized through vouchers with which to pay for training under a provider of their own choice. The program also connected demand for, and supply of, training where this was necessary. During the five-year period to 2001, the programme issued 37,606 vouchers. Access to a training provider of choice seemed to have two advantages, the first being that mutual self-selection meant the trainees and mentors were likely to be more suited to each other than if they were imposed on each other. The second advantage was that trainers found themselves in a competitive market in which they had to perform. While the scheme was adjudged to increase employment and assets compared with a control group, there were indications that its design could be complex and costly (Johanson and Adams, 2004). Second, the subsidy created a dependence that was difficult to phase out. These design problems were seen to reflect government involvement, leading to a perception they could be overcome through a strategy nurturing willingness to pay, managed by the private sector.

6.4.5 Improving links between education and the labour market, including revitalizing job-search infrastructure in the country

A strong and effective job-search infrastructure and labour market information system is critical in addressing the youth unemployment challenge in the country. However, in Kenya informal social networks potentially play an important role in matching workers to employers in labour markets. According to data presented in Table 6.13, the most frequently used method of job search in the country is informal (friends and relatives).

Table 6.13 Job-search method in the week before the survey, 1998–99

Job-search method	*Frequency*	*Percentage*
Formal	93	5.91 (6.73)
Informal	1308	83.15 (80.52)
Direct contact	172	10.93 (12.74)
Total	1573	100.00

Source: Wambugu *et al.* (2012).
Note: Weighted percentages in parentheses.

About 81 per cent of jobseekers relied on friends and relatives in their search for work; 12 per cent of jobseekers contacted employers directly, while fewer than 8 per cent used formal channels to search for work. However, informal channels have various weaknesses. They promote inequalities as those with weak or no social networks are likely to remain continuously disadvantaged in accessing decent employment, especially in the formal sector (Wambugu *et al.*, 2012). It is therefore important for the country to revitalize the formal job-search infrastructure in the country. Labour market information systems should also be strengthened while ensuring effective linkage between education and training and the labour market.

6.4.6 Improving labour market laws and regulations

The stiff regulations that had governed hiring and firing in Kenya into the 1980s were slackened considerably with the adoption of structural adjustment programs, with consequent positive impacts on market rigidity and the scope for market clearing. Along these lines, Kenya ranked 40th out of 132 countries in the Global Competitiveness Report 2009/10, an improvement of 20 places on the 2007 status.[14] The country ranked 20th out of 133 with an index of 17 in rigidity of employment measures, and an index of 4.6 out of 7—rank 23 over 133—for hiring-and-firing practices. These scores suggest the Kenyan labour market is attractive, its hiring-and-firing costs being lower than those of Korea and Malaysia, for example. However, the legal framework (including continuing minimum wage legislation) and trade union activity remain significant determinants of sector competitiveness status.

The legal frameworks for the sector were reviewed recently. The legislation covered included the Labour Institutions Act (2007), Employment Act (2007), Labour Relations Act (2007), Work Injury Benefits Act (2007), and Occupational Safety and Health Act (2007). Implementation has been constrained by inadequate budgetary and human resources available to the Ministry of Labour. Its share of public spending was only 0.26 per cent—which is a likely reflection of its weak bargaining position in a Medium Term Expenditure Framework sector working group, which also includes the Ministry of Youth Affairs and Sports. On staffing, the ministry's inspectorate staff-to-labour ratio has moved from 1: 37,284 in 1996 to 1: 121,752 in 2010, resulting in *ad hoc*, unintegrated rather than programmatic interventions. Consequently, it is premature to evaluate the impact of the new laws.

On minimum wage legislation, the Kenya Wage Guidelines and its Labour Institutions Act follow ILO guidelines and the Universal Declaration of Human Rights, in principle. Yet for the two decades to 2010, minimum wage increases have lagged behind inflation by between 6 and 20 per cent. In addition, the Ministry of Labour's resource constraints undermine the strict enforcement of wage guidelines, even in the formal sector. The Productivity Centre of Kenya has been mandated with linking labour productivity to the wage-setting process.

Trade unions have been important agencies in Kenyan history, even outside the narrow labour domain. The Global Competitiveness Report 2009–10 ranked Kenya at 80 out of 133 for a flexibility of wage determination index of 5 out of 7, implying some degree of flexibility in the arena. The literature suggests that unions have been most effective in raising wages in the manufacturing sector, but their effect in other sectors is unclear. Kingdon *et al.* (2005) have reported a strong correlation between unionization and alternative explanations for market distortions, such as regulations, monopoly rents and market size. Thus further empirical evidence is necessary to affirm the effect of unions on wages and employment.

Table 6.14 presents a summary of issues and strategies in the Kenyan labour sector's Strategic Plan for 2008–12, which are pertinent to youth unemployment.

Table 6.14 Youth unemployment issues and potential response strategies

Issue	*Response strategy*
Inadequate capacity to facilitate provision of quality services to the public and stakeholders, and to respond to emerging issues	Build adequate capacity to provide quality, efficient and effective services to the public, stakeholders and to respond to emerging issues (among other interventions): • mainstream HIV/AIDS within the Ministry • mainstream gender and youth issues within the Ministry
Lack of policy and legal framework to facilitate effective implementation of the framework for new labour laws and for MSE development	Undertake legal, policy and institutional reforms to facilitate implementation of the Ministry's mandate and functions: • develop relevant policies and legislation • fast-track enactment of pending bills and policies • operationalize labour institutions under the new labour laws mainstream public sector reforms into the Ministry's programs and activities
Ineffective public employment services, high levels of youth unemployment, underutilization of the capacity of MSEs to generate employment, disjointed coordination of MSEs and uncoordinated labour exportation	Enhance public employment services and streamline labour export: • establish modern regional employment offices and upgrade existing ones • promote and regulate labour export • facilitate job creation for the youth establish an institutional framework to tap Kenyan expertise in the diaspora • develop a website for employment interaction

(*continued on next page*)

Table 6.14 (continued)

Issue	*Response strategy*
	Develop MSEs: • enhance capacity of MSEs to promote employment creation • enhance MSEs' access to markets and marketing information • enhance coordination of policies, strategies and programmes for support of the MSE sector • enact MSE Act and establish National Council for Small Enterprise Development • develop and upgrade infrastructure for MSEs • acquire and secure parcels of land for MSEs • establish centres of excellence for MSEs to facilitate technology transfer • undertake MSE baseline and informal sector development • develop and implement entrepreneurship promotion programmes
Lack of national human resource database and an integrated human resource development policy and strategy	Establish a comprehensive national human resource database and formulate and implement an integrated human resource development policy and strategy: • develop and maintain a human resource databank • manage and coordinate national human resource development
Inadequate supplies of skilled labour at all levels of industry	Ensure adequate supply of skilled labour at all levels in industry: • strengthen linkages between industry, education training and research institutions • enhance capacity of existing industrial training institutions • establish regional industrial training centres develop national training and testing standards • transform the directorate of industrial training into a semi-autonomous government agency industrial training, trade testing and skills upgrading • sponsorship of female training in engineering courses

(*continued on next page*)

Table 6.14 (continued)

Issue	*Response strategy*
Lack of a national productivity policy and legal framework, lack of awareness of productivity and productivity culture, low national expertise capacity, lack of national productivity statistics, low national productivity levels and inadequate capacity to champion productivity practices	Develop and implement a national strategy on productivity improvement and management: • give strategic direction on productivity management in the country • strengthen institutional capacity of the productivity centre of Kenya to champion and change productivity interventions • facilitate adoption of productivity culture and practices • facilitate assessment of productivity levels and provision of guidelines for wage determination

Source: Ministry of Labour (2008).

6.5 Determinants of youth unemployment and underemployment

6.5.1 Work situation in modern, transitional and traditional economies

The unemployment literature distinguishes open or 'classical' unemployment from disguised unemployment, also termed underemployment. Chapter 2 in this volume underscores the importance of this distinction in discussing employment in Africa, a continent where poverty forces people to find employment of some kind or other for survival. Such desperation is not as common in the western world, where comparatively higher incomes enable workers to save for the future, and various benefits might be available to the unemployed, including unemployment pay, council housing, medical insurance and free education, among other welfare benefits. Whereas unemployment trends in developed economies follow business cycles, Ranis and Gollin (Chapter 2) argue that unemployment in poor countries is a factor of the structure of their economies, which undermines the ability of the labour market to clear. Yet this position should not disregard the cyclical nature of agriculture-based employment in poor countries, which is controlled by crop seasonality.

In analyzing unemployment, Ranis and Gollin (Chapter 2) refer to the well known Ranis–Fei model (Ranis and Fei, 1961), which recognizes the economic dualism inherent in developing countries, pitting a traditional low-productivity sector against a modern sector that includes the government.[15] Individuals in the traditional sector survive on an average product below which disease and death would restore the equilibrium. Consequently, underemployment is a characteristic of this sector, causing outmigration to the urban sector, the lure to which is the higher expected earnings. In the urban sector, however, unemployment and underemployment call for structural changes to enhance modern sector growth, creating new employment opportunities.

Wambugu *et al.* (2012) recognize the multi-sectoral labour model underlying the Ranis and Gollin (Chapter 2) framework. They note the non-classical, segmented nature of the labour market in developing countries. The Harris and Todaro (1970) two labour-sector model explains the migration of labour from the low-productivity rural sector to the higher-productivity urban sector. The model posits that labour escapes the low returns of rural underemployment, or open unemployment, in anticipation that any employment in the urban sector will realize greater returns. The model bases (urban) unemployment on formal sector wage rigidity above the market-clearing level. Thus employers do not hire new workers, and retrench in response to wage increases. Whereas some retrenchment victims enter the low-productivity informal sector, others prefer unemployment in anticipation of a job in future.

Ranis and Gollin (Chapter 2) report a further variant to the multi-sectoral labour market, the Jamal–Weeks model, which calls for inequality reduction. This model recognizes that in both rural and urban areas there are poor and rich people, inducing straddling for the disadvantaged.

Ranis and Gollin distinguish four broad employment sectors in a typical Sub-Saharan African economy: agriculture, rural household enterprise, urban household enterprise and the urban formal sector. This formulation is based on a conceptualization of returns to labour: whereas in the modern economy, wages reflect the marginal product of labour, this is not the case with the traditional economy, where production is based on the household rather than the individual. Given the contexts of self-employment, self-provisioning and unpaid family work, the various members contribute to a household's aggregate resources, enabling ascription of the household's average product to each member, including those who did not contribute. It is therefore easy to see that in the modern economy one is either employed or unemployed, whereas the shared responsibilities (and benefits) of the traditional economy mean that individuals often will not exploit their full potential, hence their invariable underemployment. The foregoing reality leads Ranis and Gollin to define underemployment as the 'inability to work as many hours as (one) would like'. Yet this definition is problematic: it would classify as underemployed formal sector workers wishing to go beyond the regular (eight-hour) day.

Of the labour market typology offered above, agriculture is the main employer, often accounting in regions such as Sub-Saharan Africa for more than three-fifths of all employment. Indeed, World Bank data show that out of the 18 countries under consideration, agriculture accounted for over 60 per cent of employment in at least 13 countries. Contrary to the Ranis and Gollin (Chapter 2) generalization, however, the agriculture sector is not homogenous—as implied by the recognition by Jamal–Weeks that the rich and poor are found in both rural and urban sectors. Agriculture's commercial component has the trappings of the (urban) modern sector, with a high technology component in production, and wages based on the marginal product. However, the dominant character of Sub-Saharan African agriculture—including the pastoralist component—is the household-based, self-employed and self-provisioning production unit. While migration to urban areas deprives the rural areas of youthful labour, the youth remain the dominant suppliers of labour to agriculture. Culturally prescribed gender biases that, for example, favour education of the male child over female siblings mean that migrant labour is likely to be male, so that rural agriculture labour is dominated by female youths.[16]

Population pressure impinges on often fixed or diminishing land holdings, where largely rudimentary farming methods are applied, to constrain output.[17] Coupled with the expectations developed through education and exposure, constrained agriculture livelihoods cause diversification into the rural household enterprise, for which sustainability depends, ironically, on agriculture-based incomes (or products, where barter is a mode of exchange). The livelihood activities of the rural household enterprise are as diverse as the agricultural contexts in which they are carried out, but are characteristically service-based with fledgling manufacturing (primarily of household items). Among the activities undertaken are food processing, the making of furniture, garments, and handicrafts, hairdressing, basic domestic repairs, retailing, private security and transport.

The activities of the rural household enterprise are quite similar to those of the Ranis and Gollin (Chapter 2) third employment cluster, the urban household enterprise, which they estimate to have accounted for four-fifths of all new entrants into the Sub-Saharan African urban labour force in recent years. These household enterprises primarily target each other as customers. Their operations are unregistered and unlicensed, but often pay unofficial levies to local authority inspectors. They often operate from temporary structures which are shifted as the need arises, providing informal apprenticeships to individuals who soon move to set up their own operations. Thus the urban household enterprise sector is always dynamic, absorbing new entrants with varied qualifications—or none at all—undermining the scope for full employment while also retaining (a semblance of) extensive structural and frictional unemployment. In rare instances, it loses members to the formal sector.

However, the urban household enterprise has a more lucrative market based on the comparatively wider money economy it serves. This has enabled the emergence of a subsector that is neither characteristically informal nor characteristically formal: notably, formal outlets develop backward linkages to non-formal suppliers whose technological capacities are everything except formal, operating without business licenses and unregistered by the tax authorities, but supplying (finished) goods and services to the formal sector.[18] Indeed, entrepreneurs who otherwise qualify for the formal sector take refuge in the informal sector to evade the high costs of formalization (King, 1996).[19] Operating from established premises with employees on regular payrolls, they defy categorization alongside the basic urban household enterprise. In effect, their staff can neither be described as underemployed, nor be said to produce an average (household) product. Their marginal product and consequently, their wages can be calculated as in the urban formal sector.

The final employment sector is the urban formal sector, which is reported to be small even if it is growing. This is the sector that attracts educated—and uneducated—youth from the rural areas, in anticipation of its comparatively higher, formal wages, secured not just by the value addition of output but also by legislated minimum wages. The urban formal sector also suffers from structural and frictional unemployment. However, the likely response to sustained formal sector unemployment is to straddle into the informal sector. Ranis and Gollins cite World Bank evidence that youth underemployment is more serious in urban than in rural areas, but the returns to any urban employment will be more rewarding than that in rural areas.

Ranis and Gollins (Chapter 2) offer a country typology of the nature of labour markets distinguishing coastal from landlocked and resource-rich countries. Coastal countries outdo the other two categories in terms of wage employment, with land-locked countries offering the least scope for the same. Conversely, resource-rich countries have the greatest scope for informal employment, with land-locked countries performing averagely in both contexts. While they use country data to illustrate their typology, there are many country instances that challenge the typology. For one, there are many countries that typically fall under more than one of their categories, some because they are so large. For example, the greater Sudan is resource-rich and coastal, Botswana and expansive DRC Congo are both resource-rich and landlocked, and informal employment dominates coastal Kenya (Table 6.9).

6.5.2 Unemployment models

Keynes (1936) attributes unemployment to deficiencies in aggregate demand over certain periods in the business cycle, such that jobs created are not enough for everyone who wants to work. Unemployment of this nature is involuntary as the unemployed are constrained from workplaces by limited job availability. Related to the demand deficiency idea is unemployment created by predictable seasonal variation in demand often corresponding with climatic seasons. From the perspective of Marxism, unemployment is inherent within the unstable capitalist system. Periodic crises of mass unemployment are to be expected (see McLellan, 2009) because a deliberate attempt by the capitalists to keep wages low creates an environment of surplus labour.

A mismatch between demand in the labour market and the skills and location of jobseekers tend to cause structural unemployment. This situation is related to unemployment created by technological advancement that makes the skills of some workers obsolete. The time it takes the individual to find and move into a new job, or the time and resources it takes an employer to identify and recruit suitable workers to fill vacancies, create frictional search unemployment which is of short duration. The insider–outsider labour market model (see Linbeck and Snower, 1988), efficiency wage theory (see Shapiro and Stiglitz, 1984), and the implicit contract model are some of the theories that explain unemployment.

The underlying theoretical models of studies on unemployment in Africa often focus on the supply side. Empirical studies using household-level data for most developing country studies do not find the expected inverse relationship between unemployment and education. Examples include (i) Kuepie *et al.* (2006), who find that unemployment levels generally increase with the level of education, at least until the end of the secondary level in the West African Economic and Monetary Union countries; (ii) Rama (1998), who finds that unemployment in Tunisia is concentrated among the young and relatively well educated; and (iii) others (Serneels, 2004; World Bank, 2006; Cling *et al.*, 2007) who reported related findings for Ethiopia, Rwanda, Senegal and Tanzania.

Studies on unemployment generally have focused on the impact of personal characteristics, unemployment insurance and local labour market characteristics on the probability of leaving unemployment. In addition to supply-side factors, demand-side factors such as local unemployment rates and place of residence are typically found to be significant determinants of individual unemployment duration. Other potentially significant determinants of an individual's employability include demographic characteristics such as age, ethnicity, education, health condition, own and parental education levels and previous working experience. Other significant factors are spouse employment status and family background. Many of these covariates are available in our datasets and were used in the analyses.

6.5.3 Determinants of unemployment

This section analyses the determinants of the incidence of open and other forms of unemployment among the youth in Kenya, mainly relying on a quantitative approach. The analysis focuses on both youth unemployment and quality of employment considering the dichotomy between unemployment and informality. The section investigates the determinants of an individual's incidence of unemployment and looks at the role of education in reducing unemployment.

The question of why young people remain unemployed can, to some extent, be addressed empirically. The extant empirical literature has concentrated heavily on supply-side explanations of unemployment as a function of unemployment incentives and personal characteristics. One reason for this approach may be that most data sources are not suitable for investigating demand-side influences at the level of the individual worker. Demand-side explanations of individual unemployment (usually based on profit-maximizing decisions of firms) have therefore been ignored in favour of supply-side discussions of utility maximizing labour/leisure choices.

The empirical approach uses a multinomial probit model to identify how labour supply factors affect employment status of the youth. This model (see Wooldridge, 2002) can be specified as:

$$y^*i = \beta_1' X_{i1} + \varepsilon_{i1}$$

where:

$$\varepsilon_i \approx N(0, 1)$$

where y^*_i is a discrete variable that takes on a value of 1 if the individual aged 15–35 years is underemployed, a value of 2 if fully employed, and a value of 3 if openly unemployed.

$$\beta_1$$

is a vector of parameters for the various explanatory variables including age, gender, household size and education.

$$X_{i1}$$

is a vector of exogenous factors.

$$\varepsilon_{i1}$$

is the error term which is assumed to be normally distributed with the mean of zero and constant variance.

Individual-level data are used to estimate the determinants of states of youth unemployment. The census 2009 data collected by the Kenya National Bureau of Statistics are used for the analysis. The data cover both wage-earners and the self-employed. The sample of youths aged between 15 and 35 is made up of all workers in the formal and informal sectors, public and private employees, the self-employed, the unemployed, and so on.

6.5.4 Correlates of youth employment status

Equation 6.1 is estimated using a multinomial probit model. The marginal effects estimates are presented in Table 6.15. The estimation results reported for youth unemployment and full employment should be interpreted using the underemployed youth as the reference category.

The results show that age is negatively related to the probability of being unemployed compared with being underemployed, but its coefficient is not statistically significant in the full employment category. The negative relationship between age and unemployment is seen in some literature to underscore the obligation that an individual has to work to provide for oneself or a family as

Table 6.15 Multinomial probit model of youth employment status (underemployment is the comparison category), 2009

Variables	*Unemployment (marginal effects estimates)*	*Full employment (marginal effects estimates)*
Age (years)	–0.182*** [0.0672]	0.0181 [0.0590]
Age^2 (years)	0.00183 [0.00124]	–0.000322 [0.00107]
Gender (1 = female)	0.415*** [0.0469]	0.688*** [0.0416]
Marital status (1 = married)	–0.503*** [0.0988]	–0.240*** [0.0903]
Residence (1 = rural)	–0.750*** [0.0573]	–0.825*** [0.0492]
Household size	0.0533*** [0.00787]	–0.0210*** [0.00761]
Income quintile_2	–0.255*** [0.0759]	–0.0321 [0.0751]
Income quintile_3	–0.454*** [0.0773]	–0.0748 [0.0741]
Income quintile_4	–0.462*** [0.0802]	0.145* [0.0744]
Income quintile_5	–0.422*** [0.0890]	0.437*** [0.0810]
Years of education (years)	0.0546*** [0.00869]	0.0307*** [0.00757]
Basic literacy (reading or writing)	0.198* [0.115]	0.0447 [0.106]
Central province (reference = Nairobi province)	–0.671*** [0.119]	–0.519*** [0.103]
Coast province	–0.260** [0.124]	–0.357*** [0.111]
Eastern province	–0.632*** [0.115]	–0.586*** [0.101]
North Eastern province	0.750*** [0.216]	–0.510** [0.232]
Nyanza province	–1.000*** [0.116]	–0.870*** [0.101]
Rift Valley province	–0.682*** [0.110]	–0.474*** [0.0958]
Western province	–0.876*** [0.121]	–0.879*** [0.107]
Constant	3.259*** [0.921]	–0.138 [0.825]
Observations	9,785	9,785

Source: KIPPRA computations using the Kenya Integrated Household Budget Survey (KIHBS) 2005/06 dataset *collected by (Kenya National Bureau of Statistics (KNBS))*.
Note: Standard errors in parentheses. *** significant at 1 per cent; ** significant at 5 per cent; * significant at 10 per cent.

one grows older (Wamalwa, 2009). An increase in household size raises the probability of unemployment by 5.3 per cent while lowering that of full employment by 2.1 per cent relative to underemployment probability. In other words, relative to youths from small families, youths from large families are more likely to be unemployed, and more likely not to find a full-time job.

Female youths are more likely to be unemployed but more likely to be fully employed (conditional on having work) relative to their male counterparts. Moreover, relative to male youths, female youths are more likely to be unemployed rather than underemployed. This finding suggests that female youths do not benefit from the casual employment arrangements that male youths are exposed to. Being married relative to being single is associated with a lower likelihood of being unemployed, but is also negatively correlated with the likelihood of being fully employed. That is, marriage is associated with a higher probability of underemployment. A possible explanation is that married youths are under great pressure to take up any available employment opportunities to support their dependants, raising their susceptibility to underemployment.

Results associated with area of residence indicate that the probability of being employed is higher for the rural youth. The rural youths are likely to be engaged in own account and unpaid family work in agricultural activities. In addition, urban areas in Kenya receive more migrants relative to rural areas, and the growing numbers of urban youth would be competing for limited employment opportunities. Although the rural youth are likely to be employed, they are also more likely to be underemployed whenever they are working.

In the same vein, in comparison with Nairobi region, youths from all other provinces, with the exception of North Eastern, are more likely to be employed. However, the youths from other provinces are less likely to be fully employed compared with the youths in Nairobi. A plausible explanation is that the regions outside Nairobi are less urbanized, with predominantly agriculture-based livelihoods that require all members of the household to work. It is unclear why being a youth in the arid and semi-arid North Eastern region raises the probability of unemployment relative to Nairobi. This finding is in contrast to the expectation that pastoralist livelihoods entail activities that are particularly suited to the youth, such as herding, fencing and fetching water.

The positive, statistically significant coefficient on education indicates that schooling is associated with risk of unemployment, but also with a higher probability of full employment when a job is found. Literacy also raises the probability of unemployment compared with underemployment, but the coefficient for the full employment category is not statistically significant. Consequently, besides enabling them to read or write in any language, it is important to develop employable skills among the youth to improve their employability.

The results in Table 6.15 show the effect of household income on youth employment status. Relative to youths from the lowest income quintile, belonging to any of the other income quintiles lowers the probability of unemployment below that of underemployment. However, with respect to full employment, only youths from households in income quintiles 4 and 5 have higher probabilities of being fully employed than being underemployed.

6.6 Employment creation and employment-oriented development strategies

This section focuses on employment-creation interventions in Kenya, contributions of livestock and small-scale agriculture to employment creation, and employment creation in the formal and informal sectors, among other related issues. The section also provides options for i) initiatives to improve employability of the labour force, ii) interventions towards addressing youth unemployment, and iii) identifying programs and projects towards addressing unemployment and underemployment and improving the quality of jobs in the country.

The section assesses the effectiveness of the current strategies on job creation and provides a synthesis of new ideas for improving labour market outcomes.

It includes projections of labour demand and supply, links job creation to education and training, and draws policy recommendations. These include innovative strategies that can be adopted both in the short and long term to create employment opportunities.

6.6.1 Simulating employment creation using a social accounting matrix

A KIPPRA–NESC study employed the Social Accounting Matrix (SAM) of 2003 to simulate the impacts on categories of employment of exogenous interventions (financed by Ksh1 billion injection) across Kenya's three sectors of the economy: agriculture, manufacturing and services, which respectively account for 26.4, 13.3 and 60 per cent of GDP (Wambugu *et al.*, 2012: 49–64). Using structural path analysis, the simulations found agriculture most favourably disposed to employment creation, a 100 per cent increase in maize production leading to 15.8 per cent increase in labour demand, with 26,000 jobs of Ksh6000 being created. Figure 6.12 summarizes the impacts on labour demand of subsectors across Kenya's three key production sectors, showing that the change in agriculture labour demand ranged between 10 and 24 per cent compared with a range of 2 to 12 per cent for manufacturing and 6 to 20 per cent for services.

In agriculture, the greatest labour demand would be generated by the livestock-based subsectors, ranging between 21 per cent for 'other livestock' and 24 per cent for cattle/goats. The gender differentials in labour demand are important for the design of interventions. The highest change in labour demand for men would be in rice production (17 per cent) compared with the highest for women in other livestock (18 per cent). Besides other livestock and cattle/goats, demand for women's labour exceeded that for men in the wheat and barley subsectors. In manufacturing, men had the highest labour demand in the mining subsector (9 per cent), but women dominated in wood and paper (8 per cent), textiles and footwear, and petroleum and chemicals. Finally, under services, women had the greatest impact in the hotels and restaurants subsector (13 per cent), but were dominated by men in all the other subsectors.

The simulations also enabled an evaluation of the impacts of the labour status on value addition. In agriculture, rural formal skilled labour dominated value addition only for barley (more than 80 per cent), with rural informal skilled labour accounting for more than 60 per cent of value addition for all the other activities. While the roles of the urban unskilled labour and urban formal skilled labour were marginal across the activities, the latter contributed under 10 per cent value addition to forestry. The pictures in industry (manufacturing) and the services and social sectors were more mixed, with urban unskilled and urban formal skilled labour dominating the other categories. The broad conclusion is that the urban employment subsectors require skills, which is not the case with the agriculture subsectors.

Building on the concern with skills, a further simulation presented in Table 6.16 considered the impact of education status on employment creation across

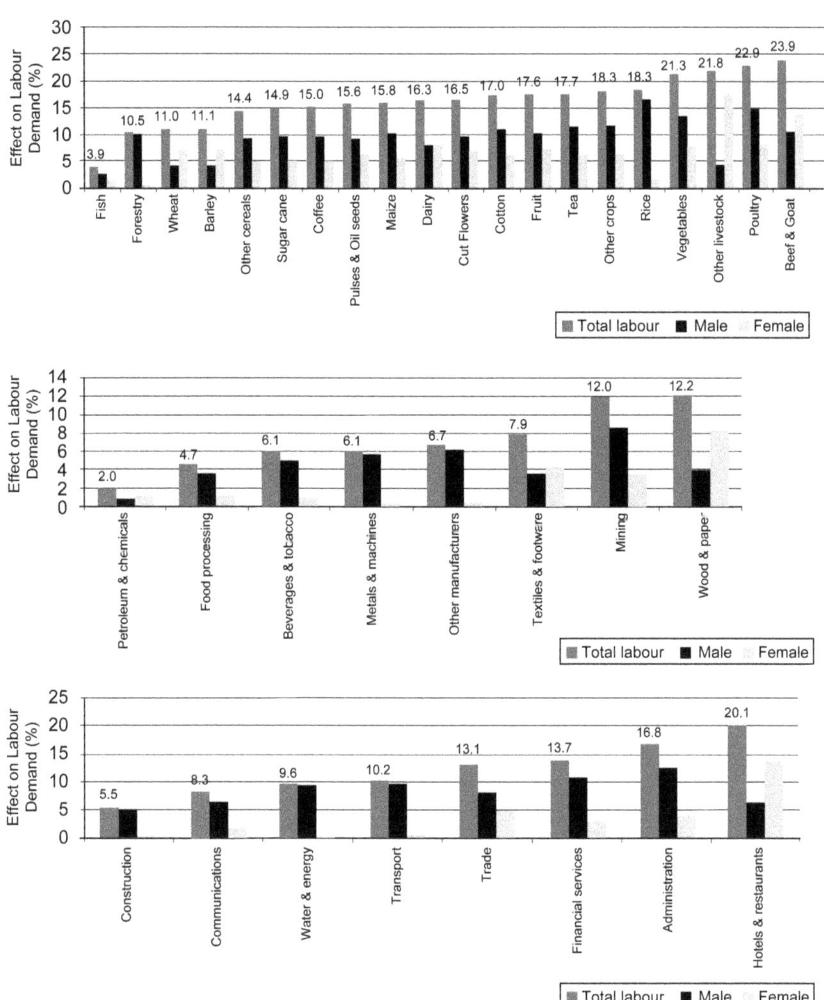

Figure 6.12 Simulations of sector employment generation
Source: NESC (2011: 56–8).

the broad areas of activity, this time including the public service, which had been excluded from the previous simulations. For aggregate employment, the latter category generated the greatest demand for employment at 25 per cent, compared with an average 17 per cent for agriculture. Two important insights arise: that the public services for which growth in employment is always constrained by policy should be dominant; and that despite wishes to expand employment in the formal sector, it is not a major employment growth area. On the gender differential, livestock remains the key expansion area for women who now lose the dominance they previously had in services.

Table 6.16 Employment effects of Ksh1 billion by labour category and by enterprise

	Crop	*Livestock*	*Food industry*	*Other manufactures*	*Services*	*Public services*
Total employment effect	16.2	18.8	5.34	7.0	11.59	24.9
Male	10.1	8.5	4.26	4.1	7.90	14.4
Female	6.1	10.3	1.08	2.9	3.69	10.4
Male no education	1.8	1.0	0.20	0.1	0.26	0.1
Male primary	6.7	6.3	1.41	1.5	1.91	1.5
Male secondary and above	1.5	1.2	2.69	2.6	5.79	12.8
Female no education	1.3	2.1	0.24	0.1	0.11	0.1
Female primary	3.8	6.4	0.50	0.6	0.85	0.4
Female secondary and above	1.1	1.9	0.34	2.3	2.74	10.0

Source: NESC (2011: 73).

The simulations offer a bleak employment outlook for males and females with no education, with women in livestock alone attaining a demand level above 2 per cent. Prospects for individuals with primary education and secondary education were better for males than females, the secondary graduates' prospects in public service employment being the greatest across the sectors. These realities surrounding educational attainment underscore the need to strengthen school enrolment, retention and school-to-work transition.

6.6.2 Multiplier effects of education on labour income and employment

The multiplier effects computed from the Kenyan SAM show that services subsectors seem to have better distribution of impact on employment creation, with exception of the unskilled rural labour. Education has the second highest impact on employment creation among the urban unskilled (0.27) after health (0.64). It also has the largest impact on employment of rural unskilled labour (0.23). The effect of an exogenous stimulus to education on labour income is 0.82 and is the third highest after health (1.14) and poultry (0.88) (Wambugu *et al.*, 2012). This implies that targeted interventions in the education subsector can have large impacts on employment while ensuring better earning. University education and technical training play critical roles in human development while reducing the risk of being poor and being either openly unemployed or underemployed through its effect in increasing individual earnings. Consequently, while increasing access to basic (primary and secondary) education is critical in laying the foundation for entry into higher education, stimulating access to primary education is effective in reducing unemployment if, and only if, individuals concerned take the initiative to undertake post-primary education, especially secondary, technical training and university education. This poses a delicate challenge in managing the flow of children across all levels of education until attainment of higher education and associated higher returns.

The number of highly skilled individuals unable to find jobs in the formal sector (which has high returns) is associated with low and unsustainable growth, urban migration, implementation of structural adjustment programs starting in the early 1990s, and reduced public investment to create required jobs in the modern economy. Although the informal sector provides substantial jobs, especially in urban areas, the sector is associated with low returns and may not assist the majority of the underemployed youth. Coupled with continued support to increase access to basic education, there is a need to increase investment and growth for the effective creation of high-quality jobs, absorption of a skilled and educated labour force, and increased productivity.

6.7 Summary of key findings, conclusions and recommendations

Finally, this section provides a summary of key findings, main conclusions and policy recommendations. It also identifies research-based projects that this study recommends for funding by government, multilateral and bilateral agencies.

6.7.1 Summary and conclusions

Kenya's population of nearly 40 million individuals is dominated by young persons under the age of 35, with those between 15 and 34—the youth—accounting for 35.3 per cent. Total employment and the number of employed individuals in the labour force has grown steadily over the years, from 2.3 million in 1990 to about 6.0 million and 11 million in 2000 and 2010, respectively. The employment-to-population ratio, which shows the minimum rate at which jobs should be created to achieve full employment, has inched upwards from 0.24 in 2003 to 0.28 in 2010. Although total employment has increased, most of the jobs created have been in the informal sector, with minimal expansion of formal sector opportunities. This resulted in the consistent decline of the share of formal sector jobs to about 19 per cent in 2010 from 58 and 30 per cent in 1990 and 2000, respectively. This trend was also true for the 2003–07 period of remarkable economic recovery.

The open unemployment rate, which is the ratio of the unemployed to the total labour force, was 8.6 per cent in 2009, not as high as would be reasonably expected. A low open unemployment rate is a characteristic of many developing countries where the majority of individuals become 'entrepreneurs by necessity' and are thus likely to be engaged in some form of survival activity, rather than being openly unemployed. Consequently, apart from measuring open unemployment, the nature of employment available should also be analyzed.

Even though the majority of the youth (about 63 per cent) fall in the category of the employed, about 77 per cent of all employed youth, and 79 per cent of those aged above 35 years, are engaged in vulnerable employment. People in vulnerable jobs comprise own account and unpaid family workers.

The youth employment and joblessness challenge can be summarized as follows:

About 24 per cent of youths (or about 3.4 million youth) have poor-quality jobs (defined to include those jobs that entail either over 65 hours per week or under 29 hours per week).

About 11 per cent of all youth—1.5 million youth—are inactive, making youth inactivity a greater challenge than open unemployment.

About 1 million youths—7 per cent of the total youth population—are openly unemployed.

In a related vein, an estimated 3.8 million children (aged 5–14 years) were reported working in the previous week to the 2009 census. About half of these children (51 per cent) worked for over 65 hours during those seven days. This implies that Kenya has a large group of children who are likely to graduate into youths without meaningful labour market skills, as their current labour participation is at the expense of being in school.

The problem of youth unemployment is worsened by the weak job-search infrastructure in the country. According to a recent study on job-search methods in Kenya, informal job-search channels are more prevalent than formal job-search methods. However, informal channels promote inequalities, and those with weak or non-existent social networks are likely to remain continually disadvantaged in accessing decent employment.

Educational attainment seems to be a good predictor of labour market activity. As an example, while about 90 per cent of employed primary school graduates were engaged in vulnerable jobs, only 21 per cent of university graduates had vulnerable jobs. In addition, the ratio of those who never attended school among the inactive and openly unemployed youth was 18 and 21 per cent, respectively—and about 11 per cent for all the youth.

6.7.2 Recommendations

A useful approach to summarize the policy implications is to adopt the World Bank's MILES framework, which identifies five broad factors that are central in affecting job creation (World Bank, 2012a, 2012b). These broad factors, giving rise to the acronym MILES, are (i) macroeconomic environment, (ii) investment, (iii) labour institutions and aspects of labour policies, (iv) education and skills, and (v) social protection. In providing the policy implications of this study, this subsection also illuminates how the government can improve the ongoing policy interventions. These factors must be viewed in the context of existing youth employment policies, as well as the employment implications of devolution of government activities to the counties.

Macroeconomic environment and investment

To a large extent, an unwavering implementation of the Constitution (2010) and *Kenya Vision 2030* have a huge potential to spur growth. The two documents contain far-reaching reforms that can effectively address the political and governance obstacles that have hindered economic growth and transformation in the past, thereby expanding employment opportunities.

Addressing the factors that impact on the investment climate will be decisive in creating jobs, especially in the formal sector. In Kenya's case, these factors include management of the perceived high political risk and measures to reduce the current political risk. There is also a need to address the factors that may hinder the creation of formal quality jobs, which have hitherto stifled growth. These factors include perceived high taxation rates, large numbers of procedures required for starting a business, and a high burden of customs procedures (Global Competitiveness Index, 2010, 2011). Other factors include the challenge posed by corruption, and the business costs of crime and violence. Significantly, the design of these measures should go beyond the general context to opening up specific opportunities for the youth.

One of the key lessons from the middle-income countries Kenya aspires to emulate is the need to transform the economy from an agricultural one to an economy based on value addition in areas of comparative advantage. In this endeavour, Kenya must implement a coherent approach to industrialization, which has been identified as one of the key challenges in the country (Onsomu *et al.*, 2009). Some of the policies that are yet to be implemented include the Master Plan for Kenya's Industrial Development (2007) and the National Export Strategy. The former included recommendations for the development of the agroprocessing and information and communications technology sectors. The more successful countries in Asia, such as China, can offer lessons on industrial policy directions. A key lesson is that these countries benefited from government intervention in industry and technology. These included efforts to help the firms avoid coordination failures by providing early investments in areas such as training, education and infrastructure.

Whereas the government and private sector have initiated various programs aimed at creating employment, most jobs have been created in the informal sector. It is imperative that all sectors of the economy are stimulated to grow at a higher and sustainable rate so as to ensure creation of quality and productive jobs in the modern economy. Further, measures must be taken to enable formal sector investments to decentralize away from the major urban centers of Nairobi and Mombasa, especially in the context of devolution to the 47 counties.

Ongoing youth-focused interventions decentralized to the counties include YEDF and the Women's Enterprise Development Fund. Apart from offering finance, a key intervention is training of the beneficiaries. Information on the impacts of these government and non-government initiatives is necessary to inform policy formulation. Education is significantly associated with high-expectation and high-growth entrepreneurs who are more highly represented in the manufacturing and service sectors. A society's view of entrepreneurship also seems to matter—implying the important role that can be played by education (Autio, 2007).

Labour institutions and aspects of labour policies

It is generally accepted that sustainable employment creation requires that macroeconomic policies be supported by employment policies. A key area for employment policy is the area of labour institutions (ILO and IMF, 2010). The three broad issues identified by the ILO/IMF report, which are also clearly relevant for Kenya, encompass wage-determination mechanisms, productivity growth and addressing income inequalities.

To a large extent, the operation of minimum wages in Kenya seems to satisfy most of what would be expected of a minimum wage policy. For example, the adjustments are done periodically and are devoid of large, abrupt movements.

The wage-setting process can be improved by ensuring compliance to the legally binding minimum wage, and providing more information and research to the wage-setting bodies.

One finding from the study and the literature is that some unemployed youth are inactive and are not searching for work (Wambugu *et al.*, forthcoming). Perhaps searching for work for a long time might be discouraged, and some individuals have left the labour force to work as unpaid family workers and in low-paid informal employment. To address this problem, various policy interventions can be explored, as follows:

Improvements in the job-search infrastructure and labour market information. This may be in the form of strengthening public employment services under the ministry in charge of labour, the public service commission, private sector employment services and others. It also may provide incentives to private employment service providers, to extend services to underserved areas.

Investing in education and training should be coupled with investment in alternative job-search and placement channels, particularly the public and private sector employment services.

Sustainable entrepreneurship and apprenticeship programs should be designed and implemented.

Employment opportunities should be increased in both rural and urban economies. In rural areas, improving the investment climate for rural non-farm enterprises and markets provides an opportunity to expand non-agricultural employment.

The Kenya National Bureau of Statistics, in collaboration with the Ministries of Education and Labour, should capture information on the incidence of job search and use of job-search methods. The information should be collected by region and profession for regular updating of the labour market information systems

Education and skills development

Educational attainment seems to be a good predictor of labour market activity, at least based on the 2009 census data. As an example, about 90 per cent of employed primary school graduates were engaged in vulnerable jobs, relative to 21 per cent for university graduates. In addition, the ratio of the youth who never attended school was 11 per cent for all youth, while for the inactive and openly unemployed youth this ratio was 18 and 21 per cent, respectively.

Given the importance of education, investment in human capital presents a key intervention. At the basic level of education, enrolment could be improved by reducing child labour, which appears to be a significant problem. The child labour problem is likely to be a manifestation of poverty, and suggests that the free primary education and the free day secondary education policies should be enhanced by additional interventions. Enhancement of well targeted social transfer programs—some already at pilot stages—could ameliorate part of the challenge. Given that out-of-pocket expenditure related to education, such as books, transportation and school uniforms, rose sharply in the two years to 2011 (based on consumer price index values), there is a need to reduce out-of-pocket expenditure, especially for the poor. In other countries, reduction of costs has been achieved by distributing vouchers for school uniforms. Access can be improved further by increasing provision of bursaries in public schools and extending the provision to private schools. School feeding programs have been successful in enhancing enrolment and retention among Kenya's pastoralists in the arid and semi-arid lands of the country. The expansion of these programs, and their modulation to include food and micronutrient supplementation, would have the additional benefit of improving the nutritional status and learning capacities of the beneficiaries.

Given that about 20 per cent of the openly unemployed youth and inactive youths never attended school, training in basic numeracy and literacy through 'second-chance education programs' would be instrumental in tackling the problems related to the quality of labour supply. For the older youths, support could be through building strong public–private partnerships in offering 'adult education' initiatives. In some countries, free tuition is provided to individuals eligible for these second-chance education programs who meet certain criteria. For the younger youths, it is possible to roll out programs in partnership with existing public and private sector institutions (such as village polytechnics) that offer subsidized basic numeracy and literacy education in a flexible manner.

Making post-primary education more accessible—including secondary and university education and technical training—is an important step for developing an employable and skilled labour force. Kenya is also one of the few African countries that has developed private–public partnerships to train the youth in the essential skills required to function in an IT-intensive economy (Africa Progress Panel, 2012). Such partnerships should be seen as important features of a broad social protection system that protects people from joblessness and from self-unemployment due to skills deficits. According to the SAM multiplier effects, education-related interventions that target the unskilled labour force in both rural and urban areas will have the highest impact. This would contribute greatly towards reducing unemployment among the educated graduates from higher learning institutions and technical education graduates.

Social protection

Employment creation and unemployment interventions should be coupled with targeted social protection initiatives for poor and vulnerable groups. Kenya has already launched various initiatives in these respects, focused on orphans and vulnerable children and the elderly. The value of that to the youth is that it reduces the dependence burden in a country where extended family responsibilities are considerable and undermine the capacities of the working youth for sustainable business planning. However, the precarious context of the business environment is such that some protection should also be afforded to the youth: in agriculture, for example, irregular rains can reduce considerable investment effort to nothing, with little scope for recovery. The enhancement of social medical insurance also can release the youth from the need to cover catastrophic medical bills. However, social protection also must be extended to the business environment, for example through the development of affordable insurance packages for informal activities.

Notes

1 According to the ILO, decent work involves opportunities for work that is productive and delivers a fair income, security in the workplace, and social protection for families, among other attributes.
2 This study recognizes the need for regional analysis to move away from the province and district to the county, in line with the new constitutional dispensation since 2010. However, the choice of province as the unit of regional analysis was driven by the desire to undertake some historical comparisons.
3 The *CIA World Fact Book* places Kenya's 2012 rate at 2.444 per cent, the 27th highest globally.
4 The traditional nomadic lifestyle of North Eastern province pastoralists explains some of their movements into and out of the province. However, extensive population movements have recently been occasioned by the turmoil in neighbouring Somalia. There is anecdotal evidence of the movement deeper into Kenya of Somalis who can speak neither Kiswahili nor English, suggesting they are recent arrivals from the Somali conflict who might originally have taken refuge in North Eastern province, but who are now moving further away from the conflict area.
5 Other provinces also have a land constraint; but, for example, Central province's surplus labour constitutes the itinerant workers who merely commute to the country's economic hub, Nairobi.
6 Indeed, a booming economy in Nyanza province would have provided a destination for Western province's surplus labour. The data are unavailable with which to estimate the net effect of population flight from, and return migration into, Nyanza precipitated by the post-2007 elections violence.
7 Since the 2009 census did not collect specific income/expenditure data, the principal components analysis method was applied to data on the ownership of assets—radio, TV, cellular phone, landline phone and access to computer service—to develop a proxy for wealth status separately for urban, rural and peri-urban areas. The overall 'asset' or 'wealth' index was a standardized measure of each of these separate indices and agreed with intuition, in being good proxies for household wealth based on correlations with other outcomes (such as schooling and labour market variables across quintiles).
8 Yet a more significant factor could be the earning rate enabling one working a few hours to have a higher gross income than one working longer hours.
9 These data are from *Strategic Review of the National Hospital Insurance Fund—Kenya* undertaken by Deloitte in 2010, for the Ministry of Medical Services and NHIF. While its various disclaimers deter its citation, the document is available at www.wbginvestmentclimate.org/advisory-services/health/upload/Kenya-Strategic-review-of-the-NHIF-final_cv.pdf.
10 The exchange rate at the time of writing is Kshs 85 to the US$.

11 This includes the upgrading of public middle-level institutions such as polytechnics and teacher training colleges into public universities. More recently, the private universities, which had been exclusively urban-based, have also established or expanded their presence in rural areas.
12 For example, research by the National Cohesion and Integration Commission has revealed extensive ethnicization of employment in public institutions (NCIC, 2011). Also see Wambugu, Onsomu and Munga (forthcoming).
13 This was a controversial policy in that 'Kenyanness' was constitutionally defined by citizenship rather than race; see Himbara (1994), for example.
14 The labour market efficiency index monitors the following: cooperation in labour–employer relations; flexibility of wage determination; rigidity in employment; hiring and firing practices; firing costs; pay and productivity; reliance on professional management; brain drain; and female participation in the labour force.
15 While this dichotomy includes the government in the higher-productivity modern sector, government productivity is characteristically low.
16 This is heightened by practices such as husbands migrating for work while spouses take care of the home and elderly parents.
17 In many traditional Sub-Saharan African tenure systems, land is subdivided for allocation to male heirs.
18 In Kenya, for instance, high street furniture is manufactured in *jua kali* (open air) settings.
19 Among the SMEs reported on by King were professionals such as accountants, doctors and engineers.

References

Africa Progress Panel (2012) *Africa Progress Report: A Twin Education Crisis is Holding Back Africa*. Geneva: Africa Progress Panel. www.africaprogresspanel.org

Autio, E. (2007) *The 2007 Global Entrepreneurship Monitor Special Topic Report: High Growth Entrepreneurship.* London: Global Entrepreneurship Research Association, London Business School. www.gemconsortium.org.

Boateng, K. (2000) 'Economics of the Labour Market and the Ghanaian Experience,' Department of Economics, University of Ghana, unpublished.

Brenthurst Foundation (2012) *Putting Young Africans to Work Addressing Africa's Youth Unemployment Crisis.* Johannesburg: Brenthurst Foundation.

CBS (2003) *Report of the 1998/99 Labour Force Survey.* Nairobi: Central Bureau of Statistics/Ministry of Planning and National Development.

Clark, K.B. and Summers, L. (1982) 'The Dynamics of Youth Unemployment,' in Freeman, R. and Wise, D. (eds) *The Youth Labour Market Problem: Its Nature, Causes and Consequences.* Chicago, IL: University of Chicago Press, pp. 199–234.

Cling, J.-P., Gubert, F., Nordman, C.J.F., Christophe, J. and Robilliard, A.-S. (2007) 'Youth and Labour Markets in Africa: A Critical Review of Literature,' *Document de Travail No 49.* Paris: Agence Française de Développement.

Curtain, R. (2001) 'Youth and Employment: A Public Policy Perspective,' *Development Bulletin*, 55: 7–11

Fares, J.M., Claudio, E. and Orazem, P.F. (2006) *How are Youth Faring in the Labor Market? Evidence from Around the World*, Policy Research Working Paper Series 4071. Washington, DC: World Bank.

Fei, J.C.H. and Ranis, G. (1964) *Development of the Labour Surplus Economy.* Irwin: Homewood.

Freeman, R. and Wise, D. (eds) (1982) *The Youth Labour Market Problem: Its Nature, Causes and Consequences*. Chicago, IL: University of Chicago Press.

Garcia, M. and Fares, J. (2008) *Youth in Africa's Labour Market*. Washington, DC: World Bank.

Gardner, L.A. (2009) 'Colonial Origins of Government Corruption? Evidence from Tax Collection in Kenya and Zambia,' preliminary draft. Oxford: University of Oxford. www2.lse.ac.uk/economichistory/seminars/gardner.pdf.

Government of Kenya (2002) *The 1998–99 Integrated Labour Force Survey Report*. Nairobi: Ministry of Planning and National Development.

——(2003) *Economic Recovery Strategy for Wealth and Employment Creation 2003–7*. Nairobi: Government Printer.

——(2005a) *Development of Micro and Small Enterprises for Wealth and Employment Creation for Poverty Reduction*, Sessional Paper No. 2 of 2005. Nairobi: Government Printer.

——(2005b) *Employment Policy and Strategy for Kenya*, Sessional Paper No. 7 of 2005. Nairobi: Government Printer.

——(2007) *Basic Report on Well-Being in Kenya. Based on Kenya Integrated Household Budget Survey (KIHBS), 2005/6*. Nairobi: Ministry of Planning and National Development.

Harris, J. and Todaro M. (1970) 'Migration, Unemployment and Development: A Two-sector Analysis,' *American Economic Review*, 60(1): 126–42.

Heintz, J. and Pollin, R. (2003) *Informalization, Economic Growth and the Challenge of Creating Viable Labor Standards in Developing Countries*, PERI Working Paper Series No. 60. Amherst, MA: Political Economy Research Institute.

Himbara, D. (1994) *Kenyan Capitalists, the State, and Development*. Nairobi: East African Publishers.

International Labour Organization (1972) *Employment, Incomes and Inequality. A Strategy for Increasing Productive Employment in Kenya*. Geneva: ILO.

——(2005) *World Employment Report 2004–2005: Employment, Productivity and Poverty Reduction*. Geneva: ILO.

ILO and IMF (2010) *The Challenges of Growth, Employment and Social Cohesion*. Discussion Document prepared for the Joint ILO–IMF Conference in Cooperation with the Office of the Prime Minister of Norway. ILO/International Monetary Fund. www.Osloconference2010.org/discussionpaper.pdf.

Johanson, R. and Adams, A. (2004) *Skills Development in Africa*, Regional and Sectoral Studies. Washington, DC: World Bank.

Kabubo-Mariara, J. (2003) *Wage Determination and Gender Wage Gap in Kenya: Any Evidence of Gender Discrimination?*, AERC Research Paper 132. Nairobi: African Economic Research Consortium.

Kenya National Bureau of Statistics (KNBS) (2002–2011), *Economic Survey*, Nairobi: Government Printer.

——(2006–2011), *Economic Survey*, Nairobi: Government Printer.

Keynes, J. (1936) *The General Theory of Employment, Interest and Money*. New York: Cambridge University Press.

King, K. (1996) *Jua Kali Kenya: Change & Development in an Informal Economy*. Nairobi: East African Educational Publishers.

Kingdon, G., Sandefur, J. and Teal, F. (2005) *Labour Market Flexibility, Wages and Incomes in Sub-Saharan Africa in the 1990s*, WPS-030. Oxford: Global Poverty Research Group.

KIPPRA (2010) *Kenya Economic Report 2009*. Nairobi: Kenya Institute for Public Policy Research and Analysis.

——(2011) *Kenya Economic Report 2010: Enhancing Sectoral Contribution towards Reducing Poverty, Unemployment and Inequality in Kenya*. Nairobi: Kenya Institute for Public Policy Research and Analysis.

Kuepie, M., Nordman, C. and Roubaud, F. (2006) *Education and Labour Market Outcomes in Sub-Saharan West Africa*, Working Paper DT/2006/16. Paris: Développement, Institutions et Mondialisation (DIAL).

Leo, B. (2012) *Africa's Employment Prospects and Challenges in a Competitive World*. Johannesburg: Brenthurst Foundation, pp. 67–83.

Linbeck, A. and Snower, D.J. (1988) *The Insider–Outsider Theory of Employment and Unemployment*. Cambridge, MA: MIT Press.

Manda, D.K. (2004) *Globalisation and the Labour Market in Kenya*, KIPPRA Discussion Paper No 31. Nairobi: Kenya Institute for Public Policy Research and Analysis.

Manda, K.D. and Odhiambo, W. (2003) *Urban Poverty and Labour Force Participation in Kenya*. Nairobi: Kenya Institute for Public Policy Research and Analysis.

Manda, D.K., Bigsten, A. and Mwabu, G. (2005) 'Trade Union Membership and Earnings in Kenyan Manufacturing Firms,' *Applied Economics*, 37(15): 1693–1704.

Manda, D.K., Kosimbei, G.K. and Wanjala, B. (2007) *Impact of Minimum Wages on Formal Employment in Kenya*, KIPPRA Discussion Paper No. 67. Nairobi: Kenya Institute for Public Policy Research and Analysis.

McLellan, D. (ed.) (2009) *Karl Marx's Capital*, abridged edn. Oxford: Oxford University Press.

Ministry of Labour (2008) *Ministry of Labour Strategic Plan 2008–12*. Nairobi: Ministry of Labour, Republic of Kenya.

Ministry of Planning and National Development (2003) *Economic Recovery Strategy for Wealth and Employment Creation*. Nairobi: Ministry of Planning and National Development, Republic of Kenya.

Ministry of Planning, National Development and Vision (2008) *Kenya Integrated Household Budget Survey, 2005–06 – Basic Report*. Nairobi: Ministry of Planning, National Development and Vision 2030, Republic of Kenya.

Moyi, E., Otieno, G., Mumo, I. and Ronge, E. (2006) *Developing a Marketing Framework for Micro and Small Enterprises in Kenya*, Discussion paper 60. Nairobi: Kenya Institute of Public Policy Research Analysis.

Mwega, F.M. and Ndung'u, N.S. (2008) 'Explaining African Economic Growth Performance: the Case of Kenya', in Ndulu, N.S. *et al.* (eds), *The Political Economy of Growth in Africa: 1960–2000*, Vol. 2. Cambridge: Cambridge University Press.

Mwiria, Kilemi (1991) 'Education for Subordination: African Education in Colonial Kenya,' *Journal of the History of Education Society*, 20(3): 261–73.

National Economic and Social Council (NESC) (2011) *Unemployment in Kenya: Proposed Interrentions*, NESC Discussion Paper No. 3/2011, Nairobi: National Economic and Social Council.

NCAPD (2011) *State of the Kenyan Population 2011 – Kenya's 41 Million People: Challenges and Possibilities*. Nairobi: National Coordinating Agency for Population and Development, Ministry of Planning.

NCIC (2011) *Towards National Cohesion and Unity in Kenya: Ethnic Diversity Audit of the Civil Service*. Nairobi: National Cohesion and Integration Commission.

Odhiambo, W. and Kulundu, D. (2003) 'Urban Poverty and Labour Force Participation in Kenya,' *paper presented at the World Bank Urban Research Symposium*, Washington, DC, December 15–17, 2003.

OECD (2009) *OECD Employment Outlook 2009: Tackling the Jobs Crisis.* Paris: Organisation for Economic Co-operation and Development.

Onsomu, E., Wambugu, A. and Wamalwa, F. (2009) *Improving Technical and Vocational Training in Kenya: Lessons from Selected Countries*, KIPPRA Discussion Paper No. 105. Nairobi: Kenya Institute for Public Policy Research and Analysis.

Pollin, R., Githinji, M. and Heintz, J. (2007) *An Employment-Targeted Economic Programme for Kenya.* Amherst, MA: Political Economy Research Institute.

Rama, M. (1998) *Wage Misalignment in CFA countries: Are Labor Market Policies to Blame?*, Policy Research Working Paper Series 1873. Washington, DC: World Bank.

Ranis, G. and Fei, J.H. (1961) A Theory of Economic Development,' *American Economic Review*, 51(4): 533–65.

Schultz, T.P. and Mwabu, G. (1998) 'Labour Unions and the Distribution of Wages and Employment in South Africa,' *Industrial and Labor Relations Review*, 51(4): 680–703.

Serneels, P. (2004) *The Nature of Unemployment in Urban Ethiopia*, CSAE Working Paper Series 2004-01. Oxford: Centre for the Study of African Economies, University of Oxford.

Shapiro, C. and Stiglitz, J. (1984) 'Equilibrium Unemployment as a Worker Discipline Device,' *American Economic Review*, 74(3): 433–44.

UNECA (2005) *Economic Report on Africa 2005: Meeting the Challenges of Unemployment and Poverty in Africa.* Addis Ababa: United Nations Economic Commission for Africa.

United Nations (2011) *The Millenium Development Goals Report 2011.* New York: United Nations.

Vandermoortele, J. (1991) 'Labour Market Informalization in Sub-Sahara Africa,' in G. Standing and V. Tockmal (eds), *Towards Social Adjustment: Labour Market Issues in Structural Adjustment.* Geneva: International Labour Organization, pp. 81–113.

Wamalwa, F.M. (2009) 'Youth Unemployment in Kenya: Nature and Covariates,' KIPPRA Discussion Paper No. 103. Nairobi: Kenya Institute for Public Policy Research and Analysis.

Wambugu, A., Munga, B. and Onsomu, E. (2009) 'Unemployment in Kenya: A Situational Analysis and What Must be Done,' a project of the Kenya Institute for Public Policy Research and Analysis in conjunction with the National Economic and Social Council, United Nations Development Programme and the Royal Danish Embassy.

Wambugu, A., Munga, B. and Onsomu, E. (2010) *Unemployment in Kenya: A Situational Analysis*, NESC Discussion Paper No. 1/2010. Nairobi: National Economic and Social Council (NESC).

Wooldridge, J. (2002) *Econometric Analysis of Cross-section and Panel Data.* Cambridge, MA: MIT Press.

World Bank (2006) *Labor Diagnostics for Sub-Saharan Africa: Assessing Indicators and Data Available.* Washington, DC: World Bank.

——(2009) *Youth and Employment in Africa: The Potential, the Problem, the Promise.* Washington, DC: World Bank.

——(2011) *World Development Indicators 2011.* Washington, DC: World Bank.

——(2012a) *A Primer on Policies for Jobs.* Washington, DC: World Bank.

——(2012b) *World Development Report 2013: Jobs.* Washington, DC: World Bank.

van Zwanenberg, R.M. (1975) *Colonial Capitalism and Labour in Kenya, 1919–1936.* Nairobi: EALB.

7 South Africa

Martin Abel, Megan Blair, Raissa Fabregas, Kamilla Gumede and Murray Leibbrandt

7.1 Introduction

South Africa's economy has undergone radical changes since the fall of apartheid and the first democratic elections in April 1994. Economic growth stagnated during apartheid due to sanctions on international trade and investment, uncompetitive local industries, rigid exchange controls, restricted skills development and high levels of poverty and inequality (Aron *et al.*, 2008). After the first democratic election, economic sanctions were dropped, labour restrictions were lifted and policies were put in place to advance the interests of African workers, who had been marginalized for many decades. Since the first democratic election, South Africa has had stable macro management and, as shown in Table 7.1, South Africa's economy has grown steadily in both real and per capita terms.

Over the same period, the schooling system transformed from one characterized by highly skewed spending across racial groups to one based on equitable government funding. School enrolment rates rose, though learning achievements remain very poor in previously disadvantaged schools (van der Berg, 2007). The new, young labour market participants have more education, on average, than their parents had a generation ago. Two in five young adults graduate with Matric degrees (the qualification awarded to those who pass nationally set, standardized exams at the end of the final years of secondary schooling).

Other countries, such as Brazil and India, have seen education gains translate into productivity and employment growth, and large decreases in poverty and inequality. Job creation in a dynamic labour market served as the key pathway through which these societies generated high social returns to improved education and second-round effects to social transfers.

South Africa has not made similar gains. Over the post-apartheid period, poverty has fallen only sluggishly. Eighteen years after the first democratic election, the share of people living below a $2 per day poverty line has declined by no more than 4 percentage points from 34 per cent in 1993 to 30 per cent in 2008. These gains are often attributed to social policy reforms (a massive expansion of cash grant transfers) rather than economic development

Table 7.1 Economic growth in constant 2005 prices, 1993–2008

Year	*GDP (R000,000)*	*GDP growth*	*GDP per capita*	*GDP per capita growth*
1993	1,065,830	1.2	28,227	–0.9
1997	1,214,768	2.6	29,582	0.5
2001	1,337,382	2.7	30,024	0.8
2005	1,571,082	5.3	33,176	3.9
2008	1,814,521	3.7	36,950	2.5
Average 1993–2008	1,400,717	3.1	31,592	1.4

Source: Leibbrandt *et al.* (2010a), using South African Reserve Bank Data, www.resbank.co.za/webindicators/EconFinDataForSA.aspx.

(Leibbrandt *et al.*, 2010). Of equal concern is the fact that inequality has risen further from its very high levels under apartheid (Leibbrandt *et al.*, 2010).

Just as the labour market was the key intermediary in the successes in Brazil and India, so the unsatisfactory performance of the labour market sits centre-stage of South Africa's disappointing development outcome. A net 2.74 million jobs were created between 1993 and 2008, 2.5 million of which were targeted at skilled labour, while unskilled workers lost a net 770,000 jobs. Over the same period, unemployment rates more than doubled from 14 per cent in 1993 to a peak of 29 per cent in 2001, before declining to 23 per cent in 2008. By the time of the economic crisis in 2010, the unemployment rate had reversed to 25 per cent, using the narrow definition of unemployment (National Treasury, 2011). If discouraged workers—who have stopped looking for work 'because they do not anticipate finding any'—are included into this definition, the figure is substantially higher at about 32 per cent (StatsSA, 2012).

Of the total population of 4 million unemployed, 75 per cent are long-term unemployed and many young jobseekers report having limited or no formal work experience, even at age 30 (National Treasury, 2011). The informal sector is small, with only 6 per cent of South Africans working in self-employment. The supply of labour is therefore directed primarily at jobs in the formal sector.

In general, the labour market has not had a positive impact on poverty because of the failure to pull individuals from poor households into employment. This unemployment situation worsened between 1993 and 2008, especially for those in the poorest households. The number of no-worker households has increased by 3 per cent in the past 15 years, pushing up the number of households relying on assistance, especially child grants, as their main form of income. Indeed, the improved aggregate poverty situation is due to increased support from social grants, not from the labour market. Even in one-worker households, the poverty incidence remains high. Because of high living costs and the fact that many workers are in low-paid employment, the presence of an employed person in a household is not a guarantee to escape poverty.

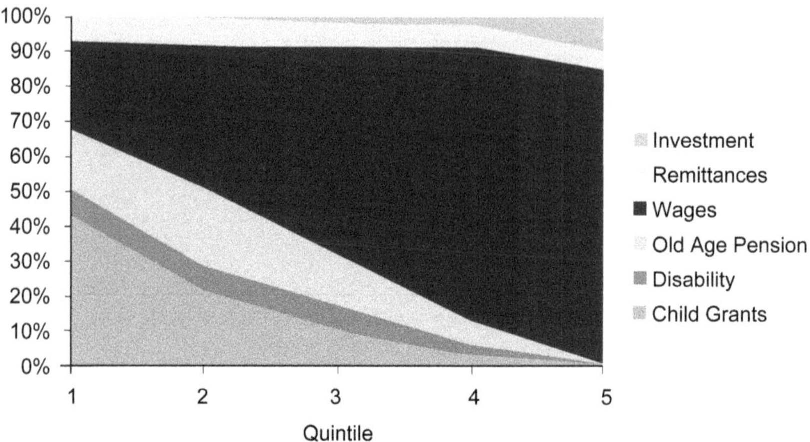

Figure 7.1 Share of household income from various sources, 2008
Source: Own calculations, using NIDS (2008).

The poverty impacts of pervasive unemployment are compounded by a social protection gap that exists for unemployed adults, as social cash grants target people who are not expected to be economically active: children, pensioners and people with disabilities. This leaves unemployed adults deeply dependent on goodwill transfers from within their community, placing a large care burden on communities and deepening poverty.

Figure 7.1 shows the share of income sources in total household income by income quintile in 2008. The proportion of income derived from wages increases linearly by income quintile. If a person is a member of a household situated in the poorest five deciles, the person is likely to receive relatively little wage income and to depend quite heavily on government grants and subsidies.

Moreover, Leibbrandt *et al.* (2010) show that labour markets play a dominant role in driving inequality. Even though the average share of wage income in total income has remained constant at around 70 per cent over the post-apartheid period, wage income has contributed between 85 and 90 per cent of the total inequality in household income over the years 1993, 2000 and 2008. In contrast, state transfers are shown to make up less than 1 per cent of the overall Gini coefficient. Reducing unemployment and creating a better-functioning labour market is the major economic and social challenge in South Africa, which is explicitly recognized by the South African government. Indeed, employment creation has emerged as a top policy priority of the ANC-led government. Its New Growth Path strategy aims to create 5 million jobs by 2020 with 'the creation of decent jobs at the centre of its economic policy.' In his 2011 State of the Nation Address, President Zuma declared 2011 to be the year of job creation, and announced the government's intention to spend 9 billion rand (R) on job creation. Later that year, a new Job Fund launched its first round of competitive bids for innovative job-creation projects to be implemented by NGOs, public–private partnerships or public institutions, and to be partially funded by the Job Fund.

Despite this commitment, and as in many other countries around the world, there is a lack of solid evidence to back this commitment. The hope is that our review of the South African evidence pinpoints imminent gaps in the South African evidence. In particular, we seek to understand better the nature of South African unemployment, the costs and benefits of current labour regulation, and the effectiveness of existing active labour market policies. This chapter reviews the conditions and causes of unemployment in South Africa (section 7.2), summarizes current labour market institutions and policies (section 7.3), discusses existing evidence and knowledge gaps (section 7.4) and concludes with a set of recommendations (section 7.5). We give special attention to barriers to employment for young adults.

7.2 Profile of labour market disadvantage: participation, unemployment and low earnings

In this section, we review the labour market participation, unemployment and earnings trends in South Africa over the post-apartheid period. This review is based on available micro-level data. In particular, we use household data from the National Income Dynamics Survey (NIDS) panel dataset,[1] the Labour Force Survey data (LFS) collected by the South African Statistical Agency (StatsSA), the October Household Survey also collected by StatsSA, and the Project on Statistics on Living Standards and Development collected by the Southern Africa Labour and Development Research Unit (SALDRU).

The legacy of apartheid was one by which South Africa entered the post-apartheid period with a labour market characterized by low participation rates, high unemployment rates and some low earnings sectors. Each of these spheres of disadvantage had strong racial markers, with black South Africans bearing the burden in each case. This section provides a record of the extent to which the policy milieu and the economy have been able to reverse this apartheid legacy.

7.2.1 Economic participation

Between 1995 and 2008, the working-age population (the number of persons aged 16–64) increased from 23 million to 29 million, and the labour force participation rate from 49 to 55 per cent. These two reinforcing factors resulted in an additional 5 million people entering the labour market over this period. Of today's population of 48.7 million and a total labour force of 16.8 million people, the level of participation in the labour market is still relatively low by international standards.[2] Though higher than for women, labour force participation rates are particularly low for men (67 per cent in South Africa compared with 81 per cent in OECD countries), with those for women (54 per cent) closer to the OECD average of 61 per cent. Between 1993 and 2008,

Table 7.2 South Africa's labour force participation rates, 1993–2008

Year	*Total*	*Male*	*Female*
1993	49.1	61.0	39.0
1997	47.0	57.1	37.7
2001	57.8	65.6	50.5
2005	58.4	66.1	51.4
2008	55.2	67.0	53.8
Percentage change 1993–2008	12.4	9.7	37.8

Sources: Leibbrandt *et al.* (2010a) using data from PSLSD (1993), OHS (1997), LFS (2001, 2005), NIDS (2008).

female labour market participation rose by 38 per cent (or four times the growth rate of men). Kingdon and Knight (2006) surmise that this is most plausibly the result of higher female education levels, loss of male employment, HIV/AIDS mortality and a greater number of female-headed households.

More young adults participate in the labour force due to a larger youth cohort and a reduction in the time spent in school relative to grade attainment. Defined as the highest school grade passed, grade attainment for youth, particularly Africans, has increased markedly since 1994, while years in school have increased only marginally. Therefore there has been little change in the delay in labour market entrance due to increased education. The large increase in youth participation suggests instead that either the youth are more actively seeking employment (perhaps due to their increased education levels), or youth who previously did not enter the job market are increasingly choosing to do so (Leibbrandt *et al.*, 2010). Taken on its own, this is a good thing. In a post-apartheid labour market characterized by a sluggish demand for labour, this flags the possibility of rising youth unemployment.

7.2.2. *Unemployment rates*

High youth unemployment is a global phenomenon that is not unique to South Africa, as young adults, on average, are about twice as likely to be unemployed as their older countrymen.[3] In South Africa, 42 per cent of people below 30 are unemployed compared with 17 per cent for older adults. Young adults are also particularly vulnerable to economic downturns, with almost all of the 1 million job losses in the most recent economic crisis affecting those under the age of 30 years with less than a grade 12 education (National Treasury, 2011). Three million, or 72 per cent of all unemployed, are youths according to the South African government's definition, which includes people between 15 and 34 years of age (StatsSA, 2012).

The official definition of unemployment (also referred to as the narrow definition) considers as unemployed only those who have actively searched for work in the past four weeks and are able to accept a job within the next week. All other 'discouraged' workers (who would like to work but are not actively

Table 7.3 South Africa's unemployment rates by narrow and broad definitions, 1993–2008

Year	*Narrow definition*	*Broad definition*
1993	13.6	31.2
1997	20.5	36.1
2001	28.9	40.8
2005	26.4	38.3
2008	23.4	28.9
Percentage change 1997–2008	14.2	–20.1

Sources: Leibbrandt *et al.* (2010a) using data from PSLSD (1993), OHS (1997), LFS (2001, 2005), NIDS (2008).

seeking work) are classified as not economically active. The broad definition includes as unemployed all those who would like to work (regardless of whether they actively sought work). As shown in Table 7.3, the difference between the broad and narrow rates is considerable, often exceeding 10 percentage points, meaning that there have historically been very high numbers of discouraged workers. However, the gap between the narrow and broad rates has narrowed dramatically recently, as the level of broad unemployment appears to have dropped between 2005 and 2008. In 2010, about 1.3 million young adults were reported as discouraged jobseekers.

There are stark differences in unemployment rates across gender and race, with black South Africans experiencing unemployment rates that are five times higher than those for whites at 30 and 6 per cent, respectively. Coloured also experience high unemployment rates, and are the only population group for whom unemployment rates have increased since 2000.

We end this subsection by providing more detail on the contemporary South African labour market using data from the first quarter of the 2011 Quarterly LFS. We see high variation across provinces, especially with

Table 7.4 Unemployment by race, 1995–2011

	1995	*2000*	*2005*	*2008*	*2009*	*2010*	*2011*
Unemployed		*(March)*	*(March)*	*(March)*	*(Q1)*	*(Q1)*	*(Q1)*
Rate (percentage)	16	27	27	24	24	25	25
Total (000s)		4333	4283	4191	4184	4310	4364
Women	21%	2179	2285	1982	2033	2146	2237
Men	12%	1983	1997	2209	2131	2036	2126
Population group (percentage):							
Black/African	20	32	32	28	28	30	29
Coloured	14	20	20	19	20	22	23
Indian/Asian	9	20	13	12	13	9	12
White	3	7	5	5	5	6	6

Source: Own calculations using OHS (1995), LFS (2000, 2005, 2008), QLFS (2009–11); strict unemployment definition.

Table 7.5 Unemployment rates across provinces in 2011

	Unemployment (percentage)	*Participation (percentage)*	*Employed/population*
South Africa	25	54.1	40.6
Gauteng	26.9	70.4	51.5
Western Cape	22.2	67.1	52.1
Eastern Cape	26.9	43.6	31.9
Northern Cape	31.3	53	36.4
KwaZulu-Natal	20.3	45.4	36.1
Free State	27.9	58	41.8
Mpumalanga	30.8	54.7	37.9
North West	25	47.4	35.5
Limpopo	19.3	35	28.2

Source: own calculations using Quarterly Labour Force Survey 2011, Q1.

participation rates but also with unemployment rates. The lowest economic participation rates are in predominantly rural Limpopo, the Eastern Cape and KwaZulu-Natal, around the former homelands, which remain the most densely populated areas in South Africa outside of city centres. Unemployment rates are also particularly high in the Northern Cape and Mpumalanga. These spatial differences are important to recognize when thinking about labour market dynamics.

Only few, very young adults enter the labour market. Those who do so face high unemployment rates. Participation rates increase after the age of 20 years, but this is not matched by higher absorption rates into employment. As shown in Figure 7.2, more than half of an entering age cohort are not in employment

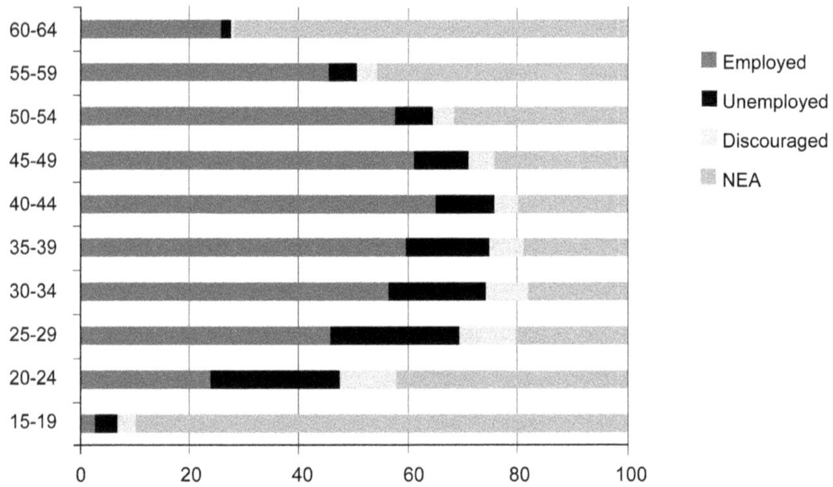

Figure 7.2 Proportion per age cohort, by labour market category in 2011
Source: Own calculations. QLFS (2011), Q1.

until their thirties. An estimated 1.2 million young people between the age of 20–24 years and 1 million between the ages of 25–30 years are unemployed. Added to this high youth unemployment rate, over 30 per cent of the employed youth were in the informal sector in 2008, leaving fewer than 29 per cent of the youth labour force formally employed, as discussed in more detail below.

Education background is an important factor in employment prospects. Looking at individuals in the 20–34-year age group, as shown in Table 7.6, those who only had primary education or less than that faced unemployment rates of 48 per cent, despite having had 15–20 years to generate work experience. Only one in three 30–34-year-olds were unemployed among individuals with some secondary education but not a complete Matric degree. This falls to one in five for individuals with a Matric degree, and 12 per cent for individuals with tertiary education. Age also plays an important role, as unemployment rates across the educational attainment categories are substantially lower for individuals aged 35–64 years than for those aged 18–24.

These interactions between cohorts and the returns to education in terms of being in employment are borne out by recent econometric work by Branson *et al.* (2012). That paper looks across the whole post-apartheid period in the labour market and decomposes the probability of being in employment into age, year and cohort effects. As intimated in Table 7.6, it finds that the returns to tertiary education remain extremely high, even for young/new labour market entrants. However, while the returns to completed Matric remain positive, they are lower for those entering the labour market now than they were for earlier cohorts on their entry into the labour market. Nonetheless, there remains a strong incentive for the youth of today to complete Matric, both because these returns remain positive and because the returns to all levels of education less than Matric have declined markedly over the post-apartheid period and are now very low for these young people.

Table 7.6 hints at the fact that many poorly educated jobseekers do find work eventually. However, the table makes it clear that there are some who do not. Also, 'eventually' seems to be from as late as age 30 and above. All of this accords with the little evidence that we have in South Africa on unemployment duration. Lam *et al.* (2011) show that for youth in Cape Town, having a Matric or tertiary education greatly reduces the duration of unemployment.

Table 7.6 Unemployment rates, across age cohorts, by educational attainment, 2011

	Age (percentage)			
	18–24	*25–29*	*30–34*	*35–64*
Primary and less	53	55	48	34
Some secondary	37	40	30	18
Matric/grade 12	29	39	21	10
Tertiary	17	18	12	4

Source: own calculations using Quarterly Labour Force Survey 2011, Q1.

For those work-seekers with lower levels of education, the proportion in employment increases slowly over time. But even after three years of job search, only 50 per cent of coloured and African females without Matric are in employment.

7.2.3 Vulnerable employment

Informal sector work is generally regarded as second best to formal sector work because it is risky and low-paid. Nonetheless, considering the extent of unemployment in South Africa, one would expect the informal sector to be fairly large, while in reality it is relatively small by international standards. Table 7.7 shows that informal employment is much higher for females than for males, at 34 and 20 per cent, respectively, in 2008.[4] The female participation rates are driven primarily by participation in domestic work. Importantly, though, the table also makes it clear that the importance of informal sector work in the labour market has grown since 1997. Conservatively put, about a quarter of the employed are in the informal sector.

Table 7.8 shows that Africans are overrepresented in the informal sector across all years. In 2008, the proportion of employed Africans working in the informal sector was sitting at around 33 per cent, by far the highest of all the race groups. The dominance of Africans in the informal sector does have inequality implications, as wages are generally much lower. The average

Table 7.7 Share of informal employment to total employment, by gender: 1997–2008

Year	*Total*	*Male*	*Female*
1997	19.8	15.3	26.9
2001	29.4	21.8	39.8
2005	30.2	23.0	39.9
2008	26.2	20.2	33.8
Change 1997–2008 (percentage)	32.3	32.5	25.5

Source: Leibbrandt *et al.* (2010a). Calculations using OHS (1997); LFS (2001, 2005, 2008).

Table 7.8 Share of informal employment to total employment, by race, 1997–2008

Year	*African*	*Coloured*	*Indian*	*White*
1997	26.1	13.4	6.1	7.2
2001	36.7	18.4	8.2	6.5
2005	37.1	14.0	7.6	5.0
2008	33.4	16.2	8.7	5.0
Change 1997–2008 (percentage)	27.6	21.3	42.9	–30.3

Source: Leibbrandt *et al.* (2010a). Calculations using OHS (1997); LFS (2001, 2005, 2008).

wage in the informal sector in 2005 was US$203 per month, while the average wage for the formal sector was 3.5 times higher at US$715 per month.

7.2.4 Earnings

It is important to at least flag the fact that the disadvantage of low earnings is borne by the same groups that bear the major disadvantages of low participation rates and high unemployment rates. In particular, even today, high wage differentials exist by race, with Africans predominantly occupying the lower deciles. As is shown by Leibbrandt *et al.*, and replicated in Figure 7.3, racial wage gaps have remained fairly steady over the past 15 years. The prevalence of such vast wage gaps may be at least partly explained by the remarkable difference in the education levels attained by different population groups, with Africans suffering the lowest levels. At the same time, though, Africans experience a lower return to Matric and tertiary education than do other population groups, which coincides with the findings of Keswell (2004). A couple of factors could account for this: quality of education and employer bias. In the post-apartheid labour market, an increase in discrimination by employers seems implausible, and Pauw *et al.* (2008) and Chamberlain and van der Berg (2002) suggest that controlling for specific tertiary qualifications and for the quality of education more generally removes a great deal of these lower returns.

Similarly, inequality can be decomposed by age, as shown in Figure 7.4. What is striking here is the low wage earned by 16–20-year-olds as compared with the other age cohorts. This is likely to be true because this age group participates more in casual and part-time labour, or is paid low wages due to their lack of experience and education. In the past three years there has been

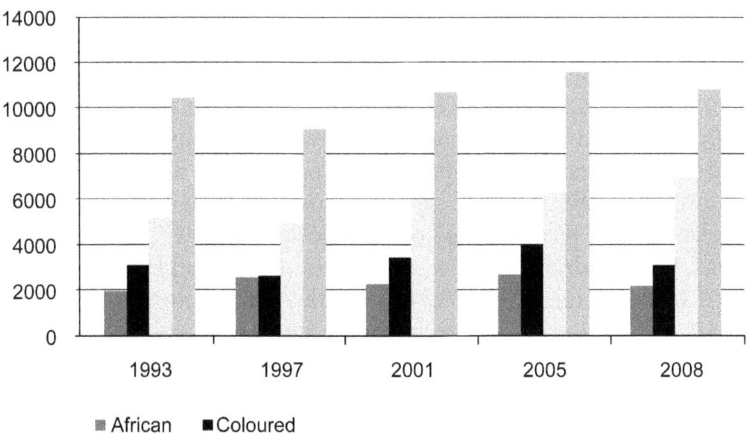

Figure 7.3 Average real wages by race, 1993–2008
Source: Leibbrandt *et al.* (2010a) using PSLSD (1003), OHS (1997), LFS (2001, 2005), NIDS (2008).

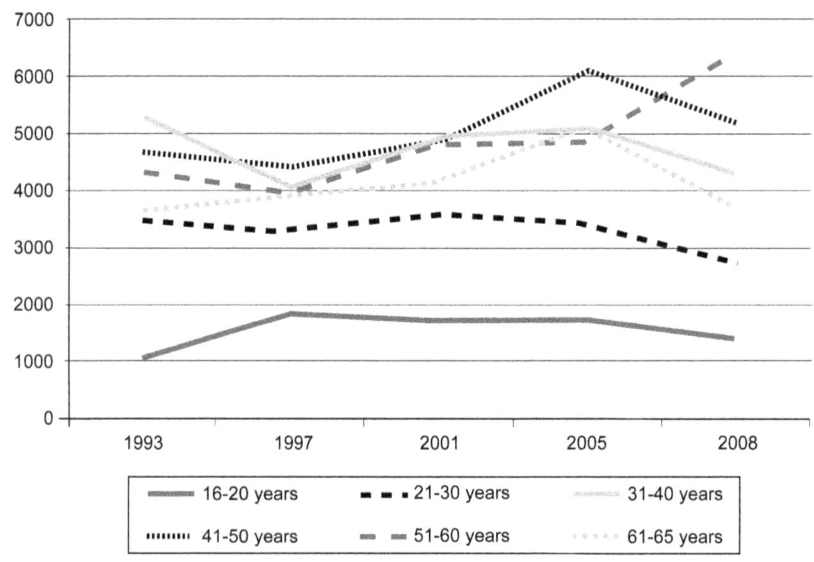

Figure 7.4 Average real wages per month, by age, 1993–2008
Source: Leibbrandt *et al.* (2010a) using PSLSD (1003), OHS (1997), LFS (2001, 2005), NIDS (2008).

a clear decrease in the real wages earned in all age groups except age 51–60. As a result, most real wage increases since 1993 have been cancelled out. This coincides with the findings of Banerjee *et al.* (2007), who found that in general, real wages in South Africa have declined.

7.2.5 Summary

At the start of the post-apartheid period, South Africa had low participation rates and high unemployment rates. Figure 7.5 provides a snapshot of the South African labour market in 2011. It is clear that South Africa still has both low labour participation rates and high unemployment rates. However, there have been some important changes in the South African labour market over the past 18 years. In this section we have shown a substantial increase in labour participation rates, especially for African females. Also there has been a decline in the portion of the unemployed who are discouraged work-seekers. 2011 reflects a South African labour market that has been battered by the global recession. Thus, as shown here, the narrow unemployment rate is notably higher than it was in the mid-2000s. There is some sensitivity of the workforce to economic growth and especially to its collapse.

Even so, it is fair to say that the contemporary labour market looks uncomfortably similar, especially by race, to the way it did at the end of apartheid. Despite substantial progress in terms of improving the levels of

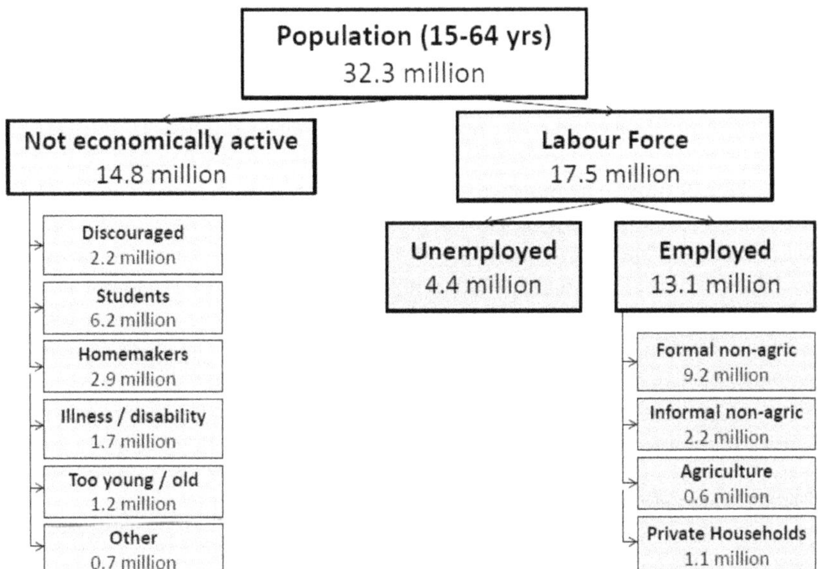

Figure 7.5 Snapshot of the contemporary South African labour market
Source: Own calculations, QLFS (2011), Q1.

education of the workforce, real earnings in the formal sector have not increased, and earnings gaps by race remain stubbornly in place. Participation in the informal sector is still the preserve of those who are most vulnerable elsewhere in the labour market. Given the centrality of changes in the labour market as drivers of change in South African society, this lack of dynamism is of concern. To some extent, this situation is the result of the labour market undergoing a classic but cruel skills twist. The education levels of workers increased, but not enough to counter the fall in the demand for all workers with education below complete secondary schooling.

We have tried to provide a detailed and subtle profile in this section. Asserting that the 2011 picture resembles the pre-1994 labour market in key dimensions is not the same as saying that the post-apartheid labour market has been ossified. There have been significant adjustments and changes, which we have touched on. The starting point for our review of the evidence (in the subsequent sections) is that the South African labour market has shown encouraging signs of transformation, though at a very slow rate. This creates room for reviewing targeted micro-reforms to complement the focus on addressing structural problems in the South African economy.

7.3 South African labour market institutions and policies

In this section we review South African's labour institutions and policies.[5] The assessment of these policies is left to section 7.4.

7.3.1 Labour market institutions

Fundamental to apartheid were labour policies that undermined the rights of black workers (Nattrass, 1997). Along with the induction of the ANC government in 1994 came the task of rewriting the labour legislation. The negotiations that gave rise to the revised legislation took place within the National Economic Development and Labour Council (NEDLAC) in that same year. It was established with representatives from government, business and labour as a means to facilitate the development of formal negotiations over labour market regulation (Benjamin and Theron, 2007). These negotiations resulted in the new Labour Relations Act and a brace of new legislation governing working conditions and employment standards. A full review of this legislation is summarized by Leibbrandt *et al.* (2010).

The evolution of post-apartheid South African collective bargaining institutions did not follow international trends and thinking. At the time, these international trends favoured increased decentralization of bargaining (Calmfors and Driffil, 1988; Soskice, 1990). In contrast, the negotiations at NEDLAC resulted in an acceptance of a sectoral or industry-level bargaining system for South Africa. Some saw this result as being little more than a consolidation of the strength of the non-racial trade union movement, reflecting a pro-labour ideology (Boccara and Moll, 1996). A more positive view of this negotiation process states that since this new legislation was founded on a tripartite process (negotiations between government, labour and employers), 'its core principles enjoy a high degree of legitimacy among the key stakeholders within the economy' (Benjamin and Theron, 2007).

In theory, the structure of the South African collective bargaining process gives significant leeway to negotiating parties in determining the influence of statutory regulations and the levels at which industry negotiations should occur. Negotiations may take place at sectoral bargaining councils or statutory councils, or outside of the statutes, or at firm and plant level or in non-statutory centralized bargaining forums (Godfrey *et al.*, 2007). In practice, though, bargaining councils have been the anchor and focus of the Labour Relations Act for union–employer negotiations, whereas statutory councils seem to have been less successful (*ibid.*).

The interaction between industry-level and firm-level bargaining is well summarized by Macun (1997). Using the South African Labour Flexibility Survey, he argued that, although bargaining levels vary considerably across sectors, there is a shift towards greater centralization of bargaining at the sector level. Plant-level bargaining remained in place, but the balance in collective bargaining in South Africa was seen as being positioned at a point closer to being centralized than decentralized (Macun, 1997). For Moll (1993), this was a predictable outcome of employers refusing to negotiate on two levels and trade unions compromising plant-level bargaining in exchange for the ability to set actual wage increases at councils. With some foresight, and given the debates that ensued, this led Moll (1993) to predict the possibility that wage hikes would thus be transferred automatically to smaller firms that might not be able to afford them, and that productivity bargaining at firm level would be seriously undermined.

South African labour unions feature prominently in bargaining at the sectoral-level bargaining councils as well as at plant-level bargaining, in addition to advising workers to resolve disputes through the Commission for Conciliation, Mediation and Arbitration (CCMA). Commentators agree that because of the history of collective bargaining in South Africa, the unions see their mandate and objectives as being fairly broad. For Moll (1995), they were driven primarily by concerns about economic justice, fair working conditions and the standardization of wages within and across firms and within occupations. This view is consistent with the view of Godfrey *et al.* (2007) that the main agenda of South African labour unions is to address the effects of the inequalities created by the racially warped labour market of the apartheid era. This includes raising wages, improving working conditions and expanding social benefits, but has no direct focus on expanding economic participation and job creation (*ibid.*).

In South Africa, the three major union federations, COSATU, the Federation of Trade Unions of South Africa (FEDUSA) and the National Council of Trade Unions (NACTU) have a vast membership majority and form the labour constituency at NEDLAC. Macun (1997) found that 86 per cent of firms had a recognized trade union, with COSATU having a 75 per cent majority of membership. Trade union membership has begun to decline in recent years, however, with a drop in actual membership of just over 600,000 workers from 2005 to 2008 (StatsSA, 2005; SALDRU, 2008). The biggest drop in membership occurred in the finance and utilities sectors. Union representation in South Africa generally also reflects a relatively narrow spectrum. Small businesses had low union participation; an overwhelmingly high percentage of unionized workers are either unskilled or semi-skilled, and black trade unions lack representation in the semi-skilled sector overall. Furthermore, it was found that union affiliation was dominated by African males.

The Basic Conditions of Employment Act (BCEA), promulgated in 1997, covers all workers who can be considered 'employees.' The BCEA also made provision for the establishment of the Employment Conditions Commission, which is responsible for conducting investigations into appropriate conditions of employment and minimum wages for workers in certain sectors with a view to making sectoral determinations for those sectors. In general, these are sectors in which no bargaining council exists. It is estimated that between 3 and 4 million workers are afforded protection via these sector-specific determinations. Sectoral determinations are in place in the following sectors: domestic work, agriculture, forestry, contract cleaning, private security, civil engineering, hospitality and tourism, the taxi sector, and wholesale and retail trade. The Minister of Labour can add additional sectors at any time if it is considered that there are significant numbers of 'vulnerable' workers in the sector. As part of the investigation into making sectoral determinations, the commission holds public hearings nationwide and obtains views from representatives of business, labour and civil society, as well as from academics and other interested parties, on various issues concerning wages and employment conditions. The annual increases in these sectoral minimum wages are usually set at 1 or 2 percentage points above inflation.

Questions have been raised with regard to the binding nature of the minimum wages imposed by bargaining councils. By the late 2000s, Godfrey *et al.* (2007) reported that most firms cited poor enforcement of bargaining council rulings as a fundamental flaw in the system and demanded more rigorous enforcement. Interestingly, small firms turned out to be far more perturbed by a lack of enforcement, as they regarded themselves as being at greater risk from unregistered competition than their larger counterparts (*ibid.*). It must be pointed out that the growing trend towards hiring labour through labour brokers in South Africa is making the enforcement of rulings a far more challenging task, as the workers are generally not registered with the relevant council (*ibid.*).

The dispute resolution function of the Labour Relations Act is carried out via the CCMA, formerly known as the Conciliation Boards, and the Industrial Court. Conflict resolution was an important new function that CCMA-accredited bargaining councils would need to perform within their designated scope and area (Godfrey *et al.*, 2007). The main objective of the CCMA is to ensure the more efficient resolution of disputes about employment issues (Benjamin and Gruen, 2006). Today, the vast majority of cases referred to the body deal with unfair dismissals, as well as unfair labour practices, collective bargaining and severance pay (*ibid.*). According to the positive view of Benjamin and Gruen (2006), the CCMA is effective at settling labour disputes and makes a considerable contribution to South Africa's solid industrial relations (Benjamin and Gruen, 2006). In addition, strike action as a means of labour retaliation has begun to decline since its implementation (*ibid.*).

However, there are strong indications of internal inefficiency within the country's main dispute-resolution mechanism (Bhorat *et al.*, 2009). There is a 'tremendous backlog' (CCMA, 2005, p. 16), the CCMA has also been accused of employing underqualified and inexperienced judges, and delays in rulings are becoming longer and more frequent (*ibid.*). In addition, the high turnover rate of acting judges makes it practically impossible for important precedents to be set (*ibid.*).

It is generally accepted that well intentioned labour regulations may sometimes have unfortunate and unintended consequences. From the outset, the key criticisms of South Africa's labour legislation have concerned its indirect effects on employment levels, equality and investment. These criticisms were most strident in the 1990s. We review the literature on the effects of labour regulation in a later section.

7.3.2 Employment promotion policies

Job-creation policies go well beyond direct labour activation policies to include more general growth, industrial and agricultural strategies, as well as education and skills development and, in the context of high HIV prevalence, also health and social protection reforms. Below we discuss the country's employment activation policies in more detail.

South Africa's active labour market policies include training programs that enhance skills; incentive schemes that provide subsidies to employers, employees, entrepreneurs and new firms; public works programs; and job-search and job-matching services. Because labour activation programs are expensive and demonstrate varying results, they need to be well designed and customized to meet national and local circumstances. Despite the existence of a portfolio of active labour market policies in South Africa, these interventions lack both depth and breadth, and the public works program receives 80 per cent of the budget allocated to active labour market programs. New policy initiatives are currently debated, including a proposal by the National Treasury for a youth wage subsidy for low-skilled, low-income young adults to target and stimulate private sector employment, and a large reform program to introduce a social insurance system and a national health insurance scheme.

Skills development

The South African government has sought to address the mismatch between skills supplied by workers and those technical and specialized skills demanded by industry, with its introduction in 1998 of the Sectoral Education and Training Authorities (SETAs) and the Further Education and Training (FET) colleges under the National Skill Development Act. With these institutions, a strong focus was placed on workplace training and the introduction of several learnership and apprenticeship programs. SETAs are funded through a levy on private and public sector employers and are expected to develop sector skills plans that identify current and future qualification needs and facilitate the provision of sector-specific training opportunities in respect of the plans. The current annual budget of the SETAs is about R7.6 billion.

After being in existence for more than a decade, these learner- and apprenticeships have suffered from low take-up, particularly among small- and micro-enterprises (SMEs), due to the burden of elaborate administrative procedures and low quality of training courses, and the workplace training programs were further undermined by resource mismanagement and low private sector buy-in. The only courses that achieved large-scale take-up and completion were those centred around basic literacy and numeracy, as opposed to technical or artisan skills (Kraak, 2008).

The New Growth Path announced by President Zuma in his State of the Nation Address in 2011 placed further emphasis on skills development as a core pillar of his administration's growth and development path, through 'a radical review of the training system to address shortfalls in artisanal and technical skills' (p. 19). Skills development is a high policy priority within trade unions and within the New Growth Path, as it is seen as an essential missing element that can enable the creation of decent jobs through productivity gains, without undermining labour protection and living standards.

Support for small and medium businesses

Support programs for SMEs were launched in the first years of the new democratic dispensation with funding from the European Union and other bilateral donors. In 2004, the South African government established the Small Enterprise Development Agency (SEDA) under the Department of Trade and Industry as a 'one-stop-shop' to support SMEs. Services provided by SEDA included information and advice on running a business, business assessments, business mentoring and technical support. SEDA services were complemented by financial support programs through Khula Enterprise Finance (urban firms) and the South African Finance Apex Fund (Samaf) (rural firms). Their coverage was limited: according to the FinScope 2010 South Africa Small Business Survey, only 3 per cent of entrepreneurs had ever heard of Khula Finance and 3 per cent of SEDA, and only 1 per cent of small businesses reported they had visited a SEDA office (Finscope, 2010).

The New Growth Path's strategy places further emphasis on support for small and micro-enterprises, including the establishment of a single funding agency by merging Khula, Samaf and various other small government finance agencies. The goal is to reduce red tape barriers and thereby increase access to micro-finance. These services continue to receive considerable national funding: the 2011 national budget allocated R600 million for enterprise investment incentives, R282 million for microfinance, and R55 million for piloting of new approach to small business lending (National Budget Speech, 2011).

Public employment programs

EXPANDED PUBLIC WORK PROGRAM

South Africa's spending on active labour market policies is currently concentrated on direct job creation through the Expanded Public Work Programme (EPWP), which absorbs 81 per cent of the active labour market policies budget. By comparison, OECD countries allocate on average 9 per cent of their active labour market policies budget to public works programs (National Treasury, 2011).

Started in 2004/05, the EPWP, led by the Department of Public Works, was launched with the goal of creating 1 million job opportunities over five years and thus providing the marginalized unemployed with work experience and training to increase their job prospects outside of EPWP. EPWP projects were developed in four categories: infrastructure, environmental, economic (income-generating projects), and social sectors. After its five years of existence, the EPWP had created 1.6 million work opportunities (of 100 days each) or the equivalent of 640,000 full-time jobs, though the program's effectiveness was 'diluted by the limited duration of jobs, lack of training, and low labour intensity' (National Treasury, 2011).

A revised program was launched in 2009 with the goal of creating a total of 4.92 million work opportunities (with an average duration of 95 days) or the full-time equivalent of 2 million jobs (DPW, 2009). The program has scaled back on its ambition to serve as a stepping stone into formal employment, and its training component is reduced to an average of nine training days per work opportunity. Implementation of the program has been decentralized to provincial authorities and carried out through municipal offices and political ward offices.

COMMUNITY WORK PROGRAMME

Further problems in the scale-up of the EPWP have been the department's inability to identify suitable public works opportunities, and the elaborate contract requirements with NGOs and private sector implementers in the program. In reaction to this, the Community Work Programme (CWP) was launched as a Special Project under President Zuma's Second Economy Initiative. The CWP is an anti-poverty program as well as an employment program. It provides guaranteed access to a minimum level of two days per week of regular public employment for 1000 individuals per site. As it is an area-based program, it is targeted at the poorest areas with high unemployment rates. Community participation is used to identify 'useful work' opportunities and prioritize services to be delivered through the program.

The program was institutionalized in the Department of Cooperative Governance and Traditional Affairs from April 2010. By March 2011 it had reached 99,230 participants and operated at 74 sites across the country. Current budgetary commitments allow the CWP to grow to 250,000 participants by 2014. Policy pressure exists for the CWP to scale up much faster, with the South African cabinet approving a proposal for the CWP to be scaled up to a million participants in the same period.

Employment services

The National Department of Labour provides employment services for South Africa (ESSA) through its 126 Labour Centres and 153 visiting points nationally, delivered by a total staff of about 5700 caseworkers, or a ratio of about 1:700 unemployed persons per caseworker (Department of Labour, 2011).

Included in these services are a computerized database of work-seekers, career information sessions and job-search workshops. In 2010, the ESSA database had 636,140 jobseekers and 48,499 employment opportunities registered. Of these registered vacancies, about 20,000 (41 per cent) were filled (Department of Labour, 2011). Over the next five years, the Department of Labour's goal is to increase the number of firms that register vacancies with ESSA from less than 2000 to 6000.

About 70,000 jobseekers received career information and counselling through government employment services in 2010. This included short briefing sessions as part of the Labour Centres' recruitment for nursing school opportunities, and other coordinated hiring campaigns. Labour Centres also fulfil roles in terms of Unemployment Insurance Fund (UIF) registration and claims.

The National Youth Development Agency (NYDA) was launched in 2009 in an effort to coordinate youth development initiatives. The NYDA provides similar services to the Labour Centres, including various services to facilitate job search and job matching, including the Graduate Development Programme and Job Preparation Services for unemployed graduates. It also includes the National Youth Service (NYS) that combines community service with skills development, provides an online database to match seekers and vacancies, and runs Youth Advisory Centres for career counselling.

Several NGOs also provide career guidance, placement services and life skills training for unemployed work-seekers, particularly to those with low levels of education and skills. Some examples of these NGOs are the Youth Development Trust, Khulisa, Business Skills Development Centre, and the Career Research Information Centre.

New policy initiatives

WAGE SUBSIDY

Following a proposal by the National Treasury, a policy proposal is in discussion between social partners at NEDLAC that. if adopted, will introduce an employment subsidy for low-wage workers. It is designed as an employer-side subsidy and is available for full-time formal jobs for a maximum period of two years.

The policy targets low-skilled youth with an income below the annual personal income tax threshold of R60,000. The value of the subsidy depends on the wage level. For newly hired workers, the subsidy provides up to 50 per cent of employment costs of R24,000. In the second year, newly hired are treated as existing workers and receive a maximum subsidy of 20 per cent. The subsidy scheme includes young existing workers to reduce the risk of a substitution effect, although this increases the deadweight loss of the program.

NATIONAL YOUTH SERVICE/YOUTH CORPS

The National Treasury has also proposed a National Youth Service or Youth Corps. The program would provide public service work opportunities for unemployed youths for a period of 12 months. To increase employability prospects after this period, the program would include 'extensive vocational training, career counselling, and placement services' (National Treasury, 2011). Job opportunities would be created in areas such as adult literacy, green economy campaigns and rural development (*ibid.*).

This plan builds on existing smaller scale schemes: the first NYS program was launched in 2001 with a pilot phase in which the government contracted demonstration projects to NGOs. During 2006–09 the NYS program was scaled up, yet only 13,000 youths participated in NYS projects. In 2010, the Department of Rural Development and Land Reform launched the National Rural Youth Service Corps, which targets youth from deep rural areas between the ages of 18 and 35. About 10,000 youths are envisioned to participate in this two-year program, which incorporates extensive training.

In its medium-term strategic plan for 2011–13, the Department of Economic Development (2010) plans to 'launch a much larger national youth service programme' but it does not provide any information on the scope and details of the program.

7.4 Review of the evidence

While the post-apartheid South African government has established institutions to oversee programs to promote SMEs, to develop skills and to counsel workers, it is generally accepted that these interventions have had mixed delivery records, and that very little rigorous evidence exists in the South African context to inform labour market policy interventions. This lack of rigorous policy evidence stands in sharp contrast to the rich empirical literature on conditions of unemployment, described in previous sections.

This section is divided into two parts: the first reviews evidence on potential constraints to labour supply and effective job-search behavior, while the second part looks at what we know about constraints to the demand for labour.

7.4.1 Constraints to supply of labour

Returns to education and human capital formation

School enrolment rates are high. Most young adults in South Africa stay in school until secondary school. Demand for young adults as labourers within the family appears to be extremely limited. Teen pregnancy rates have declined in post-apartheid South Africa but remain high, with 30 per cent of teenage girls having at least one child before the age of 20, and 30 per cent of children being born to mothers below the age of 20 (SALDRU, 2011). These high fertility rates do not translate directly into labour market constraints if extended families provide cheap and accessible childcare. They may, however, negatively affect human capital development and mobility. Qualitative fieldwork by J-PAL Africa in urban settings suggests that mothers access childcare arrangements, but (although they worry about the quality of the available care) they did not perceive childcare to be a binding constraint on their labour market participation.

Low education quality means that many young adults enter the labour market without adequate skills to prepare them for work, including basic math and English literacy skills (Kraak, 2008). Many do not obtain a Matric pass level that qualifies them for further studies at the tertiary level. Half a million to 700,000 school leavers enter the labour market each year. While they leave school with more education than in the past (Branson, 2006; Pauw *et al.*, 2008), they now have to compete against many more Matric graduates than before. Furthermore, the economy is increasingly demanding more technical and specialized skills rather than manual labour, and perceptions of falling Matric standards undermine the credibility of the qualification among prospective employers.

A Matric qualification is no longer a 'ticket to employment', but a Matric degree still is positively associated with employment prospects and earnings. Using LFS data, Branson (2006) finds that matriculants are 30–60 per cent more likely to be formally employed and their earnings are 40–70 per cent higher than those of people without similar education attainment. These patterns are further reflected in returns to tertiary education, with individuals who complete some level of tertiary education being between two and three times more likely to be formally employed compared with people without a Matric degree. The completion of a diploma or certificate increases this to 170–220 per cent compared with people with less than Matric qualification, and the differences in returns to higher education increases over time (Branson *et al.*, 2009).

Despite these higher returns, enrolment rates at tertiary education institutions remained unchanged during 2000–07. One of the reasons for stagnant tertiary education rates may be that young people are unable to pay for their education. Gurgand *et al.* (2011) find that credit constraints reduce enrolment rates into higher education by more than 20 percentage points in a population of South African student loan applicants.

In qualitative fieldwork conducted by J-PAL Africa, Matric graduates showed strong knowledge of returns to further education and training programs across universities, vocation-oriented training programs and other diplomas. Many young adults have access to information about education options through school career programs and from widespread internet access (even on mobile phones). Their main barriers to further education were seen as complicated application procedures, high costs associated with decentralized applications at each institution, and lack of access to education finance. As far as we are aware, no research has been conducted into the potential effects of time-inconsistent preferences on youth education choices and efforts.

There is some evidence that the number of discouraged jobseekers (as a proportion of active jobseekers) is negatively correlated with economy-wide employment growth, which suggests that jobseeking individuals do have access to information about job prospects and incorporate calculations of search costs and likely benefits into their behavior.

Ineffective job search

Employment agency usage is low in South Africa, as reported in questions about job search strategies in the South African Social Attitudes Survey and the NIDS. Instead, informal networks are widely used together with arguably less effective strategies such as going from door to door and handing out CVs in shopping malls (Noble *et al.*, 2008). These strategies are particularly common among new labour market entrants who do not have an extended network to help them in their job search.[6]

According to NIDS, only one in six jobseekers had registered with employment agencies, and only 3 per cent of current wage earners had found their jobs through employment agencies. Similarly, in a survey of unemployed youths, 57 per cent reported to have contacted firms directly about job openings while only 7 per cent had registered formally with employment agencies or trade unions (Kanyeze *et al.*, 2000). Private employment agencies target skilled workers and charge substantial registration fees (Surender *et al.*, 2007).

Search activity is low, with just more than half of the unemployed reporting that they are actively looking for work (LFS, 2007).[7] During 2002–06, the Cape Area Panel Study collected monthly data on school, work and job search of some 5000 youths who resided around Cape Town, and found that four months after leaving school, only 20 per cent (45 per cent) of Africans (coloured) had found work and an additional 24 per cent (18 per cent) were still searching for jobs. Eight months later, employment had increased to 34 per cent for blacks (58 per cent for coloured) and searching had dropped to 18 per cent for blacks (12 per cent for coloured); the numbers stagnate at these levels for the following 12 months (Lam *et al.*, 2008). The authors attribute the lower search activity of Africans to the lower probability of finding a job (Lam *et al.*, 2008). Among unemployed respondents in NIDS, only 17 per cent of blacks (24 per cent of coloured) believe there is a realistic possibility of finding employment in the next month (next six months) (NIDS, 2008).

Banerjee *et al.* (2007) argue that lower job-search effectiveness of Africans and coloureds may be partially accounted for by the legacy of apartheid-era spatial segregation. A substantial part of the African population lived in homelands that suffered from poor infrastructure and were located far from centres of business and industry (Banerjee *et al.*, 2007). Although South Africa has a relatively high percentage of migrant workers, the spatial separation discourages many people from leaving their home to search for jobs. Even in urban areas such as Johannesburg and Cape Town, poor households typically reside far away from where jobs are.

The average distance of African townships from the central business districts of the seven largest South African cities is 28 km. This spatial segregation adds to the cost of job search, particularly through transport costs and time. NIDS data show that people with employment spend on average R215 ($30, 7 per cent of average net salary) per month on transport to and from work (NIDS, 2009). The mean amount spent by the actively searching unemployed on transport costs related to the job search was R106 in the previous week, although 43 per cent did not spend anything. The main sources of funding for these transport costs were co-resident family members (80 per cent), savings (11 per cent) and friends (7 per cent) (NIDS, 2009).

The negative effect of search costs on search behavior may be particularly high for the youth, who have limited resources and lack of mobility (Burns, 2008). A survey among unemployed youths finds that almost a quarter of respondents reported not being able to afford the transportation cost associated with job search (Kanyeze *et al.*, 2000). Similarly, 47 per cent of respondents in the Khayelitsha/Mitchell's Plain Survey exclusively used passive search strategies (e.g. relying on their network) (Schöer and Leibbrandt, 2006). The large proportion of unemployed youth within one geographical area may also lead to negative neighborhood effects by affecting social norms and thereby disincentivizing active job search behavior. Such 'ghetto' or neighborhood effects have not received sufficient attention in the South African empirical literature, nor have evaluations of the effectiveness of programs to overcome ghetto effects.

Geographical segregation also spills over into segregated social networks and therefore has an added indirect and adverse effect on job search by restricting access to information flows through social networks about available openings (Burns, 2008). Three in five young wage-earners, interviewed in the South African Young Persons Survey and Cape Area Panel Study, report to have found their jobs through a social network, compared with only 12 per cent who found employment through job advertisements (Burns, 2008). This is in addition to other indirect social implications of negative neighborhood effects, where areas with high unemployment tend to create a culture in which work and education are less valued, and where there are few role models for youth entering the labour market. Lastly, employers may be reluctant to hire applicants from disadvantaged communities, either because of stigmatization or because employers do not want to use resources screening applicants from a pool with a high fraction of workers with low productivity (Rospabe and Selod, 2006).

Employment dynamics

Despite high levels of unemployment and many of the unemployed reporting that they have little or no work experience even at the age of 30, Banerjee *et al.* (2007) find a considerable degree of churning in the labour market, using data from a rotating panel of the LFS. Only 62 per cent of all non-economically active men remained inactive the following year, whereas 15 per cent had become unemployed, 11 per cent discouraged jobseekers and 13 per cent had entered employment in the formal or informal sector. Of the unemployed men, just more than half (55 per cent) continued to be unemployed, while 16 per cent had become discouraged jobseekers, and 23 per cent entered into employment within a year. These are considerable movements across employment status. The same is found for women. Only formal sector employment showed less instability, with a total of 83 per cent remaining in formal employment, 13 per cent moving into unemployment and 7 per cent now being employed in the informal sector (Banerjee *et al.*, 2007).[8] Such churning and mobility is not satisfactorily explained in the current literature.

Table 7.9 Reason for leaving most recent employment, percentage of individuals who left work in 2008

Reason for leaving	*Percentage*
Health reasons	9.8
Caring for own children/relatives	1.7
Pregnancy	2.8
Other family/community responsibilities	1.3
Going to school	0.6
Lost job/job ended/laid off	60.7
Changed residence	3.9
Dissatisfied with the job	18.1
Retired	1

Source: Own calculations, 2008 National Income Dynamics Study.

Such high levels of churning are inconsistent with a rigid insider–outsider understanding of the South African labour markets that would be characterized by insurmountable entry barriers into employment opportunities. The NIDS data also suggest that jobseekers execute a degree of choice in movements out of employment. When asked about the reason for leaving their most recent employment, a majority of respondents reported that they had been laid off (61 per cent). Yet a total of one in five left their employment because they were dissatisfied with it, and 10 per cent left for health reasons. Only 1 per cent retired. Another 6 per cent cited children, family or community responsibilities as their main reason for leaving employment. If there are large entry barriers to employment, it could be expected that these voluntary exits from employment would be less frequent.

Reservation wages and the social assistance system

It has also been argued that young South Africans are discouraged from looking for employment because their subsistence is supported through household income resources, in particular through a generous social grant system[9] that provides monthly cash grants to seniors of about $125 per month, or twice the median per capita income, and child caregivers about $30 per month. These cash transfers made up 73 per cent of household income in the bottom income decile in 2009, and are an important source of poverty relief for the poorest households, as reviewed earlier. Because many of the grant-eligible elderly and children reside in rural households, away from cities and job opportunities, some have suggested that young adults can become trapped in these households as they are dependent on household income for survival.

At the end of 2011, more than 15 million people (of a population of 49 million) were eligible for social grants. This is a sixfold increase from 2.5 million in 1998; and more than half of all households now benefit from social assistance. Direct spending on cash transfers now stands at 3.5 per cent of GDP, which is more than twice the medium spending (of 1.4 per cent) across

Table 7.10 Unemployment and financial support to cover costs of living, 2008

Type of support	*Searching unemployed (percentage)*	*Non-searching unemployed (percentage)*
Someone in the household has a job	54	48
Individual receives a grant	15	23
Someone in the household receives a grant	44	59
Home agricultural production (self)	5	9
Someone in the household is engaged in home agricultural production	8	13

Source: Leibbrandt *et al.* (2010a).

developing countries and emerging economies (Leibbrandt *et al.*, 2010). In section 7.2 we reviewed the role of social grants in income distributions.

Klasen and Woolard (2008) find that the young unemployed tend to delay setting up their own household and instead live with parents or other relatives and friends. As can be seen in Table 7.10, the young unemployed live mainly on income from other household members from their income-generating employment or social grants. Fifteen per cent of searching unemployed also receive grants, as do 23 per cent of discouraged jobseekers.

A more positive view on the interaction between the social grant system and labour markets has emerged recently and suggests that social grants have enabled households to invest in the wellbeing and job-search strategies for household members, rather than the converse. Ardington *et al.* (2009) finds that pension transfers to the elderly increase employment among prime-aged adults, which occurs primarily through subsidizing labour migration. On the contrary, Ranchhod (2009) finds large and statistically significant increases in employment rates for middle-aged females and males (9 and 8 percentage points, respectively) as well as for older adult females and males (10 percentage points) among households that cease receiving an old-age pension because the pensioner dies.

Entrepreneurship and informal sector work

South Africa had 2.43 million small enterprises in 2007. Of these, 595,000 were in the formal sector, 1.39 million were in the informal sector, and 431,000 were involved in subsistence farming (DTI, 2008).

It is generally argued that South Africa has a very small entrepreneurship class compared with other African and middle-income countries. It is further argued that the reasons for South Africa's relatively weak SME sector can be traced back to the apartheid era, when the state suppressed black entrepreneurs and entrenched a system of market and financial institutions, infrastructure and regulations that prevented Africans from participating in the economy beyond low-paid wage work. This not only deprived non-white South Africans

Table 7.11 Self-employment rates by race

Year	*African*	*Coloured*	*Indian*	*White*
1993	1.9	1.1	3.0	7.8
1997	9.8	3.5	13.7	15.9
2001	10.6	4.8	12.1	20.6
2005	12.9	3.9	15.3	18.5
2008	10.9	5.9	20.1	17.7
Difference 1993–2008	9.0	4.8	17.1	9.9

Source: Leibbrandt *et al.* (2010a).

of business opportunities at that time, but also removed opportunities to develop entrepreneurship skills that could be handed down to the new generation of South Africans in the post-apartheid period.

It is, however, unclear as to the magnitude of this intergenerational effect relative to other barriers to business development for previously disadvantaged South Africans in today's economy. Geographically, Africans still find themselves located relatively far from business centres, mainly in rural areas and informal townships. Other potential impediments include relatively high levels of crime and lack of access to formal credit markets. The figures in Table 7.11 suggest that the self-employed are not an insignificant share of the population. In the context of low employment rates, around one in 10 Africans and 15–20 per cent of employed Indians and whites are self-employed. This is a substantial increase from 1993 (if the data are to be believed), but has not grown in any robust way in the strong-growth period after 2000. Most of the change happened between 1993 and early 2000, and may be explained by data inconsistencies or the relaxation of apartheid legislation after 1994.

While there is generally a strong notion that self-employment is a small piece of the South African labour market puzzle, there is limited evidence on the actual role and dynamics of self-employment. It remains to be seen whether further growth would take place if South Africa could sustain a longer period of stable and stronger economic growth.

As described in section 7.3, South Africa has an elaborate support system for SMEs. There is, however, very little evidence that these services have been effective, or about what aspects of SME support have worked and what have not. This lack of data needs immediate attention to be able to provide the detailed insights needed on program effectiveness. Such data must inform the implementation of the New Growth Path, which places a strong emphasis on firm development strategies.

7.4.2 Constraints to the demand for labour

Adverse effects of labour regulation on hiring and firing

The South African labour institutions were reviewed in detail in section 7.3.2. It is clear that some of the initial fears concerning South African labour legislation have not been realized. For example, in a 2007 Small Business Project, only 20 per cent of businesses cited labour laws or government regulations in general as discouraging them from hiring more employees (Benjamin and Theron, 2007). In its 2008 Economic Assessment of South Africa, the OECD calculated South Africa's Employment Protection Legislation indicator to be less restrictive than the average for the OECD countries as a whole.

Nonetheless, this positive view is not shared by all. In its *Doing Business Report*, the World Bank ranked South Africa 23rd of 56 African countries in its employment index that captures the rigidity of regulation on hiring and firing (World Bank, 2009). Table 7.12 shows the disaggregated scores and compares them with low, lower-middle, upper-middle and higher-income countries (higher scores indicate more rigidity). It also reports the costs of hiring and firing, though such costs are not captured in the employment index. According to the *Doing Business Report*, South Africa's hiring and firing regulations are more rigid than the average of other lower-middle-income countries, while the cost of hiring and firing is considerably below average.

Using the Labour Flexibility Survey, Standing (1997) found that the preferred means to avoid escalating labour costs was to introduce technological changes. This not only decreases the demand for labour overall, but increases the demand for skilled relative to unskilled labour. In South Africa, this means a shift in demand away from a pool of unskilled labour that is abundant to a pool of skilled labour that is scarce.

Godfrey *et al.* (2007) found that a majority of firms are reluctant to increase the number of people they employ due to the negative impact of the country's labour legislation. Similarly, Rankin (2006) found that, after other business factors, the most frequently mentioned constraint on hiring new workers, especially the unskilled, was inflexible labour laws, particularly concerning the hiring and firing of employees and minimum-wage laws. In addition, the argument during the 1990s that South African's labour market legislation has a negative effect on investment levels has not disappeared. For example, according to Rankin (2006), firm surveys indicate that labour legislation is perceived to be

Table 7.12 Employment rigidity index

Age of regulation	*Low income*	*Lower middle income*	*Upper middle income*	*High income – non-OECD*	*High income – OECD*	*South Africa*	*Total*
Rigidity of hiring	44.28	33.68	29.91	27.00	20.60	44.00	34.33
Rigidity of hours	47.60	39.64	40.57	45.22	32.00	40.00	42.40
Rigidity of firing	40.00	33.04	33.43	27.39	14.00	40.00	33.26
Aggregate Employment index	43.96	35.45	34.64	33.20	22.20	41.33	36.66
Hiring costs	12.40	16.01	17.31	21.43	10.17	2.40	15.62
Firing costs	65.32	50.91	44.63	31.32	54.64	24.00	51.34

Sources: Bhorat *et al.* (2010); World Bank and International Finance Corporation (2006).

as important a constraint on investment as interest-rate levels. Some of the stronger claims about the impact of rigidities and high costs are hard to prove because they revolve around the claim that if the regulations were not so cumbersome for small firms, and if the bargaining processes within the bargaining councils were not dominated by larger firms and large unions, then there would be more firms and therefore more workers than are seen in the data.

One of the core goals of the Labour Regulation Act is equality, and some, for example Aron *et al.* (2008), believe that South Africa's labour legislation—in particular the labour market governance embodied in the Labour Relations Act, the Basic Conditions of Employment Act and the Employment Equity Act—is too rigid for a country with the kinds of unemployment conditions and labour market segmentations that currently exist. Bhorat and Lundall (2002) identified rigidities in the bargaining system based on the fact that employers speak of high transaction costs or a 'hassle factor' associated with labour legislation that extends far beyond meeting minimum-wage requirements. It includes the costs to employers of complying with wage and benefit standards, and issues such as the legal and procedural requirements on hiring and firing employees, the extension of agreements and the number of trade unions firms are required to interact with. According to the authors, this 'hassle factor' has contributed significantly to South Africa's low employment level (Bhorat and Lundall, 2002). The resources utilized in addressing these issues are considered by businesses as an increase in the implicit fixed costs of interacting with labour (*ibid.*). As with any additional costs, firms employ various methods in order to avoid such expenses. These include hiring fewer labourers, substituting capital for labour, increasing the use of temporary workers, and using subcontractors (*ibid.*). The implication here is that, as a result of stringent labour legislation, labour is being replaced by capital, workers are enduring unemployment for a substantial length of time, and firms are keeping employment levels to a bare minimum.

Finally, and importantly, the increased use of atypical (or non-permanent) workers can be seen as a reaction to the labour market institutions. This allows firms to avoid increased labour costs but may have detrimental effects on the protection and remuneration of this form of labour and may threaten the very existence of bargaining councils. According to Benjamin and Theron (2007), the use of atypical labourers in South Africa is growing at a rapid pace. Rankin (2006) found that increasing subcontracting and outsourcing was a more common response to labour regulations than labour-shedding. Generally, temporary workers are paid less than permanent workers and receive fewer or no benefits. According to Roskam (2007), casual labourers work for wages that are well below the poverty line, often work only for a few hours a day, and have no access to medical aid or retirement fund schemes. In addition, temporary workers have virtually no job security, and the supervision of labour standards by labour inspectors is more difficult (Roskam, 2007). Thus it does seem that there are some negative consequences from the legislative milieu.

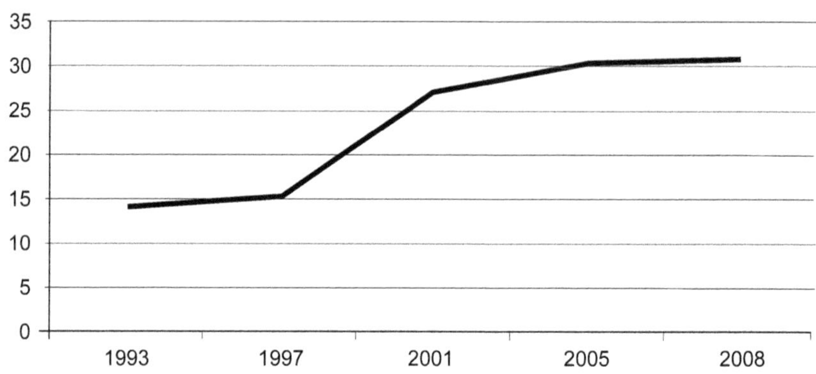

Figure 7.6 Part-time and casual workers as a share of total employment, 1993–2008
Source: PSLSD (1993), OHS (1997), LFS (2001), LFS (2005) and NIDS (2008).

Correlated with the introduction of new labour regulation has been the sharp rise in casual and part-time work, as shown in Figure 7.6. The drastic increase after 1997 in the use of part-time labour coincides with the implementation of the Labour Relations Act of 1995, the Employment Equity Act of 1998 and the Skills Development Act of the same year. These data support the argument that the implementation of firmer labour laws has contributed to the use of temporary workers and thus a fall in permanent, protected employment.

In recent years, a large labour-brokering industry has emerged with more than 3000 recruitment centres nationally and up to 500,000 placements each year. While the industry may facilitate job placements, it has come under fire from the South African government and trade unions for lack of compliance with labour regulation, underpayment of workers and insufficient contributions to worker's UIF, health insurance and pensions. Trade unions have held several large public protests against labour brokers. The government has raised concerns that labour brokers have contributed to the increase in atypical forms of employment, such as short-term work contracts, that may be more prone to violation of labour standards and fair labour practices (Department of Labour, 2011). In December 2010, the South African government passed the Employment Services Bill, which seeks to regulate the labour brokers, while labour unions continue to call for their illegalization.

Adverse effects of minimum wages and sectoral determinations

There is little evidence that South African collective bargaining institutions have provided positive benefits to offset their costs. Banerjee *et al.* (2007) estimate a union wage premium of about 15 per cent. Their analysis suggests that wage premiums for unskilled and semi-skilled workers increased over time in response to minimum wage policies, but decreased for skilled workers. Wage rigidity was further increased by the introduction of a bargaining council system (Burns *et al.*, 2010).[10] Magruder (2011) estimates that centralized bargaining reduced employment by 8–13 per cent. These adverse employment effects are concentrated in small firms, as large firms tend to agree to high wage levels with unions in order to reduce competition from smaller companies. In addition, he estimates that centralized bargaining reduces the number of entrepreneurs by 7–15 per cent.

Estimates by the South African National Treasury suggest that sectoral minimum wages contribute to unemployment, especially among labour market entrants with low productivity levels (National Treasury, 2011). The average minimum wage across all sectors is about 62 per cent of average for formal sector wage compared with an OECD average of 37 per cent. In contrast to most countries, South Africa does not differentiate minimum wages by age through inclusion of sub-minima for youths. Other researchers have found that the minimum wage is not properly enforced (Bhorat *et al.*, 2010) as only 45 per cent of covered workers are paid wages below the legislated minimum, and that the average depth of shortfall is only 36 per cent of the minimum wage.

The best-researched sector in this regard is the domestic worker sector, which employs about a million individuals, mainly women. This sector was completely unregulated prior to 1993 and had no prescribed minimum wage before 2002. When the minimum wage was introduced, there was considerable concern that massive job losses would ensue, but the data do not bear this out. Both Hertz (2004) and Dinkelman and Ranchhod (2012) find that regulations appear to increase domestic workers' wages and improve certain non-wage conditions as well, without decreasing employment. This is surprising given limitations in enforcement. Also, Benjamin (2008) found that the use of the statutory dispute-resolution mechanism (the CCMA) is heavily used by domestic workers, with over 10,000 unfair dismissals referred to it by domestic workers annually.

Adverse effects of migration policies on demand for labour

The labour regulatory effects on the demand for labour may also have second-order implications for unskilled labour employment. While there is no empirical research to quantify the relationship, some argue that skilled and unskilled labour are complementary (rather than substitutes) as skilled supervisors are required to hire unskilled labour. The shortage of skilled labour may therefore have a further effect of constraining firm growth and employment opportunities for unskilled labour. This makes intuitive sense, and led the Harvard Growth Commission to recommend that South African government consider relaxing immigration procedures for skilled labour as a means to create a growth-enabling environment and to promote employment for unskilled labour (Hausmann, 2008).

Affirmative action policies and demand for labour

Adding to this potential rigidity of doing business is the post-apartheid government's introduction of a series of programs to promote economic participation of previously disadvantaged population groups. The Broad-based Black Economic Empowerment Act of 2003 promotes direct empowerment through targets on ownership and control of businesses and assets, and indirect empowerment by means of preferential procurement, enterprise development, profit- and contract-sharing by black enterprises, local content requirements, etc. (Burger and Jaffa, 2006). Burger and Jaffa use national household surveys to assess the impact of these policies on employment, occupational attainment and wage determination. They further conclude that affirmative action policies have had no observable effect on the racial employment gap, and that the impact on the wage distribution is limited to a small narrowing of wages at the top of the income scale.[11]

Discrimination

Banerjee *et al.* (2007) argue that it is difficult to estimate the extent to which discrimination contributes to unemployment in South Africa, as it is hard to distinguish between observable characteristics such as race and unobservable attributes such as quality of education, which are correlated with race and which impact employment status.

Most of today's employers grew up in a racially segregated South Africa that prevented social interactions across racial groups and may have impaired their ability to recognize latent talent across races. This can give way to adverse selection problems—where employers demand skill levels that are unnecessarily high, exacerbate existing skills shortages, and thus lead to inefficient resource allocations within the economy. An experiment by van der Merwe and Burns (2008) underlines the role of racial identity in economic exchanges in South Africa. The researchers played dictator and trust games with students. In the dictator games, the last names of participants were made known before the game, which did not affect offers made by black students, but white students were 27 per cent less generous when their partner had an African-sounding name. The same authors found a low level of trust within and between African and coloured population groups.

In another study, Burns (2006) ran trust games with high school students in Cape Town in which photographs of participants were used to transmit information about the race of the individuals. In such experimental games, the amount sent by the proposer is an indication of trust between strangers in a one-shot interaction, while the amount returned by the trustee/responder is an indication of reciprocity or trustworthiness. Results showed that behavior differs across racial groups: black participants show no in-group favouritism, they are both less trusting and less trustworthy towards other blacks. This behavior is consistent with the very low levels of interpersonal and community trust reported by black students in the self-reported surveys. By contrast, coloured students show strong insider bias as they are making significantly higher offers and returns to coloured than to African partners. White students often choose not to engage in an interaction with black partners. If they do, however, they do not treat black proposers significantly differently from other proposers (Burns, 2006).

7.5 Conclusions and recommendations

Our review of the South African evidence has examined the current knowledge of the nature of South African unemployment, the costs and benefits of current labour regulation and the effectiveness of existing active labour market policies.

Only partial answers can be found to some of the questions we asked. While we have shown that there has been a lot of debate over labour market policies, few randomized controlled trials have been conducted outside of the public health sector, with direct implications for social policy. This stands in contrast to the extensive empirical literature on conditions of unemployment and employment that has been produced in South Africa over the past two decades. This literature sets the stage nicely for thinking about specific policy interventions to address unemployment in South Africa, and we conclude with a set of policy recommendations and suggestions for further research.

In our recommendations, we focus on interventions that target unskilled and semi-skilled poor workers, and lend themselves to be tested through randomized controlled trials. Such trials have the benefit of enabling the researcher to isolate the causal impact of a program or policy from other confounding factors that are also changing over time and across regions. Over the past few years, a wide range of tools have been developed to allow an element of randomization to be incorporated into the program of an implementing agency or group in a way that both maintains scientific rigor and allows for the practical constraints of the implementing agency. This ability to blend randomized evaluations into the everyday operations of development practitioners around the world has transformed the technique from a rare and extremely expensive operation to a more flexible and therefore commonly used approach to evaluation. Because randomized impact studies test the effectiveness of practical programs in real-life settings, the evidence is solution-oriented and helps inform policies on how to overcome barriers to employment, rather than just identifying them. This is important, as the most cost-effective way to improve employment is not always to tackle the biggest barrier. Comparisons that identify the most cost-effective way of addressing a specific policy objective are particularly useful for policymakers who work within limited budgets.

The research agenda that we outline below includes recommendations of further research on both dimensions.

Randomized controlled trials are not suitable for answering all policy questions. There is a similar gap in the availability of rigorous policy analysis using other quasi-experimental methods which also warrant further attention within the South African research community. These research agendas should and would easily complement each other.

We summarize the evidence and research recommendations under three headings to group the evidence according to how firmly we assess the knowledge base to be.

7.5.1 Area with robust evidence

Other chapters in this country case study series, especially the review of the Kenyan evidence (Chapter 6) and the micro theory review (Chapter 3), present strong evidence that early-life interventions (such as nutritional support and reduction of early childhood diseases as well as intellectual stimulation) can have long-term effects that last into early adulthood and entry into work life, affecting fertility, delinquency and adulthood wellbeing. Some of these interventions hold the potential to be comparatively cheap and effective, and critical policy options for stopping the enduring cycle of poor prevention leading to costly remediation. This body of evidence makes an important point that barriers to employment may operate well beyond the narrow dynamics of labour supply and demand. Nonetheless, they are foundational for thinking about a highly productive and well paid workforce. Without these policies in place, labour markets can become end-games of poor human development (on the supply side) and poor dynamism in the private and public sectors (on the demand side), rather than platforms for transformation.

Recommendations

These lessons from other countries have relevance to South Africa. In some cases, such as information campaigns on relative risks, similar interventions could be adopted in South Africa, while in others there is interesting work to be done to adapt the findings to the South African policy context.

7.5.2 Areas with suggestive evidence

Are the right people looking for work?

From the empirical literature there appear to be substantial economic incentives to obtain education, and limited demand (from households and social networks) on young adults to exit schools in favour of labour market participation. These returns persist across different further education options, especially universities and FET college qualifications. Young adults seem relatively well informed about these differences. Cost is a barrier to further education that existing bursary schemes have been unable to close.

RECOMMENDATIONS

It would be worth testing whether centralized, simplified and less expensive application systems to institutions of further training would enable access to further institutions for more marginalized young adults. When these young adults miss a deadline or do not get selected because of incomplete documentation, they wait a full year to reapply.

We have insufficient knowledge of the effects of social norms, role models and gender differences in school-to-work transitions.

Do jobseekers have the right means of looking for work?

Access to job-search methods differs by region, prior skills and race. It is therefore important to assess who benefits from different job aid measures and who does not.

The Department of Labour and the NYDA offer centralized databases to register jobseekers and work opportunities. Both databases are populated with thousands of jobseekers, but because a majority of jobseekers have limited prior work experience, it is challenging to capture information on these individuals that communicates work fitness to prospective employers. Also, with limited counsellor-to-jobseeker interactions, counsellors are effectively unable to recommend jobseekers to prospective employers. Some of these constraints could be remedied in potentially innovative ways through online facilities to upload reference letters onto the database, test basic skills and update contact information.

It is evident that transportation costs place a financial burden on job search and work. Subsidizing transportation costs for job search behavior may incentivize more active job searching. If there are large social benefits to active job search, it makes economic sense to subsidize job-search costs—or even to reward finding work financially—if the benefits are large enough to justify it. Despite an extensive social grant system, there is no conclusive evidence that these social transfers lead to high reservation wages that disincentivize work. As we have shown, time trends in labour supply and the share of unemployed who report themselves to be discouraged jobseekers show some correlation with economic conditions and macro-level job creation.

RECOMMENDATION

The National Treasury proposal to introduce a wage subsidy is worth testing through a randomized controlled trial. Further experimentation on a transportation subsidy and improvements to information on jobseekers is also recommended. In these instances it would be particularly useful to link such studies to broader measures of motivation and social network effects to understand better how changing labour market conditions affect behaviors in other spheres (such as skills development and school exit).

Is it possible to create more jobs?

There is some rigorous evidence that minimum wages and sectoral extensions of minimum wages negatively affect employment in some sectors. Evidence on the effects of other aspects of labour regulation (e.g. cost and complexity of hiring and firing) is more limited and relies on self-reported perceptions of constraints to doing business. These perceptions may not be grounded in reality. Further evidence is therefore needed to understand better how knowledgeable firms are of the laws and biases in their interpretation of labour regulation.

It would be interesting—though it may not be politically feasible—to test more flexible labour regulation for new labour market entrants or for young firms.

Affirmative action legislation has not been a major constraining factor on doing business in South Africa. It has been narrowly focused on needed changes to ownership structures. It may become more constraining if BEE targets are broadened to include rationing of skills development training and employment quotas.

There is some evidence that low levels of trust negatively affect social outcomes in post-apartheid South Africa, but more research is needed to understand the implications for labour market dynamics. This could include testing the effectiveness of mentoring and internship programs. These may alter the employee's job readiness and skills while simultaneously altering the employer's perceptions of young adults.

7.5.3 Areas of limited evidence

There is a general lack of evidence on the effectiveness of programs to support jobseekers. This includes the returns to job-readiness training and other short-term, vocational and technical training courses. It also includes job-placement programs, career counselling interventions and testing for prior skills. More generally, there is a need for more rigorous testing to restructure skills training programs, including through SETAs.

If the returns to job exposure are high, internship programs and civic work guarantees for school leavers may have larger benefits than costs. Holiday internship programs could expose young adults to real-life work environments and future prospective employers to new cohorts of young adults. Testing the career effects of offering a school-to-work bridging employment scheme, at a minimum salary, would improve our knowledge of how young adults can gain experience with work and enable them to establish a track record. Similar public employment schemes in France have shown positive effects for marginalized youth that could be worthwhile testing in South Africa.

There is a definite need for further research into the dynamic effects of employment prospects across social networks and neighborhoods and over time as individuals and households revise their resource allocations to changing labour market prospects.

The literature on informal and formal sector entrepreneurship can also benefit from testing the effectiveness of support services.

More evidence is needed to understand the economy-wide and societal effects of large-scale public employment schemes, including on broader measures of social cohesion, service delivery and the economic agency of program beneficiaries. While individual-level effects can be measured, it is more challenging to measure the effects of such programs on the opportunities they create for corruption and fiscal mismanagement.

There is little research on firm culture in South Africa, and further evidence is needed from business science on whether enhanced involvement of workers in firm ownership and management structures could be conducive to greater productivity, growth and employment. Countries with a strong tradition for workers to stay and develop their career within a firm also have stronger skills development cultures.

Notes

1 NIDS is collected by SALDRU at the University of Cape Town, with financial support by the South African government. The first wave was collected in 2008, the second in 2010/11 and the third in 2012, and will be followed by biannual waves going forward. For more information, see www.nids.ac.za.

2 The world labour force participation rate for 2008 was 64.1 per cent, while that for Sub-Saharan Africa was 70.8 per cent (ILO, 2008).

3 According to the *World Development Report 2007*, in the Middle East and North Africa, unemployment rates are 10 per cent on average but 32 per cent for young adults; in Europe and Central Asia, average unemployment rates are about 10 per cent with youth unemployment rates at 25 per cent; in Latin America, unemployment rates are 7 per cent on average but 18 per cent for young adults. In Sub-Saharan Africa, 14 per cent of young adults are unemployed compared with 7 per cent on average (World Bank, 2007).

4 Informal jobs are defined here as those within a business that is not registered, in addition to all domestic workers. Workers operating within the informal sector are not offered the rights and protections enshrined in South African labour law, and thus are open to exploitation in terms of wages, hours, leave, etc. The informal sector is generally considered the last preserve of the unemployed, for the reasons stated above.

5 This section is adapted from Leibbrandt and Woolard (2010).

6 Lam *et al.* (2008) argue that the importance of networks puts Africans at a particular disadvantage—at age 20 more than 88 per cent of whites worked in the past year, as opposed to 20 per cent African females and 31 per cent African males.

7 The labour force survey respondents are asked 'During the past four weeks, have you taken any action a) to look for any kind of work or b) to start any kind of business?' The SASAS asks those currently unemployed 'Do you continuously look for work?' and finds that 81 per cent of respondents are searching (Noble *et al.*, 2008).

8 More recent panel data from the NIDS have shown similar levels of churning. According to Cichello *et al.* (2012), 'while NEA and employment categories might be considered *relatively* stable states, they are not overly stable. Thirty per cent of those employed in 2008 were not employed in 2010 and over 40 per cent of those in NEA in 2008 were in the labour force by 2010.' Furthermore, as acknowledged by the authors, these dynamics capture activities only within the last three weeks of

the survey interviews, and it is possible that even further changes could have taken place between the waves, with some NEA individuals having accepted work or been actively searching for work in the two-year period between the NIDS interviews.

9 The social impact of the rise in unemployment has been dampened by an accompanying expansion of the social assistance system since the end of Apartheid, particularly at the bottom of the income distribution. In 2009, government grants make up 73 per cent of income in bottom income decile compared to 15 per cent in 1993 (Leibbrandt 2009).

10 About 25 per cent of formal sector employees are covered by bargaining council agreements (Magruder, 2011).

11 This is supported by Leibbrandt *et al.* (2010a, b) who find that while between-race inequality remains high, intra-African inequality and poverty trends increasingly dominate aggregate inequality and poverty in South Africa.

References

Adcorp (2011) 'Adcorp Employment Index, March 2011.' www.adcorp.co.za.

Aghion, P., Braun, M. and Fedderke, J. (2008) 'Competition and Productivity Growth in South Africa,' *Economics of Transition*, 16(4): 741–68.

Ardington, C., Case, A. and Hosegood, V. (2009) 'Labour Supply Responses to Large Social Transfers: Longitudinal Evidence from South Africa,' *American Economic Journal: Applied Economics*, 1(1): 22–48.

Aron, J., Kahn, B. and Kingdon, G. (2008) 'South African Economic Policy under Democracy: Overviews and Prospects,' in Aron, J., Kahn, B. and Kingdon, G. (eds), *South African Economic Policy under Democracy*. Oxford: Oxford University Press.

Banerjee, A., Galiani, S., Levinsohn, J., McClaren, Z. and Woolard, I. (2007) *Why has Unemployment Risen in the New South Africa?*, NBER Working Paper 13167. Cambridge, MA: National Bureau of Economic Research.

Benjamin, P. (2008) 'Informal Work and Labour Rights in South Africa,' *paper presented at the Conference on the Regulatory Environment and its Impact on the Nature and Level of Economic Growth and Development in South Africa*, 27–29 October. Cape Town: Development Policy Research Unit, University of Cape Town.

Benjamin, P. and Gruen, C. (2006) *The Regulatory Efficiency of the CCMA: A Statistical Analysis of the CCMA's CMS Database*, Development Policy Research Unit Working Paper No. 06/110. Cape Town: University of Cape Town.

Benjamin, P. and Theron, J. (2007) *Costing, Comparing and Competing: Developing an Approach to the Benchmarking of Labour Market Regulation*, Development Policy Research Unit Working Paper No. 07/131. Cape Town: University of Cape Town.

van der Berg, S. (2007) 'Apartheid's Enduring Legacy: Inequalities in Education,' *Journal of African Economies*, 16(5): 849–80.

Betcherman, G., Olivas, K. and Dar, A. (2004) *Impacts of Active Labor Market Programs: New Evidence from Evaluations with Particular Attention to Developing and Transition Countries*, Social Protection Discussion Paper 0402. Washington, DC: World Bank.

Bhorat, H. and Lundall, P. (2002) *Employment, Wages and Skills Development: Firm Specific Effects – Evidence from Two Firm Surveys in South Africa*, Development Policy Research Unit Working Paper No. 9654. Cape Town: University of Cape Town.

Bhorat, H., Pauw, K. and Mncube, L. (2009) *Understanding the Efficiency and Effectiveness of the Dispute Resolution System in South Africa: An Analysis of CCMA*

Data, Development Policy Research Unit Working Paper No. 09/137. Cape Town: University of Cape Town.

Bhorat, H., Kanbur, R. and Mayet, N. (2012) 'Estimating the Causal Effect of Enforcement on Minimum Wage Compliance: The Case of South Africa,' *Review of Development Economics*, 16(4): 608–23.

Boccara, B. and Moll, P. (1996) *Labour Market Flexibility and Industrial Councils in South Africa*. Washington, DC: World Bank, Africa Region.

Branson, N. (2006) *The South African Labor Market 1995–2004: A Cohort Analysis*, SALDRU Working Paper. Cape Town: Southern Africa Labour and Development Research Unit, School of Economics, University of Cape Town.

Branson, N., Leibbrandt, M. and Zuze, T.L. (2009) 'What are the Returns to Tertiary Education and Who Benefits?' in N. Cloete (ed.), *Responding to the Educational Needs Of Post-School Youth*. Wynberg: Centre for Higher Education Transformation.

Branson, N., Garlick, J., Lam, D. and Leibbrandt, M. (2012) *Education and Inequality: The South African Case*, SALDRU Working Paper No 75. Cape Town: Southern Africa Labour and Development Research Unit, School of Economics, University of Cape Town.

Burger, R. and Jaffa, R. (2006) *Returns to Race: Labour Market Discrimination in Post-Apartheid South Africa*, Working Paper. Matieland: Stellenbosch University.

Burns, J. (2006) 'Racial Stereotypes, Stigma and Trust in Post-apartheid South Africa,' *Economic Modelling*, 23(5): 805–21.

——(2008) *Reducing Youth Unemployment in South Africa: Where to Intervene?* Cape Town: University of Cape Town.

Burns, J., Edwards, L. and Pauw, K. (2010) *Wage Subsidies to Combat Unemployment and Poverty*, IFPRI Discussion Paper 969. Washington, DC: International Food Policy Research Institute.

Calmfors, L. and Driffill, J. (1988) 'Bargaining Structure, Corporatism, and Macroeconomic Performance,' *Economic Policy*, 3(6): 13–62.

Chamberlain, D. and van der Berg, S. (2002) *Earnings Functions, Labour Market Discrimination and Quality of Education in South Africa*, Economic Working Paper No. 2/2002. Matieland: Stellenbosch University.

Cichello, P., Leibbrandt, M. and Woolard, I. (2012) *Labour Market: Analysis of the NIDS Wave 1 and 2 Datasets*, Working Paper Series No. 78. Cape Town: National Income Dynamics Study, Southern Africa Labour and Development Research Unit, School of Economics, University of Cape Town.

Department of Labour (2011) *Strategic Plan for the Department of Labour 2011–16*. Pretoria.

DHET (2010) *Address by the Minister of Higher Education and Training Dr Blade Nzimande at the launch of the Quality Council for Trades and Occupations*, 23 February. Pretoria: Department of Higher Education and Training.

Dinkelman, T. and Ranchhod, V. (2012) 'Evidence on the Impact of Minimum Wage Laws in an Informal Sector: Domestic Workers in South Africa,' *Journal of Development Economics*, 99(1): 27–45.

DPW (2009) *Expanded Public Works Programme Five Year Report 2004/05–2008/09: Reaching the One Million Target*. Pretoria: Department of Public Works.

DTI (2008) 'Annual review of small business in South Africa,' Pretoria: Department of Trade and Industry.

Du Toit, R. (2005) *A Review of Labour Markets in South Africa: Career Guidance and Employment Services*. Pretoria: Human Sciences Research Council.

Fedderke, F. and Hill, A. (2006) *Industry Structure and Labour Market Flexibility in the South African Manufacturing Sector: A Time Series and Panel Data Approach*, SALDRU Working Paper No. 43. Cape Town: Southern Africa Labour and Development Research Unit, School of Economics, University of Cape Town.

Fedderke, J.W., Kularatne, C. and Mariotti, M. (2007) 'Mark-up Pricing in South African Industry,' *Journal of African Economies*, 16(1): 28–69.

FinScope (2010) *FinScope South Africa Small Business Survey 2010*. www.finscope.co.za.

Go, D.S., Kearney, M., Korman, V., Robinson, S. and Thierfelder, K. (2009) *Wage Subsidy and Labor Market Flexibility in South Africa*, Policy Research Working Paper Series 4871. Washington, DC: World Bank.

Godfrey, S., Theron, J. and Visser, M. (2007) *The State of Collective Bargaining in South Africa: An Empirical and Conceptual Study of Collective Bargaining*, Development Policy Research Unit Working Paper No. 07/130. Cape Town: University of Cape Town.

Gurgand, M., Lorenceau, A. and Melonio, T. (2011) *Student Loans: Liquidity Constraint and Higher Education in South Africa*, Agence Française de Développement Working Paper 117. Paris: Paris School of Economics.

Haroon, B., Ravi, K. and Natasha, M. (2010) *Minimum Wage Violation in South Africa*, Development Policy Research Unit Working Paper 1143. Cape Town: University of Cape Town.

Hausmann, R. (2008) *Final Recommendations of the International Panel on ASGISA*, Working Paper No. 161. Cambridge, MA: Center for International Development, Harvard University. www.hks.harvard.edu/centers/cid/programs/growth-lab/growth-research/south-africa-growth-initiative.

Hertz, T. (2004) *Have Minimum Wages Benefited South Africa's Domestic Service Workers?*, Forum Paper. Development Poverty Research Unit, University of Cape Town in association with Trade and Industrial Policy Strategies, Cornell University, African Development and Poverty Reduction.

ILO (2008) *Key Indicators of the Labour Market*, 6th edn. Geneva: International Labour Organization.

Kanyeze, G., Mhone, G. and Sparreboom, T. (2000) *Strategies to Combat Youth Unemployment and Marginalization in Anglophone Africa*, Discussion Paper 12. Harare: International Labour Office, Southern Africa Multidisciplinary Advisory Team.

Keswell, M. (2004) 'Non-linear Earnings Dynamics In Post-apartheid South Africa,' *South African Journal of Economics*, 75(5): 913–39.

Keswell, M. and Poswell, L. (2004) 'Returns to Education in South Africa: A Retrospective Sensitivity Analysis of the Available Evidence,' *South African Journal of Economics*, 72(4): 834–60.

Kingdon, G. and Knight, J. (2004) 'Unemployment in South Africa: The Nature of the Beast,' *World Development*, 32: 391–408.

——(2006) 'How Flexible are Wages in Response to Local Unemployment in South Africa?', *Industrial and Labor Relations Review*, 59(3): 471–95.

——(2008) 'Unemployment: South Africa's Achilles Heel,' in Aron, J., Kahn, B. and Kingdon G. (eds), *South African Economic Policy under Democracy*. Oxford: Oxford University Press.

Klasen, S. and Woolard, I. (2008) 'Surviving Unemployment without State Support,' *Journal of African Economies*, 18(1): 1–51.

Kraak, A. (2004) *The National Skills Development Strategy: A New Institutional Regime For Skills Formation In Post-apartheid South Africa*. Cape Town: HSRC Press.

——(2008) 'A Critical Review of the National Skills Development Strategy in South Africa,' *Journal of Vocational Education and Training*, 60(1): 1–18.

Lam, D., Leibbrandt, M. and Mlatsheni, C. (2008) 'Education and Youth Unemployment in South Africa,' *SALDRU Working Paper Number 22*. Cape Town: Southern Africa Labour and Development Research Unit, School of Economics, University of Cape Town.

Lam, D., Ardington, C. and Leibbrandt, M. (2011) 'Schooling as a Lottery: Racial Differences in School Advancement in Urban South Africa,' *Journal of Development Economics*, 95(2): 121–36.

Leibbrandt, M., Woolard, I., Finn, A. and Argent, J. (2010a) *Trends in South African Income Distribution and Poverty since the Fall of Apartheid*, OECD Social, Employment and Migration Working Papers No. 101. Paris: Organisation for Economic Co-operation and Development.

Leibbrandt, M., Woolard, I., McEwen, H. and Koep, C. (2010b) 'Better Employment to Reduce Inequality further in South Africa,' in *Tackling Inequalities in Brazil, China, India and South Africa: The Role of Labour Market and Social Policies.* Paris: Organisation for Economic Co-operation and Development, Ch. 5.

Levinsohn, J. (2008) *Two Policies to Alleviate Unemployment in South Africa*, CID Working Paper No. 166. Cambridge, MA: Center for International Development, Harvard University.

LFS (2000) *Labour Force Survey. Statistics South Africa.* Pretoria, South Africa. February.

Lundall, P. and Rospabé, S. (2002) *The South African Labour Market in Economic and Legislative Considerations*, ILO Employment Paper No. 2002/32. Geneva: International Labour Organization.

Macun, I. (1997) 'Evolving Practices in Industrial Relations and Collective Bargaining: The SALFS Results,' *presented at the Labour Market and Enterprise Performance in South Africa Conference.* Johannesburg: Sociology of Work Unit, University of Witwatersrand.

Magruder, J. (2011) 'High Unemployment yet Few Small Firms: The Role of Centralized Bargaining in South Africa,' unpublished. Berkeley, CA: University of California.

Manuel, T. (2012) *Address to the opening session of Strategies to Overcome Poverty and Inequality – Towards Carnegie III, University of Cape Town by Trevor Manuel, MP, Minister in The Presidency: National Planning Commission.* www.info.gov.za/speech/DynamicAction?pageid=461&sid=30350&tid=82285.

Meth, C. (2011) *Employer of Last Resort? South Africa's Expanded Public Works Programme (EPWP)*, SALDRU Working Paper Number 58. Cape Town: Southern Africa Labour and Development Research Unit, School of Economics, University of Cape Town.

——(2010) *Active' Labour Market Policies: Lessons for South Africa?*, Research Report No. 86. Durban: School of Development Studies, University of KwaZulu-Natal.

van der Merwe, W.G. and Burns, J. (2008) 'What's in a Name? Racial Identity and Altruism in Post-apartheid South Africa,' *SALDRU Working Paper Number 24*. Cape Town: Southern Africa Labour and Development Research Unit, School of Economics, University of Cape Town.

Mlatsheni, C. (2007) 'A Survey of Youth Labour Market Trends,' draft paper presented for the Employment Growth and Development Initiative (EGDI), Urban, Rural and Economic Development, Human Sciences Research Council, Pretoria.

Moll, P. (1993) 'Black South African Unions: Relative Wage Effects in International Perspective,' *Industrial and Labour Relations Review*, 46(2): 245–61.

——(1996) 'Compulsory Centralisation of Collective Bargaining in South Africa,' *American Economic Review*, 86(2): 326–29.

National Department of Economic Development. (2010) www.economic.gov.za/.

National Treasury (2011a) *Confronting Youth Unemployment: Policy Options for South Africa*, Discussion Paper. Pretoria: National Treasury.

——(2011b) *2011 Budget Speech*, 23 February. Pretoria: National Treasury. www.treasury.gov.za/documents/national%20budget/2011/speech/speech2011.pdf.

Nattrass, N. (1997) *Business and Employer Organisations in South Africa*, Occasional Report No. 5. Geneva: Employment and Training Department, International Labour Office.

NIDS (2008) *National Income Dynamic Survey. Southern Africa Labour and Development Research Unit*. Wave 1. Version 4. 1. Cape Town.

Noble, M., Ntshongwana, P. and Surender, R. (2008) *Attitudes to Work and Social Security in South Africa*. Pretoria: Urban Rural and Economic Development Research Programme, Human Sciences Research Council.

NSDS (2010) *National Skill Development Strategy 2011–15*. Pretoria: Department of Higher Education and Training.

OHS (1995) *October Household Survey. Statistics South Africa*. Pretoria, South Africa.

Pauw, K., Oosthuizen, M. and van der Westhuizen, C. (2008) 'Graduate Unemployment in the Face of Skills Shortages: A Labor Market Paradox,' *South African Journal of Economics*, 76(1): 45–57.

Philip, K. (2009) 'The Community Work Programme in South Africa, The Second Economy Strategy Project: An Initiative of the Presidency', *paper presented at the conference on 'Employment Guarantee Policies: Responding to the Current Economic Crisis and Contributing to Long-Term Development'*, United Nations Development Programme, Regional Bureau for Latin America and the Caribbean, and Bureau for Development Policy, in partnership with the Levy Economics Institute of Bard College, New York, June. www.levy.org/pubs/conf_june09/conf_june09_files/presentations/Session5b_Philip.pdf.

PSLSD (1993) *Project for Statistics on Living Standards and Development. Southern Africa Labour & Development Research Unit*. School of Economics, University of Cape Town. Cape Town, South Africa.

QFLS (2009–2011) *Quarterly Labour Force Survey. Statistics South Africa*. Pretoria, South Africa.

Ranchhod, V. (2009a) *Household Responses to Adverse Income Shocks: Pensioner Out-migration and Mortality in South Africa*, Working Paper 133. Cape Town: Economic Research Southern Africa.

——(2009b) *Labour Market: Analysis of the NIDS Wave 1 Dataset*, NIDS Discussion Paper No. 12. Cape Town: National Income Dynamics Study, Southern Africa Labour and Development Research Unit, School of Economics, University of Cape Town.

Rankin, N. (2006) *The Regulatory Environment and SMMEs. Evidence from South African Firm Level Data*, Development Policy Research Unit Working Paper No. 06/113. Cape Town: University of Cape Town.

Roskam, A. (2007) *An Exploratory Look into Labour Market Regulation*, Development Policy Research Unit Working Paper No. 07/116. Cape Town: University of Cape Town.

Rospabe, S. and Selod, H. (2006) 'Does City Structure Cause Unemployment? The Case of Cape Town,' in Bhorat, H. and Kanbur, R. (eds), *Poverty and Policy in Post-Apartheid South Africa*. Cape Town: HSRC Press, pp. 262–87.

SALDRU (2011) *Revisiting the 'Crisis' in Teen Births: What is the Impact of Teen Births on Young Mothers and their Children?*, SALDRU Policy Brief No. 1. Cape Town: Southern Africa Labour and Development Research Unit, School of Economics, University of Cape Town.

Schöer, V. and Leibbrandt, M. (2006) 'Determinants of Job Search Strategies: Evidence from the Khayelitsha/Mitchell's Plain Survey,' *South African Journal of Economics*, 74(4): 702–24.

Smith, C. (2006) *International Experience with Worker-side and Employer-side Wage and Employment Subsidies, and Job Search Assistance Programs: Implications for South Africa*, Employment Growth and Development Initiative. Pretoria: Human Science Research Council.

Soskice, D. (1990) 'Wage Determination: The Changing Role of Institutions in Advanced Industrialised Countries,' *Oxford Review of Economic Policy*, 6(4): 36–61.

Standing, G. (1997) 'Labour Market Dynamics in South African Industrial Firms: The South African Labour Flexibility Survey,' *paper presented to conference on Labour Markets and Enterprise Performance*, Pretoria, South Africa, 30 January.

StatsSA (2011) *Quarterly Labour Force Survey 2011*. www.statssa.gov.za/publications/P0211/P02114thQuarter2011.pdf.

——(2012) *Quarterly Labour Force Survey 2012*. www.statssa.gov.za/publications/P0211/P02111stQuarter2012.pdf.

Surender, R., Ntshongwana, P., Noble, M. and Wright, G. (2007) *Employment and Social Security: A Qualitative Study of Attitudes towards the Labour Market and Social Grants*. Pretoria: Department of Social Development.

World Bank (2007) *World Development Report 2007: Development and the Next Generation*. Washington, DC: World Bank.

——(2009) *Doing Business 2009*. Washington, DC: World Bank.

World Bank and International Finance Corporation (2006) *Doing Business in 2006: Creating Jobs*. Washington, DC: World Bank.

Yu, D. (2009) *The Comparability of Labour Force Survey (LFS) and Quarterly Labour Force Survey (QLFS)*, Working Paper 08/09. Matieland: Stellenbosch University.

Index

www.ingramcontent.com/pod-product-compliance
Ingram Content Group UK Ltd.
Pitfield, Milton Keynes, MK11 3LW, UK
UKHW052031210425
457613UK00032BA/1036

* 9 7 8 0 3 6 7 8 6 8 2 6 0 *